Glenn Randall

Dusk to Dawn
A Guide to Landscape Photography at Night
Second Edition

rockynook

Dusk to Dawn, 2nd Edition
A Guide to Landscape Photography at Night
Glenn Randall
www.glennrandall.com

Project editor: Maggie Yates
Project manager: Lisa Brazieal
Marketing coordinator: Katie Walker
Copyeditor: Maggie Yates
Layout: Anthony Paular Design
Cover design: Aren Straiger

ISBN: 979-8-88814-051-2
2nd Edition (1st printing, May 2024)
© 2024 Glenn Randall
All images © Glenn Randall unless otherwise noted

Rocky Nook Inc.
1010 B Street, Suite 350
San Rafael, CA 94901
USA

www.rockynook.com

Distributed in the UK and Europe by Publishers Group UK
Distributed in the U.S. and all other territories by Publishers Group West

Library of Congress Control Number: 2023934967

"This book is dedicated to the champions of wilderness,

both celebrated and unknown, who have fought to preserve the wild places

that inspire nature photographers to create their art."

Table of Contents

Acknowledgments

The roots of this book date back to August 2011, when I saw a slideshow by Colorado landscape photographer Grant Collier. His images of the Milky Way glowing over landscapes in Utah opened my eyes to the potential of the latest digital cameras to make stunning images at night. Thanks, Grant! Over the next 12 years I have learned from, and been inspired by, the writings and night photographs of a number of other landscape photographers, including Adam Woodworth, David Kingham, Floris van Breugel, Ian Norman, Michael Frye, Mike Shaw, Patrick Endres, and Royce Bair. Thanks to all of you for sharing your insights through your articles and books. I'd particularly like to thank Roger Clark, a professional astronomer and ardent night photographer, whose extensive website provided a great deal of technical information on the best cameras, lenses, and field techniques for night photography. Dr. Stan Solomon, senior scientist at the High Altitude Observatory at the National Center for Atmospheric Research, and Professor Scott Bailey at Virginia Tech provided helpful insight into the complex physics of airglow. Mark Zalcik graciously shared his extensive knowledge of noctilucent clouds and insights into the best shooting locations in Canada, which helped me prepare for my 2023 noctilucent clouds shoot in the Canadian Rockies. I'd like to thank the staff at Rocky Nook, particularly my editor, Maggie Yates, whose eagle-eyed, thoughtful, and meticulous editing helped make this book the best it could be. Most importantly, I'd like to thank my wife Cora, an atmospheric scientist whose perceptive questions, boundless curiosity, and insistence on scientific rigor encouraged me to go beyond a superficial understanding of whatever topic was at hand, and whose tolerance of long absences made it possible to create the images in the second edition of *Dusk to Dawn: A Guide to Landscape Photography at Night*.

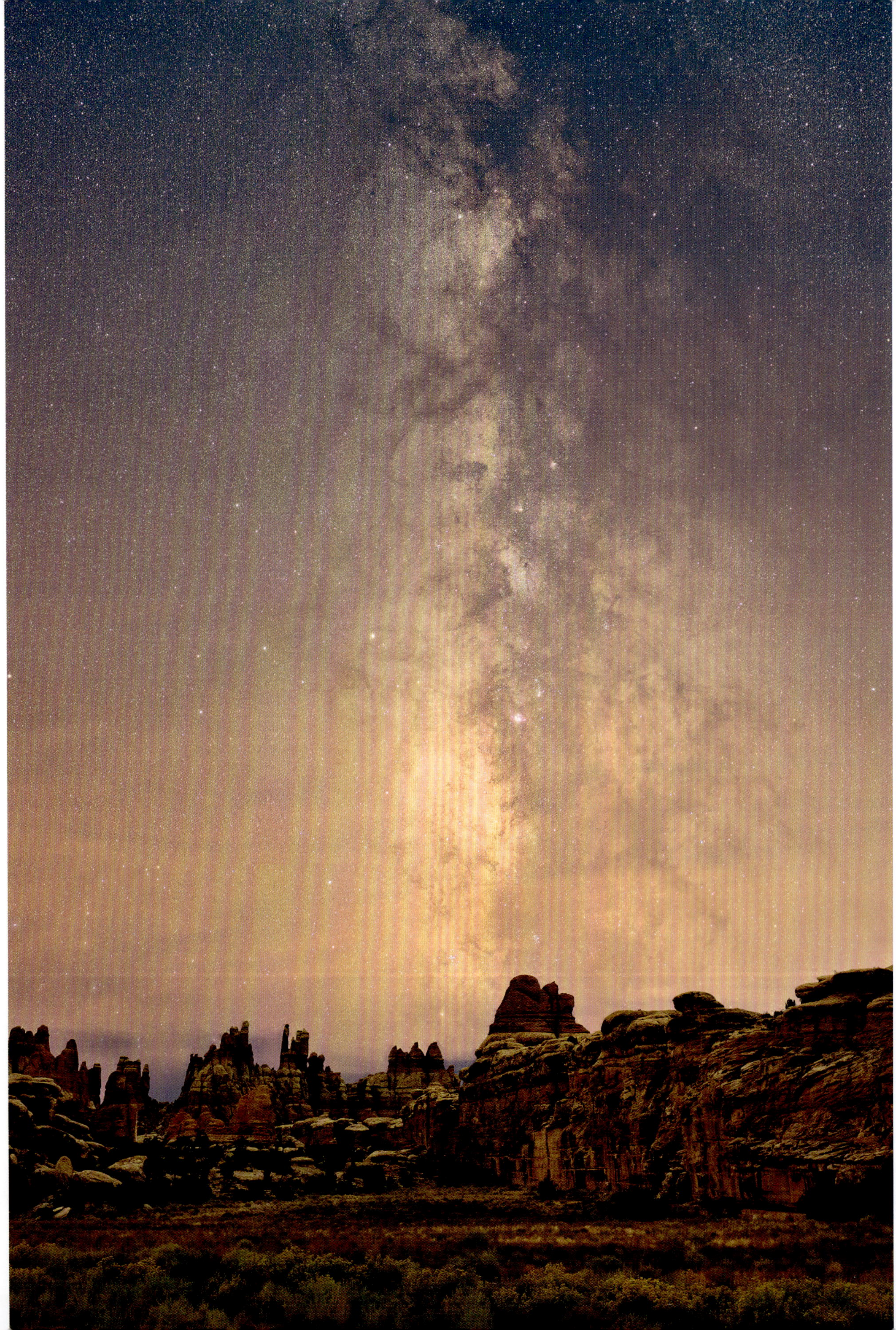

Foreword

Glenn Randall has been a long-time contributor to *Outdoor Photographer* magazine – where I served as editor-in-chief – and with good reason. His stories for OP over the years have been packed with excellent information, gorgeous imagery, and useful advice on how to become a better outdoor photographer. And with this latest edition of *Dusk to Dawn: A Guide to Landscape Photography at Night*, he brings that wealth of photographic knowledge to a subject that will be of keen interest to readers.

Shooting landscapes at night might sound simple but, of course, it's not. It can actually be rather intimidating for some photographers, which is why it's great to have Glenn as a guide in this helpful book. What I've admired about his writing and what I'm sure you'll find engaging in this deeply researched book is the way he's able to blend a strong technical expertise in photography with personal anecdotes and first-hand experience. This is exactly what's needed to fully understand how to take better night photos.

On the one hand, as Glenn points out, the tools for astrophotography have never been better, with the latest cameras, lenses, and apps making the experience of capturing landscapes at night much more enjoyable than it was even just a few years ago. (Which is all the more reason this new edition of *Dusk to Dawn* is needed right now.) But photography is more than just having the right gear. In addition to explaining the new technology, Glenn meticulously takes you through the entire process of planning a night shoot. (As a side note, Glenn's meticulousness is another one of his invaluable assets as I found out when he volunteered to proofread a story in *Outdoor Photographer* and discovered that several paragraphs had been inadvertently lopped off. Good save, Glenn!) He begins with something, I think, many photographers might take for granted: scouting a location beforehand. We are all so eager to get out there with our cameras we can sometimes forget to simply use our eyes to look around. Is there a rocky outcropping that would help to frame a shot? Is there a cliff that could pose a danger when you come upon it in the dark? Can your GPS get a signal in a remote area?

◄ Milky Way over Devils Pocket, Needles District, Canyonlands National Park, Utah. October 13, 2023, 8:30 p.m. Sony Alpha 7R IVa, Sony FE 35mm f/1.4 GM. Land: one camera position, nine frames, images stacked in Photoshop, noise reduced with Stack Mode>Median, 40 seconds, f/1.4, ISO 6400. Sky: one camera position, one frame, camera mounted on iOptron SkyTracker Pro equatorial mount, 81 seconds, f/1.4, ISO 800.

From there, Glenn breaks down the essential skills in night photography and ways to not only plan and shoot the Milky Way, for example, but how to process the images afterward so they come out the way you truly saw them. In this latest version of the book, he adds tips on how to capture several wonders of the night sky not included in the first edition including comets, zodiacal light, and noctilucent clouds. Which proves there's always something new to learn when capturing landscapes at night. And as this latest edition of Glenn's book shows you, there's no reason to be afraid of the dark.

– Dan Havlik, former editor in chief of *Outdoor Photographer* magazine; current editor in chief of *Wild Eye* magazine (www.wildeyemagazine.com).

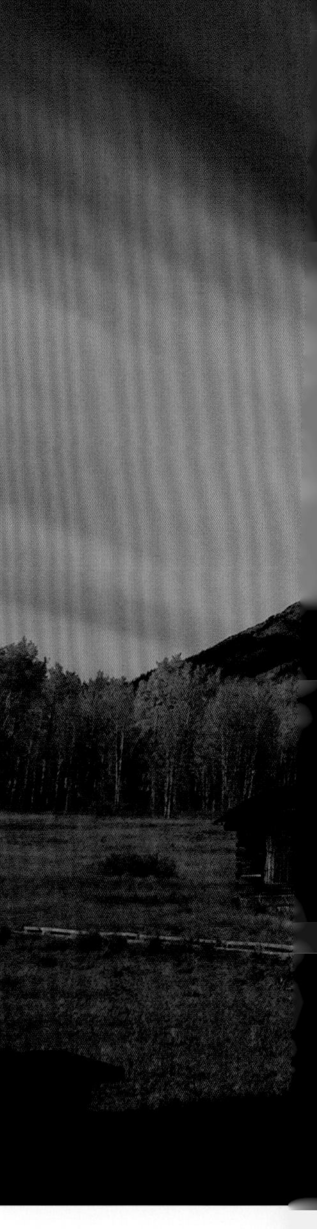

▸ The ghost town of Ashcroft by the light of the full moon, near Aspen, Colorado. September 27, 2007, 10:28 p.m. Nikon D70s, Nikkor 18-70mm f/3.5-f/4.5 at 22mm (33mm full-frame equivalent). 272 seconds, f4.8, ISO 200. During the long exposure I ran into each cabin and lit the interior with one pop of a Nikon SB24 flash unit with an orange filter over the flash head.

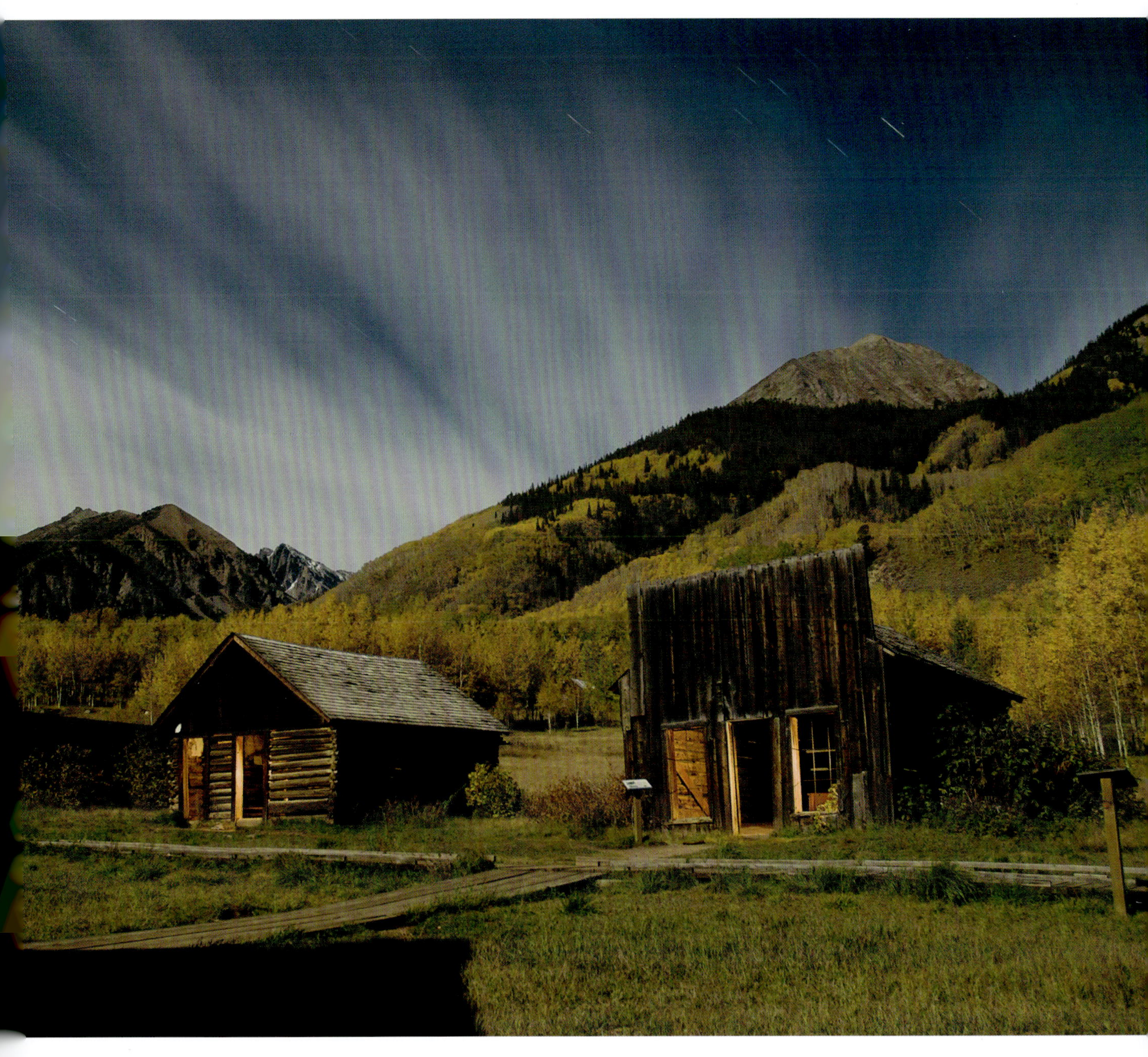

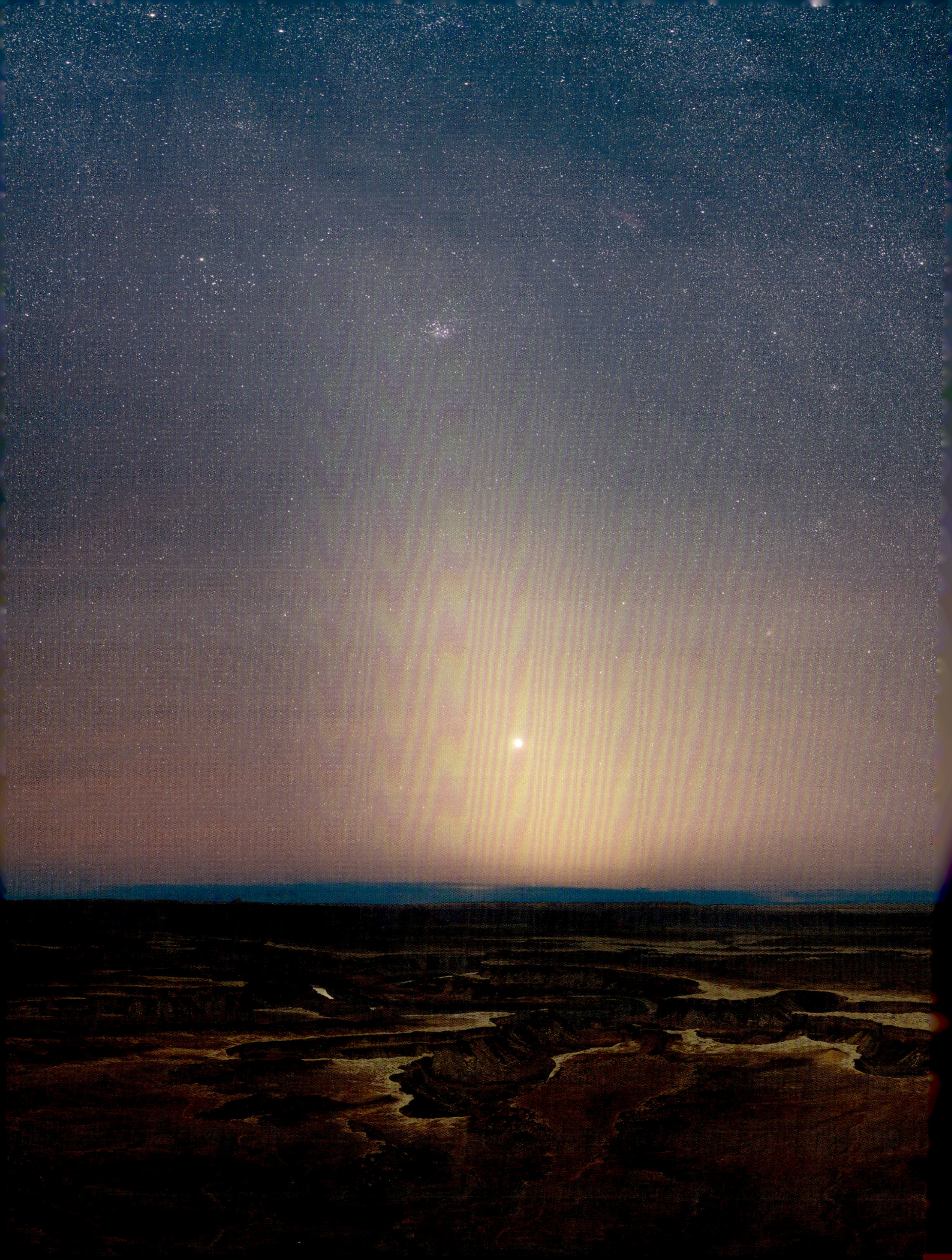

Introduction

Six years have passed since I finished writing the first edition of *Dusk to Dawn: A Guide to Landscape Photography at Night*. During that time, interest in night photography has exploded. Manufacturers have responded by producing still better cameras and lenses. Software developers have created even-better apps both for planning night images and for processing them. My techniques have evolved, and I've tackled exciting new subjects that I didn't discuss in the first edition. It's time for a second edition. Here's what's new.

Mirrorless cameras, while certainly popular in 2017, have now taken the digital-photography world by storm. It's unlikely that any new DSLRs will be introduced by the major manufacturers. The new mirrorless cameras provide night photographers with new capabilities. The last six years have also seen the introduction of a new generation of "focus-by-wire" lenses designed specifically for mirrorless cameras. These new lenses are superb optically, but their design has complicated the problem of focusing at night. This book will cover the best way to focus with these new lenses, including a discussion of Bahtinov masks, focusing aids that can help ensure critically sharp images.

New and improved apps for both desktop computers and mobile devices now make the task of planning night photographs even easier and more fun. For example, you can now open an app in a web browser, select a date, time, and location, and see a realistic 3D model of the land with the position of the sun, moon, and galactic center, the brightest and most photogenic part of the Milky Way, positioned correctly above the land. The model even shows you how the land will be lit by either the sun or moon as you adjust the time, with the intensity of the moonlight adjusted for the phase of the moon and with the color of sunlight adjusted for the time of day. You can now stand at a prospective shooting location, open a different app on your mobile device and see projected on your device's screen a live view of the land in front of you with the starry band of the Milky Way superimposed on the sky as it will appear on the date and time of your choosing. This edition will discuss these amazing new apps in detail.

◄ The zodiacal light, Venus (the bright planet near the center of the frame), and Soda Springs Basin from Murphy Point, Island in the Sky district, Canyonlands National Park, Utah. March 16, 2023, 9:28 p.m. Sony Alpha 7R IVa, Sony FE 35mm f/1.4 GM. Land: one row, three camera positions, four frames per camera position, images stacked in Photoshop, noise reduced with Stack Mode>Median, 40 seconds, f/1.4, ISO 6400. Sky: two rows, three camera positions per row, four frames per camera position, images aligned and noise reduced in RegiStar, 10 seconds, f/1.4, ISO 6400.

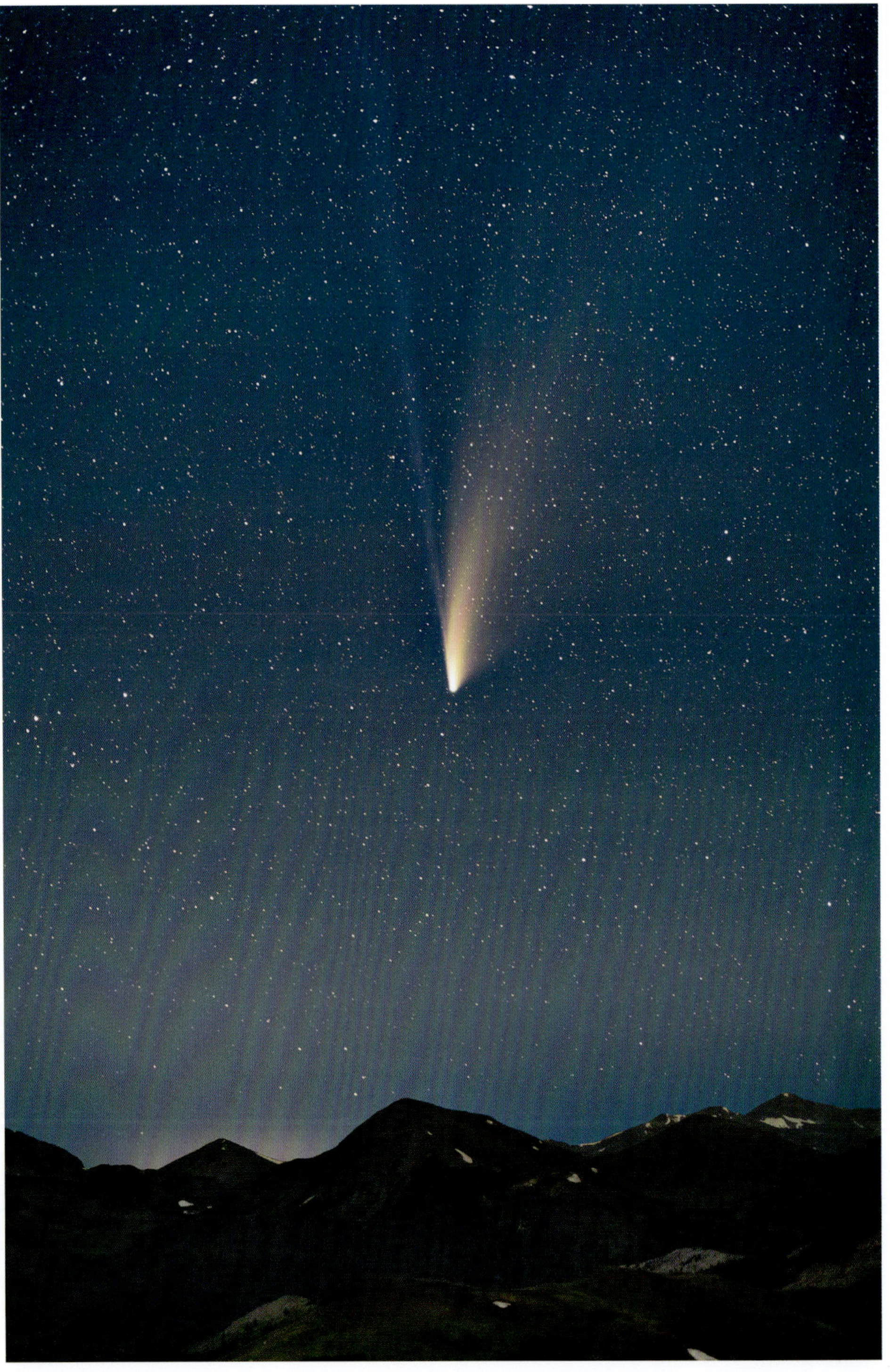

► Comet NEOWISE over the Never Summer Range, Rocky Mountain National Park, Colorado. July 20, 2020, 11:38 p.m. Canon EOS 5D Mark IV, Canon EF 85mm f/1.4L IS USM. Land: four frames, images stacked in Photoshop, noise reduced with Stack Mode>Median, 40 seconds, f/1.4, ISO 6400. Sky: nine images, images aligned and noise reduced in RegiStar, 10 seconds, f/1.4, ISO 6400.

This edition also covers several fascinating subjects for night photographers that the first edition neglected: comets, the zodiacal light, and noctilucent clouds. Bright comets are rare, but contrary to what you might think, a telescope is not necessarily required to photograph them; my best shots of comets were taken with lenses from 35mm to 85mm in focal length. The zodiacal light is a gauzy pyramid of light. In the Northern Hemisphere, it's seen to the west an hour or more after sunset in the spring, and to the east well before dawn in the fall. Noctilucent clouds are shimmering veils of ice crystals that form around particles of meteor dust on the very edge of space. They're found in the mesosphere some 50 miles above the earth's surface. They can only be seen well after sunset or before sunrise, when the sun is 6 to 16 degrees below the horizon.

I've replaced all of the instructional photos in the sections discussing digital noise and dynamic range with photos from the most recent cameras. And I've included all the best new night landscapes I've made over the last six years.

What hasn't changed in the last six years is the lure of exploring a mysterious and fascinating new world with your camera. In the past, landscape photography largely ended when the last light of dusk faded from the sky. Today, it's only beginning. The latest digital cameras have made it easy to create images of the landscape at night that film and early digital photographers could only dream of. Equipped with off-the-shelf cameras, more and more photographers are venturing into the night, far beyond the comforting glow of city lights, and returning with spectacular images unlike anything seen before. *Dusk to Dawn: A Guide to Landscape Photography at Night* is your trail map for this new photographic wilderness. In addition to the topics I mention above, it will teach you how to plan, shoot, and process professional-quality images of the Milky Way, auroras, lunar eclipses, meteor showers, star trails, and landscapes lit solely by moonlight. Throughout the book, I'll emphasize ways to integrate beautiful depictions of the night sky with equally compelling renditions of the land below it to create landscape images that evoke a sense of place—and a sense of wonder. Equipped with the knowledge in this book, readers will be prepared to create their own nocturnal masterpieces.

I clearly remember my own introduction to the amazing capabilities of these new cameras. It was August 2012. I was about three-quarters of the way through my "Sunrise from the Summit" project, a seven-year quest to photograph sunrise (or occasionally sunset) from the summit of all 54 of Colorado's Fourteeners, peaks reaching 14,000 feet in height. Now it was time to put my new digital SLR, a Canon 5D Mark III, to the test on a very different kind of image: a shot of the Milky Way taken from the summit of 14,267-foot Torreys Peak.

I waited for a day with good weather that would be followed by a night with no moon. When a weather window arrived, I drove to the trailhead in the afternoon and hiked the steep, strenuous trail to the summit. I met a few people heading down as I was heading up, but when I reached the summit, I was alone. I shot sunset, then settled down to wait, trying hard to stifle an instinctive sense of unease. Old mountaineering habits die hard, and I'd never deliberately lingered on the summit of a high peak as the light vanished from the sky. Slowly, the few remaining clouds dissipated, and the stars began to come out. Then the glowing heart of the Milky Way, the center of our galaxy, emerged from the darkening sky directly over Grays Peak, another Fourteener.

Never before had I seen the most spectacular part of the Milky Way from such a dark and elevated perch. The sight was breathtaking. I left the summit about midnight as the best part of the Milky Way set to the southwest. Two hours later, I reached my truck. Two hours after that, I collapsed into bed after a 21-hour day.

I examined my images later that afternoon and saw for myself how the latest generation of digital cameras had opened up a whole new photographic genre: landscape photography at night. Images that were close to impossible in the film era were now within the grasp of any knowledgeable and reasonably well-equipped photographer willing to venture into the dark. Today, as I look back at the images from that first effort, I can see how improved cameras and lenses, better software, and a deeper knowledge of planning, shooting, and processing night images (all of which are described in this book) would allow me to make a much better image from the same location.

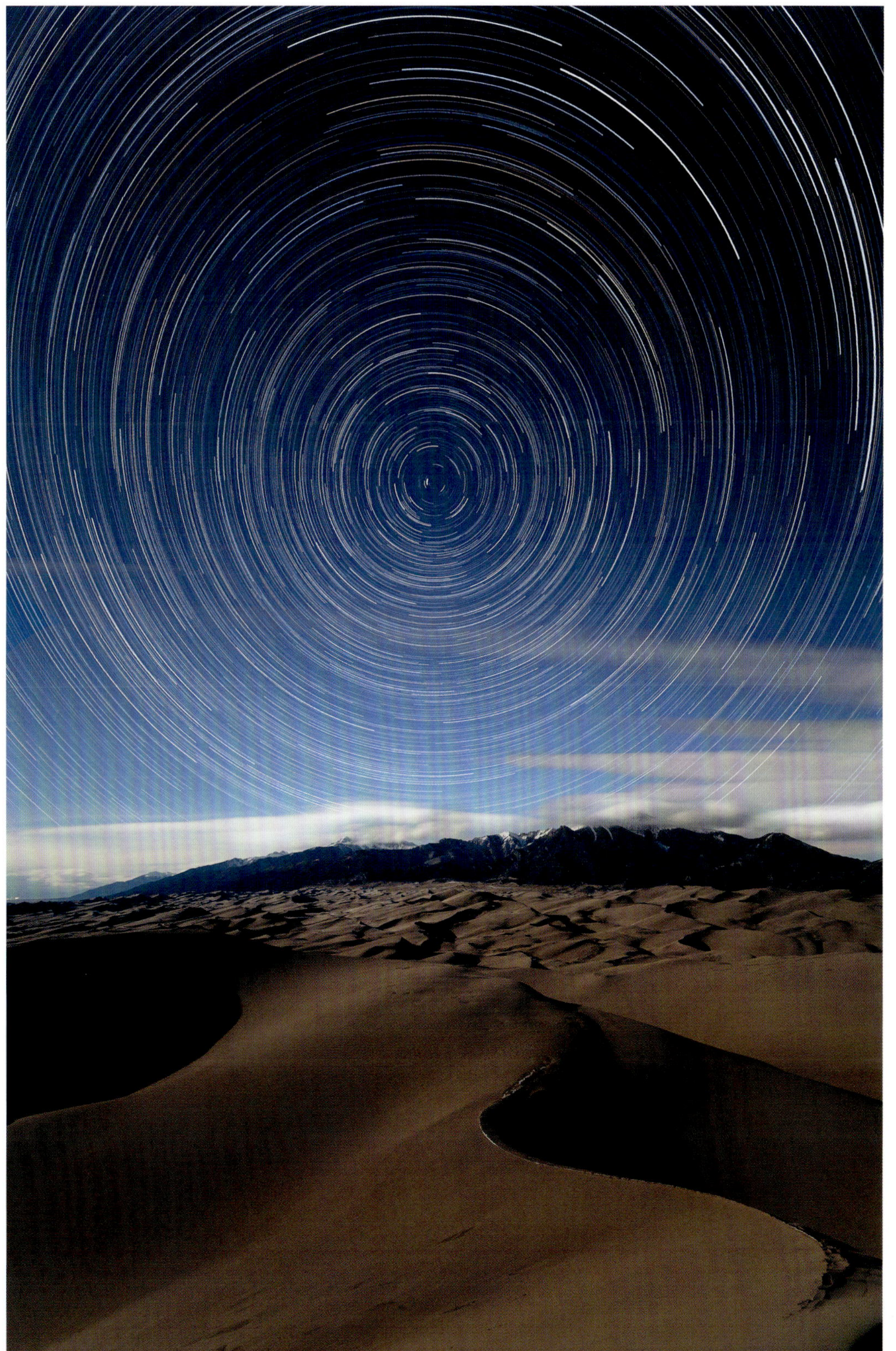

◄ Star trails over the moonlit Sangre de Cristo Range from High Dune, Great Sand Dunes National Park, Colorado. December 13, 2016, 1:57 a.m. to 5:00 a.m. Canon EOS 5D Mark III, Canon EF 16-35mm f/2.8L III USM at 16mm. 291 frames, 30 seconds, f/2.8, ISO 400. A full moon (over 99 percent illuminated) provided the light on the land.

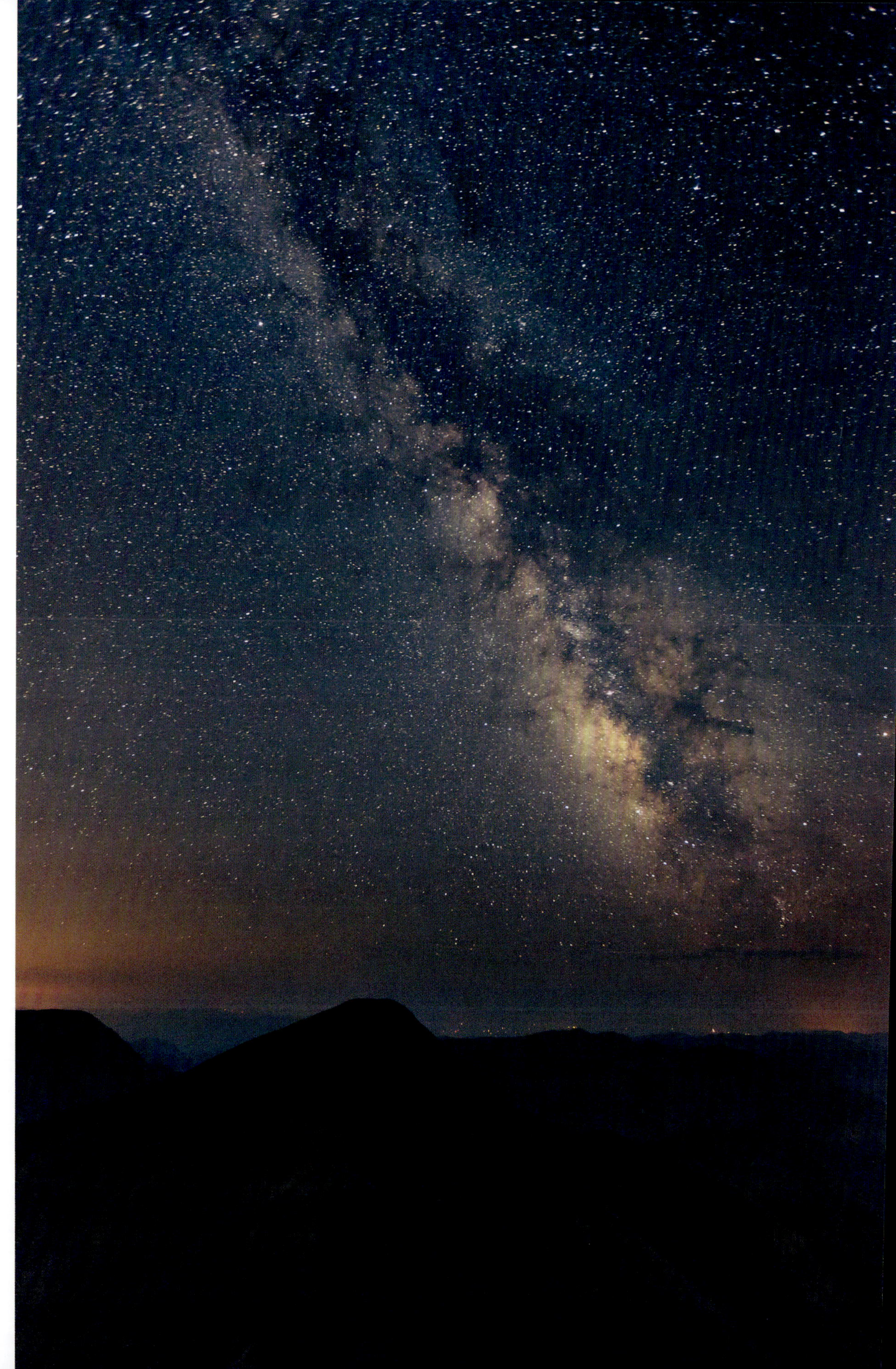

This book will prepare you for your first photographic journey into the night and for many adventures beyond that. It is not, however, a book for complete beginners. I'll assume readers know the fundamentals of photography and the basics of image storage, organization, and editing. I use Adobe Lightroom Classic (the desktop version) for cataloging and RAW editing, and Adobe Photoshop for more advanced techniques like combining two different exposures of the same scene. I'll show you how to use those two programs to perfect your night images, but this book will not be a complete guide to either program. I will provide sidebars on some key topics to help bring less-experienced readers up to speed.

This book details techniques for shooting grand landscapes at night. These are images where the land and sky are equally significant. This book will not cover astrophotography, the proper name for photographs of deep-space objects taken through telescopes. Astrophotography is a specialty all its own. It requires a significant additional investment in hardware. If you have a relatively recent DSLR or mirrorless camera, a fairly fast, wide-angle lens, and a tripod, on the other hand, you can probably get started in night photography without purchasing any additional equipment.

Your photographic voyages of exploration will be more successful if you have a clear sense of your destination. For daylight landscape photography, my destination always seemed obvious: an authentic image that captured the magnificence of the natural world the way I saw it. I wanted my viewers to know that what they saw in my prints was what I saw through the lens. When I began photographing at night, however, I realized that my photographic path had grown misty. My eyes, no matter how well dark-adapted they were, could barely glimpse the colors and details my camera so easily recorded. Should I suppress those colors and create near-monochrome images that resembled what I actually saw? Or should I celebrate the camera's ability to reveal an unseen world and show night scenes in color as the camera recorded them? I experimented with desaturating my night images or converting them to black-and-white and concluded that while they might be closer to a literal representation of what I saw, they came nowhere close to evoking the emotions I felt when I was standing there.

◄ The Milky Way over 14,270-foot Grays Peak, seen from the summit of 14,267-foot Torreys Peak, near Georgetown, Colorado. August 8, 2012, 10:07 p.m. Canon 5D Mark III, Canon EF 16-35mm f/2.8L II USM at 16mm. 30 seconds, f/2.8, ISO 6400.

I returned to the idea of rendering night scenes in color, but quickly ran into another conundrum. The colors my camera recorded sometimes seemed jarringly out of sync with what I imagined those colors ought to be. We all have a lifelong association of the sky with the color blue. Sky blue is a memory color, one of those colors where we tend to substitute what we want to see (e.g., an idealized, pure blue) for what we actually saw. It's also a color we tend to have strong opinions about in terms of what looks "right." Look straight up on a clear day at noon and the sky is always some shade of blue. Look straight up as the light fades from a clear sky after sunset and the last color we see is blue. When light returns with the onset of dawn, the first color we see in the sky straight above us is blue. Naturally, we imagine that the night sky must be blue, even if we can't actually see the color. Indeed, on a night with a full moon, the sky really is blue, and your camera will record it as such. On a moonless night, however, the sky is not blue. Its exact color varies, depending on atmospheric conditions and the distance to major cities, but it is often some shade of green. You may be shocked at the color of the sky that your camera records on a moonless night since it is so wildly at odds with what a lifetime on this planet would lead you to expect. Do you continue to celebrate your camera's ability to record the unseen, or do you change the color of the sky to the blue you were expecting, a color that feels "right"?

These are tough questions that I will answer in detail later. For now, I'll leave you with this thought: photographing in color at night is like shooting in black-and-white during the day. It is an inherently subjective process. At high noon, what shade of gray should the sky be? Any shade of gray that looks good! At midnight, what shade of blue should the sky be? You can't see the color of the midnight sky, so you once again have broad artistic latitude.

My goal when shooting at night is to create an image that captures the feeling I had as I stood there under a magnificent starry sky. You can choose to follow my lead or take a different path entirely. Regardless of your decision, I promise that your journey into the night will be an exciting and rewarding adventure.

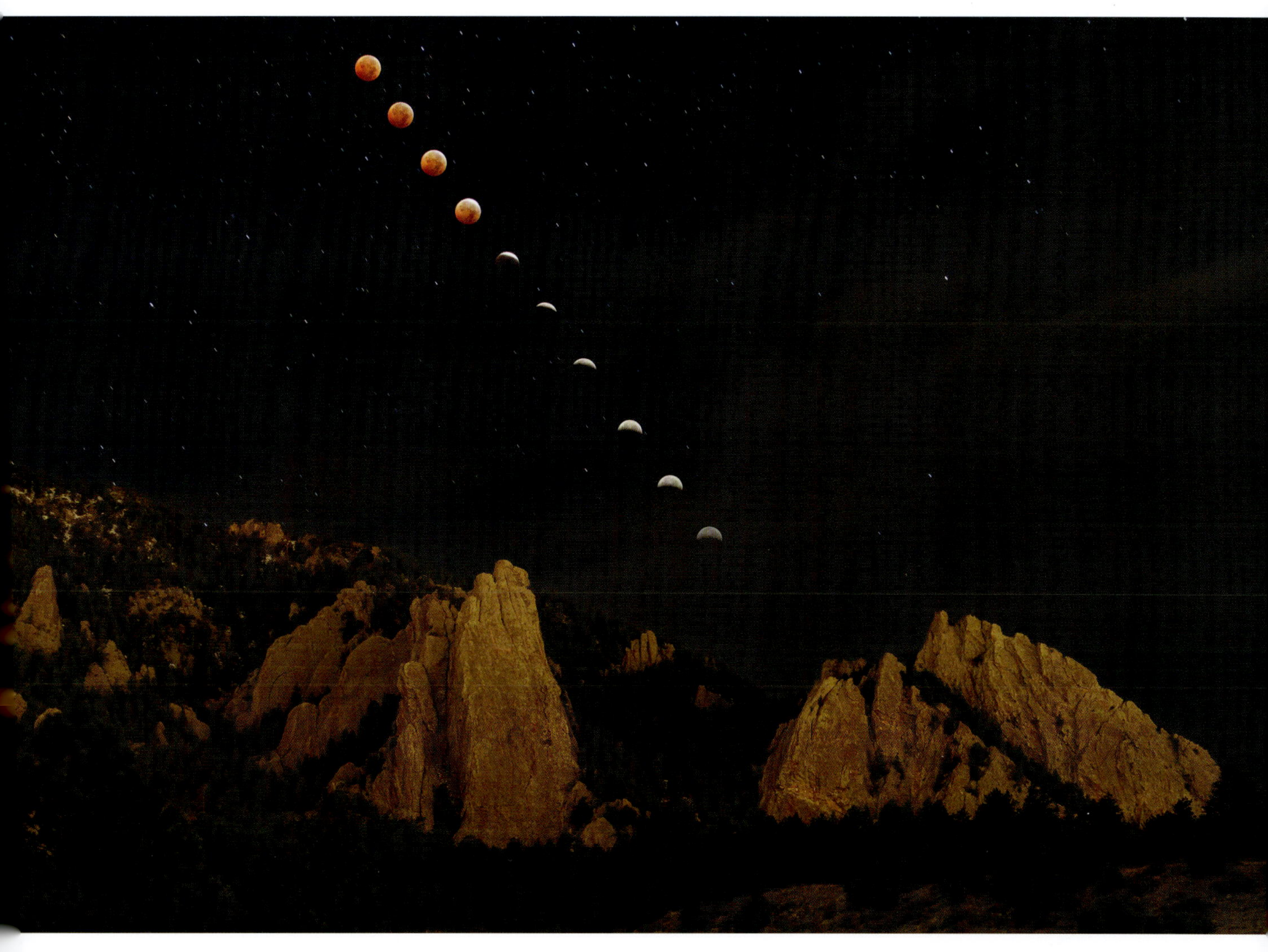

▲ Lunar eclipse over the Flatirons, Boulder Mountain Park, near Boulder, Colorado. November 8, 2022, 4:31 a.m. to 5:26 a.m. Sony Alpha 7R IVa, Canon EF 70-200mm f/4L IS USM at 70mm with Metabones EF-E mount T adapter (fifth generation). Land and sky: 15 seconds, f/4.0, ISO 3200. The city lights provided the light on the land. Moon: 12 moon images, with exposures ranging from 4 seconds, f/11, ISO 800 (moon fully eclipsed) to ¼th, f/11, ISO 200 (moon partially eclipsed). The setting moon vanished into thickening clouds near the horizon shortly after I made the lowest moon exposure.

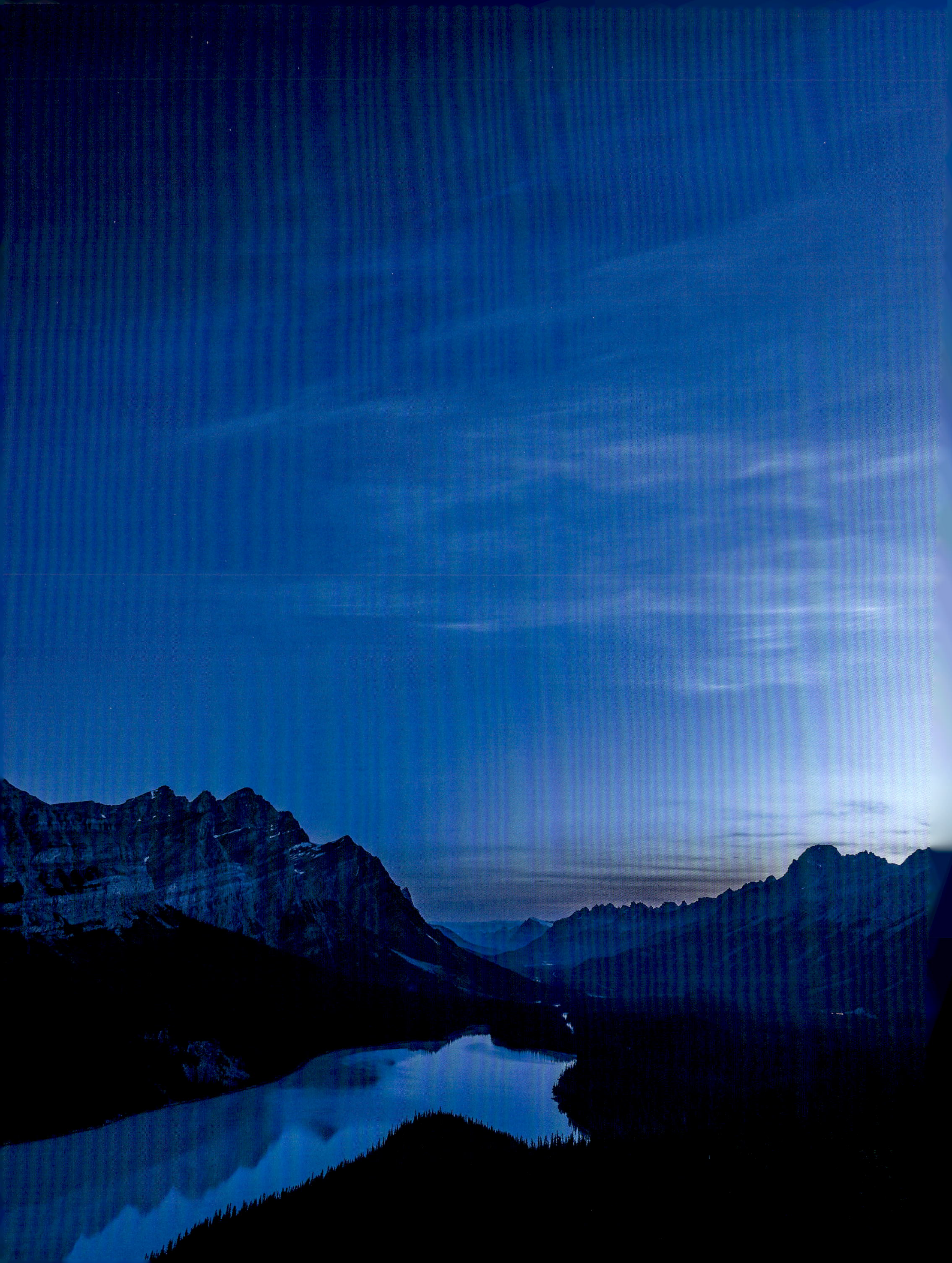

Preparing for Night Photography

For many people, the idea of photographing at night is intimidating. We all have an instinctive fear of the dark. Making the best photographs of the night sky requires getting away from city lights—and all the services cities provide. Some good locations for night photography can be reached by road, but many of the best locations can only be reached by hiking. The prospect of even a short hike at night can be frightening if you've never done it before. With the right preparation and equipment, however, your journey into the night can be magical rather than scary.

Hiking at Night

One of the best ways to reduce fear is to visit prospective shooting locations in daylight. Seeing a location at high noon makes shooting there at night seem a lot more feasible. While you're scouting, look for hazards that might be less obvious at night, such as cliff edges or the slippery embankments of streams. Pay close attention to landmarks along the trail leading to your location. Remember that you don't have eyes in the back of your head. The trail will look very different on the return trip than it did when you were hiking to your shooting location. Turn around periodically during the hike to your shooting location and memorize what key junctions and landmarks will look like when heading back to your car. Learn how to use a compass and a detailed topographic map, and always carry these items with you. If you own a GPS receiver, record a waypoint at your vehicle, at key junctions, and at your shooting location. There are many good smartphone apps these days that can provide similar capabilities. Just be sure to conserve battery power so you'll have it when you really need it. If reaching your shooting location requires traveling off-trail at night, the demands on your navigational skills will increase tenfold. Regardless of your destination, be sure to let someone know where you are going and when you plan to return. For a detailed discussion of wilderness navigation, including the use of altimeters and GPS receivers, see my book, *Outward Bound Map & Compass Handbook, Fourth Edition*, published by Falcon Guides.

◄ FIGURE 1-1: Noctilucent clouds over Mt. Patterson and Peyto Lake, Banff National Park, Canada. July 3, 2023, 4:27 a.m. (1 hour 7 minutes before sunrise; solar depression angle 8 degrees). Sony Alpha 7R IVa, Sony Vario-Tessar T* FE 16–35 mm f/4 ZA OSS at 16mm. 1.6 seconds, f/4.0, ISO 100.

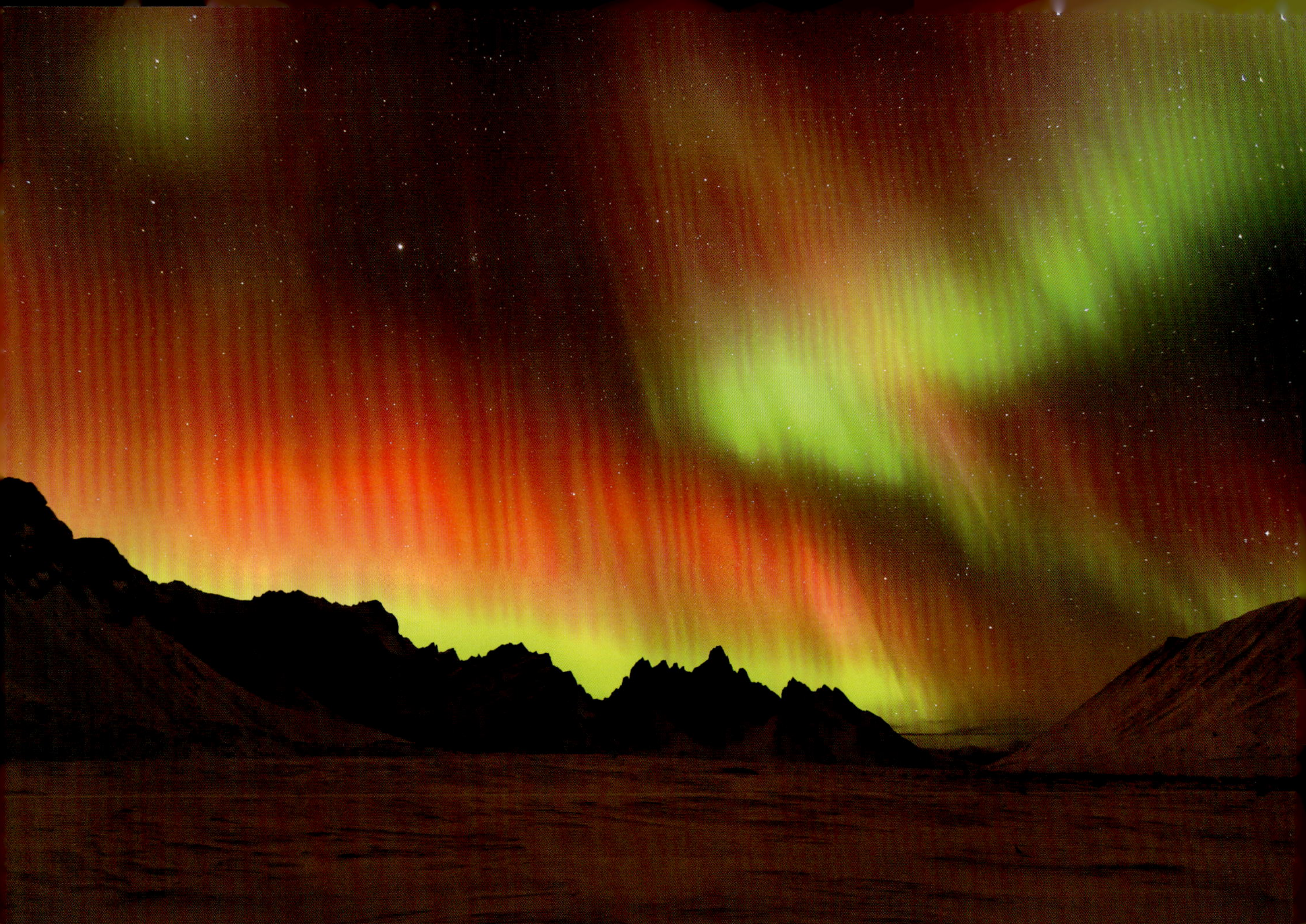

Whenever possible, bring a companion when shooting at night. Simply the sound of another human voice is very reassuring when you're startled by a dry branch cracking underfoot. Two heads are better than one when you need to assess risks and weigh the best approach to problems that may arise. Having a companion can help if you sprain an ankle or twist a knee. And from a photographic perspective, two photographers working together can share ideas about composition and technical tips on camera settings.

If you're hiking by yourself or traveling into really remote country, consider buying a personal locator beacon. These small, battery-driven devices can broadcast an emergency distress signal, along with your GPS coordinates, to a network of satellites. No cellular service is required. From there, the SOS goes to a central clearinghouse, then on to the nearest search-and-rescue team. I've been routinely carrying an emergency locator beacon for many years. My current unit, a Garmin GPSMAP 66i, combines full-fledged GPS navigational capabilities with two-way satellite communication via short texts. It also gives me detailed, hour-by-hour weather forecasts for my current location.

When the terrain is rough, turn back the evolutionary clock and reinvent yourself as a quadruped by using a pair of trekking poles. I've been hiking with trekking poles, day and night, for more than 20 years. They help prevent tripping and make it far easier to rock-hop across streams. They also reduce wear-and-tear on your knees and transfer some of the effort of hiking uphill to your arms and shoulders. On many occasions, using trekking poles has saved me from twisting my ankles, skinning my knees, and soaking my feet.

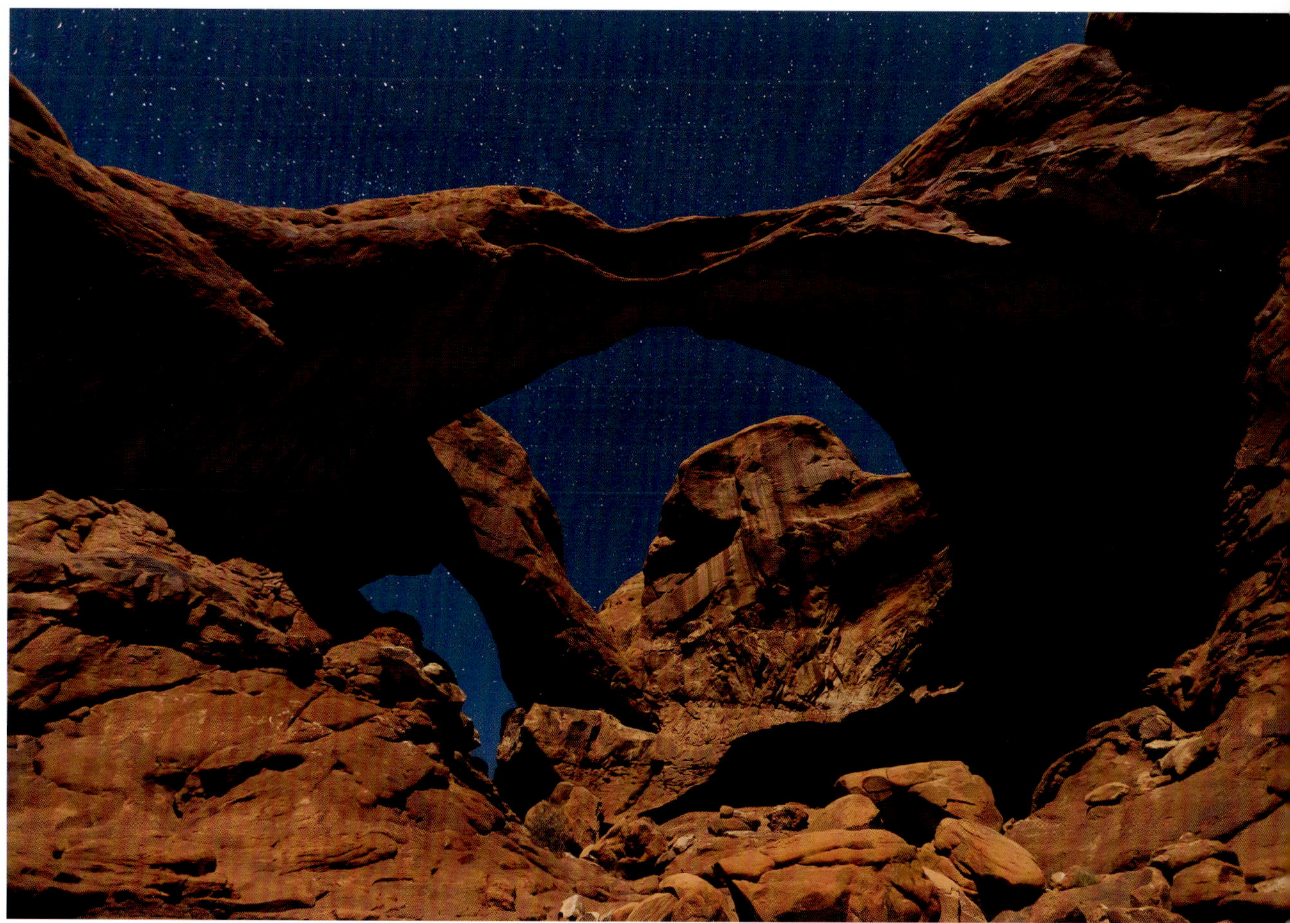

▲ FIGURE 1-3: Double Arch by moonlight, Arches National Park, Utah. November 8, 2008, 7:38 p.m. Canon EOS 5D Mark III, Canon EF 16-35mm f/2.8L II USM at 16mm. 20 seconds, f/2.8, ISO 1600. A waxing gibbous moon (78 percent illuminated) provided the light on the land.

A bright headlamp is another important piece of safety equipment for night photography. I use a model that will throw a usable beam of light for 100 yards with fresh batteries. When traveling by myself, I always carry a smaller backup headlamp for emergencies. Nothing dispels irrational fears about imaginary lions, tigers, and bears faster than the ability to see clearly what's out there in the dark. Headlamps are better than flashlights for hiking at night and night photography because they leave your hands free to handle trekking poles or camera gear. They do have one disadvantage, however. Having the light source right near your eyes creates a nearly shadow-free light no matter which way you look. Our visual system needs shadows to see dimension and depth. If you find that you're having a hard time seeing the bumps and hollows along a particularly difficult section of the trail with the headlamp on your head, try carrying the headlamp in your hand. Better yet, wear the headlamp on your head and clip a second light, such as a bike light, to your belt. Positioning a light source away from your eyes will produce the shadows that reveal the contours of the trail clearly. I'll have more to say about the specifics of choosing a headlamp in the next chapter.

An attack by a wild animal is a common fear for novice night hikers (and photographers). It's also one of the most irrational. I've been banging around in the mountains and deserts of Colorado and Utah for nearly 50 years and have yet to feel threatened by a mountain lion or black bear. In fact, my scariest wildlife encounter involved neither. I was hiking out from Lost Remuda Basin in the Maroon Bells-Snowmass Wilderness, alone, at night, when I was suddenly terrified by the thunder of pounding hooves. An entire herd of elk had bedded down next to the trail and been spooked by my approach. The herd leaped to its feet and sprinted across the trail in front of me. I was astonished that elk could run so fast in the dark without breaking their legs. When the last elk crossed the trail, I resumed my solitary trek back to my tent, my heart still thumping loudly in my chest.

The threat from wild animals is not zero, but it is much smaller than most people imagine. Approximately 27 people have been killed by mountain lions in North America since 1868, according to Wikipedia. Wild black bears killed about nine people and grizzlies killed about 17 in the 2010s in North America, again according to Wikipedia. While that may sound alarming, you need to keep that in perspective. For example, only eight people have been killed by bears (seven grizzly-bear attacks, one undetermined attack) in Yellowstone National Park since its establishment in 1868, according to the National Park Service. During that time, over 191 million people have visited the park. To further put that in perspective, on average about 28 people were killed by lightning *every year* from 2006 to 2021, according to a report from the Centers for Disease Control. Now, I grant you that grizzlies are more dangerous than black bears. If you plan to shoot at night in grizzly country, extra precautions are advisable. Travel in a group, make lots of noise to avoid startling a bear, and carry bear spray. However, grizzlies are only found in Alaska, Canada, and parts of the northern Rocky Mountains, and they're only active in the warmer months. You have nothing to fear if you're shooting the aurora in mid-winter.

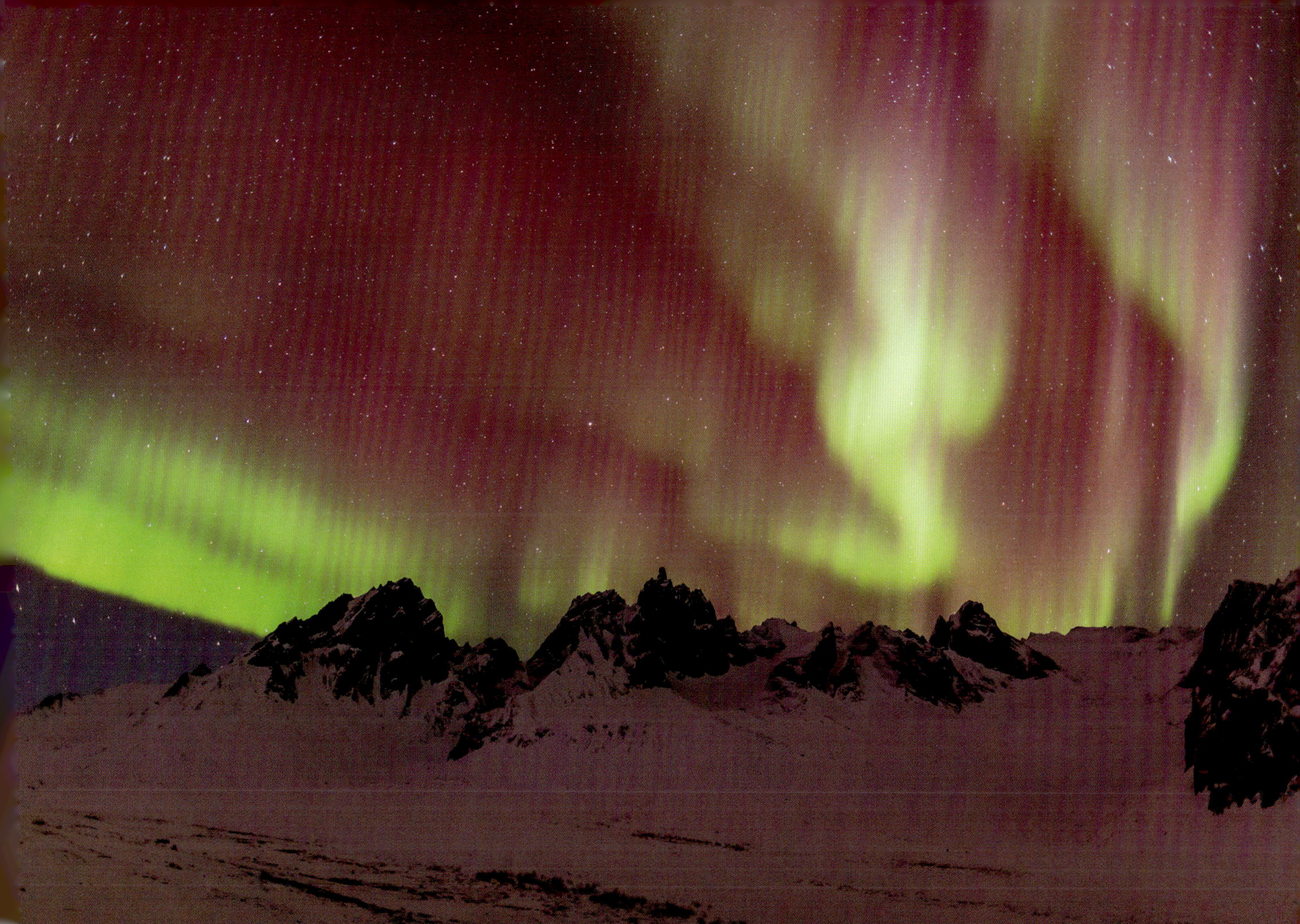

Staying safe at night includes learning to stay warm. Novice night photographers frequently underestimate how cold it will feel working under the stars. Your body produces about five times as much heat when you're moving at a sustainable pace as when you're standing still. Standing around for hours next to your tripod can be chilly. Even on a cold day, sunlight warms you more than you realize. Without sunlight, the same temperature feels much colder. On clear nights, without clouds to hold in the earth's heat, the temperature plunges after sunset. Of course, those are the very nights when you're most likely to be shooting.

Staying warm starts with bringing more clothes than you think you'll need. Be sure to insulate your head and neck as well as your torso. I like wearing a fleece hat, a hooded fleece garment, and a down jacket with hood, in addition to whatever other layers I need. Keeping your head and neck warm is that important. Be sure you also insulate your legs. Don't make the mistake of thinking you can throw a warm jacket over a pair of blue jeans and stay warm in temperatures below freezing. You need multiple layers on your legs as well as your torso when the temperature plunges. Even a little

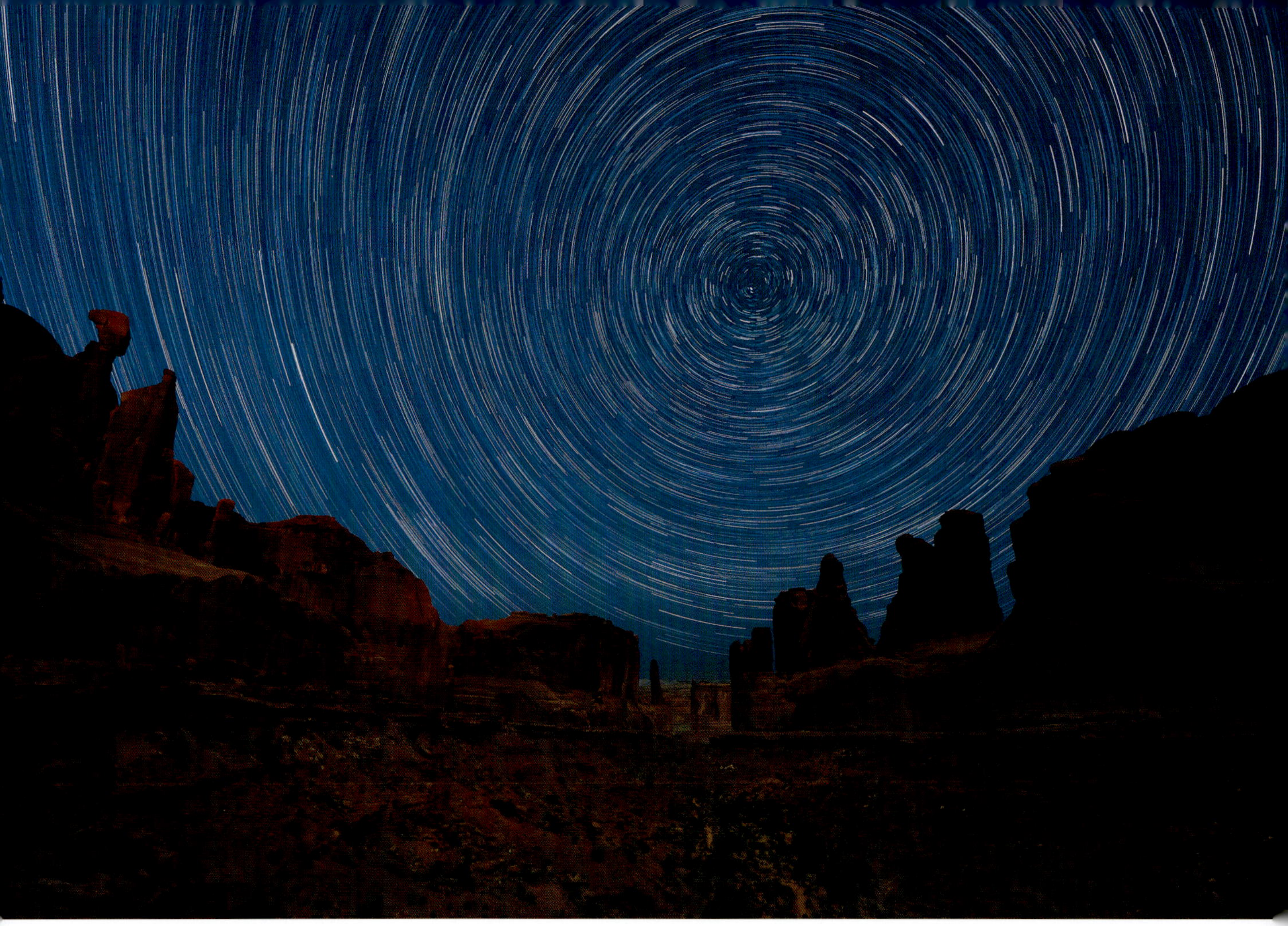

▲ Figure 1-5: Star trails over Park Avenue, Arches National Park, Utah. April 19, 2023, 10:37 p.m. to 11:37 p.m. Sony Alpha 7R IVa, Sony FE 14mm f/1.8 GM. Land: four frames, images stacked in Photoshop, noise reduced with Stack Mode>Median, 1 minute, f/1.8, ISO 6400. Sky: 31 frames, 2 minutes, f/2.8, ISO 400.

bit of wind makes a big difference at night. Bring windproof layers for both your legs and your torso.

Be sure to regulate your temperature when hiking to your destination so that you don't work up a sweat. That sweat will evaporate and chill you to the bone the moment you stop moving. The fastest way to get cold is to get too hot first. Always stop and peel off a layer at the first sign of perspiration.

There is no such thing as gloves that are both thin enough to let you push your camera's buttons easily and thick enough to keep your fingers toasty in sub-zero weather. My solution is to wear heavy gloves and bring an unsharpened, new pencil with a good eraser. Before your trip, drill a hole through the leaded end and tie a thin piece of string through the hole so you can hang the pencil from your tripod. It's easy, even with heavy gloves on, to use the eraser end of the pencil to push a button. Heavy gloves do allow you enough dexterity to spin the dials found on most modern cameras. I made it easier to use my wired cable release with heavy gloves on by gluing a short piece of dowel rod to the shutter-release button. With patience and practice, and with the possible exception of changing batteries and memory cards, you can do almost an entire shoot while wearing heavy gloves. I also always put chemical hand warmers inside my gloves if the temperature is below zero.

You can keep the trigger end of a wired cable release handy by attaching some peel-and-stick hook-and-loop (Velcro is the most common brand name) to the back of your cable release and attaching the mating part of the hook-and-loop to the top of a tripod leg. That way you can park the cable release on your tripod to keep it in easy reach rather than letting it dangle and get tangled around a tripod leg or get damaged by mud, sand, or water.

No matter how much clothing you're wearing, it's hard to stay warm if you neglect basic body maintenance. Don't hike so hard that you exhaust yourself. Bring snacks to stay fueled and enough fluids to stay hydrated. If you're shooting near your car, bring a thermos of hot coffee or tea. On a cold night, hot liquids are the nectar of the gods. If you get up at 2 a.m. to shoot, you *deserve* two breakfasts. One final tip: never eat breakfast before midnight. If you have to get up before midnight to get the shot, eat dessert.

Before leaving your shooting location, inspect the ground carefully for small items you might have dropped that could easily get overlooked in the dark.

Don't forget to build recovery time into your trip planning. Staying up all night is debilitating. Allow time for a nap during the day after your shoot.

▾ Figure 1-6: Milky Way over the Rock Cut, near Trail Ridge Road, Rocky Mountain National Park, Colorado. July 1, 2017, 2:56 a.m. Canon 5D Mark III, Canon EF 16-35mm f/2.8L III USM at 20mm. Land: four frames stacked in Photoshop, noise reduced with Stack Mode>Median, 2 minutes, f/2.8, ISO 6400. Sky: two rows, one camera position per row, four frames per camera position, camera mounted on iOptron SkyTracker Pro equatorial mount, images aligned and noise reduced in RegiStar, 2 minutes, f/2.8, ISO 1600.

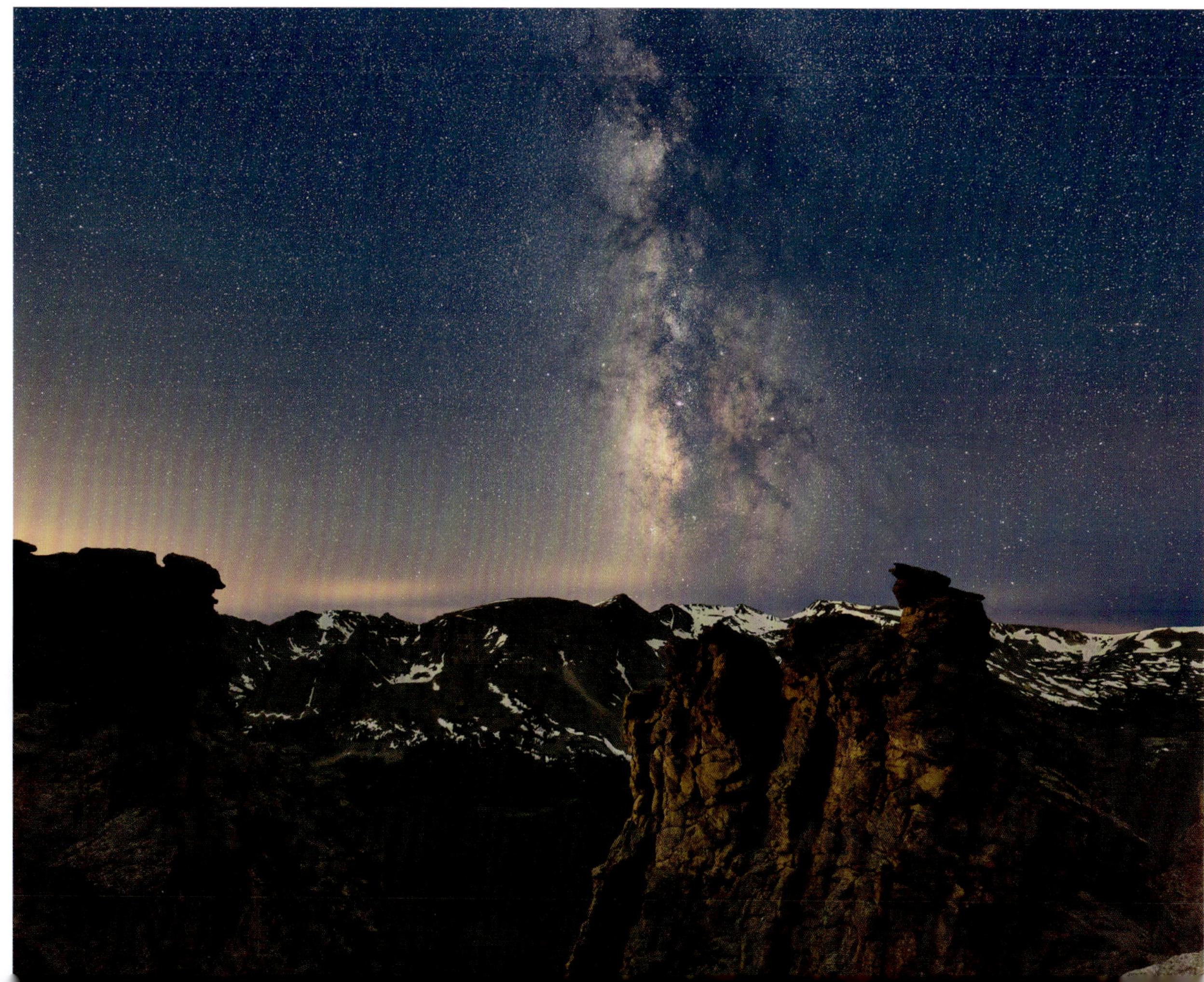

Finding Clear, Dark Skies

Making great night images requires getting as far away from city lights as possible. A number of websites publish maps that use a color-coded scale to indicate the amount of light pollution in a location. A search for "maps of light pollution" should kick out the ones that are currently available. If possible, plan your shoot to be looking away from major cities. The light dome of a big metropolitan area can easily be visible on the horizon from 50 miles away or more. Clouds over the city will be lit from below by the city lights, brightening the sky in that direction further.

▾ Figure 1-7: Aurora over the Tombstone Range, Tombstone Territorial Park, Yukon Territory, Canada. March 19, 2015, 12:06 a.m. Canon EOS 5D Mark III, Canon EF 16-35mm f/2.8L II USM at 35mm. 2 seconds, f/2.8, ISO 3200.

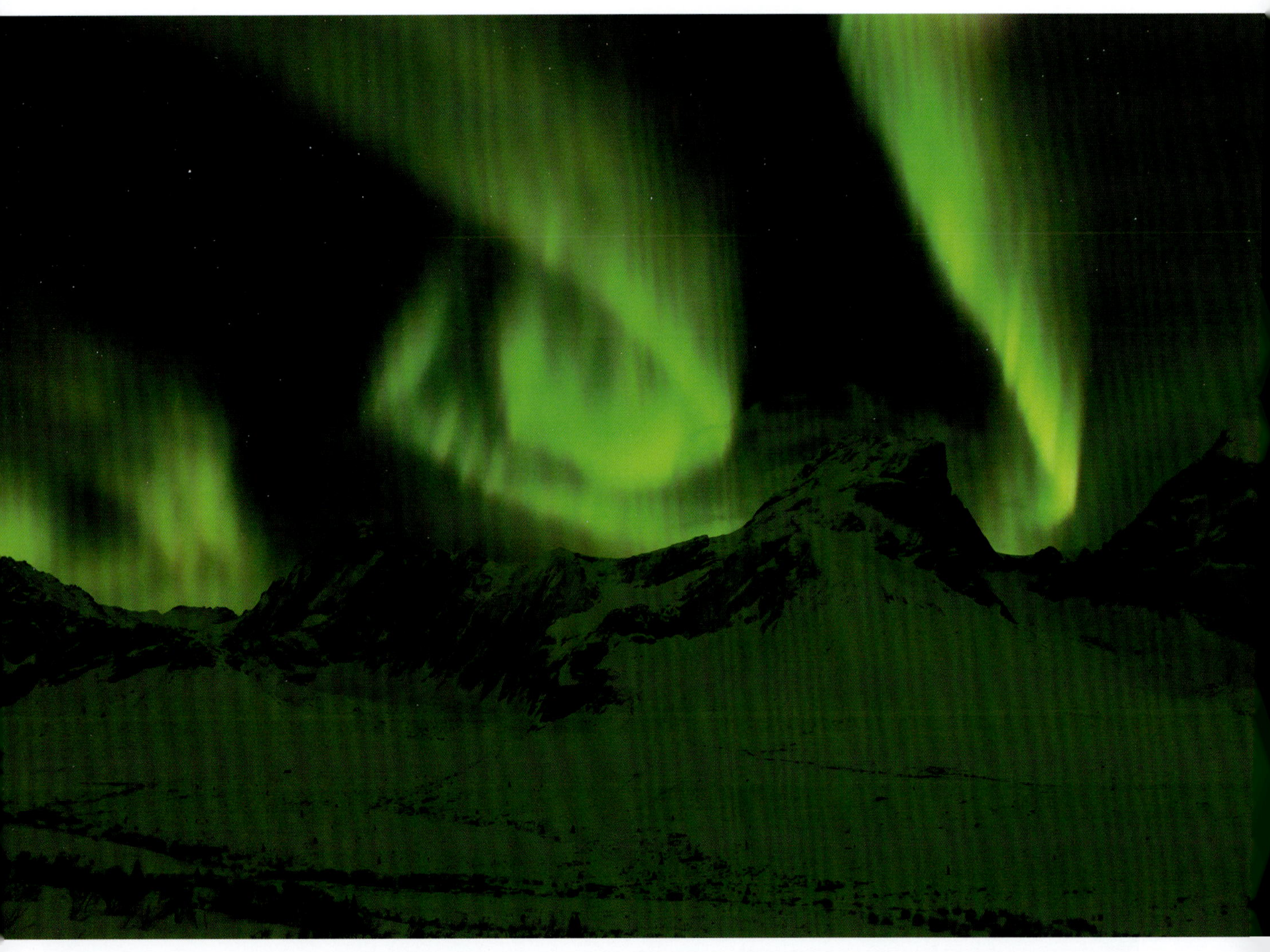

Once you've identified a promising dark-sky location, check the weather forecast. Partly cloudy skies can work at night, particularly if the moon will be illuminating those clouds. Most of the time, however, you'll be looking for clear skies and brilliant stars. There are many weather sites on the internet these days, but I like to go to the horse's mouth: the National Weather Service (NWS). I particularly like the point forecasts it makes available. These are forecasts for very small geographic areas, as small as a square measuring 1½ miles on each side. In level country, the forecast will probably differ very little over a distance of a few miles. In mountainous country, however, a distance of a few miles horizontally can be the difference between a valley floor at 7,000 feet and the summit of a Fourteener. From a weather perspective, those two locations might as well be on different planets.

As of this writing, you can find the home page for the NWS at www.weather.gov. If that URL no longer works, search for "National Weather Service." On the home page, look for the local forecast search box and enter a city and state or a zip code. Next, locate the map with a green square showing the region for which the forecast is valid. Scroll across the map and click to reset the green square on a new region of interest, such as a nearby mountain. Dig a little deeper on the local forecast page and you can find a link to an hourly weather forecast, complete with graphs showing temperature, wind speed, chance of precipitation, and, most importantly for our purposes, what percentage of the sky will be covered by clouds—all on an hour-by-hour basis. Clouds are notoriously hard to predict, so don't be surprised if the actual cloud cover differs somewhat from the forecast. Remember that you don't need perfectly clear skies in every direction to get good images. A forecast for anything less than 20 or 30 percent cloud cover will give you a reasonable chance of success.

For a second opinion on likely sky conditions, consult a specialized astronomer's forecast, available at a number of sites on the web. One of the most comprehensive is www.cleardarksky.com. It offers forecasts for thousands of sites in the United States, Canada, and parts of Mexico. In addition to forecasting the percentage of cloud cover, it offers forecasts for transparency and seeing. Transparency is just what it sounds like: the opacity of the atmosphere from the ground to outer space. It is primarily related to the moisture content of the air. Seeing refers to the amount of turbulence in the atmosphere, which is related to wind speed and temperature differences. Both transparency and seeing are very important to astronomers trying to photograph faint, low-contrast objects with large telescopes. They are of much less importance to photographers shooting wide-field landscape photographs at night. In my experience, the cloud-cover forecasts on cleardarksky.com tend to be rather optimistic, while the NWS's cloud-cover forecasts are sometimes excessively glum.

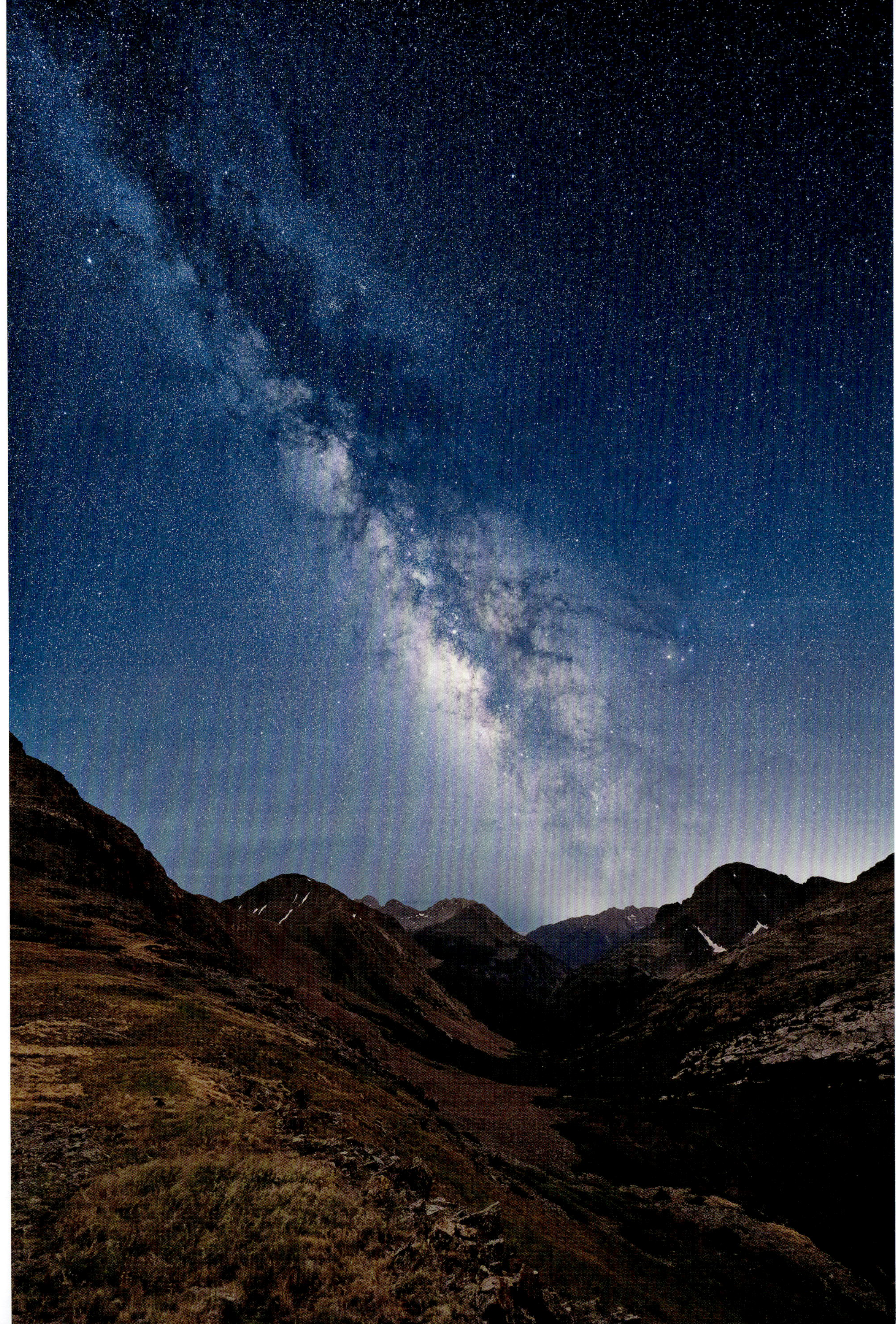

Now that you've located a dark location and identified a promising weather window, you need to decide what time of night to visit. Astronomers define three different types of twilight, with specific times that mark the end of one period and the beginning of the next. These times are called civil, nautical, and astronomical dusk (or dawn).

At the middle latitudes, civil dusk occurs about 30 minutes after sunset when the sun is six degrees below the horizon. It marks the end of civil twilight and is often the time when you are required to turn on your car's headlights. Nautical dusk, the end of nautical twilight, occurs about an hour after sunset when the sun is 12 degrees below the horizon. At nautical dusk, sailors can no longer distinguish water from sky at the horizon. Astronomical dusk, the end of astronomical twilight, occurs about an hour and a half after sunset when the sun is 18 degrees below the horizon. It marks the time when the sky becomes as dark as it is going to get and astronomers can start observing.

Many phone and tablet apps and websites list the times of the various types of dusk. The cycle repeats itself in reverse as dawn approaches. Some night subjects, such as noctilucent clouds (wispy, shimmering clouds 50 miles above earth's surface, visible only from high latitudes) can be photographed as soon as civil dusk arrives. Most, however, are best shot between astronomical dusk and dawn, when the sky is as dark as possible.

The final consideration when planning a night shoot is moon phase. The same apps that give you the times of civil, nautical, and astronomical dusk will also give you the times and directions of moonrise and moonset, as well as the percentage of the moon's surface that is illuminated. Some night subjects, such as the Milky Way, comets, and meteor showers, are best photographed when the moon is below the horizon. Others, such as the aurora, star trails, and, of course, moonlit landscapes, can be shot when the moon is visible. Lunar eclipses only occur when the moon is full. I'll have more to say about moon phase when I discuss each nocturnal subject in detail.

◄ FIGURE 1-8: Milky Way over the valley of Vallecito Creek from Hunchback Pass, Weminuche Wilderness, Colorado. August 7, 2023, 9:54 p.m. Sony Alpha 7R IVa, Sony FE 14mm f/1.8 GM. Land: four frames, images stacked in Photoshop, noise reduced with Stack Mode>Median, 1 minute, f/1.8, ISO 6400. Sky: 20 frames, images aligned and noise reduced in RegiStar, 6 seconds, f/1.8, ISO 6400.

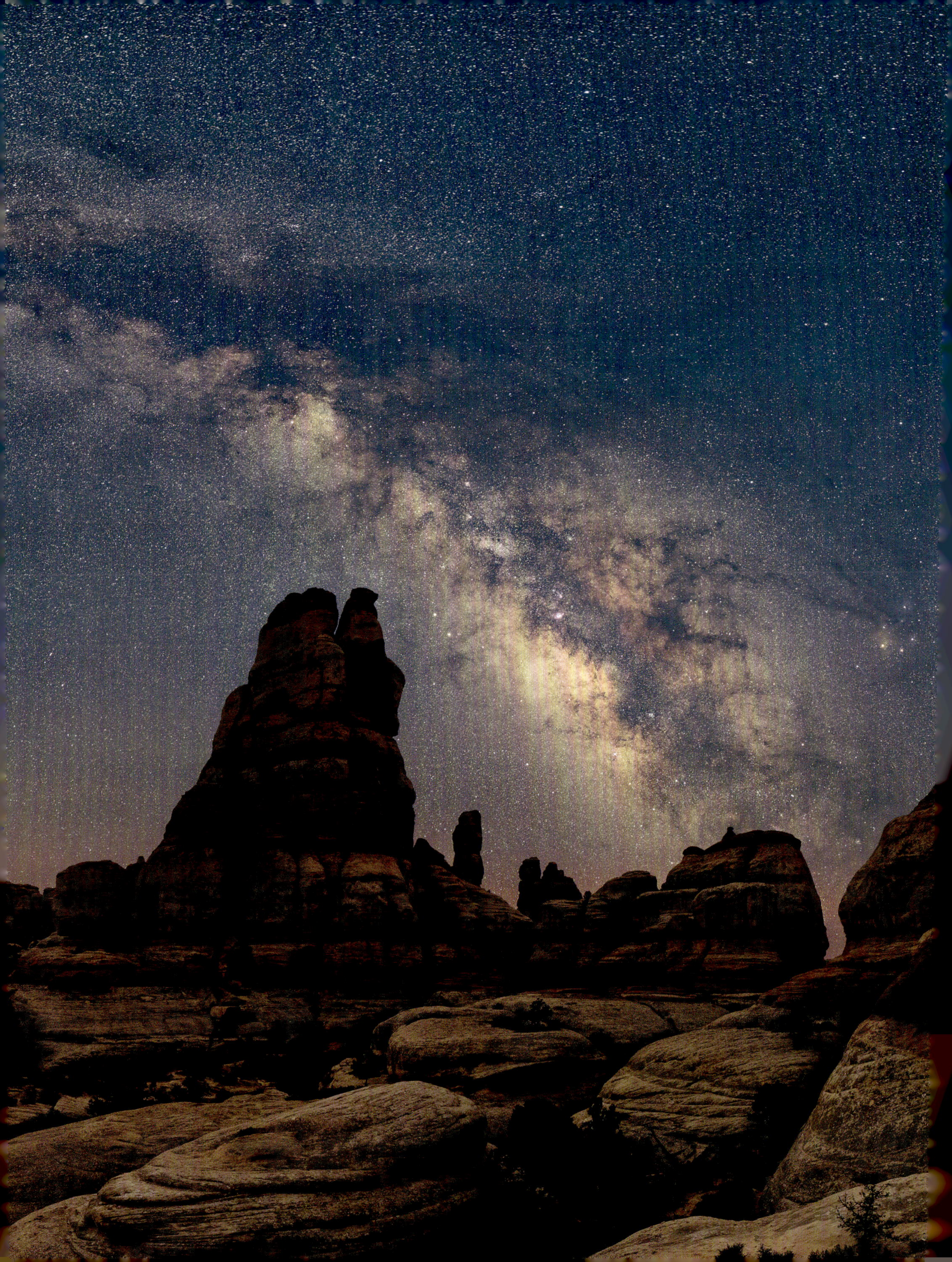

Tools for Night Photography

Shooting at night puts much greater demands on your equipment than does shooting during the day. Photographing in such dim light requires a camera that can make images at high ISOs with manageable noise. Photographing stars requires lenses that are sharp edge to edge and that can render stars as round rather than distorted by optical aberrations, all while shooting wide-open. Photographing when exposure times are measured in seconds or minutes requires a tripod that is sturdy enough to hold the camera steady even in high winds. This chapter will cover these three key pieces of equipment as well as some accessories that will make your nighttime excursions more efficient, safe, and enjoyable.

Fortunately, the low-light performance of even mid-range cameras has improved since I wrote the first edition, and more and more lenses have become available that perform well when shooting stars.

Camera and Sensor

Let's start with cameras. Phone cameras and small, fixed-lens compact cameras are getting better and better, but for the best results at this time you'll still want a mirrorless camera or DSLR that offers interchangeable lenses.

The most important characteristic for a good night-photography camera is low noise during long exposures at high ISOs.

The fundamental task of the sensor in your camera is to collect photons at each of the millions of light-sensitive elements, called *photosites*, which make up the sensor. Each photosite converts incoming photons into electrons, which form a tiny current flowing off the photosite. The strength of the current is proportional to the amount of light reaching the photosite. Each photosite corresponds to a single pixel in the image on your screen.

Noise is unwanted, random fluctuations in that electronic signal. The noise you see in your images comes in two broad categories: *luminance noise*, random, unwelcome variations in brightness; and *color noise* or *chrominance noise*, random, unnatural variations in color. Excessive noise gives the image a grainy appearance, as if it was taken with a high-speed film in the days of yore. In extreme cases (figure 2-2) it can introduce many red, green, and blue dots into the image. In addition to luminance and color noise, sensors can have *hot photosites*, faulty photosites that generate a stronger electric charge than they should, given the amount of light reaching them. After processing,

◄ FIGURE 2-1: Milky Way over towers near the Joint Trail, Needles District, Canyonlands National Park, Utah. April 14, 2018, 5:07 a.m. Canon EOS 5D Mark IV, Canon EF 35mm f/1.4L II USM. Land: one row, three camera positions, four frames per camera position, images stacked in Photoshop, noise reduced with Stack Mode>Median, 2 minutes, f/2.8, ISO 6400. Sky: two rows, three camera positions per row, four frames per camera position, images aligned and noise reduced in RegiStar, 10 seconds, f/1.4, ISO 6400.

▸ FIGURE 2-2: Extreme example of digital noise, taken with a Sony Alpha 7R IVa at 15 seconds, f/1.8, ISO 25,600. All noise reduction, including Lightroom's default color noise reduction, turned off.

hot photosites show up as hot pixels in your image. Hot pixels exhibit a fixed, rather than random, pattern. Virtually every step in the process of creating a digital image generates its own type of noise. Even the best sensors produce some noise.

When you take pictures in bright daylight, the noise makes up a small fraction of the overall data flowing off the sensor, so the image is largely free of noise. In engineering terms, you have a good signal-to-noise (SNR) ratio. As night falls, light levels drop, and the strength of the image-forming signal coming off the sensor drops as well. Only two factors control how much light reaches the sensor: the shutter speed (also called the exposure time) and the aperture. At night, the longest shutter speed you can use is limited by the

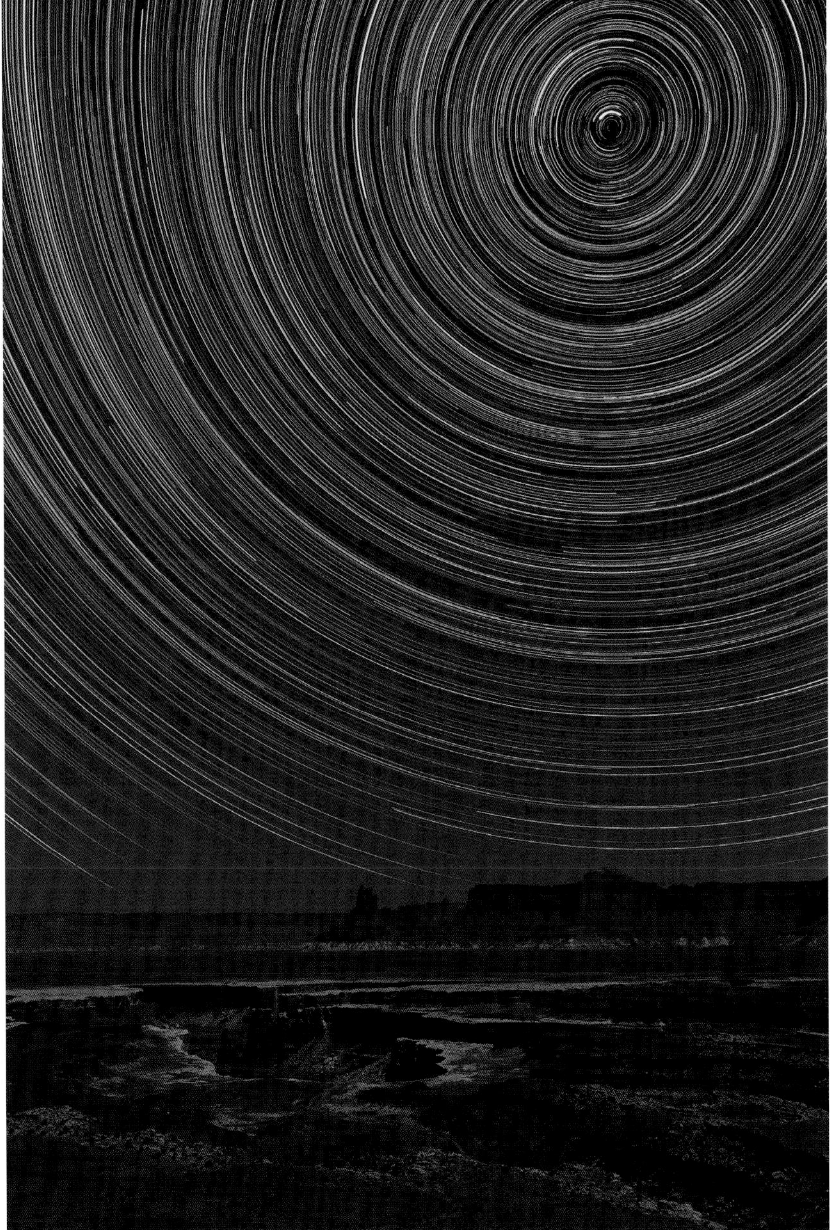

constant motion of the stars unless you're using a star tracker (see chapter 7). The widest aperture you can use is determined by the design of the lens. To achieve a correct exposure at night without the stars creating long streaks, you need to increase the ISO. Raising the ISO does *not* increase the sensitivity of the sensor. In other words, raising the ISO does not make the sensor convert a larger fraction of incoming photons into electrons. It merely increases how much the signal is amplified. To understand why that's a problem, you need to know a bit more about noise.

Noise has many sources, but one of the largest is called *photon noise* or *shot noise*. It occurs because there are random fluctuations in the rate at which photons strike each photosite on the sensor. Photon noise equals the square root of the signal. If the signal has a value of 4, then the signal-to-noise ratio is 2 (4 divided by 2, the square root of 4). That's poor. If the signal has a value of 100, then the signal-to-noise ratio is 10 (100 divided by 10, the square root of 100). This is much better.

Images taken in very low light have a worse signal-to-noise ratio than images taken in strong light. As the light reaching the sensor decreases, noise makes up an increasingly large fraction of the overall data flowing off the sensor. When you amplify the image-forming signal to achieve a correct exposure, you also amplify the noise. Since the signal is weak and the noise is relatively strong, your signal-to-noise ratio deteriorates and the image becomes noisy.

Good night-photography cameras employ a variety of strategies to combat all kinds of noise. The details of those strategies are proprietary, but there are various companies that do extensive independent testing of high-ISO performance and publish the results online or in a magazine. DxO Labs is one well-respected source. The test procedures are not identical, and results from the various testing methods don't always rank cameras in the same order. To make matters still more confusing, the relative contribution of the various types of noise changes from day to night. Nonetheless, the reviews are still a good starting point when researching the capabilities of a particular camera.

Sensor technology is improving all the time. Not surprisingly, more recent and more expensive cameras generally exhibit less noise both during the day and at night. For daylight photography, cameras with full-frame sensors the size of a 35mm film chip have some strong advantages over cameras with smaller sensors. Larger sensors can accommodate more photosites if photosite size is held constant. That translates into better resolution. Or, if the megapixel count is held constant, a larger sensor can allow for larger photosites, which can collect more light than the same number of smaller photosites on a smaller sensor. Let's say you're shooting wildlife or outdoor sports at dusk or dawn. You need a fast shutter speed, and your lens is already wide open, so you must raise the ISO to attain correct exposure. Since some types of noise are relatively constant on a per-photosite basis, and since the larger photosite can collect more light in the same amount of time, the camera with larger photosites should have a better signal-to-noise ratio than a camera with smaller photosites in that scenario.

The situation at night is a bit different. Another large source of noise is thermal noise, also called dark current. A perfect sensor would only kick out an electron when struck by a photon. In reality, sensors produce some electrons even if kept in total darkness. The number of electrons produced is proportional to the sensor's temperature and the length of the exposure. According to Dr. Roger Clark, a professional astronomer and expert on photographing the night sky, this kind of noise is actually the dominant type during the long exposures that are inescapable at night. Thermal noise increases in proportion to photosite size. Larger photosites collect more light but also exhibit more thermal noise, so the ratio of signal to thermal noise isn't necessarily better for large photosites than for smaller ones. The bottom line is that larger photosites are not always an advantage in night photography. Cameras with sensors smaller than a 35mm film chip, often called sub-full-frame sensors, crop sensors, or APS-C sensors, can work well at night if they can effectively suppress thermal noise.

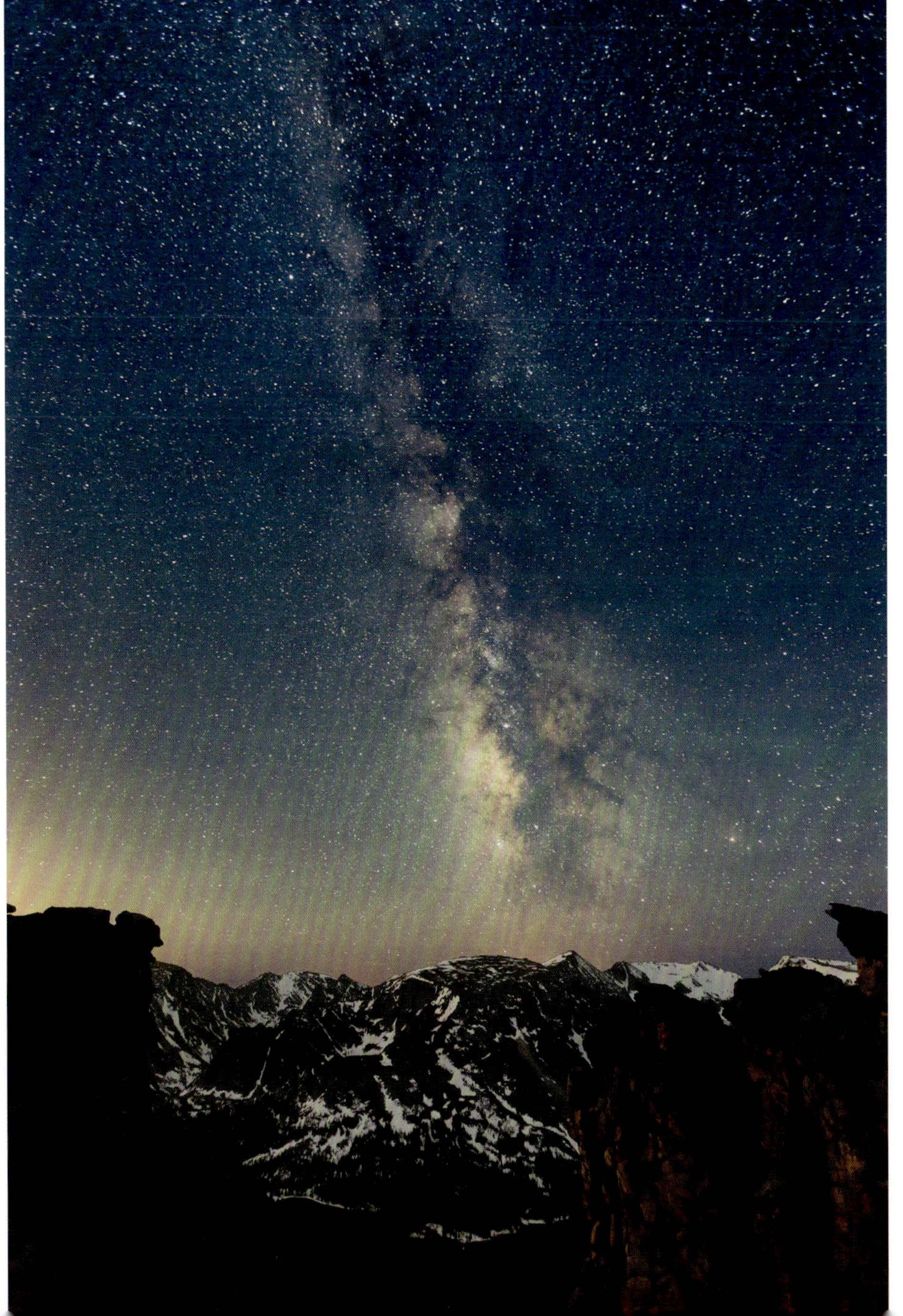

◄ FIGURE 2-4: The Milky Way over the Continental Divide from the Rock Cut, Trail Ridge Road, Rocky Mountain National Park, Colorado. June 4, 2014, 3:45 a.m. Canon 5D Mark III, Canon EF 16-35mm f/2.8L II USM at 16mm. Land: 2 minutes, f/2.8, ISO 6400. Sky: 30 seconds, f/2.8, ISO 6400.

At a minimum, look for a camera with a top ISO rating of at least 6400. Today even the least expensive new models easily meet that criterion; you'll only find cameras with that low a top ISO in the used market. If the camera offers still-higher ISO ratings without going into the menus and choosing High 1 or High 2 or words to that effect, all the better, even if you're unlikely to actually use the higher settings. Shooting at the highest ISO a camera offers is likely to produce images of marginal quality. If the highest ISO is several steps above 6400, then shooting at 6400 is more likely to produce acceptable results.

The mirrorless cameras that have swept the photographic world over the last five years aren't necessarily better than DSLRs of comparable age and price when it comes to the quality of their sensors, but they do have other advantages for night photography. For one thing, they tend to be smaller and lighter, always an asset at any time, and even more of one when you're trying to avoid tripping over a root in the dark. Of equal importance, in my view, is the abundance of information available in the electronic viewfinder. Photographers of a certain age, like yours truly, sometimes have a hard time using the LCD to focus at night or to critically examine an image. I often find it easier to focus on an enlarged live-view image seen through the viewfinder than on the same live-view image displayed on the LCD. Although not an issue at night, I also prefer to change menu settings while looking through the viewfinder rather than trying to read an LCD awash in bright sunlight.

Even the most in-depth review is a poor substitute for actually shooting with a new camera, then examining the results closely on a big, well-calibrated monitor. Before buying a new camera, consider renting it for a couple of days. If there's no store that rents cameras near you, consider working with an internet-based outfit. The price may be less than you think, and when you do eventually settle on a camera you can be confident that you'll be pleased with it for years to come.

Lenses for Night Photography

The best lens for your first ventures into the night is an ultra-wide-angle lens whose biggest aperture is as large as possible. The Milky Way is big in an angular sense. You need a lens with an expansive angle of view to capture it. When the aurora is active, it fills the sky; again, you'll want the widest lens available. Meteors can appear in any part of the sky. To capture as many as possible, you'll once again need a wide-angle optic.

Wide-angle lenses also have a less obvious advantage. Stars appear to move constantly as the earth rotates. To render stars as points, or at least as very short streaks that will still resemble stars in a print, you must keep

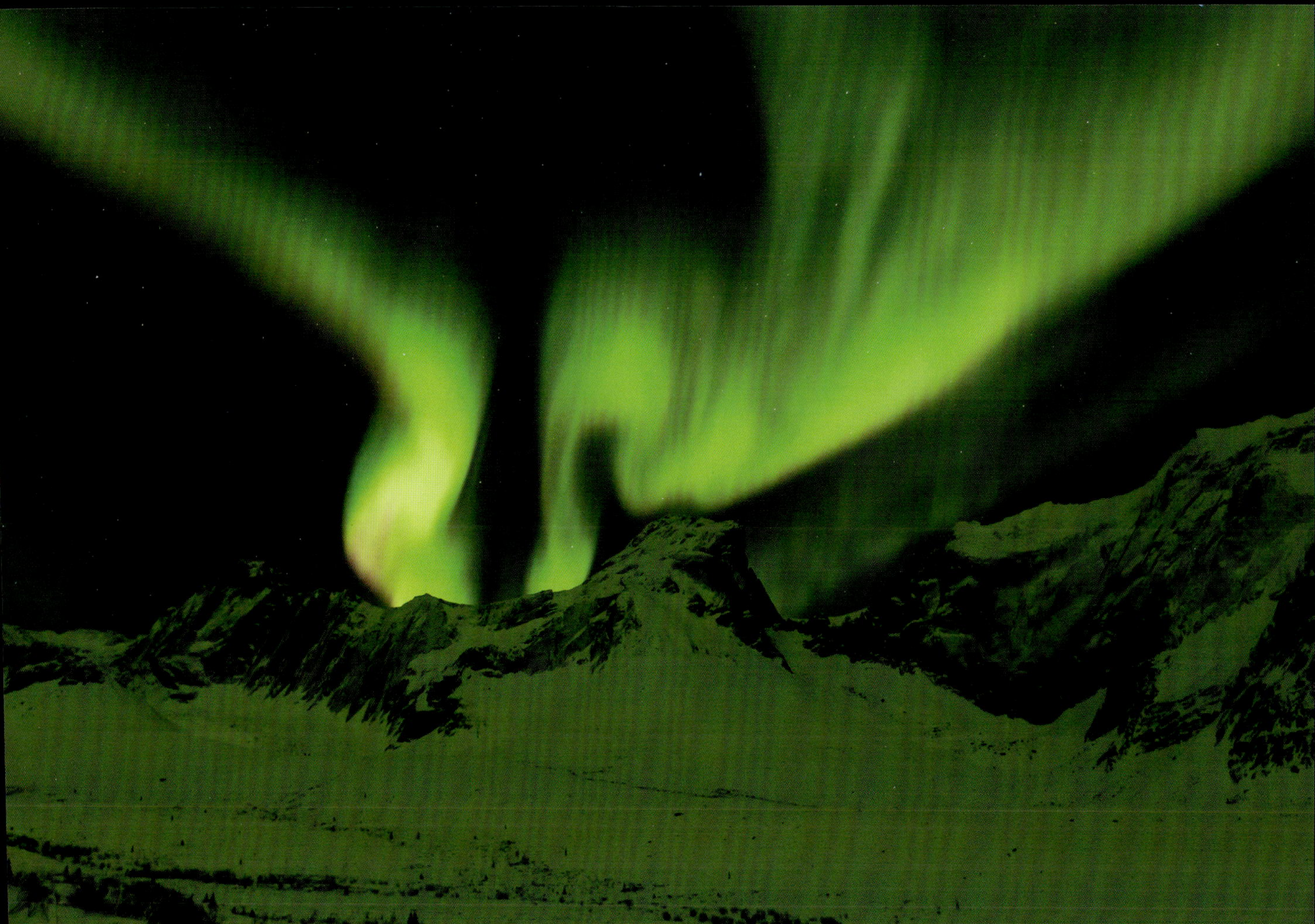

▲ FIGURE 2-5: Aurora over the Tombstone Range, Tombstone Territorial Park,
Yukon Territory, Canada. March 18,
2015, 11:39 p.m. Canon EOS 5D Mark
III, Canon EF 16-35mm f/2.8L II USM at
27mm. 2 seconds, f/2.8, ISO 3200.

the shutter speed to a minimum. The wider the angle of view of the lens, the longer you can leave the shutter open before the stars make visible streaks. Here's an example: Imagine a star near the celestial equator, the imaginary line in the sky you'd see if you could project the terrestrial equator onto the celestial sphere. During a 30-second exposure, that star travels $\frac{1}{8}$th of a degree. If you were shooting with a super-telephoto lens with a one-degree angle of view, the star would travel $\frac{1}{8}$th of the way across the frame in a 30-second exposure, creating a highly visible streak. If the field of view of that super-telephoto was a football field, the star would have made a 12-yard run and notched a first down. If you were shooting with a 16mm lens with a 97-degree angle of view, that same star would only travel $\frac{1}{776}$th of the way across the frame, creating a much shorter streak. To extend the football analogy, the star would have been stopped five inches past the line of scrimmage. Now you can see why ultra-wide, fast lenses are ideal for shooting the stars.

I'm assuming that you're using a full-frame camera—an assumption I'll be making throughout the book. Readers with crop-sensor cameras will need to multiply the focal lengths I discuss by the appropriate crop factor for their camera, as explained in the sidebar.

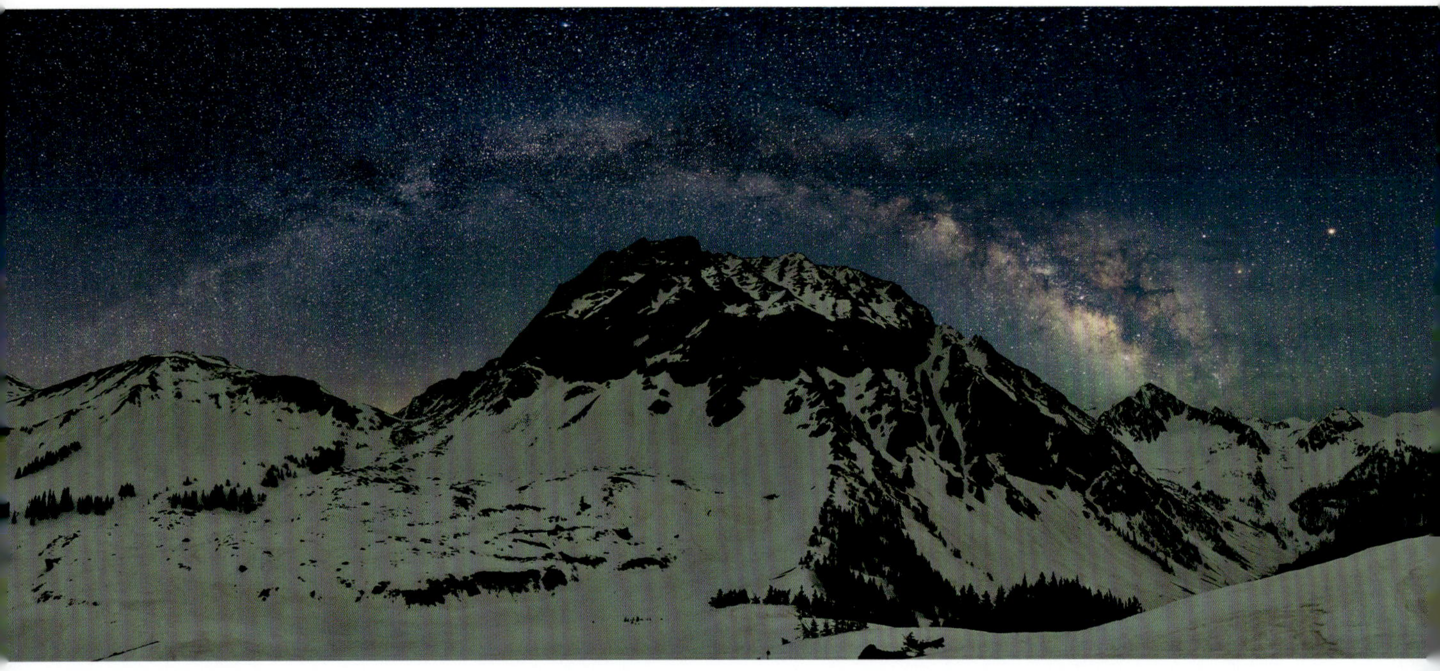

▲ Figure 2-6: Milky Way panorama over Capitol Peak, Maroon Bells-Snowmass Wilderness, Colorado. June 5, 2016, 12:23 a.m. Canon EOS 5D Mark III, Canon EF 16-35mm f/2.8L II USM at 16mm. Land: one row, four camera positions, one frame per camera position, 2 minutes, f/2.8, ISO 6400. Sky: one row, four camera positions, one frame per camera position, 30 seconds, f/2.8, ISO 6400. For this panorama I shot the first pair of sky and land frames back to back, then moved the camera to the next camera position, shot the second pair of sky and land frames, etc.

The longer shutter speeds you can use with ultra-wide-angle lenses compared to moderate wide-angles help you achieve correct exposure without using excessively high ISOs. But how wide a lens do you really need? One good way to answer that question is to look at what's required to shoot the Milky Way, one of the most popular night-photography subjects and also one of the dimmest.

A good starting-point exposure for shooting the Milky Way is 30 seconds, f/2.8, ISO 6400. To use a 30-second exposure without the stars streaking noticeably, you must have a 16mm or wider lens (or a zoom lens that goes to at least 16mm at the wide end of the range). If you're just getting into night photography and don't yet have a suitable lens, look for one that goes to 16mm or wider, with a maximum aperture of f/2.8 or larger.

Such a lens is an excellent choice for many kinds of night images, but you certainly don't need to drop a bundle on expensive glass before shooting the night sky for the first time. Take the widest lens you have and go out and play. Note, too, that shooting star trails can be done successfully with longer-focal-length lenses that don't have such a large maximum aperture. Such lenses are typically much less expensive than fast, ultra-wide models. In fact, you probably already own a lens that will work well for star trails.

As I mentioned previously, only two factors control how much light reaches your sensor: the shutter speed and the aperture. We've seen how

Clearing up Crop Factors

A full-frame camera has a sensor the same size as a frame of 35mm film, 24 x 36 millimeters. A crop-sensor camera has a smaller sensor, often measuring around 14.9 x 22.3 millimeters. Exact dimensions vary, and there is no standard adhered to by all manufacturers. Many crop-sensor cameras have an APS-C size sensor, a term derived from a now-obsolete line of film cameras.

All lenses produce a circular image. The sensor captures a rectangular portion of that image. A crop-sensor camera, with its smaller sensor, records data from a smaller rectangle within that image circle than a full-frame camera would when used with the same lens. The effect is that the crop-sensor camera provides a narrower angle of view than a full-frame camera does when used with the same lens. To calculate the focal length of the full-frame equivalent to a crop-sensor lens, you must multiply the focal length of the crop-sensor lens by the crop factor. The exact factor for APS-C sensors varies slightly, but 1.5 is usually close enough. Just divide the focal length of the crop-sensor lens in half and add that value to the focal length. For example, let's say you're using a 16mm lens on a camera with an APS-C sensor. To calculate the focal length of the full-frame lens with the same angle of view, divide 16 in half to get 8, then add 8 to 16 to get 24. A 16mm lens on an APS-C camera has about the same angle of view as a 24mm lens on a full-frame camera. Throughout this book, when I speak of lens focal lengths, I'll be referring to full-frame lenses.

One final note: you can put a lens designed for a full-frame camera on a crop-sensor camera without a problem, but the opposite is not true. Images taken with a full-frame camera and a crop-sensor lens will have dark or black corners because the image circle created by the crop-sensor lens isn't big enough to cover the entire area of the full-frame sensor.

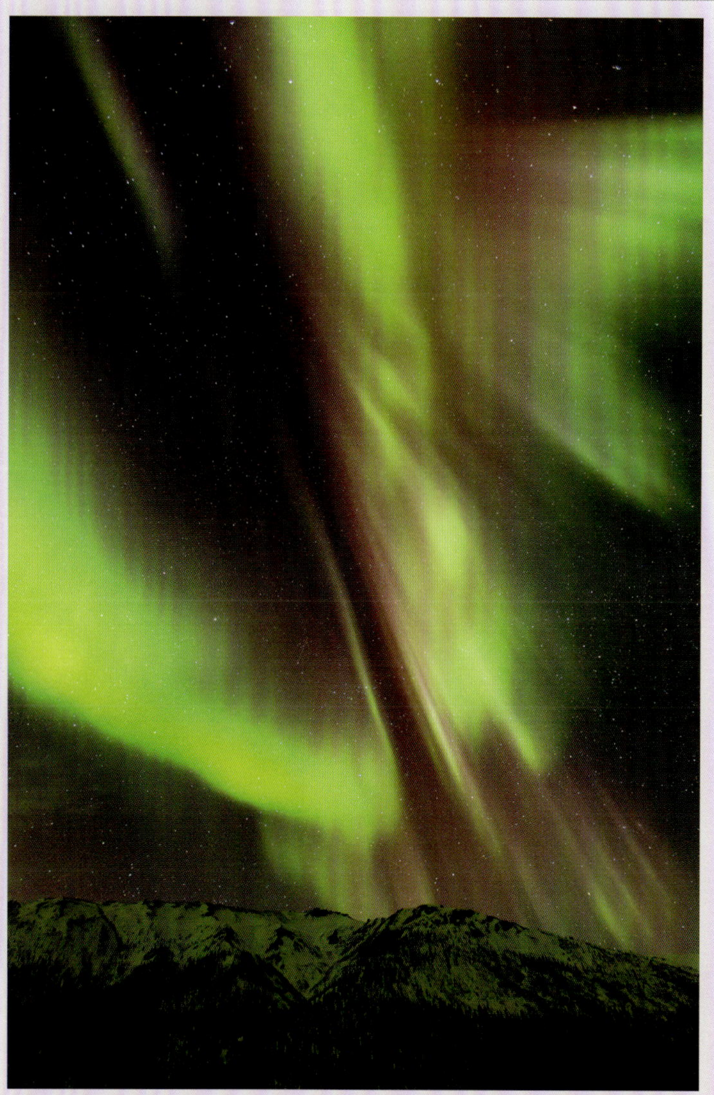

▲ Figure 2-7: Aurora over the Brooks Range, near Wiseman, Alaska. March 11, 2016, 12:13 a.m. Canon EOS 5D Mark III, Canon EF 16-35mm f/2.8L II USM at 16mm. 13 seconds, f/2.8, ISO 3200.

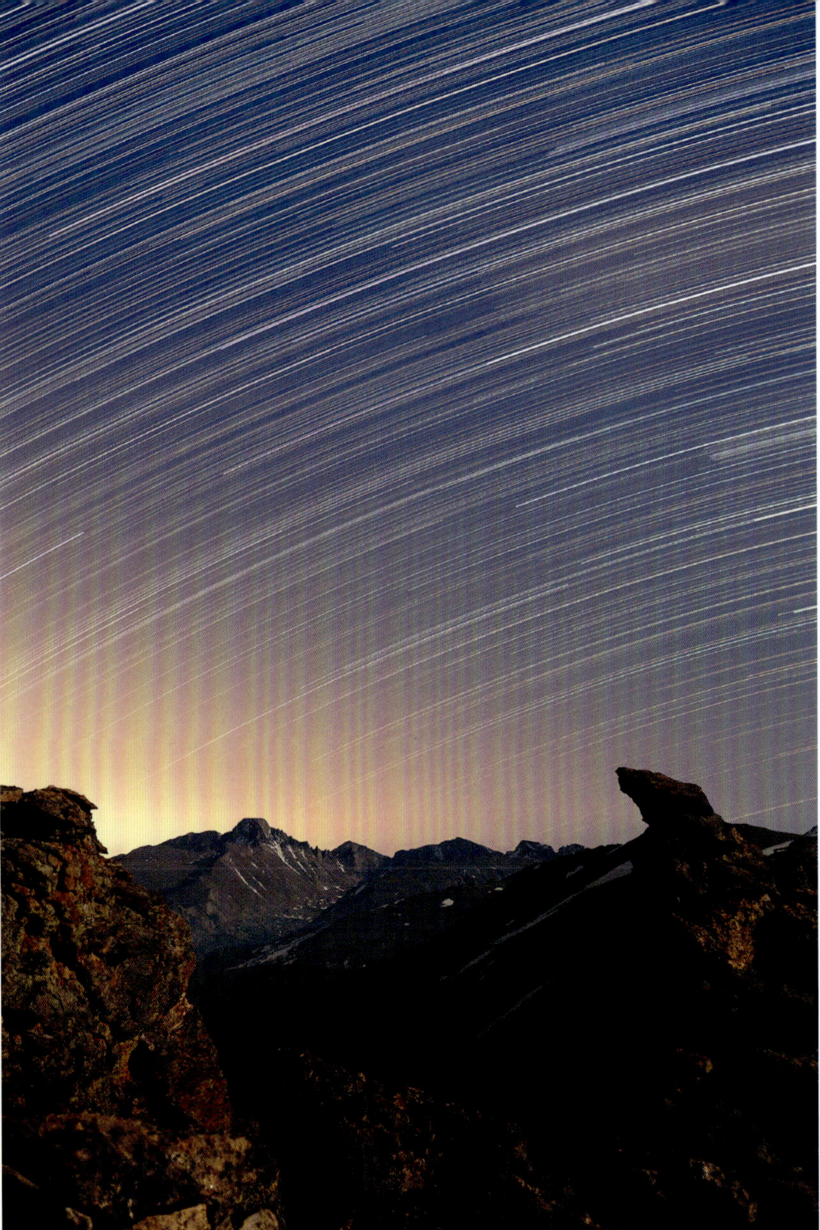

▸ FIGURE 2-8: Star trails over the Rock Cut and Longs Peak, Rocky Mountain National Park, Colorado. June 30–July 1, 2017, 10:46 p.m. to 2:31 a.m. Canon 5D Mark III, Canon Compact-Macro EF 50mm f/2.5 USM. 213 frames, 1 minute, f/2.8, ISO 400. The first-quarter moon (48 percent illuminated) provided the light on the land.

wide-angle lenses allow longer shutter speeds while still keeping the appearance of the stars reasonably round. But what about the aperture? How does your choice of aperture affect the appearance of the night sky? Here things get a bit tricky.

First, recall that the f-number is the ratio of the focal length of the lens to the diameter of the aperture, or to be more precise, the diameter of the entrance pupil, the apparent diameter of the aperture when viewed through the front of the lens. So if you set a 50mm lens to f/2.0, the diameter of the aperture is 25 millimeters ($50 \div 2 = 25$).

One of the fundamental principles of photography is that pictures of the same subject, taken at the same shutter speed, f-stop, and ISO, in the same light, will all have the same exposure, regardless of the focal length of the lens you use. Imagine, for example, that you're photographing a gray card. You may need to walk up close to the subject if you're using a wide-angle lens or walk far away if you're using a telephoto in order to fill the frame with the gray card, but the resulting images will have the same density. In other words, the total amount of light reaching your sensor will be the same, and the gray card will be the same shade of gray in both images.

This principle holds true for photographs of ordinary scenes, but it requires qualification when you're photographing stars. Stars are point sources that radiate light in all directions. The larger the aperture, the more light you can gather per second from that star, as shown in figure 2-9. The diameter of the aperture for a 16mm lens set to f/2.8 is 5.7 millimeters. The diameter of the aperture for a 35mm lens set to f/2.8 is 12.5 millimeters. What we're really concerned about is the *area* of the aperture, not its diameter, since it's the area that determines how much light, per second of exposure, actually reaches the sensor. The area of the aperture of a 16mm lens at f/2.8 is 26 square millimeters. The area of the aperture for a 35mm lens at f/2.8 is 123 square millimeters—almost five times as much as the 16mm lens. Granted, to avoid star trails you have to use a shorter shutter speed with the 35mm lens (about 14 seconds) than you do with the 16mm lens (about 31 seconds), but the net gain in light-gathering power is still significant.

For the moment, let's assume you hold the shutter speed, aperture, and ISO constant. An image of the night sky shot with the 35mm lens at f/2.8 will show more stars than an image of the night sky taken with the 16mm lens after cropping the 16mm shot to the 35mm angle of view. The 35mm shot will also show a bit better separation of the Milky Way from the background sky. In other words, the Milky Way will appear brighter in the 35mm shot than in the 16mm shot in relation to the background, which will have about the same density in both images. Most importantly (and most obviously) the 35mm shot will exhibit less noise. This is true even though the two exposures would be equivalent for ordinary terrestrial subjects.

How can that be? The key to understanding this apparent paradox is to think of the subject, the stars and the Milky Way, as being composed of a very large number of very small points. Each point sends out light in all directions. The larger the aperture, the more rays can be captured from each of these points. The 35mm lens at f/2.8 captures more light from each point than the 16mm lens at f/2.8, but its field of view is smaller, so it gathers light from fewer points. The result

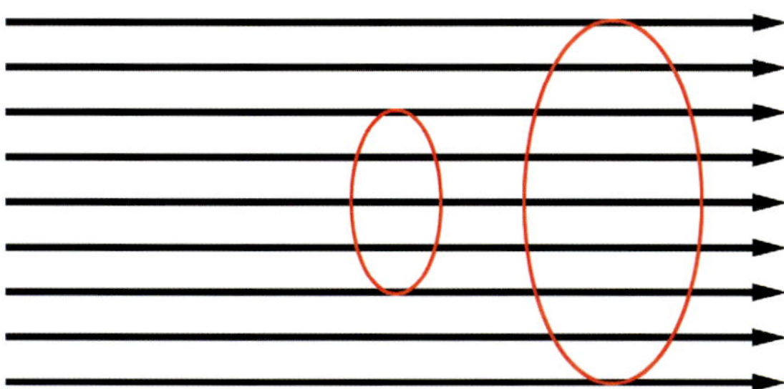

▼ FIGURE 2-9: Stars are effectively point sources, but they are so distant that the rays of light from a star can be considered parallel as they enter a lens. A large aperture gathers more light per second of exposure than a small aperture.

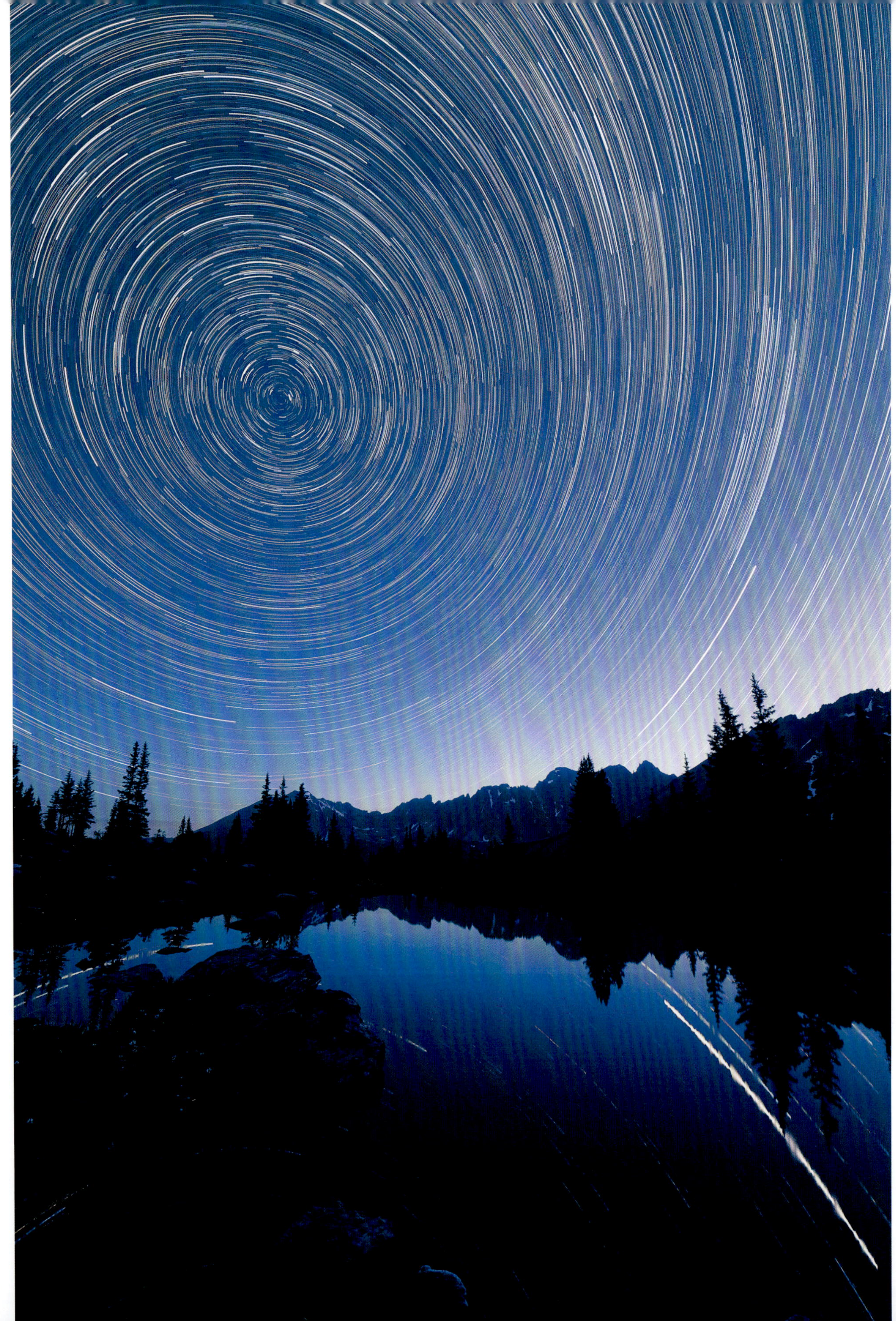

is that overall exposure—total number of photons gathered—for the two lenses is the same when the f-number, ISO, and shutter speed are kept constant. However, the amount of light gathered from each point—the signal—is stronger for the 35mm shot, which means the signal-to-noise ratio is better as well, since the SNR increases in proportion to the square root of the signal.

The difference in signal-to-noise ratio between the two lenses is imperceptible during the day, when the signal is so strong that the SNR is excellent regardless of the diameter of the aperture. At night, however, the difference is quite significant. Here's an admittedly oversimplified example that will make the point clear. Assume for the moment that the only source of noise in your image is photon noise. Let's say you're trying to capture an image of a faint star that is only slightly brighter than its background. With a 16mm f/2.8 lens, you might gather only 100 photons of light from the star and 90 from the background at a particular shutter speed. The signal-to-noise ratio for the starlight would be 10 (the square root of 100), meaning you could expect a random fluctuation in the brightness of that star of plus or minus 10 photons. That's the same as the actual difference in brightness between the star and its background. The difference in brightness between the star and its background is lost in the noise. The star can't be seen in the image.

Now imagine trying to photograph that star using a 35mm f/2.8 lens. The ratio of star brightness to background brightness hasn't changed, but the signal is much stronger, so the signal-to-noise ratio is much better. To use the example above, holding shutter speed and ISO constant, the 35mm lens at f/2.8 would gather almost five times as much light from that star as the 16mm lens at f/2.8. The sensor would collect about 500 photons from the star and 450 photons from the background. The SNR would be 22 (the square root of 500) instead of 10, meaning you would expect a random fluctuation of plus or minus 22 photons. The difference between star and background—50 photons—now rises above the noise floor. The star can be seen.

The same principle applies to photographing the dust and gas clouds that make up the Milky Way. The lens with the larger aperture captures more light from each point of the Milky Way. That improves the signal-to-noise ratio and creates better separation of tones between the Milky Way and the background sky.

The situation may become clearer if you think about it in a different way. The angle of view of a 35mm lens is just over half that of the 16mm lens. To cover the same area of the sky included in the 16mm shot, you'd have to shoot four frames with the 35mm lens, arranged in two rows of two. Since each exposure with the 35mm lens gathers the same amount of light, overall, as the single exposure with the 16mm lens, the total amount of light gathered in the four-frame 35mm array is four times as much as is gathered in the single 16mm frame, even though the area of sky included in the image

◄ FIGURE 2-10: Star trails over pond near Caribou Lake, Indian Peaks Wilderness, Colorado. July 16, 2020, 2:41 a.m. to 4:19 a.m. Canon EOS 5D Mark IV, Canon EF 16-35mm f/2.8L III USM at 16mm. Land: 2 minutes, f/4.0, ISO 400 at 4:48 a.m., 59 minutes before sunrise. Sky: 50 frames, 2 minutes, f/4, ISO 400.

▸ Figure 2-11: The relative sizes of the aperture for fast, wide-angle lenses.

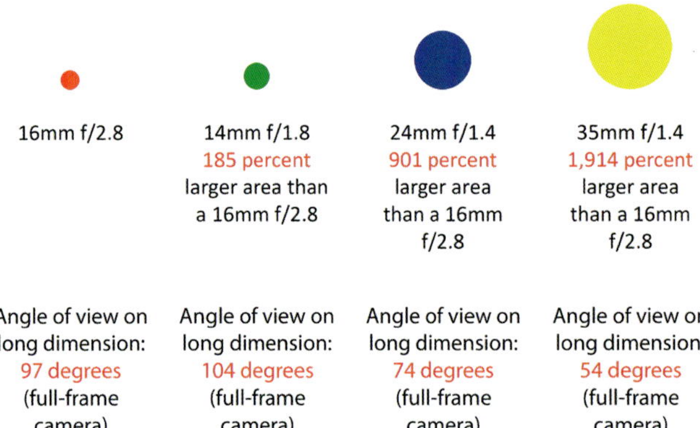

is the same. The signal is four times stronger, which means the signal-to-noise ratio has doubled. You'll have less noise and will be able to see fainter stars and more detail in the Milky Way in the composite image taken with the 35mm lens.

I provided the above example to make my point clear, but as a practical matter I'm not urging you to shoot the Milky Way with a 35mm lens at f/2.8. Several manufacturers make 35mm lenses that have a maximum aperture of f/1.4. The area of the aperture of a 35mm lens at f/1.4 is 491 square millimeters—nearly 19 times greater than the area of the aperture for a 16mm lens at f/2.8. Again, you have to consider the shorter shutter speeds required to keep the stars from streaking, but the gain in light-gathering power is still huge. Add one of the star-tracking devices I'll discuss in chapter 8 to your kit, and you can use the same shutter speed with the 35mm lens that you do with the 16mm lens. Now the additional light-gathering power of the 35mm f/1.4 lens is truly impressive. In my testing of my Sony FE 14mm f/1.8 GM, the most obvious difference between an image shot with that lens at f/2.8 and one shot with a Sony FE 35mm f/1.4 GM lens at f/1.4 is the greatly reduced noise (see figure 2-12). Using the 14mm lens wide open, at f/1.8, only reduces noise slightly compared to using the same lens at f/2.8. (I did the comparison at f/2.8 because many more photographers own 14mm or 16mm f/2.8 lenses (or f/2.8 zooms that go that wide) than own a 14mm f/1.8, which is a rather specialized and expensive piece of glass.)

So why not use a 35mm f/1.4 lens for all of your night photographs? The answer is that a 35mm lens is often not wide enough to capture everything you want in a single frame. One solution to that problem is to shoot a stitched panorama, a technique that adds complexity but can produce superb results.

▸ Figure 2-12: I shot the upper image with a Sony Alpha 7R IVa and Sony FE 14mm f/1.8 GM lens at 30 seconds, f/2.8, ISO 6400. I shot the lower image with a Sony Alpha 7R IVa and Sony FE 35mm f/1.4 GM as a panorama, three rows, three frames per row, at 10 seconds, f/1.4, ISO 6400 (an essentially equivalent exposure in terms of the density of the image). I then resized the panorama to the same width in pixels as the single frame shot with the 14mm. Finally, I enlarged both images to 100 percent to show the difference in noise between the two images.

I'll discuss night panoramas fully in chapter 5. A 35mm lens set to f/1.4 also has much worse depth of field than a 16mm lens at f/2.8. Focused at infinity, a 35mm lens set to f/1.4 renders everything sharp from 142 feet to infinity. A 16mm lens set to f/2.8 renders everything sharp from 15 feet to infinity.

To sum up, the simplest way to make great night images is to use an ultra-wide-angle lens, 16mm or wider, with a maximum aperture of f/2.8 or larger. As you venture deeper into night photography, you may want to add a 35mm f/1.4 or other moderately wide, super-fast lens to your arsenal, along with panorama hardware.

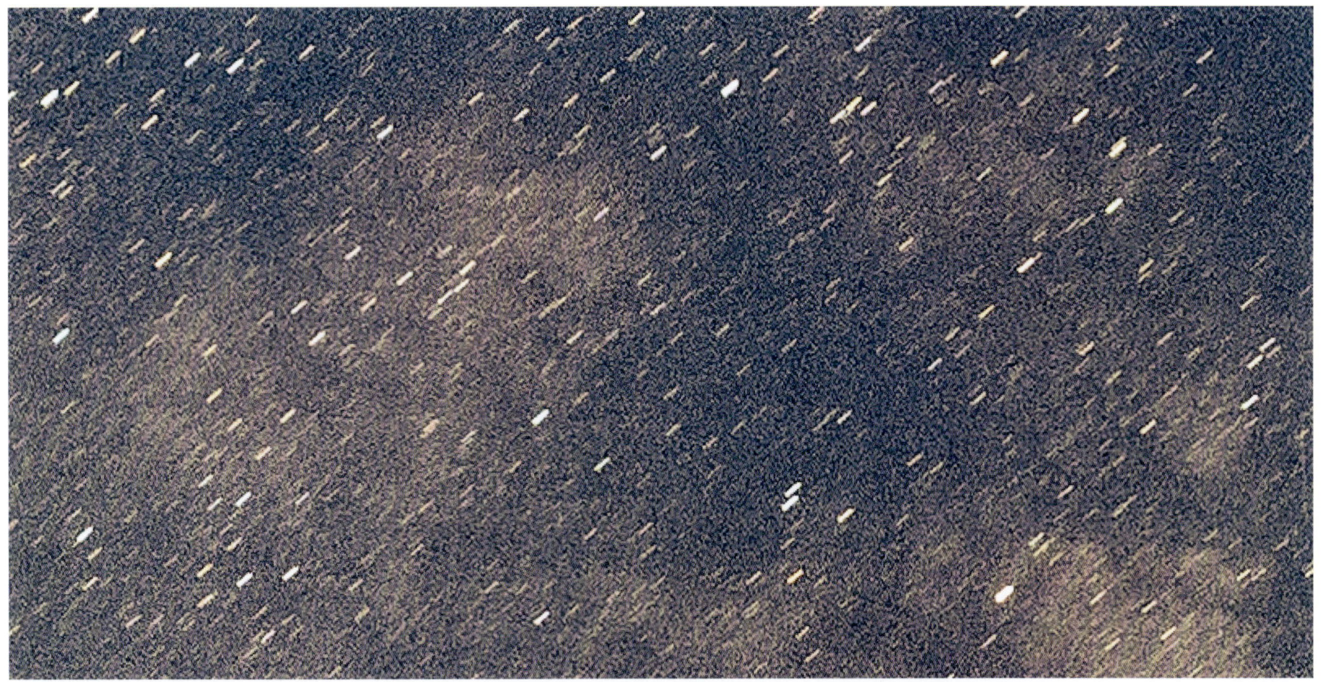

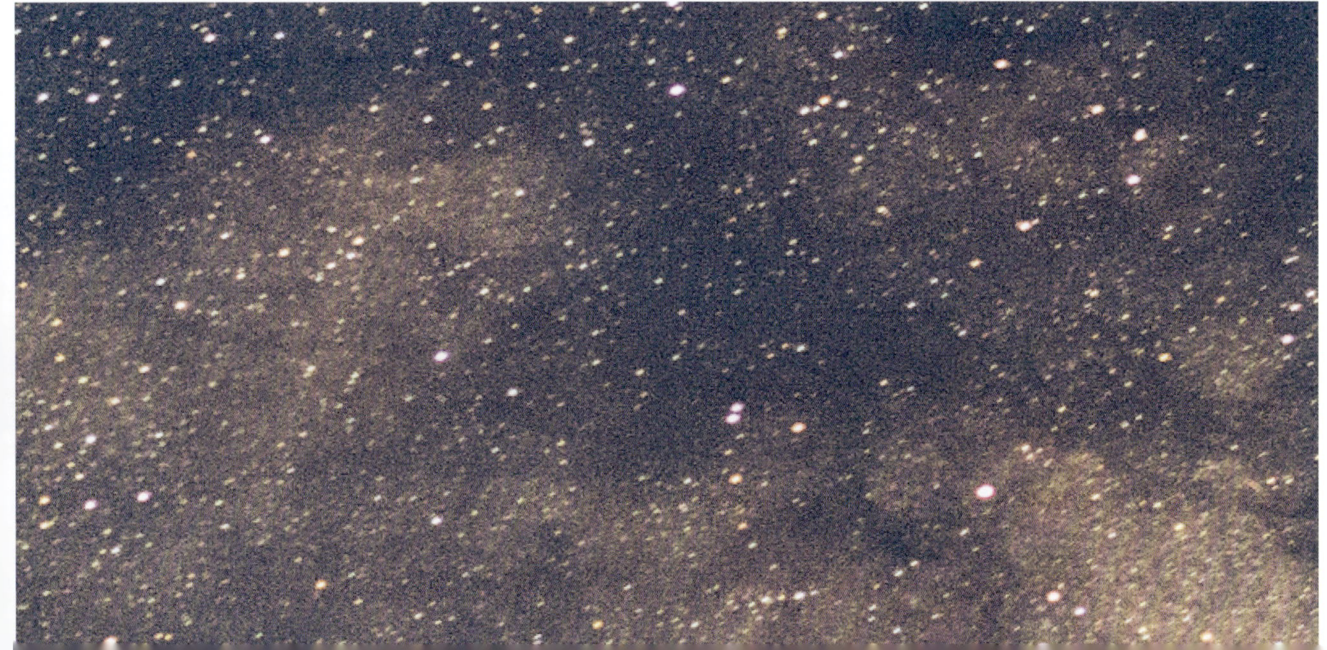

Not all fast wide-angle lenses are created equal. Even very expensive lenses can exhibit optical aberrations when shooting wide open that cause stars in the corners of the frame to grow little bat wings that are perpendicular to a line leading from the star to the center of the frame, as seen in figure 2-13. It's become commonplace in some corners of the web to refer to these aberrations as coma. To an optical engineer, however, coma is a different problem, in which stars grow a single tail that can point either toward or away from the center of the image. Coma is most commonly found in telescopes that use mirrors to create a folded light path. According to Dr. Clark, the astronomer, the actual cause of the bat-wing problem in wide-angle lenses is usually some combination of astigmatism and spherical aberration.

These bat wings are an annoyance in single-camera-position images because they are clearly unnatural. They are a bigger problem in panoramas stitched together from multiple frames because the stars with bat wings form an arch-like shape in each frame. When you stitch multiple frames together, you can get an obvious and unnatural pattern, with multiple arches stretching across the sky. This pattern is very difficult to hide with retouching.

There are many specialized night-photography websites that test various lenses for these optical aberrations when shooting stars. Before buying a new lens for night photography, be sure to check out their reviews. Better yet, rent a lens you're considering buying and put it through its paces before laying down the big bucks.

Tripods

Many photographers hate their tripods, and for good reason: their tripods are often flimsy, prone to breaking, and so short that the center post must be extended to get the camera to eye level—which makes them shakier still. In many cases, these photographers exhausted most of their photo budget buying good cameras and lenses. With only a little money left over, they purchased the cheapest tripod they could find, which means that they really aren't getting the full benefit of their investment in their camera and lenses. Even the sharpest lens, mounted on the best camera body, will still not produce a quality image if you mount your gear on a flimsy tripod. These photographers fail to realize that a good tripod is easily as important as a good lens—and may cost just as much. Here are some tips on selecting a three-legged companion you'll love to use both day and night.

First, a hard truth: all tripods are either too heavy or too flimsy. There are no super-light, super-sturdy tripods.

◄ Figure 2-13: Detail of image shot with Canon EF 24mm f/1.4L II USM lens showing stellar aberrations in the upper-right corner of the frame.

Next, a caution: don't go overboard. A quality tripod is required to produce the sharpest possible images, but if the tripod you buy is so big and heavy that you can't carry it more than 10 feet from your car, then you've bought the wrong tripod.

At the higher end of the market, tripod legs and heads are normally sold separately. Here's what to look for in tripod legs.

If possible, get a set of legs that extend higher than your head without raising the center post (if your tripod has one—you're better off without). You'll need that extra leg length when setting up on a steep slope. The leg on the downhill side of the tripod must extend longer than your height to position the camera at eye level. The ability to position the camera close to the ground is just as important as the ability to place it high; buy tripod legs that can be splayed out so that you can position the camera near ground level. Avoid tripod legs with center posts, which restrict your ability to place the camera low. Center posts can also cause other problems. If it's windy, extending the center post makes the camera wobble like a flower atop its stalk. Some top-quality tripods have removable center posts, which solves the problem of placing the camera low, but doesn't solve the problem of camera vibration in the wind with the center post extended.

Carbon-fiber legs are light but expensive. Aluminum works just fine, at the cost of more weight. Tripods with three leg sections are a bit sturdier and set up faster than tripods with four leg sections, but don't pack down as small. If you travel with your gear by air, look for a tripod that will fit inside your suitcase or carry-on bag. If you're interested in shooting panoramas, be sure that your tripod has a bubble level on the chassis, the part where the three legs come together. As I'll explain in chapter 5, being able to level the chassis makes it easier to set up a panorama shot accurately.

Now let's take a look at tripod heads. Your first choice is between a three-way pan/tilt head and a ball head. I prefer ball heads because they're faster to use and lighter for the amount of support they provide. Loosen one knob, and you can re-position the camera with complete freedom.

Inexpensive tripod heads come with flat quick-release plates that attach to the bottom of the camera with a single bolt. The major disadvantage of this design is that the quick-release plate can easily rotate in relation to the camera body. The plate is constantly trying to unscrew itself from the camera. This can happen if you pan the camera left or right without loosening the pan lock on the tripod head. It's virtually guaranteed to happen when

▾ Figure 2-14: Panorama of the Milky Way over the Maze, Maze District, Canyonlands National Park, Utah. April 3, 2017, 4:23 a.m. Canon 5D Mark III, Canon EF 35mm f/1.4L II USM. Land: one row, seven camera positions, one frame per camera position, 90 seconds, f/1.4, ISO 6400. Sky: two rows, seven camera positions per row, one frame per camera position, 10 seconds, f/1.4, ISO 6400.

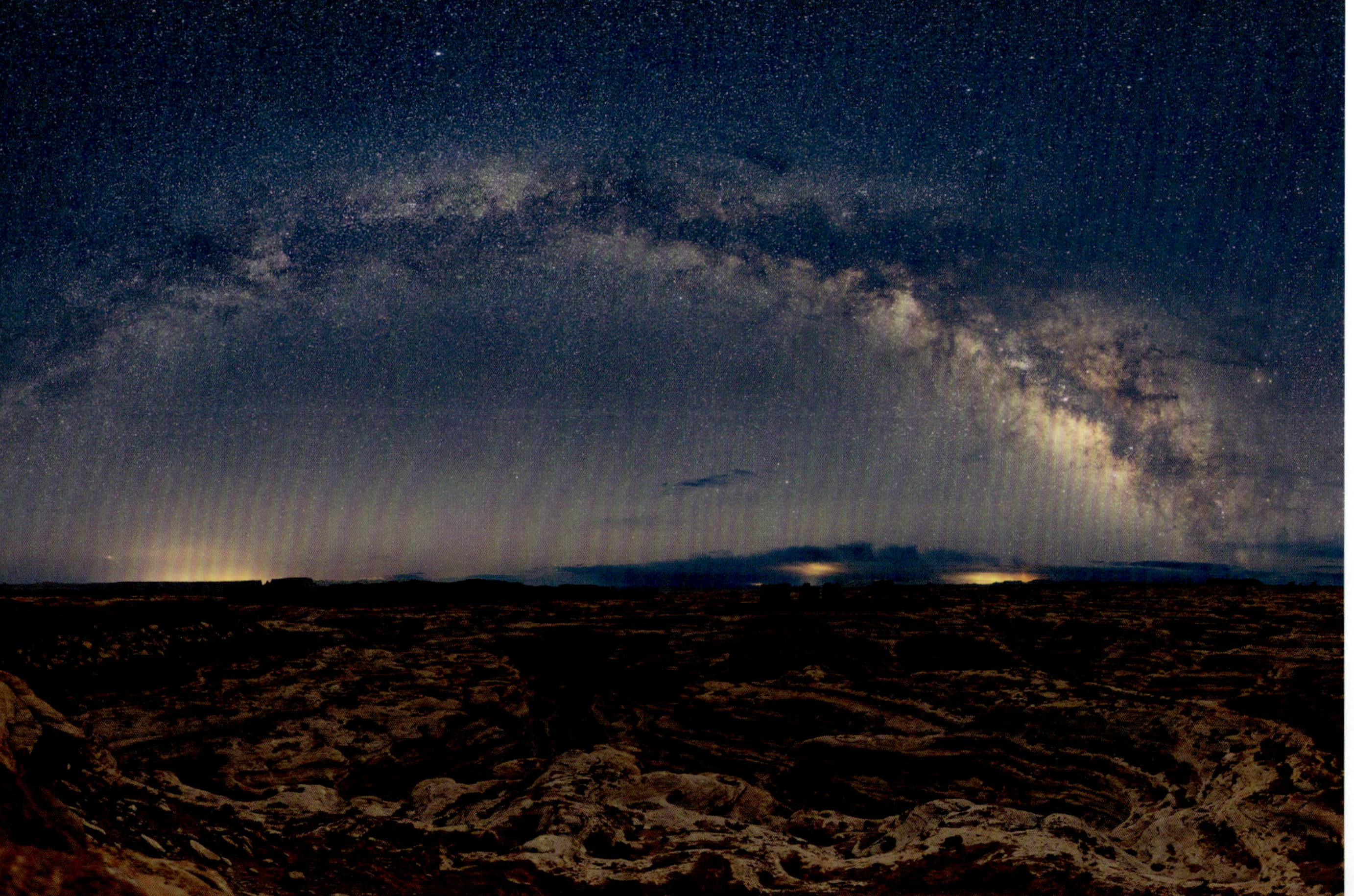

you shoot a vertical image, particularly with a long lens, because you must tip the tripod head onto its side. The nose-heavy camera/lens combination tends to rotate in relation to the plate until the lens is pointing straight down. The only way to really beat that problem is to buy a custom-fitted camera plate for your specific camera body from Really Right Stuff, Kirk Enterprise Solutions, Acratech, or another supplier. These camera plates are designed to cup the bottom of the camera so that they cannot rotate in relation to the camera. The plates have a dovetail that fits into the dovetail clamp on certain tripod heads. The best plates are built to the Arca-Swiss standard, which means they fit the dovetail clamps on Arca-Swiss heads as well as the many heads that conform to the Arca-Swiss standard.

An even better solution than a custom-fitted straight plate is a custom-fitted L-plate (also called a L-bracket), so called because it has a dovetail running along both the bottom and the side of the camera body. Like good straight plates, good L-plates are built to the Arca-Swiss standard and are fitted to your camera body so they can't twist loose. To switch the camera from horizontal to vertical orientation, release the bottom dovetail from the tripod head's clamp and position the side dovetail in the clamp instead. You no longer need to tilt the tripod head onto its side to shoot a vertical image. This keeps the weight of the camera and lens centered over the tripod head, which increases stability. L-plates also make it easier to maintain the same

▾ FIGURE 2-15: Aurora over the Tombstone Range, Tombstone Territorial Park, Yukon Territory, Canada. March 17, 2015, 2:13 a.m. Canon EOS 5D Mark III, Canon EF 16-35mm f/2.8L II USM at 16mm. 15 seconds, f/2.8, ISO 3200.

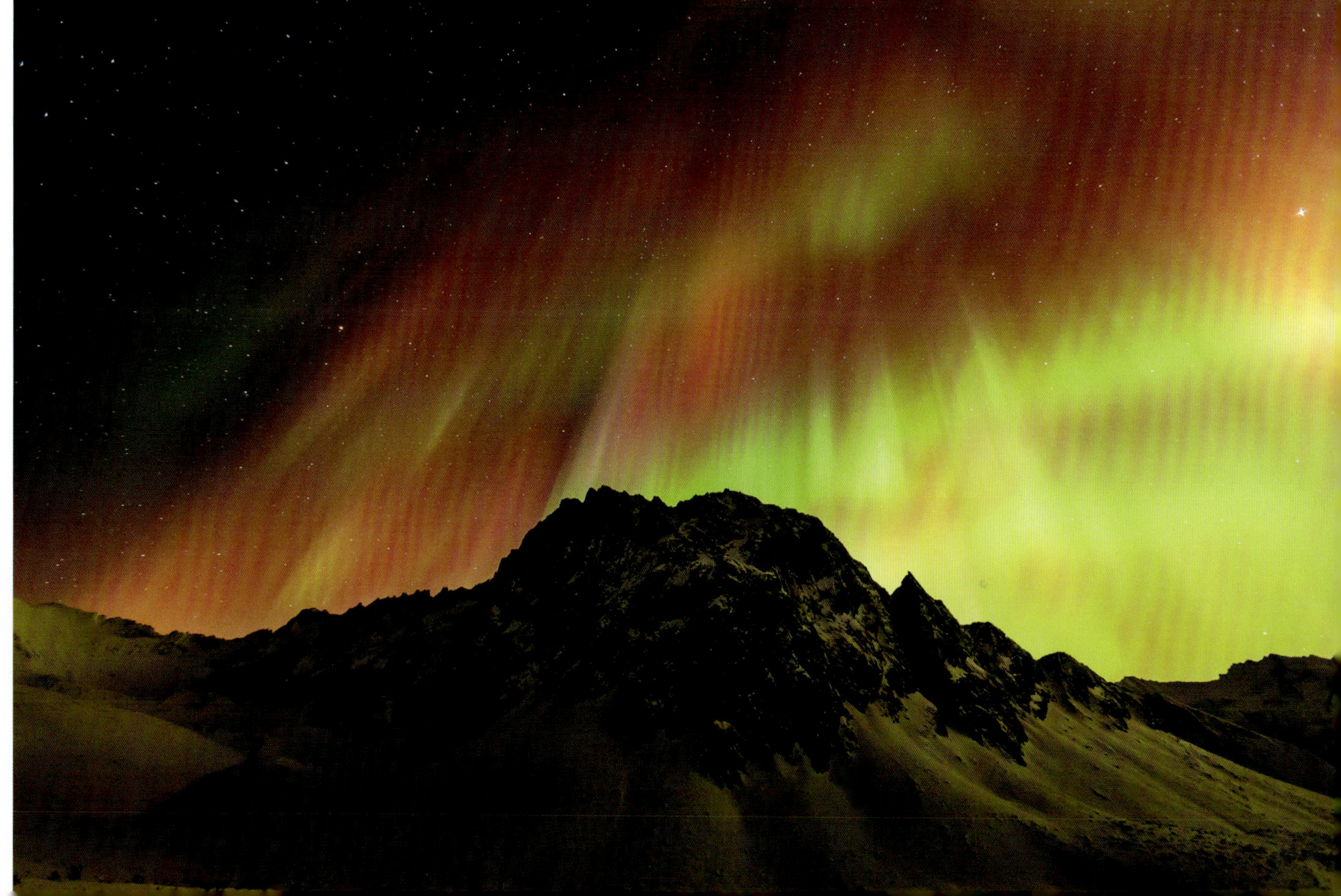

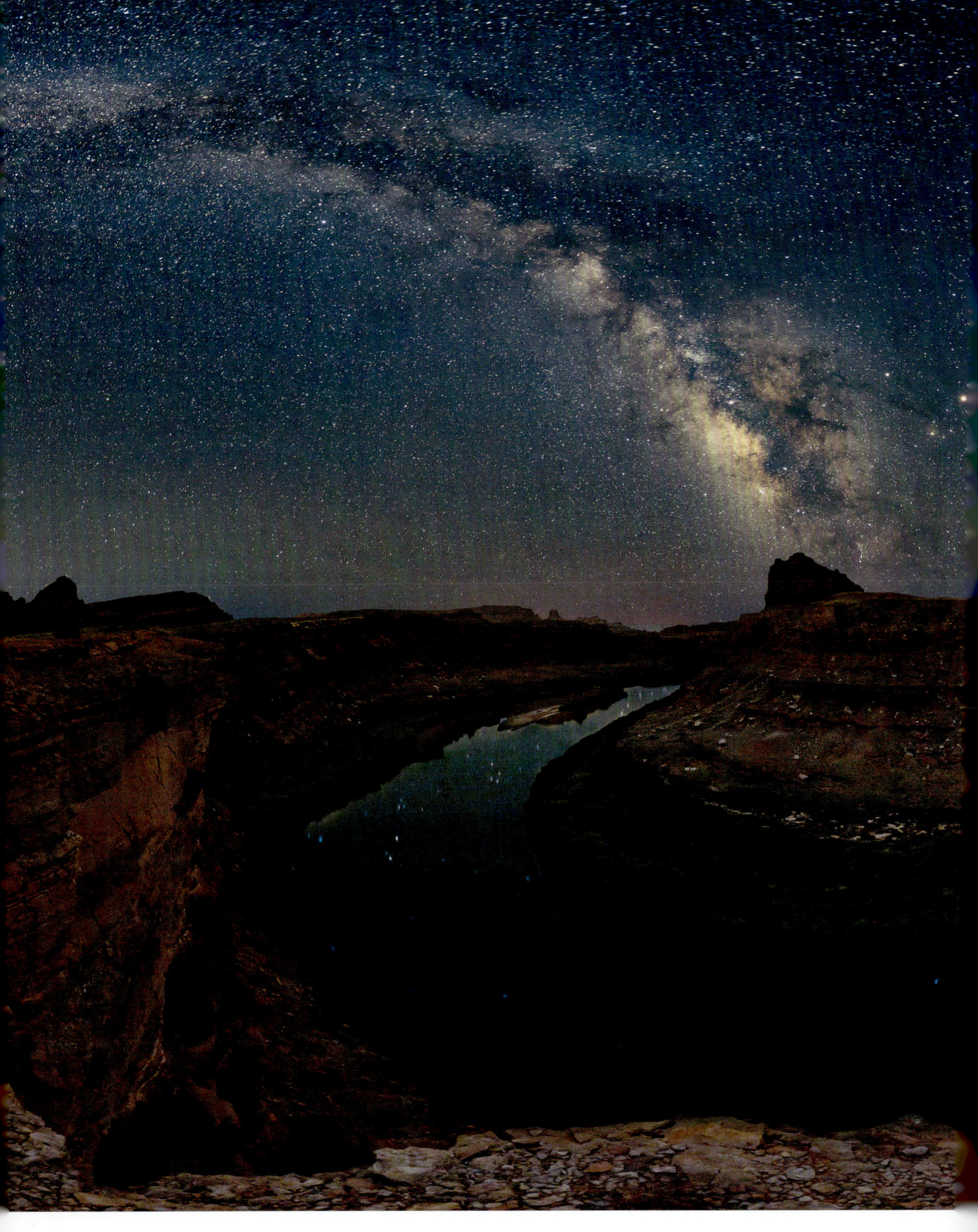

relationship between foreground and background elements in your composition. Let's say you set up a horizontal composition such that the tallest flower in your foreground is directly beneath the summit of a peak. Switching to a vertical composition when using a straight plate will move the camera either right or left when you flop the camera onto its side. That moves the flower away from its ideal position in relation to the peak. Switching to a vertical composition using a L-plate keeps the camera in the same position left-to-right, which in turn keeps the flower where it belongs. A number of companies now make tripod heads that are Arca-Swiss compatible, but not all of these companies offer custom-fitted plates that won't rotate against the bottom of the camera. Whether you buy a straight plate or a L-plate, be sure it's custom-fitted to your camera.

Accessories for Night Photography

Cameras, lenses, and tripods are the most important pieces of equipment for night photography, but there are a number of accessories that will make your nighttime photo adventures more productive and trouble-free.

A reliable headlamp should be your next purchase. You'll need it both for the hike to and from your shooting location and for working on location with your gear. To fully appreciate the beauty of the night sky, however, you'll want to let your eyes adapt to the dark, a process that takes about 30 minutes. How then to reconcile these two conflicting needs? The answer is to buy a headlamp that puts out a dim, red light in one of its modes and a bright, white light in a different mode. Understanding why a dim, red light is useful requires a brief digression into the physiology of vision.

Your eyes have two basic types of photoreceptors: cones and rods. There are three types of cones, each sensitive to a different region of the visual spectrum. We compare the response of our cones to distinguish different colors; we use the sum of the response from our cones to determine brightness or luminance. Cones are relatively insensitive, so they are most active in bright light. Cones are packed close together in the very center of our retina, a region called the *fovea*, which provides us with our high-resolution vision.

Rods provide us with our night vision. There is only one type, so they cannot distinguish different colors, but they are much more sensitive to light than cones. That sensitivity comes at the cost of resolution. Our rods are too widely spaced to let us see sharply. To see the buttons on your camera clearly, for example, you need enough light to stimulate your cones.

The fundamental first step in vision occurs when a photon of light enters the eye and strikes a light-sensitive protein in your photoreceptors. In your

◄ Figure 2-16: Milky Way panorama over the Goosenecks of the Colorado River, along the Potash Road just outside Canyonlands National Park, Utah. May 4, 2016, 3:51 a.m. Canon 5D Mark III, Canon EF 16-35mm f/2.8L II USM at 16mm. Land: 2 minutes, f/2.8, ISO 6400. Sky: 30 seconds, f/2.8, ISO 6400. Two rows, three frames per row. For this panorama I shot the first pair of sky and land frames back to back, then moved the camera to the next camera position, shot the second pair of sky and land frames, etc.

rods, that photopigment is called rhodopsin. Embedded within the rhodopsin molecule is a smaller molecule called retinal. When struck by a photon, the retinal changes shape permanently. That change in shape triggers a chain of events that ultimately triggers a neural impulse. The spent retinal molecules disassociate from their parent rhodopsin molecules, which cannot respond to another photon of light until they recombine with the light-sensitive form of retinal.

During the day, rods are overwhelmed by all the bright light. All of their retinal is used up in a process called *photobleaching*. Regeneration of the rods' light-sensitive rhodopsin is too slow for them to become active again so long as the light is strong. Once darkness falls, the process of regeneration can recharge the rods and make them active once again. That process of regeneration is what allows our eyes to become dark-adapted.

Once your eyes have become fully dark-adapted, which takes about 30 minutes, you don't want to destroy that adaptation by exposing your rods to bright light. The peak sensitivity of rods occurs in the blue-green region of the spectrum. They are relatively insensitive to red light. By using a very dim, red light, you can stimulate your cones enough to see how to change the settings on your camera without bleaching your rods. If too bright, however, even a red light will deplete your rods enough to temporarily compromise your night vision.

Now you know what to look for in a headlamp intended for night photography. First, you want a bright, white setting for hiking, scouting, and dispelling irrational fears about things that go bump in the dark. Many good headlamps actually have two white settings: one that provides a broad, low-intensity beam to illuminate a large, nearby area, such as the inside of your tent; and one that creates a narrow, bright beam to spotlight small, distant objects. The broad beam typically uses less battery power than the spotlight. You also want a dim, red setting that will give you just enough light to set essential camera functions without compromising your night vision. The best headlamps offer adjustable brightness in both the white and red modes and let you go straight to the red setting without cycling through the white settings first. The very best headlamps even have a brightness memory feature that causes the headlamp to remember your last-used settings. You may find that the default brightness of the red mode is still too bright to preserve your night vision as well as possible. The brightness memory feature lets you turn on the headlamp with the ideal brightness already set. Without it, you have to dial back the brightness of your headlamp every time you turn it on, potentially compromising your night vision each time. A brightness memory feature is a great convenience because you'll probably be turning your headlamp on and off repeatedly.

▸ FIGURE 2-17: Aurora over Mt. Monolith, Tombstone Territorial Park, Yukon Territory, Canada. March 17, 2015, 11:12 p.m. Canon EOS 5D Mark III, Canon EF 24mm f/1.4L II USM lens. 10 seconds, f/2.0, ISO 3200.

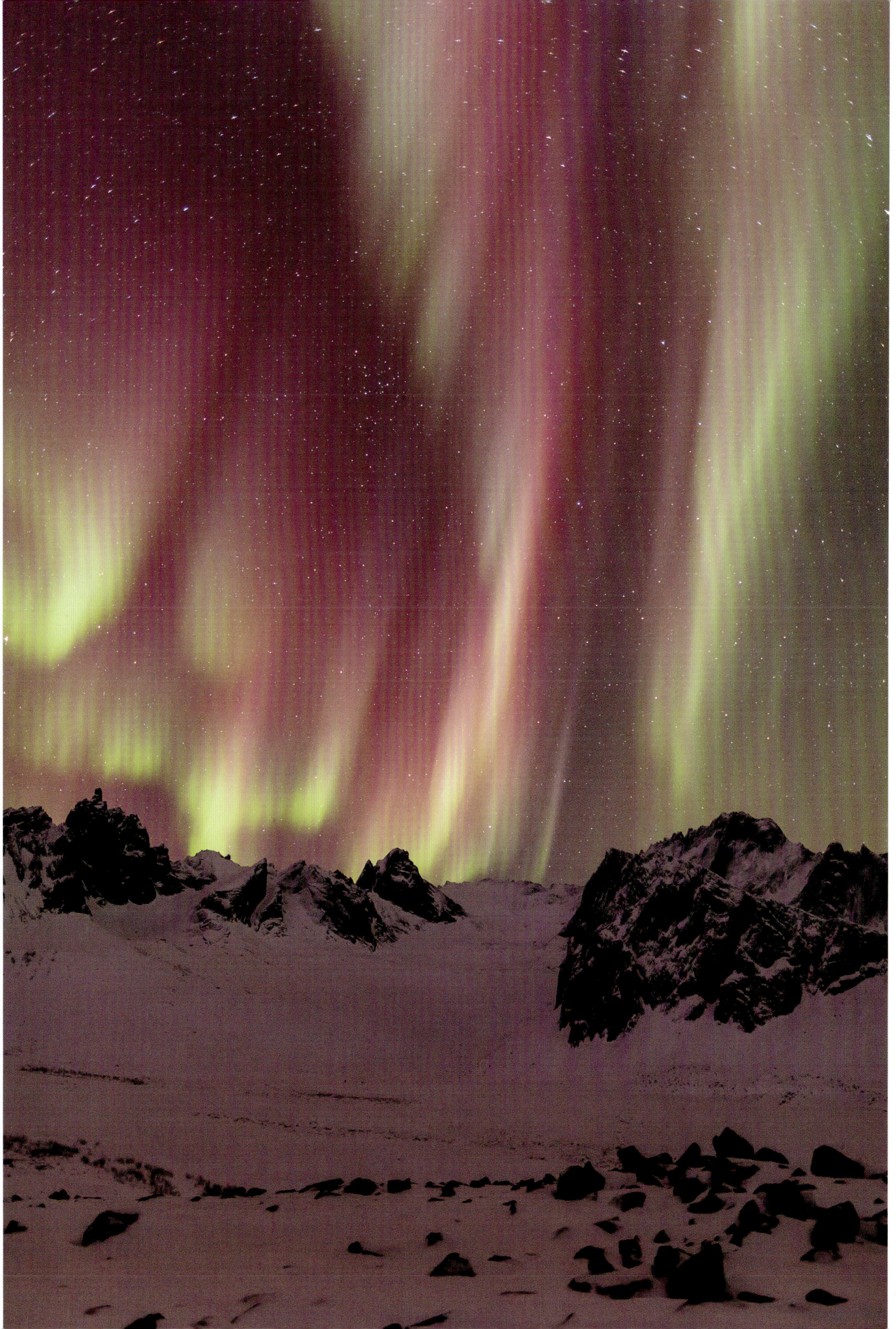

The next item to consider purchasing is an intervalometer. Virtually all DSLRs and mirrorless cameras will let you set shutter speeds up to 30 seconds, but at night, shutter speeds longer than 30 seconds are often required. Most cameras do offer a bulb mode, which lets you hold down the shutter-release button on the camera or on a remote release for the duration of the exposure, regardless of length. Using bulb mode in this manner is a hassle, however. Holding down the shutter release on the camera is likely to make the camera shake, which will ruin sharpness. Holding down the shutter release on a remote release prevents that problem but makes it difficult to time your exposures. How are you going to see your watch at night with your headlamp off? Yes, you can use the timer on your phone, but the light from the screen can bleed into your foreground, ruining the shot. In a pinch, you can set a timer on your watch and close the shutter when the chime sounds, but there's a better way: using an intervalometer.

An intervalometer is basically a fancy cable release that gives you control over four key parameters: the delay before the first shot is taken; the length of the exposure; the interval between frames; and the number of frames

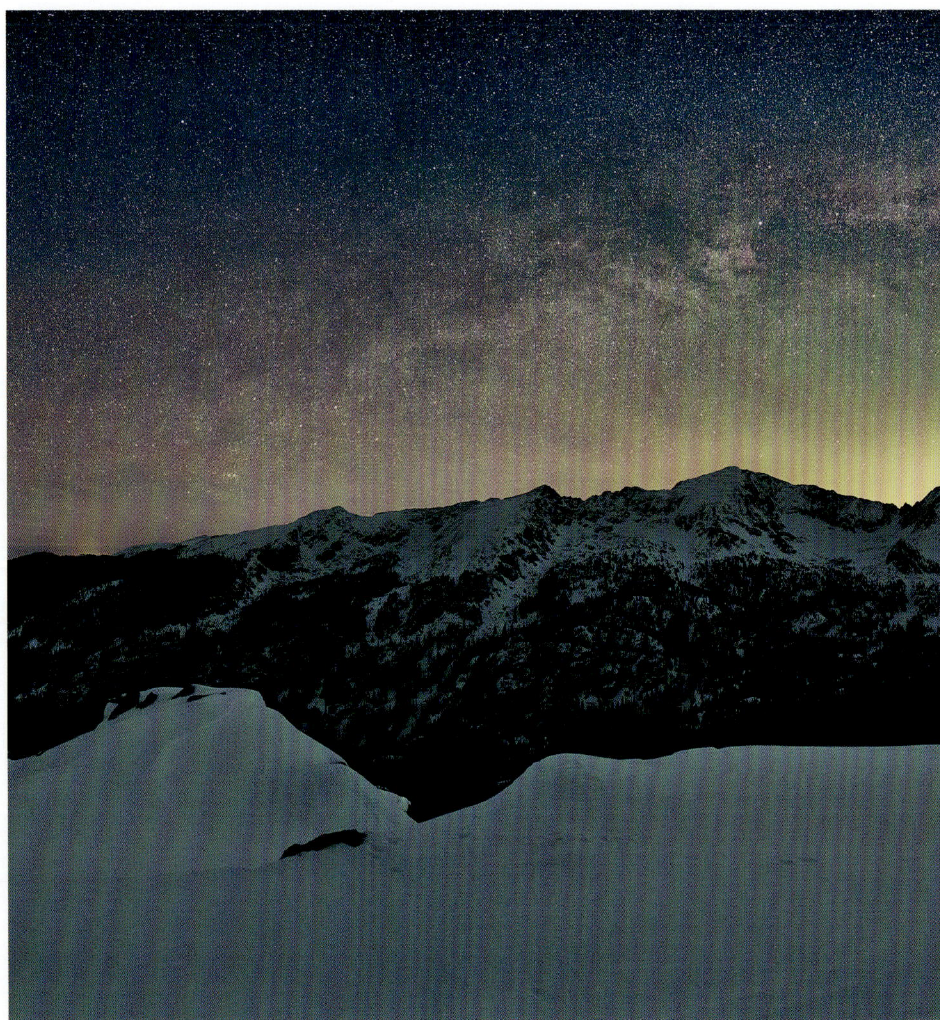

▶ FIGURE 2-18: Milky Way panorama over Gold Dust Peak from the ridge south of Charles Peak, Holy Cross Wilderness, Colorado. March 2, 2022, 4:27 a.m. Sony Alpha 7R IVa, Sony FE 14mm f/1.8 GM. Four camera positions, four frames per camera position, 15 seconds, f/1.8, ISO 6400. I was able to capture all the detail I needed in both sky and land using one exposure setting because the land was predominantly covered with snow, which made it approximately the same brightness as the sky. I processed each group of four images twice, once for land color and detail (images stacked in Photoshop, noise reduced with Stack Mode>Median), and once for sky color and detail (images aligned and noise reduced in RegiStar). I stitched the good-sky and good-land images together separately in Lightroom, then composited the two panoramas in Photoshop.

to be taken in a row. You'll find yourself using all of these settings as you dive deeper and deeper into night photography. In one common scenario, you'll make one exposure for the sky and a second, longer, exposure for the land. Using an intervalometer lets you change shutter speeds without touching the camera, eliminating the possibility of jarring the camera or tripod and causing misalignment of the two images. In another common scenario, you'll make multiple exposures with the same camera settings. Later, you can stack the images in Photoshop or specialized astronomical software and blend them in a way that reduces noise. Intervalometers make these procedures and many others much more convenient. If your camera manufacturer doesn't make one, you can probably find a model from a company such as Vello that makes camera accessories.

Long exposures and cold temperatures deplete batteries quickly. Bring at least one spare battery (I carry three). Batteries gradually lose charge if stored for a long time; be sure your batteries are freshly charged before heading into the field.

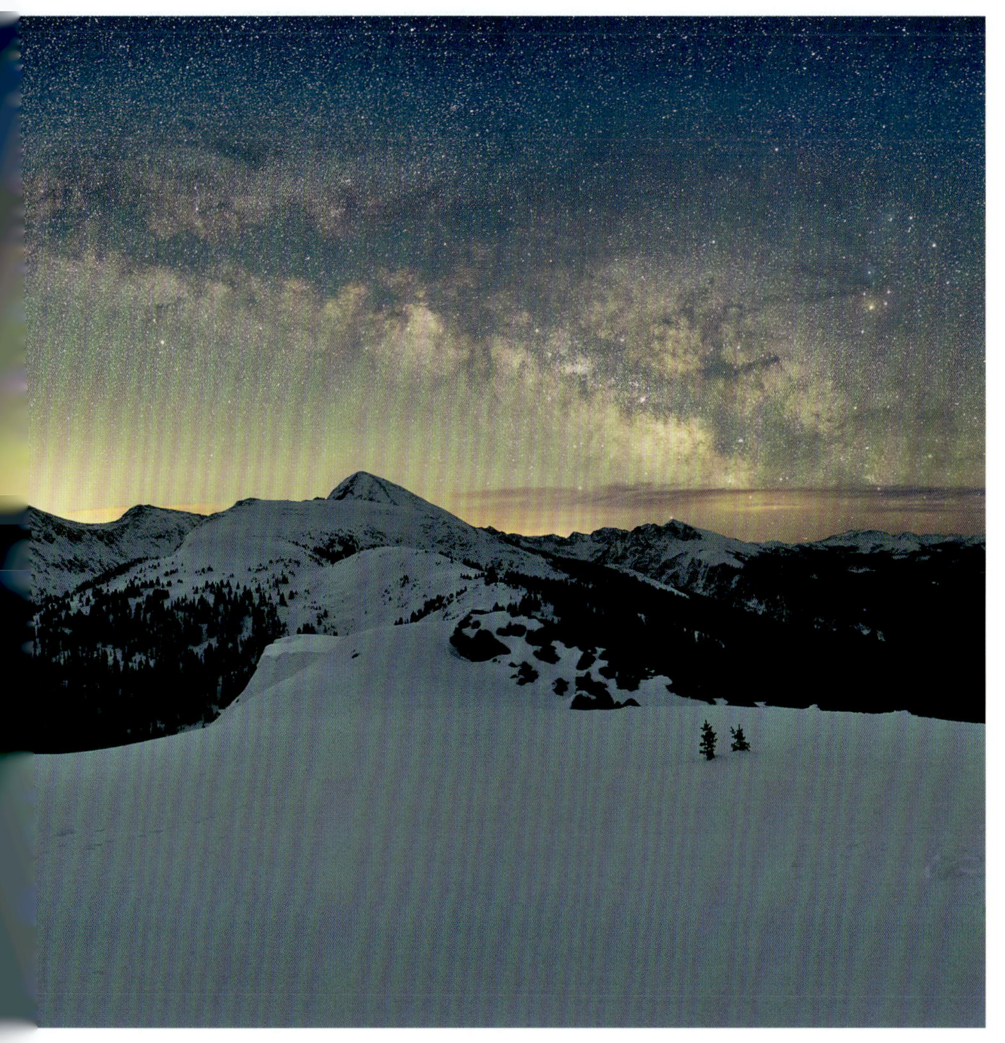

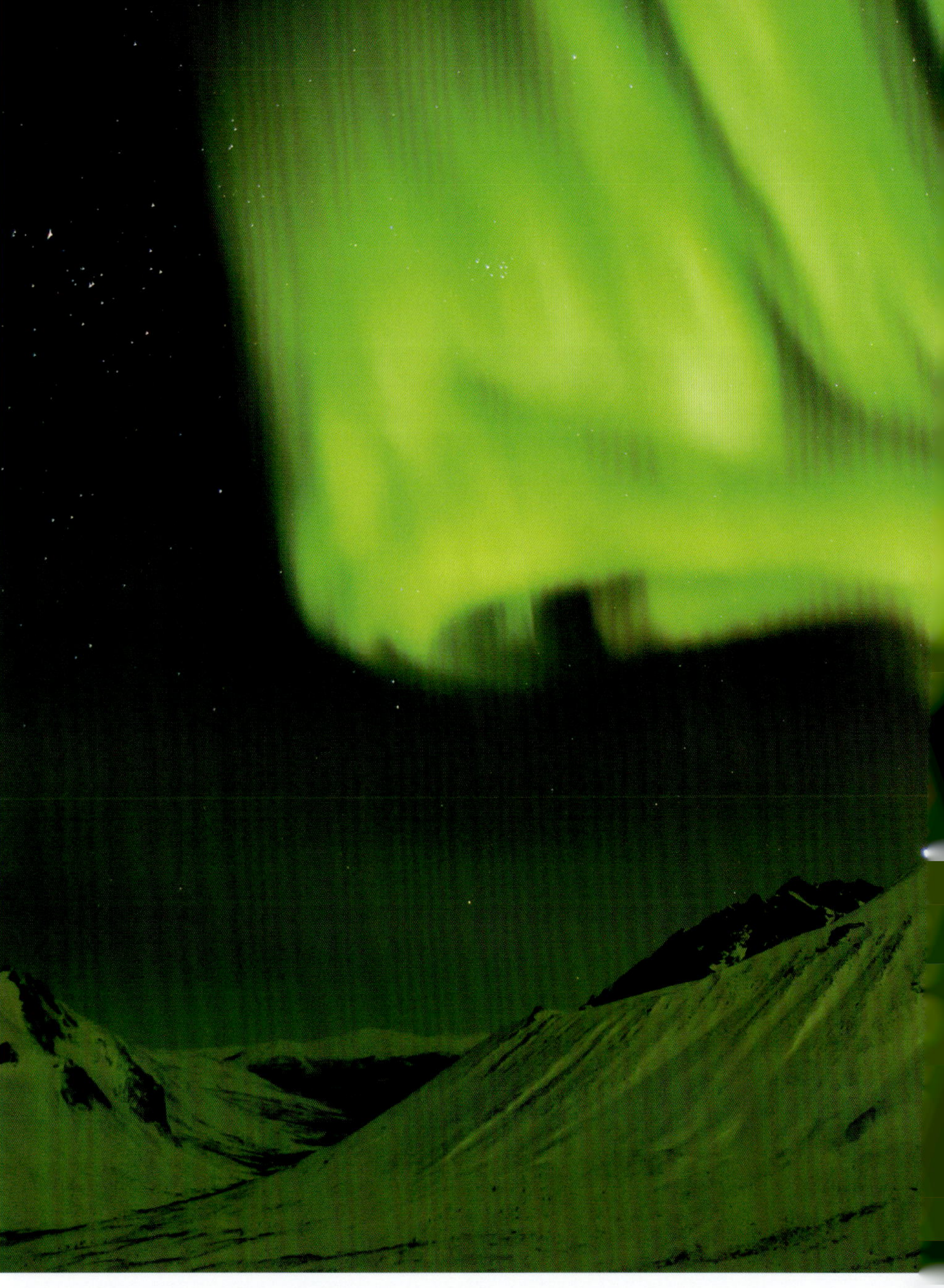

▸ FIGURE 2-19: Aurora over the Cloudy Range, Tombstone Territorial Park, Yukon Territory, Canada. March 19, 2015, 11:20 p.m. Canon EOS 5D Mark III, Canon EF 16-35mm f/2.8L II USM at 27mm. 3.2 seconds, f/2.8, ISO 3200.

One final accessory to consider: a lens heater. When the sun goes down, the temperature drops and cameras and lenses cool. If the temperature of the lens drops below the dew point, condensation can form on the front element, ruining your image. I once shot the Perseid meteor shower under conditions so humid I had to wipe moisture off the lens with an absorbent lens tissue after every single shot. Several manufacturers offer lens heaters. The simplest are just fabric strips with pockets for chemical hand warmers (the

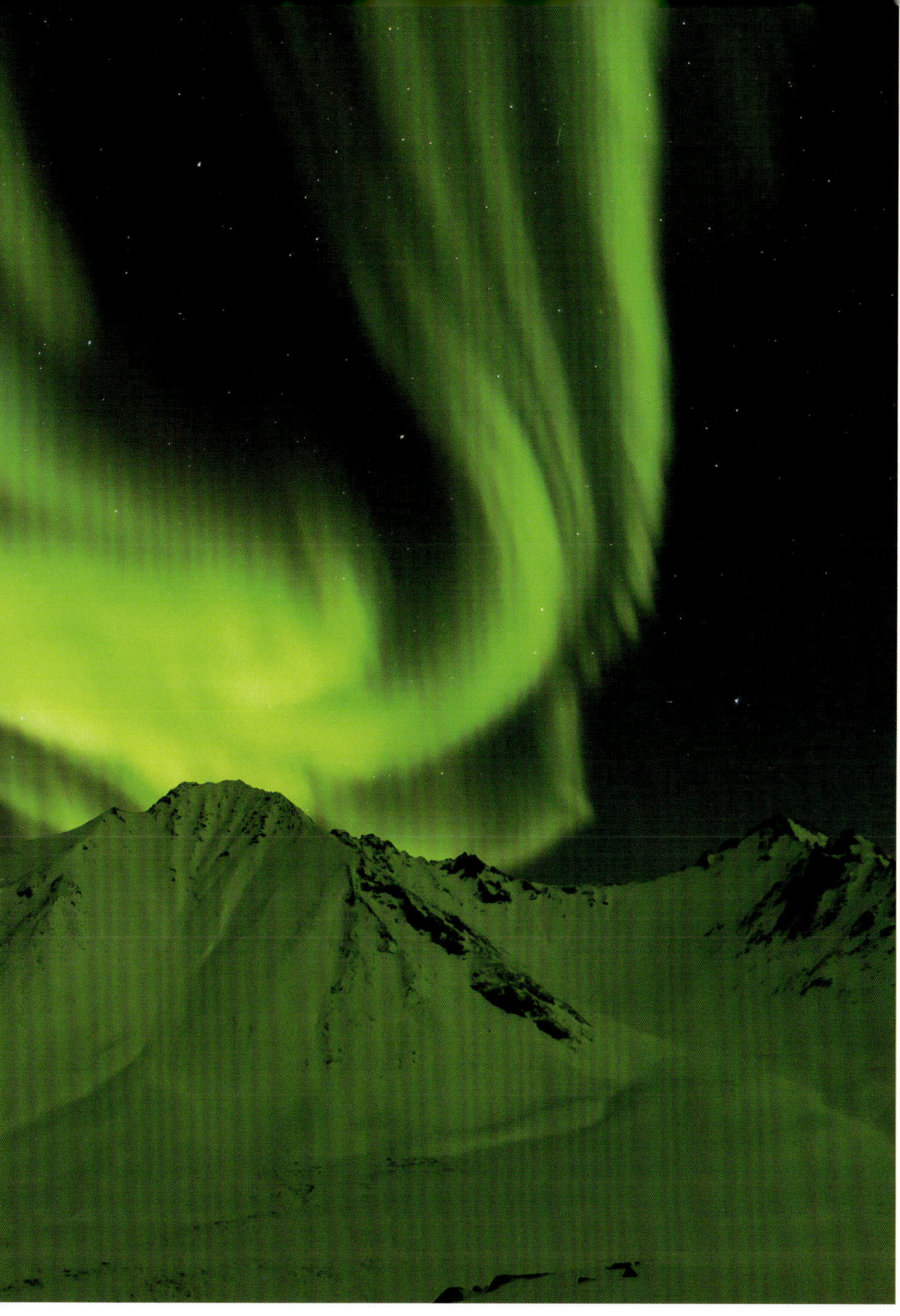

kind skiers use inside their gloves). The fabric strip wraps around the lens and attaches with hook-and-loop. Heavier but more effective lens warmers are fabric or Neoprene strips that have electric heating elements embedded in them. These plug into an external battery pack with a standard USB cable. Be sure you attach your lens warmer at the first sign of condensation. If you wait until the lens is thoroughly coated, it will take time for the lens to warm up again and the condensation to dissipate.

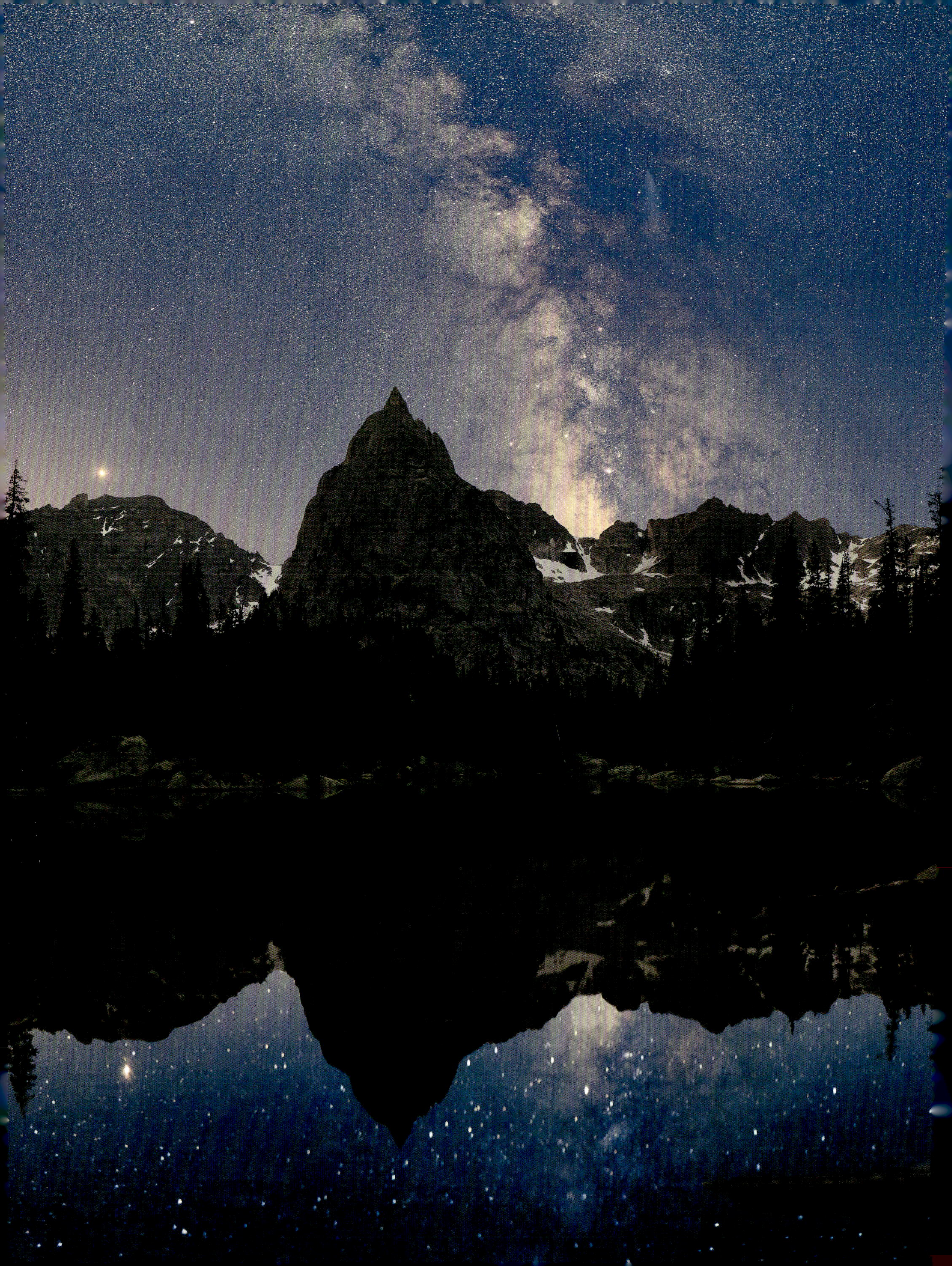

Essential Skills for Night Photography

No matter what subject you choose to photograph at night, you'll need to master certain skills. Among those skills are focusing at night, composing when you can barely see anything through the viewfinder, achieving the correct exposure when you can't get a meter reading, holding detail everywhere in the frame, controlling noise, and more. Let's start with focusing at night.

Achieving Critical Focus

In 2011 I had a once-in-a-lifetime opportunity to photograph from the summit of 14,014-foot North Maroon Peak by the light of the full moon. North Maroon Peak is one of the hardest Fourteeners in the state to climb. I climbed it in the dark, by headlamp, and arrived so early in the morning that only moonlight lit the vast expanse of the Maroon Bells-Snowmass Wilderness. Unfortunately, in my sleep-deprived, hypoxic mental fog, I missed the focus. Fortunately, I was able to shoot a beautiful 360-degree panorama of moonset at sunrise an hour later. Still, I had lost some unique images. Don't let a priceless opportunity like that one slip away from you. Here's how to achieve perfect focus in any situation.

When shooting grand landscapes during the day, you'll usually focus on something in between the closest part of your subject and the distant skyline. When shooting grand landscapes at night, however, you'll be shooting with your lens wide open, which means your depth of field will be very shallow. In theory, you could look up the hyperfocal distance for your lens at your shooting aperture and focus there to gain additional depth of field. In practice, however, such a strategy is difficult to implement, particularly with fast, moderately wide lenses. For example, the hyperfocal distance for a 35mm lens at f/1.4, using a strict standard for sharpness of .02 mm for the circle of confusion, is 142 feet. How are you going to figure out which part of your subject is 142 feet away, and how are you going to focus accurately on that subject in the dark? (For more on hyperfocal distance, see the sidebar on page 59.)

◄ FIGURE 3-1: Milky Way over Lone Eagle Peak and Mirror Lake, Indian Peaks Wilderness, Colorado. July 11, 2018, 1:34 a.m. Canon EOS 5D Mark IV, Canon EF 35mm f/1.4L II USM. Land: Two rows, four camera positions per row. For the upper row I shot four frames per camera position and reduced noise with Stack Mode>Median. For the lower row I shot only one frame per camera position because I didn't think I could realign the stars using RegiStar, given the slight rippling of the water surface. Land exposures: 40 seconds, f/1.4, ISO 6400. I shot one row for the sky, 10 seconds, f/1.4, ISO 6400, four frames per camera position, images aligned and noise reduced in RegiStar. I processed the land images twice, once for land color and once for water color. There are three major layers in the file: the sky; the land; and the reflection of the sky.

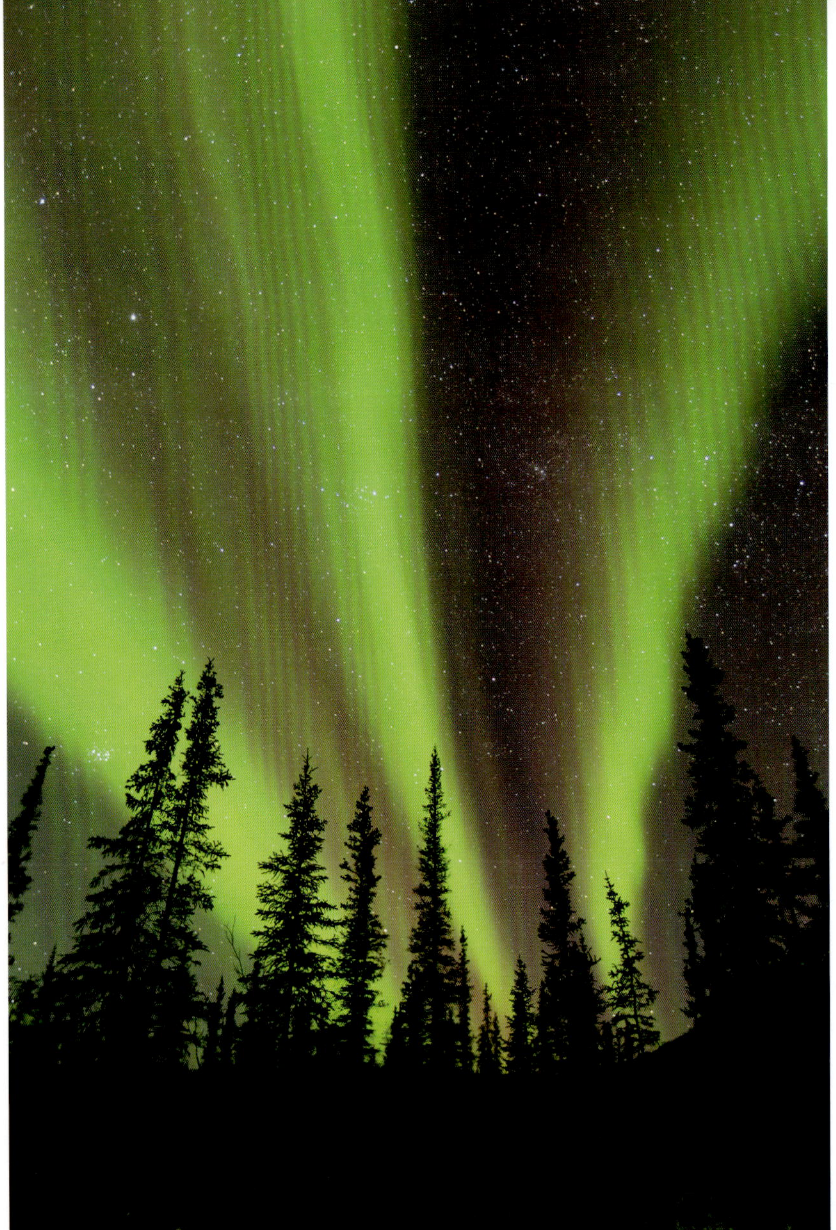

▸ FIGURE 3-2: Aurora over black spruce and the Brooks Range, near Wiseman, Alaska. March 8, 2016, 11:24 p.m. Canon EOS 5D Mark III, Canon EF 16-35mm f/2.8L II USM at 22mm. 25 seconds, f/2.8, ISO 3200.

At night, I always start by focusing on infinity; then I compose so all the critical parts of the foreground are within the depth of field. For most night landscapes, infinity is the only distance at which you'll need to focus. If you need greater depth of field than you can achieve in a single frame, you can try shooting the sky with the lens wide open to minimize star trailing, then stop down the lens and shoot a second frame for the land (more on this approach later in this chapter). Or you can try focus stacking, which I'll cover in chapter 7.

If you've arrived during the day, then focusing is easy. Turn on auto-focus, and set your camera to use a single, central auto-focus point. The central auto-focus point is usually the one that delivers the greatest accuracy. Auto-

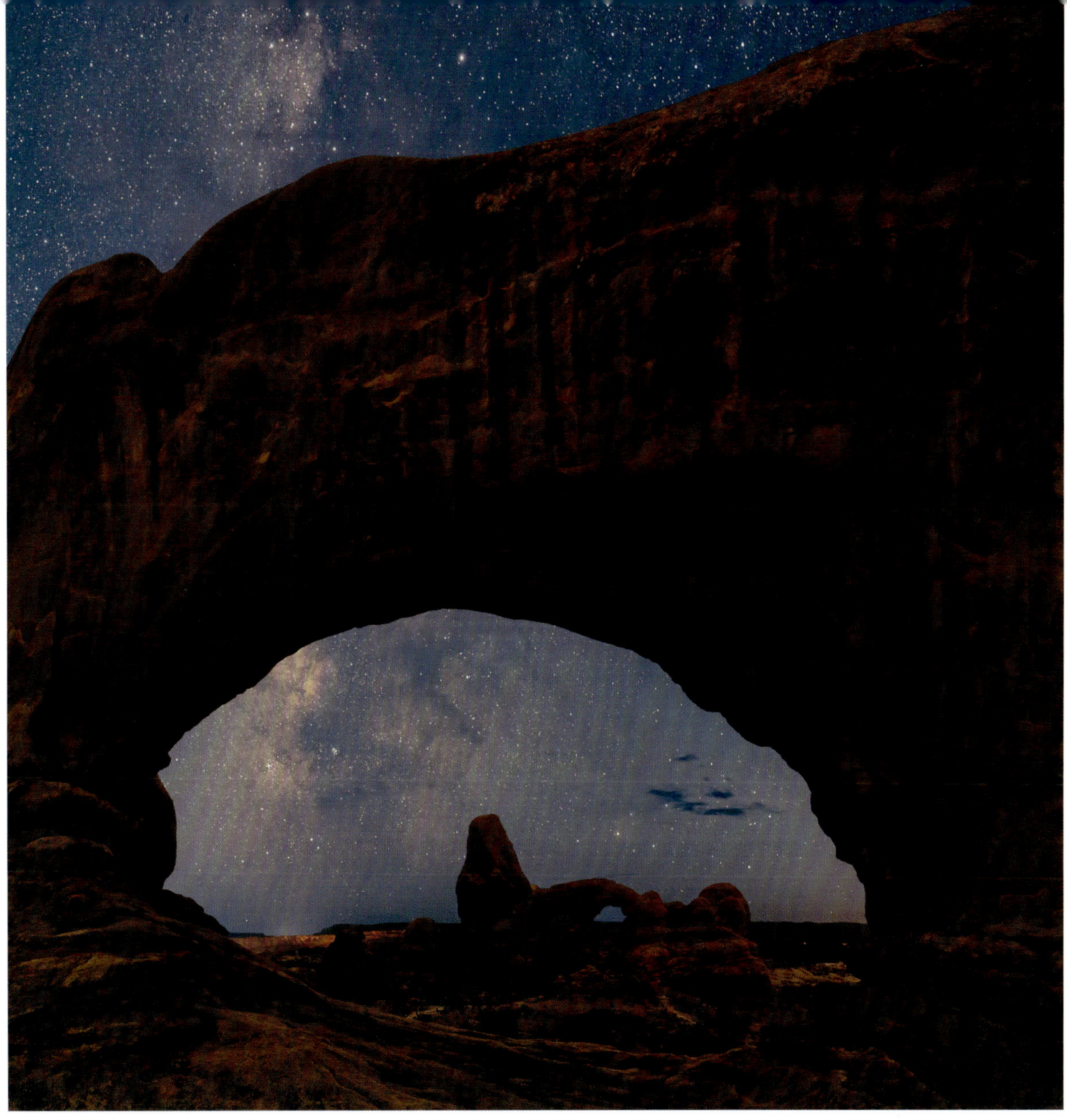

focus on a distant object. If you're using a wide-angle lens, as is likely, any-thing beyond 50 yards away is essentially at infinity. Most older lenses have a distance scale, including an infinity symbol, and an index mark. If you're using such a lens, examine it to see where the index mark lined up with the distance scale. Auto-focus on something nearby, then focus again on the same distant object. Is your auto-focus repeatable? Does the distance scale line up next to the index mark in the same way every time? If so, you're good. If the lens barrel comes to a stop at a different place each time you auto-focus on a distant object, try this: turn off auto-focus and turn on Live View. Zoom in to a magnification of 10x. Beware: some cameras allow an even

▲ FIGURE 3-3: Milky Way over Turret Arch through North Window, Arches National Park, Utah. October 13, 2020, 8:37 p.m. Canon EOS 5D Mark IV, Canon EF 35mm f/1.4L II USM. Land: one row, two camera positions per row, one frame per camera position, 40 seconds, f/1.4, ISO 5000. Sky: one row, two camera positions per row, one frame per camera position, 10 seconds, f/1.4, ISO 3200. I tried to shoot four frames per camera position but so many people were exploring the area with their flashlights that I was lucky to get just one frame that was not ruined by bright light on an arch.

higher degree of magnification—so much so that everything looks blurry even if you've focused the camera perfectly. You may need to zoom back out a step or two from the maximum zoom level. Carefully focus manually on a distant subject. Once you've achieved critical focus, be sure you don't bump the focus ring! Better yet, use a bit of gaffer tape, which doesn't leave a residue unless you let it bake in the sun, to tape the lens at infinity focus.

Modern, focus-by-wire lenses designed primarily for mirrorless cameras usually lack a distance scale. These lenses don't have a mechanical connection between the focusing ring and the lens elements. The focusing ring on older lenses reaches a hard stop at each end of the focus range (closest possible focus and infinity focus). These lenses are referred to as "mechanical" lenses. Focus-by-wire lenses, on the other hand, have no such mechanical stops; you can rotate the focus ring indefinitely in either direction. Auto-focus still works, of course, so you can still focus at infinity during the day. However, taping the lens does no good. Some mirrorless cameras will retain the last-used focus setting even if you turn them off, then turn them on again. However, some mirrorless cameras "park" the lens when you turn off the camera, changing the distance at which the lens is focused. This behavior can sometimes be disabled by changing a menu setting. These cameras will then retain the focus distance when you turn off the camera. Regardless of whether your camera parks the lens when you power off, you may find you lose the focus distance if you change lenses or change batteries. Dig into your owner's manual and experiment with your particular camera to be sure you understand how it behaves.

Focusing is more difficult if you've arrived at your shooting location at night. With mechanical lenses, you might think you could simply rotate the focus ring until the infinity symbol lines up with the index mark. Unfortunately, that's usually not accurate enough to achieve critical focus wide open. Nor can you simply twist the focus ring until it reaches its mechanical limit. Many older lenses let you focus *past* infinity. One reason is to permit critical focus at infinity even as the lens expands and contracts in extreme heat and cold. Another is to protect the auto-focus mechanism. Lens designers don't want the focusing mechanism to bang into a hard stop when the user focuses on infinity.

Much night photography is done on moonless nights. If the moon is above the horizon, however, your camera may be able to auto-focus on it. You might also be able to auto-focus on distant city lights. If you have a very bright flashlight or headlamp, you may be able to shine it on a detailed object 50 yards away and auto-focus on that object. Or you can walk into the scene, place a flashlight at the correct distance, return to your camera, and focus on it. Some photographers carry a bright laser pointer. They point the laser

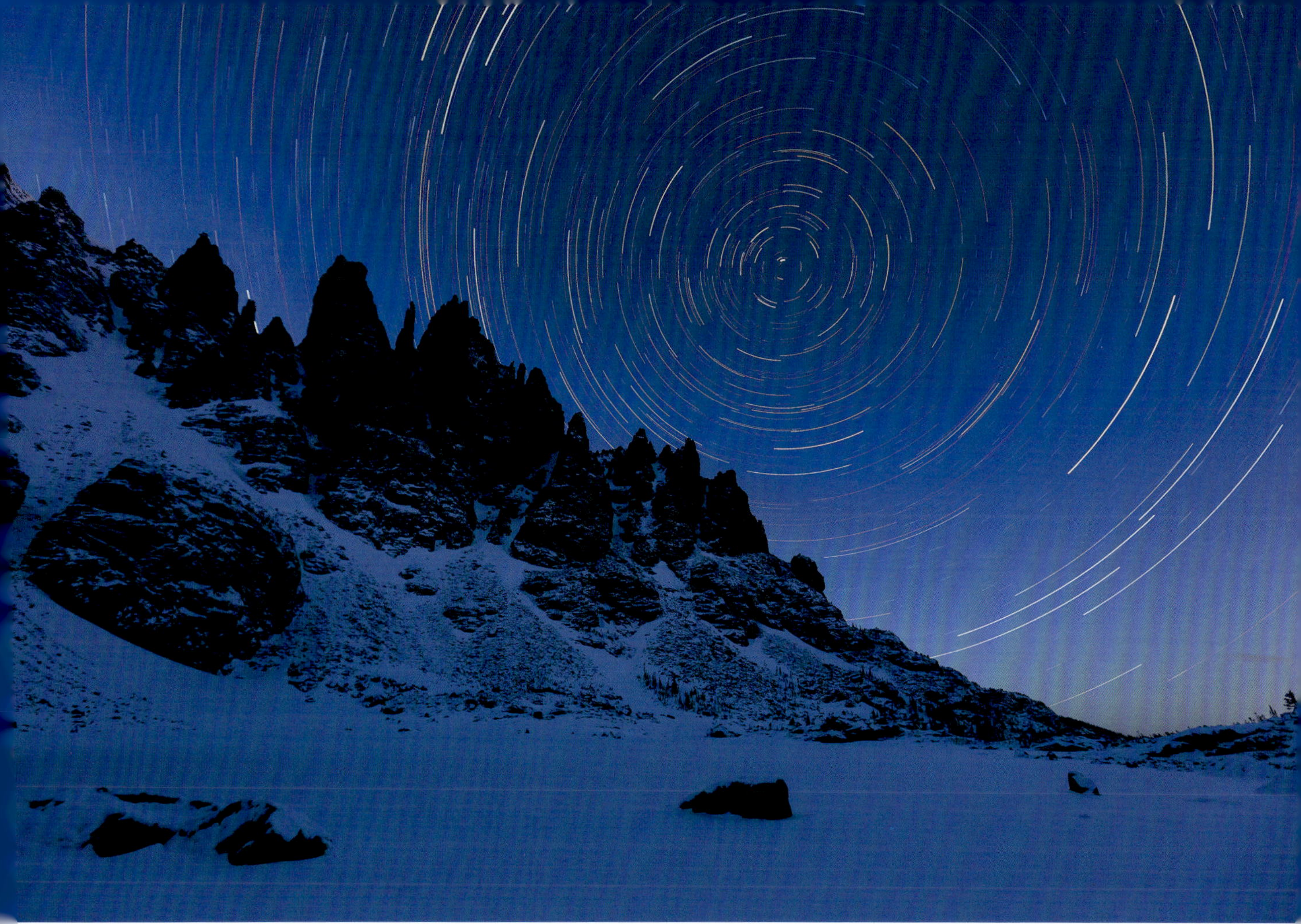

at a distant object, then use auto-focus or the Live View technique described above to focus. Inexpensive laser pointers designed for PowerPoint presentations may not be bright enough. Look for a model designed for amateur astronomers, who use it to point out stars and constellations.

Once you've achieved infinity focus, be sure to turn auto-focus off completely if you haven't already. This is important even if you have removed control of auto-focus from the shutter release and assigned it to a button on the back of the camera. It's all too easy to hit that button by mistake, particularly in the dark, while wearing gloves, and while wearing warm hats and hoods that muffle the whirr of the auto-focus motor as the lens hunts futilely for something to focus on.

If all these techniques fail, try this: turn off auto-focus. Point the camera toward a bright planet or star. If you have a mechanical lens, rotate the focus ring until the infinity symbol is opposite the index mark. This will give you an approximation of infinity focus. If you neglect this step, the stars may be so blurry that they disappear completely. Slowly rotate the focus ring on focus-by-wire lenses until the first stars pop into view. Some cameras will

▲ FIGURE 3-4: Star trails over the Saber, Petite Grepon, Sharkstooth, and Sky Pond, Rocky Mountain National Park, Colorado. January 22, 2015, 6:08 p.m. to 8:01 p.m. Canon 5D Mark III, Canon EF 16-35mm f/2.8L II USM at 16mm. 30 frames, 4 minutes, f/4.0, ISO 200.

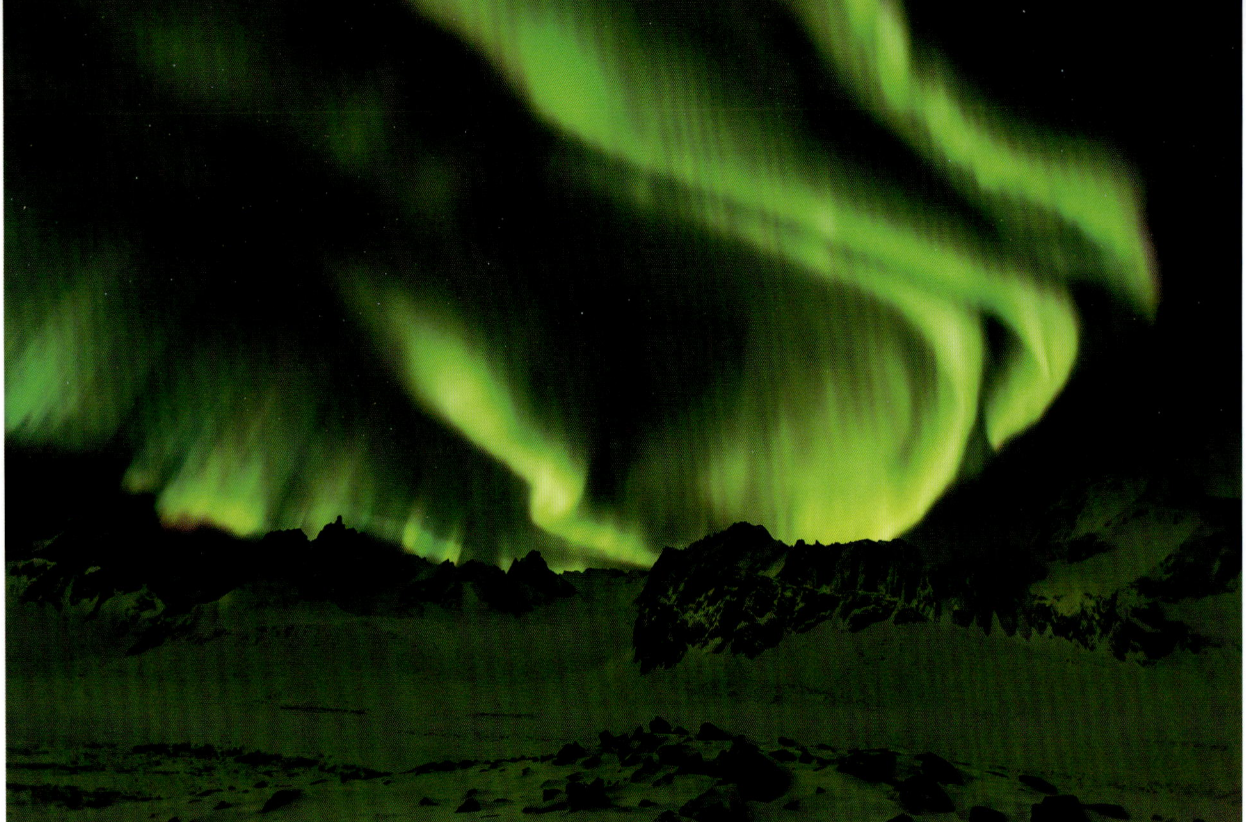

show an approximate distance scale in the viewfinder when you are focusing manually. Now engage Live View (if you're using a DSLR), magnify the view to 10x, and focus manually on a bright planet or star. A star is sharp when its image is as small as possible and pure white, with little or no color fringing. As you focus on a bright star, keep an eye out for dimmer ones nearby, which appear at their brightest when you've achieved critical focus. Canon users may need to disable exposure simulation in their live-view menu to actually see a star. Nikon DSLR users may need to set the lens to the largest available aperture before turning on Live View.

Regardless of which method you use, be sure to check focus by shooting a test frame. Include a bit of the skyline when testing at night. It's easier to check the sharpness of the skyline than the sharpness of a star because a slightly out-of-focus star looks just like a slightly larger star. A perfectly focused image should show not only the bright stars, but lots of dimmer stars as well, all rendered as small, sharp points.

No matter how carefully you focus and no matter how closely you examine the test image on your camera's LCD screen, it can still be hard to be certain you've achieved perfect focus. This is particularly true for ultra-fast, moderate wide-angle lenses like a 35mm f/1.4, which are much less forgiving than ultra-wide-angle, slower lenses like a 16mm f/2.8. If you want to be absolutely sure you've nailed the focus, you can use a filter called a Bahtinov mask to confirm focus. These filters were invented by an amateur Russian astronomer named Pavel Bahtinov in 2005 to aid in focusing small telescopes. Today several companies have taken his idea, refined it, and produced filters for use with the wide-angle lenses typically used for night photographs of grand landscapes. In its simplest form, a Bahtinov mask has a pattern of lines like those shown in figure 3-6. By placing a bright star or planet at precisely the midpoint of the grid, a diffraction pattern is formed. The photographer adjusts the focus until the pattern is symmetrical (figure 3-7). The filter is placed in a filter holder which screws onto the front of the lens with an adapter ring (figure 3-8). Be sure to remove the filter before you begin shooting in earnest.

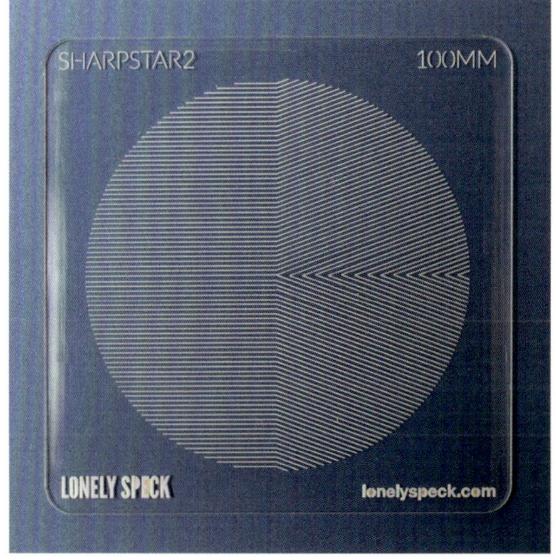

▲ FIGURE 3-6: A Bahtinov mask made by Lonely Speck showing the diffraction grating that allows precise focusing.

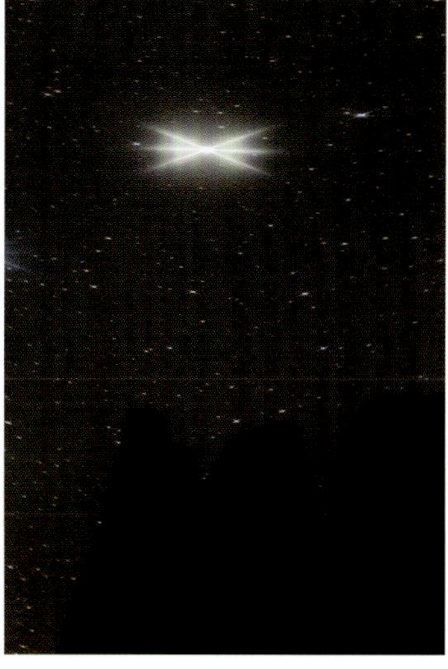

▲ FIGURE 3-7: Photo taken with a Canon EF 35mm f/1.4L II USM lens at f/1.4 and a Bahtinov mask made by Lonely Speck showing the pattern that results when focus is perfect.

◄ FIGURE 3-8: A Bahtinov mask made by Lonely Speck in a Lee filter holder attached to a lens.

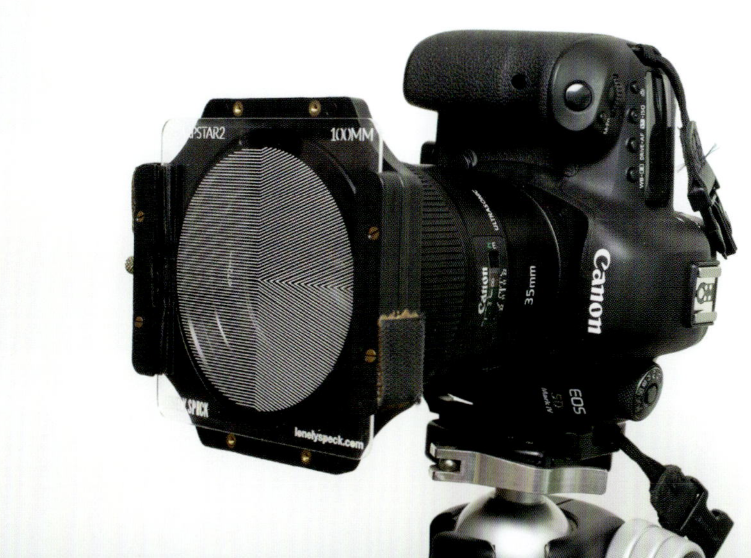

Bahtinov masks are easiest to use when the target planet or star is very bright. They're also easiest to use with fast, moderate wide-angle lenses like a 35mm f/1.4—precisely the type of lens that is least forgiving of small focus errors since the depth of field is so shallow when the lens is wide open. They're harder to use with ultra-wide, slower lenses like a 14mm or 16mm f/2.8. For one, the pattern is dimmer because less light can come through the smaller aperture. For another, the pattern is smaller because the angle of view of the lens is so large.

Most Bahtinov masks have a single pattern of horizontal and diagonal lines, which means that the diffraction pattern only appears if the target star is precisely centered. If you don't see the pattern, it can be hard to know which way to move the filter (up or down in the filter holder or left to right by panning the camera on the tripod). The Focus on Stars filter, created by Gabor Takacs, solves this problem by having a large number of tiny Bahtinov patterns arranged in a grid. That gives you many more opportunities to place the target star at the center of a Bahtinov pattern.

To be effective with wide-angle lenses, the grid lines must be very thin and very tightly spaced. If the grid pattern is too coarse, the target star can either fall into the gap between the lines or be completely blocked by one of the lines, so no pattern appears. According to Takacs, the Focus on Stars filter has grid lines only a few microns apart. As of this writing, the Focus on Stars filter is the only Bahtinov mask I've used that will work well with a 16mm f/2.8 lens.

Here's a depth-of-field table for certain lenses mounted on full-frame cameras and focused at infinity. The circle of confusion (CoC) is .02mm. The circle of confusion refers to a standard of sharpness. A CoC of .02mm is a tighter standard for sharpness than that used by many phone apps, which often use .03mm. Check a phone app or online hyperfocal distance calculator if you're using a camera with a sensor smaller than full frame.

Focal length	Aperture f/1.4 or f/1.8	Aperture f/2.0	Aperture f/2.8
14mm	18 feet to infinity at f/1.8	16 feet to infinity	11 feet to infinity
16mm	Not available at this time	21 feet to infinity	15 feet to infinity
20mm	46 feet to infinity at f/1.4	33 feet to infinity	23 feet to infinity
24mm	67 feet to infinity at f/1.4	47 feet to infinity	33 feet to infinity
35mm	142 feet to infinity at f/1.4	100 feet to infinity	71 feet to infinity
50mm	290 feet to infinity at f/1.4	205 feet to infinity	145 feet to infinity

Hyperfocal Distance and Depth of Field

Depth of field refers to the zone of sharpness in an image from near to far. For example, you might say that the depth of field in a particular landscape print extends from two feet to infinity. All objects two feet away or farther appear to be sharp.

The hyperfocal distance is the distance at *which you focus* to get the best possible depth of field at a particular focal length and aperture. Depth of field extends from one-half of the hyperfocal distance to infinity. For example, the hyperfocal distance for a 24mm lens on a full-frame camera at f/22 is 51 inches (CoC .02mm). If I focus the lens at that distance, depth of field will extend from 25.5 inches to infinity.

That's the basic idea. Now let's dive in a little deeper.

In a sense, depth of field is an optical illusion. You can actually only focus a lens at one particular distance. Only objects at the focused distance will truly be as sharp as the lens and camera can deliver. Objects closer than the focused distance, as well as those farther away, will become more and more blurry as the distance between them and the focused distance increases. But our eyes do not have infinite resolving power. As long as the width of the blurry edge of the object is narrower than a certain limit, we still see the object as sharp. One widely accepted standard for "sharp" is that the blurry edge cannot be more than $\frac{1}{100}$th of an inch wide in the print. Since all prints require enlarging the tiny image captured by the sensor, the blurry edge on the sensor must be still narrower.

With that background information, you can now understand that all hyperfocal and depth-of-field tables are based on a series of assumptions, in particular on how big a print you want to make and how closely you want to view it. A particular image may have a depth of field from two feet to infinity when printed at 8x10 inches and viewed from a foot away. That same image may have a depth of field from four feet to infinity if you make a 30x40-inch print and view it from a foot away. View that 30x40-inch print from five feet away, however, and once again it has a depth of field from two feet to infinity. Our ability to resolve fine detail steadily declines as we get farther from the subject. For example, you can easily read a book held at arm's length. Place the book 20 feet away, and the task is impossible.

You should think of hyperfocal tables as optimistic. They provide a minimal level of sharpness that will be acceptable in magazine-size prints but may not deliver the sharpness you need if you plan to make a big print. If your composition requires that you obtain the maximum

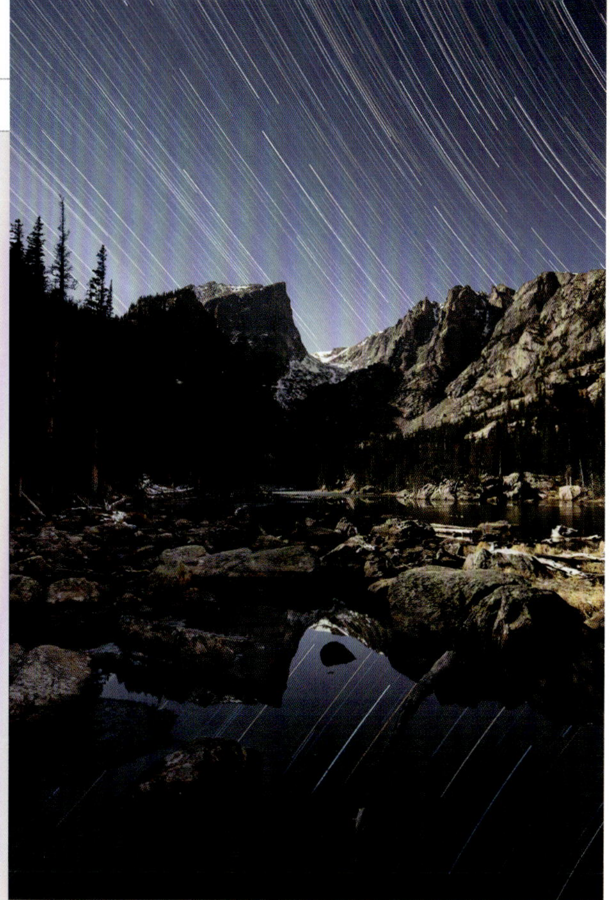

▲ FIGURE 3-9: Star trails over Dream Lake and Hallett Peak, Rocky Mountain National Park, Colorado. November 7, 2016, 6:52 p.m. to 8:32 p.m. Canon EOS 5D Mark III, Canon EF 16-35mm f/2.8L II USM at 22mm. Land and sky: 32 frames, 3 minutes, f/5.6, ISO 1600. A first-quarter moon (53 percent illuminated) provided the light on the land.

depth of field possible, then by all means use them. If, on the other hand, you're shooting with a wide-angle lens and the closest object in your composition is 50 feet away, don't focus on the hyperfocal distance. Instead, focus on the closest object, which will essentially be at infinity with a wide-angle lens, stop down to f/8 or f/11 (usually your sharpest apertures), and fire away.

All of these calculations can seem rather befuddling when you're hypoxic and sleep-deprived. To double-check that you've got it right, shoot a test frame, enlarge it on your LCD by a factor of 10, and scroll back and forth across the image to be sure everything is sharp. If you have an older camera, the image may look fuzzy everywhere at 10X, limiting the usefulness of this approach, but newer cameras have better LCDs that should let you evaluate sharpness even when the image is enlarged. When in doubt, compare sharpness at the focused distance (which should be razor-sharp if you're on a good tripod) with sharpness at the near and far limits of your composition.

Composition at Night

The principles of good composition in daylight still hold true at night. The trick is implementing them when you can't see through the lens.

The best way to choose the ideal composition for your nocturnal landscape is to visit it in daylight first. Scouting during the day, when you can see a considerable distance in any direction, makes it much easier to locate great foregrounds. It also makes it easier to spot distracting elements you might overlook at night, such as distant powerlines or roads. Such flaws may be nearly impossible to see on your camera's LCD display, but all too obvious when you view your image on a big monitor.

Daylight scouting lets you plan your shot in advance rather than trying to figure it out on the fly in the dark. What focal-length lens will you need? Will your widest lens be wide enough, or will you need to shoot a panorama? How important is detail in the land to the success of your image? If it's important, you'll probably need to shoot two frames, one exposed for land, one exposed for sky. What depth-of-field challenges will you face? All of these questions are easier to answer in daylight than at night.

If you can't visit your location in advance during the daytime, you'll be forced to rely on guess-and-check to get the composition right. When your eyes are dark-adapted, you'll probably be able to distinguish land from sky as you look through the viewfinder—but not much else. Use the built-in level your camera may offer or a small bubble level inserted in your camera's hot shoe to be sure the camera is level from left to right. Estimate the right exposure and shoot a compositional study frame. If you plan to use a shutter speed that will extend into minutes for the final image, consider boosting the ISO to a very high value to speed up the process of refining your composition. It

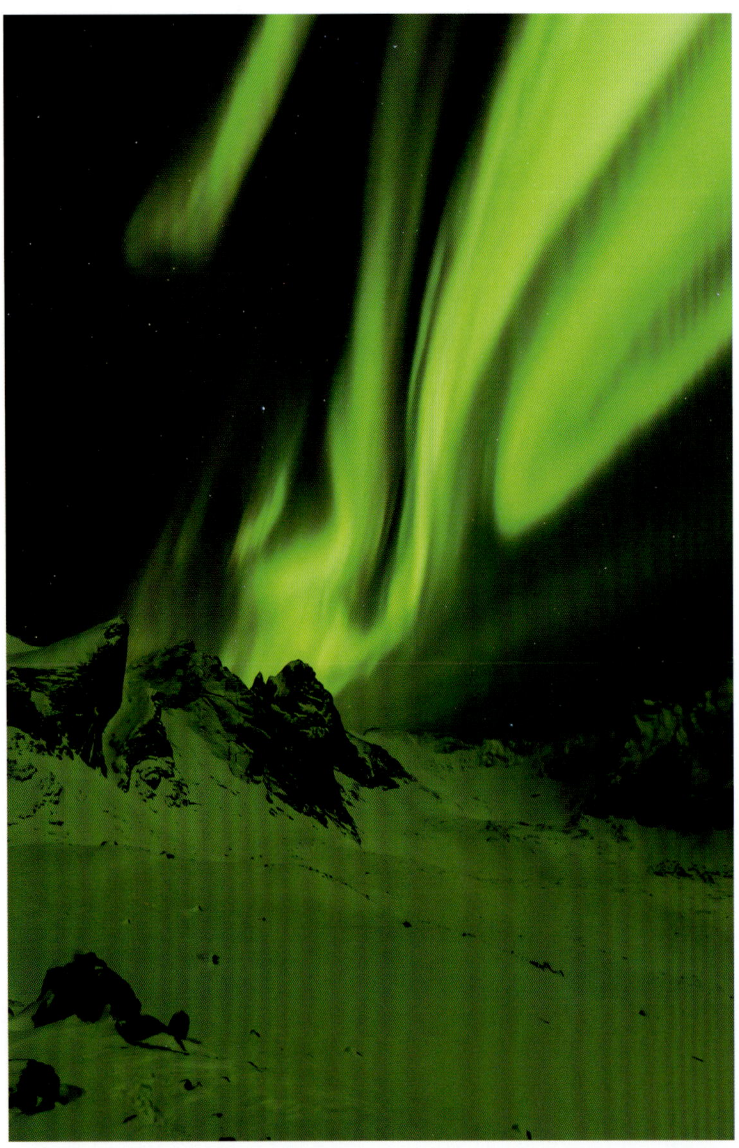

▲ FIGURE 3-10: Aurora over the Tombstone Range, Tombstone Territorial Park, Yukon Territory, Canada. March 20, 2015, 1:48 a.m. Canon EOS 5D Mark III, Canon EF 16-35mm f/2.8L II USM at 23mm. 3.2 seconds, f/2.8, ISO 3200.

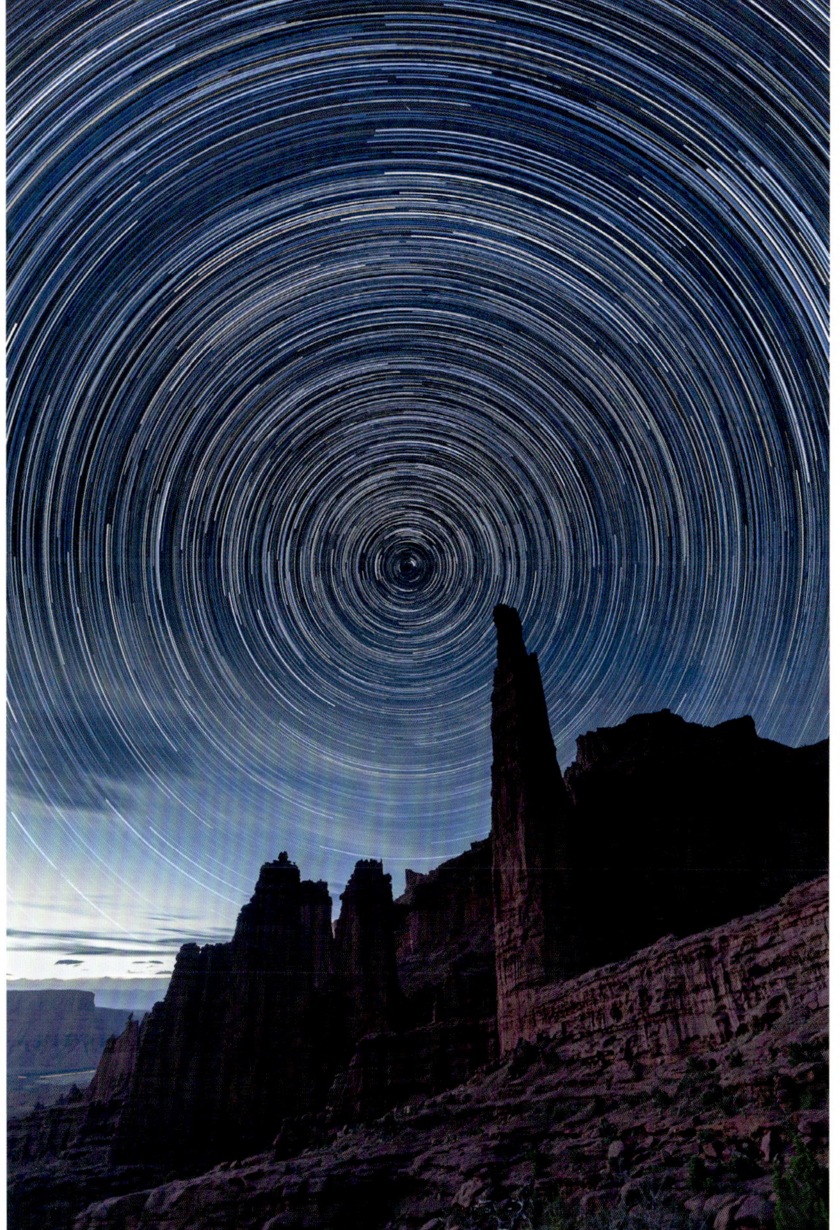

◄ FIGURE 3-11: Star trails over the Titan, Fisher Towers, Utah. August 10-11, 2016, 9:44 p.m. to 3:28 a.m. Canon 1Ds Mark III, Canon EF 16-35mm f/2.8L II USM at 16mm. Land: 6 seconds, f/11, ISO 200 (shot at 8:33 p.m., 18 minutes after sunset). Sky: 339 frames, one minute, f/2.8, ISO 200.

doesn't matter if the test image is noisy since it's only a compositional study frame. Dial the ISO back down for the final shot.

The process of composing an image begins when you have a gut reaction to a prospective subject—"That's cool! I want to shoot that!" The first step is emotional, but the next two steps are analytical. What is it about the scene that makes you think it is worth photographing? What are the key elements that must be included to convey the emotion you are feeling? Include those elements, and no others. The novelist Antoine de Saint-Exupéry wrote, "Perfection is achieved, not when there is nothing more to add, but when there is nothing left to take away."

The final step in achieving a good composition is arranging the key elements within the frame. Now you need to compose with your feet (and your knees and elbows). Examine the subject from all angles and all possible camera heights: ground level, knee level, waist level, eye level. Move left and right to decide how foreground elements should line up with background elements. The perspective of your photograph is determined by camera placement, not by focal length. By perspective I mean the size of your foreground elements relative to the background. Move forward to put more emphasis on the foreground. Move backward to give the background more visual weight. The final step is adjusting the focal length of your lens to once again include only those elements that will generate maximum emotional impact.

Exposure at Night

Achieving correct exposure at night is more challenging than during the day. For starters, you probably won't be able to get a meter reading, even under the light of a full moon. In addition, your exposure choices are more limited at night than they are during the day. In daytime you can choose the aperture you need to achieve the depth of field you want and still keep shutter speeds within reason, all without resorting to high ISOs. At night you'll be shooting with your lens wide open and begging for every photon you can get. Shutter speeds are limited by the motion of the stars, and ISOs are limited by the ability of your camera to control noise.

It's helpful to remember a few rules of thumb to get you close to correct exposure. For example, the correct exposure for the Milky Way, one of the dimmest night-photography subjects, using a lens with a maximum aperture of f/1.4, is about 10 seconds, f/1.4, ISO 6400. With an f/1.8 lens, it's 15 seconds, f/1.8, ISO 6400. And with an f/2.8 lens, it's 30 seconds, f/2.8, ISO 6400. That assumes you're shooting on a moonless night far away from city lights. The correct exposure for a landscape lit by the full moon is about four stops down from that, or about 30 seconds, f/2.8, ISO 400. The correct exposure for the aurora varies widely. The variation in exposure in my own collection of aurora photos goes from 2 seconds, f/2.0, ISO 800, all the way to 30 seconds, f/2.8, ISO 6400—a difference of six stops. My starting-point exposure, however, is 10 seconds, f/2.8, ISO 3200. Finding exactly the right exposure within the ranges suggested here is a matter of making test exposures, then checking your histogram. See the sidebar if you need help reading a histogram. Important note: these recommendations ignore, for the moment, the effect of these shutter speeds on the appearance of stars, which will vary dramatically depending on the focal length of the lens you use.

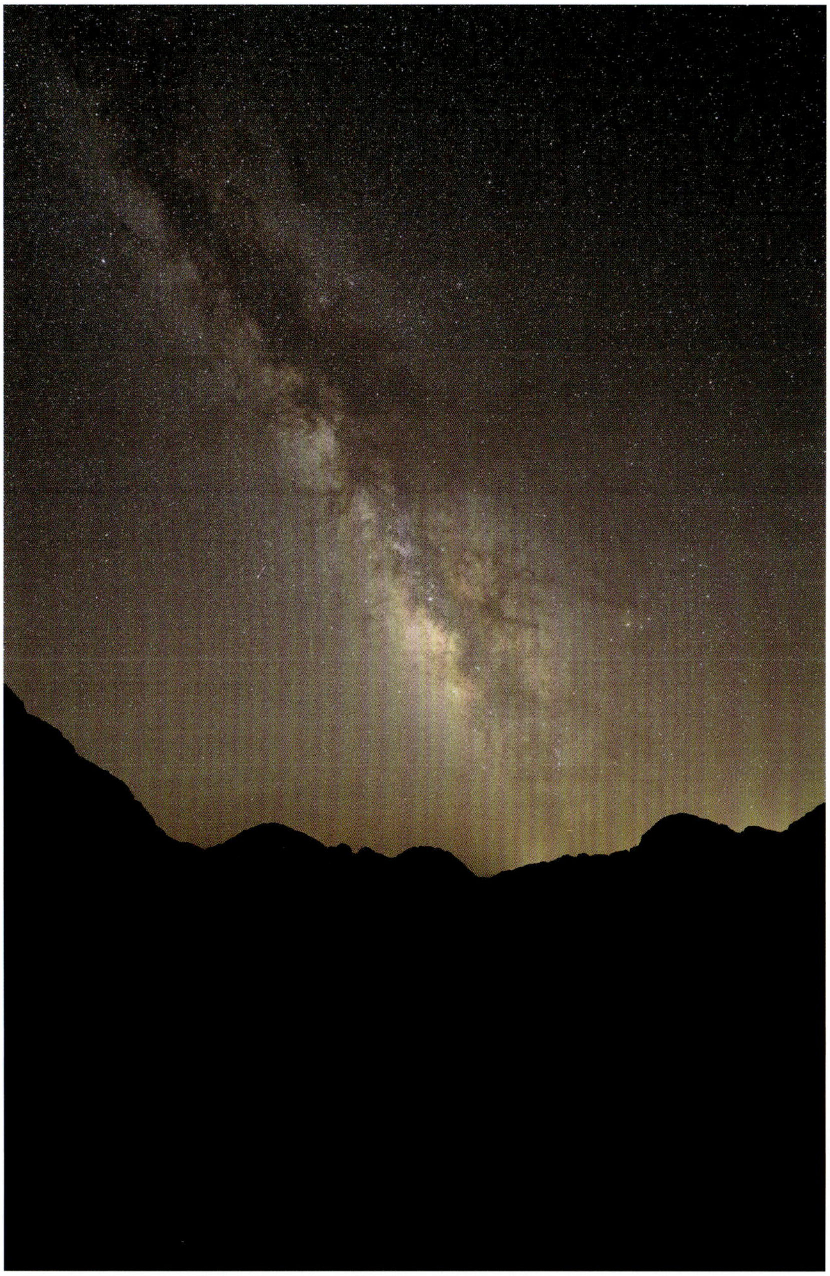

◄ FIGURE 3-12: Milky Way from Hunchback Pass, Weminuche Wilderness, Colorado. This is a single Milky Way shot, not yet composited with a land image, shown as it would look on the back of the camera when shot with a daylight white balance. August 7, 2023, 10:01 p.m. Sony Alpha 7R IVa, Sony FE 14mm f/1.8 GM. 15 seconds, f/1.8, ISO 6400.

▼ FIGURE 3-13: The histogram for the image in figure 3-12, showing how the peak of the rounded hump in the data that represents the Milky Way and sky (excluding stars) is roughly one third of the way in from the left side of the histogram.

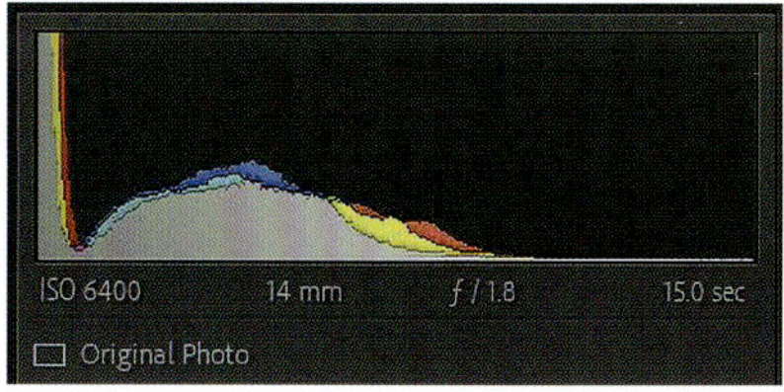

The exposures I'm recommending here assume you want to achieve a correct exposure right out of the camera. However, some recent cameras are said to be "ISO-invariant." This means that you can deliberately under-expose the image in the field by reducing the ISO, then restore the correct brightness to the image by using the exposure slider in Lightroom's Develop module. In some cases, this approach will actually reduce the amount of noise in the image. Before trying this approach, you should test your own camera at night to see if it is ISO invariant. Hold aperture and shutter speed constant, and expose the first image at ISO 6400, the second at ISO 3200, the third at ISO 1600, and the fourth at ISO 800. When you return home, increase the exposure for the ISO 3200 image by one stop, the ISO 1600 image by 2 stops, and the ISO 800 image by 3 stops. Compare the results at 100 percent magnification to see which image gives you the lowest noise and the best highlight detail.

As in daylight, you should never use the image on the LCD to judge exposure. Instead, use the histogram. Once your eyes are dark-adapted, the image on your LCD, if displayed at a brightness level suitable for viewing in daylight, will be deceptively bright. It's likely to mislead you into believing you have more shadow detail than you actually do. Dive into your menus and turn down the brightness of your LCD. Then remember to turn it back up again when you're done shooting for the night. If you forget, you may find that the LCD looks so dim in bright daylight that you can't see it well enough to turn the brightness back up without taking the camera indoors or into deep shade.

Histograms

Your best tool for understanding exposure in the field is the histogram you can display on your camera's LCD screen. In its simplest form, a histogram is a black-and-white graph of the tones in your image, as shown in figure 3-14. The horizontal axis is brightness, from black on the left to white on the right. Although the scale is not marked on the histogram, it runs from zero (black) to 255 (white). For the moment, think of the vertical axis as the number of pixels at each brightness level (I'll provide a more rigorous definition later).

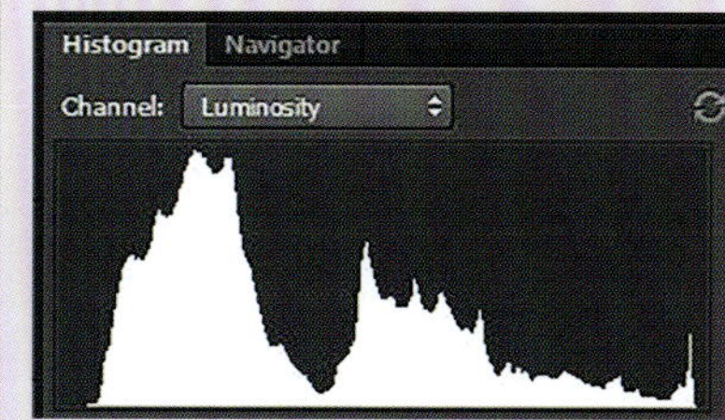

◄ Figure 3-14: A screenshot from Photoshop of a histogram for a properly exposed, moderately high-contrast image.

The most important information you can glean from the histogram is found at the far-right side of the graph. The mountain of data should terminate along the bottom of the graph and not run into the far-right side. If the mountain is cut off by the right side of the graph, the image has lots of pixels that are pure white. No amount of Photoshop wizardry will restore good color and detail to areas of pure white. Such an image is said to be clipped in the highlights. Figure 3-15 shows a histogram for an overexposed image with clipped highlights.

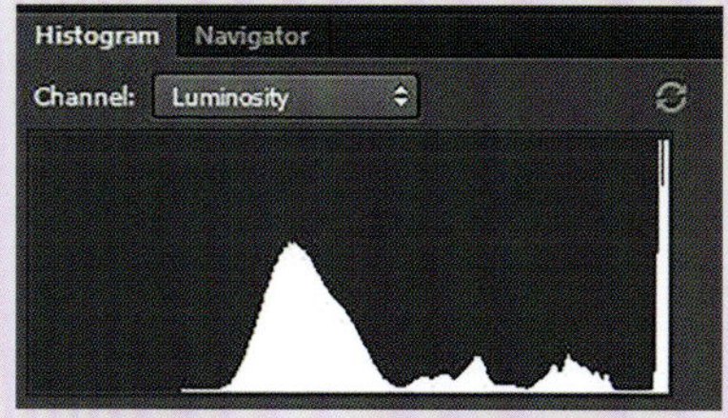

◄ Figure 3-15: A screenshot from Photoshop of a histogram for an overexposed image with clipped highlights.

Images can also be clipped in the shadows, meaning you have a number of pixels that are pure black. As with the highlights, it's impossible to restore good color and detail to regions of pure black. A small amount of black is actually an asset in most landscapes. Highlights look brighter because the eye has something pure black to compare them to. For most images, however, even night images, large areas of pure black are undesirable. Figure 3-16 shows a histogram for an underexposed image with clipped shadows.

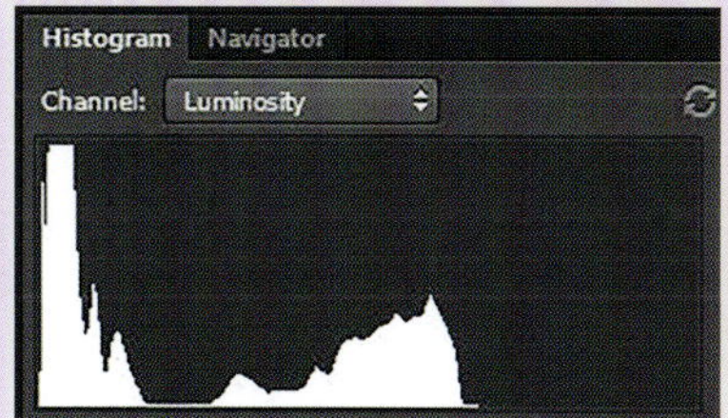

◄ Figure 3-16: A screenshot from Photoshop of a histogram for an underexposed image with clipped shadows.

Your camera can display a simple black-and-white histogram like the ones shown in figures 3-14 to 3-16. It can probably also display three separate histograms, one for each color channel (red, green, and blue). Lightroom and Adobe Camera Raw (ACR—the raw processing engine that ships with Photoshop) display a histogram that combines the three color channels into one graph. The histogram at the top of figure 3-17 shows an example of the combined histogram you'll find in Photoshop. As of this writing, the histogram you'll find in Lightroom and ACR is similar in concept, but slightly different in the way the three color channels are displayed. The other histograms in figure 3-17 show the individual channels as you might see them on your LCD.

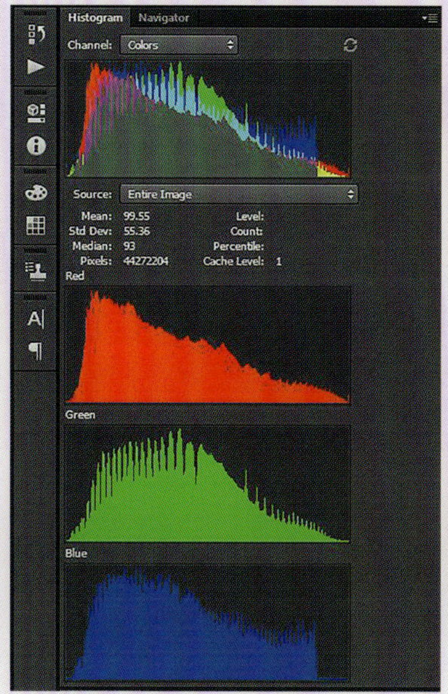

◄ Figure 3-17: The histogram at the top of figure 3-17 shows an example of the combined histogram you'll find in Photoshop. As of this writing, the histogram you'll find in Lightroom and ACR is similar in concept, but slightly different in the way the three color channels are displayed. The remaining three histograms show each color channel separately as you might see them on your LCD.

Histograms *(continued)*

To understand the style of histogram found in Lightroom and ACR, consider first the appearance of a histogram for only one channel. The red histogram, for example, plots the number of pixels with each red value. If there are 50 pixels with a red value of zero, it plots a count of 50 at the zero position at the far-left side of the graph. If there are 65 pixels with a red value of 255, it plots a count of 65 at the 255 position on the far-right side of the graph, and so on. The other two histograms, for blue and green, are plotted the same way. Lightroom and ACR then stack all three histograms on top of one another. Areas where all three histograms overlap are shown in gray. Areas where two of the three histograms overlap are shown in the color the two channels would make if mixed together. Areas where the blue and green histograms overlap are shown in cyan; the red-green overlapping area is shown in yellow; the red-blue overlapping area is shown in magenta. Areas where only one channel is present are shown in that channel's color.

Why should you care about the brightness of the individual channels? Because clipping in even one channel is an early warning sign that you may be on the verge of clipping the highlights or shadows overall.

I mentioned previously that the vertical axis on Photoshop's RGB histogram does not, strictly speaking, represent the number of pixels at each brightness level. In other words, the software doesn't simply take the average of the red, green, and blue values for a particular pixel and plot that on the histogram. Instead, the histogram plots *counts*: one count is recorded at each level for every pixel where the red, green, or blue value is equal to that level. In other words, a pixel with red, green, and blue values of 255, 240, and 225 provides one count at the 255 level, as well as one count each at the 240 and 225 levels.

The RGB histogram is designed this way so that if any channel reaches 255 for a given pixel, you'll see it on the histogram as a count at 255. If the software simply averaged the red, green, and blue values for each pixel, pixels that were clipped in one or two channels wouldn't appear at the far-right side of the graph even though they might be dangerously close to clipping overall.

Photoshop actually offers two black-and-white histograms: the RGB histogram I just described; and a luminosity histogram like the ones shown in figures 3-14 to 3-16. The luminosity histogram takes into account the fact that human vision is not equally sensitive to all colors. We are much more sensitive to green light than we are to red and blue light. Luminosity histograms, also called brightness histograms, attempt to capture the perceived brightness of the scene. Your camera may also offer you a choice between the two types of histograms. I prefer to display the luminosity histogram because it gives me a better sense of the overall distribution of tones in the image. I then check the individual red, green, and blue histograms to see if I'm clipping any of the channels. As a practical matter, RGB and luminosity histograms only differ significantly when photographing subjects more saturated than the typical landscape.

As I mentioned in the previous chapter, the longest shutter speed you can use on a stationary camera (one not mounted on a star-tracker), is determined by the focal length of the lens. One handy rule of thumb for estimating the longest shutter speed you can use for a particular focal length is called the 500 rule. The basic idea is simple: the longest exposure, in seconds, that you can use before the stars make visible streaks in your image equals 500 divided by the focal length of the lens. For example, the longest exposure you can use with a 20mm lens is about 25 seconds (500 ÷ 20 = 25).

The chart below assumes you are using a full-frame camera. If you are using a camera with a sub-full-frame or APS-C sensor, multiply the focal length printed on the lens by the appropriate crop factor, then use the result as the focal length for the purpose of this chart. For example, if you are using a 16mm lens on a camera with a 1.5 crop factor, multiply 16 by 1.5 to get 24. The longest exposure you can make with that lens without visible star motion is 21 seconds. Note that this chart assumes you are viewing a print made at normal resolution for high-quality output (file resolution of 240 ppi). If you zoom in to 100 percent on your monitor you will see very short star trails.

The 500 Rule			
Focal length	Angle of view (horizontal dimension in landscape mode)	Angle of view (vertical dimension in land-scape mode)	Maximum shutter speed to avoid visible star motion in a print (per the 500 rule)
14mm	104°	81°	36 secs
16mm	97°	74°	31 secs
20mm	84°	62°	25 secs
24mm	74°	53°	21 secs
28mm	65°	46°	18 secs
35mm	54°	38°	14 secs
50mm	40°	27°	10 secs
85mm	24°	16°	6 secs

The 500 rule is admittedly a compromise. If you use shorter shutter speeds, your stars will exhibit less trailing, but you'll either need to increase the ISO in the field or increase the exposure in Lightroom to achieve correct exposure. Both increasing the ISO and increasing the exposure in Lightroom can generate more noise. If you insist on pinpoint stars, you can use the 200 rule: divide 200 by the focal length of the lens in use to get the longest acceptable shutter speed for pinpoint stars. Alternatively, you can use the Spot Stars calculator in a mobile app for iOS and Android devices called PhotoPills. I'll discuss advanced techniques for managing the noise that can result in chapter 7.

Controlling Noise

Noise is an implacable foe when photographing at night. Even the best cameras exhibit noise when making long exposures at high ISOs. Your DSLR or mirrorless camera probably offers two means of reducing noise in-camera: high-ISO noise reduction and long-exposure noise reduction (LENR).

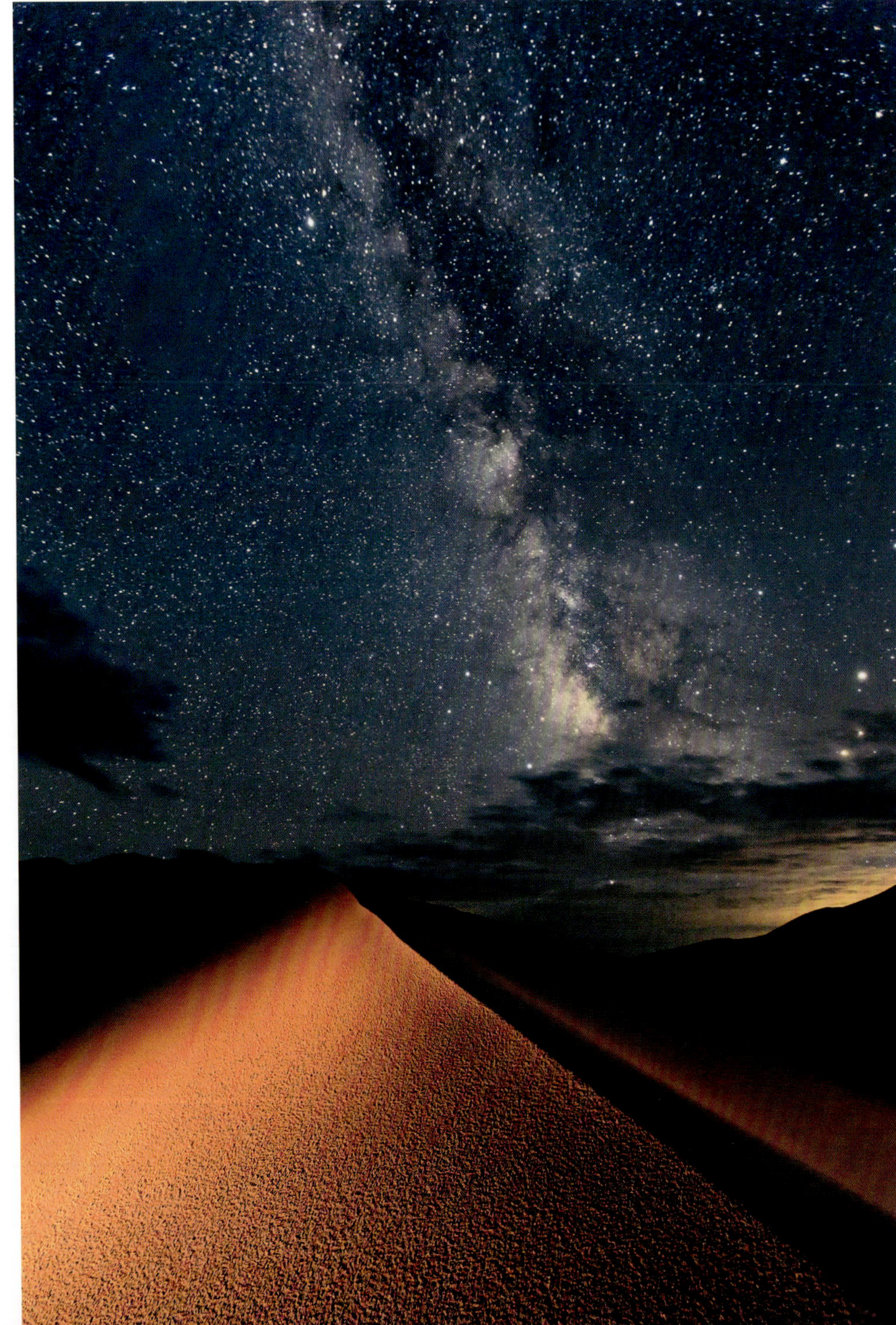

► FIGURE 3-18: Milky Way over dunes at Great Sand Dunes National Park, Colorado. August 22, 2016, 10:06 p.m. Canon 5D Mark III, Canon EF 16-35mm f/2.8L II USM at 16mm. Focus stacked: seven focus positions, focus-stacked images aligned and blended in Photoshop, 30 seconds, f/2.8, ISO 6400. Two F&V HDV-Z96 flat-panel LED lights fitted with 85B warming filters provided the light on the foreground.

Lightroom and Adobe Camera Raw ignore high-ISO noise-reduction settings in the camera. The only way to get any value from this feature when editing your images is to use the camera manufacturer's RAW conversion software. Since both Lightroom and ACR are much more full-featured editors than the camera manufacturers' software, I recommend using them instead. Fortunately, both Lightroom and ACR offer excellent noise-reduction utilities. I keep high-ISO noise-reduction turned on in my camera only because it makes it easier to assess sharpness in the JPEG-rendered preview of the captured image that I see on the camera's LCD. I'll explain how to reduce noise in Lightroom in chapter 6.

LENR tackles a different form of noise. As I mentioned in chapter 2, one of the biggest sources of noise in night images is dark current or thermal noise. Unlike photon noise, thermal noise appears in the same fixed pattern on the sensor, and therefore in your image, so long as the temperature and shutter speed are the same. When you engage LENR, you tell the camera to make a second exposure with the shutter closed immediately after the first exposure. That dark frame should be completely dark except for the thermal noise. The camera subtracts the *dark frame* from the actual exposure, which eliminates the thermal noise. The catch is that the second exposure takes just as long as the first, which can really slow you down. Recent cameras do a much better job than earlier models in controlling thermal noise without engaging LENR. My preference is generally to leave LENR off and just use the Spot Removal tool in Lightroom to deal with any hot pixels.

White Balance

Imagine a wedding. The bride is wearing a white dress. Her dress looks white when she's standing in the parking lot in the sun at noon on a clear day. It also looks white when she walks into the shade of the church, and still looks white when she says her vows at the altar, then walks into the reception hall to celebrate.

Daylight-balanced slide film would record those moments very differently. The bride's dress would be rendered as white when she was standing in the sun, but it would take on a strong bluish cast when she walked into the shade because the light source would become the blue sky. Her dress would be rendered as orange when she is standing at the altar lit by tungsten (incandescent) bulbs, and green when she entered the reception hall, which is lit by cheap fluorescents. The bride's skin tones would be radiant when she stood in the sun, but she would look cold and dead in the shade, badly sunburned at the altar, and rather seasick at the reception.

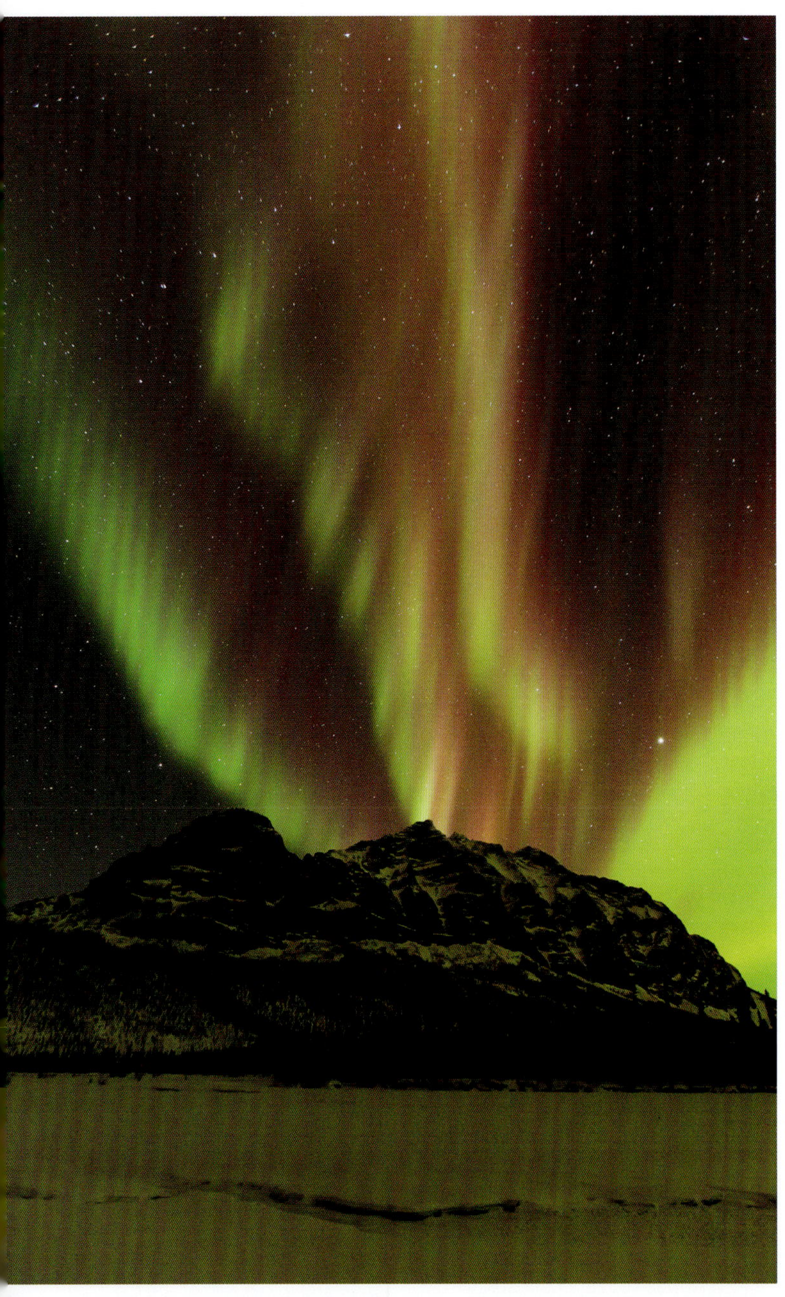

Your visual system's ability to give objects a consistent color, regardless of the color of the light, is called color constancy. Your camera's auto white balance (AWB) feature tries to mimic this property and render colors accurately without your intervention. When set to AWB, your camera will try to render that white dress as white regardless of the color of the light. In other words, it shifts the colors actually present in the scene and shows you the scene as if it was lit by white light. AWB is a great choice when shooting events where the color of the light is unknown or is changing constantly and the priority is preserving accurate skin tones.

Setting the white balance to daylight, on the other hand, causes the camera to record the colors that are actually present in the scene, without altering them. It is the digital equivalent of a daylight-balanced film. I always use a daylight white balance when I'm shooting daylight landscapes. If I am so fortunate as to see wonderful warm light bathing a snow-covered peak at sunrise, I want to capture that glow. Using AWB in that situation would cause the camera to think I wanted to eliminate that warmth and render the snow as white, just like the camera would render the bride's dress as white when she stood at the altar bathed in orange tungsten light.

So what about shooting at night? I always use a daylight white balance for night landscapes just like I do for daytime ones. I want to start by recording the wavelengths that reach my sensor without altering their color. Then, if I choose, I'll alter the color of certain parts of the scene to more powerfully evoke the emotions I felt when I was standing there. I'll explain my approach in detail in chapter 6. If you're shooting RAW, you probably already know that the white balance on RAW files can be changed in processing with virtually no degradation in quality. This is not true if you're shooting JPEGs. (If you're not shooting RAW, please read the sidebar on why you should.)

Why You Should Shoot RAW

RAW files have numerous advantages over JPEGs. Most importantly, a RAW file gives you greater flexibility in editing. You can recover much more highlight and shadow detail from a RAW file than you can from a JPEG (see figures 3-20 and 3-21). RAW files also give you greater freedom to adjust the contrast in the image. JPEGs have a certain level of contrast baked in. It's easy to add more contrast to an image, but it can be hard to reduce contrast in a pleasing way. You can also make more changes to the color of a RAW file without creating banding or *posterization*, an abrupt transition from one region to the next rather than a smooth gradient. The white balance setting you choose in-camera can be changed without penalty when you process a RAW file, but not when you process a JPEG. Shoot some JPEGs outdoors with a fluorescent white balance, as I once did, and you've just saddled yourself with a time-wasting digital-darkroom project.

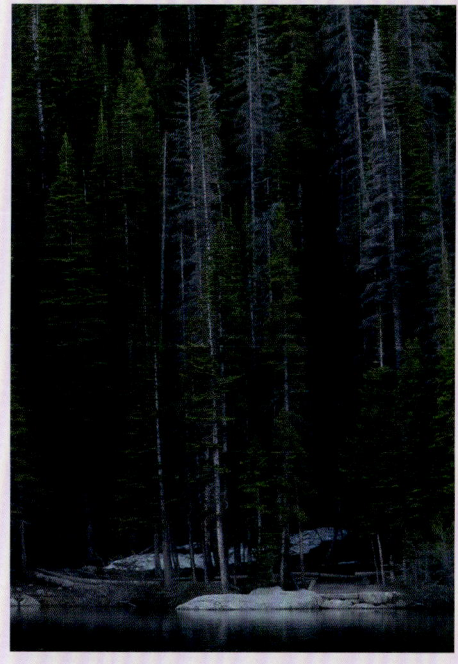

◄ FIGURE 3-20: I shot both images with a Sony Alpha 7R IVa. On the left is the RAW file; on the right is the JPEG. I underexposed the trees by about three stops, then opened up the exposure by three stops in Lightroom to show how much more shadow detail can be recovered from a RAW file than a JPEG.

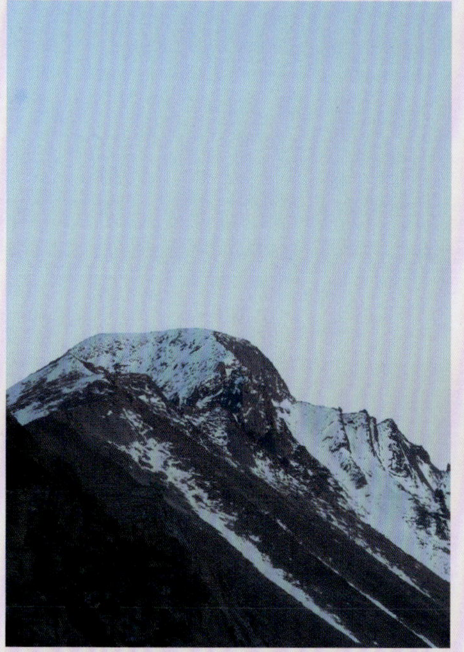
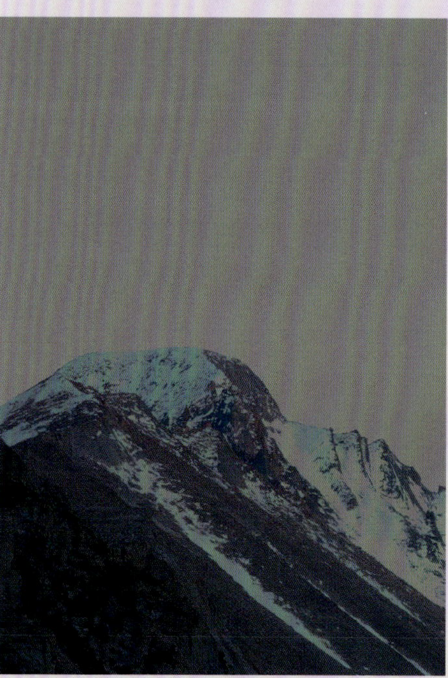

◄ FIGURE 3-21: I shot both images with a Sony Alpha 7R IVa. On the left is the RAW file; on the right is the JPEG. I overexposed the sky by about three stops, then reduced exposure in Lightroom by three stops to show how much more highlight detail can be recovered from a RAW file than a JPEG.

Why You Should Shoot RAW *(continued)*

All edits you make to a RAW file are non-destructive. In fact, you can't actually make changes to the RAW data, which is always protected. When you edit a RAW file, you're actually creating an instruction set that will be applied to that RAW data when you export the image from Lightroom as a JPEG for the web or a TIFF for printing. In fairness, Lightroom does let you make non-destructive edits to JPEGs, but the range of changes you can make before the image degrades is small. Opening a JPEG in Photoshop and saving it repeatedly will eventually damage the file. RAW files are not compressed or are compressed in a lossless way; JPEG files use a compression scheme that discards some data every time the image is saved in that format. No sharpening or noise reduction is applied to a RAW file, giving you the ability to fine-tune those parameters as needed for each image. Sharpening and noise-reduction are baked into JPEGs.

Some photographers prefer shooting JPEGs because they feel that the image is ready to go straight out of the camera. With no editing required, it takes less time to send pictures to friends or post them on social-media sites. Some photographers who are used to shooting JPEGs think RAW files are too low in contrast and too dull in color to be pleasing. It's true that RAW files, by design, are relatively low in contrast and color saturation. If that's not the look you want, it's easy to create a Develop preset in Lightroom that mimics the look of your JPEGs (snappy contrast, saturated colors) and apply it automatically to every RAW image you import. My feeling is that all images can be improved in processing. Why would you ever show someone anything less than your best work? For me, that means shooting RAW files, perfecting them in Lightroom and, sometimes, Photoshop, then creating JPEGs to post to the web or TIFFs to send to my printer.

RAW files do have a couple of disadvantages. The first, a minor one, is that RAW files are considerably bigger than JPEGs. They eat up space on your memory card and hard drive more quickly. The ever-decreasing cost of memory cards and storage, however, has largely nullified this disadvantage. A second, more significant drawback is that RAW files, because they are larger, will fill your camera's buffer faster when you're shooting a burst of frames than JPEGs will. Once the buffer fills, you must wait until the camera moves the data from the buffer to the memory card before you can shoot again. That's never an issue when shooting landscapes but could be a problem when shooting wildlife or fast-moving sports.

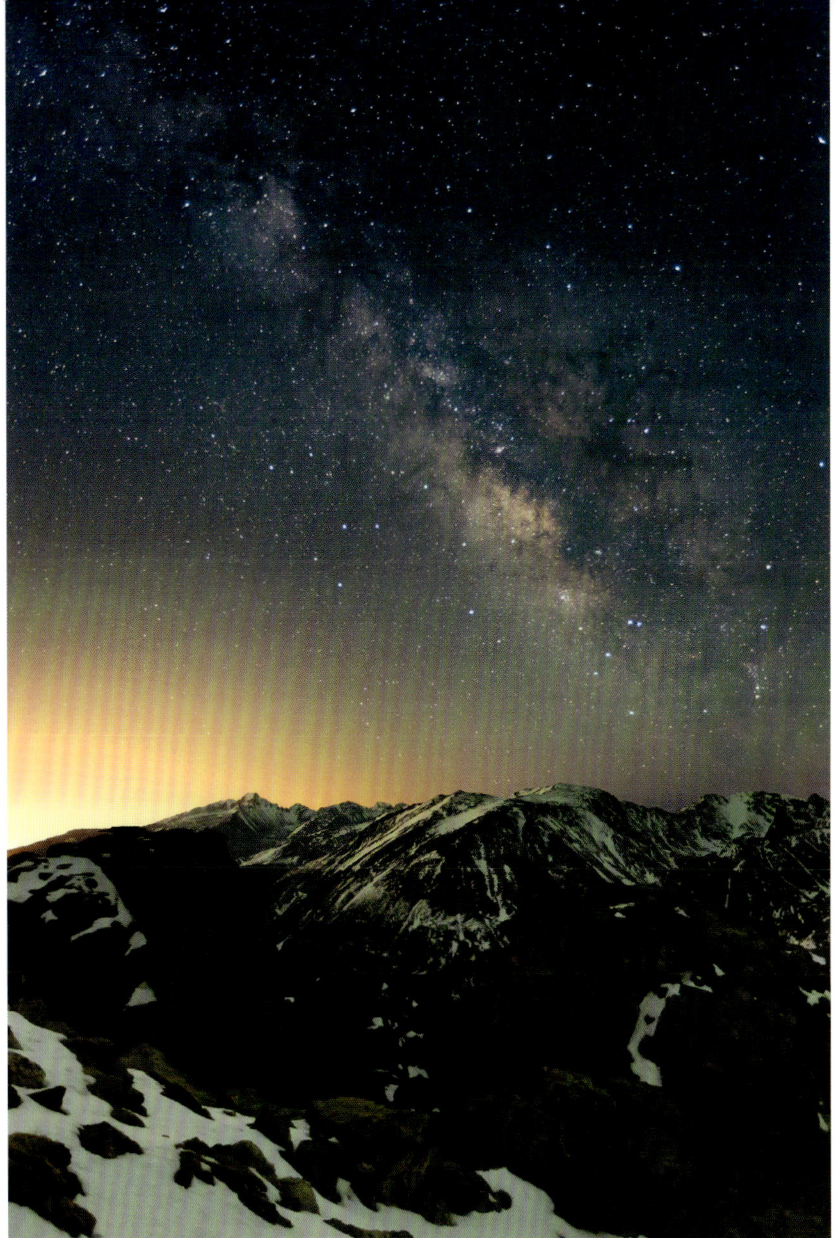

◄ FIGURE 3-22: Milky Way over Longs Peak from the Rock Cut on Trail Ridge Road, Rocky Mountain National Park, Colorado. May 28, 2014, 1:59 a.m. Canon EOS 5D Mark III, Canon EF 16-35mm f/2.8L II USM at 24mm. Land: one frame, 81 seconds, f/2.8, ISO 6400. Sky: one frame, 15 seconds, f/2.8, ISO 6400.

Holding Detail in the Land

The sky is always brighter than the land, particularly near the horizon. This is true at night as well as during the day. In daytime, the dynamic range of your camera can easily cover the difference in brightness between sunlit land and clear sky. The high ISOs required to shoot at night, however, not only increase noise, the most obvious problem, but also decrease dynamic range. That means it can be difficult to hold detail in the land with an exposure short enough to render the stars as points. When editing daytime images you can often open up shadows by as much as two stops to restore

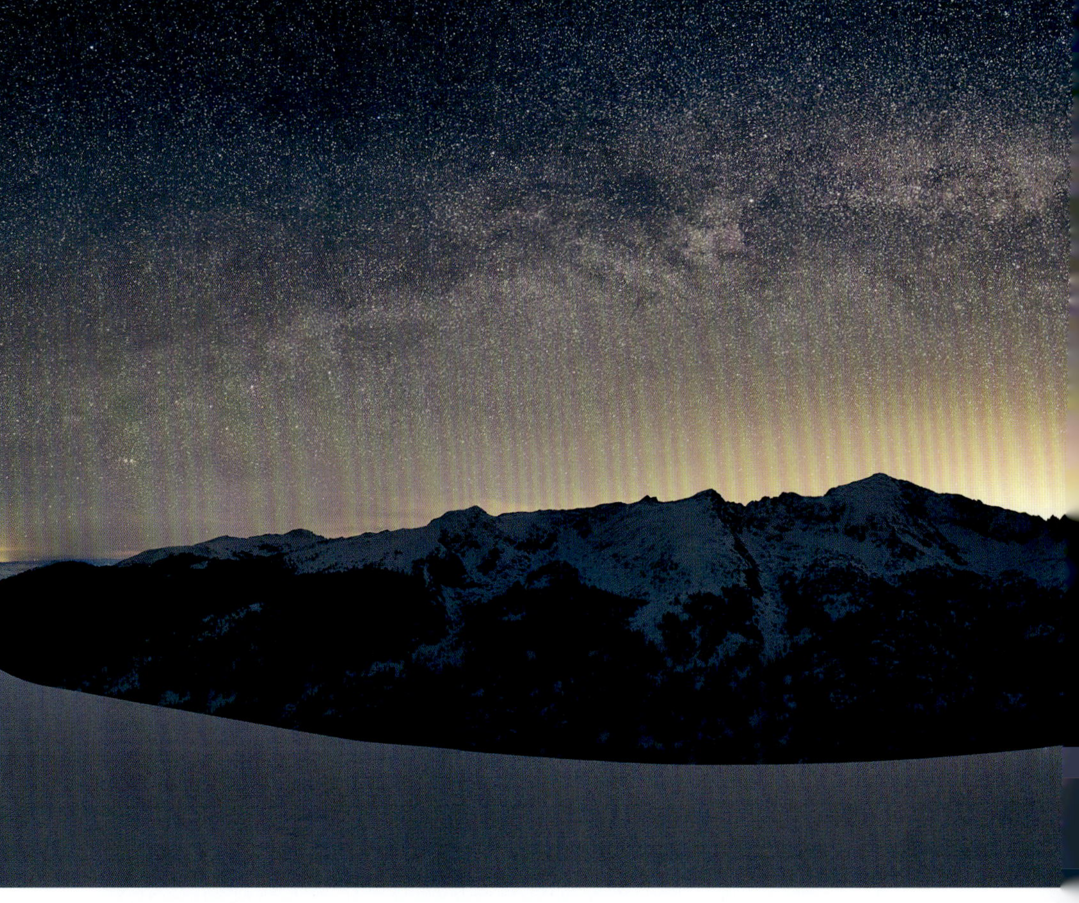

▸ Figure 3-23: Milky Way panorama over Gold Dust Peak from Charles Peak, Holy Cross Wilderness. March 1, 2022, 4:15 a.m. Sony Alpha 7R IVa, Sony FE 14mm f/1.8 GM. Land and sky: 16 seconds, f/1.8, ISO 6400. I shot this image as a single-row panorama, four camera positions, four frames per camera position. I processed each group of four images twice, once in RegiStar to reduce noise in the sky, and once using Photoshop's Stack Mode>Median to reduce noise in the land, then composited the two panoramas in Photoshop.

the detail you want. Attempting the same strategy at night usually creates unmanageable noise. Depending on the camera and the image, you may only be able to brighten the deep shadows by a half-stop or so.

One solution, of course, is simply to compose so that the image works when the land is a black silhouette. Old, wind-warped trees, saguaro cactuses, sea stacks, and sandstone towers in the desert can all make for foregrounds that are interesting enough when seen in silhouette to carry the shot. You'll have far more compositional options, however, if you learn to record good detail in the land.

The easiest way to hold good detail in the land in a single exposure is to shoot when there's snow on the ground. Snow reflects about four

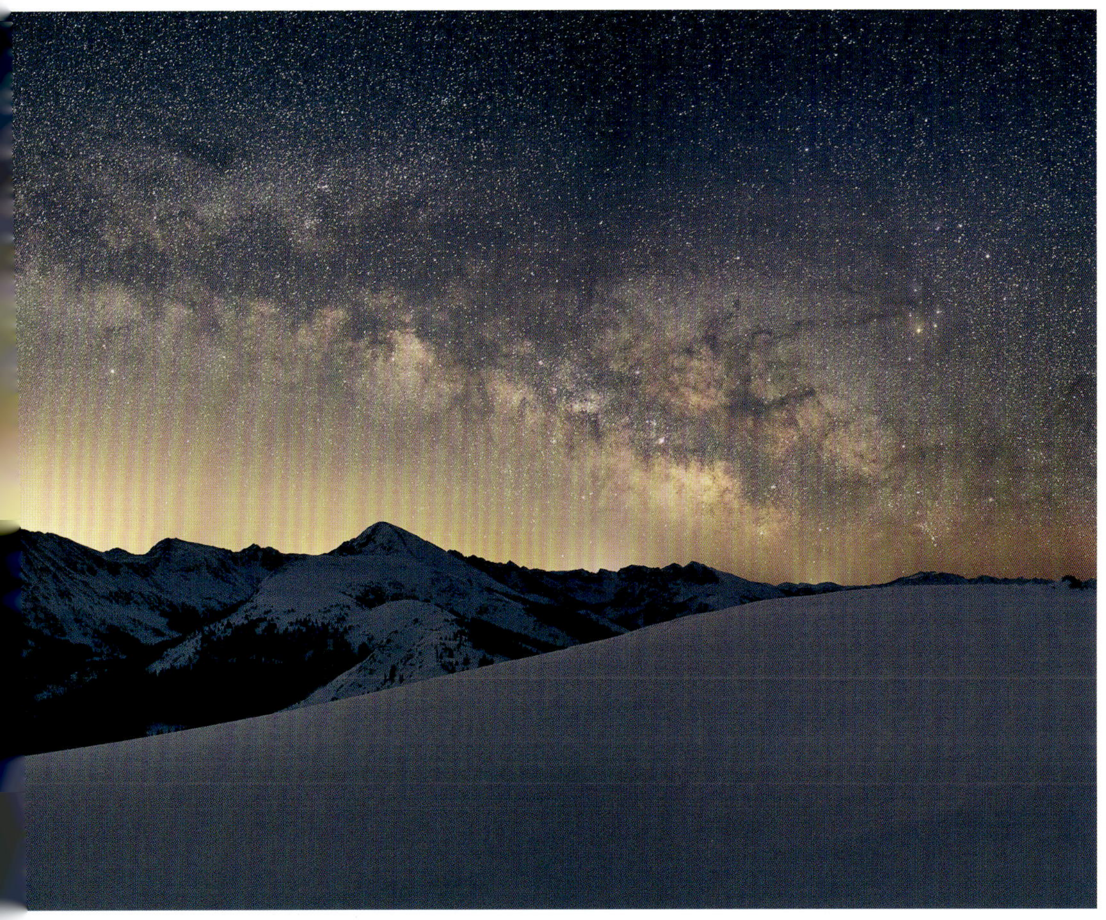

times as much light as midtone rock. That's a two-stop difference, which, coincidentally, is about the same as the average difference in brightness between night sky and snow-free land. In other words, if the landscape is snow-covered, the difference in brightness between sky and land is often within the limited dynamic range of an image shot at a high ISO. In many situations, you can capture all the detail you want in a single frame.

If your composition includes foreground elements that are relatively close to the camera (less than 100 feet away), you may be able to capture all the detail you want in a single frame by "painting" the foreground with light from a flashlight or flat-panel LED light. I'll describe this approach in detail in chapter 7.

Another strategy is to shoot as much as 20 minutes before astronomical dusk or after astronomical dawn. Figures 3-24 to 3-26 are examples of images shot at various times after astronomical dawn. The faint glow on the western or eastern horizon will provide a bit of detail in the land without completely washing out the stars. Starlight is very soft and can make the land look flat. Shooting the land in twilight puts a soft but still directional light on the land. This can be an asset when shooting sand dunes or other subjects when there is very little variation in brightness or color in the land by itself.

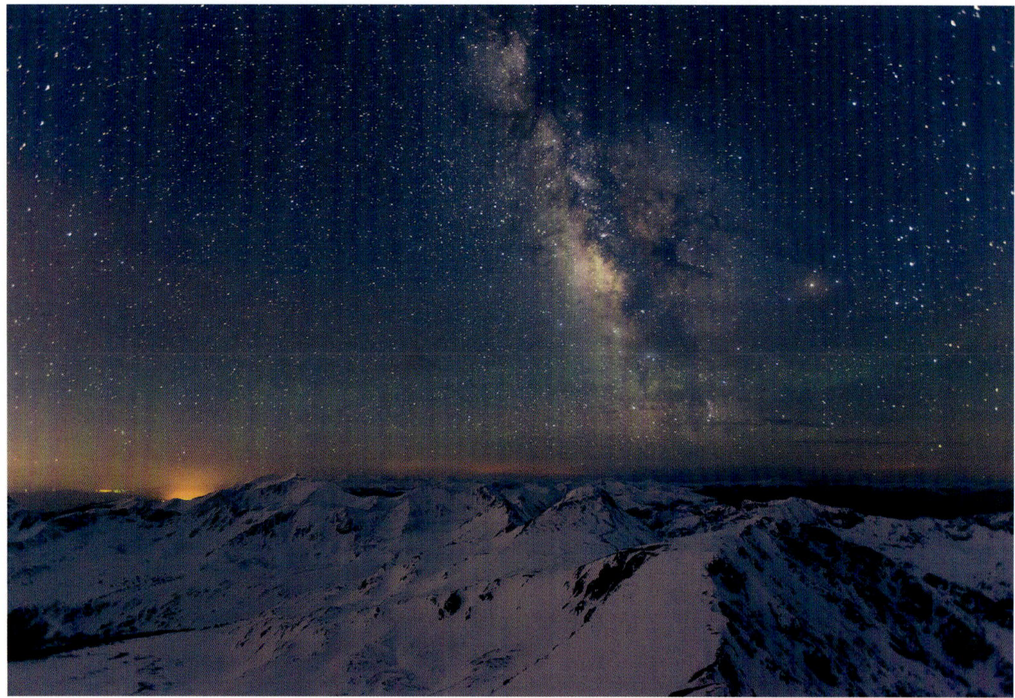

► FIGURE 3-24: Looking south at the Collegiate Peaks and the Milky Way from the summit of Missouri Mountain, Collegiate Peaks Wilderness, Colorado. May 13, 2013, 4:17 a.m. (about 10 minutes after astronomical dawn). Canon 5D Mark III, Canon EF 16-35mm f/2.8L II USM at 17mm. 30 seconds, f/2.8, ISO 6400.

Yet another strategy is to shoot on nights when the moon is above the horizon. A full moon will provide great detail in the land, but it will make it impossible to see the Milky Way and the fainter stars. Shooting when only 15 to 30 percent of the moon's surface is illuminated can be a good compromise. A crescent moon can provide enough light to record adequate detail in the land without completely losing dim stars and the Milky Way. If possible, shoot when the moon is low in the sky and illuminating the scene from the side. Avoid backlighting, which will cast very harsh shadows at night, and avoid including the moon in the frame. If you use an exposure that is correct for the sky, the moon will turn into a grossly overexposed white blob. Shooting just before astronomical dusk and just after astronomical dawn, as well

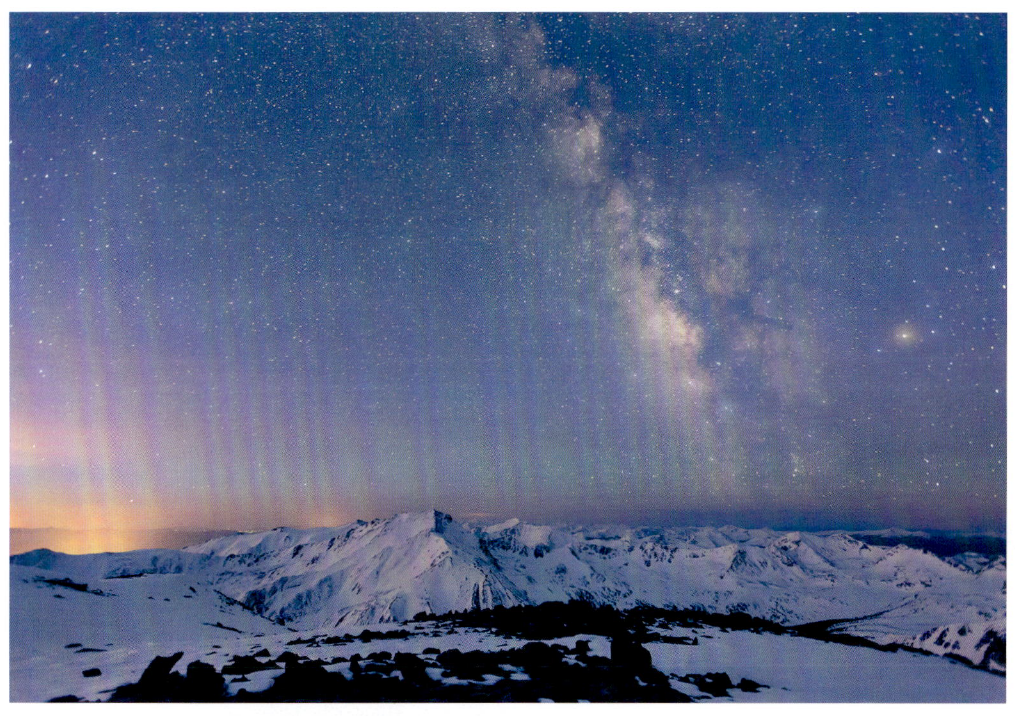

◄ FIGURE 3-25: Milky Way over Mt. Harvard from the summit of Mt. Oxford, Collegiate Peaks Wilderness, Colorado. May 14, 2013, 4:26 a.m. (about 20 minutes after astronomical dawn). Canon 5D Mark III, Canon EF 16-35mm f/2.8L II USM at 16mm. 30 seconds, f/2.8, ISO 6400.

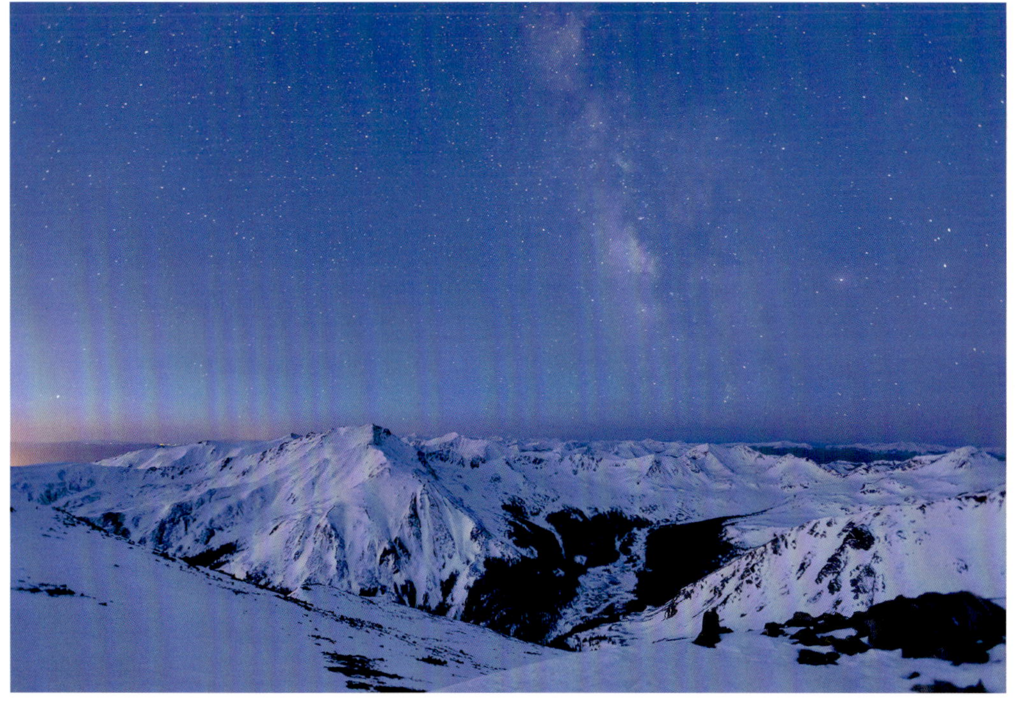

◄ FIGURE 3-26: Milky Way over Mt. Harvard from the summit of Mt. Oxford, Collegiate Peaks Wilderness, Colorado. May 14, 2013, 4:36 a.m. (about 30 minutes after astronomical dawn). Canon 5D Mark III, Canon EF 16-35mm f/2.8L II USM at 16mm. 30 seconds, f/2.8, ISO 6400.

as shooting under a crescent moon, are all compromises that trade off detail in the land for detail in the Milky Way.

You can try to capture all the detail you want in both land and sky in a single frame by pushing your ISO to extreme levels. Unfortunately, with today's technology, you're likely to get unacceptable noise and color shifts. You may also render the sky so bright it's hard to bring it back down to a realistic-looking density.

You might think that the best way to hold detail throughout a night scene is to use high-dynamic-range (HDR) techniques in which you shoot a bracketed series of images, then combine all the frames in HDR software. Unfortunately, HDR only works when there's nothing moving in the frame. The long exposure required to hold detail in the land also causes the stars to record as long streaks. When combined with the shorter sky exposure, the streaks become obvious and unacceptable.

The best way to hold detail in the land when there's no snow on the ground and when you're shooting on a moonless night between astronomical dusk and dawn is to shoot one frame for the sky and one frame for the land using precisely the same composition. Usually the difference between the two exposures will be about two stops. If the correct exposure for the sky is 30 seconds, f/2.8, ISO 6400, then the correct exposure for the land will usually be about two minutes, f/2.8, ISO 6400. Use a solid tripod and be sure not to bump the tripod or camera between exposures. It's best to use an intervalometer to change the exposure so that you don't need to touch the camera at all.

A variation on this approach is to shoot the land while the moon is above the horizon, then wait until the moon sets to shoot the sky (figure 3-27); or you can shoot the sky first, then wait until moonrise and shoot the land (more on that in the next chapter). One drawback to this approach is that it can look unnatural to put a landscape lit by bright moonlight beneath the Milky Way. Somehow our brains know that the Milky Way is only visible on moonless nights.

Yet another variation is to shoot the land portion of the image during civil or nautical twilight, perhaps 15 to 45 minutes after sunset, then wait until astronomical dusk to shoot the sky. You can also use this strategy in reverse, shooting the Milky Way first, then waiting until 15 to 45 minutes before sunrise to shoot the land. This approach has the advantage that you'll have enough light when shooting the land image to use a small aperture to get full depth of field without using an inordinately long shutter speed. The disadvantage is that the color of the light on the land will usually be more blue than the color if you shoot the land with a long exposure in total darkness. Another potential problem concerns the direction you're facing. If

▸ FIGURE 3-27: Two views of the Milky Way over Goblin Valley, Goblin Valley State Park, Utah. April 5, 2017. Canon EOS 5D Mark III, Canon EF 35mm f/1.4L II USM. The upper image shows the Milky Way over Goblin Valley by moonlight. I shot the land portion of this image at 2:18 a.m., about an hour and a half before the waxing gibbous moon (68 percent illuminated) set behind me. I shot the land as a single-row panorama, six camera positions, four frames per camera position, images stacked in Photoshop, noise reduced with Stack Mode>Median, 30 seconds, f/1.4, ISO 1000. I shot the Milky Way shown in this image at 4:18 a.m., about 25 minutes after moonset, again as a panorama, two rows, six camera positions per row, four frames per camera position, images aligned and noise reduced in RegiStar, 10 seconds, f/1.4, ISO 6400. For the lower image, I composited the same Milky Way panorama with a panorama of the starlit land shot at 4:35 a.m., six camera positions, four frames per camera position, images stacked in Photoshop, noise reduced with Stack Mode>Median, 1 minute, f/1.4, ISO 6400.

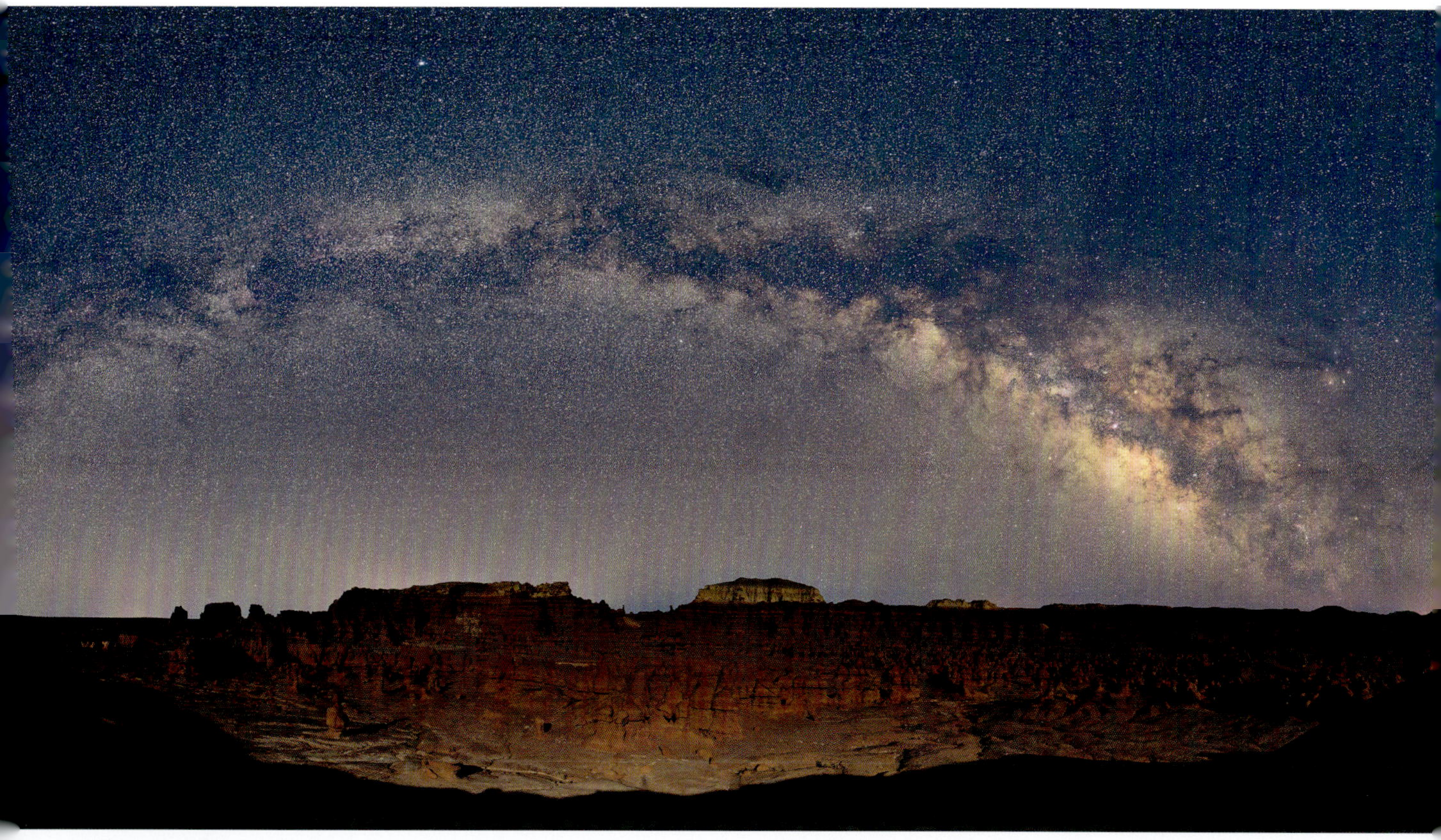

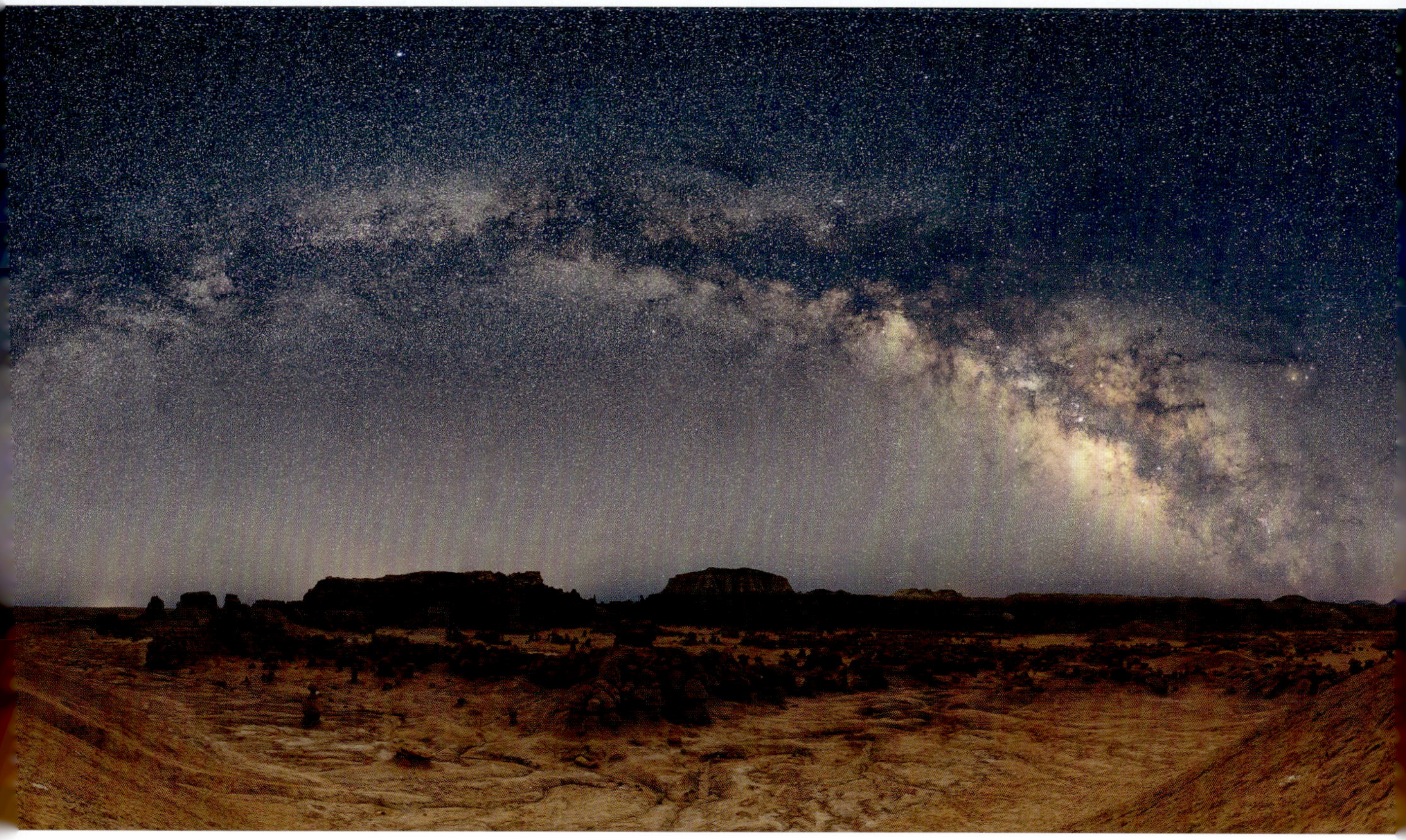

▸ FIGURE 3-28: Geminid meteor shower from High Dune, Great Sand Dunes National Park, Colorado. December 13-14, 2020. Canon EOS 5D Mark III and Mark IV, Canon EF 35mm f/1.4L II USM and Canon EF 24mm f/1.4L II USM lenses. This composite panoramic image contains 59 meteors, shot from the summit of High Dune over a nine-hour period during the night of December 13-14, 2020. Land: I shot the land images about 50 minutes after sunset with the 35mm lens, six camera positions, one frame per camera position, 13 seconds, f/2.8, ISO 400. Sky: two rows, six camera positions per row, four frames per camera position, 10 seconds, f/1.4, ISO 6400. I shot the sky images at 10:04 p.m. with the 35mm lens when the radiant for the Geminid meteor shower was positioned as shown in the image. Meteors: two Canon EF 24mm f/1.4L II USM lenses mounted on two cameras (Canon EOS 5D Mark IV and Canon EOS 5D Mark III) and positioned on a bracket on a single tripod so their fields of view just barely overlapped, 20 seconds, f/1.4, ISO 2000. I made back-to-back exposures all night, then selected the 59 frames with the brightest meteors.

you're facing east, for example, then trying to shoot the land portion of the image 20 minutes or so before sunrise means dealing with an extremely bright sky that may bleed into the land at the horizon, giving you endless grief when you try to combine the good-sky image with the good-land image. The same problem occurs if you're facing west and trying to shoot the land portion 20 minutes after sunset. I generally prefer to shoot the land portion of the image between astronomical dusk and dawn using only starlight as my light source.

I made an exception to that rule when I shot the Geminid meteor shower from the summit of High Dune in Great Sand Dunes National Park. The sand is so uniform in color that without directional light each dune crest tends to merge with the next. I shot the land portion of the image 50 minutes after sunset, then shot back-to-back sky images all night to capture as many meteors as possible. It was a good thing, too: shortly after I finished shooting the land, a boisterous group of backpackers appeared over a dune and proceeded to set up two tents in the sandy valley at the bottom of High Dune, right in my line of sight. They had every right to be there, of course, and probably didn't even know I had set up my tripod high above them. Nonetheless, I was glad I had a people-free set of land images to composite with the best meteor images.

Regardless of how you come up with the good-land and good-sky images, you'll need Photoshop to combine them. I'll explain how to merge the two images in a way that our visual system finds believable in chapter 6.

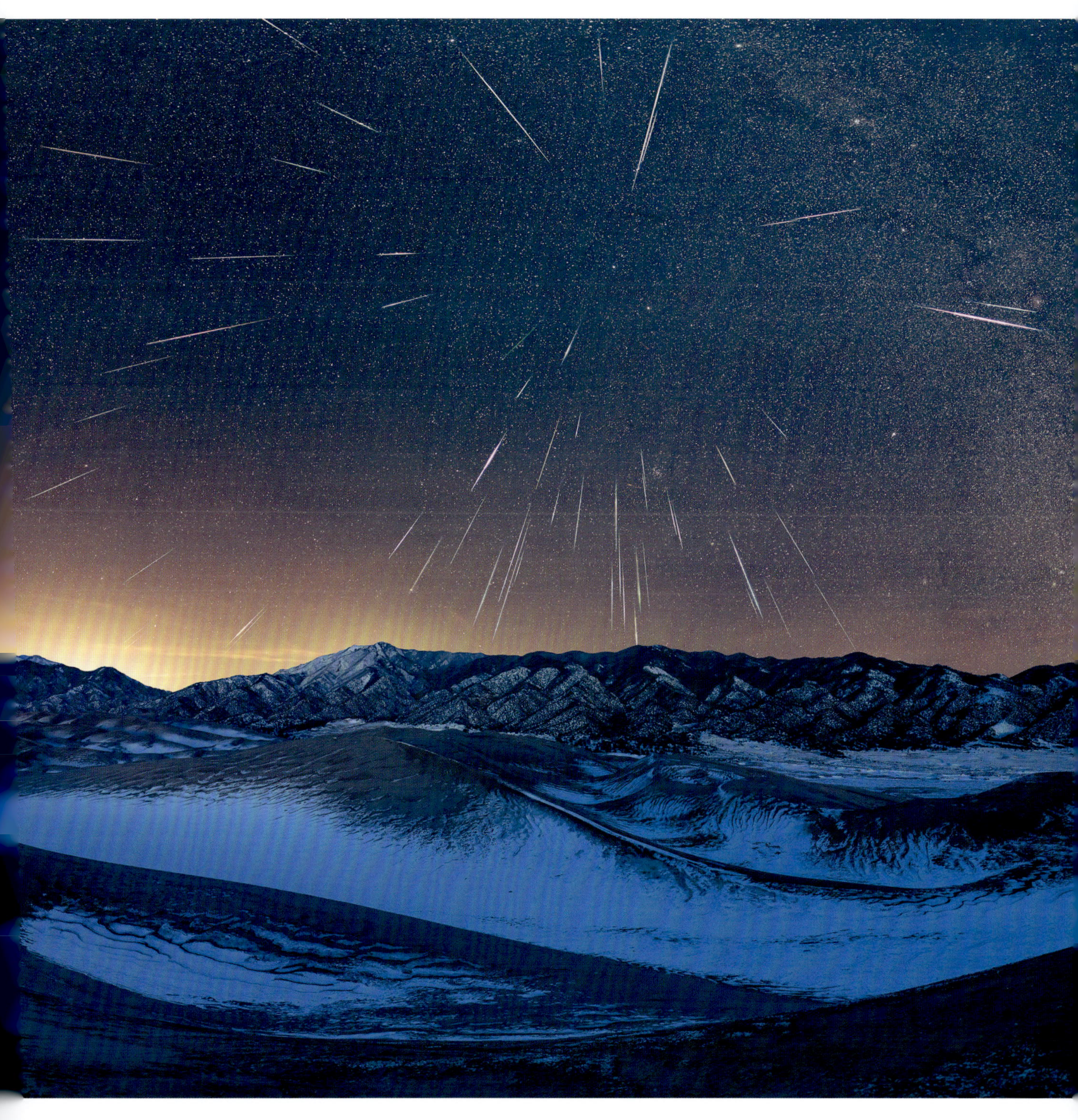

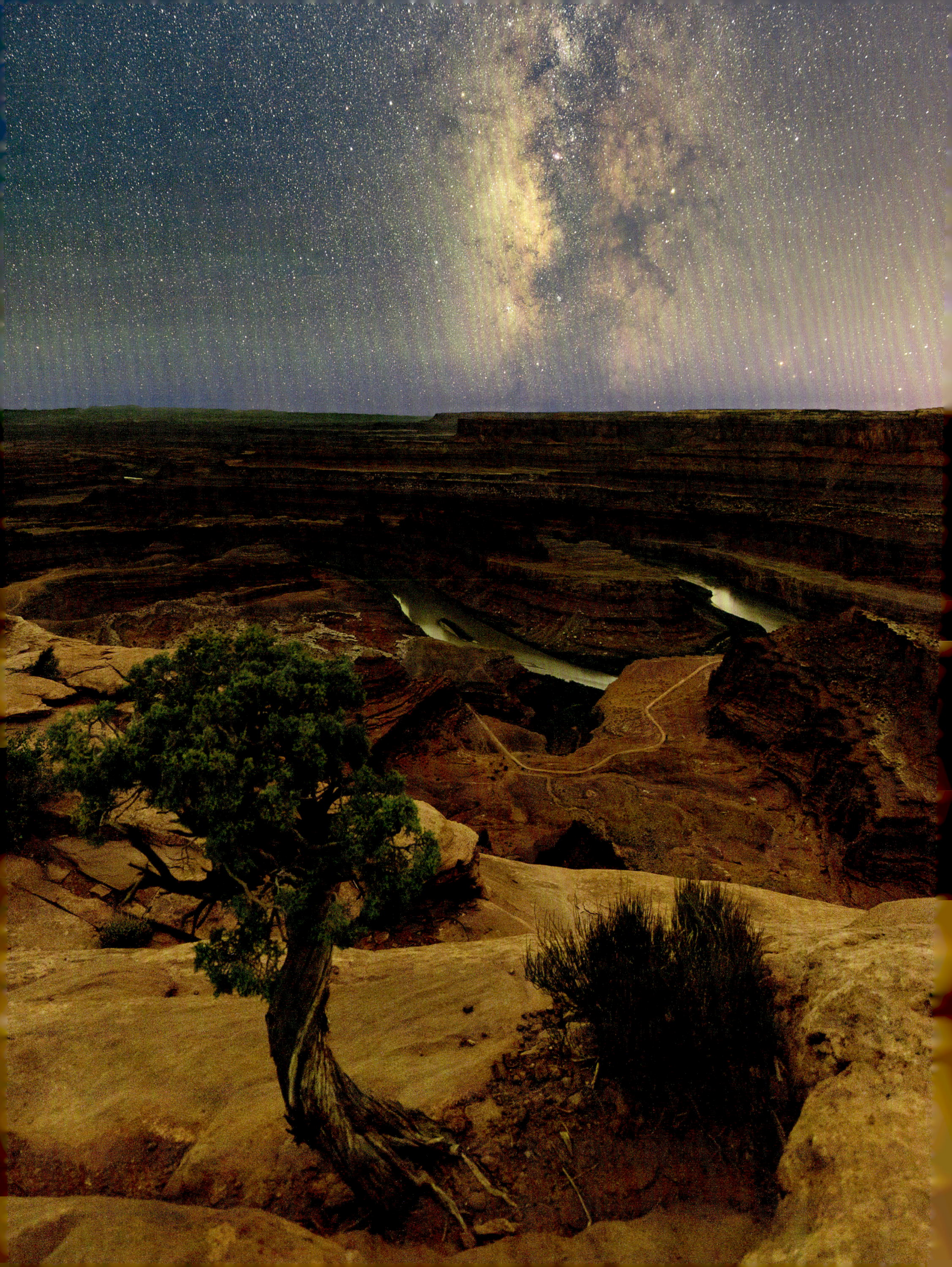

Planning a Milky Way Shoot

Of all the wonders of the night sky, the most spectacular and accessible subject for photographers who lack a telescope is surely the Milky Way. Meteor showers and lunar eclipses, while amazing to witness, are rare events; the aurora is an astonishing sight, but you must travel to the Arctic to see it. This chapter will teach you how to plan a successful Milky Way shoot.

Let's start with a refresher on your college astronomy class. We live in the Milky Way Galaxy, which is shaped like a plate, not a sphere, as seen in figure 4-2. Our solar system lies part way between the center and the rim of the galaxy, which contains between 100 and 400 *billion* stars. The Milky Way is the band of light formed by billions of very distant stars that you see as you look along the galactic plane. You can see the Milky Way every clear, moonless night of the year, but it's not equally bright in all directions. If you look away from the center of the galaxy, you are looking through a region with relatively few stars. If you look toward the center of the galaxy, however, your line of sight leads past many more stars, so the Milky Way is much brighter and has more interesting structure.

The center of our galaxy and the most photogenic part of the Milky Way lies between the constellations Sagittarius and Scorpius. Like most celestial objects, the galactic center appears to rise and set as the earth rotates. The galactic center always rises at an *azimuth* (compass bearing) of 128 degrees (southeast) and sets at an azimuth of 232 degrees (southwest) at the latitude of Denver, but the time of rising and setting varies throughout the year. In the middle latitudes, the galactic center is most prominent in spring, summer, and early fall, and is not visible in winter because it is only above the horizon during the day. In Colorado, where I live, the Milky Way season runs from about March 1 to October 1. Regardless of where you live, the Milky Way appears in the same part of the sky on the same day every year. (This is unlike the moon, whose position in the sky varies tremendously on the same day each year.)

Even the brightest part of the Milky Way is relatively dim. For the best images, get as far away from city lights as possible, and shoot on a clear, moonless night during the interval between astronomical dusk and astronomical dawn, when the sky is as dark as it will get. As I mentioned in chapter 1, many websites and phone and tablet apps provide moonrise and moonset times and the times of astronomical dusk and dawn. You don't need to confine your shooting to the night of the new moon. So long as

◄ FIGURE 4-1: The Milky Way and the Colorado River from Dead Horse Point, Dead Horse Point State Park, Utah. October 14, 2017, 9:33 p.m. Canon 5D Mark III, Canon EF 16-35mm f/2.8L III USM at 16mm. Land: two focus positions, four frames at each focus position, each set of four images stacked in Photoshop, noise reduced with Stack Mode>Median, 3 minutes, f/2.8, ISO 6400. Sky: four frames, camera mounted on iOptron SkyTracker Pro equatorial mount, images aligned and noise reduced in RegiStar, 2 minutes, f/2.8, ISO 1600.

▸ FIGURE 4-2: An artist's illustration of the Milky Way Galaxy, viewed from above. If you look away from the center of the galaxy from our position on Earth (near the sun), you are looking through a region that contains relatively few stars, and the Milky Way is faint. If you look in the opposite direction, through the center of the galaxy and toward the far rim, the Milky Way is much brighter because you are looking through a region that contains many more stars, as well as the fascinating gas and dust clouds that shroud the galactic center.

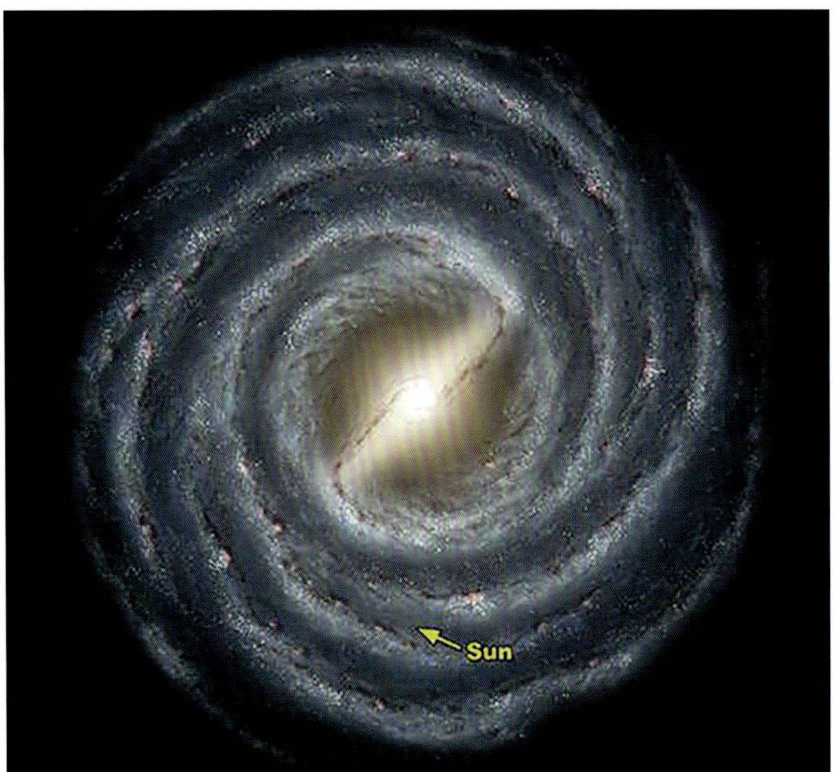

▸ FIGURE 4-3: Lone Eagle Peak and the Milky Way reflected in Mirror Lake, Indian Peaks Wilderness, Colorado. I planned the shot so that the galactic center would be just to the right of Lone Eagle Peak. June 18, 2015, 3:27 a.m. Canon 5D Mark III, Canon EF 16-35mm f/2.8L II USM at 16mm. Land: 2.5 minutes, f/2.8, ISO 6400. Sky: 30 seconds, f/2.8, ISO 6400.

the moon is well below the horizon, the sky will be dark enough to shoot. Even with a nearly full moon, you should be able to begin shooting 30 minutes after moonset or continue shooting until 30 minutes before moonrise. Remember that one strategy for holding detail everywhere in the image is to shoot two identical frames, one exposed for the land and one exposed for the sky. You may want to shoot the land portion of the image while the moon is above the horizon, then shoot the sky after the moon has set, or shoot the sky first, then wait for the moon to rise so you can shoot the land.

As I mentioned in the previous chapter, the sky is always brightest near the horizon. It gets darker as you look higher into the sky. That's true at night as well as during the day. To make the Milky Way stand out against a dark sky, shoot when the galactic center is as high in the sky as possible. The galactic center reaches its highest point above the horizon, an *altitude* (angular elevation) of 21 degrees as seen from the latitude of Denver, when it transits, that is, when it is due south.

The maximum altitude of the galactic center varies with latitude. As you head south, the galactic center reaches a much greater altitude, and the Milky Way season is correspondingly longer. In Miami, Florida, for example, the maximum altitude is 38 degrees. As you head north, the maximum altitude of the galactic center becomes lower, and the Milky Way season is correspondingly shorter. At the latitude of Fairbanks, Alaska, the galactic center never rises at any time of year, and the best part of the Milky Way is

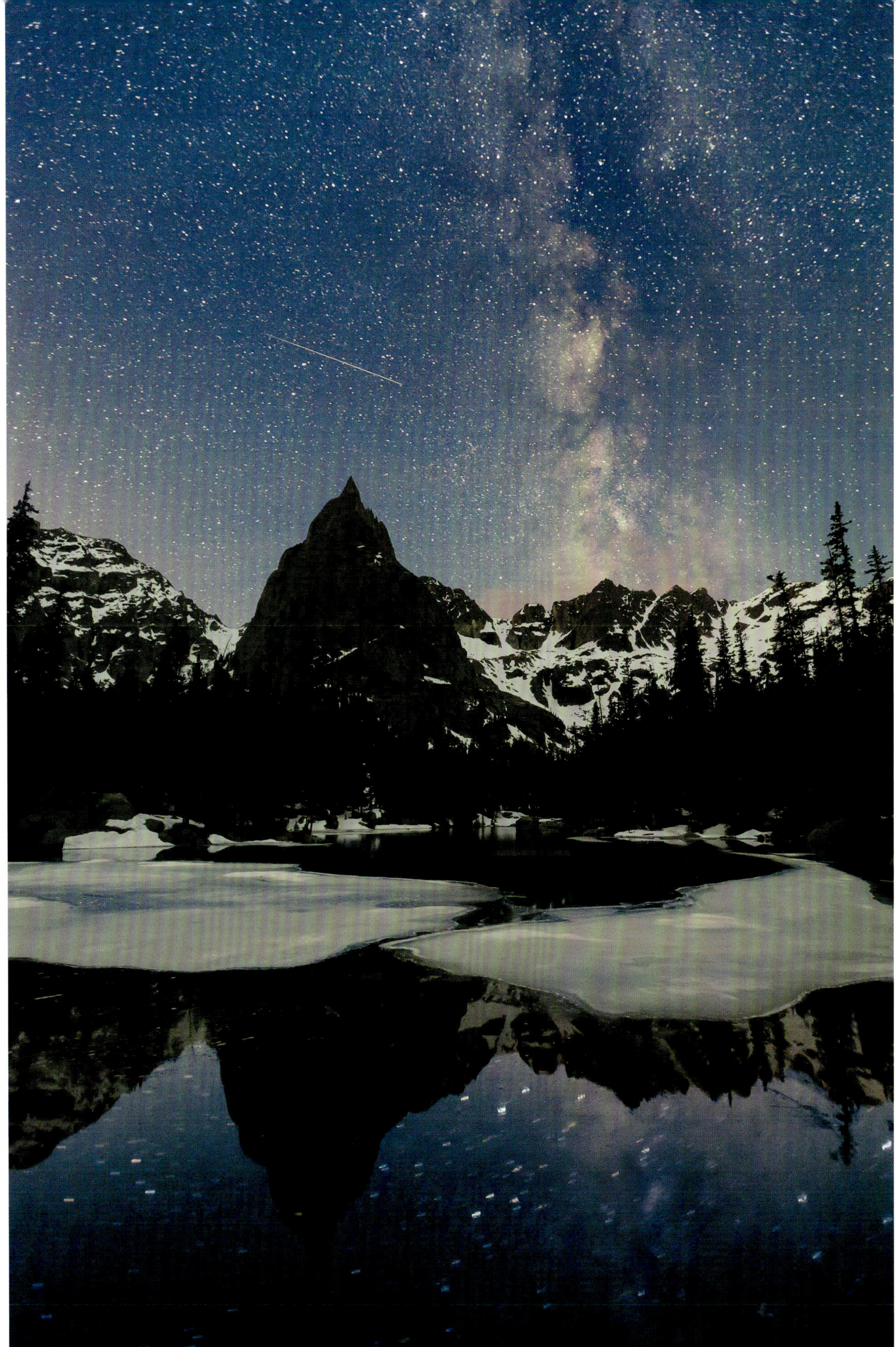

never visible. That doesn't mean you can't see and shoot the Milky Way in Fairbanks, but it does mean you won't be able to shoot the photogenic gas and dust clouds that are close to the galactic center.

The best time of night to shoot the Milky Way varies. In the spring, the galactic center rises in the wee hours of the morning and doesn't transit until after astronomical dawn. The best time to shoot is just before astronomical dawn, when the galactic center is as high in the sky as possible but the sky is still dark. During that period, the galactic center will be rising to the southeast. If you want to shoot the land portion of your image by moonlight, look for a night when the moon sets an hour or two before astronomical dawn. Shoot the land just before moonset, when the moon will be approaching the western horizon and providing good texturing light on the land as you look southeast toward the Milky Way, then shoot the Milky Way after moonset.

During the summer, the galactic center is above the horizon most of the night, giving you a much longer window of opportunity to shoot the best part of the Milky Way. Shooting during the summer also gives you more flexibility in terms of composition, since the Milky Way will be in the southeast region of the sky at astronomical dusk, due south around midnight, and in the southwest region of the sky at astronomical dawn. If you want to shoot the land by moonlight, choose a time near moonrise, when the moon in the eastern sky will provide texturing light on the land as you look south, or near moonset, when the moon in the western sky will again provide texturing light.

In the fall, you'll want to shoot right after astronomical dusk, since the galactic center will have already passed transit and will be rapidly setting to the southwest. If you want to shoot the land portion of the image by moonlight, look for nights when the moon rises an hour or two after astronomical dusk. The moon in the eastern sky will provide texturing light on the land as you look southwest. Regardless of when you use moonlight to illuminate the land, avoid situations where the moon is backlighting the scene and producing harsh contrast, and particularly avoid situations where the moon is in the frame. If you expose the sky properly, the moon will cause unmanageable flare. If you expose the moon properly, everything else in the frame will be black.

The angle between the Milky Way band and the horizon also varies, depending on both time of night and season. In the spring, at mid-latitudes such as Denver, the Milky Way slopes up and left from the point where it intersects the horizon. In mid-summer it slopes up and left when it first rises (figure 4-4), then becomes more vertical as the night progresses. In the fall, the Milky Way is nearly perpendicular to the horizon, or slopes slightly up and right (figure 4-5).

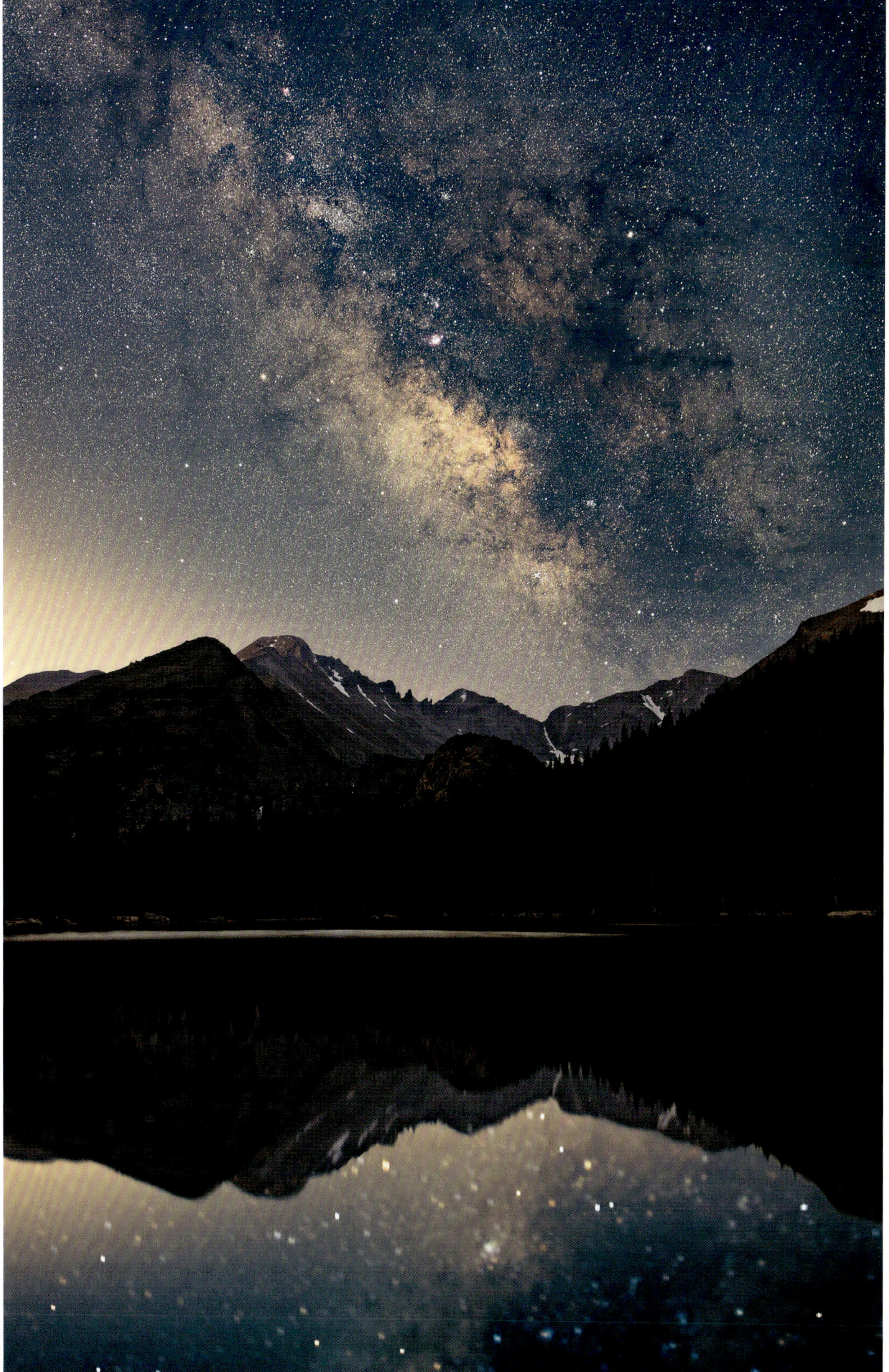

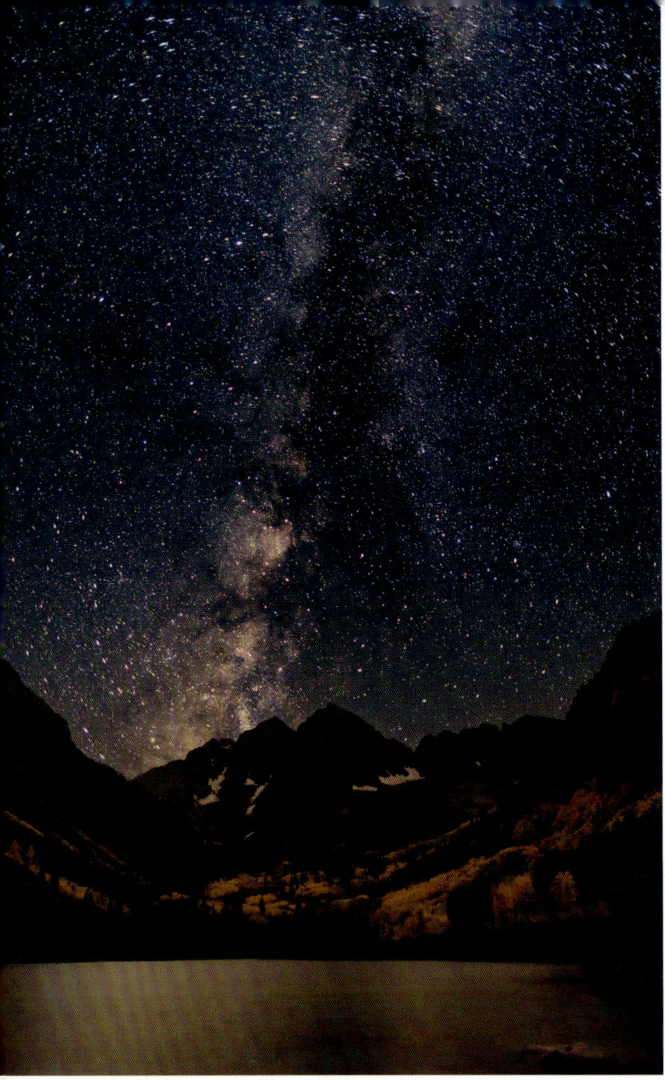

The varying shape and position of the Milky Way affect the planning process. As with any landscape, the best Milky Way photographs include more than sky. When planning your shoot, think about compositions in which something interesting lies in an arc from southeast to southwest. Arches, sea stacks, sandstone towers, and dramatic peaks make good land elements. At least at the beginning, don't worry much about the immediate foreground; the depth of field is so shallow at the wide-open aperture you'll be using that you won't want anything in the frame closer than about 15 feet even with a 16mm lens. See the chart in chapter 3 for the depth of field of selected lenses focused at infinity.

In the spring and early in the night during the summer, when the Milky Way arcs up and left from the horizon, you'll probably want to compose your shot so that the galactic center is near the lower-right side of your frame and your land elements are to the left of the Milky Way. That way the Milky Way band forms part of an arch over the peak or tower you've chosen to anchor the shot. Later during the night in the summer and at any time in the fall, when the Milky Way rises nearly vertically from the horizon, you'll probably want to position the Milky Way closer to the center of the frame with the important land elements distributed on either side of it.

There are a number of free or low-cost astronomy programs available for desktop and laptop computers that make it easy to visualize the shape and position of the Milky Way at different times of night and different times of year. As of this writing, two leading contenders are Starry Night and Stellarium. By the time you read this, there may be others. All provide a map of the sky that you can configure for location, date, time of night, and the direction you are looking. Starry Night, my current favorite, lets you search for constellations such as Sagittarius, then center them on the screen and show whether they are above or below the horizon at the time of night you've selected. Starry Night's Info panel provides data on the selected object, such as rise and set times, azimuths, time and altitude at transit, etc.

Starry Night and Stellarium will help you visualize the appearance of the Milky Way band in the sky, but they don't really offer the precision you'll want when you're planning a Milky Way shoot. For accurate planning you'll

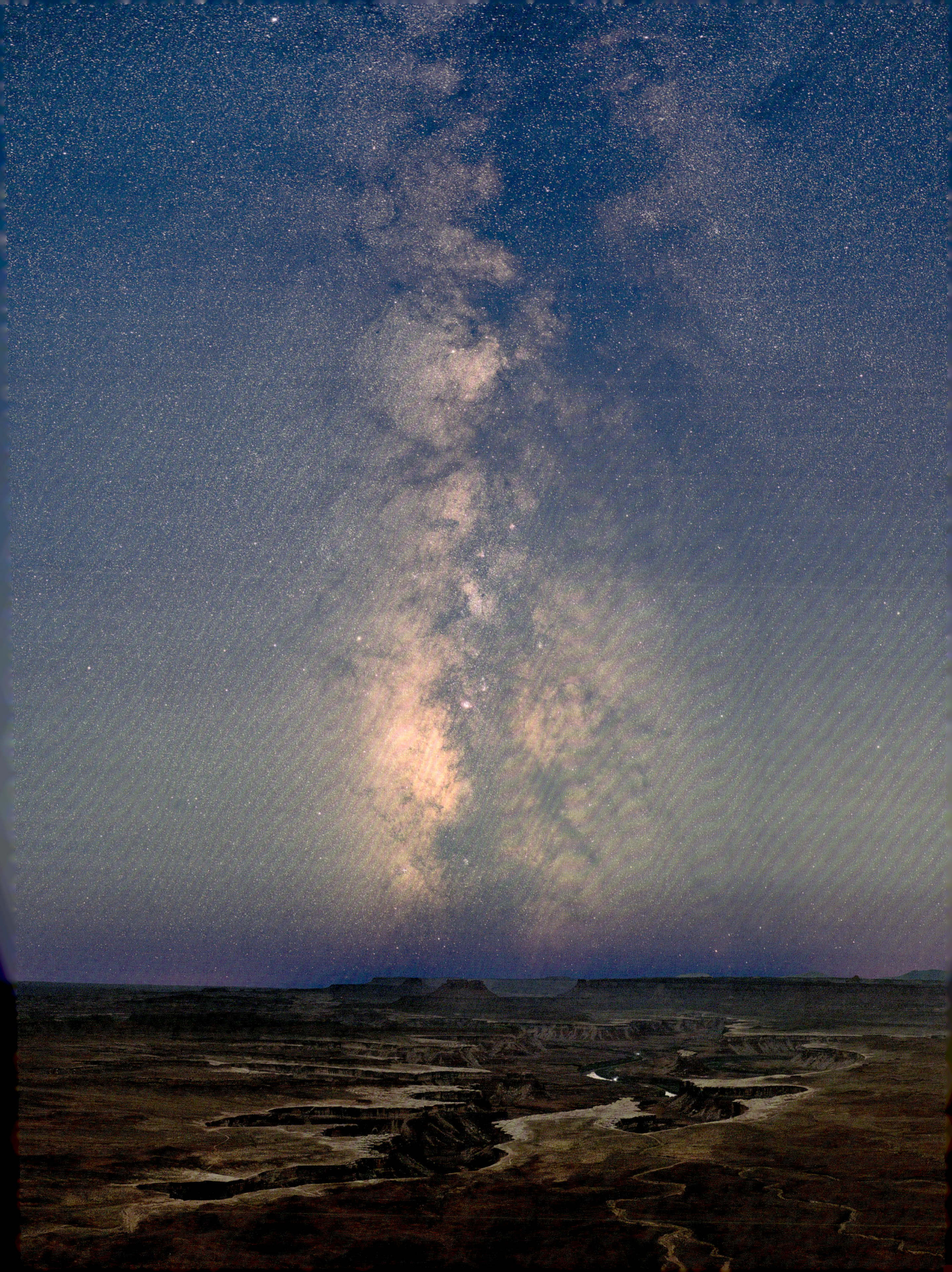

▸ FIGURE 4-7: Screenshot from the Planner module in PhotoPills. I placed the red pin on the north shore of Bear Lake. I placed the black pin on the summit of Longs Peak. The date is set to July 15, 2023; the time is set to 10:27 p.m., the same day of year and time as the image in figure 4-4. Six broad lines radiate from the red pin. The yellow line indicates the direction to sunrise; the orange line indicates the direction to sunset. The light and dark blue lines indicate the direction to moonrise and moonset, respectively. The light gray line (almost hidden beneath the broad white line) indicates the direction to the galactic center at astronomical dusk; the dark gray line indicates the direction to the galactic center when it sets. The broad white line passing through the largest white dot indicates the direction to the galactic center at the time set. The thin white lines indicate the points where the Milky Way arch intersects the horizon. The geodetics panel (top-right corner of the interface) provides the distance and direction of the black pin from the red pin, as well as the difference in altitude in both feet and degrees.

want to consult one of the many superb apps that have been developed to help you plan both nighttime and daytime landscape photographs.

During the six years since the publication of the first edition, the power of photo-planning apps like Photo Ephemeris Web, Sun Surveyor, PhotoPills, and PlanIt Pro has increased tremendously. No one has an infinite amount of time to spend in the field. Mastering one or more of these programs will greatly increase the odds that you'll be able to create a compelling image during your next shoot.

At the heart of all four programs is a topographic map or, optionally, a satellite image. All four programs provide a way to position a primary marker or pin at one location on the map (usually your shooting location). Colored lines radiating out from the primary marker show the direction to sunrise, sunset, moonrise, moonset, and galactic center rise and set for the date you specify. Additional lines show the direction to the sun, moon, and galactic center at the specific time you set. You can also drop a secondary marker on your main subject. The app then calculates the distance between the two pins, the change in elevation (measured in feet), the change in altitude (how much the secondary pin is higher or lower than the primary pin, measured in degrees), and the direction of the secondary pin as seen from the primary pin. In addition, these apps provide a wealth of data on the time and direction of sunrise, sunset, moonrise, moonset, galactic-center rise, and galactic-center set. They also provide information on the position in the sky of the sun, moon, and galactic center. All of this data is available for any time of day or night, any day of the year, for almost anywhere in the world.

These tools help you visualize where the sun, moon, and galactic center will be in relationship to your subject at any time of day or night. Knowing the position of the sun during the day and the moon at night helps you visualize what portions of your subject will be lit, and what parts will be in shadow. These capabilities alone would make these apps invaluable for planning landscape images. At this time, two apps, Photo Ephemeris Web and PlanIt Pro, include 3D models of Earth's surface. The 3D module in Photo Ephemeris Web (formerly called the Sphere module) shows you what portions of the terrain will be lit by the sun as you adjust the time from sunrise to sunset; it also shows you what portions will be lit at night by the moon, and even adjusts the intensity of the virtual lighting depending on moon phase. It also shows you the path of the sun, moon, and galactic center across the sky and the position of the Milky Way band, including where it intersects the horizon.

PlanIt Pro offers a feature called VR (Virtual Reality) Viewfinder. After dropping the primary marker on your shooting location and the secondary marker on your main subject, you turn on VR Viewfinder and see a 3D model of the world. For example, the 3D model can show you what Longs Peak and

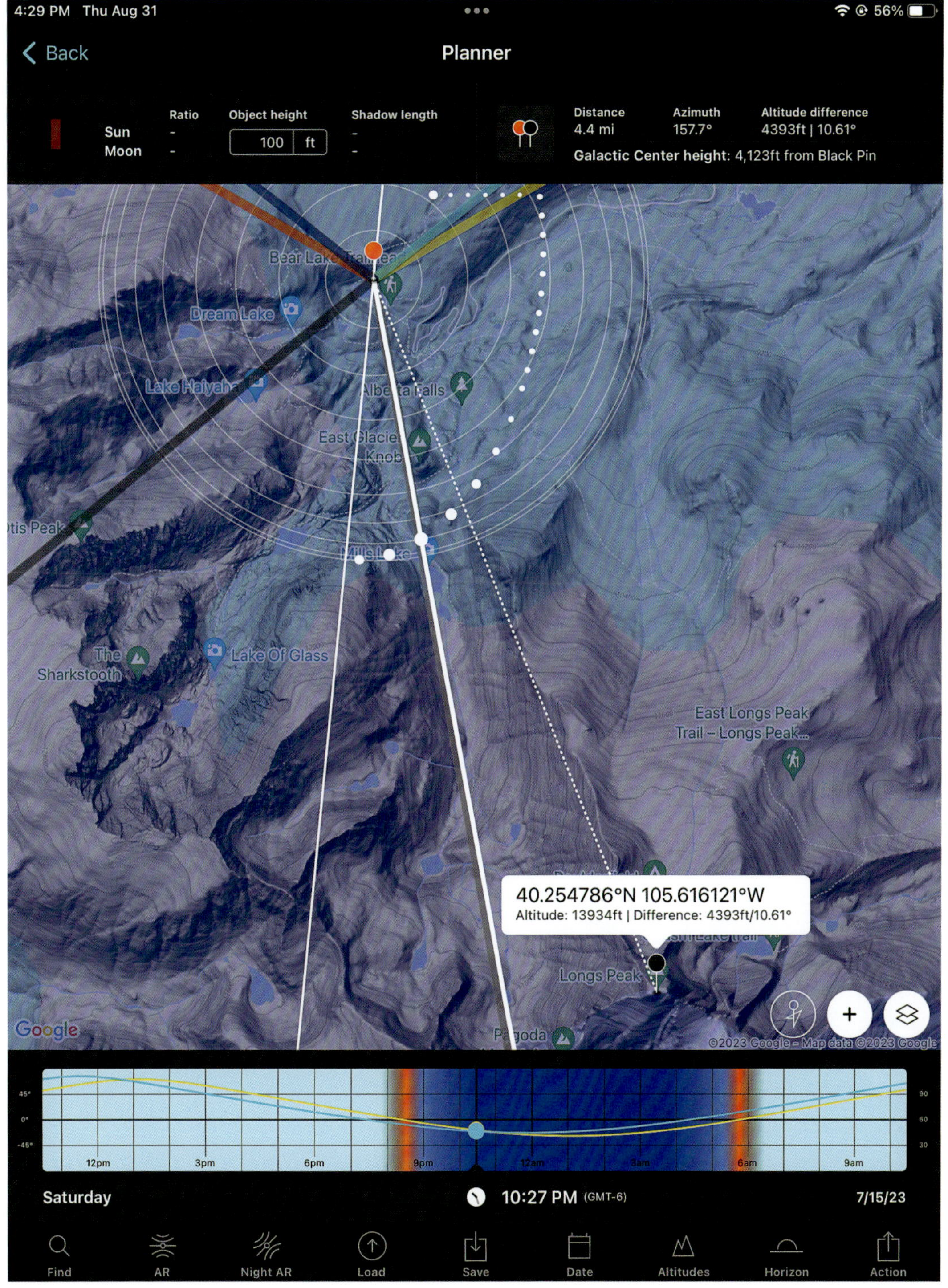

4:29 PM Thu Aug 31
Back
Planner
56%
Sun
Moon
Ratio
-
-
Object height
100 ft
Shadow length
-
-
Distance
4.4 mi
Azimuth
157.7°
Altitude difference
4393ft | 10.61°
Galactic Center height: 4,123ft from Black Pin
Bear Lake Trailhead
Dream Lake
Lake Haiyaha
Albeta Falls
East Glacier Knob
Otis Peak
Mills Lake
The Sharkstooth
Lake Of Glass
East Longs Peak Trail – Longs Peak...
40.254786°N 105.616121°W
Altitude: 13934ft | Difference: 4393ft/10.61°
Longs Peak
Pagoda
Google
©2023 Google - Map data ©2023 Google
45°
0°
-45°
12pm
3pm
6pm
9pm
12am
3am
6am
9am
90
60
30
Saturday
10:27 PM (GMT-6)
7/15/23
Find
AR
Night AR
Load
Save
Date
Altitudes
Horizon
Action

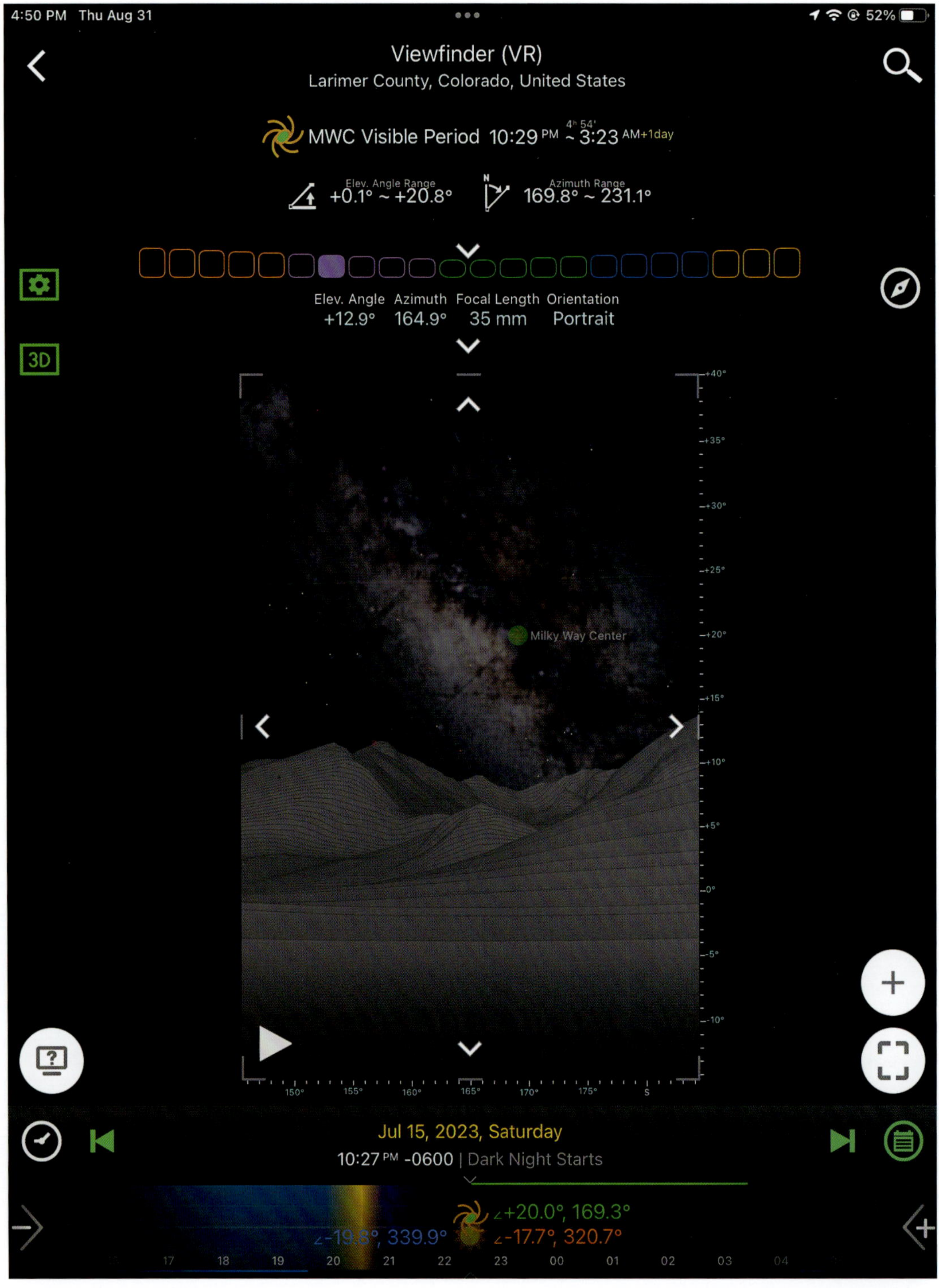
4:50 PM   Thu Aug 31
52%
Viewfinder (VR)
Larimer County, Colorado, United States
MWC Visible Period 10:29 PM ~ 3:23 AM+1day
Elev. Angle Range
+0.1° ~ +20.8°
Azimuth Range
169.8° ~ 231.1°
Elev. Angle   Azimuth   Focal Length   Orientation
+12.9°   164.9°   35 mm   Portrait
Milky Way Center
+40°
+35°
+30°
+25°
+20°
+15°
+10°
+5°
0°
-5°
-10°
150°   155°   160°   165°   170°   175°   S
Jul 15, 2023, Saturday
10:27 PM -0600 | Dark Night Starts
+20.0°, 169.3°
-17.7°, 320.7°
-19.8°, 339.9°
17   18   19   20   21   22   23   00   01   02   03   04

the surrounding mountains look like as seen from the north shore of Bear Lake. You can then specify the focal length of the lens you are using and the visible region of the model adjusts to correspond to the angle of view of the lens. You can then adjust the date and time to see if and when the sun, moon, or Milky Way will appear in your chosen composition (figure 4-8).

All four apps also offer some variation of "position search." By this I mean the ability to search for the day and time when the sun, moon, or galactic center will be in a specific position in the sky. For example, you might want to know the best day and time to shoot the full moon setting over Longs Peak at sunrise as seen from the summit of Twin Sisters in Rocky Mountain National Park. Or you might want to know when the galactic center will be just to the right of Lone Eagle Peak as seen from Mirror Lake in the Indian Peaks Wilderness.

Photo Ephemeris Web is the only app of the four that will run natively on a desktop or laptop computer. That gives it a major advantage over the other apps: the ability to run it on a large screen. Maps are most useful when they're big. Photo Ephemeris Web lets you display detailed maps and satellite images on even the biggest monitor. It's a web app, which means that there's nothing to download or install. You simply go to app.photoephemeris.com, create an account, and start using the software. The basic version is free; the Pro version, which I recommend and which is necessary to access all the features I describe below, is available as a subscription for a modest price. The other three apps, which run on both the iOS and Android platforms, are mobile-only. The mapping features of the mobile apps are most useful if you run them on a tablet since it has a much larger screen than the largest phone. An internet connection is required to use maps on a mobile device.

I usually start my planning by displaying a topographic map, which has contours (lines of equal elevation) showing the elevation of the terrain. However, there are situations where switching to a satellite image of the terrain gives you insights the map cannot. Zoom in too far on a map, and you lose the contours that define elevation. Satellite images are often far more detailed and withstand a much greater degree of enlargement than a topographic map. Small features, like sandstone towers in the desert or sea stacks along the coasts, can get lost between the contours of a topographic map, yet they stand out clearly in the satellite image. The length of a shadow cast by a tower in the satellite image gives you a relative idea of its height as compared to adjacent towers. Satellite images can also help you "ground-truth" the map. For example, the 4wd road to Marlboro Point, near Dead Horse Point State Park in Utah, is not marked on any map I can find, yet it shows up clearly on the satellite image.

◄ FIGURE 4-8: This screenshot from PlanIt Pro uses virtual reality and a 3D model of the world to show the position of the Milky Way and Longs Peak from Bear Lake at 10:27 p.m. on July 15, 2023, the same day of year and time as the image in figure 4-4.

▶ FIGURE 4-9: A screenshot from Photo Ephemeris Web with the red primary marker positioned on the north shore of Bear Lake and the gray secondary marker positioned on the summit of Longs Peak. The geodetics panel (black band just below the map) shows the azimuth of Longs Peak as seen from Bear Lake (157.80 degrees), along with other information about the relationship between the primary and secondary markers, such as distance, change of elevation in feet, and altitude (angular elevation) in degrees. Photo Ephemeris Web uses many of the same color-coded lines as PhotoPills: yellow for the direction to sunrise, orange for the direction to sunset, light blue for the direction to moonrise, and dark blue for the direction to moonset. The Milky Way indicators are slightly different: in Photo Ephemeris Web, the broad light-gray line points in the direction where the galactic center will rise; the broad dark-gray line indicates where it will set. The thin gray line indicates the direction of the galactic center at the date and time you set, which in this case is July 15, 2023, at 10:27 p.m., the same day of year and time as the image in figure 4-4. Note that Photo Ephemeris Web shows that the galactic center is just to the right of Longs Peak as seen from the north shore of Bear Lake.

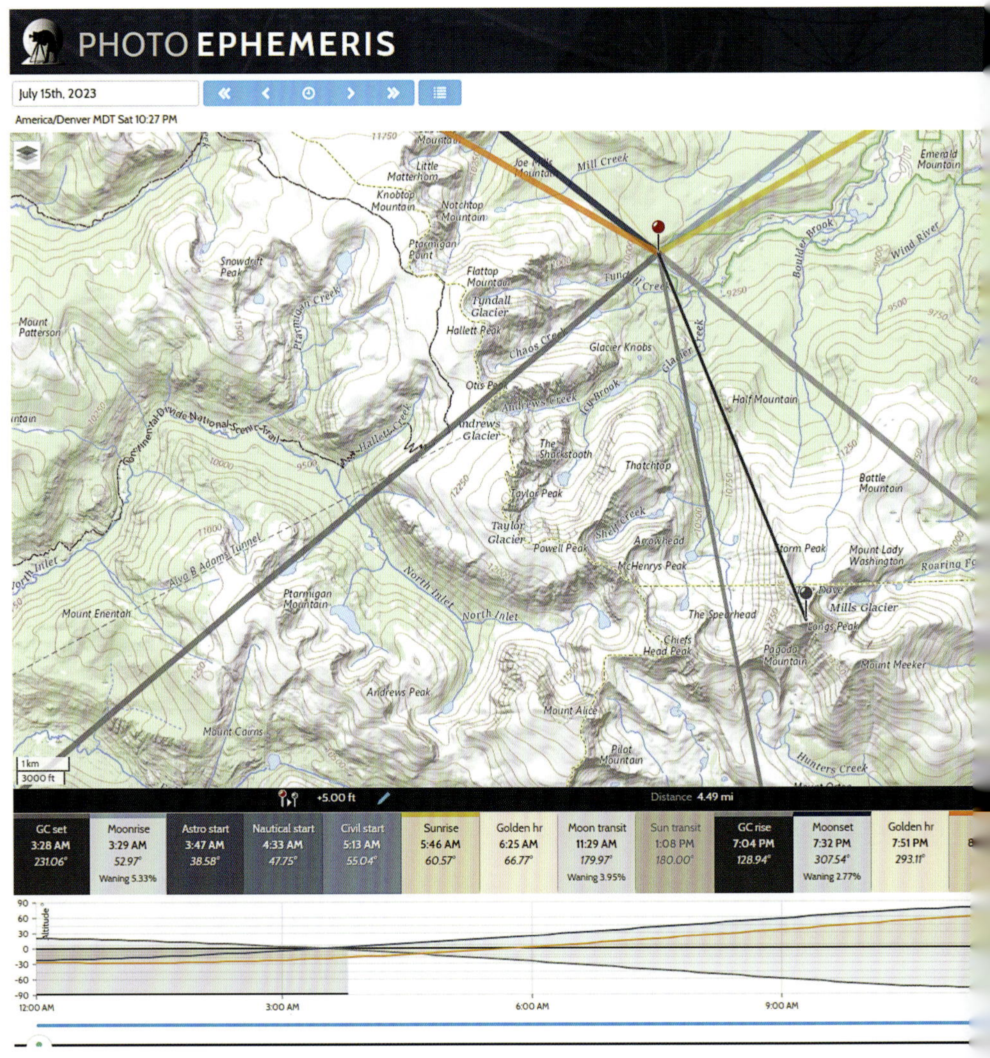

Planning a Shoot of the Milky Way over Longs Peak

Let's use Photo Ephemeris Web to plan an image of the Milky Way over Longs Peak, the highest peak in Rocky Mountain National Park. Longs Peak has a dramatic profile when seen from many angles, but the best part of the Milky Way only appears in the southeast to southwest region of the sky. We need to find a location to the north of Longs Peak that offers a good view. Fortunately, Bear Lake lies roughly to the north, and there are no tall peaks blocking the view of Longs Peak as you look south from the lake.

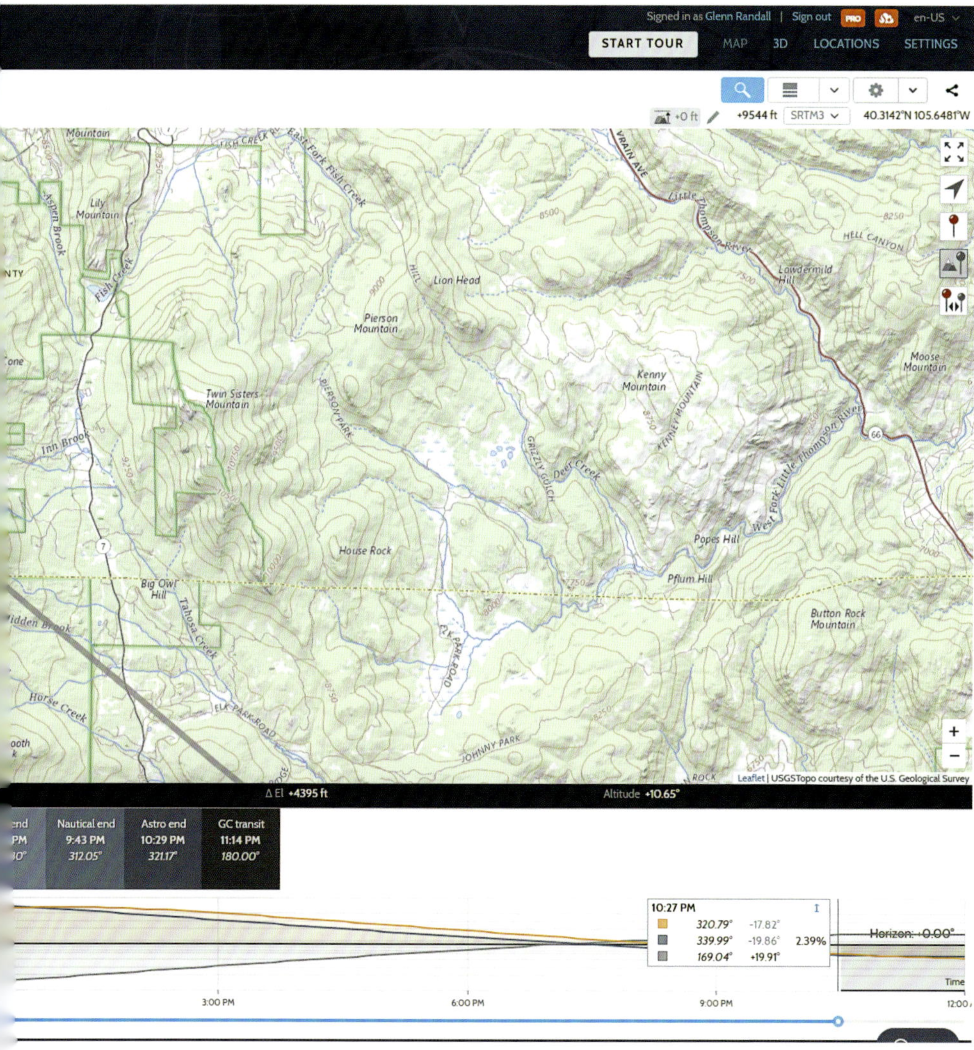

The software will open with the Map module active. Click the search icon (the magnifying glass) and search for Bear Lake, Colorado. There are many Bear Lakes in the state; choose the one in Larimer County. The software will drop the primary (red) pin in the middle of the lake. Drag the primary pin to the north shore of the lake. Now deploy the secondary (gray) marker by clicking its icon on the right side of the screen (don't try to drag the icon onto the map; just click once on the icon). The pin will appear on the map. Drag the pin to the summit of Longs Peak.

Photo Ephemeris Web will calculate the azimuth of the secondary marker as seen from the primary marker and display the results in the geodetics panel at the base of the map. In this case, that's the azimuth of Longs Peak seen from Bear Lake. I get 158 degrees, or a bit east of due south, as shown in figure 4-9. We'd like the best part of the Milky Way to be to the west (right) of Longs Peak so that the band of light arcs up and over the mountain, but there is a range of acceptable azimuths. Let's say the acceptable range is from 165° to 175°. That will position the galactic center somewhere over the dramatic peaks to the west of Longs Peak. This range is just an estimate to narrow down the number of results our search will produce.

Next, open the 3D module. For the moment, ignore the spherical model within that module, and look on the right side of the interface for the Visual Search dialog box. (Visual Search is the developer's name for position search.) If the Visual Search dialog box is not visible, click the Visual Search icon in the top-right corner, as shown in figure 4-10.

Set the various parameters as shown in figure 4-11. Don't click Use Current Position or Use Geodetics. Be sure the Range box is checked and leave Target Height blank. In this example, the altitude of the galactic center doesn't really matter. It will never exceed 21 degrees in any case, so a range of zero to 25 degrees covers all the possibilities.

Now click Search. You'll find that all the criteria we've set so far are matched on every single day of the coming year. Now you need to filter the results to show only times between astronomical dusk and dawn on nights with the moon well below the horizon.

Click Filters, then click Total Darkness and Moonless Night. The app shows you how Total Darkness is defined: with the sun 18 degrees or more below the horizon. Remember that astronomical dusk is defined as the moment when the setting sun reaches 18 degrees below the horizon; astronomical dawn is defined as the moment when the rising sun once again reaches 18 degrees below the horizon. The darkest period of night is between those two times. The app also shows you how a moonless night is defined: the time when the moon is 6 degrees or more below the horizon. You can modify those parameters if you wish, but the defaults normally work perfectly (figure 4-12).

Click Apply, then open the Results tab. You now have a list of 54 days and times when all criteria are met.

Click the blue highlighted "10:09 p.m." in the first search result (July 15) and examine the 3D model. Adjust the time forward to 10:27 p.m. to match the time I shot the Milky Way in figure 4-4. The land will be dark, so click the work-light icon just below the Visual Search icon in the top-right corner. This puts an artificial light on the land so you can

▲ Figure 4-10: Click the Visual Search icon to open the Visual Search dialog box.

▼ Figure 4-11: The Visual Search dialog box showing the settings to search for the nights when the galactic center will be just to the right of Longs Peak as seen from the north shore of Bear Lake.

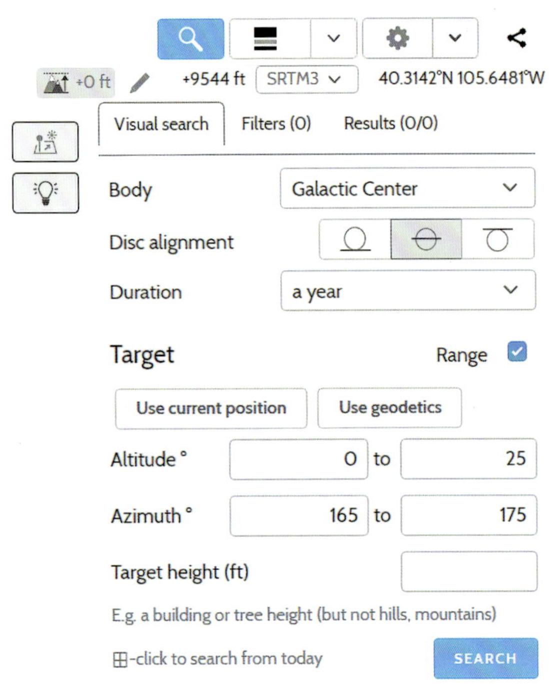

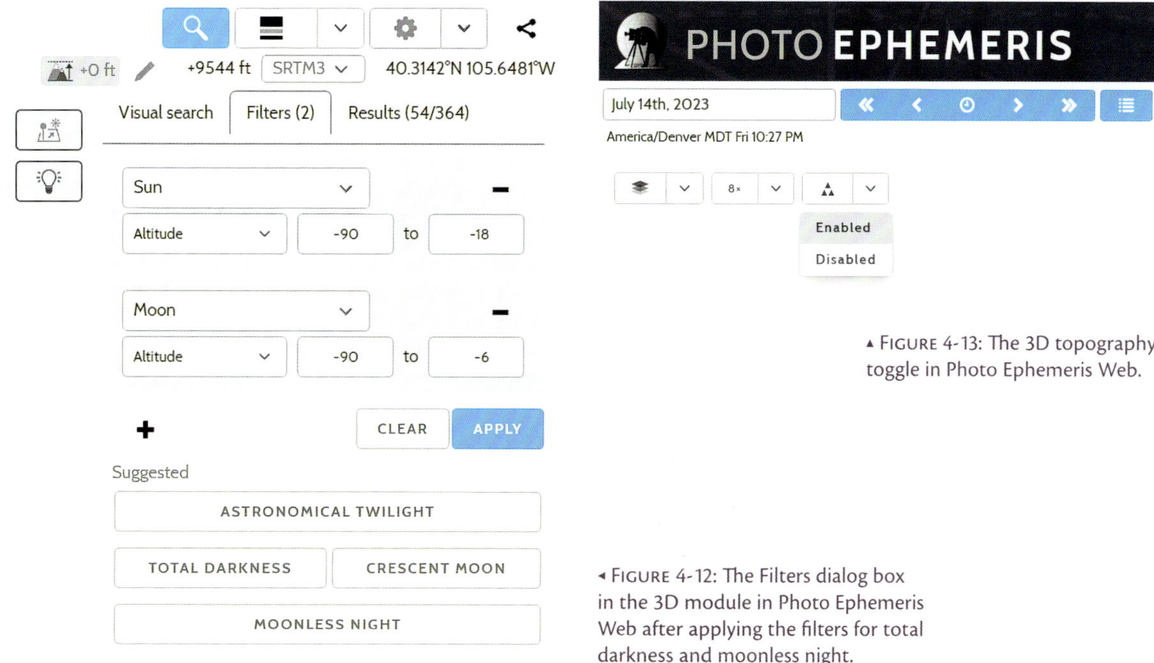

▲ Figure 4-13: The 3D topography toggle in Photo Ephemeris Web.

◀ Figure 4-12: The Filters dialog box in the 3D module in Photo Ephemeris Web after applying the filters for total darkness and moonless night.

see what you're doing. Be sure to turn on the 3D topography toggle (figure 4-13). Adjust the zoom level on the sphere to make sure the black pin on the summit of Longs Peak is within the confines of the 3D model of the land. The line of gray dots represents the Milky Way. The largest dot represents the galactic center. At 10:27 p.m. on July 15, 2023, the azimuth of the galactic center is 169 degrees. Its altitude is 20 degrees. This puts the Milky Way just to the right of Longs Peak (figure 4-14). As the night continues, the Milky Way will move farther to the right and begin to set, which gives you additional compositional possibilities.

Up to this point I've been discussing planning Milky Way photographs as you sit in the comfort of your home. Once you're in the field, you can confirm your plans using a handheld compass and data on the position of the galactic center from one of the mobile apps. For additional confirmation, you can deploy the augmented reality feature built into Sun Surveyor (figure 4-15), PhotoPills, and PlanIt Pro. This feature uses your device's built-in camera to display a live view of the scene in front of you. As you adjust the date and time, the app displays a simulated Milky Way over the live view. Note that the accuracy of this display relies on the accuracy of the compass built into your device. As a rule, it won't be quite as accurate as an old-fashioned compass with a magnetized needle, assuming you correct for declination properly.

▸ FIGURE 4-14: A section of the 3D model in Photo Ephemeris Web showing the Milky Way over Longs Peak from Bear Lake on July 15, 2023, at 10:27 p.m. The red pin is on the north shore of Bear Lake. The black pin is on the summit of Longs Peak. The largest white dot represents the galactic center; a black line connects that dot to the red pin. The gray rectangle represents the search area you defined (azimuth 165 to 175 degrees, altitude 0 to 25 degrees). The Results tab shows the days and times when the galactic center will appear within that rectangle during the period between astronomical dusk and astronomical dawn when the moon is 6 degrees or more below the horizon.

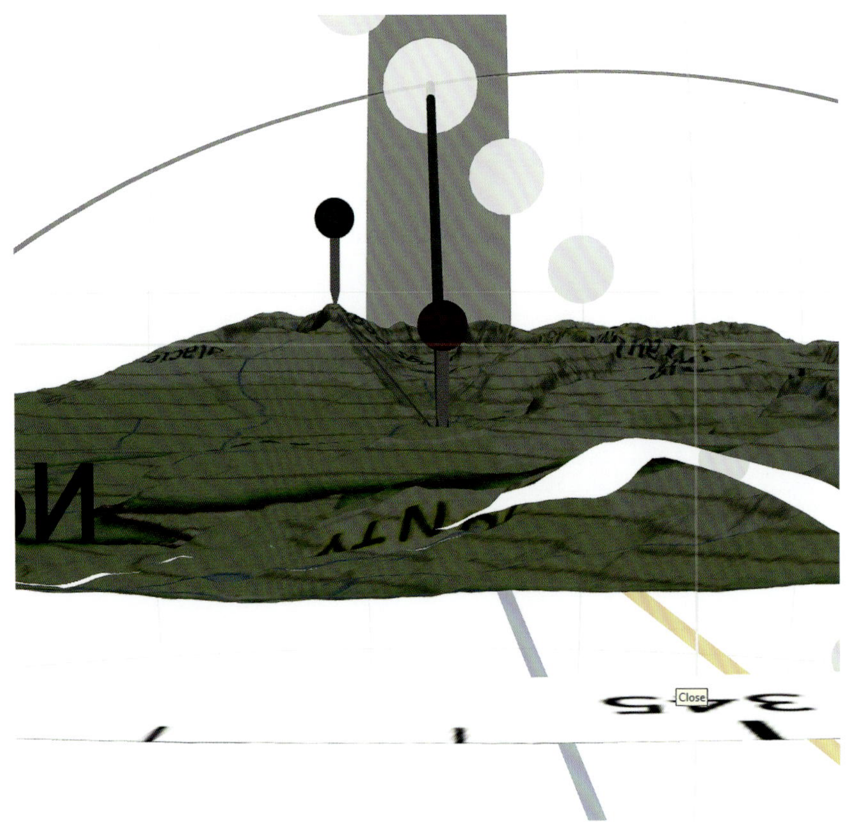

Despite this limitation, augmented reality can still be a quick and intuitive way to confirm a plan you've already made or to create a new one.

Planning Milky Way Panoramas

So far we've been talking about single-camera-position shots of the Milky Way. Such images are beautiful, but the Milky Way offers additional photographic possibilities. Look closely with dark-adapted eyes, and you'll see that the Milky Way forms a gigantic arch in the sky that extends from horizon to horizon. This arch is far too large to be captured in a single frame even with the widest rectilinear (non-fisheye) lens available. The best way to shoot it is as a stitched panorama with a multi-row panorama head. I'll describe shooting Milky Way panoramas in chapter 5. I'll discuss planning such images right here.

The best time of year to shoot a Milky Way panorama is around the time of new moon during March, April, May, and June. At that time of year, at the right time of night, the highest point of the arch formed by the Milky Way will be relatively low in the eastern sky. You'll want to start shooting when the galactic center has an altitude of about 10 degrees—high enough to be above the bright band of sky just above the horizon. At that moment, at middle latitudes, the altitude of the crest of the arch will be about 30 degrees. Try to finish shooting by the time the crest of the arch has reached an altitude of about 45 degrees. At that time the galactic center will have an altitude of about 18 degrees. This window of opportunity lasts about an hour and a half.

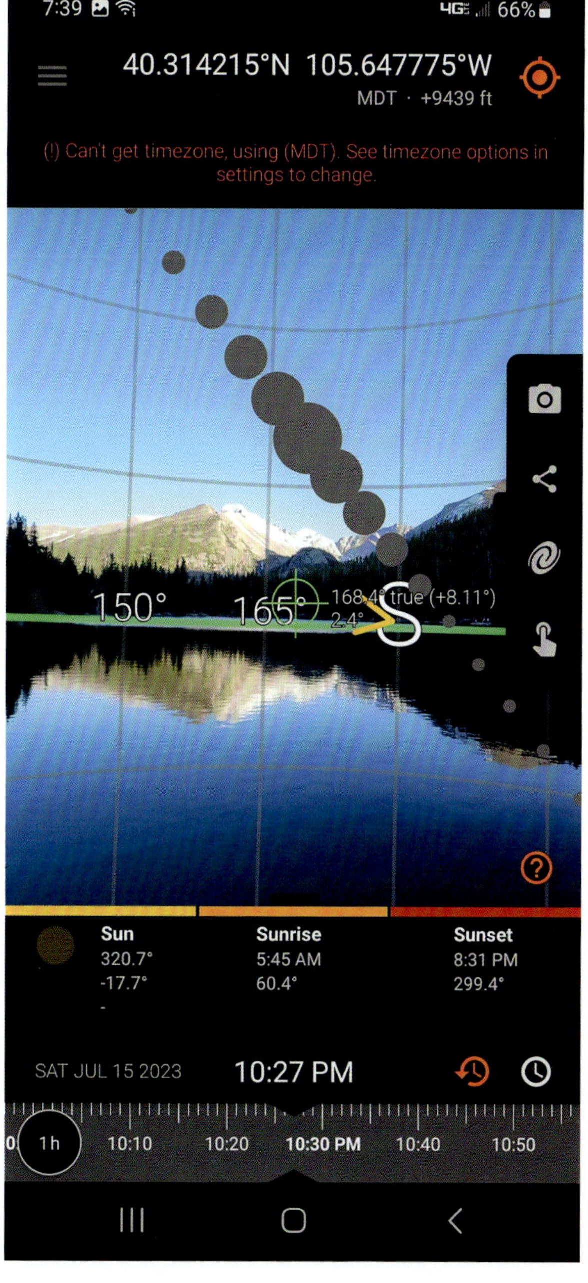

◄ Figure 4-15: Screenshot of the augmented reality view in Sun Surveyor running on a Samsung Galaxy S22 smartphone showing where the Milky Way would appear at 10:27 p.m. on July 15, 2023, as seen from the north shore of Bear Lake. The largest gray dot represents the galactic center. Compare this screenshot to figure 4-4, the image I shot at 10:27 p.m. on July 15, 2017.

▸ Figure 4-16: Milky Way panorama over Capitol Peak, Maroon Bells-Snowmass Wilderness, Colorado. June 4, 2016, 12:12 a.m. Canon 5D Mark III, Canon EF 16-35mm f/2.8L II USM at 19mm. Land: 2 minutes, f/2.8, ISO 6400. Sky: 30 seconds, f/2.8, ISO 6400. Land and sky: one row, four camera positions. I shot the land and sky exposures back to back at the first camera position, then moved the camera to the next camera position and repeated the process.

As the night progresses, the crest of the arch gets higher and higher. That makes it more difficult both mechanically and aesthetically to shoot a full Milky Way panorama. For starters, you'll have to point the camera nearly straight up, which can be awkward, depending on your tripod head and what panorama gear you're using. Second, it's challenging aesthetically because you have an enormous amount of relatively uninteresting sky between the horizon and the Milky Way band.

By late summer and fall, the crest of the Milky Way arch is already high in the sky at astronomical dusk, the earliest time it's dark enough to see it. By September 1st in the middle latitudes, for example, the top of the arch has an altitude of 73 degrees at astronomical dusk—nearly straight overhead. The best part of the Milky Way sets soon after astronomical dusk, making it impractical to shoot Milky Way panoramas in the latter half of the Milky Way season, at least in the middle latitudes.

The geometry of the Milky Way changes as you move south. At the latitude of Miami, for example, the crest of the arch is much lower in the sky when the galactic center reaches an altitude of 10 degrees. The Milky Way appears as a band almost parallel to the horizon rather than an arch whose ends touch the horizon and whose crest rises high into the sky. It assumes more of an arch shape as it rises higher. Rather than trying to memorize all these azimuths and altitudes, consult the 3D module in Photo Ephemeris

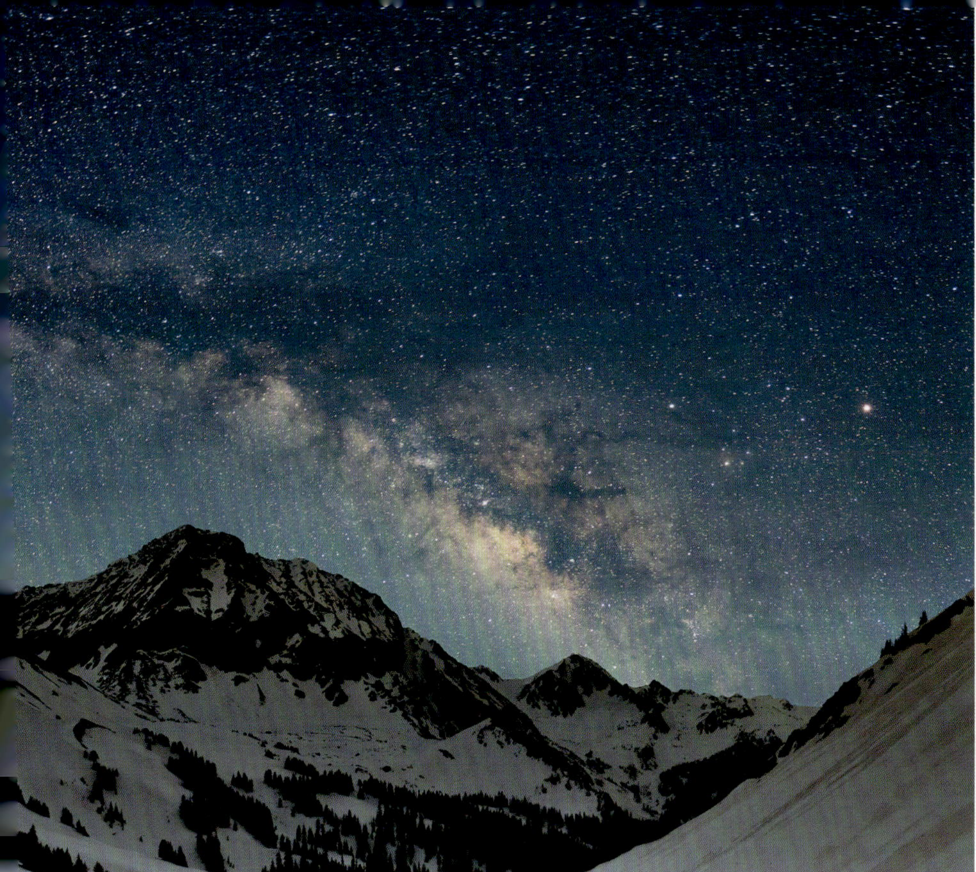

Web, which will show you graphically where the Milky Way band intersects the horizon and the altitude and azimuth of the high point of the band. If you just need data, consult the Ephemeris module in Sun Surveyor or the Planner module in PhotoPills, which list the azimuth and altitude of both the galactic center and the high point of the Milky Way band. All three apps provide information for any date, time, and location.

The crest of the Milky Way arch lies roughly to the east. The best compositions, therefore, have dramatic land elements to the east that the arch will frame. It's easy when you're in the field to underestimate just how big the Milky Way arch will be. For example, on April 1st in Rocky Mountain National Park, at 4:52 a.m. when the galactic center is 18 degrees above the horizon, the right end of the arch intersects the horizon due south. The center of the Milky Way arch has an azimuth of 90 degrees and altitude of 45 degrees. The left end of the arch intersects the horizon due north. Granted, the left end of the Milky Way arch is much dimmer than the right end, and for many compositions, it is acceptable to exclude some of the arch's left side. Still, when you compose to include a little extra sky at either end of the arch to avoid crowding the Milky Way band against the edge of the frame, you can easily end up with a composition stretching 180 degrees horizontally or more.

The details of the planning procedure for both single-camera-position shots and panoramas differ from one app to the next, but all offer some way to plan Milky Way shots in great detail. I find all of these planning tools essential. All four apps are produced by small companies. Although it's possible one or more will have disappeared by the time you read this, it's likely some other developer will have stepped forward to offer something similar. The interfaces will undoubtedly change, older apps will fade away, and newer ones will take their place, but it's unlikely the whole category of mapping and planning applications for photographers will disappear. It

▸ Figure 4-17: Milky Way panorama over Mesa Arch, Canyonlands National Park, Utah. April 12, 2016, 4:59 a.m. Canon 5D Mark III, Canon EF 16-35mm f/2.8L II USM at 16mm. Land: 2 minutes, f/2.8, ISO 6400. Sky: 30 seconds, f/2.8, ISO 6400. Land and sky: one row, four camera positions. I shot the land and sky exposures back to back at the first camera position, then moved the camera to the next camera position and repeated the process.

will be well worth your while to seek out the latest apps and spend the time necessary to master them.

Today many people never get the opportunity to see the Milky Way. The sky where they live is so polluted with artificial light that it simply never gets dark enough. Don't let yourself be one of those people. Use the information provided in this chapter to plan a shoot in a truly dark location. The experience will be well worth the effort.

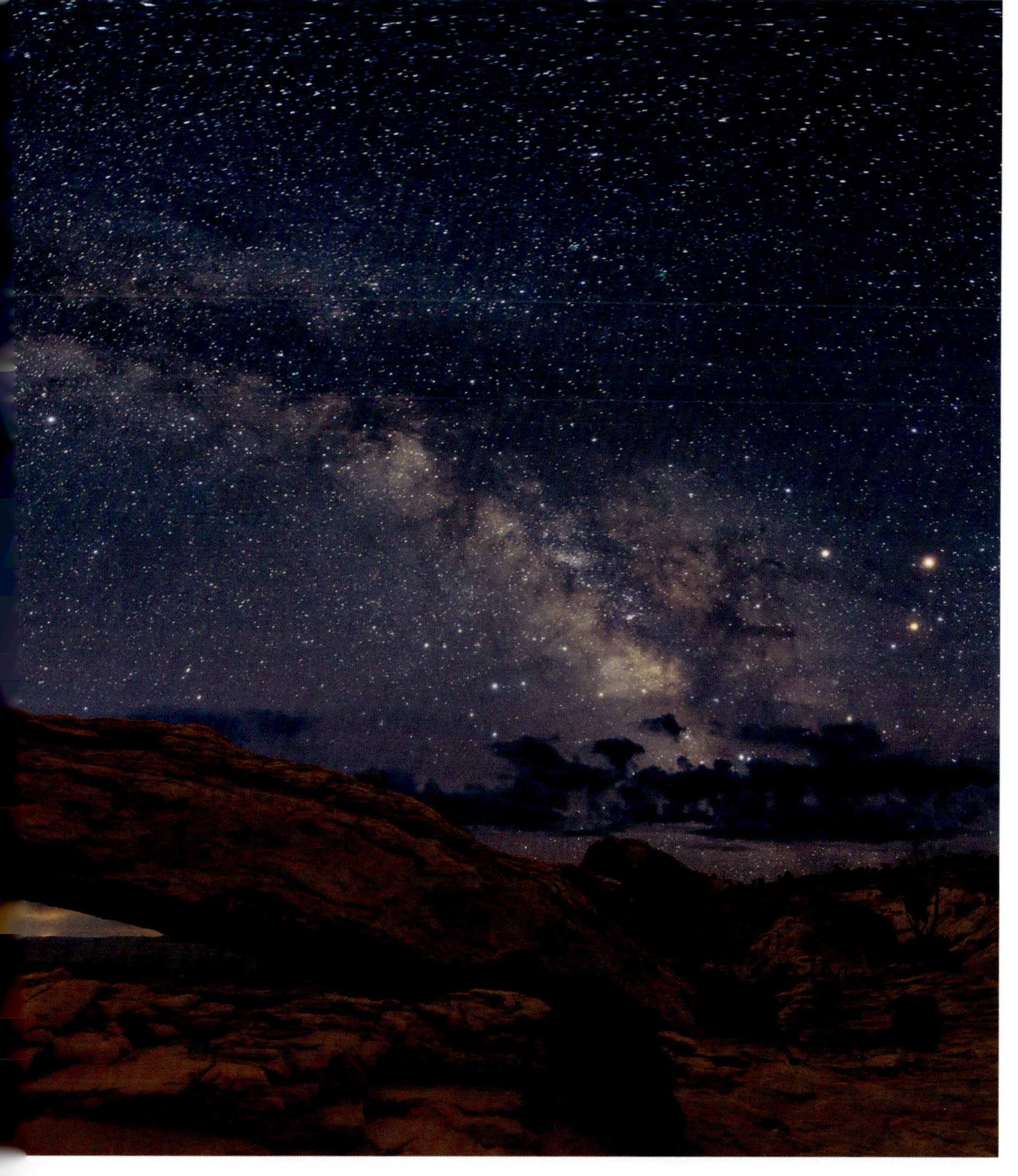

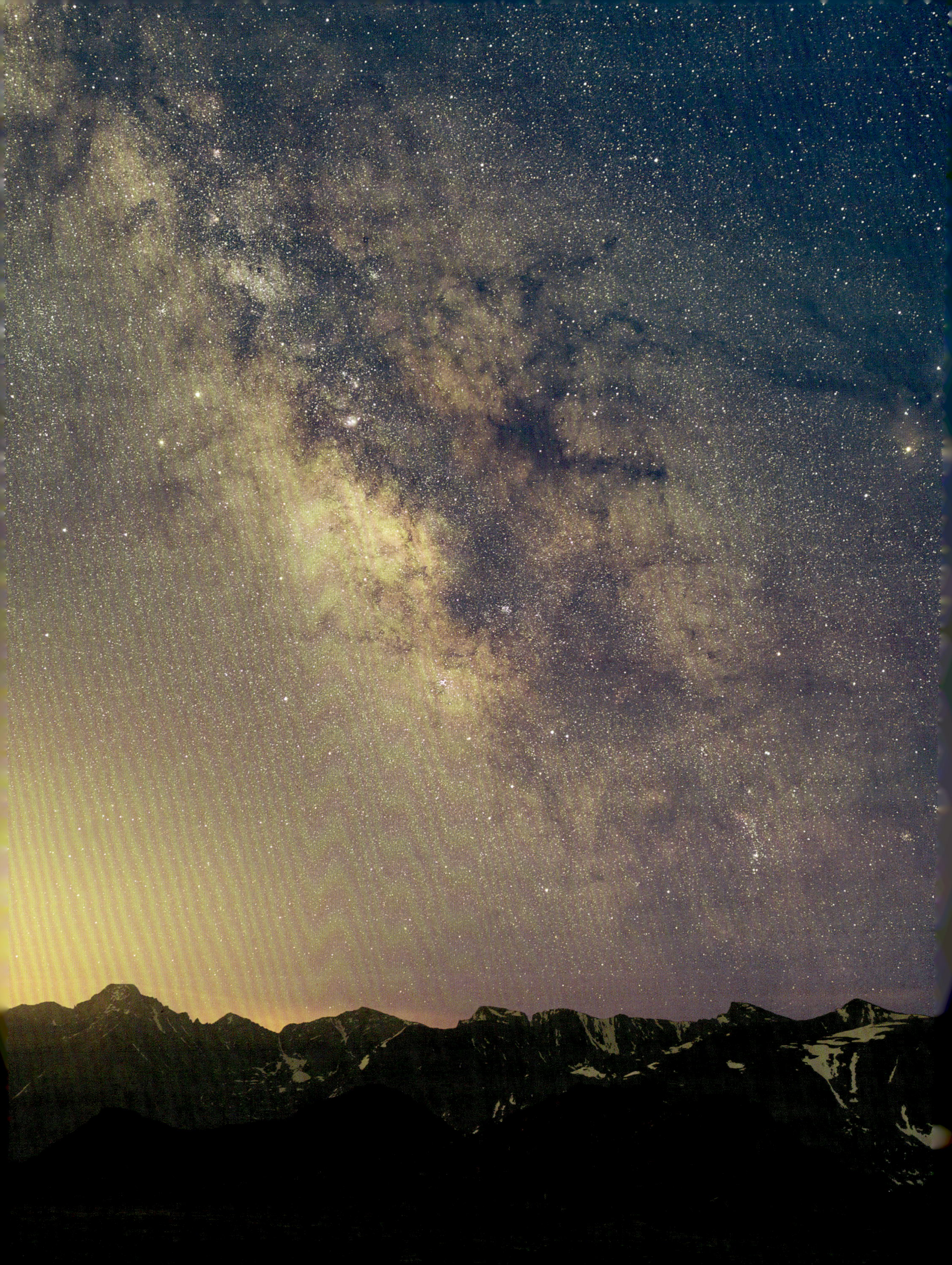

Shooting the Milky Way

After meticulous planning and scouting in daylight, you've finally arrived at a dark-sky location at the right time of year and the right time of night. The stars are glowing brightly in a clear sky. Now you're ready to capture great images of the Milky Way rising above a dramatic landscape. This chapter will begin by describing ways to shoot compositions where the lens you've chosen is wide enough to include the entire subject in a single frame. I'll call these compositions single-camera-position images rather than single-frame images because you will often shoot two frames at that one camera position (one exposed for sky, one exposed for land) that you'll later combine to achieve good detail throughout the frame. You may even shoot multiple identical frames at the correct sky exposure, then multiple identical frames at the correct land exposure, then merge each set to reduce noise before compositing the good-sky and good-land images into the final work of art.

Next, I'll describe ways to create Milky Way panoramas by shooting one or more frames at multiple camera positions, then stitching the component images together using Lightroom or a specialized panorama-stitching program. Panoramic methods are appropriate for compositions where even your widest lens can't include everything in a single frame. These compositions include panoramas spanning 180 degrees or more that reveal the complete arc of the Milky Way stretching from horizon to horizon. Multi-camera-position compositions also include images of smaller sections of the Milky Way stitched together from frames taken with moderate wide-angle lenses, such as a 35mm f/1.4. These images don't necessarily have a traditional panoramic aspect ratio (2:1 or 3:1) and may even be square. Although these images could be shot from a single camera position with an ultra-wide-angle lens, such as a 14mm or 16mm, and although these images are more complicated to shoot and edit than a single-camera-position image, the results can be even better.

Shooting the Milky Way from a Single Camera Position

The easiest way to shoot the Milky Way is to use an ultra-wide-angle lens and to shoot a single frame from one camera position. Focus the lens at infinity using one of the methods described in chapter 3. Choose an exposure that gives you a bright Milky Way but doesn't destroy star colors. When viewed on your camera's histogram, a correct exposure will generally place the peak of the data representing the Milky Way about one-third of the way in from the left side of the frame. A long tail representing the stars will extend to the right of that peak.

◄ FIGURE 5-1: The Milky Way over Longs Peak and Glacier Gorge from Timberline Pass, Rocky Mountain National Park, Colorado. June 12, 2018, 12:52 a.m. Canon EOS 5D Mark IV, Canon EF 35mm f/1.4L II USM. Land: one camera position, 12 images, images stacked in Photoshop, noise reduced with Stack Mode>Median, 40 seconds, f/1.4, ISO 6400. Sky: one camera position, 10 images, images aligned and noise reduced in RegiStar, 10 seconds, f/1.4, ISO 6400.

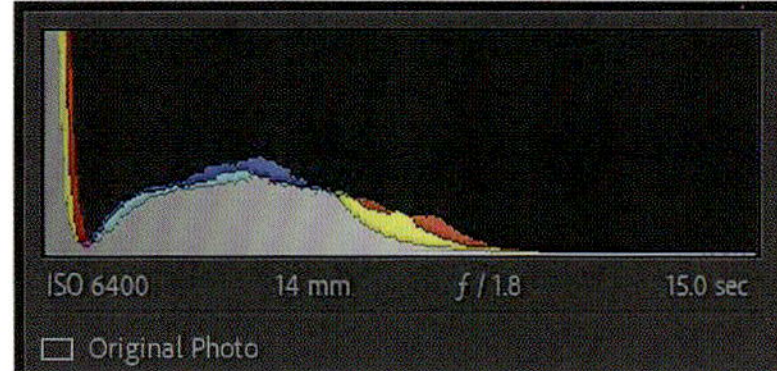

▲ FIGURE 5-2: A histogram for a properly exposed image of the Milky Way, showing how the peak of the rounded hump in the data that represents the Milky Way and sky is roughly one third of the way in from the left side of the histogram.

▼ FIGURE 5-3: Milky Way over dunes at Great Sand Dunes National Park, Colorado. September 25, 2016, 9:32 p.m. Canon 5D Mark III, Canon EF 16-35mm f/2.8L II USM at 16mm. Land and sky: Six focus positions, 30 seconds, f/2.8, ISO 6400. Two F&V HDV-Z96 flat-panel LED lights fitted with 85B warming filters provided the light on the foreground.

For a lens with a maximum aperture of f/1.4, a good starting-point exposure is 10 seconds, f/1.4, ISO 6400. For a lens with a maximum aperture of f/1.8, a good starting-point exposure is 15 seconds, f/1.8, ISO 6400. For a lens with a maximum aperture of f/2.8, a good starting-point exposure is 30 seconds, f/2.8, ISO 6400. These recommendations assume a dark-sky location far from any city lights. If your composition forces you to include the glow of a distant city, you may find that these recommendations cause the city glow to blow out to blank white. If that happens, reduce the ISO and try again. Remember that the length of your exposure will be constrained by the need to keep stars from making obvious streaks. See chapter 3 for information on the 500 rule, which will help you calculate the longest non-streaking exposure for a particular focal-length lens.

This method of shooting the Milky Way will make the land portion of the image very dark or even black. As I describe in chapter 3, that can be pleasing if you've chosen a composition with land elements that look good in silhouette, such as wind-warped trees, saguaro cactuses, sandstone towers, or dramatic peaks. If you want significant detail in the land, however, you'll need to refine your approach using one of the methods described in the section of chapter 3 titled *Holding Detail in the Land*.

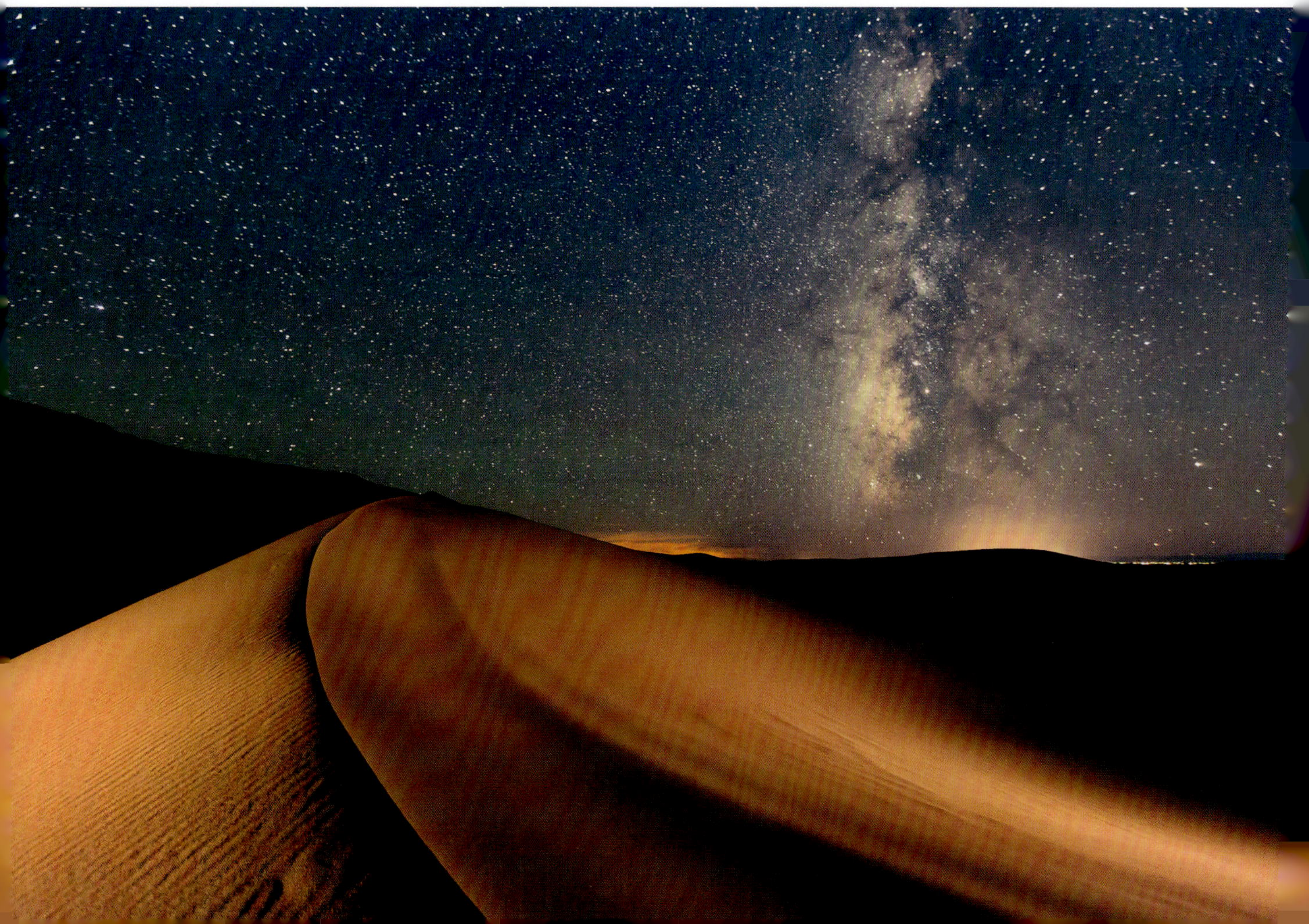

Often the best solution for capturing detail in the land when shooting the Milky Way is to shoot two frames at precisely the same camera position, one exposed for sky using the exposures recommended above, the second exposed for the land. The land exposure will usually be about two stops lighter than the sky exposure. If the correct exposure for the sky is 30 seconds, f/2.8, ISO 6400, then the correct exposure for snow-free land will usually be about two minutes, f/2.8, ISO 6400. In exceptionally dark locations, or if the land is darker than midtone, you may need an even longer exposure time. In many situations, you may want to stop the lens down for greater depth of field, then increase the shutter speed to maintain the same exposure. For example, if the correct exposure is two minutes, f/2.8, ISO 6400, but the depth of field is inadequate at that aperture, you could shoot at eight minutes, f/5.6, ISO 6400 and get the same density in the image. If the land is entirely covered with snow, which is highly reflective, you may be able to capture all the detail you want in a single exposure. I will describe two methods of combining the two frames in the next chapter. One method is simple and sometimes adequate; the other is more complicated but produces better results. I'll also discuss Photoshop's Sky Replacement tool, which for a select few images can make compositing a snap.

Shooting Milky Way Panoramas

With the right lens and composition, single-camera-position images of the Milky Way can be stunning. So why bother with shooting and stitching together multiple frames from different camera positions?

The first reason is to shoot the full arch of the Milky Way as it stretches from horizon to horizon. Such images encompass an angle of view greater both horizontally and vertically than any rectilinear (non-fisheye) lens can provide. The second reason is to shoot a composition that includes only the elements contained in a single-camera-position shot taken with an ultra-wide-angle lens, but to shoot it with a fast, moderate wide-angle such as a 35mm f/1.4. As I explained in chapter 2, this approach can produce an image with lower noise, better stars, and more detail in the Milky Way. Using a 35mm f/1.4 lens, for example, you might shoot three rows with three images in each row, then stitch them together. After accounting for the necessary overlap between images, this will give you a completed image covering approximately the same angle of view as a single image shot with a 16mm lens, but with higher quality.

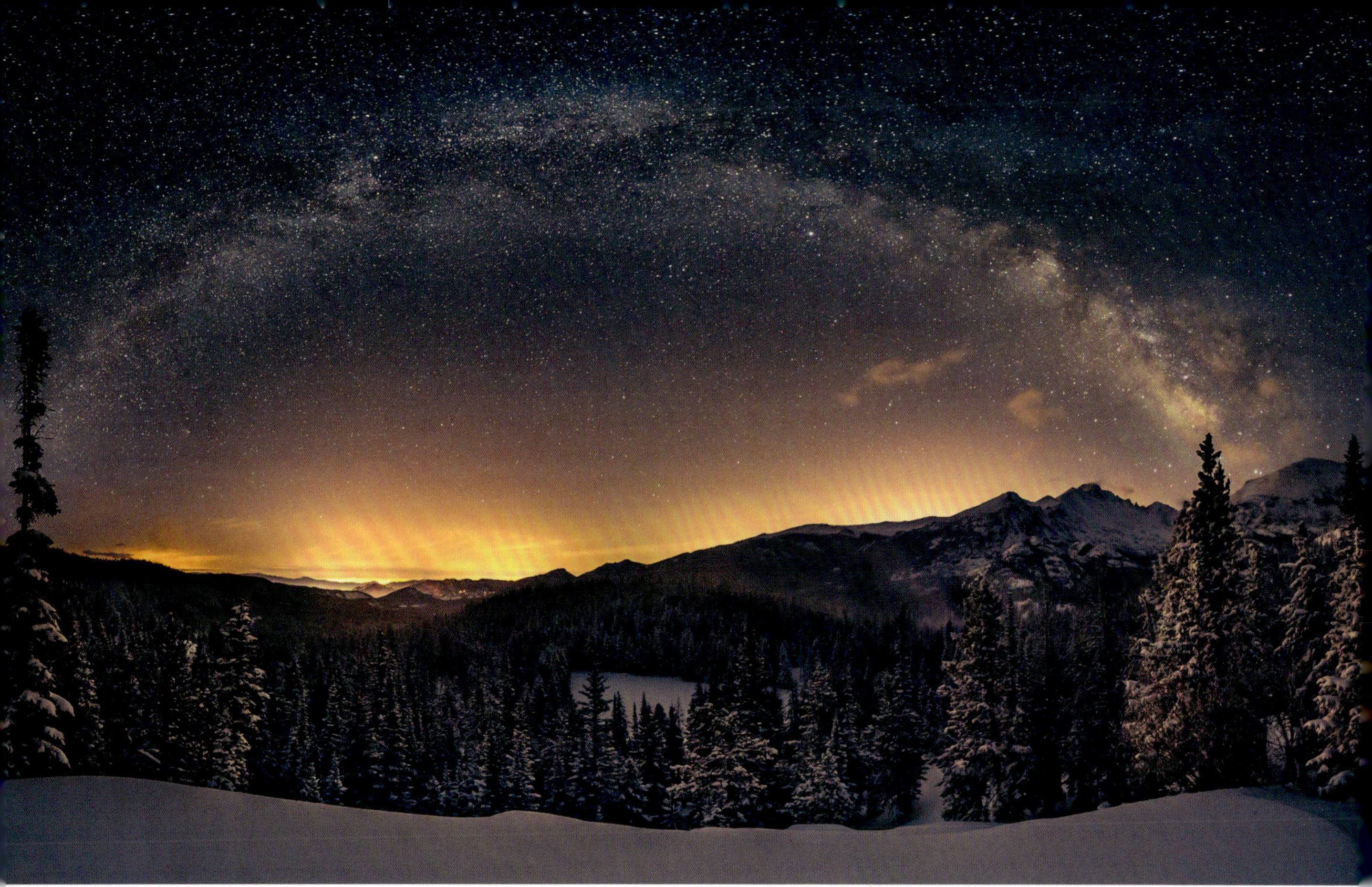

Let's start with the simplest approach to panoramas, one you can employ using only a standard tripod head.

Stitching a panorama successfully is a simple process if you've done your job right in the field. Your setup must meet three essential requirements. First, the plane of rotation as you pan across the scene must be level. This means that the chassis, the part at the top of the tripod legs where the three legs join, must be level. If it's not, your camera will be pointing down at one end of your panorama and up at the other end. That means that the horizon in the finished panorama will not be level. If you shoot an ultra-wide panorama with the chassis not level, a horizon that should be straight will look like a roller-coaster track. To level the chassis, you must adjust the length of the tripod legs. Many tripods include a bubble level mounted on the chassis that makes it easy to know when the chassis is level. If your tripod doesn't include a bubble level, you may be able to place a small level on some part of the chassis that should be parallel to the ground. Or you may be able to remove the tripod head temporarily, which will probably expose a flat surface where you can place the level.

The second requirement is that the camera must be level left to right. Many cameras today include a level that can be displayed on the LCD or in the viewfinder. If your camera doesn't include such a feature, pick up a bubble level designed to fit in the camera's hot shoe. Note that it's not essential with today's stitching software that the camera be level front to back *so long as the chassis is level*. It is essential that the camera's *pitch* (the number of degrees it is pointed up or down) be the same at all camera positions.

The final requirement is that the individual frames making up the panorama must overlap by approximately 30 percent. The amount of overlap doesn't need to be precisely the same for each pair of images.

Here's a workaround if there's no way to ensure that the chassis is level. Most cameras have both a level to ensure the camera is level left to right and a level to ensure the camera is level front to back. Start by composing the image that will become the left side of the panorama. Level the camera left to right and front to back. Shoot the first frame. Pan the camera to the right, being sure there's a 30 percent overlap with the first frame. Re-level the camera left to right and front to back. Shoot the second frame. Continue until you've shot the frame that will become the right side of the panorama. This

▾ FIGURE 5-5: The Milky Way, Turks Head, and the Green River, Canyonlands National Park, Utah. A rafter's campfire illuminates the canyon walls beyond Turks Head. October 11, 2017, 8:59 p.m. Canon 5D Mark III, Canon EF 35mm f/1.4L II USM. Land: one row, five camera positions, four frames per camera position, images stacked in Photoshop, noise reduced with Stack Mode>Median, 40 seconds, f/1.4, ISO 6400. Sky: two rows, five camera positions per row, four frames per camera position, images aligned and noise reduced in RegiStar, 10 seconds, f/1.4, ISO 6400.

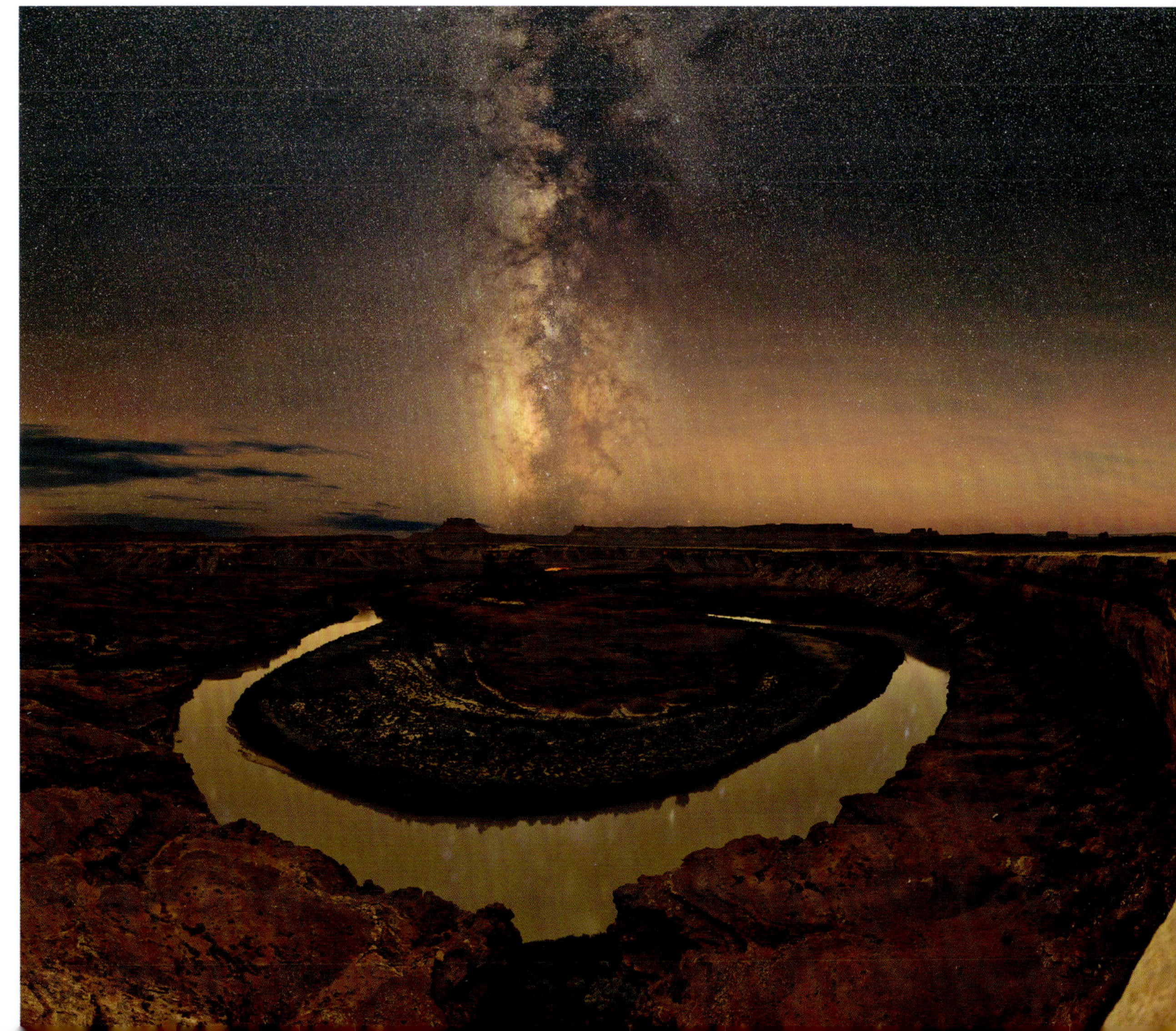

method works for single-row panoramas so long as your lens is wide enough to include the high point of the Milky Way arch when the camera is level front to back. Use a 14mm or 16mm lens, set vertically, when the high point of the Milky Way arch is no more than about 30 degrees above the horizon.

All this assumes that the closest part of your subject is at least 100 feet away. If it's closer, you need to consider parallax. The easiest way to understand parallax is to close one eye, hold up one finger in front of your face, and rotate your head side-to-side. Your finger will appear to move in relation to the background. That's parallax. It occurs because your eye is not centered on the axis of rotation of your head, which is somewhere in your neck.

▾ FIGURE 5-6: The Milky Way over Mt. Sneffels, Mount Sneffels Wilderness, Colorado. May 2, 2014, 4:35 a.m. Canon 5D Mark III, Canon EF 50mm f/1.4 USM. Three rows, five camera positions per row, 13 seconds, f/1.4, ISO 6400.

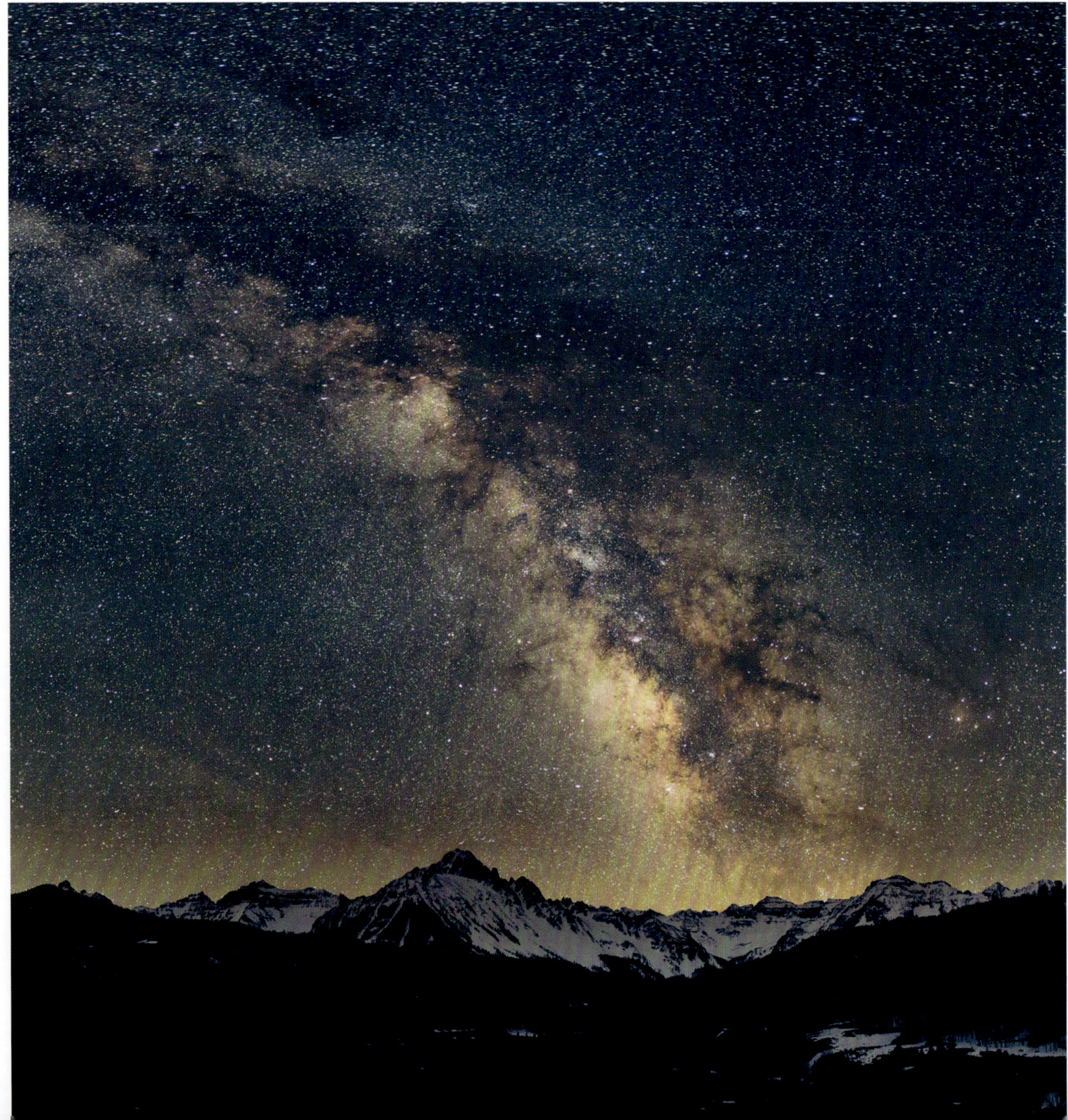

The "eye" (the lens) of a camera mounted on a conventional tripod is not centered on the axis of rotation of the tripod head. That creates parallax errors, in which the same foreground element appears in front of different parts of the background in the overlapping parts of two adjacent frames. You've just thrown a curve ball at your stitching software. It may strike out, and report that the component frames can't be stitched. Or it may stitch them, but with errors, such as weird, out-of-focus offsets in lines that should be straight or smoothly curved. In extreme cases, entire chunks of your foreground may disappear.

In my testing of the parallax problem, I found gradually diminishing errors as the closest part of the subject was farther and farther away from the camera. At three feet, the parallax problems would have required hours of retouching to repair if they could have been repaired at all. At 50 feet, I found parallax errors in only one of six trials. And at 100 feet, I found no parallax errors in six trials. My conclusion: if the closest part of the subject is 100 feet away or more, you can shoot panoramas with a standard tripod head without worrying about parallax.

My 100-foot standard is conservative. If I come across a great panorama with foreground elements closer than 100 feet and don't have any panorama hardware with me, I always go ahead and shoot and hope I can correct any stitching errors in Photoshop.

To solve the parallax problem for compositions where the closest part of the subject is less than 100 feet away, you'll need some kind of specialized panorama hardware. At a minimum, you need a *nodal slide*, an aluminum rail that lets you position the camera so that the axis of rotation of the tripod head passes through the nodal or no-parallax point on the lens, as shown in figure 5-7. You'll also need a straight dovetail plate or, much better, a L-plate (also called a L-bracket) so you can attach your camera to the nodal slide (see chapter 2 for more details).

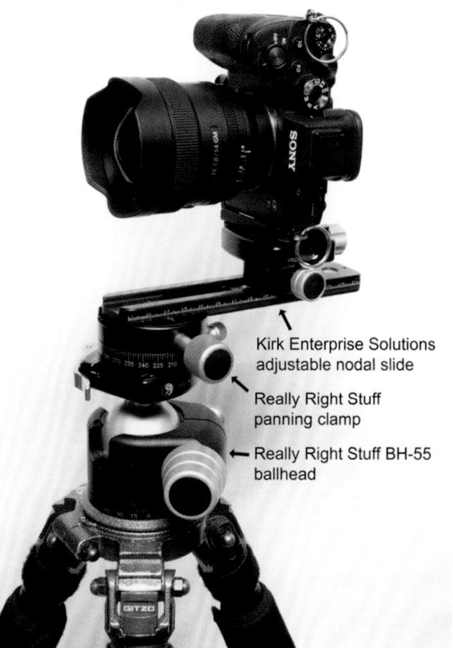

◄ Figure 5-7: A Sony Alpha 7R IVa camera and Sony FE 14mm f/1.8 GM lens mounted with a Kirk Enterprise Solutions L-plate on a Kirk adjustable nodal slide, which is mounted on a Really Right Stuff panning clamp atop a Really Right Stuff BH-55 head.

Finding the Nodal Point

Before you can use your nodal slide, you must do a one-time test, at home, to determine the nodal point for your various lenses. First, find (or create) a situation where some part of the subject is close to the lens, say 18 inches or two feet away, while the background is at least 50 yards away. One easy setup is to tie a string to a branch, the roof of your garage (with the garage door open), or some other high support where you can see past the string to a well-defined landmark like a building, streetlamp, or tree. Hang a weight from the string to keep it from blowing in the wind. Now set up your tripod. Be sure the chassis is level and your camera is level left to right and front to back. Adjust the nodal slide until you've positioned the center of the lens approximately over the axis of rotation of your tripod head. Now rotate the camera left to right. If the string appears to shift to the right in relation to the background, slide the camera forward (away from you as you stand behind the camera). If the string appears to shift to the left in relation to the background, slide the camera backward (toward you as you stand behind the camera). Find the position of the nodal slide that allows the string to remain stationary in relation to the background as you pan the camera from left to right.

If you're working with a zoom, you should test several focal lengths, say, 16mm, 20mm, 24mm, 28mm, 35mm, and 50mm. You don't need to test every millimeter change in focal length. You may find that you don't have enough travel on the nodal slide to rotate a 70mm lens around the nodal point, but you're not likely to be shooting panoramas with very close-in foregrounds with a 70mm lens because you won't be able to achieve full depth of field. Write the results on a small card and put the card in your camera bag.

The clamp for the camera bracket is fixed on some nodal slides. This can create problems if you want to shoot panoramas with a wide variety of focal lengths. A slide that is long enough to work with a 24-70mm lens set to 70mm may be too long for a 14mm lens, which has such a wide angle of view that the end of the nodal slide protrudes into the frame. One solution is to buy two nodal slides, one short, one long. A better solution is to buy a nodal slide with an adjustable clamp that can be positioned at various points along the nodal slide, as shown in figure 5-7.

Equipped with a nodal slide, you can tackle compositions where the closest part of the subject is only a few feet from the camera, bearing in mind the depth of field of your lens at the aperture you need to shoot the Milky Way.

During the day, it's easy to determine how much to pan the camera between shots by looking through the lens. If you're panning left to right, you pick some point in the subject on the far-right side of the frame, then pan until that object is about one-third of the way in from the left side of the

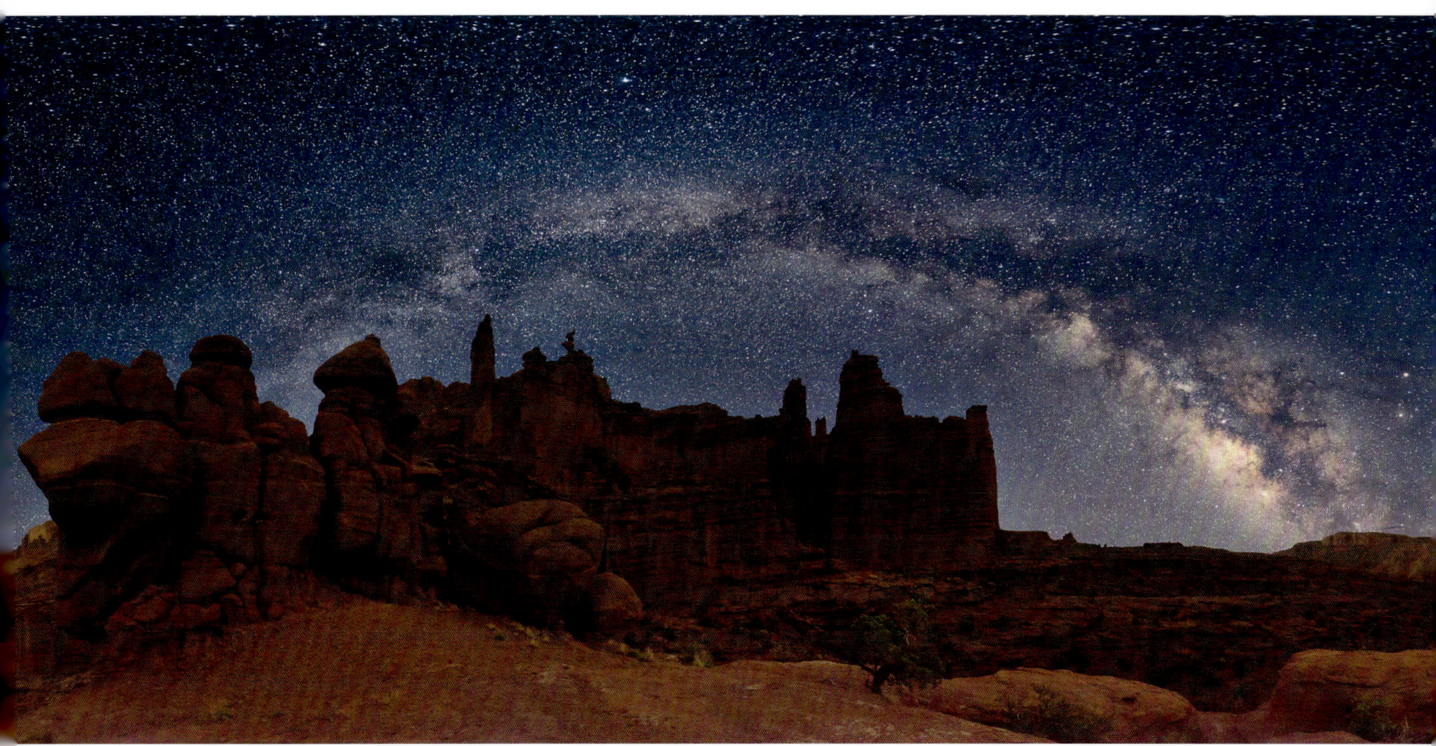

frame. At night, however, it's hard to see clearly through the lens, even when your eyes are dark-adapted. My solution was to calculate the number of degrees of pan I needed for each focal-length lens (see accompanying table). I always set the camera vertically so I can shoot the maximum number of frames possible as I pan across the scene. That, in turn, gives me the largest pixel dimensions and the best resolution possible. With that approach, the correct value for the panning angle (the number of degrees of rotation as you pan the camera to a new position) will be about two-thirds of the angle of view of the lens, measured on the short dimension. You can find angle-of-view tables on the web as well as in mobile apps like PhotoPills. For example, the angle of view of a 16mm lens on the short dimension is 74 degrees. The panning angle, therefore, is 50 degrees, or about two-thirds of the angle of view. I chose a panning angle that is a multiple of five to make the math easy as I move to each new camera position. I added that information to the table I created of nodal-slide positions. I always set up my panorama so the degree scale on my tripod head's pan control is set to zero for the first camera position and always shoot left to right because the degree scale on the panning control increases in a counterclockwise direction. That allows me to reposition the camera quickly, since I can calculate the next camera position in my head, without digging out a calculator. With a 16mm lens, for example, I use 0 degrees, 50 degrees, 100 degrees, etc. (If I shot right to left, I'd have to calculate 360 − 50 = 310, then 310 − 50 = 260, etc., all while in a hurry and sleep deprived.)

▲ FIGURE 5-8: Milky Way over the Fisher Towers, Utah. April 13, 2016, 4:35 a.m. Canon 5D Mark III, Canon EF 16-35mm f/2.8L II USM at 16mm. Land: 2.5 minutes, f/2.8, ISO 6400. Sky: 30 seconds, f/2.8, ISO 6400. Land and sky: single row, five camera positions. For this panorama I shot the first pair of sky and land frames back to back, then moved the camera to the next camera position, shot the second pair of sky and land frames, etc.

Focal length of lens on a full-frame camera. Users of crop-sensor cameras should use the full-frame equivalent focal length of the lens in use.	Panning angles for a vertically oriented camera to produce a one-third overlap with the adjacent frame
16mm	0° 50° 100° 150° 200° 250° 300°
20mm	0° 40° 80° 120° 160° 200° 240°
24mm	0° 35° 70° 105° 140° 175° 210°
28mm	0° 30° 60° 90° 120° 150° 180°
35mm	0° 25° 50° 75° 100° 125° 150°
50mm	0° 20° 40° 60° 80° 100° 120°
70mm	0° 15° 30° 45° 60° 75° 90°

Leveling the chassis by adjusting the length of the tripod legs is tedious. As with all photographic problems, you can solve this one by throwing money at it. Buy a panning clamp, such as those made by Really Right Stuff, then mount it atop the tripod head. The nodal slide then attaches to the panning clamp (figure 5-7). With this setup, you can level the plane of rotation as you pan across the scene by leveling the panning clamp using the standard tripod controls. This is much faster than leveling the chassis by adjusting the tripod legs. Once the panning clamp is level, you can lock down the tripod head and not touch it throughout the shooting sequence. You use the panning clamp to rotate the camera from one position to the next, not the pan control on the tripod head. Leveling the panning clamp also levels the camera left to right.

Adding a panning clamp to your panorama kit greatly simplifies setup, but it has the disadvantage for night photography that it also levels the camera front to back. The highest object in your frame will have an altitude of half the angle of view of the lens; the lowest object will have a negative value equal to the same altitude. For example, a 16mm lens has an angle of view, measured on the long dimension, of 97 degrees. The highest star in your frame will have an altitude of 48.5 degrees; you'll be looking down at the lowest part of the foreground at the same angle. This limitation means you can't point the camera upward to take in the highest part of the Milky Way arch.

To understand this, consider the situation in Colorado or other locations with a similar latitude of about 40 degrees. Let's say you'll be shooting on April 15. By the time the galactic center has reached an altitude of 10 degrees, which puts it above the bright sky near the horizon, the center of the highest part of the Milky Way arch will have an altitude of about 28 degrees—barely within range of a 16mm lens set vertically and leveled front to back. Remember that the upper edge of the Milky Way band is roughly 10 degrees above

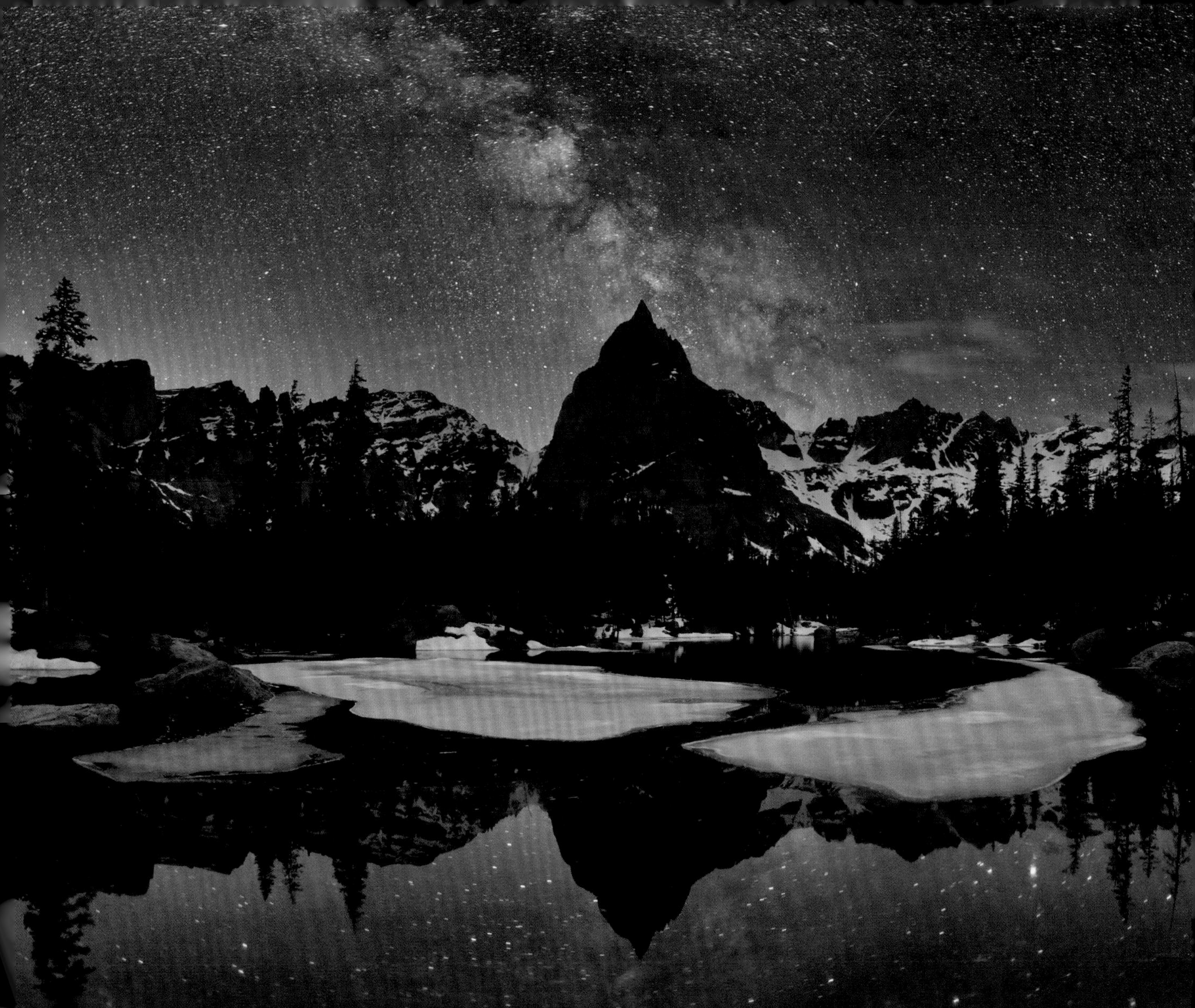

the altitude of the galactic equator, which is the centerline of the Milky Way band. (Apps normally provide the maximum altitude of the galactic equator when displaying the altitude of the high point of the Milky Way arch.) Remember also that you'll need to have some sky visible above the band to avoid crowding the band against the top of the frame. By the time the galactic center reaches an altitude of 20 degrees, the highest point of the Milky Way arch will have an altitude of 51 degrees—beyond what you can shoot even with a 16mm lens set vertically, unless you are pointing the lens upward.

The least expensive solution to this problem is to restrict the use of a panning clamp to panoramas where you can include everything you want

▲ FIGURE 5-9: Lone Eagle Peak and the Milky Way reflected in Mirror Lake, Indian Peaks Wilderness, Colorado. June 18, 2015, 1:51 a.m. Canon 5D Mark III, Canon EF 24mm f/1.4L II USM. Land: 80 seconds, f/1.4, ISO 6400. Sky: 20 seconds, f/1.4, ISO 6400. Land and sky: two rows, three camera positions per row. For this panorama I shot the first pair of sky and land frames back to back, then moved the camera to the next camera position, shot the second pair of sky and land frames, etc.

in the composition by shooting a single row with the camera level front to back. When the highest point of the Milky Way arch is too high in the sky for that approach, remove the panning clamp, level the chassis by adjusting the tripod legs, point the camera up at the right angle, and level the camera left to right with the in-camera level or a hot-shoe level. This will allow you to shoot a single-row panorama of the complete Milky Way arch up to the time when the highest point of the arch is so high in the sky that you can't include it and your foreground in a single frame even with your widest lens.

Multi-Row Panoramas

If you're like me, you'll eventually chafe at the restrictions imposed on your panoramic compositions by the necessity of shooting them in a single row with an ultra-wide-angle lens. You may want a wider angle of view vertically than can be encompassed in a single row with such a lens, or you may want the additional quality that can be achieved by using a fast, moderate wide-angle lens such as a 35mm f/1.4. In both situations, you'll need to shoot multiple rows to capture a complete Milky Way panorama.

It's theoretically possible to shoot a multi-row panorama without using multi-row panorama hardware, or any panorama hardware at all if the closest part of the subject is more than 100 feet away. You could, for example, level the chassis, then level the camera front to back and left to right, shoot the first row, then point the camera up, check that the camera is still level left to right, and shoot a second row. The problem, potentially, is that the starting point for the two rows would not be exactly the same. That could cause problems when you try to stitch the panorama together.

Today's panorama-stitching software is amazingly good at finding the common elements in the overlapping part of each pair of frames and stitching everything together into a seamless whole—amazing, but not invincible. The most precise and reliable way to shoot a multi-row panorama is to invest in multi-row panorama hardware such as that manufactured by Really Right Stuff, Acratech, Nodal Ninja, or other manufacturers. Figure 5-11 shows one example. With that hardware you can point the camera up or down as much as necessary to include the top of the Milky Way arch in the highest row and the closest foreground elements in the bottom row. By shooting multiple rows of images, you can cover whatever angle of view you need, regardless of the focal length of your lens. The starting point of each row is the same, which makes it much easier for your stitching software to put everything together without stitching errors.

▶ Figure 5-10: The Milky Way over Big Spring Canyon, Needles District, Canyonlands National Park, Utah. April 30, 2017, 4:50 a.m. Canon 5D Mark III, Canon EF 35mm f/1.4L II USM. Land: one row, four camera positions, four frames per camera position, images stacked in Photoshop, noise reduced with Stack Mode>Median, 40 seconds, f/1.4, ISO 6400. Sky: two rows, four camera positions per row, four frames per camera position, images aligned and noise reduced in RegiStar, 10 seconds, f/1.4, ISO 6400.

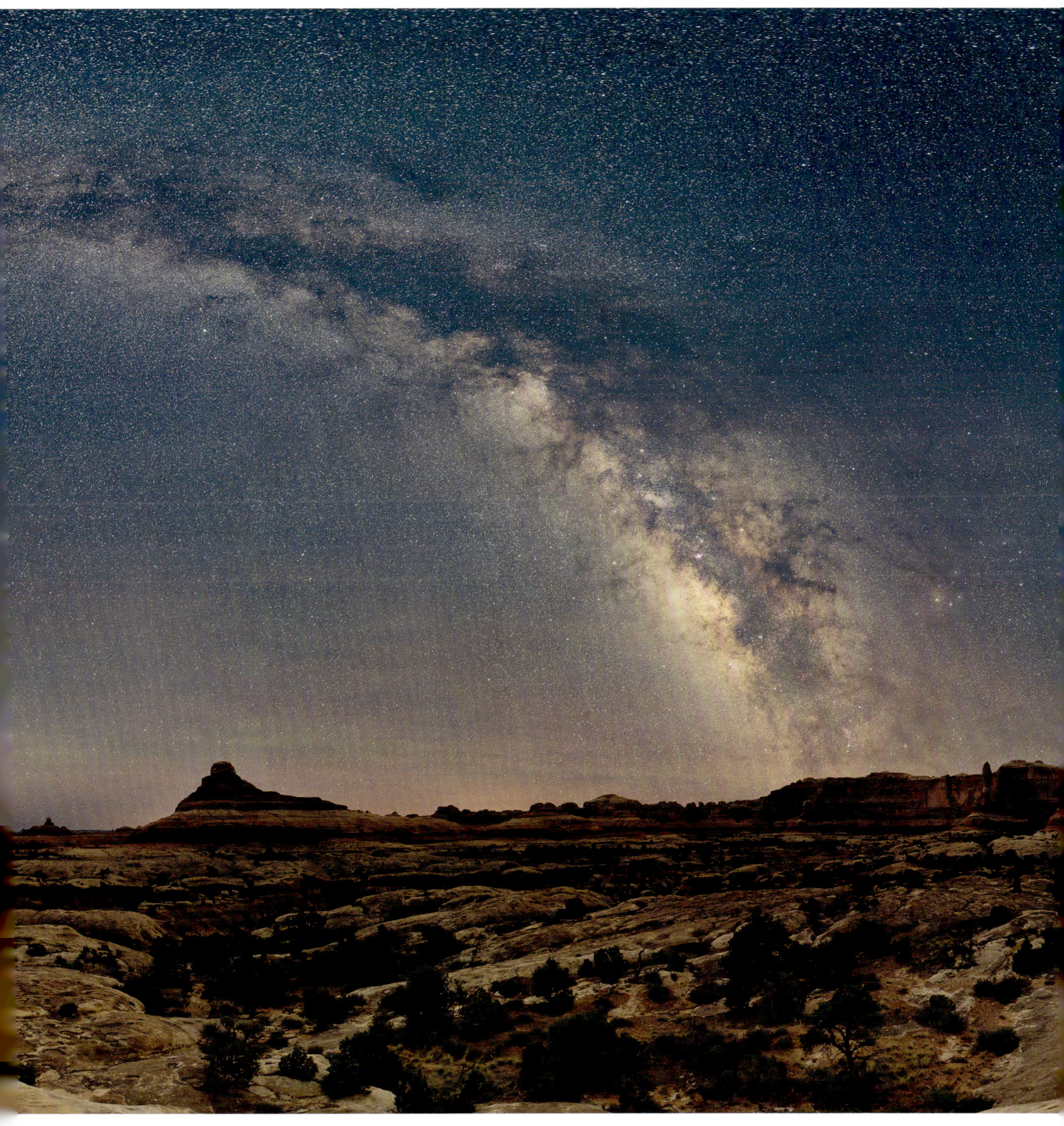

As with single-row panoramas, you'll need to use a nodal slide to ensure the camera pans around the nodal point. In addition, you'll also need to position the camera correctly left to right, so the pivot point of the rotating base passes through the center of the lens. It will be easier to stitch together your multi-row panorama if you use precisely the same panning angle as you pan the camera left to right and the same *pitch angle* (the change, in degrees, as you pivot the camera upward to start a new row). I always start at the bottom-left corner of the panorama, shoot all the frames in that row from left to right, then change the camera's pitch and shoot the next row, again going from left to right. Be sure you jot down the panning and pitch angles you use, as well as the pitch of the bottom row. Some stitching programs can use this information to perform a rough alignment of the images before stitching, which helps eliminate stitching errors.

Camera Settings for Panoramas

With the tripod setup complete, consider the camera settings. Determine exposure for your single-row or multi-row panorama the same way you calculate exposure for single-camera-position images. Be sure you use the same exposure for all of the component frames by using manual-exposure mode or by using an intervalometer to set the same exposure for each frame. You should also set focus, ISO, and white balance manually. No camera setting should change as you pan from one camera position to the next.

If you shoot just one frame at each camera position, choose an exposure that will render the sky correctly. Inevitably, that will mean that the land will be very dark unless it is completely snow-covered. If you want to shoot one frame with the correct land exposure and one frame with the correct sky exposure at each camera position, you face a choice.

One approach is to shoot the two frames one after the other without moving the camera. You then pan the camera to the next camera position and shoot the next pair of frames. With this approach, you'll need to merge each pair of frames seamlessly, then stitch each composite pair together. This is the approach to use if you're planning to use Photoshop's Sky Replacement tool to blend the two images (more on that in chapter 6). It's also the approach to use if your skyline has complex shapes, such as trees, projecting into the sky. You may need to do additional work on the completed

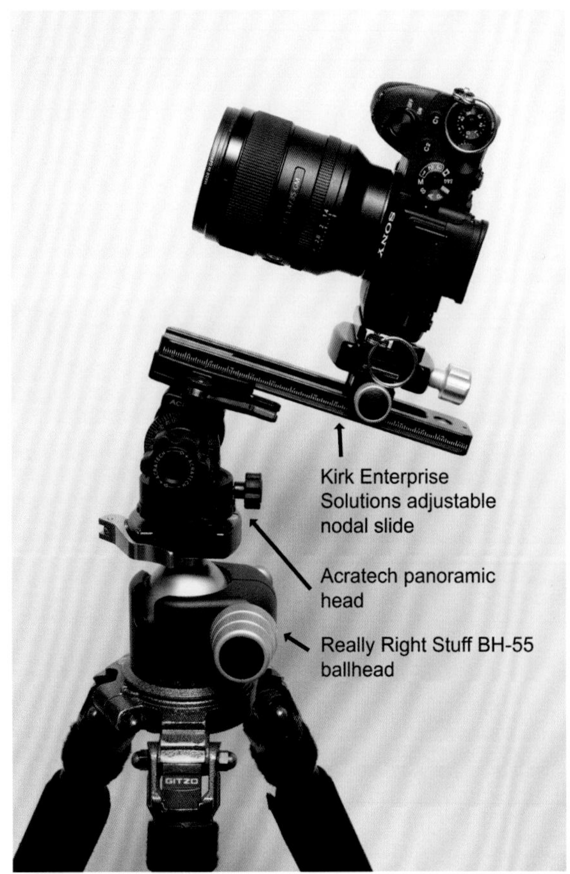

▾ FIGURE 5-11: Sony Alpha 7R IVa camera with Kirk Enterprise Solutions L-bracket and Sony FE 35mm f/1.4 GM lens mounted atop a Kirk Enterprise Solutions adjustable nodal slide attached to an Acratech panoramic head. The panoramic head is mounted atop a Really Right Stuff BH-55 ballhead. As with all panorama setups, the plane of rotation as you pan across the scene must be level. Attaching the panoramic head to the BH-55 ballhead lets me use the ballhead to level the base of the panoramic head. The panoramic head could also be mounted directly to the chassis, saving some weight, but I would then need to level the chassis by adjusting the length of the tripod legs, a tedious step I usually try to avoid.

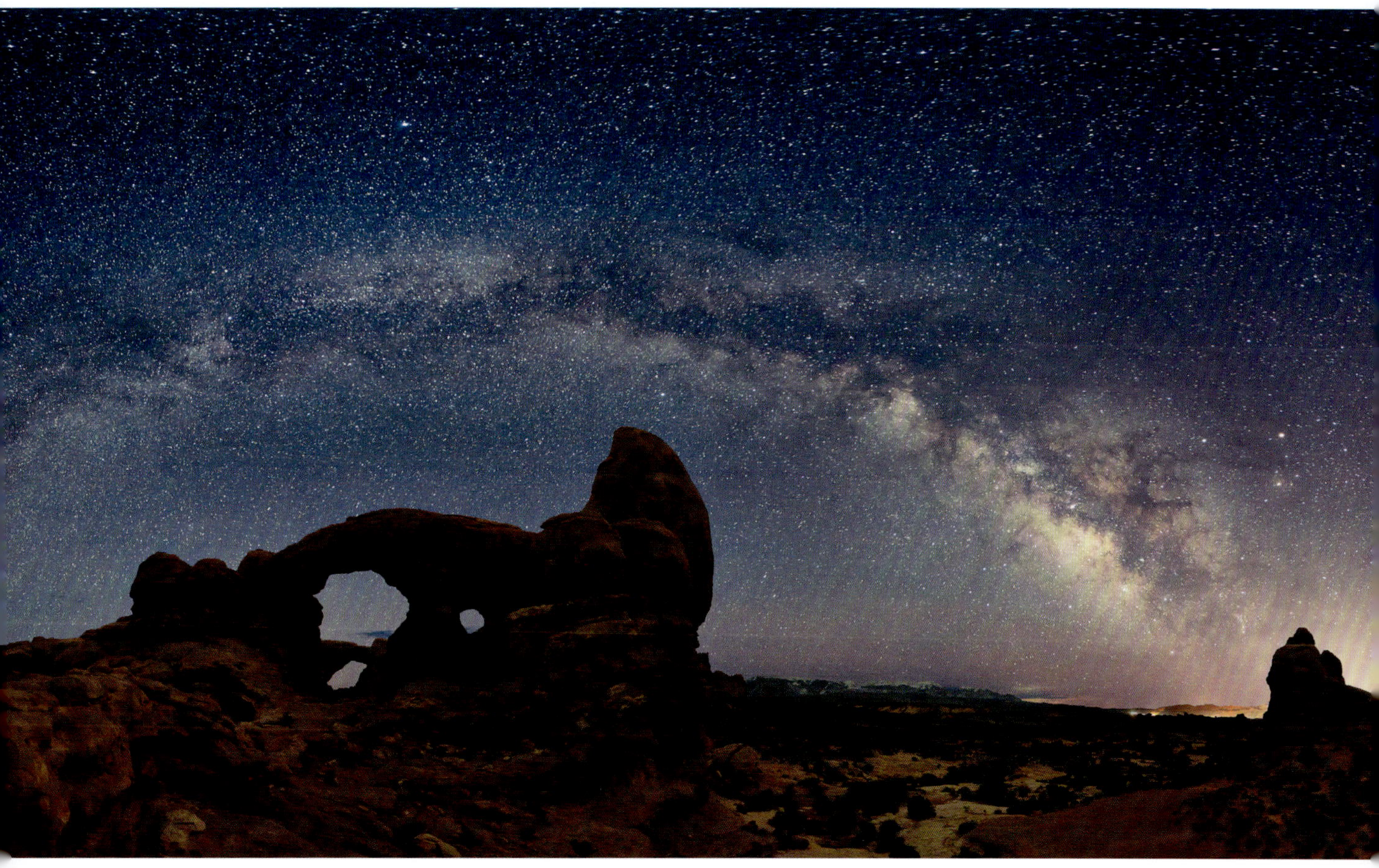

panorama to blend the land and sky regions in a way our visual system finds believable. The advantage of this approach is that each pair of images will fit together perfectly since you shot them back to back without moving the camera in between frames. The disadvantage is that it can take a lot of time to shoot both the land and sky frames at each camera position. If you take too much time, the stars may move so much between frames that the panorama may not stitch accurately. In my experience, it's possible to use a 16mm lens to shoot a 30-second sky exposure and a two-minute land exposure at each camera position, composite each pair, then stitch everything together without stitching errors.

The other approach is to shoot all the sky images first, moving the camera after each sky frame, then shoot all the land images in a second round. You then stitch all the sky images together into a complete panorama, stitch the land images into a complete panorama, then merge the two panoramas in Photoshop. One advantage of this approach is that it takes much less time

▲ FIGURE 5-12: Milky Way arch over Turret Arch and South Window, Arches National Park, Utah. April 11, 2016, 4:21 a.m. Canon 5D Mark III, Canon EF 16-35mm f/2.8L II USM at 16mm. Land: 2 minutes, f/2.8, ISO 6400. Sky: 30 seconds, f/2.8, ISO 6400. Land and sky: one row, four camera positions. For this panorama I shot the first pair of sky and land frames back to back, then moved the camera to the next camera position, shot the second pair of sky and land frames, etc.

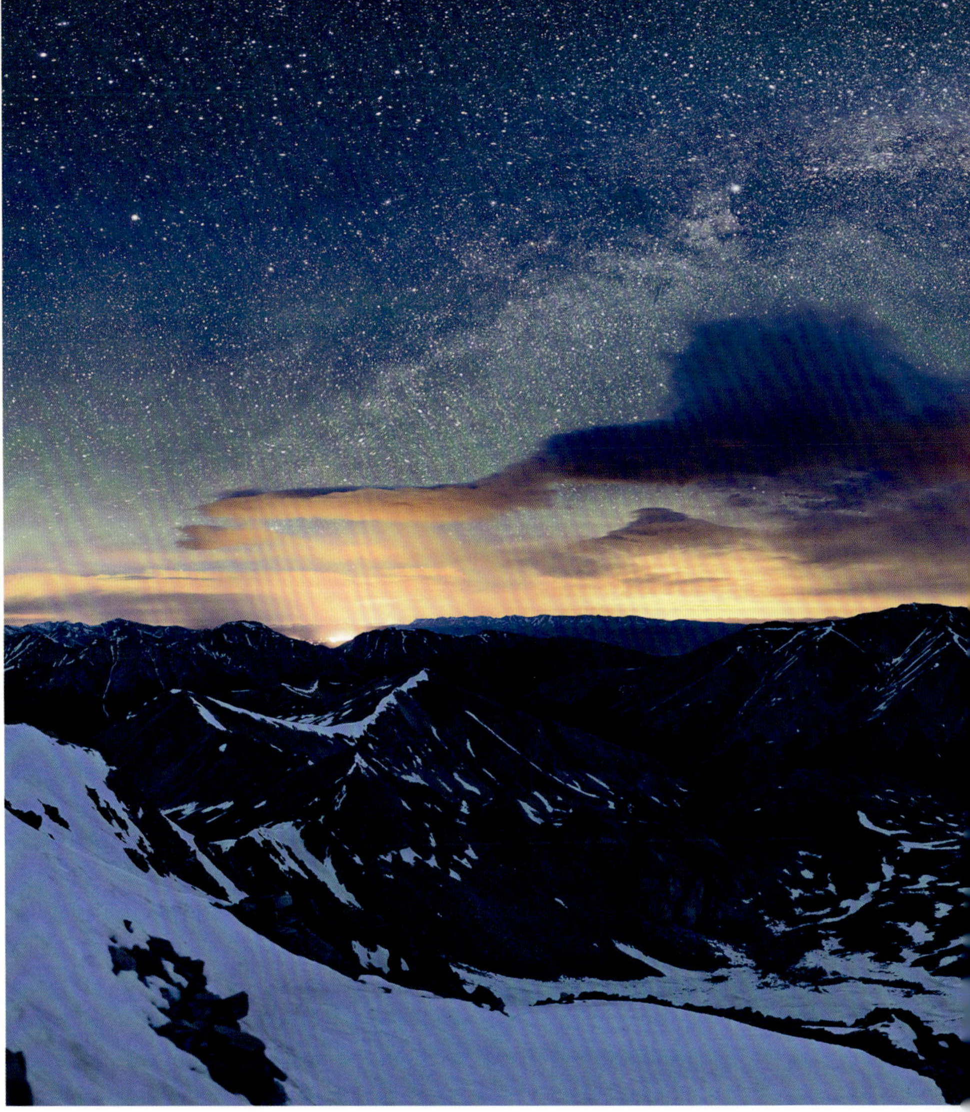

▶ FIGURE 5-13: Milky Way panorama over Missouri Mountain and the Sawatch Range from the summit of Huron Peak, Collegiate Peaks Wilderness, Colorado. June 12, 2013, 11:35 p.m. Canon 5D Mark III, Canon EF 50mm f/1.4 USM. Four rows, 10 camera positions per row, 13 seconds, f/1.4, ISO 6400.

to capture the sky images. That greatly reduces the risk that the stars will move so much in between frames that they won't match up when you stitch the panorama. A second advantage is that you can probably shoot the land in a single row even if the sky portion of the image requires two rows. The panorama sequence you shoot for the land need only include the land, plus a thin strip of sky. The panorama sequence you shoot for the sky need only include sky, plus a thin strip of land. This is the only feasible approach if you are shooting multiple identical frames at each camera position and stacking them to reduce noise. It's also the best approach if you're shooting your panorama using a star tracker. See chapter 7 for details on both techniques. With this approach it's guaranteed, however, that the sky and land panoramas will not match up perfectly. That means you'll need to do a lot of cloning along the skyline to make the two panoramas fit together seamlessly. If the scene

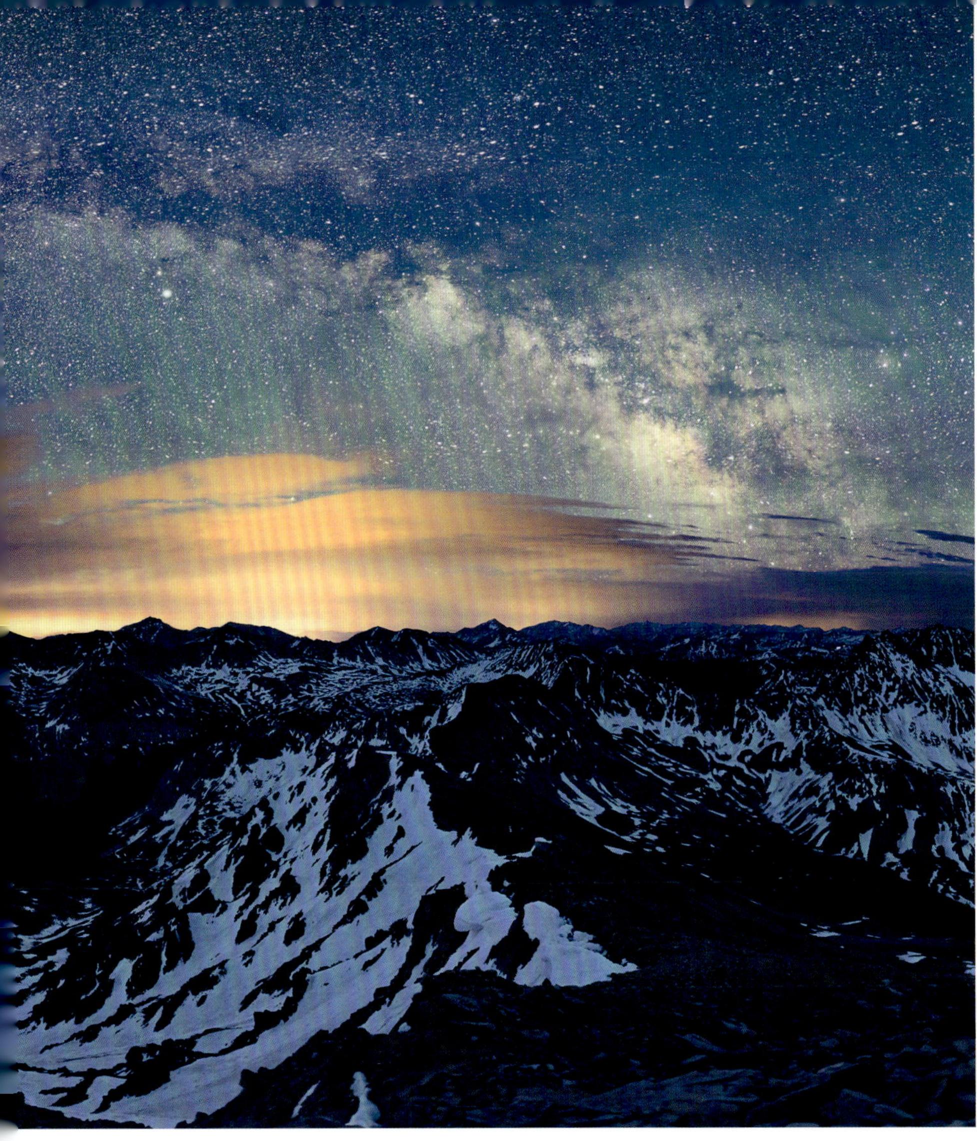

is complex—you have trees projecting upward into the sky, for example—the blending process will be tricky and time-consuming.

My recommendation is this: if you're using an ultra-wide-angle lens such as a 14mm or 16mm and planning on shooting only one sky frame and one land frame at each camera position, shoot the two frames back to back at each camera position (one for sky, one for land), then move the camera to the next camera position and shoot the next pair. Such lenses are so wide that you'll need relatively few camera positions to cover the whole panorama, and you may be able to shoot everything in a single row. You'll need two rows at most.

If you're shooting with a 35mm f/1.4 lens, shoot the sky images first, moving the camera after each frame, then do a second pass shooting the land images. You'll need many more frames per row, perhaps as many as eight or nine, and you'll need at least two rows to encompass an entire Milky Way panorama, one for land and one or two for sky. If the Milky Way arch is low in the sky and you don't own or don't want to carry multi-row panorama equipment, try this. Level the chassis by adjusting the length of the tripod legs. If your composition includes nearby foreground elements, attach the camera to the tripod with a nodal slide. Compose the land panorama so it includes only a thin strip of sky. Include much more subject matter at both the left and right ends of the panorama than you'll want in the final composition. Compose the sky panorama so it includes only a thin strip of land. Again, shoot a much wider panorama than you'll want in the final image. You won't be able to start the two panoramas at exactly the same camera position, but it won't matter, since you'll have lots of extraneous image area to crop away when you composite the two panoramas.

Your choice of lens will depend in part on how much depth of field you need. Remember that a 16mm lens focused at infinity and set to f/2.8 has depth of field from about 15 feet to infinity. A 35mm lens focused at infinity and set to f/1.4 only has depth of field from 142 feet to infinity. If you need depth of field, reach for an ultra-wide-angle lens and accept that the sky will have more noise than you can achieve with a fast, moderate-wide-angle lens. If no part of the subject is closer than 142 feet, reach for the fast, moderate-wide-angle lens to gather as much light as possible with each exposure, reducing noise and improving local contrast. In some situations, you can shoot the sky with a 35mm f/1.4 lens wide open, then stop the lens down to f/2.8 to shoot the land, giving you depth of field from 71 feet to infinity.

If you need depth of field but still want the highest possible quality image, you can try shooting the sky with a fast, moderate wide-angle like a 35mm f/1.4 and the land with an ultra-wide 14mm or 16mm. The sky panorama will have far more pixels than the land panorama over the same angle of view. That means you'll need to use Free Transform in Photoshop to compress the

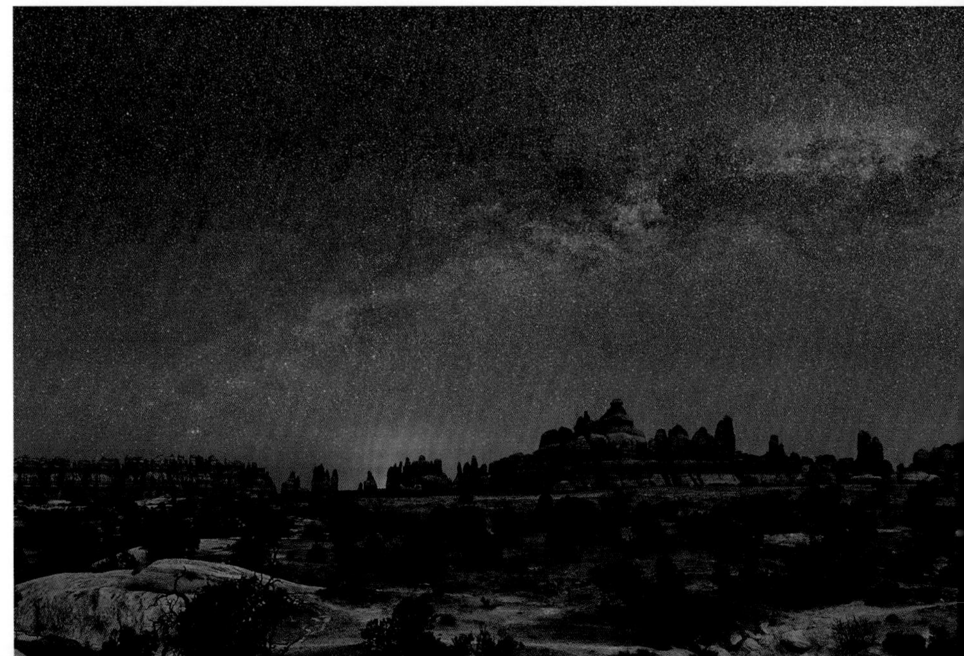

▸ Figure 5-14: Milky Way panorama over Chesler Park, Needles District, Canyonlands National Park, Utah. April 14, 2018, 3:51 a.m. Canon EOS 5D Mark IV, Canon EF 35mm f/1.4L II USM. Land: one row, eight camera positions per row, four frames per camera position, images stacked in Photoshop, noise reduced with Stack Mode>Median, 40 seconds, f/1.4, ISO 6400. Sky: one row, eight camera positions per row, four frames per camera position, images aligned and noise reduced in RegiStar, 10 seconds, f/1.4, ISO 6400.

sky panorama to fit atop the land panorama and probably need to do a lot of cloning to make the boundary between the two panoramas seamless. This approach works best if the skyline is simple, such as a row of mountains or distant cliffs. Trees breaking the skyline can make the task of compositing the two panoramas very challenging.

Regardless of whether you're shooting a single-row or multi-row panorama, be sure to compose generously. Include extra image area on all sides of the panorama you envision. Since you're stitching together a group of rectangular images, you might expect the stitched panorama to be a big rectangle. In fact, you'll find that your panorama has scalloped edges that must be cropped away. Be sure you include some unwanted subject matter on all sides that can be cropped off without ruining your composition. It's true that Lightroom's panorama-stitching utility includes a Boundary Warp slider that will warp the image to eliminate the scalloped edges. It also contains a Fill Edges slider that will invent pixels to fill in the scallops. While both tools can be a lifesaver in a pinch, it's better to compose generously and crop away the scalloped edges.

The greatest reward for learning to shoot panoramas is the compositional freedom it gives you. No longer are you restricted to the rigid 2:3 aspect ratio of the typical viewfinder on a DSLR or mirrorless camera or the angle of view of your widest lens. You can compose images in any shape, covering any angle of view you choose. Master the craft of shooting panoramas, and you'll be one step closer to creating art.

Don't let the technical details of a complex night shoot overwhelm the experience of being there. Take a moment during the shoot to step away from your camera and soak in the beauty of the night sky. It's the best way I know to truly appreciate the immensity of our universe.

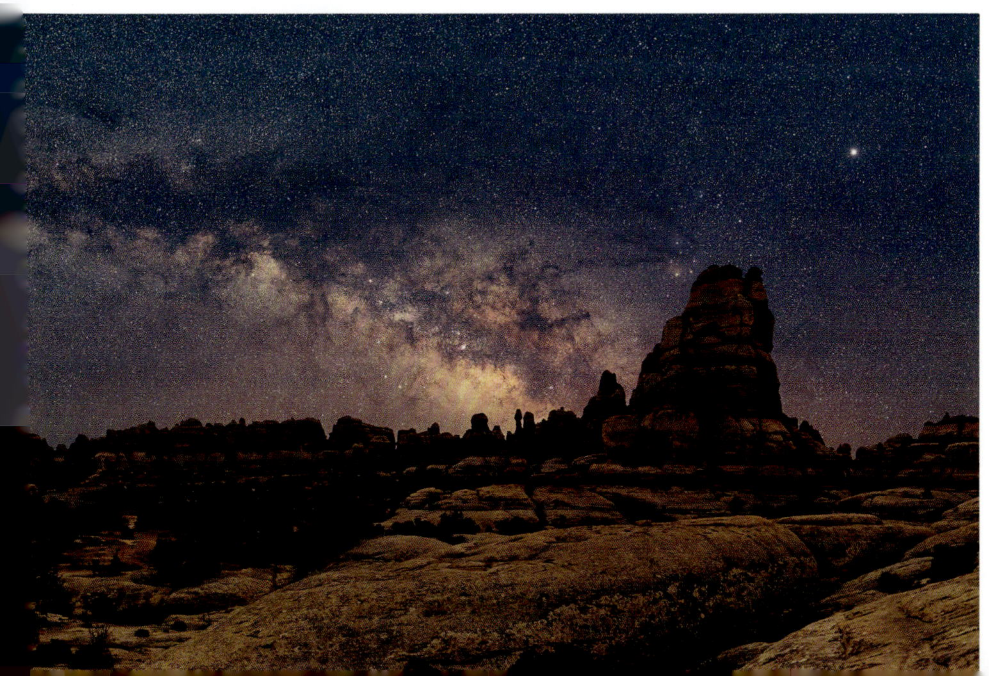

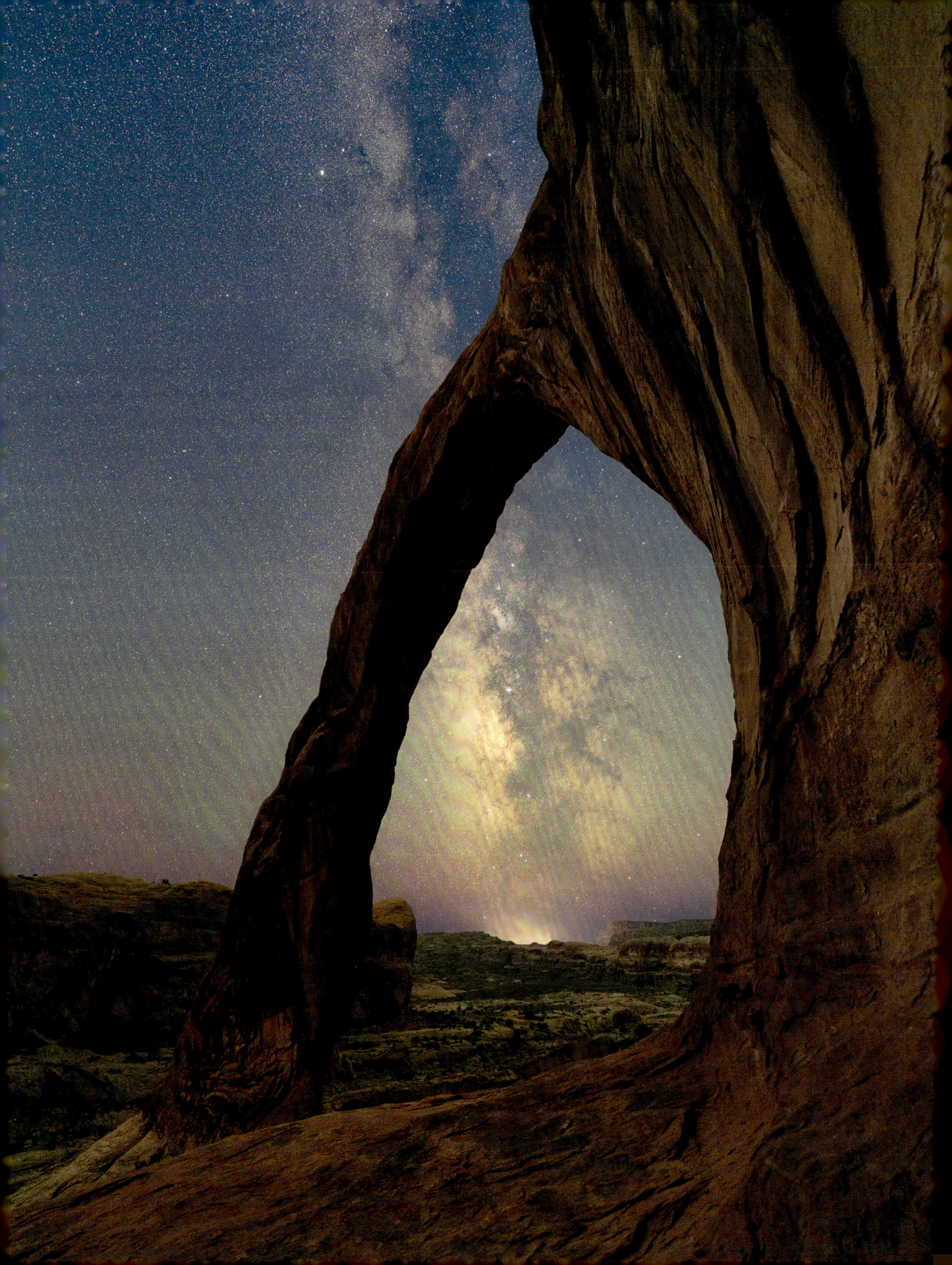

Processing Night Landscapes

Night photographers operate at the bleeding edge of both lens and sensor technology. Images taken with wide-angle lenses shot wide open are always much darker in the corners than they are in the center, a problem called *falloff* or *vignetting*. Images taken at high ISOs are inherently noisy. They also suffer from diminished resolution and decreased dynamic range, the difference in brightness between the darkest detailed shadow and the brightest detailed highlight. The lack of dynamic range means it's often necessary to shoot two frames at each camera position, one exposed for the sky, the second exposed for the land. Compositing those two images in Photoshop often requires making precise selections, but Photoshop's selection tools are less effective with noisy, high-ISO images than they are with clean images shot at ISO 100. Inevitably, night images require more processing to solve these problems than images taken during the day.

The techniques I'll discuss in this chapter apply to any night image taken at a high ISO with a wide-angle lens shot wide open. I'll use images of the Milky Way as examples, but the techniques you'll learn for correcting falloff, reducing noise, and compositing two exposures of the same scene work just as well when shooting star trails, meteor showers, and lunar eclipses.

The Color of the Night Sky

A lifetime of experience on this planet leads us to believe that a clear sky is always blue. Certainly the clear daytime sky is always some shade of blue. As day ebbs into night and our color vision fades away, the last color we see in the sky directly above us is blue; as night gives way to dawn, the first sky color we see above us is once again blue. On nights with a full moon, the sky and landscape seem to have a bluish tinge. Indeed, the sky when the full moon is up really is blue, and an image taken with a daylight white balance (which sets the camera to record the wavelengths actually present, without altering them) will record it as blue. We can't see color in the moonless night sky, but it seems logical to assume it must be blue as well.

For decades, filmmakers have exploited our belief that the night sky, and therefore the landscape, must always be blue. They use a technique called *day for night* to shoot "nighttime" scenes during the day. To create the illusion of night they underexpose their footage and shift it blue, either by using a blue filter over the lens or by changing the white balance in post-production.

◂ FIGURE 6-1: The Milky Way and Corona Arch, near Moab, Utah. September 19, 2022, 9:33 p.m. Sony Alpha 7R IVa, Sony FE 14mm f/1.8 GM. Land: seven frames, images stacked in Photoshop, noise reduced with Stack Mode>Median, 1 minute, f/1.8, ISO 6400. Sky: four frames, camera mounted on iOptron SkyTracker Pro equatorial mount, images aligned and noise reduced in RegiStar, 1 minute, f/1.8, ISO 1600.

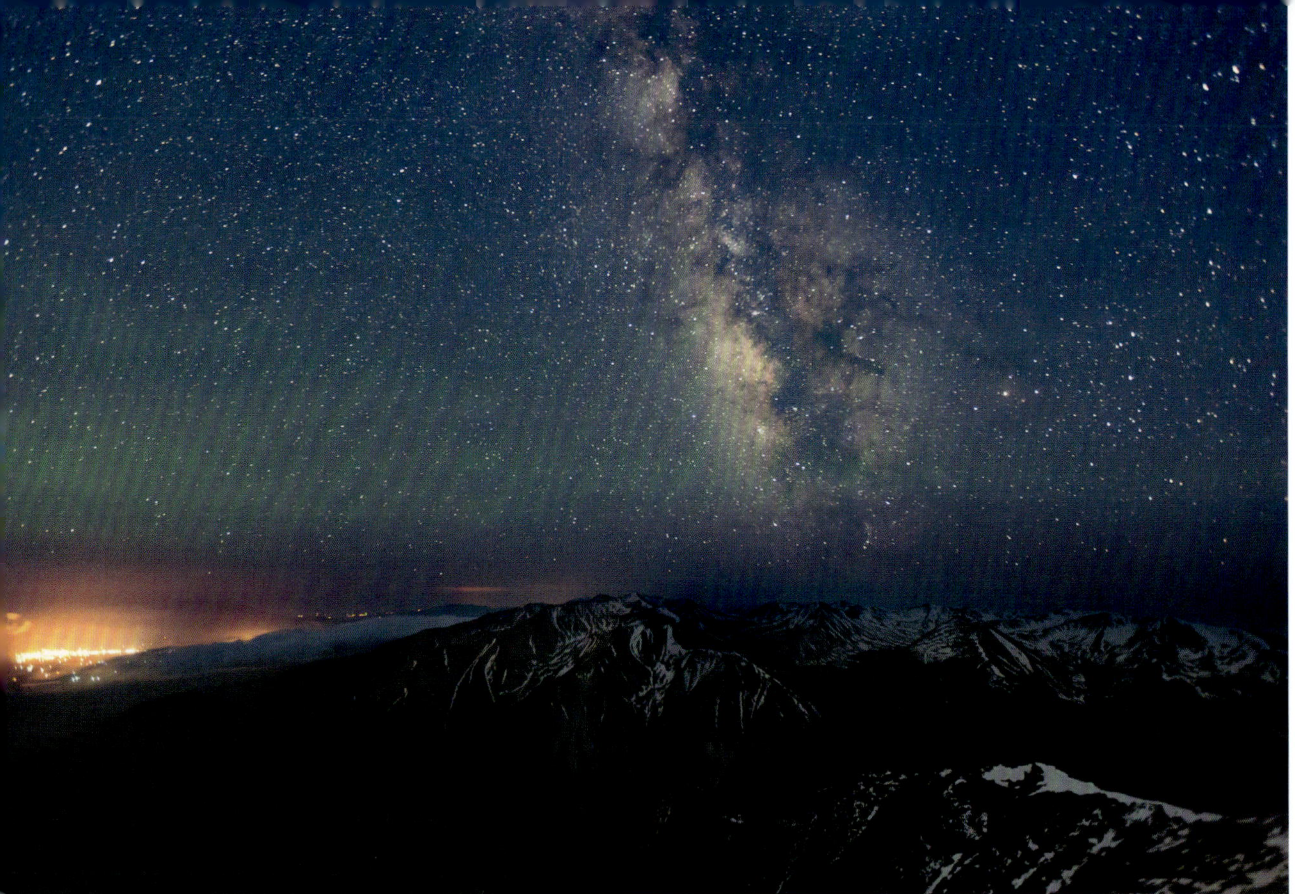

Our experience and expectations, reinforced by the many movies and TV shows we've seen, lead us to the wrong conclusion. The sky is not always blue. For starters, although the color of the moonlit sky really is blue, moonlight itself isn't blue; in fact, it's slightly yellower in hue than noon daylight. The land in a photograph taken under a full moon will actually appear warmer in tone than a photo of the same scene taken at 12 noon. In any case, even the light of a full moon isn't bright enough to directly excite our cones, the cells in our retinas that allow us to see color. So why do we see the moonlit world as bluish? Saad M. Khan and Sumanta N. Pattanaik, two researchers at the University of Central Florida, have advanced the theory that this apparent bluish tinge is essentially a perceptual illusion. As I explained in chapter 2, the light-sensitive cells in our retinas called cones come in three types, each sensitive to a different region of the visual spectrum. One type detects red light; another detects green light; the third detects blue light. At night our cones become inactive, and the rods in our retinas take over. Rods are much more sensitive to light than cones but cannot distinguish colors. Khan and Pattanaik cite evidence that some rods have neural connections with cones, so that stimulation of the rods by moonlight actually causes some activation in nearby cones as well. They then hypothesize that these interconnected rods interact primarily with blue-sensitive cones. Your brain interprets this cone activation as bluish light striking your eyes, so the world

appears to have a blue tinge even though the light reaching your eyes from the land is not actually bluish. You conclude that if the world looks bluish in moonlight, then the sky on a moonless night must be blue as well.

When you shoot with a daylight white balance you are essentially telling the camera to record the colors actually present in the scene. If you set the white balance to daylight and shoot photographs during a night with a bright moon, you will see that the sky is indeed blue for the same reason a clear daytime sky is blue: Rayleigh scattering. Moonlight is simply sunlight that has bounced off the moon's surface and traveled to Earth. Sunlight is originally composed of all wavelengths. When it hits Earth's atmosphere, however, the blue light tends to scatter out of the beam while the warmer tones tend to travel straight through. The sky looks blue during a clear day and records as blue during a moonlit night because that scattered blue light has traveled from the sky to your eyes or your camera.

Moonless nights are a different story. In fact, you may be startled by the greenish color of the sky in the first shots you take on a moonless night. Even on the darkest night, the sky is never completely black. Instead, it often exhibits airglow, a faint glow caused by a variety of complex processes in the upper atmosphere. (Technically speaking, airglow occurs 24 hours a day, so some authorities use the term nightglow for the glow we see at night.) The most common nighttime airglow color is green, but airglow can also be red,

▲ Figure 6-3: Another version of the Milky Way over Mt. Antero, seen from the summit of Mt. Princeton, San Isabel National Forest, Colorado. I used a daylight white balance for this image, which caused the camera to record the colors actually present in the scene. Intense green airglow gave the sky its startling color. June 5, 2013, 3:07 a.m. Canon 5D Mark III, Canon EF 16-35mm f/2.8L II USM at 16mm. 30 seconds, f/2.8, ISO 6400.

blue, or yellow. As Scott Bailey, a professor of atmospheric science, explained it, "To get this green line [emission] at night, we need to find a place in the atmosphere where molecular and atomic oxygen are both relatively large in abundance. This rare mixture occurs about 95 km above Earth's surface in a very narrow layer only 10 km thick. Excited O2 molecules collide with O, exciting the atoms, which relax by emitting green photons." This 557.7 nanometer Wizard-of-Oz green light has the same color as the most common type of aurora, but the mechanism of excitation of the atoms is different.

We don't see the sky on a moonless night as green, of course; in fact, we only see color if we're looking at an object, such as a bright star or a planet, that's bright enough to excite the cones in our retinas. If you look closely, you can see that certain stars exhibit color. Antares, Aldebaran, Arcturus, and Betelgeuse, along with the planet Mars, all exhibit a reddish hue; Rigel and Sirius are blue-white. A few photographers show the night sky as their cameras record it when set to a daylight white balance. While this approach is certainly accurate in showing the colors actually present in the scene, it produces a sky color that most viewers find distinctly odd. I choose to change the color of the sky to restore the deep blue color we imagine the night sky to be. However, I also choose to preserve the star colors captured with a daylight white balance, since those are colors I can actually see. I shift the color of the land slightly toward blue to help preserve a nighttime feel.

▾ Figure 6-4: Airglow is most commonly green, but it can be a variety of other colors, as seen in this image of the Milky Way over Wilson Peak from Last Dollar Road, San Juan Mountains, near Telluride, Colorado. I shot the image with a daylight white balance and didn't alter the color in processing. September 25, 2014, 8:37 p.m. Canon 5D Mark III, Canon EF 24mm f/1.4L II USM. 20 seconds, f/1.4, ISO 6400.

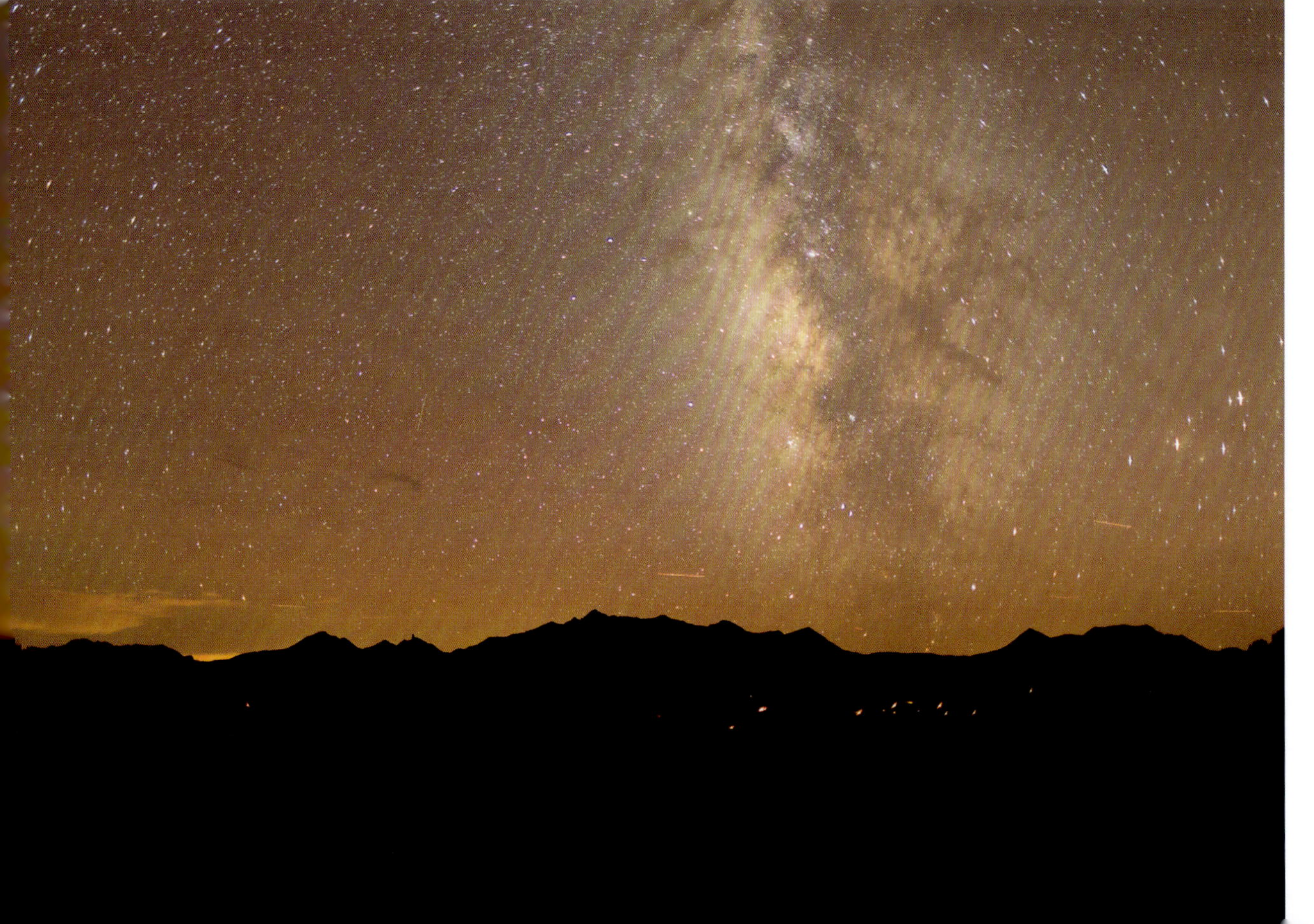

The bottom line is this: shooting in color at night is like shooting in black-and-white during the day. What shade of gray best represents a clear sky at noon? Any shade of gray that looks good! And what shade of blue (or green) best evokes the feeling of gazing awestruck at a sky full of stars? Any hue that satisfies your artistic intentions! Since you can't see the true color of the night sky regardless of whether there is moonlight or not, your choice of sky color is inherently subjective.

Editing Images Taken on a Moonless Night

I use Lightroom Classic (the desktop-based version of Lightroom) and Photoshop to edit all of my images. Both programs are constantly evolving. New features are added, and the performance of older features is improved. It's rare, however, for older features to disappear completely. In this book I'll describe methods and show screenshots from the most recent versions of the software available today. You may find that the details of the interface have changed by the time you read this book. However, with a little poking around, you should be able to relocate the tools I describe and apply them to your images successfully.

Here are the basic steps I follow when editing a photograph of the night sky in Lightroom and Photoshop. Following these steps in Lightroom may be all that's needed to perfect your image if you were able to capture adequate detail in both the land and sky in a single frame. If, however, you shot two frames at each camera position, one exposed for the sky, the other for the land, then use the procedure I'll describe next to edit the good-sky image. I'll provide instructions for editing the good-land image and compositing the two images later. Please note that all keyboard shortcuts I mention assume you're using a PC. Mac users can generally substitute the Command key for the Control key and the Option key for the Alt key.

1. Virtually all images shot at night will exhibit noise. When I wrote the first edition of this book, noise reduction was always an unsatisfying tradeoff. An effort to suppress the high-frequency variation in color and brightness that is undesirable noise inevitably suppressed some of the high-frequency variation in color and brightness that is desirable texture. If you suppressed all the noise, the land would look preternaturally smooth. Today a number of programs, including Lightroom, employ artificial intelligence to reduce noise while retaining detail and texture. These AI programs usually deliver much more satisfying results. Lightroom's

version is found in the Detail panel in the Develop module. Click the Denoise button to open the Denoise dialog box. There is only one slider, which controls Amount. I find settings between 25 and 50 usually work well. If the result looks too smooth, like the land was made of injected-molded plastic, try a lower amount in the Denoise dialog box. Alternatively, you can add a small amount of Clarity and Texture in the Basic panel. Is the photo still so noise-free it looks unnatural for a night image? Consider adding some grain in the Effects panel. The output from Denoise will be saved as a new DNG file (Adobe's RAW file format), so it will still have all the editing flexibility of any RAW file. The original RAW file will be untouched. I find Lightroom Denoise to be a significant improvement over Lightroom's older noise-reduction tool. If you want to compare the two, select the original RAW file and adjust the Luminance slider in the Manual Noise Reduction section of Lightroom's Detail panel while examining the image at 100 percent magnification. The goal is to minimize noise while still retaining as much fine detail as possible. The exact value you need will vary depending on your camera and the ISO value you set in the field. Use the lowest value that reduces noise to an acceptable level. The default setting of 25 for color noise reduction usually works well.

2. All lenses produce an image that is brighter in the center and darker in the corners. The problem gets worse as the angle of view of the lens gets wider. It also gets worse with larger apertures. At night you'll be using wide-angle lenses wide open, so the corners of the image will be much darker than the center. Fortunately, Lightroom provides a good solution. In the Lens Corrections panel, Profile tab, check Enable Profile Corrections. Double-check that Lightroom has recognized your lens. If not, find the closest equivalent in the drop-down list. Checking Enable Profile Corrections eliminates most of the vignetting found in images taken with wide-angle lenses, particularly when shot wide open. It also corrects geometric distortion, the way some lenses bend straight lines, either bowing them inward ("pincushion distortion") or outward ("barrel distortion"). Some of the latest cameras apply profile corrections to images when they're shot, so checking Enable Profile Corrections has no further effect. Lightroom provides a note at the bottom of the Lens Corrections panel informing you if the camera you used applies profile corrections automatically.

3. While you're in the Lens Corrections panel, also check Remove Chromatic Aberrations. Chromatic aberrations are thin, colored fringes that can appear where dark objects are silhouetted against bright backgrounds. Checking Remove Chromatic Aberrations usually has little effect when shooting with high-quality lenses and cameras but does no harm and may help with images from lower-quality equipment. Some recent cameras automatically remove chromatic aberrations from images when they're captured, so checking the Remove Chromatic Aberrations checkbox has no further effect. Again, Lightroom provides information at the bottom of the Lens Corrections panel informing you if the camera you used applies this correction automatically.

4. The next step is to use the Tone Curve panel in Lightroom to shift the sky color toward blue by manipulating the individual red, green, and blue channels. Note that the Tone Curve panel has two modes. If you see the word Region underneath the graph, with four sliders below that, click the white circular icon at the top of the dialog box (circled in red) to switch from Parametric Curve mode to Point Curve mode (figure 6-5).

5. Set the Point Curve preset to Linear. Next, click the red circular icon just to the right of the Point Curve icon to select the red channel. Click to place a point on the curve about two-thirds of the way up, but don't move the point in any direction. This point serves to anchor the top part of the red curve, preserving the color of the highlights (the stars and Milky Way) as captured in the original file. Next, click to place a point about one-quarter of the way up the curve and drag downward a bit. Switch to the green channel and place the same two points. Again, drag the lower point down a bit. Finally, switch to the blue channel, place the same two points, but this time drag the lower point upward a bit. Figure 6-6 shows screenshots of the three channels.

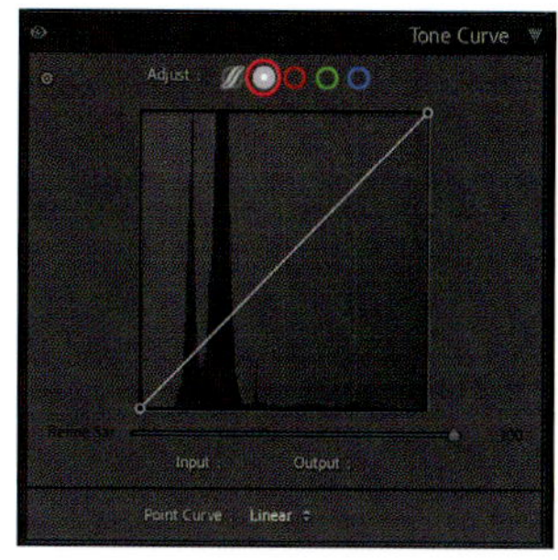

▲ Figure 6-5: Click the white circular icon (circled in red) at the top of the Tone Curve panel to select Point Curve mode.

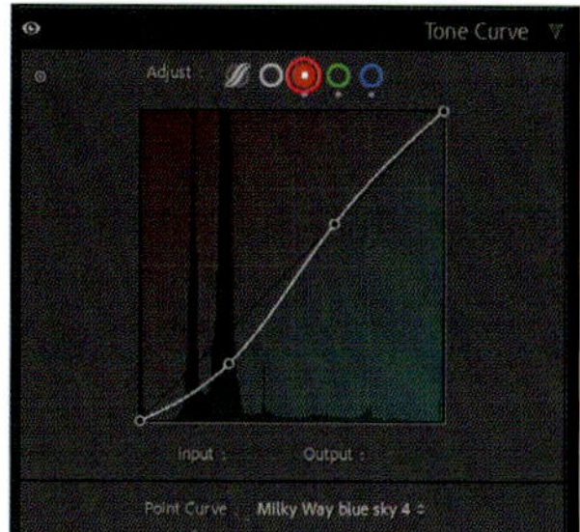
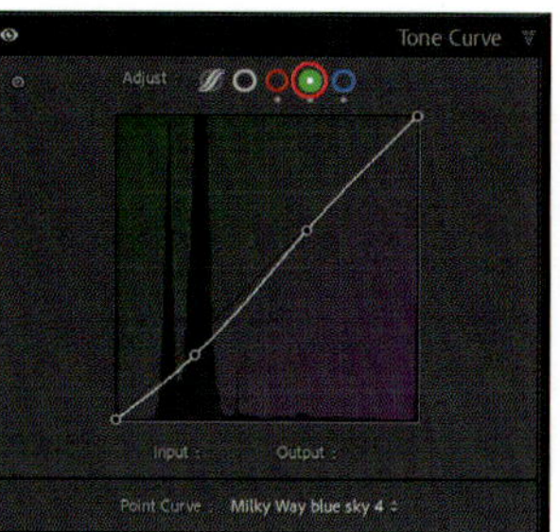
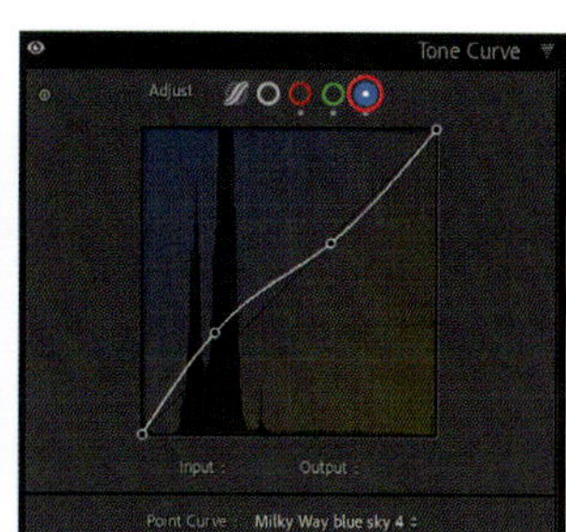

◄ Figure 6-6: Three views of the Tone Curve panel in Lightroom showing settings for the three channels that will shift the sky color toward blue.

6.   If you find that it's hard to make small, precise adjustments to the curve, hold down the Alt key while you drag the point. The point will now move a smaller distance for a given mouse movement, giving you better control. The goal is to shift the color of the sky to a pleasing blue while preserving the original colors of the stars and the Milky Way. It can take a lot of trial and error to get this right. Once you have a group of settings you like, click the disclosure triangle next to Point Curve: Custom and click Save to create a preset. Give it a name like "Milky Way blue sky 1." You'll probably find you need different settings for different images, so you may want to create a series of presets you can click through to see which one gets you closest. You can then perfect your settings if necessary. On nights when the airglow is particularly strong, you may find it impossible to completely eliminate the green cast without shifting some portions of the sky purple. Your best compromise may be to shift the upper regions of the sky blue while allowing the sky near the horizon to retain its greenish hue.

7.   The next step is to increase contrast in the sky to make the Milky Way stand out a bit more. Don't increase contrast globally; that just makes the dark land even darker. Instead, add additional contrast to the sky alone using the Masking panel. Open the Masking panel by clicking the far-right icon in the toolbox just above the Basic panel, as shown in figure 6-7. Under Add New Mask, click Sky (figure 6-8). Lightroom will use AI to select the sky. As a starting point, set Contrast to 30. Adjust the Contrast slider until you like the result (figure 6-9).

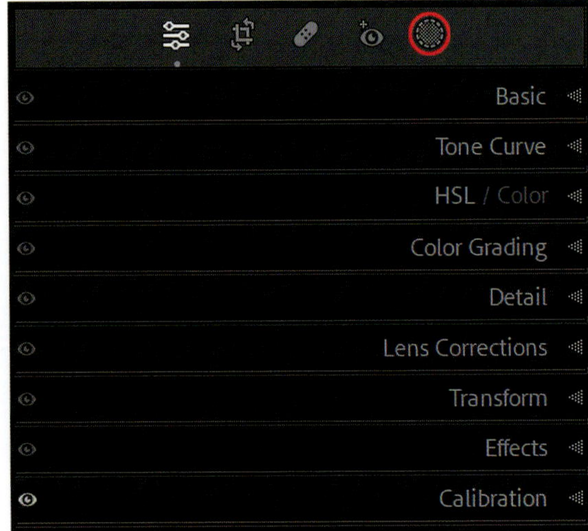

▲ Figure 6-7: The toolbox above Lightroom's Basic panel with the Masking panel icon circled.

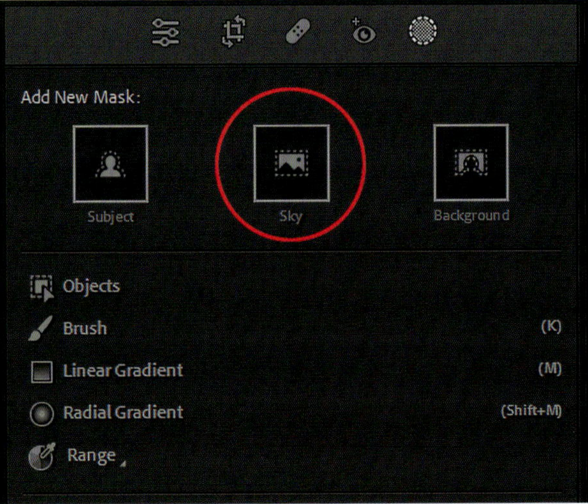

▲ Figure 6-8: The Masking panel with the Select Sky icon circled.

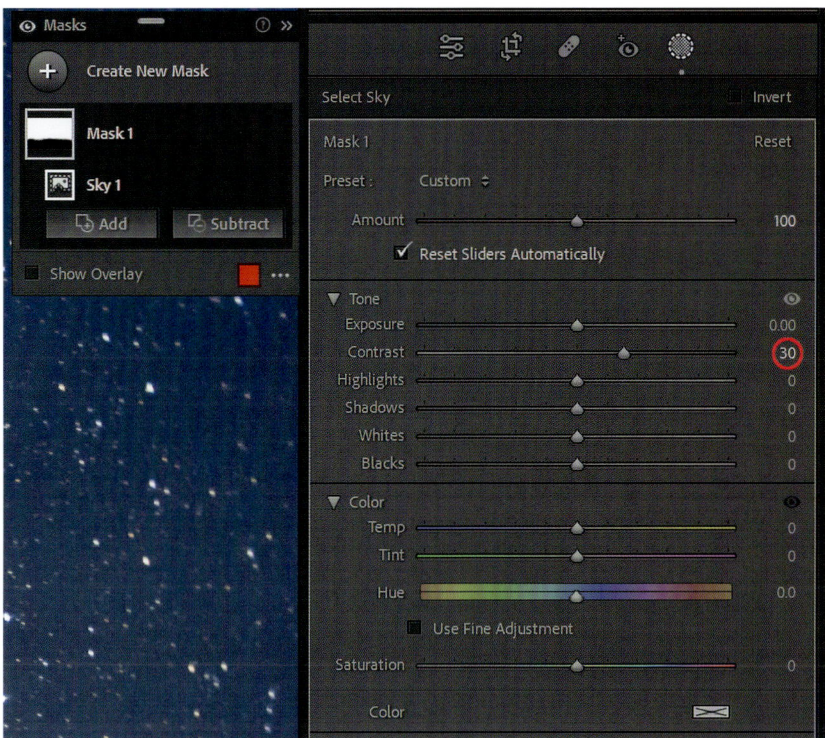

◄ FIGURE 6-9: The Masking panel after selecting the sky with the Select Sky tool and setting the Contrast to 30 (circled).

8. If Lightroom's AI sky-selection tool fails, delete the sky mask by clicking the three-dot icon to the right of Mask 1 and choosing Delete "Mask 1." Next, choose the Brush tool. Choose an appropriate brush size. It will be easiest to hide the transition between areas where you paint and unaffected areas if you choose a soft-edged brush, so set Feather to 100. Flow controls how much of the effect is laid down in one stroke over an area. A setting of 100 percent means you will apply the full effect in a single stroke. Reduce the Flow setting to build up the effect with multiple brush strokes over an area, even with the mouse button held down continuously. With enough strokes you will eventually apply the full effect. Density controls what percentage of the effect will be laid down regardless of how many passes you make over an area with the mouse button held down or how many additional strokes you apply after releasing the mouse button. I normally leave this set to 100. Leave Auto Mask unchecked. Set Contrast to 30. Once you've painted the effect into the image, you can adjust the Contrast setting (and any of the other sliders) to taste.

9.   Adding a bit of Clarity, either globally in the Basic panel, or locally with the Brush, can make the stars pop and add interest to the land. A modest dose of Dehaze can also help the Milky Way stand out.

This procedure will not only shift the color of the sky toward blue while preserving the colors of the stars, planets, and Milky Way; it will also strongly shift the color of the land toward blue, often to excess. If you have a separate exposure for the land, then you can ignore the dark, blue-tinted land in your good-sky image because you're never going to show that land to anyone. The land portion of the final image will come from the frame you exposed for the land.

If, on the other hand, you were able to capture adequate detail in both the land and sky in a single frame, then you may wish to confine your sky-color changes to the sky. Fortunately, Lightroom now makes it possible to apply the Curves preset you just created either by using the AI-powered Sky selection tool or by brushing it on. First, open the Tone Curve panel and reset the Point Curve to Linear. Next, open the Masking panel. Under Add New Mask, click Sky. Scroll down to the Curves section of the Masking panel. Click the drop-down arrow next to Presets and choose one of the Milky Way presets you created, which will be applied to the sky, leaving the land untouched (figure 6-10).

If the Sky selection tool doesn't work perfectly, delete the sky mask by clicking the three-dot icon to the right of Mask 1 and clicking Delete "Mask 1." Choose the Brush tool. Reselect your Milky Way preset from the Curves section of the Masking panel and paint in the blue-sky correction.

To help preserve a nighttime feel, I recommend cooling the land slightly. The easiest way to do this is to create a new mask (click Create New Mask at the top of the Masking panel), choose the Brush tool, move the Temp slider to the left, toward the blue end of the range, and paint over the land.

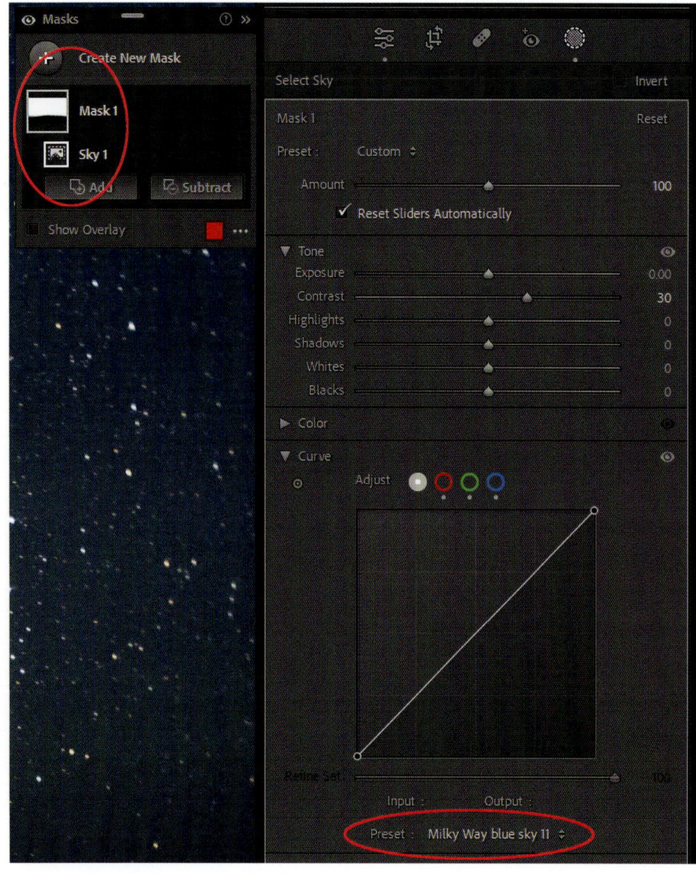

▼ FIGURE 6-10: The Masking panel showing the settings to apply a Milky Way preset to the sky using the Sky selection tool. The Tone Curve preset is circled, as is the mask and the type of tool used to create the mask (the Sky selection tool). White on the mask represents the area selected by the tool, in this case, the sky.

The Basics of Layers and Masks in Photoshop

Layers are one of the most powerful features in Photoshop. In the simplest configuration of a layered file, each layer is completely opaque, which means only the top layer is visible. The power of layers comes from the many ways in which the layers can interact with one another.

To temporarily hide a layer, click the eye icon next to the layer name. To make a layer partially transparent, revealing some of the layer beneath, change the layer's Opacity. To combine two layers in any number of ways, change the Blend mode of the upper layer to anything besides Normal. Figure 6-11 shows all these features.

To conceal part of one layer and reveal the corresponding part of the layer below, add a layer mask. Understanding layer masks is crucial to unlocking the potential of Photoshop. To add a mask to a layer, target that layer by clicking it, then click the layer-mask icon at the bottom of the Layers panel (figure 6-11). Layer masks can only be black, white, or some shade of gray. Remember this mnemonic: white reveals, black conceals. White areas on a layer mask reveal the corresponding part of the layer to which the mask is attached (not the layer underneath). Black areas conceal the corresponding part of that layer, allowing the layer beneath to show through. Shades of gray make the top layer partially transparent, allowing the two layers to blend. You can think of gray areas on a mask as a selective way to change the opacity of the layer to which the mask is attached.

Layer masks can be edited using many of the same tools you can use on any black-and-white image. You can also paint on a layer mask using the Brush tool set to white, black, or any shade of gray. If you have the layer *mask* targeted, you can press D (for default) to set the foreground color to white and the background color to black (with the layer thumbnail targeted, the default foreground color is black and the background is white). (Photoshop has the peculiar habit of sometimes switching the foreground and background colors automatically when you target the layer thumbnail instead of the layer mask thumbnail and vice-versa.) Press X to reverse the foreground and background colors. To paint on a layer mask, first target the layer-mask icon in the Layers panel by clicking it. With the Brush tool selected, move the cursor into the image window, press and hold the left mouse button, and paint.

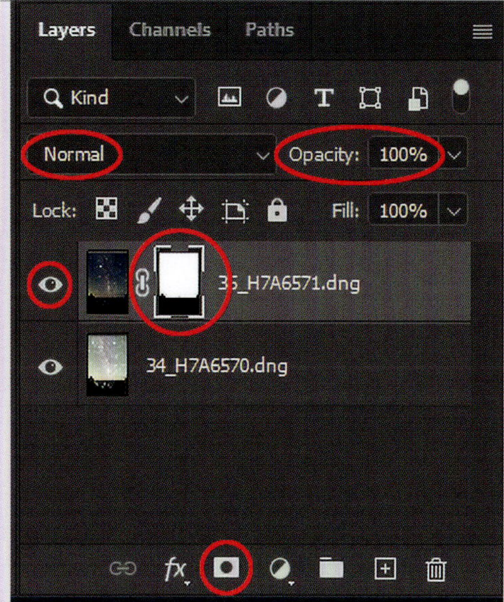

▲ Figure 6-11: The Layers panel with two layers. The eye icon, which temporarily controls visibility, is circled, as is the layer mask for the top layer. The blend mode (circled) is currently set to Normal. The Opacity (circled) is currently set to 100 percent. The Add Layer Mask icon at the bottom of the Layers panel is also circled.

The options bar that appears at the top of the screen after choosing the Brush tool lets you control the Opacity and Flow of the brush. Opacity refers to how much of the effect will be laid down in total, regardless of how many times you paint over an area with the mouse button held down continuously. However, if you release the mouse button, then press it again and paint over the same area, you will increase the effect. Releasing the mouse button, then painting again over the same area is like dipping your paintbrush in the paint bucket a second time and applying more paint. (Note that the Density of a brush in Lightroom and the Opacity of a brush in Photoshop are not exactly the same thing.) Painting with black with the Opacity set to 50 percent is like painting with middle gray. Flow refers to how much of the effect will be laid down in a single stroke. Painting with black with the Flow set to 50 percent will apply half the effect in a single stroke. Painting a second time over the same area, regardless of whether or not you release the mouse button in between strokes, will increase the effect to full strength.

The Basics of Layers and Masks in Photoshop *(continued)*

Layer masks and selections are two sides of the same coin. Photoshop provides a variety of tools for selecting part of an image so you can work on just that part. If you have a selection active and add a layer mask, the mask will automatically take on the contours of the selection and the marching ants marking the selection boundaries will disappear. Selected areas will become white on the mask; non-selected areas will become black. Partially selected areas will be rendered as shades of gray. Conversely, you can always convert a layer mask into a selection by holding down Control and clicking the layer mask, which will cause the marching ants to reappear while retaining the existing mask. Alt-clicking a mask loads the mask into the image window, allowing you to examine it closely; Alt-clicking again restores the normal view. Shift-clicking a mask temporarily disables it; Shift-clicking again re-enables it.

To save a selection, choose Select>Save Selection.

Adjustment layers are special layers that offer a non-destructive way to change the appearance of an image without permanently changing the underlying pixels. They contain no pixels themselves. You can return to an image and modify an adjustment layer as many times as you like. Curves, Levels, and Hue/Saturation are three of the most commonly used Adjustment layers. Curves and Levels adjustment layers are most often used to adjust the brightness and density of an image, but they can also be used to adjust color. Hue/Saturation adjustment layers are used to adjust the overall hue and saturation of an image as well as the appearance of individual colors. Adjustment layers are always accompanied by their own layer mask, so you can apply the effect only to those regions that require it.

Combining Two Images in Photoshop

Capturing all the detail you need in a single frame is great when it's possible. Most of the time, however, you'll need to combine two images of the same scene, one exposed for land, one exposed for sky. Combining those two frames requires Photoshop since Lightroom doesn't support layers.

Many people are intimidated by Photoshop because they believe it has a steep learning curve. Rest assured that such fear is unnecessary. Think of Photoshop as a gigantic cookbook. Mastering every recipe in the cookbook is indeed the work of a lifetime. But you don't need to master every recipe to cook yourself a satisfying meal. You just need to learn to follow one simple recipe. Soon you'll learn another, and another. Pretty soon you'll be mixing ingredients from different recipes to get different effects. Before you know it, you'll have become a master Photoshop chef.

The easiest way to combine the good-sky and good-land images in Photoshop is to use Photoshop's Sky Replacement tool. This tool is most often used to replace the boring sky from a daylight image with a more interesting sky. While that's not my style—I like to be able to tell people viewing a daylight image, "What you see in my prints is what I saw through the lens"—I admit that the tool can work pretty well for that purpose. Unfortunately, the same can't yet be said for its effectiveness when combining night images. You might think you could simply open the good-land image (which has an overexposed sky with stars that have become long streaks) and replace that sky with the sky from the good-sky exposure, which you took either moments before or after the good-land exposure. To understand the problems you might encounter, you first need to realize that the tool does not make a hard-edged selection of the overexposed sky, then drop in the correctly exposed sky. The tool instead blends the two images along the skyline, which sometimes lets unwanted parts of the sky bleed through into the land. For example, you might find faint stars popping out through your snowy peaks. The tool also moves the good-sky image downward in the frame to tuck it behind the good-land image. That can position the Milky Way or other sky subject matter much closer to the skyline than you want. The software does have tools to try to correct these problems, which are sometimes effective enough to give you a usable result. It's worth experimenting with this tool to learn its strengths and weaknesses. It will also undoubtedly get better with each new version and may someday supplant the methods I'll teach you now.

Before we continue, let's make sure we're reading from the same recipe book. Open Photoshop and choose Window>Workspace>Photography to make the arrangement of tools and panels in your version of Photoshop look similar to the screenshots that follow.

Here's the first Photoshop recipe you should learn. Let's assume you followed my instructions in chapter 3 and exposed two frames of exactly the same scene, one for the sky and one for the land. The difference in exposure will typically be two stops. Let's call the frame with correctly exposed sky and dark land the good-sky frame. Let's call the frame with correctly exposed land but very bright sky the good-land frame.

The sky at the horizon is always brighter than the land just beneath. This is true at night as well as during the day. The key to combining your two images in a pleasing but believable way is to maintain that brightness difference across the boundary between sky and land. If the sky at the horizon and the land just beneath are the same density, then it looks like you just pasted in the sky. Here's one simple way to solve this problem.

1. Start by opening the good-sky image in Lightroom's Develop module and editing using steps 1-6, described earlier. Don't add contrast to the sky in Lightroom.

2. Now open the good-land image in the Develop module. To help preserve a nighttime feel, I usually cool the good-land image slightly by setting Temp (short for temperature, in degrees Kelvin) in the Basic panel to between 4,200 and 4,800.

3. Reduce noise in the good-land image as described in step 1 for editing the good-sky image.

4.   In the Lens Corrections panel, Profile tab, check Enable Profile Corrections and Remove Chromatic Aberrations.

5.   The next task is to stack the two images as layers in Photoshop. If you're starting from Lightroom, select both images, then choose Photo>Edit In>Open as Layers in Photoshop. If you don't use Lightroom, start from Bridge (which ships with Photoshop). Select both images, then choose Tools>Photoshop>Load Files into Photoshop Layers. And if you don't use Bridge, then start from Photoshop itself. Choose File>Scripts>Load Files into Stack and navigate to the appropriate files.

6.   Whichever method you use, the next task is to drag the good-sky layer to the top of the layer stack if it's not already there. If necessary, click and hold on the good-sky layer and drag it upward until two thin blue lines appear. Release the mouse button.

7.   Now choose the Quick Selection tool, click and hold, and paint over the sky to select it. The Quick Selection tool will attempt to recognize the boundary between sky and land automatically. It's sometimes helpful to turn off visibility of the good-sky layer temporarily and make your selection on the good-land layer because it will often exhibit greater contrast between the sky and the land. If necessary, zoom in to 100 percent, choose a small Quick Selection brush in the options bar, and refine the selection. Hold down Alt while you paint to subtract from the selection. You don't need to get too fussy about making a perfect selection, as shown in figure 6-12.

Next, choose Select>Modify>Expand. I usually expand the selection by 250 to 500 pixels, but you will need to experiment to see what value works best for your particular image and for the resolution of your camera. The maximum you can expand the selection in one pass is 500 pixels, but if need be, you can expand the selection twice to achieve an expansion greater than that. Don't check the box labeled Apply Effect at Canvas Bounds.

Target the top layer (the good-sky layer) by clicking it and add a layer mask by clicking the third icon from the left at the bottom of the Layers panel (the one shaped like a square with a circle inside, shown in figure 6-11). The image will look awful.

With the new mask targeted, open the Properties panel (if it's not visible, choose Window>Properties) and feather the mask by the same amount you expanded the selection, as shown in figure 6-13. That should blend the good-sky and good-land images in a believable way, as shown in figure 6-14.

▸ FIGURE 6-12: The tool bar showing the Quick Selection tool (circled), the image with the sky selected with the Quick Selection tool, and the Layers panel showing the good-sky (dark) layer on top.

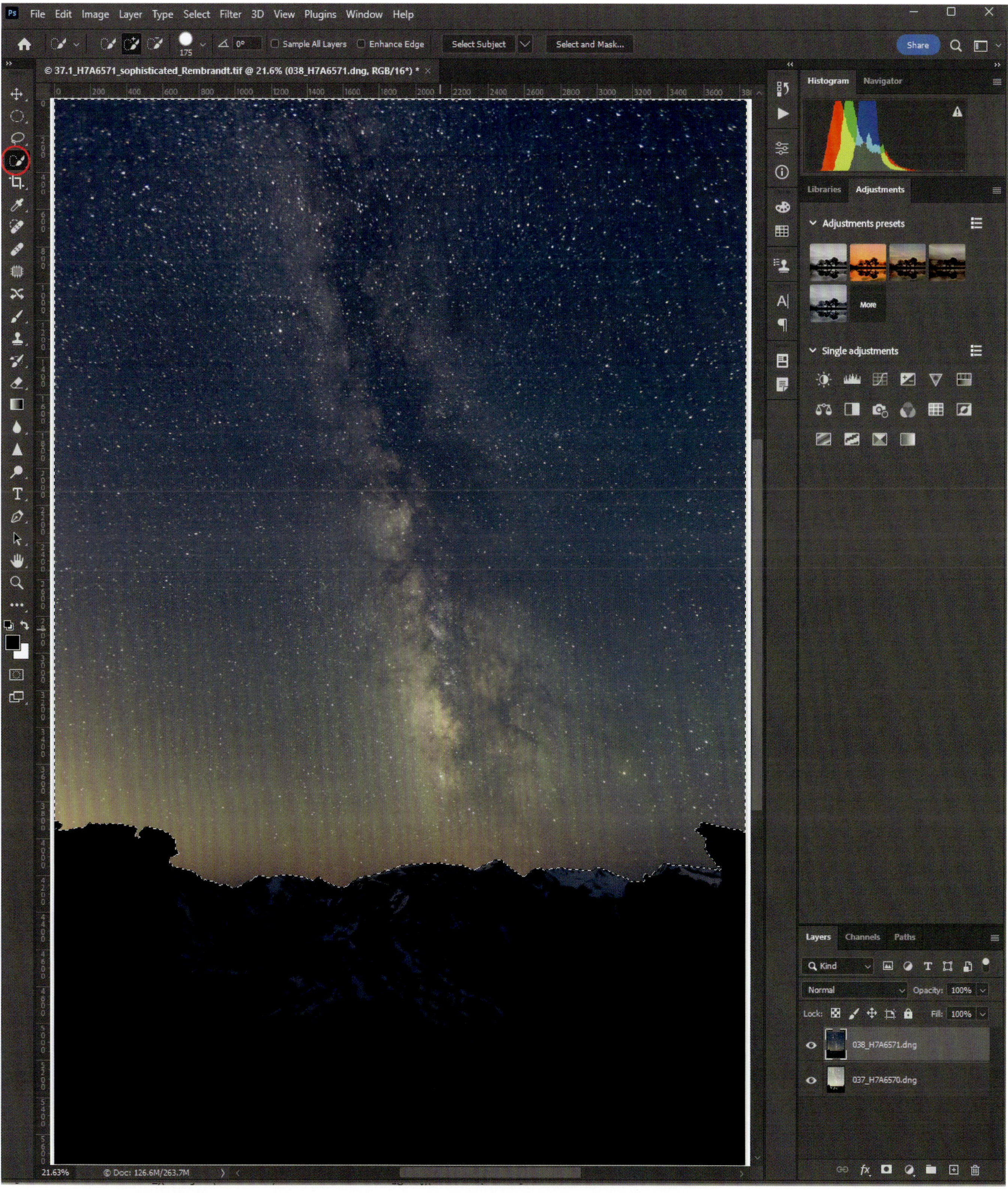

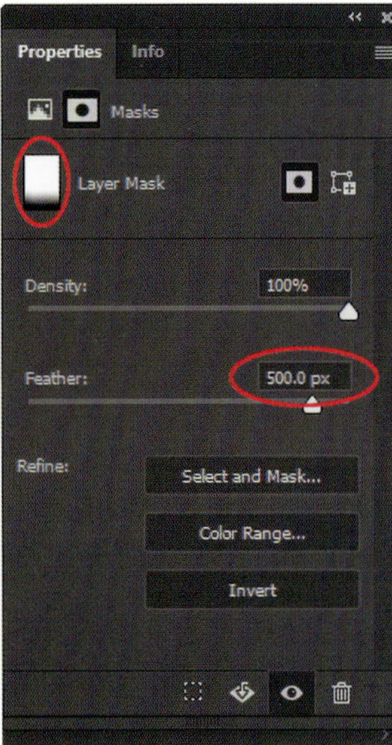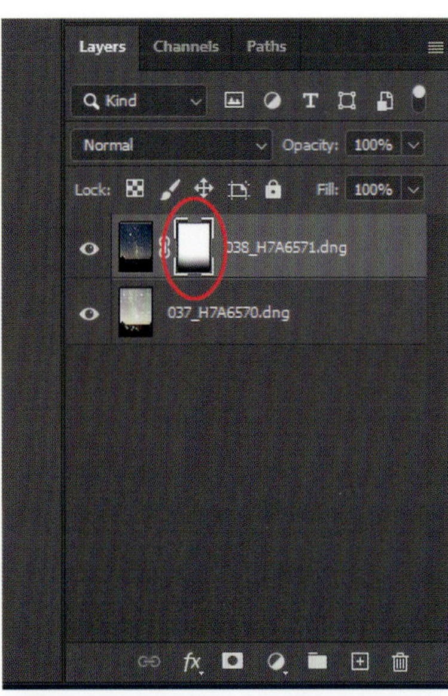

▸ FIGURE 6-13: The Properties panel showing a setting of 500 pixels for Feather and the Layers panel with the layer mask circled. Both panels show how the layer mask has a gradual transition from black to white.

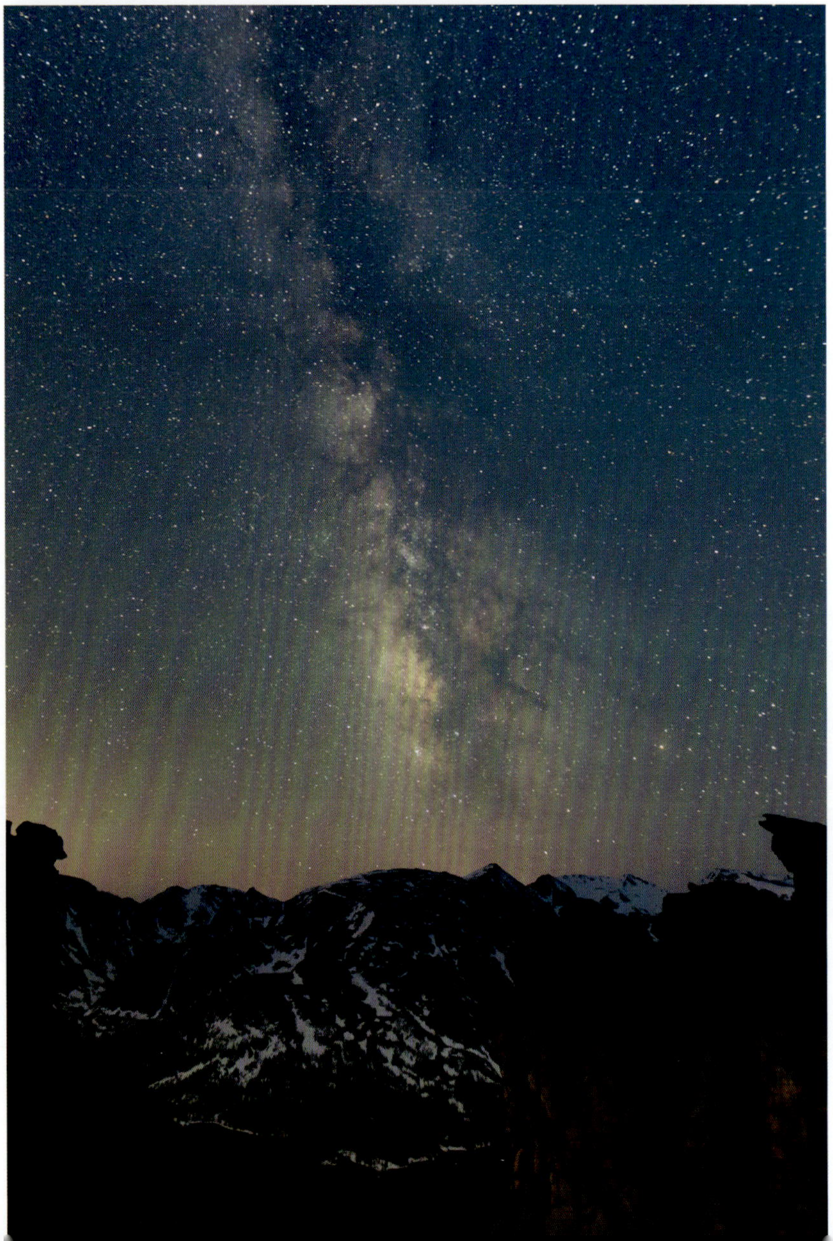

▸ FIGURE 6-14: The Milky Way image after using the simplified blending method. The next step would be to add contrast to the sky and Milky Way.

The advantage of using this approach to feathering the mask is that you can reopen the image later and adjust the feathering if need be. The disadvantage is that you can't effectively refine the mask by painting on it. The same feathering value that you've applied to the mask as a whole will also apply to the brush you choose to paint on the mask. If you choose a 30-pixel brush, for example, it will have a 250- to 500-pixel feather applied to it. That makes the edge of the brush so soft as to be nearly useless.

If you decide you need to refine the mask by painting on it, you'll need to take a different approach. Instead of feathering the mask in the Properties panel, choose Filter>Blur>Gaussian Blur. Set a radius equal to the value you used to expand the selection. Now you can paint on the mask with predictable results. The only disadvantage of this approach (a minor one) is that once you save and close the image, the mask can only be modified by further painting and/or blurring.

This method of combining two images has the advantage that it is quick and easy. It does not require any precise selections. It is by far the simplest way to deal with an image where the skyline has complex shapes, such as trees, protruding into the sky. The disadvantage is that all of the change in density required to create a believable transition from sky to land is confined to the land. In other words, we darkened the land just beneath the horizon (which often makes it too dark) but didn't brighten the sky just above the horizon. If you brighten the sky just above the horizon *and* darken the land just below the horizon, you can keep the land near the skyline from becoming too dark while preserving the brightness difference between land and sky that is essential to producing a natural look. The disadvantage of this more sophisticated approach is that you must make a precise selection of the sky. Here's how.

1. Start as before by opening the two images in Photoshop as layers.

2. If necessary, drag the dark (good-sky) layer to the top of the layer stack.

3. Now select the sky with the Quick Selection tool. This time you'll have to make the selection as close to perfect as possible.

4. Save the selection (Select>Save Selection), specifying how the selection was created with a name like *Quick Selection Sky*.

5. Next, test the quality of the selection you just made by adding a layer mask. If you examine the image at 100 percent, you're likely to see a thin white halo along part or all of the skyline, as shown in figure 6-15. This halo is a product of "anti-aliasing," Photoshop's attempt to build smooth curves using square pixels. No amount of

fiddling with the Quick Selection tool will fix it. If you see a white halo, the test has failed. The selection is not yet good enough. Delete the mask.

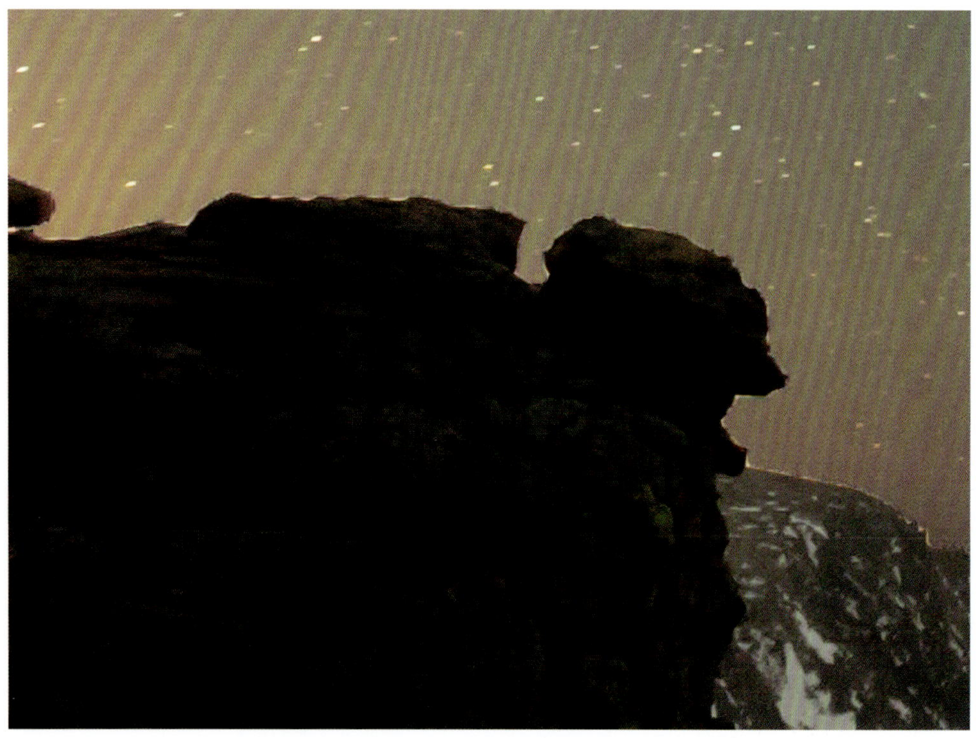

6. Here's how to minimize the halo. Reload the *Quick Selection Sky* selection (Select>Load Selection).

7. Now choose Select>Modify>Expand and expand the selection by one pixel. Don't check the box labeled Apply Effect at Canvas Bounds.

8. Next, choose Select>Modify>Feather and feather the selection by 0.5 pixels. Even the sharpest lens produces edges that are slightly softer than the edges produced by a non-feathered selection. Feathering the sky selection slightly softens the skyline, which helps the skyline match the slightly soft edges of the rest of the land. That, in turn, helps the land and sky portions of the image blend together into a believable whole.

9. Save the selection with a name that helps you remember what you did. I like to use abbreviations, such as *QS + 1 px Ex + 0.5 px Fth*.

10. Now add a layer mask again. This step should reduce or eliminate the white halo but it will probably replace it with a black halo. As you'll soon find, it's easier to remove a black halo than a white one.

11. The most reliable solution I've found for eliminating the last bit of halo is to patch it with the Clone Stamp tool. Here's how. Start by targeting the top layer and invoking the Stamp Visible command by pressing Shift+Control+Alt+E (Shift+Command+Option+E on Mac). Press all four keys simultaneously. This creates a new layer at the top of the layer stack containing all the layers beneath it.

12. Select the Clone Stamp tool. In the options bar, set Sample to Current Layer. Set Opacity and Flow to 100 percent. Uncheck Aligned. Open the Brush Preset picker. Click the disclosure triangle next to General Brushes and choose a soft round brush. Set brush size to 30 or 40 pixels and brush Hardness to zero. Figure 6-16 shows all these controls. Load the selection named *QS + 1 px Ex + 0.5 px Fth* (Select>Load Selection). Hide the marching ants temporarily by pressing Control+H. Zoom in to 100 percent. With the Clone Stamp tool selected and the Stamp Visible layer targeted, press and hold the Alt key and click in the sky near the horizon to choose the source pixels, then release the Alt key and click the skyline to clone sky up against the selection boundary. If necessary, adjust the brush size with the bracket keys (left bracket for a smaller brush, right bracket for a larger brush.) The selection boundary acts like a fence, preventing you from cloning sky onto the good land. Continue cloning sky along the entire skyline.

▼ FIGURE 6-16: The options bar with the controls set correctly for cloning sky against the selection boundary.

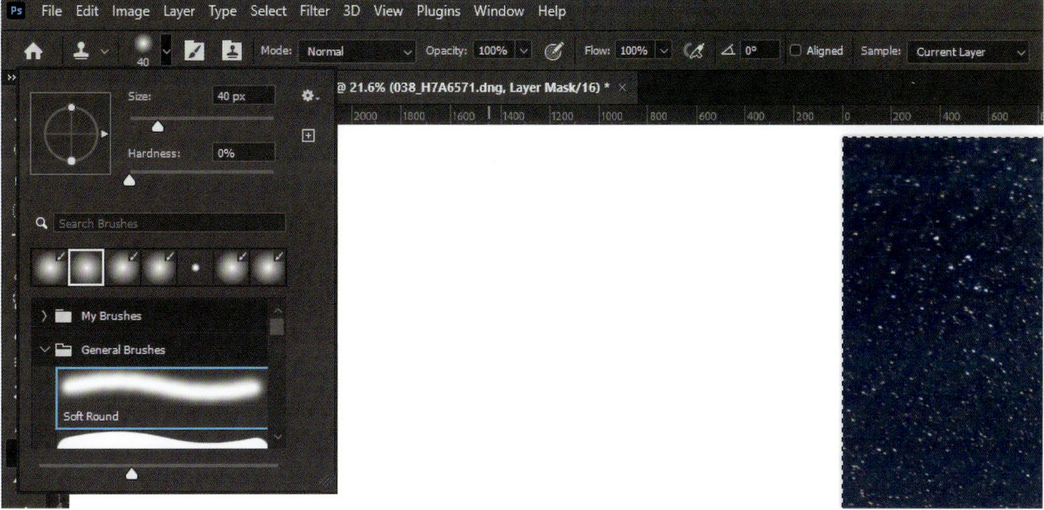

13.   If that doesn't completely eliminate the halo, invert the selection (Control+Shift+I) to include only land. Now clone land up against the selection boundary. Deselect and examine your handiwork closely. You need to get this step right because it can be hard to go back and fix errors later. Figure 6-17 shows the result. You'll find that it's easier to clone sky than land up against the selection boundary because the sky is relatively uniform in color and texture. It's harder to clone land against the selection boundary because the land will exhibit far more variations in color and texture, which makes it harder to conceal what you're doing.

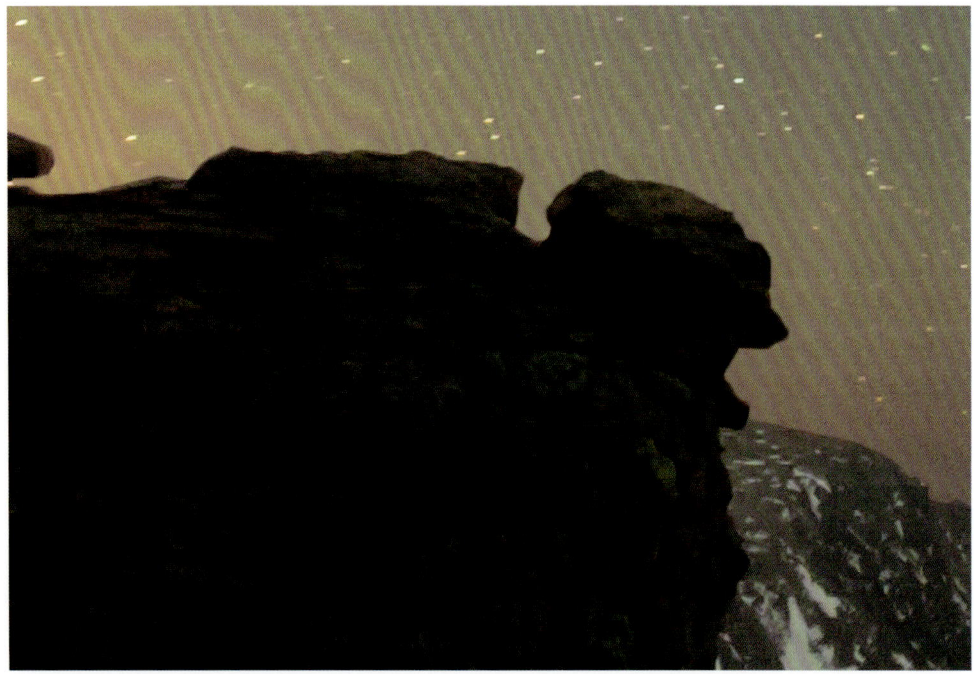

▶ FIGURE 6-17: Detail of the skyline after using the Clone Stamp tool to repair the halo created by the Quick Selection tool.

Selecting Complex Shapes in Night Images

If the skyline in your image is simple—distant peaks, plains, cliffs, the ocean—then you can skip down to the section labeled **Brightening the Sky and Darkening the Land Near the Horizon**. If, on the other hand, a complex shape such as a tree projects into the sky, then making a precise selection of the sky can be challenging. Here's how. This procedure works best if you shot a good-sky and a good-land image back to back, without moving the camera, so the two frames match up perfectly.

1. Start by selecting the sky roughly with the Quick Selection tool. Zoom in to 100 percent and refine the selection along the skyline and around the tree as much as you can, recognizing that perfection is impossible.

2. Save this selection under the name *Quick Selection Sky* (Select>Save Selection).

3. Next, expand the selection by 1 pixel (Select>Modify>Expand).

4. Now feather the selection by 0.5 pixels (Select>Modify>Feather).

5. Save the selection under a name like *QS + 1 px Ex + 0.5 px Fth*.

6. Test the selection by adding a layer mask. As you can see in figure 6-18, you'll probably find that the Quick Selection tool by itself will not produce an adequate selection. If the test fails, delete the layer mask.

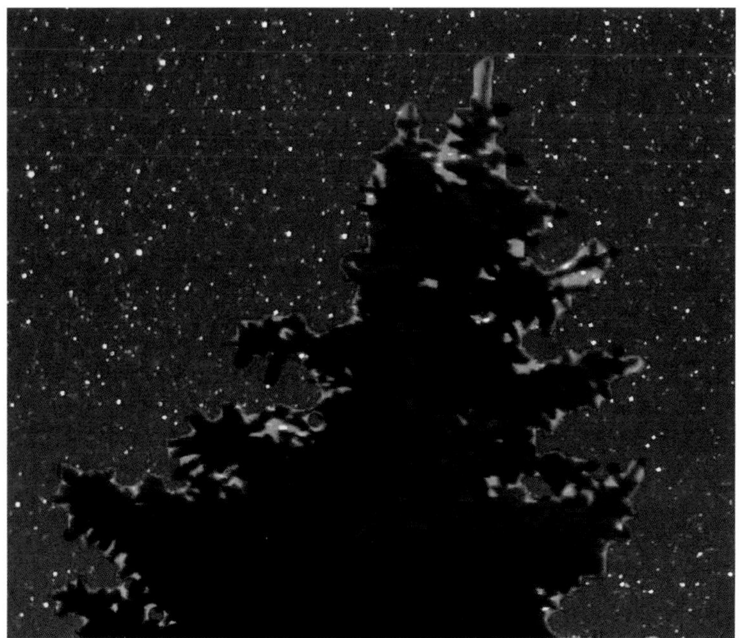

◄ FIGURE 6-18: Detail of a tree selected with the Quick Selection tool alone after adding a layer mask.

7. Reload your *QS + 1 px Ex + 0.5 px Fth* selection (Select>Load Selection).

8. Open the Select and Mask workspace by clicking its icon in the options bar. Under View Mode, choose Onion Skin and set the

transparency to 100 percent. This reveals the good-land layer underneath the good-sky layer in all the non-selected areas. Do not check Smart Radius, which is designed to distinguish hard from soft edges and adjust the softness of the selection automatically. Leave Smooth, Feather, Contrast, and Shift Edge at their default values. Uncheck Decontaminate Colors.

9. Select the Refine Edge Brush from the toolbar on the left and paint over the edges of all the branches. If the selection still isn't perfect, reduce the size of the brush and try again. Press-and-hold the Alt key to remove the effect as you paint. Don't use the Refine Edge Brush along the skyline. This tool often mistakes noise for image detail in high-ISO images and produces a fuzzy boundary where you actually want a crisp edge. Set the output to Selection and click OK.

10. Save the selection under a new name, such as *QS + 1 px Ex + 0.5 px Fth + REB*, so you can remember how you created it.

11. With the selection active, check your handiwork by adding a layer mask. You should see a better selection of the tree against the sky. Close examination, however, may reveal a subtle halo around the tree, as shown in figure 6-19. This mask is a keeper, but it needs refinement.

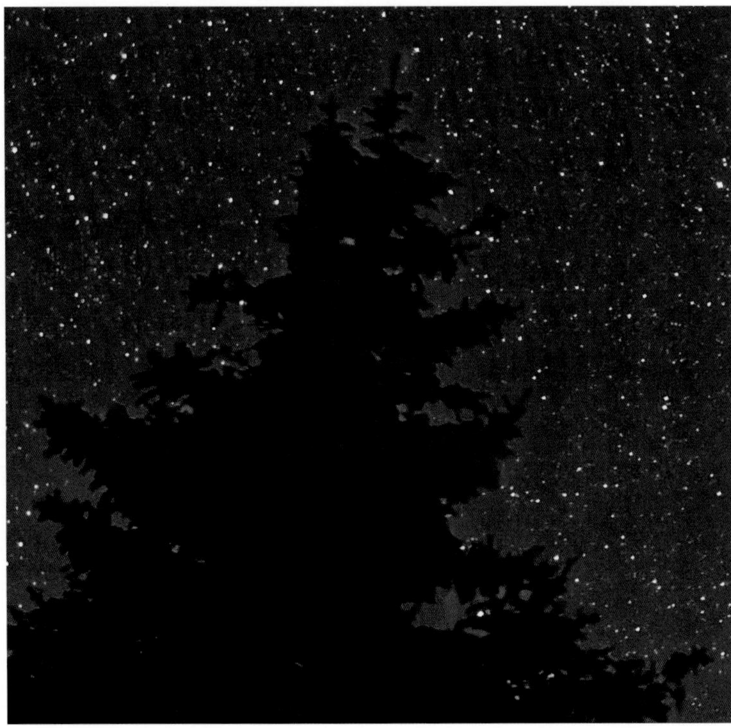

▶ Figure 6-19: Tree after selecting the sky with the Quick Selection tool and the Refine Edge Brush in the Select and Mask workspace. Note the subtle halo around the tree.

12. Examine figure 6-20, the layer mask that produced the image in figure 6-19, and you'll see a light gray speckled halo around the tree limbs. Remember that white on the mask reveals the layer to which the mask is attached. Black conceals that layer. Shades of gray partially reveal the layer underneath. In this case, the mask is attached to the good-sky layer. Pure white reveals the good sky and hides the excessively bright sky from the good-land layer underneath—exactly what we want. Light gray, therefore, partially reveals the unwanted bright sky in the layer below, creating the halo.

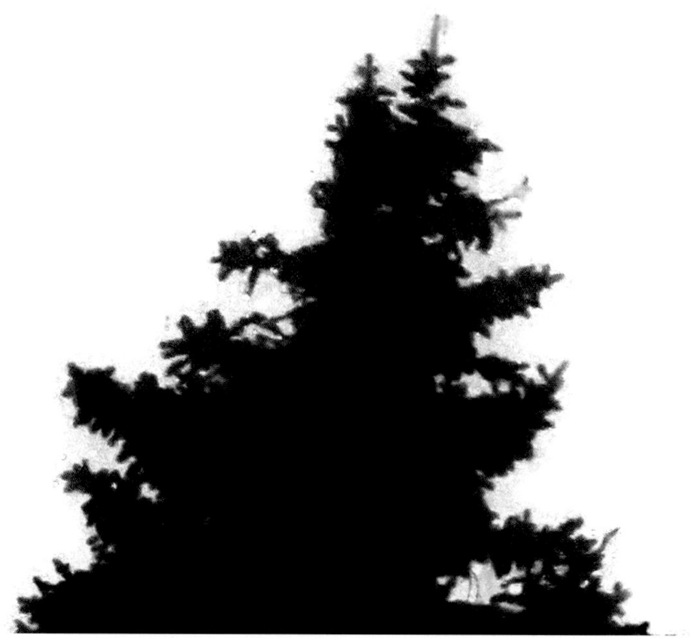

◄ Figure 6-20: An enlarged version of the layer mask that produced the halo around the tree limbs seen in figure 6-19.

13. To eliminate that halo, we need to make the light gray areas on the mask white. The easiest way to do this is to *clip the whites*—in other words, to tell Photoshop to find all pixels brighter than, let's say, an RGB value of 225 and to make those pixels pure white. Photoshop will then distribute all the remaining tones evenly across the tonal scale to prevent harsh transitions.

14. You can't apply a Curves adjustment *layer* to a layer mask without a great deal of convoluted Photoshop work. You can, however, apply a Curves *adjustment* directly to the mask. Unlike adding an adjustment *layer*, applying a Curves adjustment directly to the mask creates a permanent change in the mask. Once you've saved

and closed the file, that adjustment is fixed. To preserve your options, be sure to save the mask as a selection before applying the Curves adjustment. To do this, first Control-click the mask itself to load it as a selection. Then choose Select>Save Selection. Be sure to deselect (Select>Deselect) after saving the selection. If you need to recreate the mask as it existed before applying the Curves adjustment, do this: first, delete the current mask by dragging it to the trash can. Then load the selection you saved just before applying the Curves adjustment (Select>Load Selection). Now click the Add Layer Mask icon. The new mask will take on the shape of the selection.

15. To apply a Curves adjustment directly to the layer mask, first target the mask. Then choose Image>Adjustments>Curves. Drag the top-right end of the curve to the left. You may find it helpful to add a point to the curve in the highlight region and push it up and left, as shown in figure 6-21. Don't overdo it. Excessive clipping will make the problem worse. Click OK. You can see the result in figure 6-22.

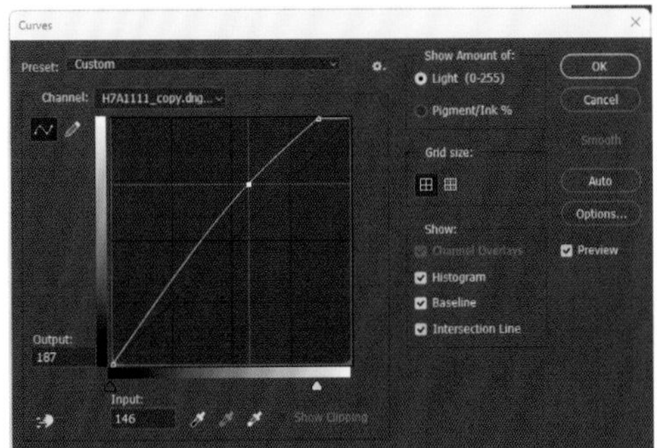

▲ Figure 6-21: A Curves adjustment applied to the layer mask to reduce the halo surrounding the tree.

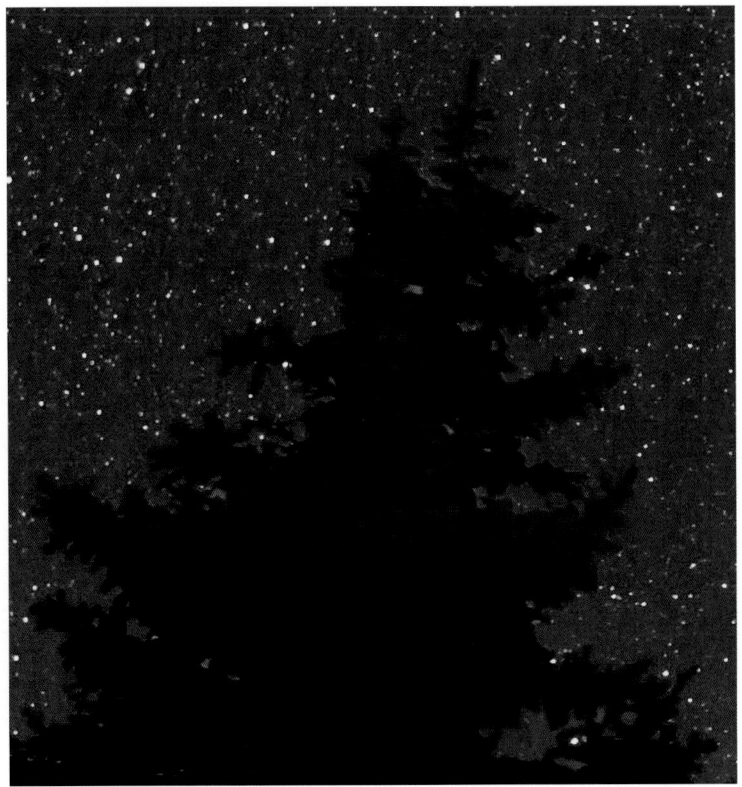

▶ Figure 6-22: The tree after selecting the sky with the Quick Selection tool, refining the selection with the Refine Edge Brush, adding a layer mask, then clipping the highlights in the mask with a Curves adjustment. Note that the halo around the tree seen in figure 6-19 is largely gone.

16. If the mask is still imperfect, select the Brush tool, set the fore-ground color to white, and paint over the light gray areas. This requires a good deal of time and care. You can speed the process by changing the blend mode in the options bar to Overlay. This partially protects the darker areas of the mask, but still doesn't give you a license to be careless.

17. When you've made the final tweaks to your mask, load it as a selection by Control-clicking the mask and choosing Select>Save Selection. Name it Sky Selection Final.

18. As before, clean up any imperfections along the skyline by cloning sky and/or land up against the selection boundary.

19. If thin branches have become wispy or translucent, you may find it helpful to invert the final sky selection and clone bits of tree over the branches to thicken them. This step is often essential when tall, nearby trees form the skyline.

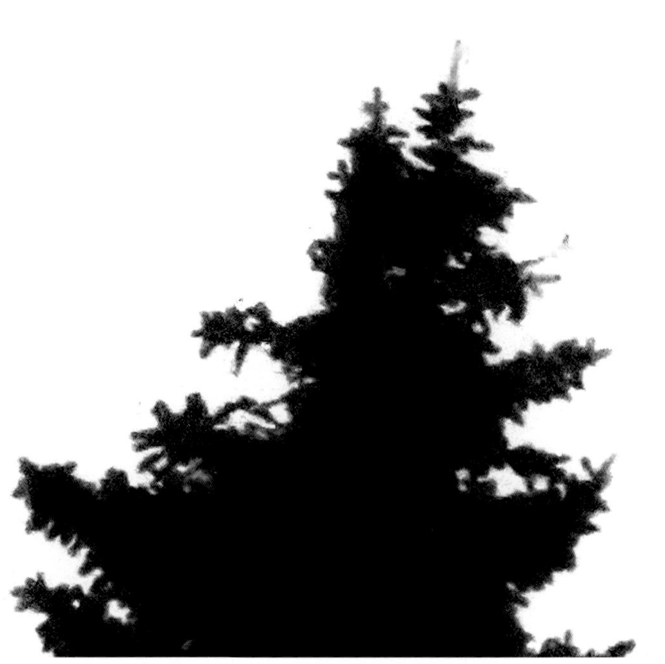

◄ FIGURE 6-23: The mask that produced the selection revealed in figure 6-22. Note that the light gray halo around the tree is mostly gone.

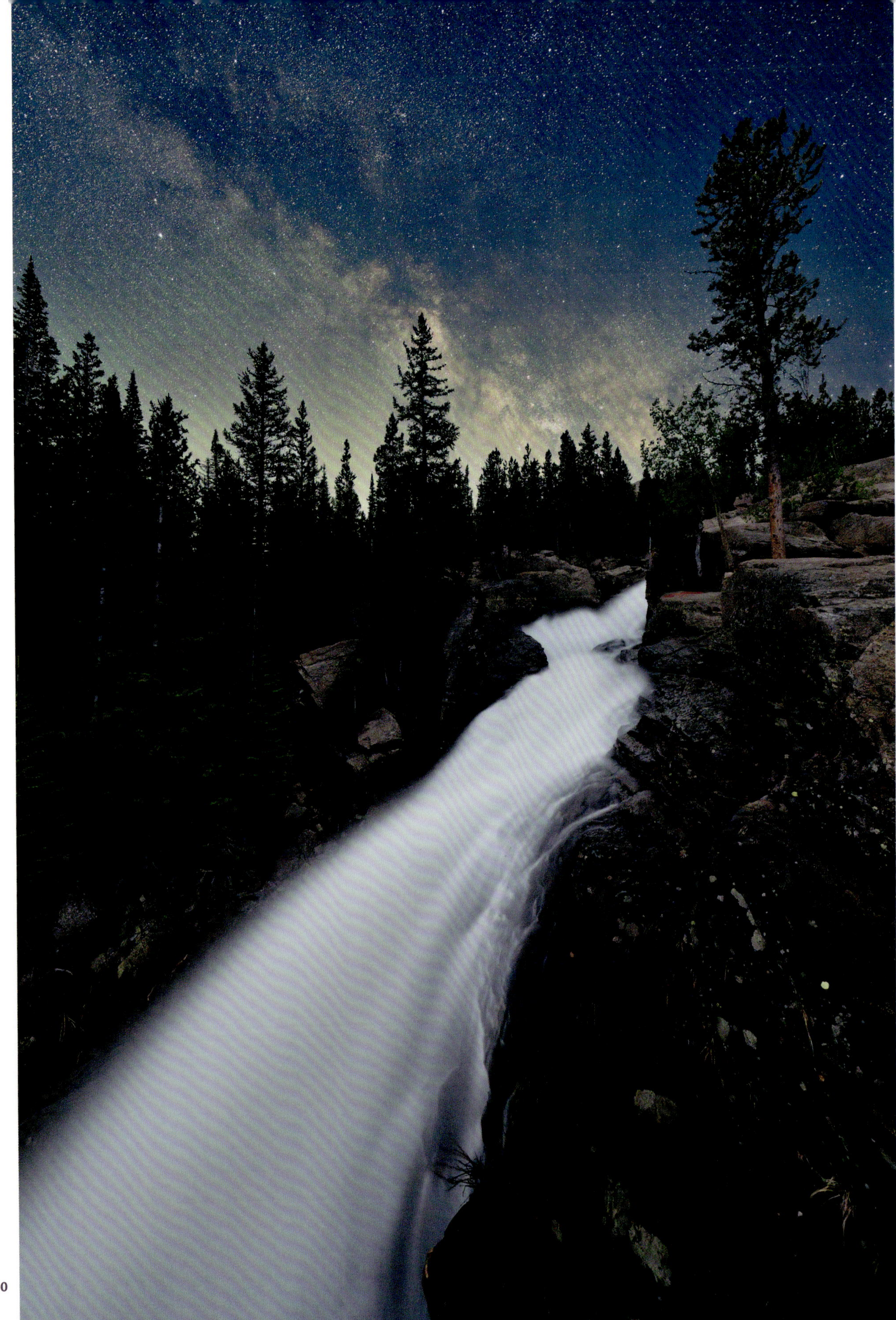

Brightening the Sky and Darkening the Land Near the Horizon

Whew! As you can see, it can be a lot of work to make a perfect selection of the sky. Before writing the second edition of this book, I spent a long time trying to find a better way to handle complex selections at night. The technique I just described is still the best way I know.

With the task of selecting the sky finally accomplished, let's brighten the sky just above the horizon and darken the land just below the horizon. This will restore a natural appearance to the image.

1. With the Stamp Visible layer targeted, load the selection named *Sky Selection Final* and add a Curves adjustment layer, which will appear at the top of the layer stack. Name it *Brighten sky just above horizon*. The Layers panel should now look like figure 6-25.

2. Be sure the layer thumbnail (not the layer-mask thumbnail) on the Curves adjustment layer is targeted, as shown in figure 6-25. Next, open the Properties panel (Choose Window>Properties if it's not visible) and brighten the sky by dragging up and left on the center of the curve. To confine this brightening to the sky just above the horizon, choose the Gradient tool from the toolbar on the left. Choose Gradient (not Classic Gradient) from the drop-down list on the left side of the options bar. Choose Perceptual as the method on the right side of the options bar. Click the drop-down arrow next to the Gradient icon in the options bar, open the Basics panel and click the leftmost icon to select Foreground to Background as the gradient type. Also check that the Linear Gradient icon is chosen. Set the other options as shown in figure 6-26. Finally, reload Sky Selection Final (Select>Load Selection or Control-click the Curves layer mask). By reloading the sky selection you will confine the effect of the gradient to the sky, leaving the land untouched.

3. Target the Curves layer mask and set the foreground and background colors to black and white, respectively (press D to make the foreground color white and the background color black, then press X to reverse them). Now click, hold, and drag downward within

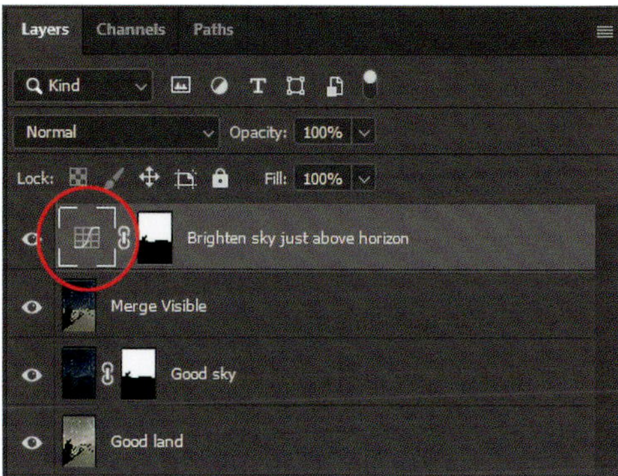

◄ FIGURE 6-24: Milky Way over Alberta Falls, Rocky Mountain National Park, Colorado. June 20, 2023, 10:18 p.m. Sony Alpha 7R IVa, Sony FE 14mm f/1.8 GM. Land: one frame, noise reduced with Lightroom Denoise, 5 minutes, f/4.0, ISO 6400. Sky: one frame, noise reduced with Topaz Denoise AI, 15 seconds, f/1.8, ISO 6400.

▲ FIGURE 6-25: The Layers panel after adding the first Curves adjustment layer. The layer thumbnail (circled), not the layer-mask thumbnail, is targeted.

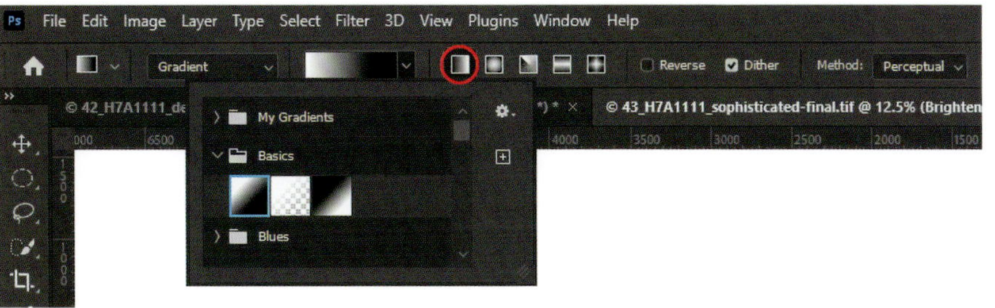

◄ FIGURE 6-26: Set the options in the options bar as shown and be sure Foreground to Background is chosen as the gradient type. Also, make sure the Linear Gradient icon (circled) is active.

the image window from an inch or two above the skyline to just below the skyline. This will drag out a gradient on the layer mask. Remember that white reveals, black conceals. The Curves layer we just added brightens the sky. We want to conceal that brightening for the upper part of the sky but reveal it near the horizon. All of the gradient above the start of your drag will be black, concealing the brightened sky; all of the gradient below the end of your drag will be white, revealing the brightened sky. The region in between will fade from black to white, creating a gradual transition from dark sky that is unaffected by the Curves layer to brighter sky that reveals the full effect of the Curves layer.

4. If you don't like the results, just click, hold, and drag another gradient, which will replace the original one. You can further adjust the gradient by dragging either the dot marking the beginning of your drag or the dot marking the end. The white diamond alongside the line connecting the two dots represents the midpoint of the transition from black to white. By default, it will be positioned midway between the two dots, which usually works well. Fiddle until you have confined the brightening of the sky to the region just above the horizon and created a gradual, believable transition to the remainder of the sky.

5. Next, invert the selection (choose Select>Inverse or press Shift+Control+I) and add another Curves adjustment layer, which should appear just above the first Curves layer. Name it *Darken land just below horizon*. With the layer thumbnail on the new Curves layer targeted, go to the Properties panel and drag the center of the curve down and right to darken the land.

6. To confine that adjustment to the land just beneath the skyline, reselect the land by Control-clicking the Curves layer mask, choose the Gradient tool, make sure the options are set as before, with the foreground color set to black and the background color set to white, then click, hold, and drag upward from an inch or so below the skyline to just above the skyline. As before, you may need to drag out several gradients, with various starting and stopping points, until you achieve the look you want. The goal is to create a believable transition from land to sky. The Layers panel should now look like figure 6-27. The gradient controls will remain visible atop your image until you choose a different tool or target the layer thumbnail rather than the layer mask thumbnail.

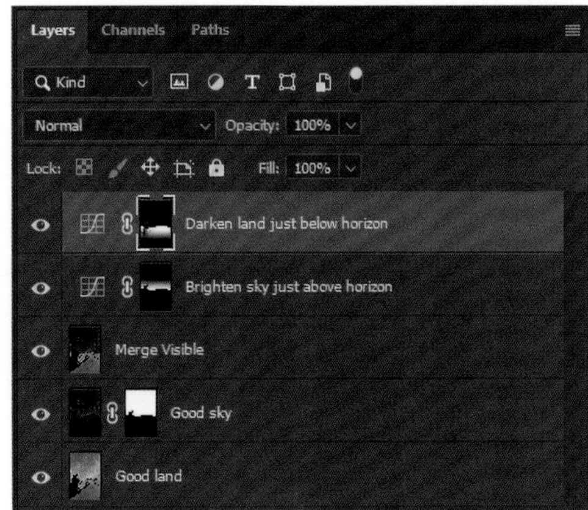

▾ Figure 6-27: The Layers panel with the first two Curves adjustment layers added.

Close examination of the image I used as an example reveals a problem: darkening the land just below the skyline also darkened the tree, rendering it nearly black. To fix this, reload *Sky Selection Final* then invert the selection so only the land is selected. Target the layer mask for the Curves layer named *Darken land just below horizon*. Choose the Brush tool and set the foreground color to black. Now paint over the dark tree. The selection boundary acts like a fence, preventing you from painting outside the line. That means you can paint over the portion of the tree projecting above the skyline without worrying that you will also affect the sky. You can also paint over dark portions of the tree below the skyline, but you must be careful not to paint over parts of the land where you want to preserve the darkening created by the *Darken land* Curves layer.

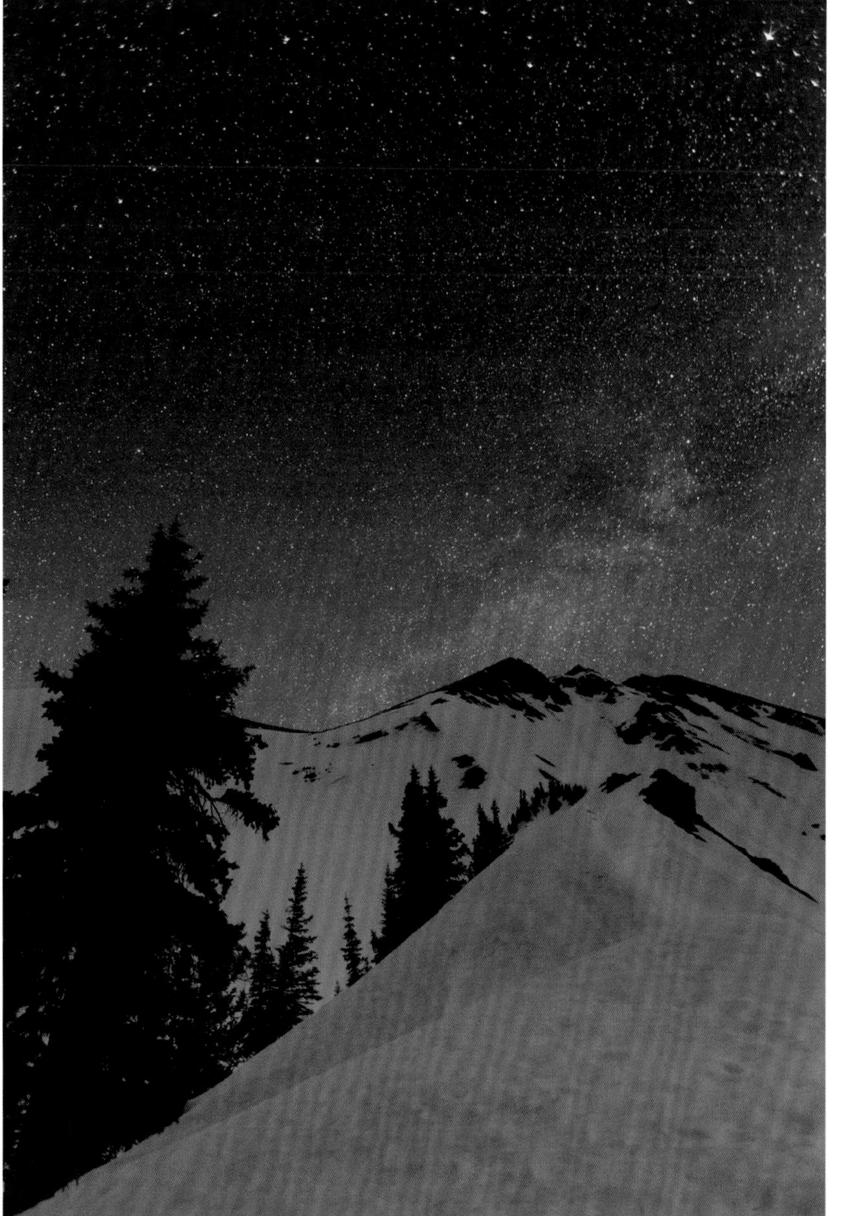

◄ FIGURE 6-28: The image after using the sophisticated blending method and lightening the tree but before adding contrast to the sky and the Milky Way.

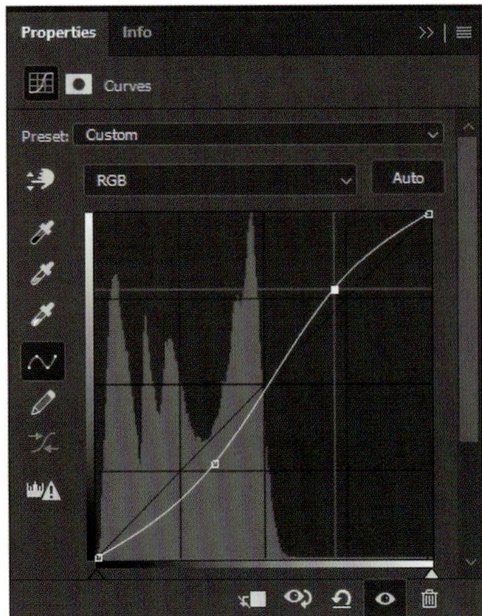

▲ FIGURE 6-29: The Properties panel showing a Curves Adjustment layer with a contrast-enhancing curve.

▼ FIGURE 6-30: The Smart Object layer in the Layers panel with the Blending Options icon circled.

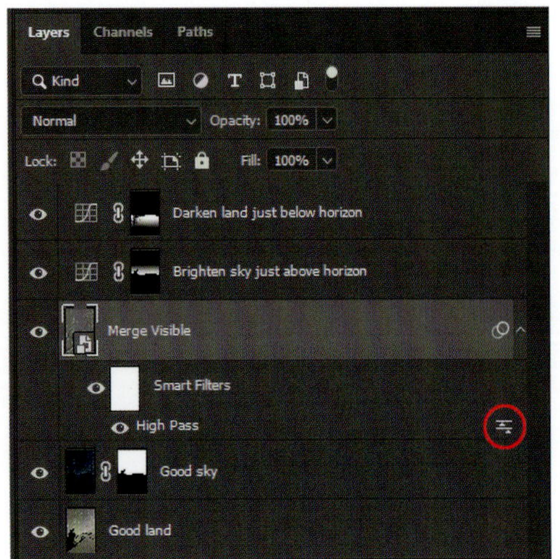

Now that you've achieved a sophisticated blending of the land and sky, you may want to add an additional Curves layer to add contrast to the sky and make the Milky Way pop. Once again, reload *Sky Selection Final*, target the top layer in the layer stack, and add a Curves adjustment layer. Pull the shadow portion of the curve down and push the highlight region up to add contrast, as shown in figure 6-29.

While in Photoshop, you may wish to brighten the stars with Unsharp Mask (Filter>Sharpen>Unsharp Mask) using a low Amount and a high Radius. I find that a setting of 30 for each value often works well. Be sure you target the Stamp Visible layer before applying the filter. To confine the adjustment to selected regions of the image, convert the Stamp Visible layer to a Smart Object first (right-click the layer and choose Convert to Smart Object). Now when you apply the filter, it will be applied as a Smart Filter, which will be accompanied by its own mask. This Unsharp Mask technique sometimes produces a halo along the skyline. Remove the halo by painting on the mask with a soft black brush.

An alternative to the Unsharp Mask technique for adding local contrast is to use Photoshop's High Pass filter. As before, target the Stamp Visible layer, right-click, and choose Convert to Smart Object. Now choose Filter>Other>High Pass. Set a high radius. Around 180 pixels often works well. The image will look awful. In the Layers panel, double-click the tiny icon in the bottom-right corner of the Smart Object layer (figure 6-30). Change the Mode to Soft Light. Adjust the Opacity to taste. I find a setting between 50 and 75 percent is often pleasing. (For a really strong effect that is usually over the top, try changing the Mode to Overlay and setting the Opacity to 100 percent.) If necessary, use the layer mask that comes with the Smart Filter to restrict the effect to the desired areas. Use the Brush tool and paint on the layer mask with black to hide the effect.

Checking Enable Profile Corrections in the Lens Corrections panel in Lightroom sometimes lightens the corners of the image so much that the colors in the corners shift toward purple. To eliminate that color cast in Photoshop, add a new, empty layer at the top of the layer stack (Layer>New>Layer). Change the blend mode for the new layer to Color (figure 6-31). Select the Brush tool and choose a large, soft-edged brush. Reduce the Brush opacity to 25–50 percent. Hold down the Alt key and click in the image to sample the color you want to apply over the purple-shifted area. Paint over the purplish region. The Color blend mode retains the color of the area you sample while preserving the density and contrast of the area where you paint. You may need to resample colors repeatedly to create a natural effect. This technique can also be used to remove the color cast caused by you or a nearby photographer accidentally turning on a red headlamp during your exposure so long as the headlamp light isn't too bright.

Processing Night Panoramas

Processing night panoramas uses many of the same techniques as processing single-camera-position images. If you were able to capture all the detail you want in a single frame at each camera position, then processing is easy. Lightroom now offers the ability to stitch together single-row and multi-row panoramas. Select all the images, right-click one and choose Photo Merge>Panorama. Lightroom will automatically apply lens corrections. In the Panorama Merge Preview dialog box, shown in figure 6-32, choose the panorama projection you find gives you the most pleasing result: Spherical, Cylindrical, or Perspective. I find Cylindrical often works best for single-row panoramas shot with moderate wide-angle lenses; Spherical is often the better choice for single-row panoramas shot with ultra-wide-angle lenses and for multi-row panoramas. Perspective often fails or produces something unusable. Check Auto Crop to get rid of the scalloped edges around the image, or leave it unchecked and crop it later, which is my preference. Either way, it's non-destructive. Experiment

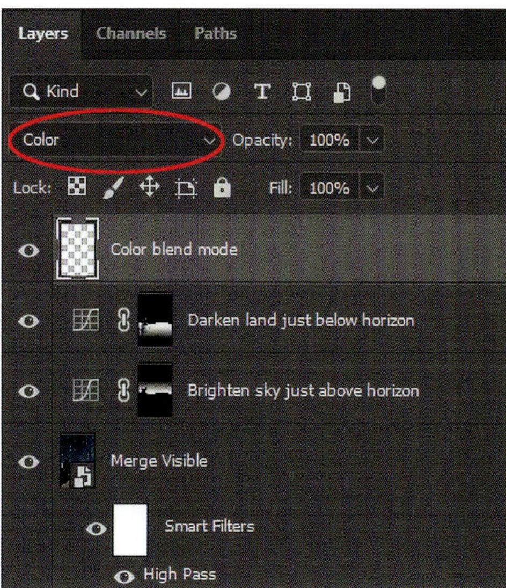

▲ FIGURE 6-31: The Layers panel showing the blend mode for the new blank layer set to Color (circled).

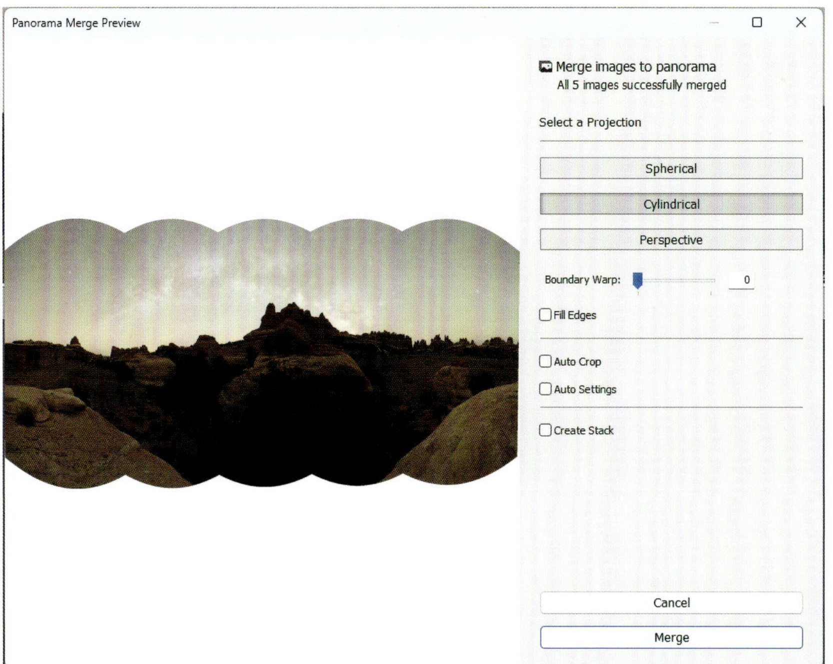

◄ FIGURE 6-32: Lightroom's Panorama Merge Preview dialog box, showing the options for stitching panoramas.

with the Boundary Warp slider if you want to distort the image to eliminate the scalloped edges. This may be helpful if key subject elements will be too close to the edge of the frame once you crop off the scalloped edges, but it's better to compose generously in the field, leave Boundary Warp set to zero, and crop off the scalloped edges. The same advice applies even more strongly to Fill Edges, which invents pixels to fill in the scallops. Once you click Merge, Lightroom will stitch the panorama and add it to your Lightroom catalog automatically. The completed panorama is still a RAW file, with all the flexibility that implies. Edit the image to taste, and you're done.

Things get more complicated if you shot two frames at each camera position to record all the detail you want in the highlights and shadows.

Try this procedure if you shot the two frames back to back, without moving the camera, then moved the camera to the next camera position, shot another pair, etc.

After downloading your images, use the procedure described above to stack each pair in Photoshop, select the sky with the Quick Selection Tool and, if you have a complex object projecting upward against the sky, the Select and Mask workspace, and add a layer mask. Don't expand the selection by 1 pixel or feather it by 0.5 pixels, and don't bother cloning out any imperfections in the selection at this stage. Save each composited pair of images as a TIFF, then use Lightroom to stitch together all of the composited frames. If Lightroom fails or produces stitching errors such as out-of-focus offsets along the skyline or along the boundaries between two frames, try a different stitching program. My current favorite is PTGUI (Panorama Tools Graphical User Interface), a high-end dedicated stitching program, but there are several others available. Now you can follow the rest of the procedure described above, re-selecting the sky, expanding the selection by one pixel, feathering the selection by 0.5 pixels, cloning out imperfections in the selection, brightening the sky above the horizon, darkening the land below the horizon, etc.

You'll follow a different procedure if you shot all the sky images in the panorama first, including only a thin strip of land in your composition, then shot all the land images, including only a thin strip of sky in your composition.

1.   Edit all the sky images as described earlier, then stitch them together. Edit all the land images as described earlier, then stitch them together. You'll now have two separate panoramas, one for the sky (with a thin strip of underexposed land) and one for the land (with a thin strip of overexposed sky). Open the good-land panorama in Photoshop and make a perfect selection of the sky using the procedure described earlier. Save your selection.

2. You'll probably need to extend the Canvas vertically. Choose Image>Canvas Size. Click the down-facing arrow in the middle of the bottom row of the Anchor section of the dialog box (figure 6-33). This will cause Photoshop to extend the canvas vertically rather than in all directions. In the Height field, enter a number equal to the width of your image. This number is arbitrary; you're just creating additional room in your image to accommodate the sky you'll be dropping in. If the canvas proves to be too large, just crop away the excess. If it's too small and your good sky won't fit, you'll have to extend the canvas farther. Click OK.

3. Reload your saved sky selection. Now extend the selection to the upper limits of the new canvas by choosing the Rectangular Marquee tool. Set the mode to Add to Selection (figure 6-34). Draw out a rectangle that includes all of the new canvas plus a strip of the existing sky selection. You should now have a perfect selection of the sky in the good-land panorama plus all of the new canvas. Save your selection.

4. Open your good-sky panorama. Select the entire image (choose Select>All or press Control+A). Copy your selection to the Clipboard (choose Edit>Copy or press Control+C). Switch back to the good-land panorama. Choose Edit>Paste Special>Paste Into. By choosing Paste Into you ensure that only the parts of the good-sky panorama that will fit within the selection boundaries will be visible. Choose the Move tool and move the new, good-sky layer until the skyline of the good-sky layer lines up with the skyline of the good-land layer as well as possible. It may be helpful to tuck the good-sky layer's horizon just below the good-land layer's horizon. You're unlikely to get a perfect match.

5. It may be helpful to target the good-sky layer and use Free Transform (choose Edit>Free Transform or press Control+T). Free Transform lets you stretch and rotate the good-sky layer to make it fit

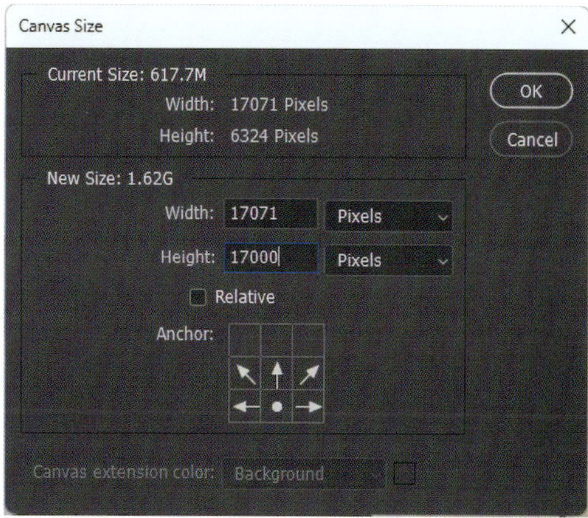

▲ FIGURE 6-33: The Canvas Size dialog box showing how to extend the canvas vertically.

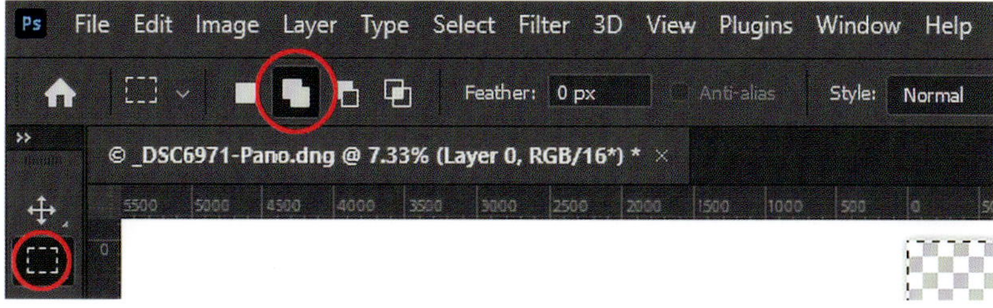

◄ FIGURE 6-34: The Rectangular Marquee tool and Add to Selection option are circled.

the good-land layer as well as possible. Stretch or compress the good-sky layer by dragging the edges of the layer with your mouse. Rotate the layer by positioning your cursor outside the layer boundary near a corner of the layer. When the cursor changes to a curved, double-headed arrow, click, hold, and drag to rotate the layer. Inevitably, you'll need to load your final sky selection and clone sky up against the selection boundary to fix the remaining imperfections. When the two panoramas fit together perfectly, you're ready to brighten the sky just above the horizon and darken the land just below the horizon using the procedure described earlier.

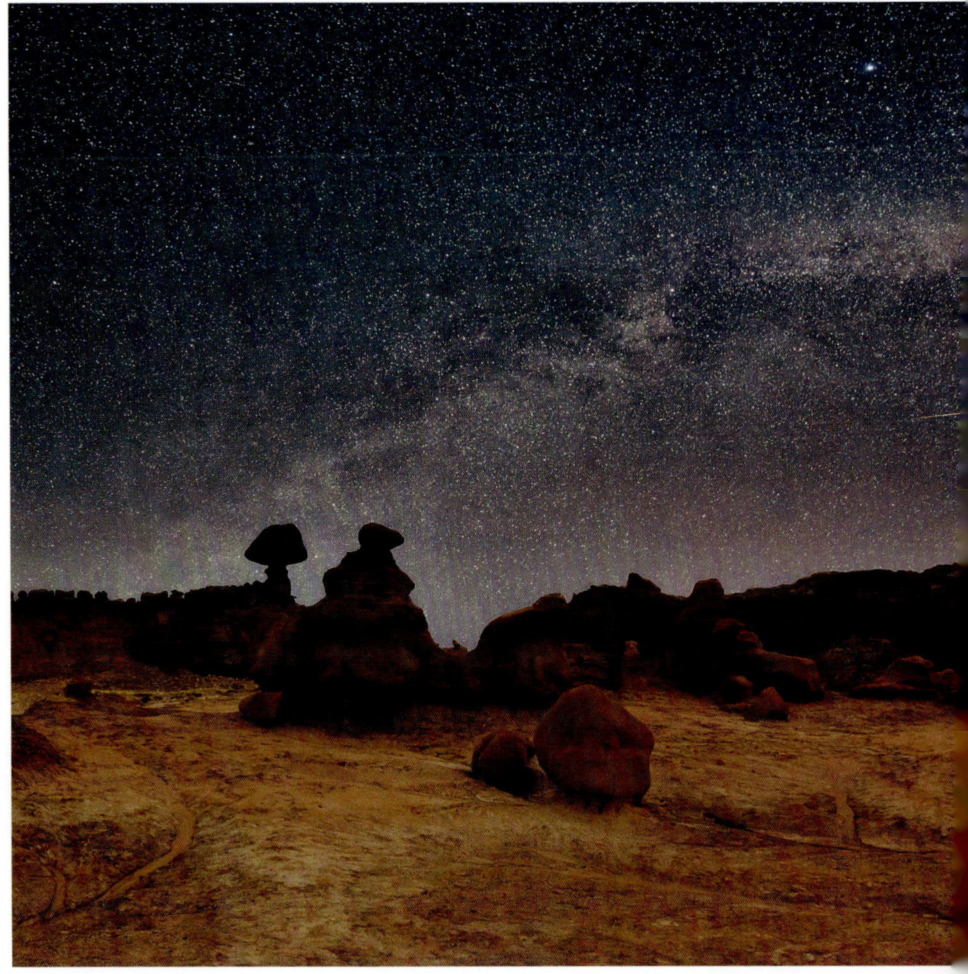

▶ Figure 6-35: Milky Way panorama over Goblin Valley, Goblin Valley State Park, Utah. April 2, 2017, 4:26 a.m. Canon EOS 5D Mark III, Canon EF 16-35mm f/2.8L III USM at 16mm. Land: one row, four camera positions, one frame per camera position, 2.5 minutes, f/2.8, ISO 6400. Sky: one row, four camera positions, one frame per camera position, 30 seconds, f/2.8, ISO 6400. For this panorama I shot the first pair of sky and land frames back to back, then moved the camera to the next camera position, shot the second pair of sky and land frames, etc.

Processing a Milky Way panorama using this method is admittedly complex and time-consuming. Despite all the advances in software over the last six years, and despite spending many hours trying to find a better way to composite two night panoramas before writing this second edition, I still haven't found a better method. In my view, the quality of the result makes the effort worthwhile. This is the method I now use for all of my Milky Way panoramas that don't have close-in foregrounds. Take the time to master this procedure, and I think you'll agree that all the work was worthwhile as soon as you hang a huge, spectacular print of a Milky Way panorama in your living room.

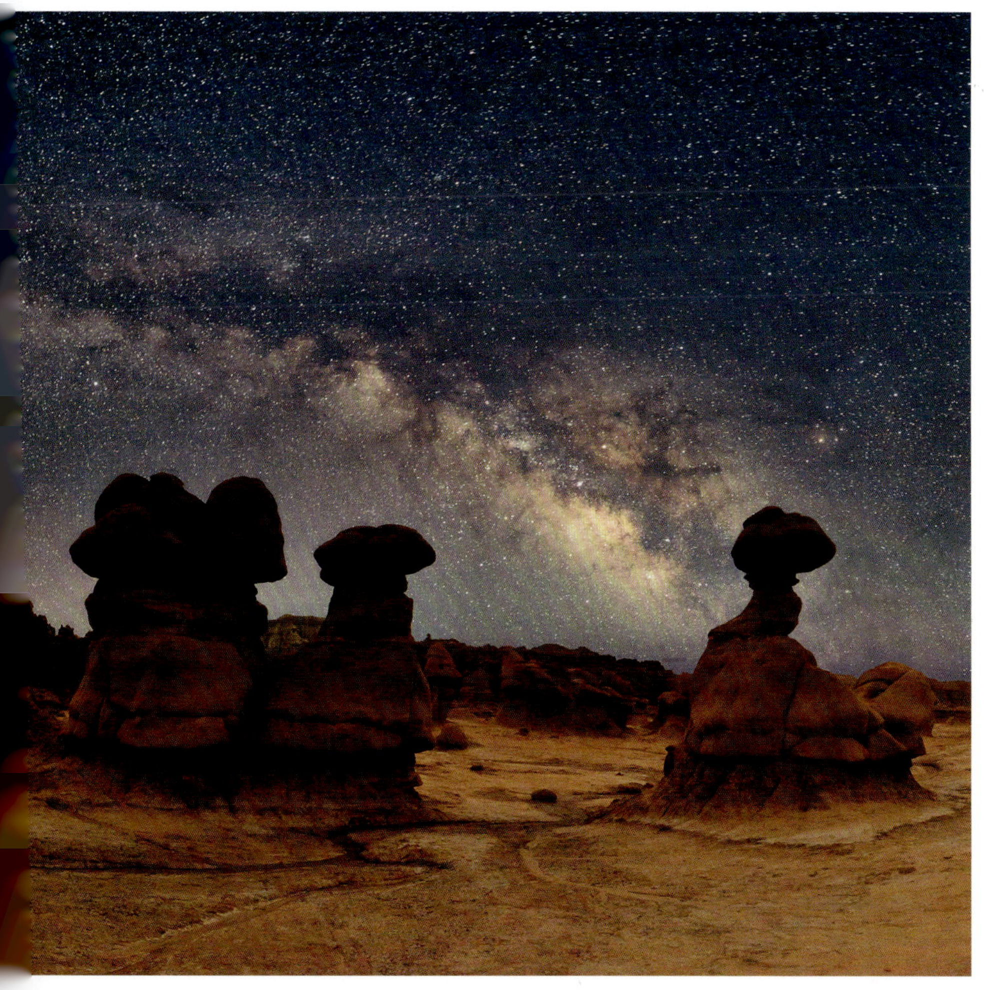

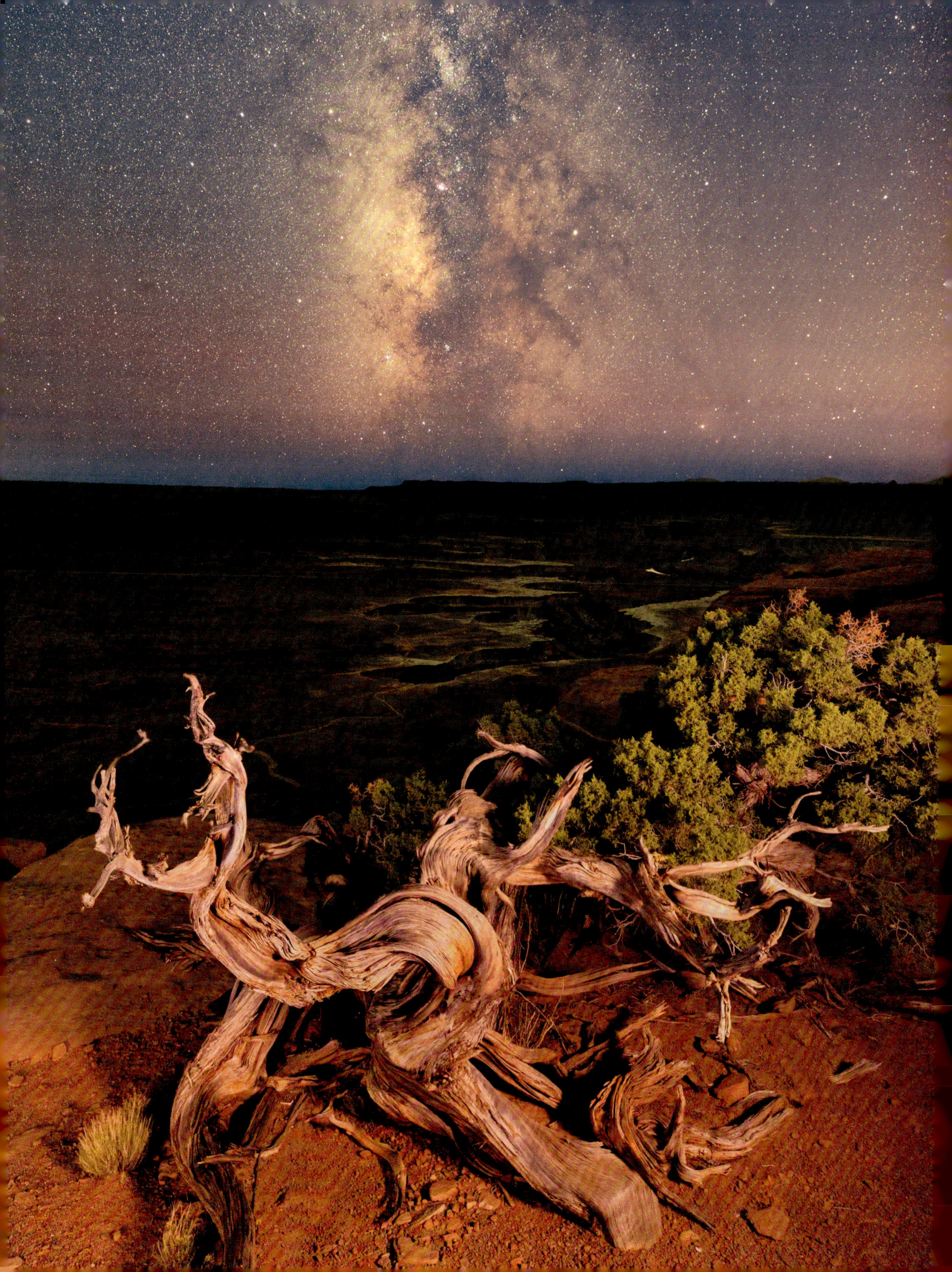

Advanced Techniques for Night Landscapes

7

The techniques you've learned in the previous chapters will enable you to make excellent images of the night sky. In this chapter I'm going to show you how to take your images still further. I'll talk about *light painting*, the technique of adding light to the foreground with flashlights, flash units, and flat-panel LED lights. Adding light to the foreground can create a unique look and simplify processing by allowing you to capture all the detail you want in a single frame. I'll provide detailed instructions for *focus stacking*, a technique that allows you to create tremendous depth of field by shooting multiple frames of the same subject with different points of focus, then combining the images in Photoshop. I'll show you how to reduce noise by shooting multiple frames with exactly the same exposure and focus setting, then combining the images using Photoshop's *Stack Mode>Median* utility and specialized astronomical software. And I'll show you how to use motorized star-tracking camera mounts, called *equatorial mounts*, to create the very best quality images of all.

Light Painting

You can use virtually any light source to add light to your foreground. Simple, inexpensive flashlights and headlamps, battery-operated tea lights, photographic flash units either on-camera or off, and flat-panel LED lights designed for videographers can all be employed to light key features in an endless variety of ways. Some light sources are easier to control than others, however.

It takes surprisingly little light to properly expose the foreground if you have set the correct exposure for the Milky Way (typically 30 seconds, f/2.8, ISO 6400 when using a 16mm or wider lens in a dark-sky location). While you may think you need to buy the biggest, most powerful flashlight available, you'll probably find that your million-candlepower searchlight is actually way too powerful unless the subject you are light painting is very distant. LED flashlights and headlamps are very bright for their size and weight and use batteries very efficiently, but they often produce an unpleasantly bluish light. One solution is to buy an 85B (orange) warming filter and hold or tape it over the head of the flashlight. The combination of warmly lit foreground and deep blue night sky is often very pleasing. Your headlamp's red LEDs,

◄ FIGURE 7-1: The Milky Way and Soda Springs Basin from the Green River Overlook, Canyonlands National Park, Utah. October 13, 2017, 10:03 p.m. Canon 5D Mark III, Canon EF 16-35mm f/2.8L III USM at 20mm. Land: three focus positions, four frames per focus position, images stacked in Photoshop, noise reduced with Stack Mode>Median, focus-stacked images aligned and blended in Photoshop, 2 minutes, f/2.8, ISO 6400. Sky: four frames, camera mounted on iOptron SkyTracker Pro equatorial mount, images aligned and noise reduced in RegiStar, 2 minutes, f/2.8, ISO 1600. Two F&V HDV-Z96 flat-panel LED lights fitted with 85B warming filters provided the light on the foreground. As of this writing, artificial lights such as these are no longer allowed when photographing in Canyonlands National Park.

while helpful for preserving your night vision, create a very strong red cast that can completely overpower the natural color of the subject. In my view, the red setting on your headlamp is best reserved for special effects.

Both flashlights and headlamps tend to produce a strong hot spot in the middle of the beam. Keep the flashlight moving during the exposure to paint your foreground uniformly. It can take many attempts to light your subject evenly, if indeed that's your goal. Sometimes uneven lighting can produce interesting effects. If possible, move around during the exposure and light your subject from different angles. Standing in one place will create inky black shadows in areas the light can't reach. On occasion, I've used the double-exposure mode on my camera when light painting. I'll stand to the right of the camera and close to the subject for the first exposure, then stand to the left of the camera and farther away for the second, producing an effect like using key and fill lights in the studio.

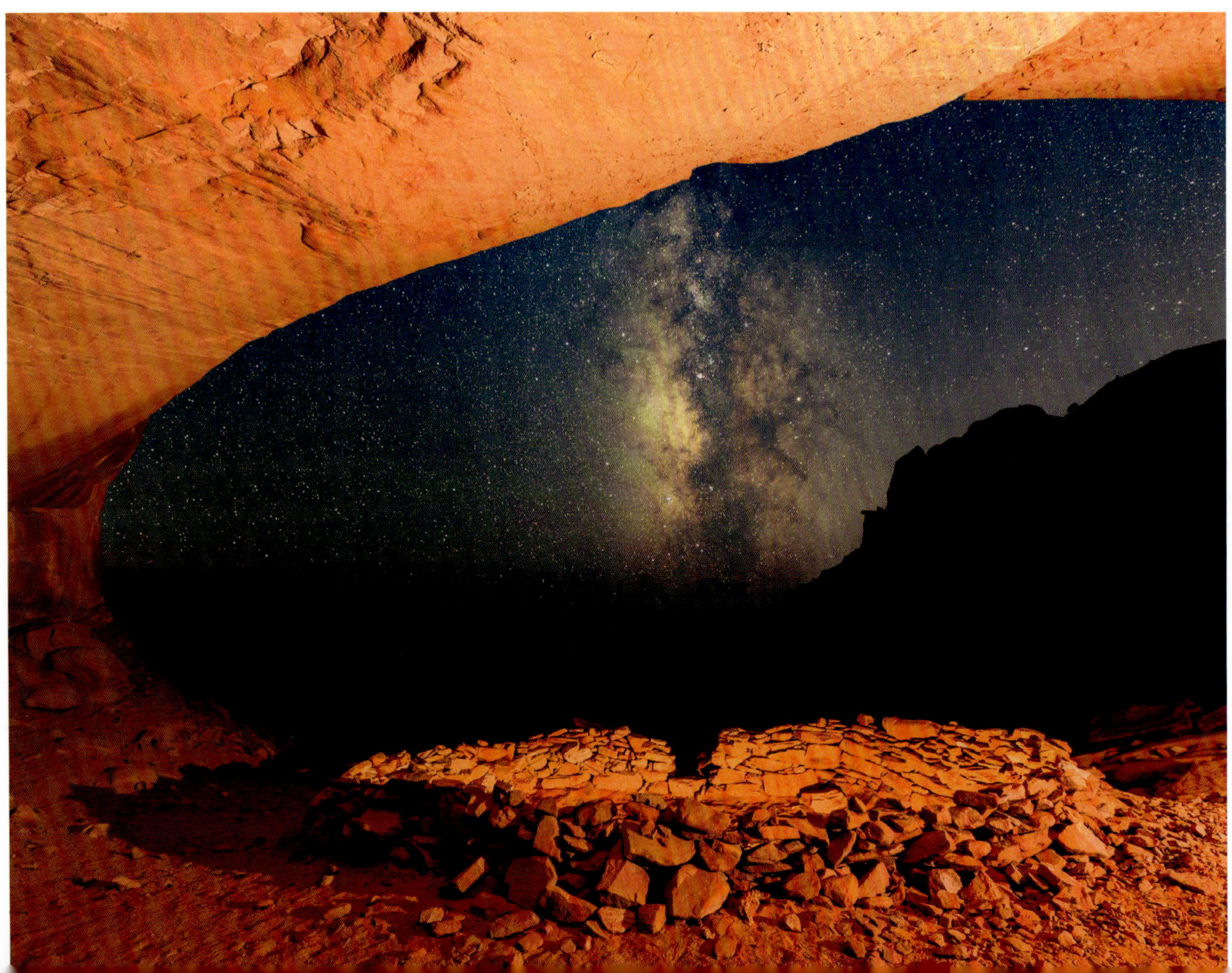

▾ FIGURE 7-2: False Kiva and the Milky Way, Island in the Sky district, Canyonlands National Park, Utah. October 10, 2017, 8:13 p.m. Canon 5D Mark III, Canon EF 16-35mm f/2.8L III USM at 16mm. Foreground land (lights on): two focus positions, four frames per focus position, images stacked in Photoshop, noise reduced with Stack Mode>Median, focus-stacked images aligned and blended in Photoshop, 2 minutes, f/2.8, ISO 6400. Background land (lights off): four frames, images stacked in Photoshop, noise reduced with Stack Mode>Median, 2 minutes, f/2.8, ISO 6400. Sky: four frames, camera mounted on iOptron SkyTracker Pro equatorial mount, images aligned and noise reduced in RegiStar, 2 minutes, f/2.8, ISO 1600. Two F&V HDV-Z96 flat-panel LED lights fitted with 85B warming filters provided the light on the foreground. I made this image when this site was open to the public and the use of artificial lighting when shooting landscape photos was allowed. As of this writing, this site can only be viewed from a distance and artificial lights such as these are no longer allowed when photographing in Canyonlands National Park.

Achieving the right exposure usually requires lots of trial and error, since you can't accurately meter the light from a flashlight that is moving constantly. You'll need to hold the shutter speed, f/stop, and ISO constant to maintain the correct exposure for the Milky Way or moonlit sky. Vary the exposure from the flashlight by changing the number of seconds you paint with the light. You may find that your flashlight is so bright it takes only a second or two to expose the foreground correctly. That makes it nearly impossible to light the subject evenly. In that situation, you may need to stop down the lens and/or reduce the ISO to give yourself more time to achieve even lighting. You'll then need to blend the properly lit land image with a correctly exposed sky image in Photoshop.

Flash units are point sources that create strong shadows both indoors and out. The light is particularly harsh outdoors because there are no light-colored ceilings or walls to bounce light into the shadows. The burst of light lasts only a fraction of a second, so you can't move around during the burst to soften the light like you can when using a flashlight. One advantage of flash units used in manual mode is that they produce a consistent amount of light with each burst. Firing the flash multiple times from different angles will soften the light by filling in the shadows. If you have a hand-held flash meter and can walk up to the subject, you can estimate how many pops of the flash you'll need based on the correct exposure for a single pop. Lacking such a meter, exposure once again becomes a matter of guess-and-check.

The best way to add light to your foreground is to use a small, flat-panel LED video light. The ones I own have 96 LEDs. They weigh about a pound and are roughly the size of my hand. A dial on the back controls brightness. My lights came with a diffusion panel and an 85B warming filter that attach with magnets. I can dim my lights to the point where the foreground exposure matches the correct exposure for the Milky Way, so I can capture all the detail I want in a single frame. On occasion I've even had to wrap the light in a white handkerchief to reduce the light still further. Best of all, the light output is constant and even, which makes it possible to shoot panoramas or to use focus-stacking techniques.

Whatever light source you use, try to move it away from the camera. Both flash units and video lights can be mounted on your camera's hot shoe, but the result is frontal lighting that makes the subject look flat, since it lacks the shadows our visual system needs to see depth. Positioning the light to the side, or, better yet, positioning two lights, one on each side of the subject at different distances, will create a much more three-dimensional look.

One final note: check with local land managers before using light-painting techniques. As I write this, some national parks have banned light-painting because it can disturb other visitors and disrupt the natural wake and sleep cycles of wildlife.

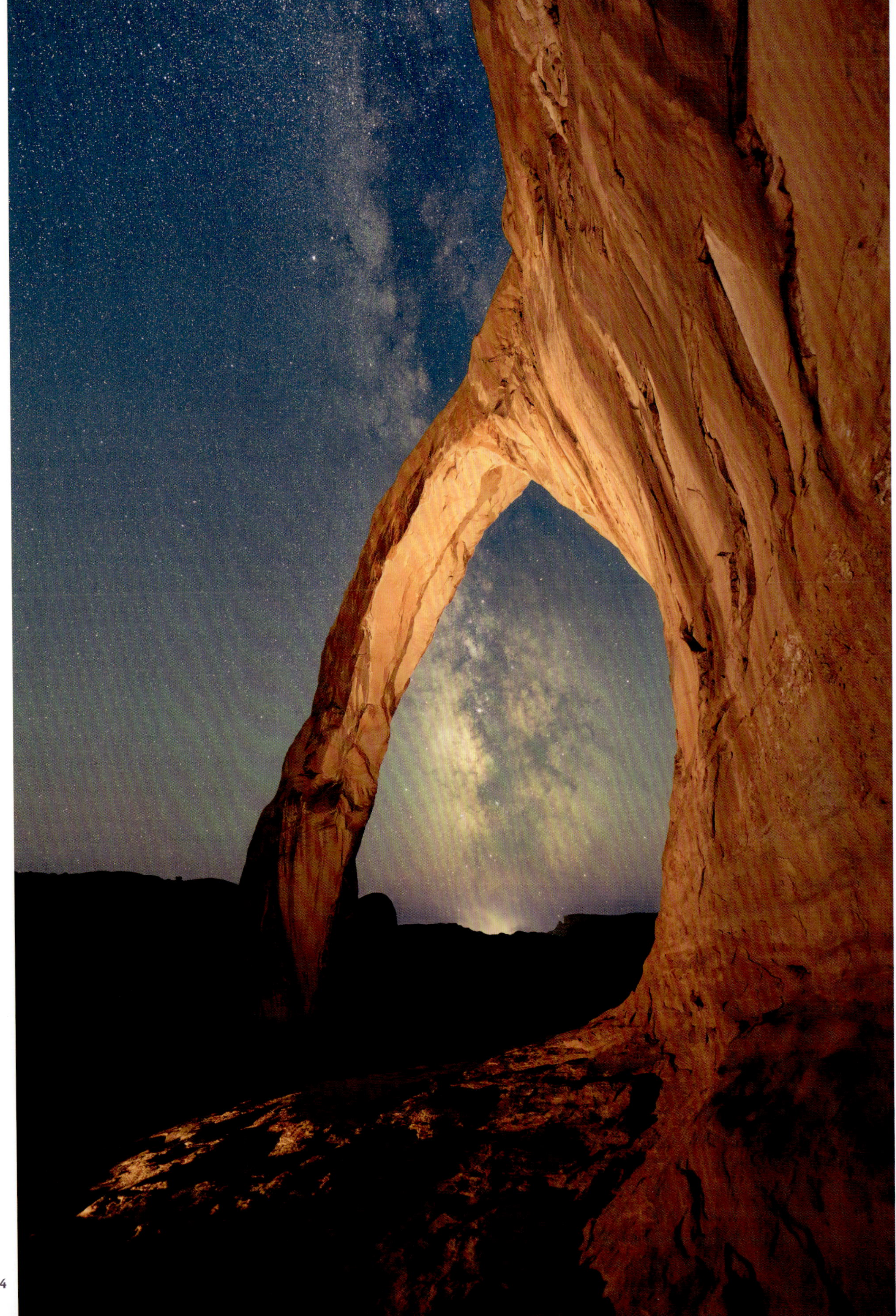

Focus Stacking at Night

Achieving full depth of field at night is a challenge because you'll normally be shooting wide open. One solution when shooting the land is to stop the lens down and do a single very long exposure. For example, the depth of field of a 16mm lens set to f/2.8 and focused at infinity is about 15 feet to infinity (circle of confusion set to .02mm). The correct exposure for the land with those settings would usually be about 2 minutes, f/2.8, ISO 6400. If, however, you stop the lens down to f/5.6 and focus at the hyperfocal distance of 7 feet 6 inches, your depth of field will extend from about 3 feet 10 inches to infinity. That depth of field will provide good sharpness with a wide variety of compositions. The catch is that your exposure time will quadruple to 8 minutes.

◄ FIGURE 7-3: The Milky Way and Corona Arch, near Moab, Utah. September 19, 2022, 9:16 p.m. Sony Alpha 7R IVa, Sony FE 14mm f/1.8 GM. Land: one camera position, 10 frames, images stacked in Photoshop, noise reduced with Stack Mode>Median, 15 seconds, f/1.8, ISO 3200. Sky: one camera position, one frame, camera mounted on iOptron SkyTracker Pro equatorial mount, 1 minute, f/1.8, ISO 1600. Two F&V HDV-Z96 flat-panel LED lights fitted with 85B warming filters provided the light on the foreground.

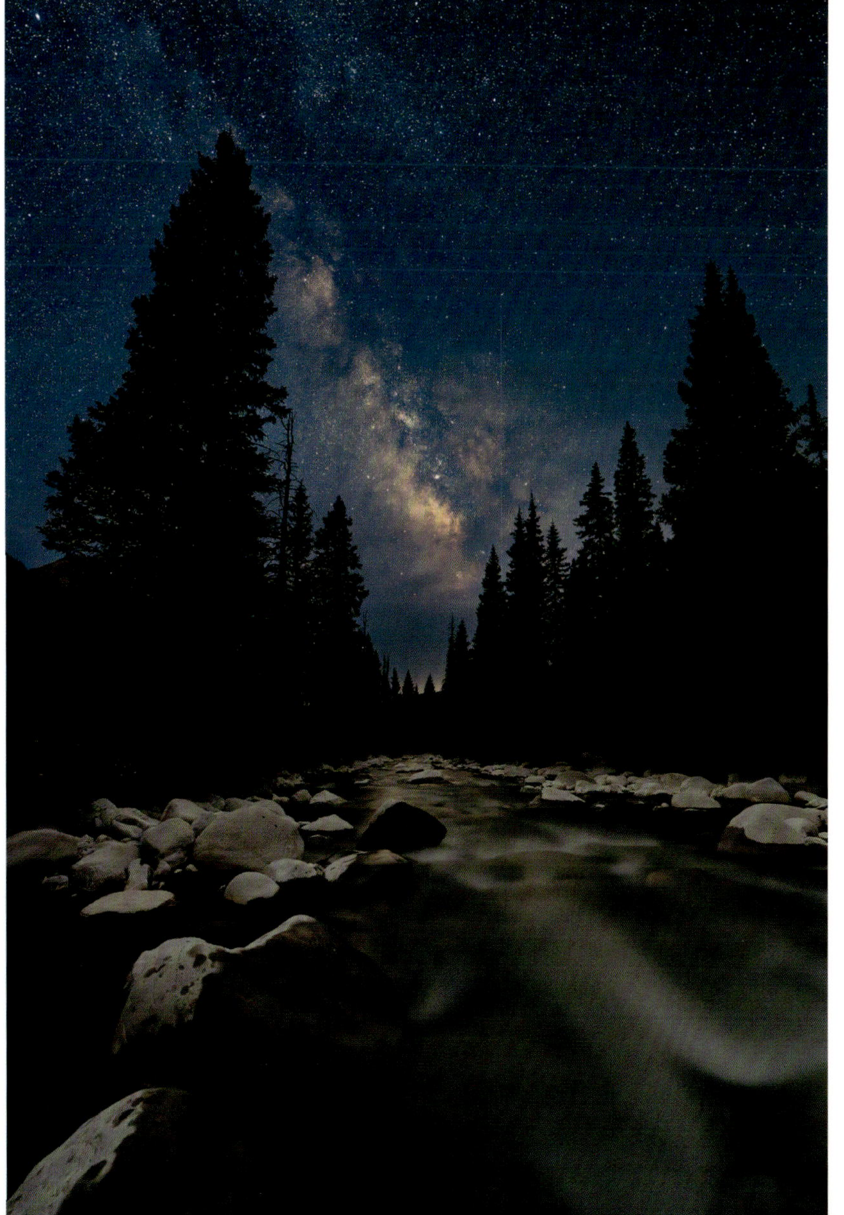

◄ FIGURE 7-4: Milky Way over Vallecito Creek, Weminuche Wilderness, Colorado. August 8, 2023, 10:23 p.m. Sony Alpha 7R IVa, Sony FE 14mm f/1.8 GM. Land: one camera position, four focus positions, one frame per focus position, noise reduced with Lightroom Denoise, focus-stacked images aligned and blended in Photoshop, 2 minutes, f/2.8, ISO 6400. Sky: one camera position, one frame, noise reduced with Lightroom Denoise, 10 seconds, f/1.8, ISO 6400.

Your camera may produce unacceptable levels of noise with such a long exposure. Such a long exposure can also be impractical if you are shooting in a place where car headlights or passersby occasionally light up your foreground, ruining your shot. It may be easier to get a clean 2-minute exposure than an 8-minute one. If an 8-minute exposure time is problematic, you may wish to try focus stacking.

The basic idea of focus stacking is simple. Place the camera on a solid tripod, compose the shot, focus at infinity, set exposure, white balance, and ISO manually, and shoot a frame. Focus a little bit closer and make another exposure. Repeat the process until you have focused on the closest part of the subject and made the final exposure. Be sure the sharp zone of each frame overlaps the sharp zones of the adjacent frames. Dump the frames into Photoshop or a specialized focus-stacking program, and let the software combine the sharp portions of each frame.

Focus stacking often works well when shooting close-ups with macro lenses and when shooting grand landscapes with wide-angle lenses rather than telephotos. Focus stacking also works better when the out-of-focus background is only a short distance beyond the point of focus. For example, it works well when shooting a field of flowers (assuming the wind is dead calm). The out-of-focus flower will only be a foot or two away from the focused flower, and therefore not too far out of focus, particularly if you're using a wide-angle lens. Focus stacking works poorly when shooting a weathered tree if the background is a mountain a mile away. The frame focused on the tree will have a blurred mountain background—no problem. The frame focused on the mountain will have a blurry tree in the foreground—a big problem because the blurry version of the tree is larger than the sharp version of the tree. That enlarged blurry tree blocks the camera's view of a part of the background. Neither frame contains sharp background in that region. Combine the two images, and you get a sharp tree against a mostly sharp background, with a thin halo of out-of-focus tree surrounding the sharp tree. The only solution is to go into Photoshop, select the sharp tree, invert the selection to protect the sharp tree, and clone the sharp background up against the selection boundary.

Focus stacking at night adds another wrinkle. Since you will probably be shooting wide-open, at f/2.8 or even wider, the depth of field in each frame will be shallow. That means you will need more frames than you would with a daylight shot taken at, say, f/16, to ensure that every part of the subject is sharp in at least one frame.

Focus stacking at night is easiest with ultra-wide-angle lenses such as a 16mm f/2.8 because you only need a few frames to create depth of field from three feet to infinity. It's much more difficult with very fast, moderate wide-angles, such as a 35mm f/1.4. For the 16mm lens at f/2.8, you can achieve

▶ FIGURE 7-5: Milky Way over Marlboro Point, near Dead Horse Point State Park, Utah. September 23, 2022, 10:15 p.m. Sony Alpha 7R IVa, Sony FE 14mm f/1.8 GM. Land: two focus positions, four frames per focus position, images stacked in Photoshop, noise reduced with Stack Mode>Median, focus-stacked images aligned and blended in Photoshop, 1 minute, f/1.8, ISO 6400. Sky: one camera position, four frames, images aligned and noise reduced in RegiStar, 15 seconds, f/1.8, ISO 6400.

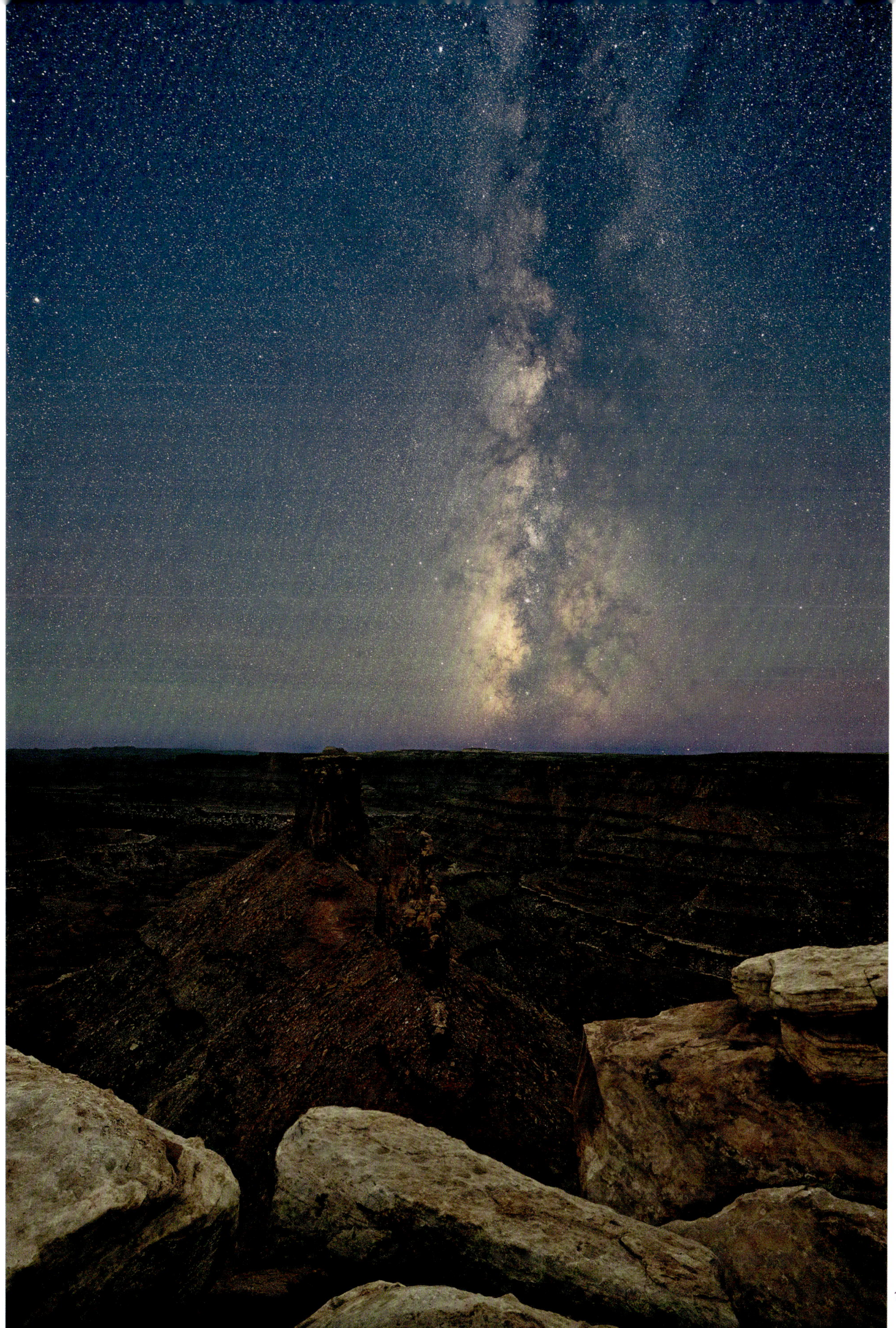

depth of field from 2 ft. 10 in. to infinity in just four frames if you focus the frames at infinity, 8 ft., 5 ft., and 3 ft. 6 in. With a 35mm lens at f/1.4 you would need 10 frames just to achieve depth of field from 8 ft. 5 in. to infinity. In addition, you would need to focus accurately, in the dark, at 75 ft., 40 ft., 28 ft., etc. If you need depth of field at night, try to find a composition that works with an ultra-wide-angle lens. Table 7-1 shows the various distances at which you must focus and the minimum number of frames you must shoot to ensure that the sharp zone of each frame overlaps the sharp zones of the adjacent frames.

	Focus distance for 1st frame	Focus distance for 2nd frame	Focus distance for 3rd frame	Focus distance for 4th frame	Focus distance for 5th frame
14mm lens at f/1.8	Infinity (18' to infinity)	10' (6'5" to 22'4")	5' (3'11" to 6'11")	3'6" (2'11" to 4'4")	2' (2'2" to 2'11")
16mm lens at f/2.8	Infinity (15' to infinity)	8' (5'3" to 17'3")	5' (3'9" to 7'6")	3'6" (2'10" to 4'7")	2'6" (2'2" to 3')
20mm lens at f/2.8	Infinity (23' to infinity)	12' (7'11 to 24'9")	6' (4'9" to 8'1")	4' (3'5" to 4'9")	3' (2'7" to 3'5")
24mm lens at f/2.8	Infinity (33' to infinity)	17' (11'3" to 34'5")	9' (7'1" to 12'3")	6' (5'1" to 7'4")	5' (4'4" to 5'10")
28mm lens at f/2.8	Infinity (45' to infinity)	23' (15'4" to 46'4")	12' (9'6" to 16'3")	8' (6'10" to 9'8")	6' (5'4" to 6'11")
35mm lens at f/2.8	Infinity (71' to infinity)	36' (24' to 73')	20' (15' to 28')	14' (12' to 17')	11' (9'6" to 13')
35mm lens at f/1.4	Infinity (142' to infinity)	75' (49' to 158')	40' (31' to 55')	28' (23' to 34')	20' (17' to 23')
35mm lens at f/1.4 continued	**6th frame** 16' (14' to 18')	**7th frame** 13' (11'11" to 14'4")	**8th frame** 11' (10'2" to 11'10")	**9th frame** 10' (9'4" to 10'8")	**10th frame** 9' (8'5" to 9'7")

If you don't mind shooting a few extra frames and you're using an ultra-wide-angle lens, you actually don't have to focus at an exact distance for the frames focused closer than infinity. Use manual focus, and rotate the focus ring a very small amount between frames. With a 16mm lens at f/2.8, you can shoot a half-dozen frames as you incrementally change your focus point from infinity to three feet and be confident you've covered the full range.

Regardless of which lens you use, the time required to make all those long exposures adds up, and the stars will move enough during the series of exposures that the images won't align properly without some extra effort. Here's my procedure for focus stacking at night using Auto-Align Layers and Auto-Blend Layers in Photoshop.

1. Shoot your focus-stacked series in the field. I always shoot the frame focused at infinity first. Use a daylight white balance. Be sure to use manual exposure. Turn off auto-ISO. The only parameter that should change between frames is the focused distance.

2. In Lightroom, select all the images, then open one of the images in the Develop module. Be sure Auto Sync is chosen so that changes applied to one image will automatically be applied to all.

3. See chapter 6 for detailed instructions on editing the series of images in Lightroom.

4. In Lightroom, in the Library module, with all the images still selected, right-click and choose Edit In>Open as Layers in Photoshop.

5. If the first image you shot was the one focused at infinity, as I recommend, and you've sorted your Library view in Lightroom by file name or capture time, that image should be at the top of the layer stack. If it's not, drag it there.

6. Turn off the eye icon for the top layer. Target the first layer below the top layer. Choose the Quick Selection tool as shown in figure 7-6 and drag the tool across the sky to select it. You don't need to be precise because you still have a completely intact layer (the one focused at infinity) that will provide the pixels to fill in any imperfections in the selection. Press the Delete key to delete the sky. Deselect and turn off the eye icon for the active layer. (In most situations I'd recommend adding a layer mask to temporarily hide the sky rather than deleting it. Using a layer mask to hide the sky gives you the option to return to the image to modify the mask at a later date. As you'll soon see, however, in this situation deleting the sky permanently simplifies the rest of the procedure. Should you ever need that sky for any reason, you can always retrieve it from the original RAW file.)

7. Target the layer below, select the sky, delete it, deselect, and turn off that layer's eye icon. You must select the sky each time because it will occupy a slightly different part of the frame as you focus closer for each image.

8. Continue down the layer stack until you have deleted the sky from all layers but the top layer. Re-enable the eye icons on all the hidden layers (right-click the eye icon for the active layer and choose Show/Hide all other layers). The layer stack should now look like figure 7-7.

▼ FIGURE 7-6: A portion of the toolbar with the Quick Selection tool circled.

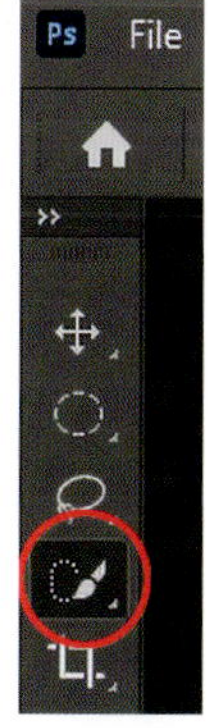

▼ FIGURE 7-7: The layer stack after deleting the sky from all images except the top one, the one focused at infinity.

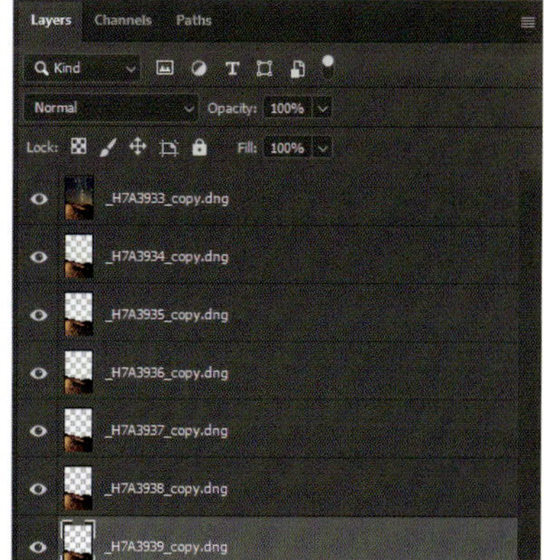

9. Select all the layers by clicking the top layer, then Shift-clicking the bottom layer. Choose Edit>Auto-Align Layers. In the dialog box that opens, under Projection, choose Auto, as shown in figure 7-8. You've already removed vignetting and corrected for geometric distortion in Lightroom, so leave both boxes under Lens Correction unchecked. Click OK. Using Auto-Align Layers is necessary even though you shot your images on a tripod because the size of the subject in each frame will vary with the focused distance. When focused on infinity, the image of the main subject may actually be smaller or larger than when you focused on the closest part.

▶ FIGURE 7-8: The Auto-Align Layers dialog box showing the correct settings.

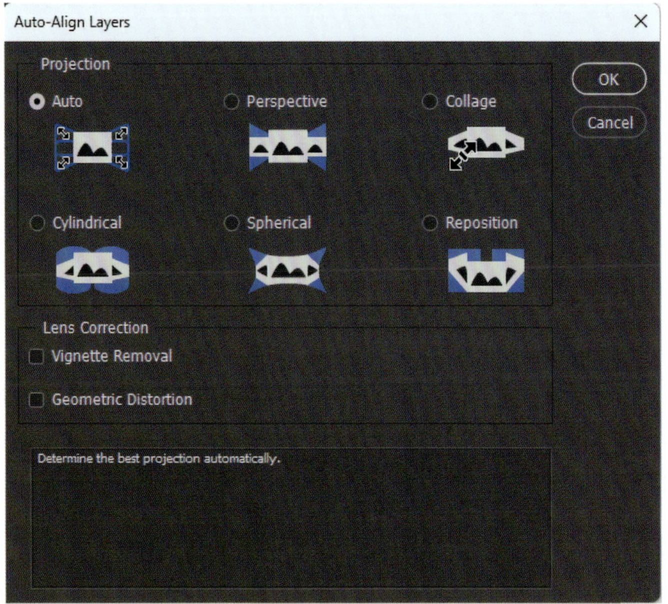

▶ FIGURE 7-9: The Auto-Blend Layers dialog box showing the correct settings.

10. With all the layers still selected, choose Edit>Auto-Blend Layers. In the dialog box that opens, under Blend Method, choose Stack Images and check Seamless Tones and Colors, as shown in figure 7-9. I prefer to leave Content Aware Fill Transparent Areas unchecked, choosing

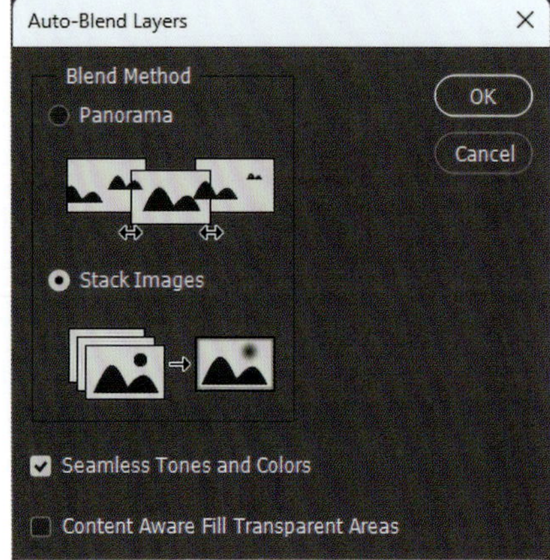

instead to simply crop away the transparent areas as well as any areas near the edges where the blending didn't work perfectly.

11. Refer to chapter 6 for detailed instructions on the final steps needed to perfect the image. These involve adding contrast to the sky to make the Milky Way stand out and enhancing local contrast using either Unsharp Mask or the High Pass filter with the Soft Light blend mode. Shifting the sky color blue (step 3) will also shift the land color toward blue. There are a number of ways to restore the original color to the land, if desired. One way is to select the land with Photoshop's Quick Selection tool, then add a Photo Filter adjustment layer (figure 7-10). In the Photo Filter Properties panel, check the radio button labeled Filter, then choose Warming Filter (85) from the drop-down menu. Check Preserve Luminosity and adjust the density to taste. Another way is to bring the completed image back into Lightroom and use the Brush in the Masking panel to paint a Temp and Tint color correction onto the land. Figure 7-11 shows the completed image after restoring the original warm tone to the foreground.

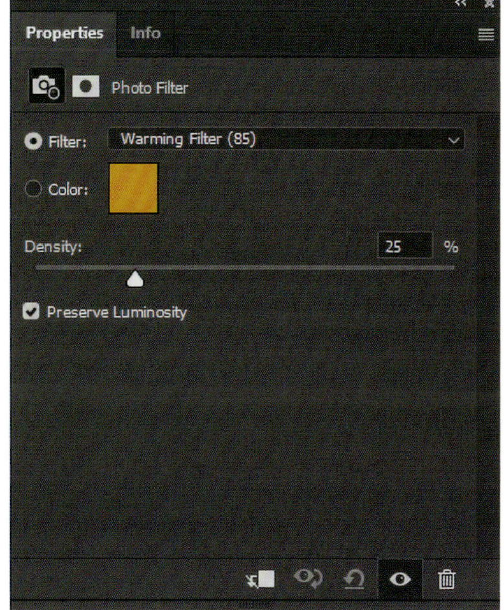
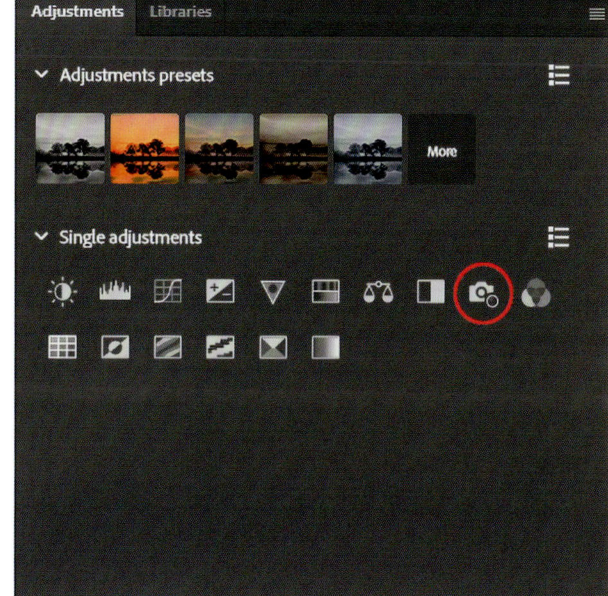

▾ FIGURE 7-10: The Adjustments panel with the Photo Filter icon circled, along with the Properties panel showing the Photo Filter settings required to restore a warm tint to the land.

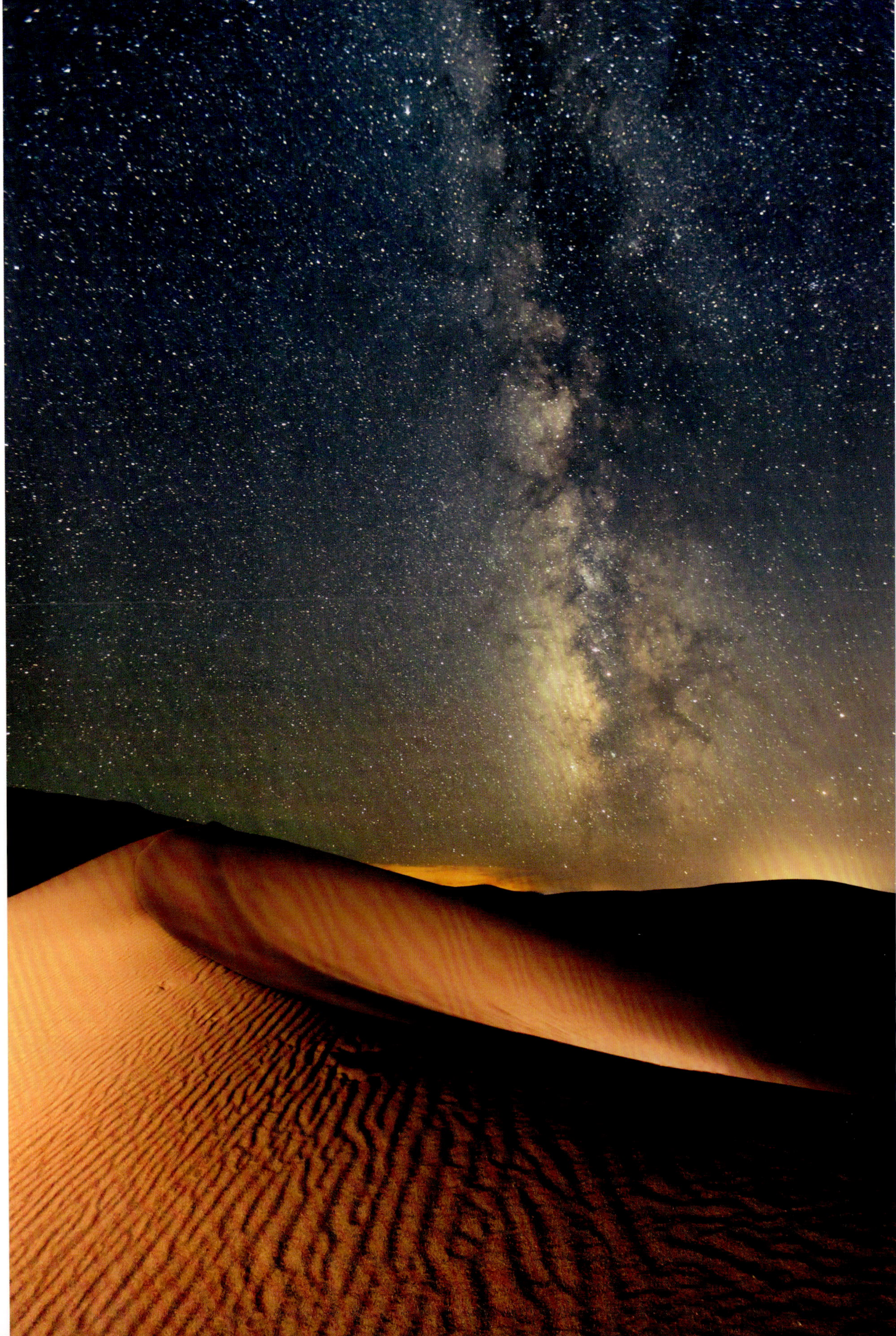

Reducing Noise with Stack Mode>Median

Noise is the great enemy of night photographers. AI-powered noise reduction utilities are often an improvement over the manual noise-reduction sliders in the Detail panel in Lightroom. Nonetheless, the result can still be a compromise. Noise-reduction software attempts to suppress the high-frequency variation in brightness and color that is unwanted noise while preserving the high-frequency variation in brightness and color that is desirable texture and detail. Inevitably, the more you reduce noise, the more you lose fine detail.

Instead of attempting to smooth out noise, delete it using Photoshop's Stack Mode>Median. The basic idea is to shoot a series of identical frames and stack them as layers in a Photoshop file. Photoshop can then drill down through the layer stack, comparing the value of each pixel to the value of all the other pixels directly above and below it. Photoshop then chooses the median value—the number in the middle of the range—and displays it.

Here's a simplified example. Let's say you shoot five identical images. As Photoshop drills down through the layer stack at a particular point in the scene, it finds five pixels. After averaging the RGB values of each pixel and arranging them in ascending order, the results are 95, 98, 100, 103, 107. The pixel with an average RGB value of 100 shows the correct brightness and color. The other pixels exhibit noise—a random and undesirable variation from the true value you want to capture. The median value of that set of five numbers is 100, so that is the value Photoshop displays. Instead of smoothing out the noise, you've removed it.

In the real world, of course, the effect isn't quite that dramatic. In my testing, I've found that shooting four frames at ISO 6400, then reducing noise with this method, produced an image that looks like it was shot at ISO 1600. Shooting 10 identical frames at ISO 6400 then stacking them to reduce noise produced an image that looked like it was shot at ISO 800 or even lower. Results from your camera may be different, of course.

It's easiest to apply this technique to the land, rather than the sky, since the land doesn't move between frames. Fortunately, the land portion of a night image is usually the part that shows the most noise. Noise is always worse in the deep shadows, and the land will always be darker than the sky. In addition, noise-reduction software does a better job with the sky than it does with the land. Usually you can find a setting that will smooth the sky while also preserving faint stars. Applying heavy noise reduction to the land, on the other hand, can easily smooth out textures to the point that the land looks like injection-molded plastic.

You can also shoot multiple frames using the correct exposure for the sky, but the stars will move enough between frames that they won't align when you stack the images in a layered Photoshop file. Photoshop's Auto-

◄ FIGURE 7-11: The Milky Way over dunes at Great Sand Dunes National Park, Colorado. September 25, 2016, 8:51 p.m. Canon 5D Mark III, Canon EF 16-35mm f/2.8L II USM at 16mm. Seven focus positions, focus-stacked images aligned and blended in Photoshop, 30 seconds, f/2.8, ISO 6400. Two F&V HDV-Z96 flat-panel LED lights fitted with 85B warming filters provided the light on the foreground.

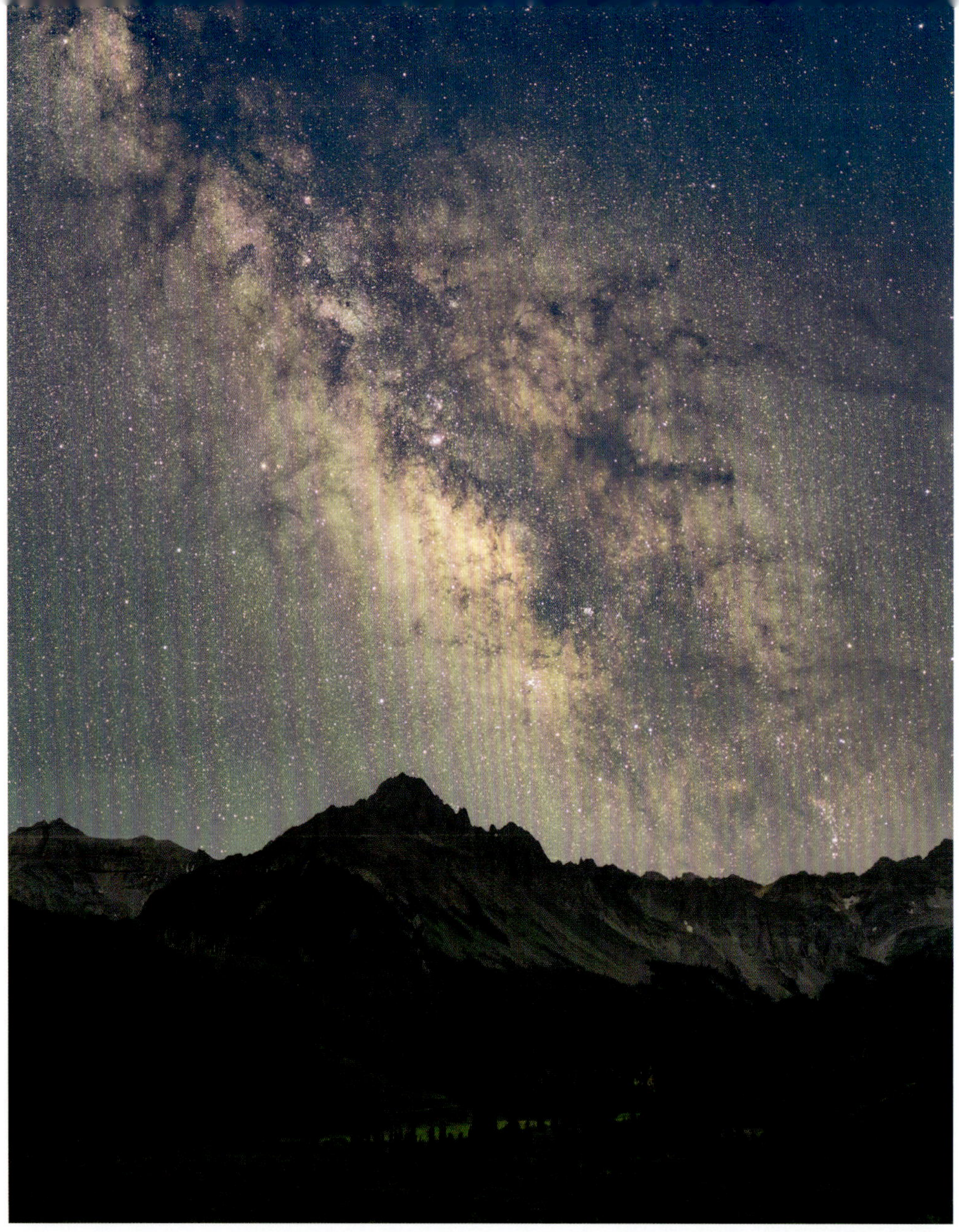

Align Layers utility is designed to identify features in the land portion of the frame and make them align. It won't work consistently to align stars. Registering the stars requires specialized astronomical software. As I write this, the best programs I've found for this purpose are RegiStar from Auriga Software (PC only), Sequator (also PC only), and Starry Landscape Stacker (Mac only). There may be other programs available by the time you read this. Once the stars are aligned, you can use the stacking utilities built into these programs to reduce noise. You'll then need to bring the good-sky and good-land images into Photoshop and blend them.

With recent cameras, you may be able to get good results by shooting 10 or 20 frames of the sky using the exposure recommended by PhotoPills' Spot

Stars calculator (which will give you pinpoint stars) even though the images will be underexposed as they come from the camera. For example, the correct exposure straight out of the camera for the Milky Way with a 14mm f/1.8 lens is about 15 seconds, f/1.8, ISO 6400. Very short star trails will be visible in the image when viewed at 100 percent. PhotoPills recommends 6 seconds for pinpoint stars. If you expose 20 frames for the sky at 6 seconds, f/1.8, ISO 6400, each frame will be about 1.3 stops underexposed. With my Sony Alpha 7R IVa I can increase the exposure for the RAW files by 1.3 stops in Lightroom, apply a Tone Curve preset to shift the sky color to blue, export the images at TIFFs, stack them in RegiStar, and get an image with very low noise and pinpoint stars. The land will be very blurry, which can be a problem if the skyline

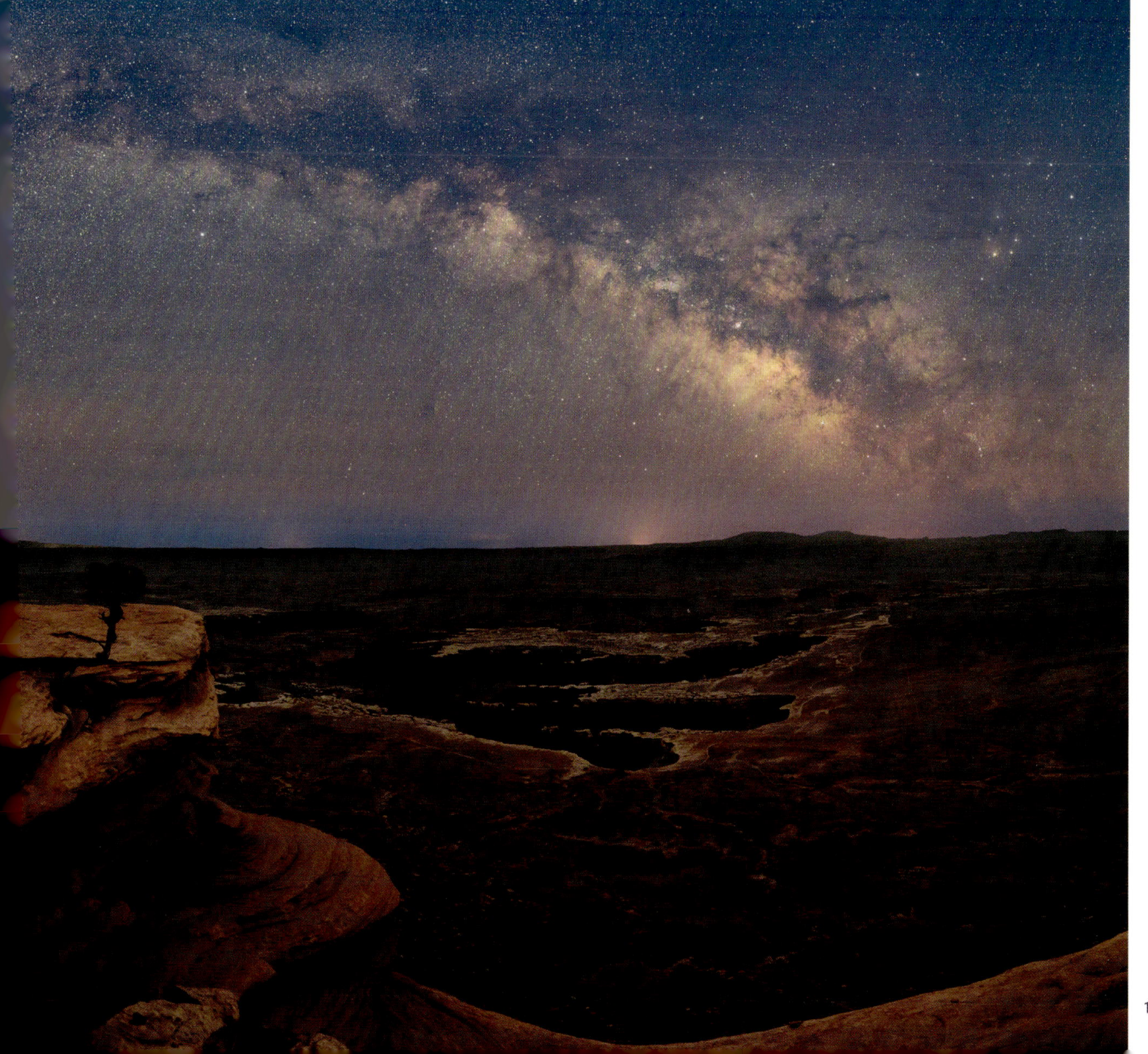

▾ Figure 7-13: The Milky Way over Monument Basin from Grand View Point, Island in the Sky district, Canyonlands National Park, Utah. April 30, 2022, 2:24 a.m. Sony Alpha 7R IVa, Sony FE 14mm f/1.8 GM. Land: 2 camera positions, five frames per camera position, images stacked in Photoshop, noise reduced with Stack Mode>Median, one minute, f/1.8, ISO 6400. Sky: two camera positions, one frame per camera position, camera mounted on iOptron SkyTracker Pro equatorial mount, two minutes, f/1.8, ISO 800.

is complex. With a simple skyline, however, compositing the good-sky and good-land images is usually straightforward, giving you an excellent result without spending all day working in Photoshop.

Here, in detail, is the procedure for using Stack Mode>Median to reduce noise in the land. Start by shooting at least four, and preferably more, identical frames using the correct land exposure. The more frames you shoot, the more you'll be able to reduce the noise. Once you've collected the necessary frames, download them to Lightroom, select all of them, and open one in the Develop module. Be sure Auto Sync is enabled so that a change applied to one will be applied to all, then edit the good-land images to taste. Don't use Lightroom's AI-based Denoise utility, and don't apply any luminance noise reduction at this stage. Experiment with turning off color noise reduction as well, then applying it again once you've created the finished image. You may find this helps preserve additional detail. With all the images still selected, right-click one of them and choose Edit In>Open as Layers in Photoshop. In Photoshop, select all the layers by clicking the top layer and Shift-clicking the bottom layer. Right-click one of the layers and choose Convert to Smart Object. Then choose Layer>Smart Objects>Stack Mode>Median. Choose Layer>Flatten Image and you're done. As a side-benefit, stacking images will remove jet streaks and satellite trails automatically, no cloning or spot-healing required.

You can also use Stack Mode>Median to reduce noise in panoramas. Let's say you're shooting the full Milky Way arch with a 35mm f/1.4 lens. Such images often require shooting two rows with as many as nine images in each row to cover a field of view that can be 180 degrees wide. To use Stack Mode>Median, you'll need to shoot a complete sequence of sky images, then a complete sequence of land images to avoid having the stars move so much that the component frames won't stitch together. In most situations, you'll want to shoot the sky first so you can capture the Milky Way when it is in the ideal position in the sky. Shooting the land takes a lot of time, and you don't want to be in the middle of shooting the land when the Milky Way reaches the perfect position.

Choose the pitch of the bottom row of your sky images so that land takes up about one-quarter of the frame. Don't worry about including everything you want in the foreground because you're only going to use the sky portion of those images. Shoot four frames at each camera position. An exposure of 10 seconds, f/1.4, ISO 6400 is usually about right with a 35mm f/1.4 lens. Then shoot the land. Again, shoot four frames per camera position. An exposure of 40 seconds, f/1.4, ISO 6400 is a good starting point. Use the same pan angle (azimuth) that you used for the sky images as a starting point for the land images but choose the pitch of the bottom row to include all the foreground

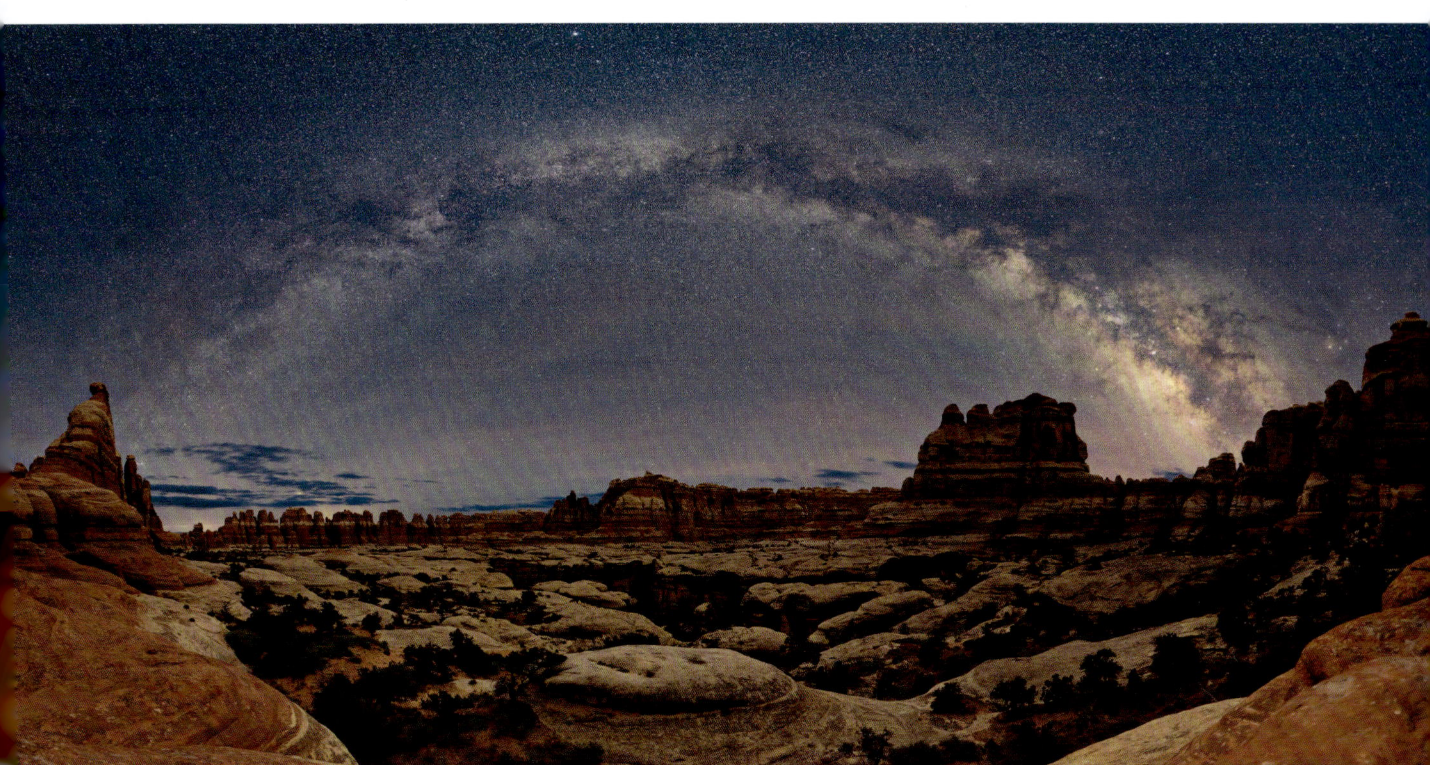

you want. When you return home, use RegiStar, Sequator, or Starry Landscape Stacker to align and reduce noise in each group of sky images, then stitch the merged images together in Lightroom. Use Stack Mode>Median in Photoshop to reduce noise in each group of land images, then stitch the merged land images together. Finally, combine the sky panorama with the land panorama in Photoshop.

Shooting panoramas with this approach obviously takes a lot of work. The result, however, is a high-resolution, low-noise image that can be used to make big prints. For example, I shot a panorama of the Milky Way over Elephant Canyon in Canyonlands National Park that will print seven feet wide at 240 pixels per inch—a printing resolution that provides superb quality (figure 7-14).

▲ Figure 7-14: Panorama of the Milky Way over Elephant Canyon, Needles District, Canyonlands National Park, Utah. April 26, 2017, 3:29 a.m. Canon 5D Mark III, Canon EF 35mm f/1.4L II USM. Land: two rows, nine camera positions per row, four frames per camera position, images stacked in Photoshop, noise reduced with Stack Mode>Median, 40 seconds, f/1.4, ISO 6400. Sky: two rows, nine camera positions per row, four frames per camera position, images aligned and noise reduced in RegiStar, 10 seconds, f/1.4, ISO 6400.

Using Star-Tracking Camera Mounts

The Earth's rotation means the stars appear to be in constant motion. Near the celestial equator, the imaginary line in the sky that represents the projection of Earth's equator onto the celestial sphere, the stars move one degree every four minutes. That imposes severe limits on how long the shutter on a stationary camera can remain open before the stars turn into streaks.

The obvious solution is to move the camera to counteract the apparent motion of the stars. To do this, one axis of such a star-tracking mount has to be aligned with Earth's axis of rotation. Before the invention of cameras capable of recording the night sky as we see it, star-tracking mounts, called equatorial mounts, were mostly big, heavy, and expensive devices designed to support a bulky telescope. You could certainly use them for shooting wide-field images of the landscape at night, but few photographers bothered.

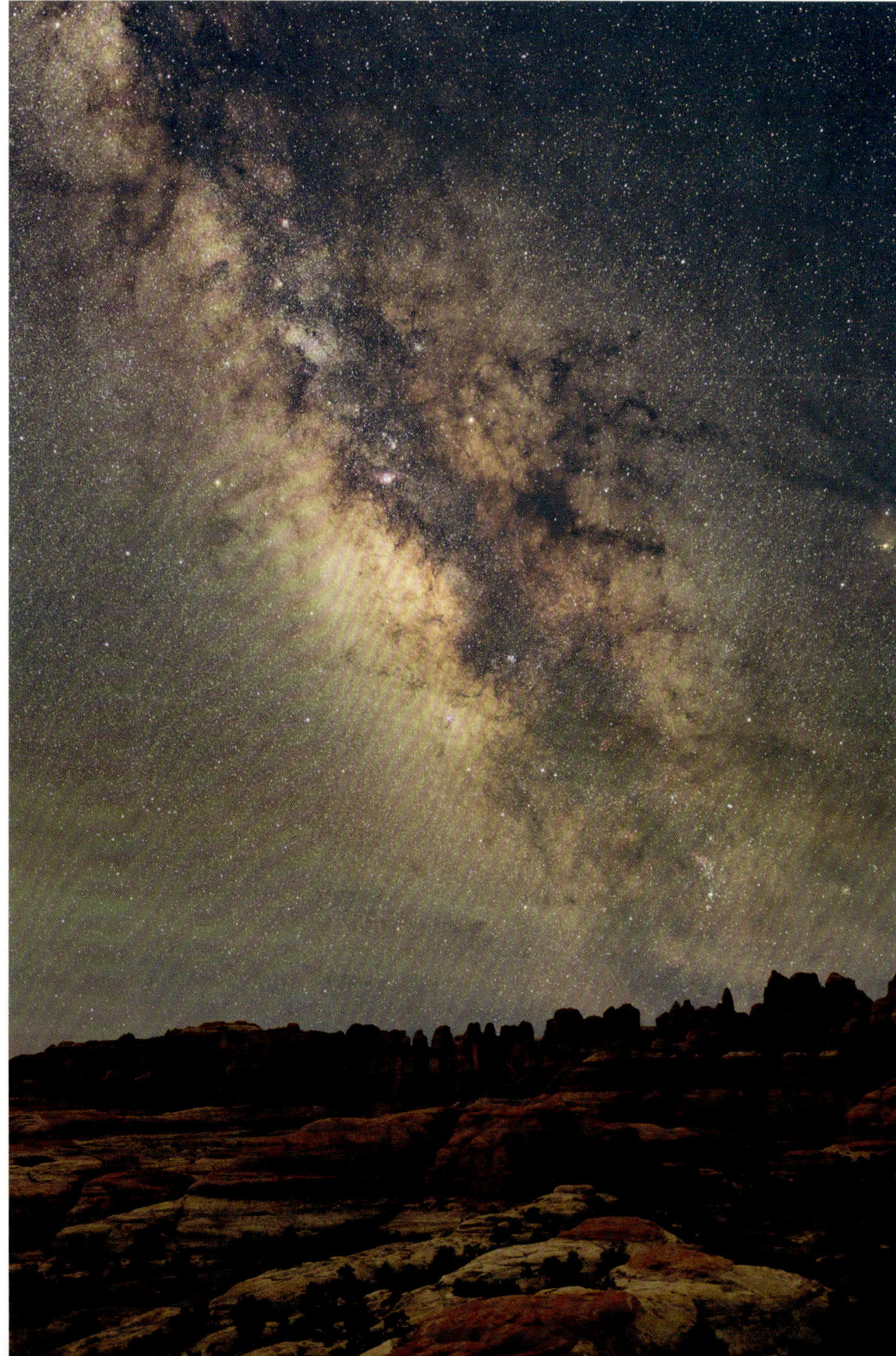

▸ FIGURE 7-15: Milky Way over towers above Elephant Canyon, Needles District, Canyonlands National Park, Utah. April 28, 2017, 4:43 a.m. Canon 5D Mark III, Canon EF 35mm f/1.4L II USM. Land: four frames, images stacked in Photoshop, noise reduced with Stack Mode>Median, 40 seconds, f/1.4, ISO 6400. Sky: four frames, camera mounted on iOptron SkyTracker Pro equatorial mount, images aligned and noise reduced in RegiStar, 40 seconds, f/1.4, ISO 1600.

The explosion of interest in landscape photography at night has led manufacturers to produce much smaller, lighter, and less expensive equatorial mounts designed specifically for supporting a DSLR or mirrorless camera with a wide-angle lens. Using one lets you create truly pinpoint stars. It also lets you use lower ISOs, which means less noise. Using my iOptron SkyTracker Pro and a 35mm f/1.4 lens, I can photograph the Milky Way using an exposure of 40 seconds, f/1.4, ISO 1600. That's two stops lower in ISO value than my

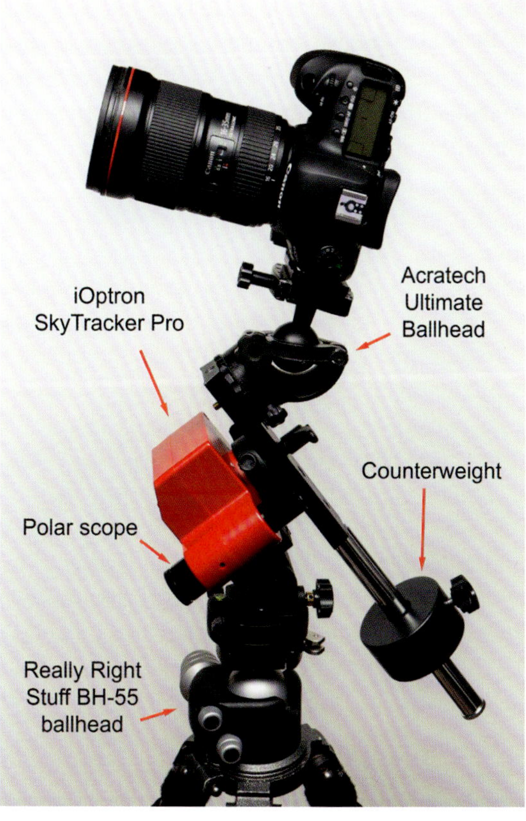

◂ Figure 7-16: A Canon EOS 5D Mark IV and Canon EF 16-35mm f/2.8L III USM lens mounted on an Acratech Ultimate Ballhead, which in turn is mounted on an iOptron SkyTracker Pro equatorial mount atop a Really Right Stuff BH-55 ballhead.

normal Milky Way exposure with that lens of 10 seconds, f/1.4, ISO 6400. Already the image is much cleaner. If I shoot four frames at 40 seconds, f/1.4, ISO 1600, then combine them and reduce noise using RegiStar, I can create an image that looks like it was shot at ISO 400. That allows me to make big prints that exhibit superb quality.

Today's lightweight equatorial mounts are smaller than those of yore, but they're still not light. You'll need a second tripod head, mounted to the equatorial mount, to support your camera. Depending on the weight of your camera and lens and the design of your tracker, you may need a counterweight kit as well. You need a very solid tripod to support that kind of weight. This is not a setup you're going to carry far from the road.

To track the stars accurately, the equatorial mount must be aligned with Earth's axis of rotation. Polaris, the North Star, is almost exactly aligned with that axis. Your first task is to identify Polaris. Use a compass, corrected for magnetic declination, to determine which direction is north. The altitude of Polaris is always equal to your latitude, which you can get from a topographic map (easiest), GPS receiver, Photo Ephemeris Web, or some hiking-oriented phone apps such as Gaia GPS. Or you can use the Big Dipper, an *asterism* (well-known group of stars) to guide you to Polaris, as shown in figure 7-17. You can also use Cassiopeia, as shown in figure 7-18.

Orient the mount by looking through the small spotting scope that comes with most trackers and adjusting the azimuth and altitude of the mount so that the scope points at Polaris. That gets you close to the correct alignment, but because Polaris is about two-thirds of a degree away from perfect alignment with Earth's axis, a correction is required if you want the best possible accuracy. Polar scopes often have a reticle (in this case, a series of concentric circles inscribed in the viewfinder). By consulting a phone app or table, you can determine where on the reticle you need to place Polaris for best accuracy. For example, when using my iOptron polar scope between 2 a.m. and 3 a.m. on April 1st, I place Polaris at the 12 o'clock position on the middle of the three inner circles in the reticle.

Achieving precise polar alignment takes time. Fortunately, perfect alignment is not essential when using a wide-angle lens. Roger Clark, the astronomer, has calculated that simply centering Polaris in the polar scope should allow one-minute exposures with a 50mm lens and two-minute exposures with a 24mm lens before the stars begin to blur.

The other tricky part of using an equatorial mount is finding the correct position on the counterweight shaft for the counterweight (if one is required). That position will vary depending on the weight of your camera

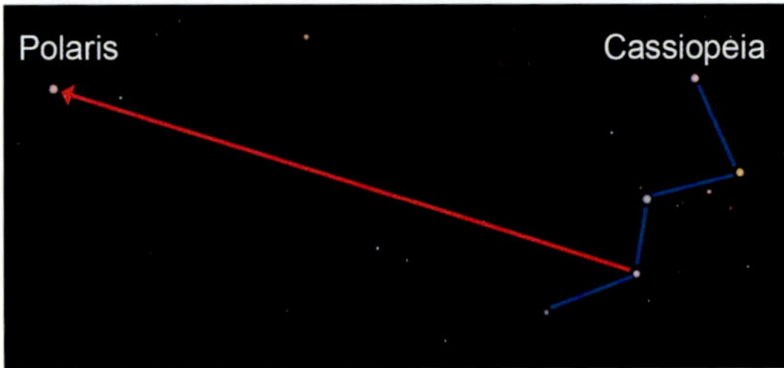

▲ FIGURE 7-18: A line drawn at 90 degrees to a line connecting the appropriate two stars of Cassiopeia leads to Polaris. The orientation of Cassiopeia in the sky is shown as of 10 p.m. on September 1st as seen from Boulder, Colorado, latitude 40 degrees N.

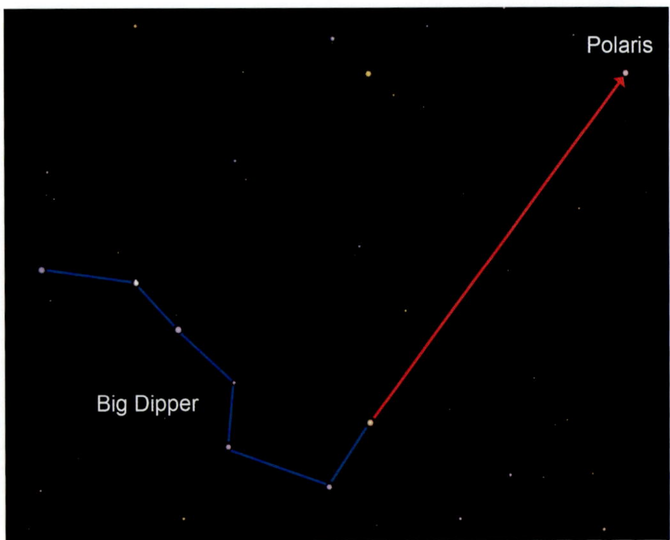

▲ FIGURE 7-17: The two stars that form the lip of the ladle in the Big Dipper point to Polaris. The orientation of the Big Dipper in the sky is shown as of 10 p.m. on September 1st as seen from Boulder, Colorado, latitude 40 degrees N.

and lens and the direction you point the camera. Position the counterweight incorrectly, and the tracker's motor can stall, ruining your shot. Be sure to examine a test frame closely to double-check that the tracker is indeed tracking accurately on the stars.

One good use of an equatorial mount, in my view, is for compositions with close-in foregrounds that require the use of an ultra-wide-angle lens to achieve adequate depth of field. Remember that a 16mm f/2.8 lens, focused at infinity and shot wide open, offers depth of field from 15 feet to infinity. A 35mm f/1.4 lens, focused at infinity and shot wide open, only offers depth of field from 142 feet to infinity. As I discussed in chapter 2, the area of the aperture for a 16mm f/2.8 lens shot wide open is only $\frac{1}{19}$th the area of the aperture of a 35mm f/1.4 lens shot wide open. The best way to compensate for that paltry light-gathering power is to use a longer exposure. Keeping stars round when using a longer exposure requires a tracking mount.

What about compositions that don't require extensive depth of field? If the composition fits within the field of view of a 35mm lens, I reach for my 35mm f/1.4 because of its superb light-gathering capability, then mount the camera on an equatorial mount. What if the composition requires a wider angle of view, one that calls for shooting a panorama if I use my 35mm lens?

My solution today is to use an Acratech panoramic head mounted atop a V-Mount from Move Shoot Move (figure 7-19). This hardware is relatively light and compact, and its design positions the weight of panorama head, camera, and lens directly over the rotating spindle of the tracker. That makes a counterweight unnecessary, at least with relatively light mirrorless equipment such as my Sony Alpha 7R IVa and Sony 35mm f/1.4 lens. Leveling the upper half of the V-plate levels the base of rotation of the panorama head, making it possible to shoot single- and multi-row panoramas with precision.

The final drawback to using an equatorial mount is that it forces you to shoot the sky and land separately. The camera is moving during the sky exposure, so by definition the land will be blurred. You'll have to shoot the scene a second time with the equatorial mount turned off to create a sharp land image. Combining the two images requires using the procedure for making a perfect selection of the sky described in chapter 6. If you have complex shapes projecting into the sky, compositing the two images will be laborious.

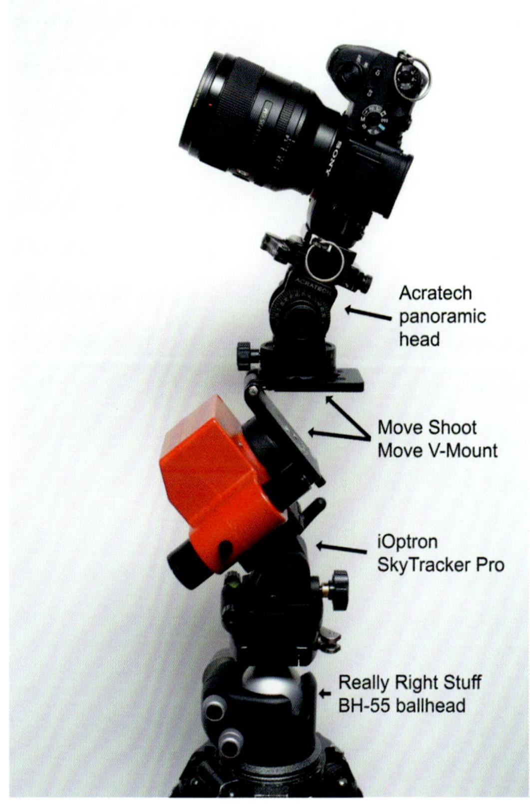

▲ FIGURE 7-19: Sony Alpha 7R IVa and Sony 35mm f/1.4 mounted on an Acratech Panoramic Head attached to a Move Shoot Move V-Mount, which is mounted in turn on an iOptron SkyTracker Pro equatorial mount atop a Really Right Stuff BH-55 ballhead. This setup enables me to shoot Milky Way panoramas while using a star-tracker. Re-leveling the upper arm of the Move Shoot Move V-Mount after each tracked shot keeps the base of the Acratech Panoramic Head level. That, in turn, lets me move the camera to the next position in the panorama sequence without disturbing the iOptron Sky-Tracker Pro's polar alignment.

The reward for all this extra expense, weight in your camera bag, setup time in the field, and time spent on the computer is beautiful, noise-free photographs of landscapes at night with pinpoint stars. Combine an equatorial mount with the focus-stacking and Stack Mode>Median techniques described elsewhere in this chapter, throw in a little light painting if desired, and you can make the most spectacular night landscapes achievable with today's digital cameras.

▸ FIGURE 7-20: Milky Way panorama over the Maze and the South Fork of Horse Canyon from Brimhall Point, Maze District, Canyonlands National Park, Utah. April 17, 2023, 2:53 a.m. Sony Alpha 7R IVa, Sony FE 14mm f/1.8 GM. Land: five camera positions, four frames per camera position, images stacked in Photoshop, noise reduced with Stack Mode>Median, 2 minutes, f/2.8, ISO 6400. Sky: five camera positions, one frame per camera position, camera mounted on iOptron SkyTracker Pro equatorial mount, 1 minute f/1.8, ISO 1600. The complete hardware setup I used is shown in figure 7-19.

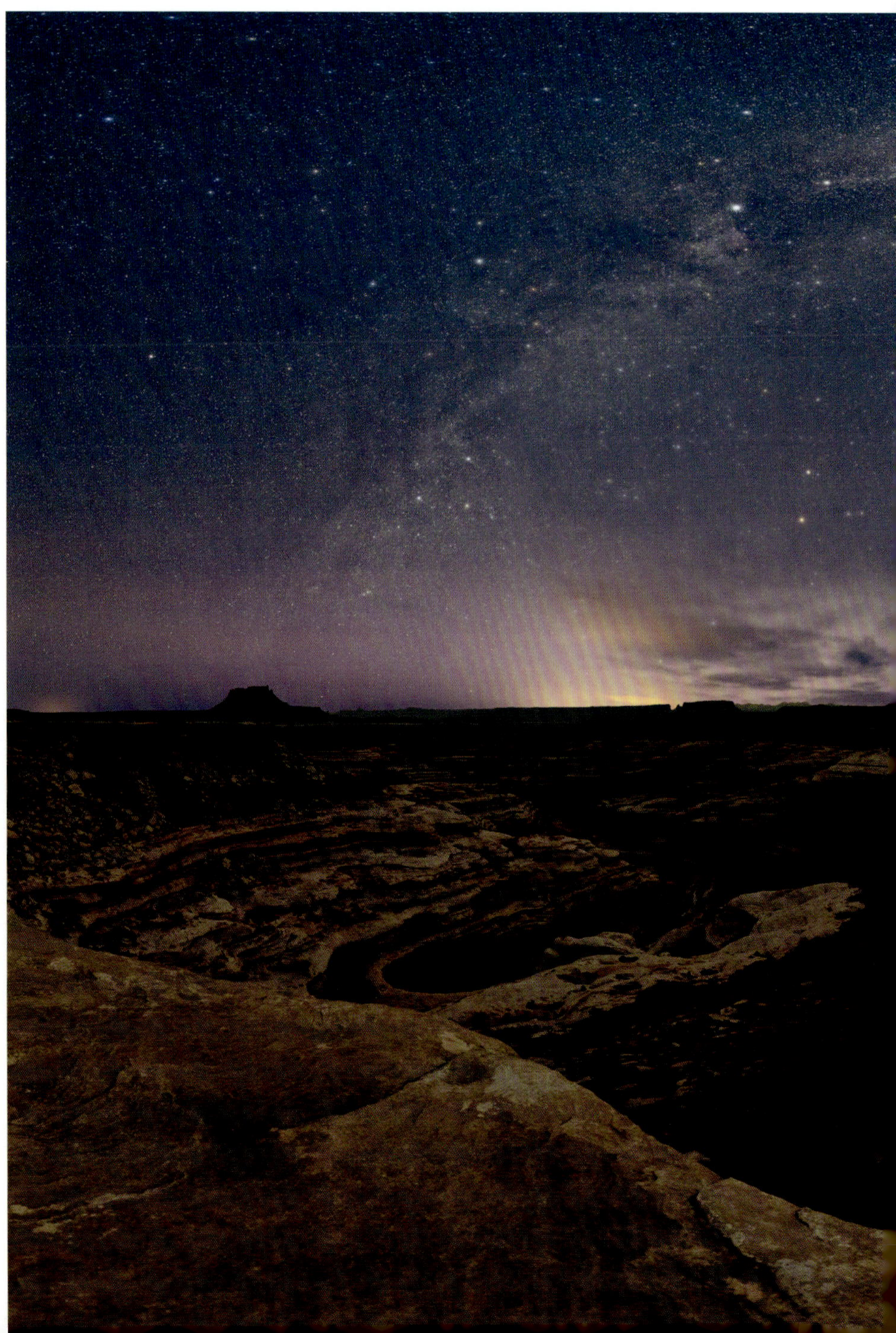

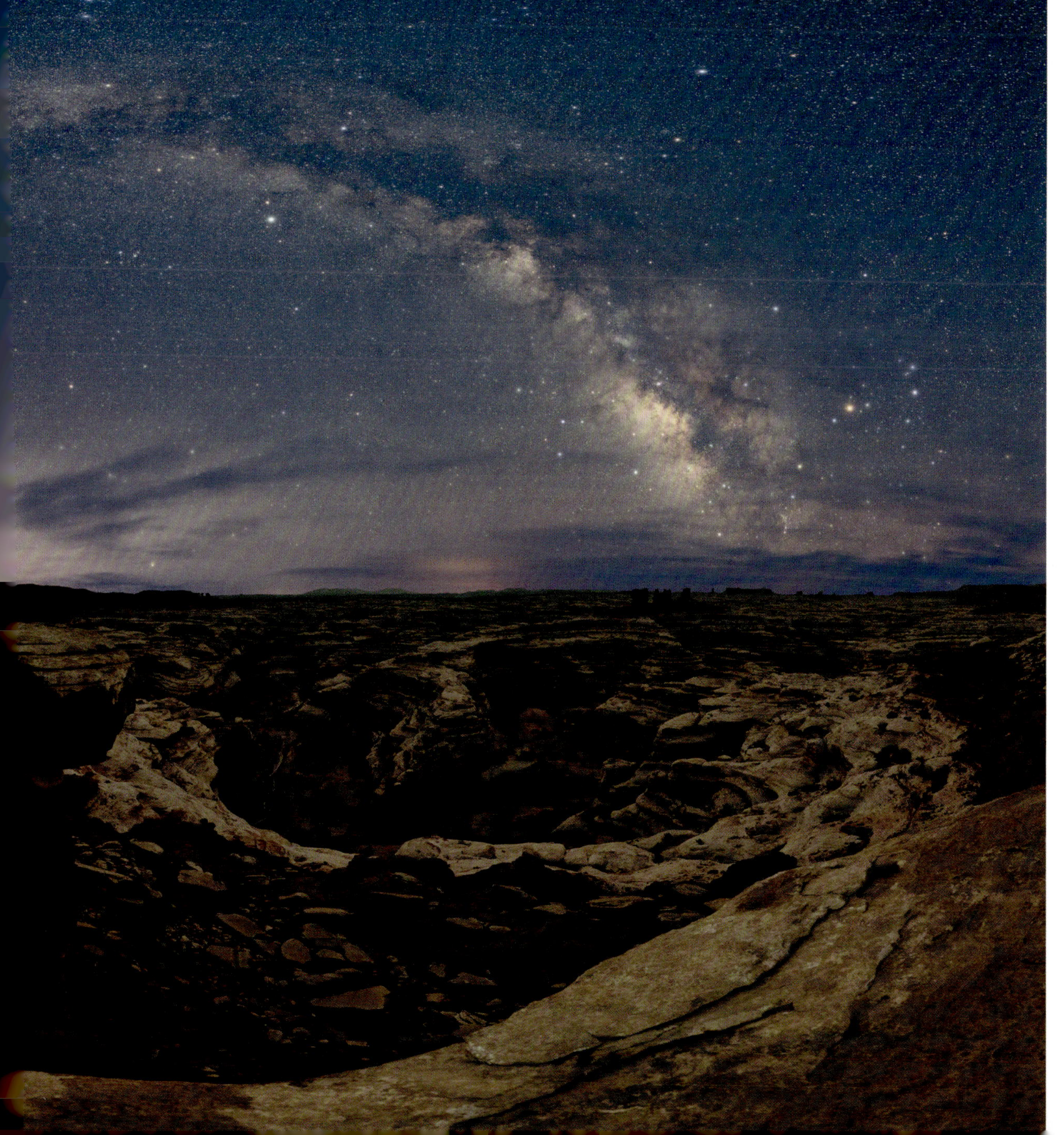

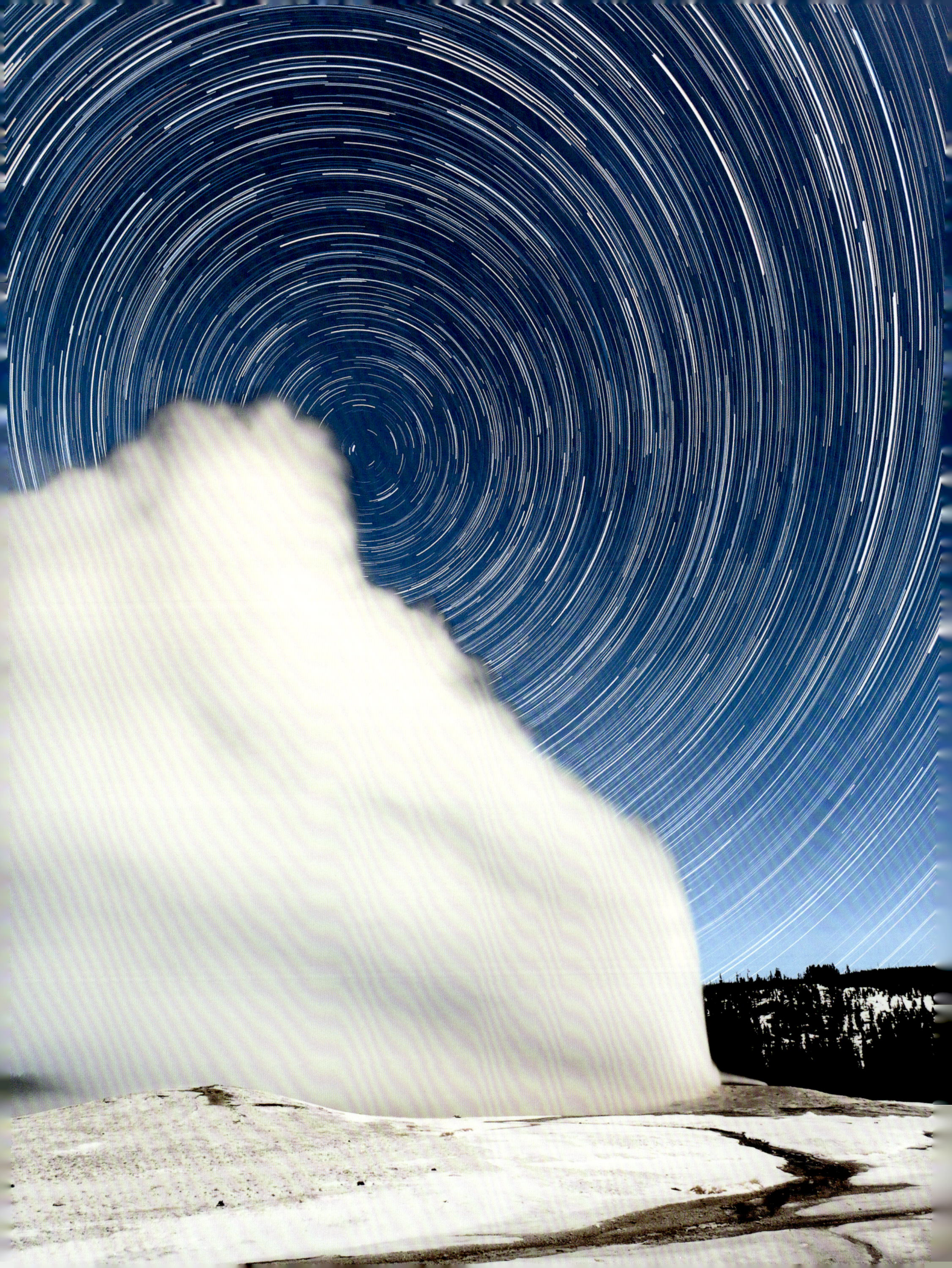

Photographing Star Trails

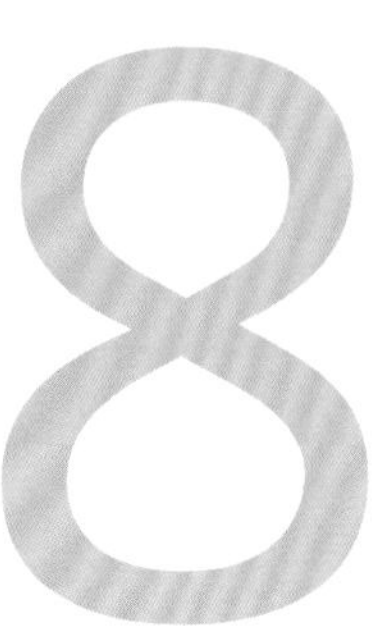

Back in the film era, the only way to capture the night sky without employing a telescope with a tracking mount was to open the shutter and leave it open for a very long time. During that long exposure, which could extend for hours, the stars would make graceful streaks across the film as the earth rotated. Although recent digital cameras can now capture the night sky as we see it, with stationary stars, it's still lots of fun to create photos of star trails.

Alas, the simple technique that worked with a film camera generates unmanageable noise if you try it with a digital camera. The standard digital approach is to make many exposures with the shortest possible time interval between each exposure, stack the exposures in appropriate software, then blend them together so the star trails show through. Although you can make star-trails exposures totaling any amount of time, I generally try to shoot continuously for at least two hours to get adequately long trails, particularly with the wide-angle lenses I normally use.

Composing Star-Trails Images

The direction you point your camera dramatically affects the appearance of your star trails. If you're in the Northern Hemisphere and point your camera north, your star trails will make concentric circles centered on Polaris, the North Star (figure 8-1). See chapter 7 for directions on finding Polaris in the northern sky. Be sure you choose a wide enough lens to include Polaris comfortably. As I mentioned in chapter 7, in the Northern Hemisphere the altitude of Polaris is always equal to your latitude, which you can get from a topographic map (easiest), GPS receiver, Photo Ephemeris Web, or some hiking-oriented phone apps such as Gaia GPS. I use the field-of-view calculator in PhotoPills to determine what focal-length lens I need to include Polaris with 10-20 degrees of sky above it and all the foreground I plan to include. Most often that means I use lenses from 16mm to 24mm.

◄ Figure 8-1: The full moon illuminates an eruption of Old Faithful as the stars circle Polaris, Yellowstone National Park, Wyoming. February 20, 2016, 9:21 to 11:14 p.m. Canon 5D Mark III, Canon EF 16-35mm f/2.8L II USM at 18mm. 615 frames, 10 seconds, f/2.8, ISO 1250.

► FIGURE 8-2: Star trails over a bristlecone pine on Windy Ridge, Windy Ridge Bristlecone Pine Scenic Area, near Alma, Colorado. March 2, 2017, 7:02 p.m. to 7:57 p.m. (land shot at 6:46 p.m., eight minutes before nautical dusk). Canon 5D Mark III, Canon EF 16-35mm f/2.8L II USM at 20mm. Land: 4 minutes, f/11, ISO 400. Sky: 55 frames, 1 minute, f/4.0, ISO 400. Images combined in Floris Van Breugel's Photoshop star-stacking script.

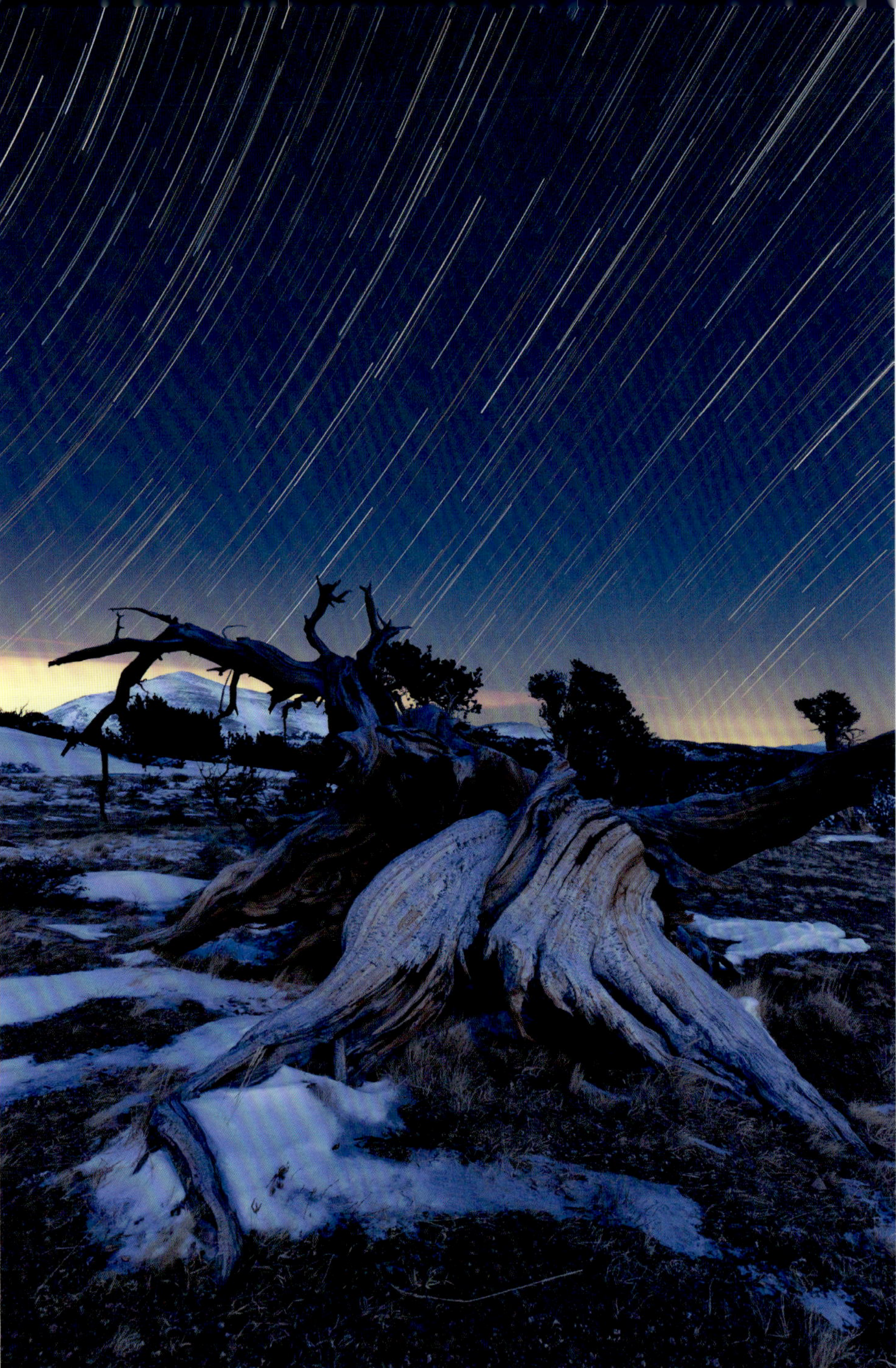

Point your camera east and the stars will make diagonal streaks leading up and right across the frame (figure 8-2). Point it south and the stars along the celestial equator, the imaginary line in the sky representing the projection of the actual equator onto the celestial sphere, will form nearly a straight line (figure 8-3). The star trails above and below the line will curve gently away from the celestial equator. In the Northern Hemisphere, the highest point of the celestial equator is always due south; its altitude in degrees is always equal to 90 minus your latitude. Point the camera west and the stars will make diagonal streaks leading down and right across the frame (figure 8-4). The Night AR module in PhotoPills shows the paths the stars will make as you point your phone or tablet in different directions, making it easy to visualize how your star trails will look.

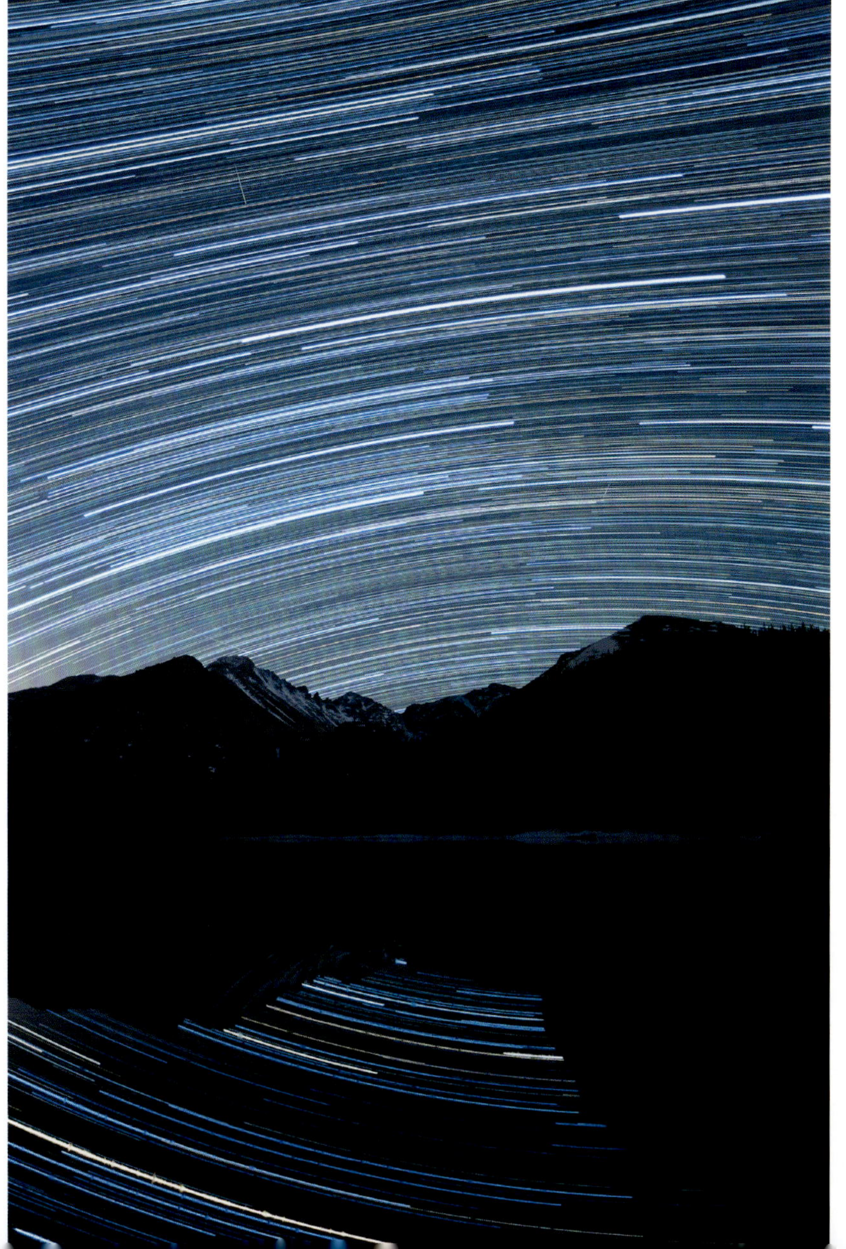

◄ Figure 8-3: Star trails over Longs Peak reflected in Bear Lake, Rocky Mountain National Park, Colorado. June 1-2, 10:07 p.m. to 12:12 a.m. Canon 5D Mark III, Canon EF 16-35mm f/2.8L II USM at 24mm. 243 images, 30 seconds, f/2.8, ISO 1600. A waxing crescent moon provided the light on the land. Images combined in Floris Van Breugel's Photoshop star-stacking script.

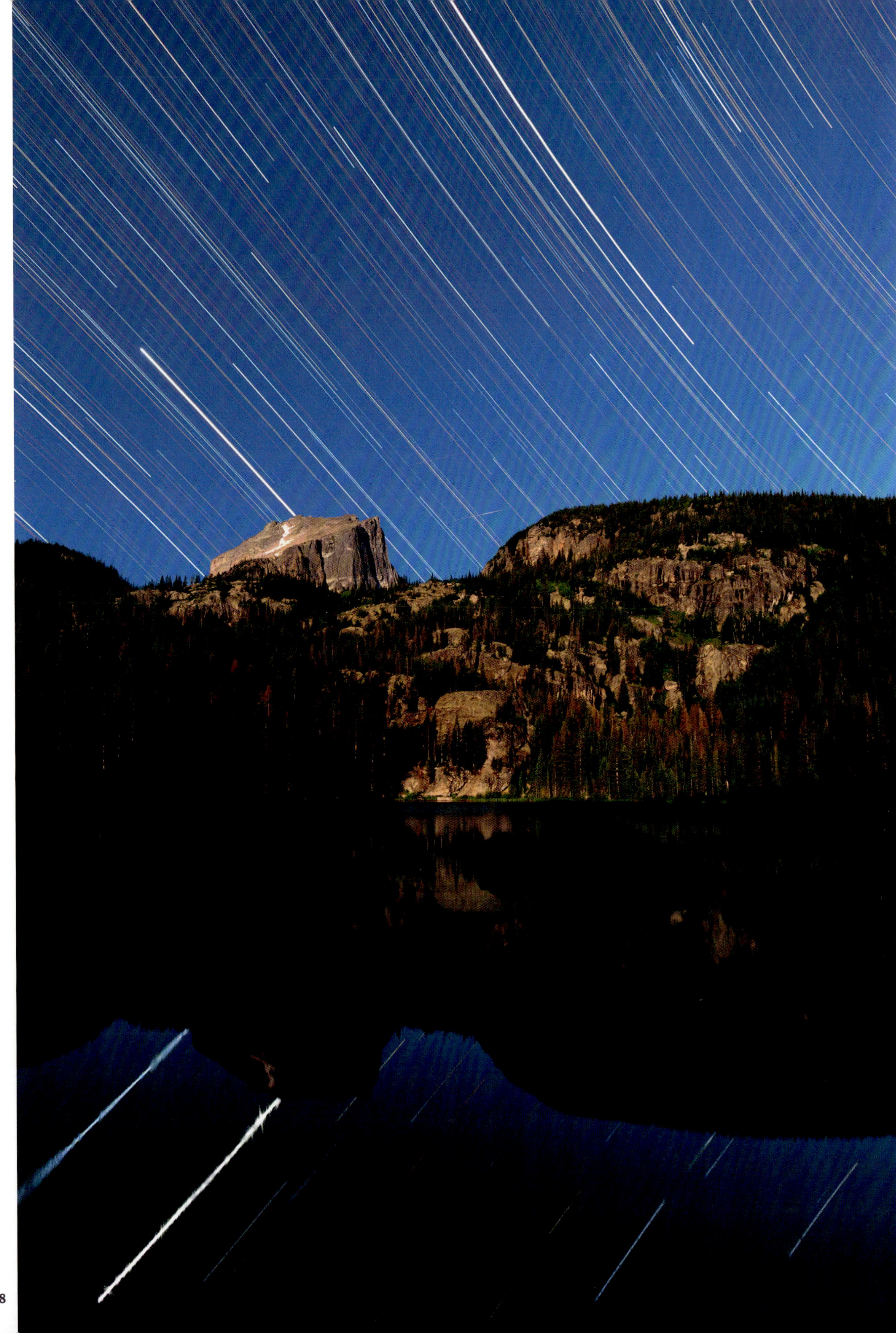

Exposure for Star Trails

There are a number of variables involved in choosing the correct exposure for the component images. On a moonless night, the shutter speed, aperture, and ISO you choose create only a small difference in the appearance of your star trails so long as the overall exposure is equivalent. In other words, you'll see about the same number and brightness of star trails at 30 seconds, f/1.4, ISO 100, as you do at 30 seconds, f/5.6, ISO 1600, as you can see in figures 8-5 and 8-6. The f/1.4 shot will have lower noise because of the low ISO than the f/5.6 shot, but it will also have shallower depth of field. Choose the combination that gives you the right compromise between noise and depth of field.

If you hold shutter speed constant on a moonless night, you will see more and brighter star trails with larger apertures (smaller f-numbers) and higher ISOs, at least up to the point where the sky is no longer black. Think of it this way: a sky that is underexposed by six stops looks the same as a sky that is underexposed by five stops—they're both black. But opening up the aperture by one stop, or doubling the ISO, will make additional faint stars visible and brighten the already-visible stars up to the point where the stars burn out to pure white. On a moonless night I generally choose an aperture between f/2.8 and f/4.0 and an ISO between 200 and 400. Shooting at f/2.8, ISO 1600 will generate so many star trails that you'll practically have more stars than sky, which you may find undesirable. Figure 8-3 shows an example. Push the ISO even higher and open the aperture farther and you'll get something like figure 8-7. Before starting a two-hour star-trails sequence, shoot a test frame and zoom in to get a sense of how the stars will look.

◂ FIGURE 8-4: Star trails over Hallett Peak and Bear Lake, Rocky Mountain National Park, Colorado. July 15-16, 2017, 9:40 p.m. to 12:20 a.m. (land shot at 12:54 a.m. after the moon rose). Canon 5D Mark III, Canon EF 24mm f/1.4L II USM. Land: one frame, 60 seconds, f/2.0, ISO 3200. Sky: 158 frames, 59 seconds, f/2.8, ISO 400. A waning gibbous moon (56 percent illuminated) provided the light on the land. Images combined in Floris Van Breugel's Photoshop star-stacking script.

▲ FIGURE 8-5: On a moonless night, star trails look about the same if overall exposure is held constant. Compare this image, shot at 30 seconds, f/1.4, ISO 100, to figure 8-6, shot at 30 seconds, f/5.6, ISO 1600.

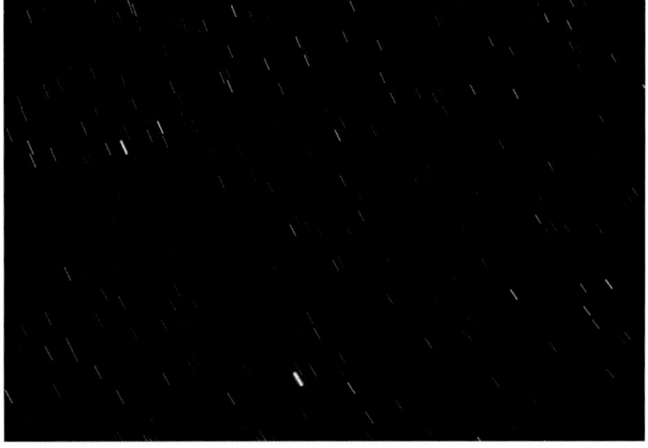

▲ FIGURE 8-6: Compare this image, shot at 30 seconds, f/5.6, ISO 1600, to figure 8-5, shot at 30 seconds, f/1.4, ISO 100.

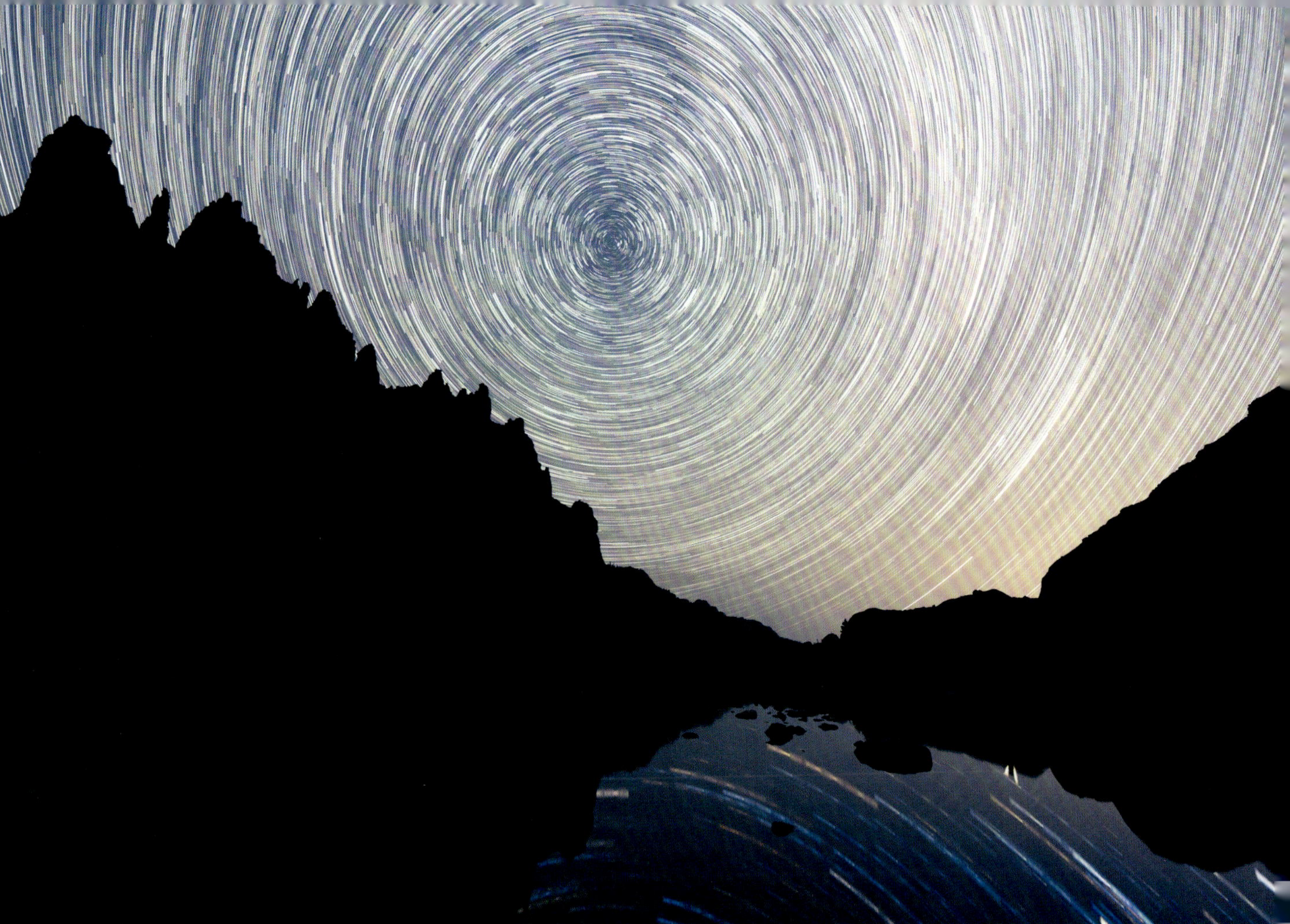

The night sky is busier than you might think. During a two-hour star-trails sequence, jets and satellites will leave long streaks through many of the component images. The longer the exposure for each frame, the fewer frames you'll need to shoot to total two hours. That means fewer frames to clean up before you stack all your images and create the trails. Although you can certainly retouch jet streaks after combining all the images, it's difficult and tedious because each jet streak will cross multiple star trails. It's better to remove the jet streaks from the individual RAW files before combining the images. On moonless nights, you'll simplify your life if you use the longest exposures your camera will tolerate without generating unacceptable noise. If possible, use exposures in the two- to four-minute range. Test your own gear to determine the longest reasonable exposure.

Your exposures will need to be shorter on nights when the moon is bright (50 percent or more illuminated). The image of a star is only centered on one pixel for a few seconds. Once the star moves, that pixel gathers light from the sky during the remainder of the exposure. The longer the exposure, the more light the pixel gathers from the sky. That's no problem on a moonless night when the sky is essentially black, but it becomes a problem on moon-lit nights because the sky is much brighter. If the amount of light gathered from the star is small in relation to the total amount of light gathered during the exposure, the star trail becomes faint or even invisible. The difference between the star streak and the background is too small. On nights with a moon, shorter exposures reveal more stars, as can be seen in figures 8-8 to 8-10. These three images are all details of star-trails images shot under a first-quarter moon (50 percent illuminated). Total exposure time for all three images was 4 minutes, so the star streaks are of equal length, but shooting 16 15-second exposures back to back revealed far more stars than shooting one 4-minute exposure. On nights with a full moon, use exposures of 10 to 30 seconds. Limit exposures to one minute or less when the moon is 50 percent illuminated.

The goal on nights with a moon, in addition to maximizing the brightness of the star trails, is to choose exposure settings that provide good detail in the land without washing out the stars. After setting the shutter speed, choose an aperture and ISO that give you a pleasing overall exposure, adequate depth of field, and minimal noise.

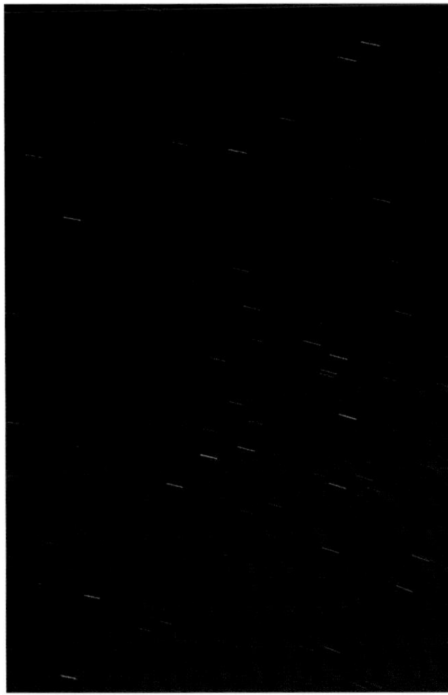

▲ FIGURE 8-8: One frame, 4 minutes, f/4.0, ISO 100.

▲ FIGURE 8-9: Four frames stacked in Photoshop and combined using the Lighten blend mode, 1 minute, f/4.0, ISO 400.

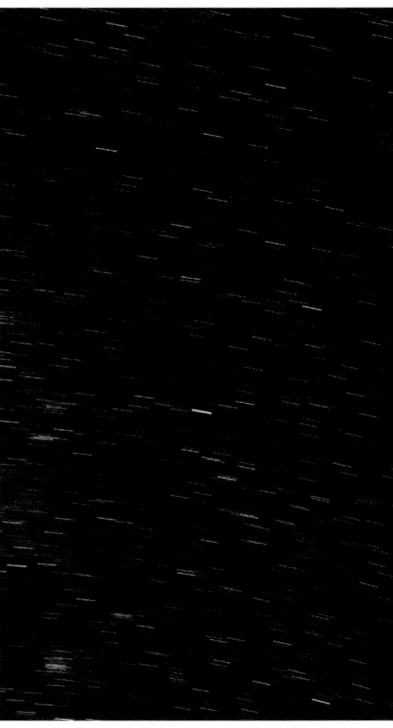

▲ FIGURE 8-10: Sixteen frames stacked in Photoshop and combined using the Lighten blend mode, 15 seconds, f/4.0, ISO 1600.

On moonless nights, if you want a frame with some detail in the land, start your star-trails sequence around nautical dusk, before the sky is totally dark. Alternatively, shoot some frames 10 or 15 minutes after sunset or before sunrise, exposing correctly for the land and ignoring the overexposed sky. Shooting the land exposures at that time lets you use small apertures for deep depth of field. You can then composite these good-land exposures with the completed star-trails exposure using the techniques described in chapter 6. A final alternative is to shoot one or more frames during the night that are exposed correctly for the land rather than the sky, then composite the good-land exposure(s) with the completed star-trails image.

An intervalometer will allow you to program the exposure length, number of exposures, and interval between exposures, which should be as short as possible. Some intervalometers will let you set an interval of zero, but your camera may respond by only making one exposure even though you set the total number of frames to a much larger number. Test your camera to see. You will probably need to set the interval to 1 second.

Editing Star-Trails Images

After downloading all your exposures to your computer, edit them to produce the sky color you want. On moonless nights the sky is not blue, but rather some shade of green. See chapter 6 for instructions on how to shift the sky color toward blue, if desired. If you use the exposures I recommend for a moonless night, the sky will be nearly black. You may find it helpful to temporarily increase the exposure in Lightroom by 2 stops so you can see more clearly the effect of your blue-sky correction. Reset the exposure increase to zero before using one of the tools described later for combining the images to reveal the star trails. On nights with a moon the sky will be a shade of blue that is closer to what we expect the sky to look like.

Retouching Jet Streaks

Close examination of your component images will probably reveal lots of jet and satellite streaks, as seen in figure 8-12. Wingtip lights on airplanes often create double streaks, sometimes punctuated with brighter flashes. Satellites high above the atmosphere can reflect sunlight even when an observer on the ground is in total darkness. Satellites usually create thin streaks that can be hard to distinguish from meteors. Satellite streaks are always of uniform width; meteors usually taper to a point at each end. I regard jet and satellite streaks as unnatural intruders that destroy the beautiful patterns made

▶ FIGURE 8-11: Star trails over Balanced Rock, Arches National Park, Utah. April 20, 2023, 10:17 p.m. to 11:27 p.m. Sony Alpha 7R IVa, Sony FE 35mm f/1.4 GM. Land: four minutes, f/4.0, ISO 6400. Sky: 36 frames, two minutes, f/4.0, ISO 400. Images combined in Floris Van Breugel's Photoshop star-stacking script.

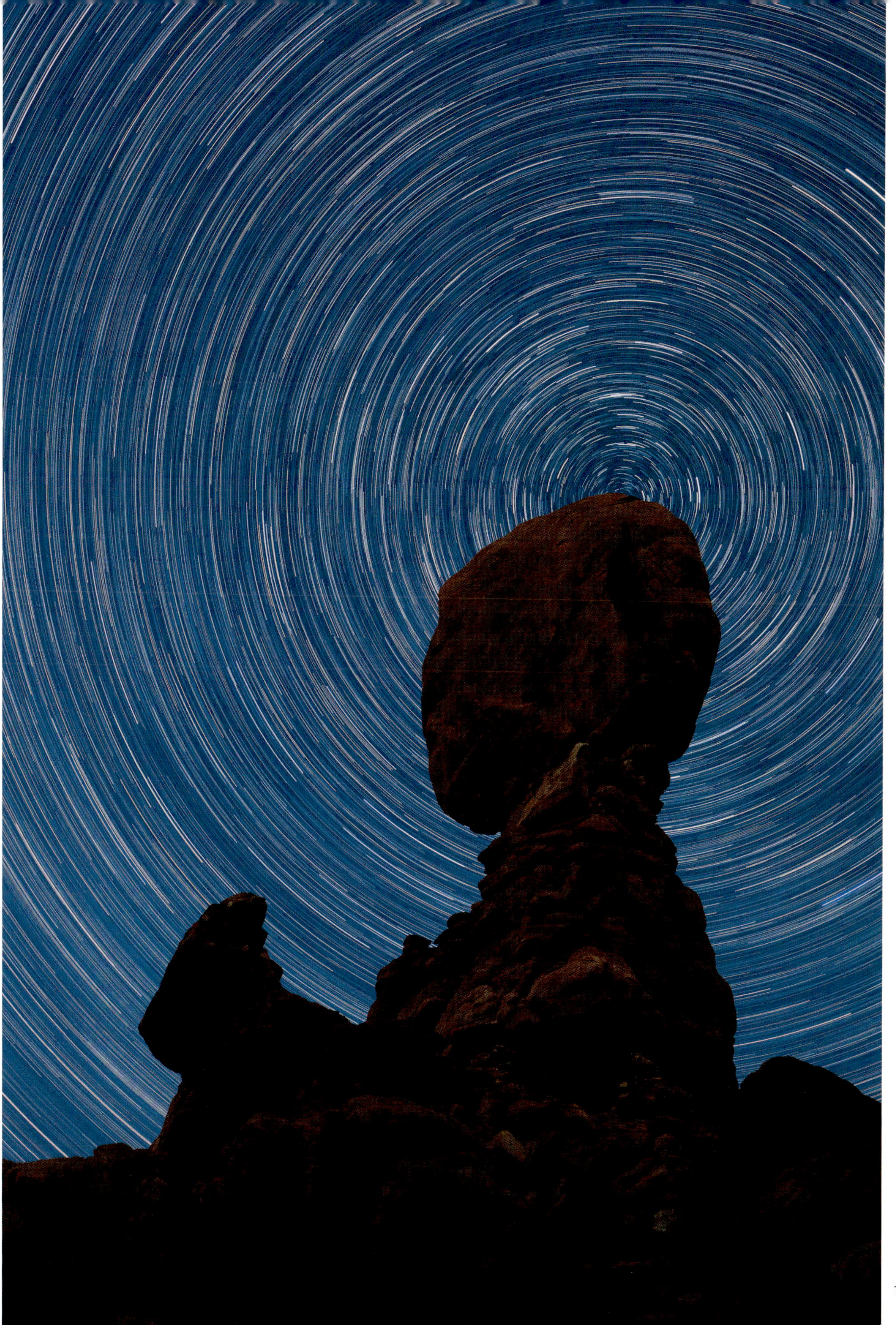

by the star trails, so I choose to remove them. As I mentioned above, it's best to remove them one at a time from each component image rather than trying to retouch the completed star-trails image. Start by selecting the Healing tool (formerly called the Spot Removal tool) from the tool bar above the Basic panel in Lightroom. The tool offers three modes: Content-Aware Remove, Heal, and Clone. Try Content-Aware Remove first. Set Opacity to 100 percent. Although you can click, hold, and drag along the streak, it often works better to click once at the beginning of the streak, then Shift-click at the end of the streak. Lightroom will draw a straight path with the Healing tool between your two clicks. If the streak is straight, this will often remove it. If the streak is curved, try removing the streak in short, straight segments. Examine the

▸ Figure 8-12: An example of a jet streak.

result closely. If the jet streak crosses prominent star trails, this technique may create gaps in those trails. Try removing the jet streak in two segments, one on either side of the star trail. Lightroom also sometimes picks up bits of star trails from the region that provides the pixels that Lightroom pastes over the streak. These random bits of star trails don't connect to other star trails, so they stand out as obvious flaws. If the results from Content-Aware Remove are unsatisfactory, try Heal, then Clone.

Blending the Images to Create the Star Trails

Your next task is to blend the images to reveal the complete star trails. If you shot just a few dozen frames, you can create a basic star-trails image by following a simple recipe in Photoshop. If you shot more than that, you'll probably need a more sophisticated approach. The upper limit on the number of frames will depend on the resolution of your camera (higher-resolution cameras create larger files) and how much RAM and processing power your computer possesses. You can find lots of free or low-cost star-trails software out there that will handle large numbers of component images. StarStaX and Startrails.exe, as well as a Photoshop script written by Floris van Breugel, are among the current possibilities. There may be others by the time you read this.

Here's how to use Photoshop to put together a star-trails image. It's easiest to start the procedure in Lightroom. Choose all the component images, then choose Photo>Edit In>Open as Layers in Photoshop.

In the Layers panel, select all the layers (click the top layer, then Shift-click the bottom layer) and change the blend mode to Lighten. The Lighten blend mode compares the pixel in the target layer to the pixel directly underneath. If the pixel underneath is lighter, Photoshop allows that pixel to shine through. This will make the star trails appear.

You can paint directly on your component images with black to remove unwanted elements in the land portion of the image, such as hikers who pass through your shot with their headlamps. There's no need to be fussy when painting, since everything black will be ignored by the Lighten blend mode. Identify the files with issues in Lightroom, then return to your layered file in Photoshop and locate the offending file. Turn off the eye icon for all layers but the target layer. You can usually Alt-click the target layer's eye icon to turn off all other layers with one click. Alt-click again to turn them on again. If that doesn't work, right-click the eye icon and choose Show/Hide All Other Layers.

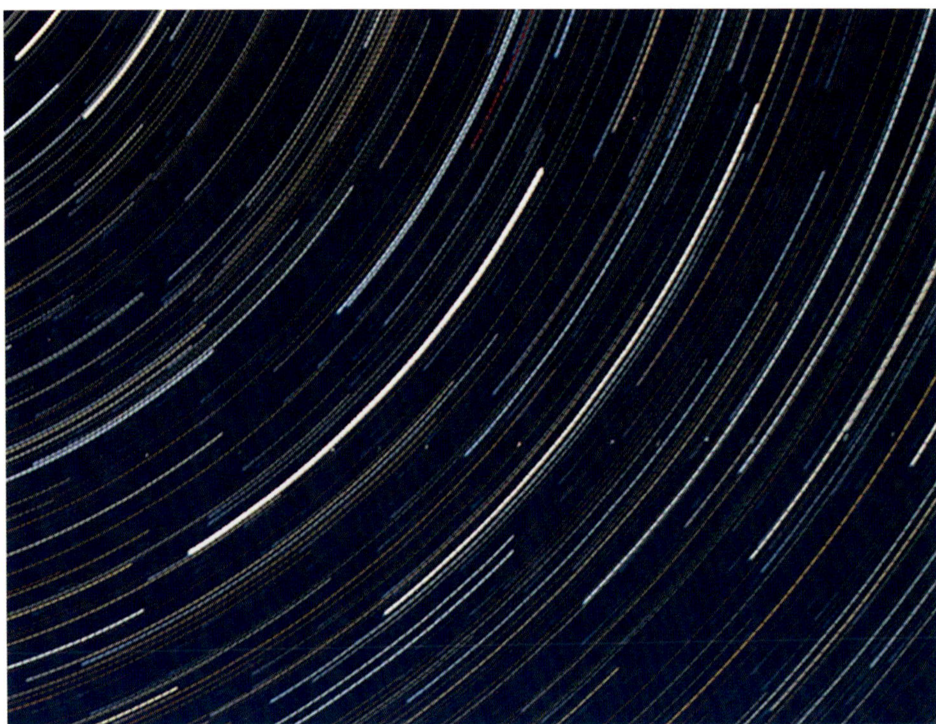

Closing the Gaps

This easy Photoshop procedure has one disadvantage. Every star trail will show a tiny gap between exposures (figure 8-13). These gaps are not noticeable on the web or in a small print but are rather annoying in a large print.

You might think that these gaps are inevitable; after all, there is a one-second interval between each exposure. However, nature photographer Floris van Breugel has pointed out that these gaps will disappear if you use the Screen blend mode instead of Lighten. He has developed a slick technique for eliminating the gaps and coded his technique as a free Photoshop script that you can download from his website at www.artinnaturephotography. com/gallery/twilightarticle/. There are actually two versions of the script. One preserves the layers but creates a very large file; the other (my favorite) flattens the layers, creating a file of reasonable size. The scripts work well but be sure to read the directions on preparing your files before running them. First, you'll need to set all your RAW files to neutral settings, with all settings in the Basic panel set to zero, and the Tone Curve set to Linear. Do apply lens profile corrections and remove chromatic aberrations if your camera doesn't do that automatically. Then you'll need to convert your RAW files to TIFFs. Put the TIFFs in a separate folder. The image that emerges from the scripts

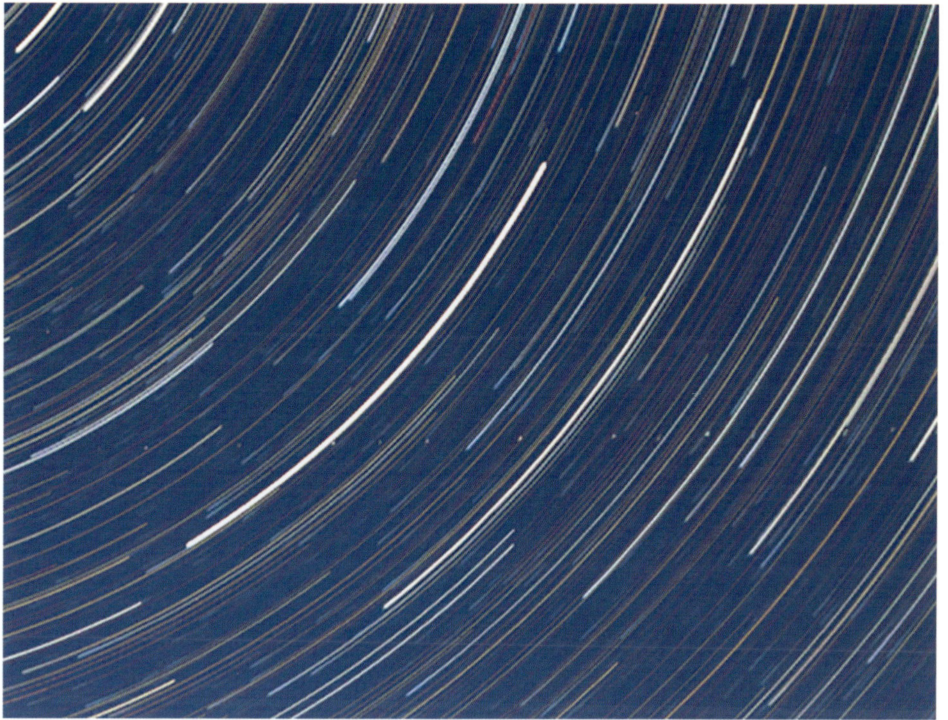

will initially look too flat and too light, so you'll need to do some processing afterwards to restore pleasing contrast and density. If the highlights in the completed file are too washed out to recover, you may want to reduce exposure in your component RAW images by one-half or one full stop, recreate the TIFFs, and try again. (This is another reason to retouch jet streaks on the RAW files. If you have to re-output TIFFs, you won't have to retouch the files again.) You can run either script directly from Photoshop by choosing File>Scripts>Browse and navigating to the folder where you saved the scripts. Figure 8-14 shows the result.

Some of the dedicated star-trails programs also offer ways to eliminate the gaps.

Here's how to remove the gaps manually if you'd rather not mess around with new software. First, prepare your RAW files the same way you would prepare them before using van Breugel's script, but don't convert them to TIFFs. Select all the images. Choose Photo>Edit In>Open as Layers in Photoshop. Make the first layer above the bottom layer of the stack active. Press Control+J to make a copy. Choose the next layer above the new copy layer and make a copy of it. Continue making a copy of every other layer in the stack except the top layer. Do not make a copy of the top and bottom layers.

Now target the top layer in the layer stack. Change the blend mode to Screen. You should see the star trails lengthen and the image get lighter. Hold down Shift and click the next layer below to highlight both the top and next-to-top layers simultaneously. Press Control+E to merge the two highlighted layers. Change the blend mode of the new merged layer to Lighten. Target the next layer below the new merged layer and change the blend mode to Screen. Again the star trails should lengthen. This time, however, the image will not get lighter. It will only get lighter during the first execution of this procedure. Hold down Shift and click the next layer below so you have two layers selected simultaneously. Press Control+E to merge the two layers. Change the blend mode of the new merged layer to Lighten.

Repeat this procedure all the way down the stack. Each time you change the blend mode to Screen at the start of another repetition of this procedure, the star trails should lengthen. If they don't, you've done something wrong. Back up in the History panel until you know you're above where you made the mistake and try again. When you've completed the procedure on the final pair of layers, at the bottom of the layer stack, flatten the layers to reduce file size (Layer>Flatten Image). The photo at the end of the procedure will look flat and dull. Increase contrast and adjust color and density to taste.

Star-trails images may seem like a throwback to an earlier time, before advanced digital cameras were invented that could capture the night sky as we see it, with stationary stars. Despite their retro quality, star-trails images are still astonishing in their ability to capture an unseen phenomenon. Our visual system cannot integrate the light that enters our eyes over a period of hours and create one coherent image. Cameras can. Star-trails images reveal the paths of the stars and planets through the heavens in a graceful, graphic way that is still intriguing, even today.

▶ FIGURE 8-15: Star trails over the Titan, Fisher Towers, Utah. August 11-12, 2016, 8:44 p.m. to 2:28 a.m. Canon 1Ds Mark III, Canon EF 16-35mm f/2.8L II USM at 16mm. 340 frames, one minute, f/2.8, ISO 200. A waxing gibbous moon (65 percent illuminated) provided the light on the land. Images combined in Floris Van Breugel's Photoshop star-stacking script.

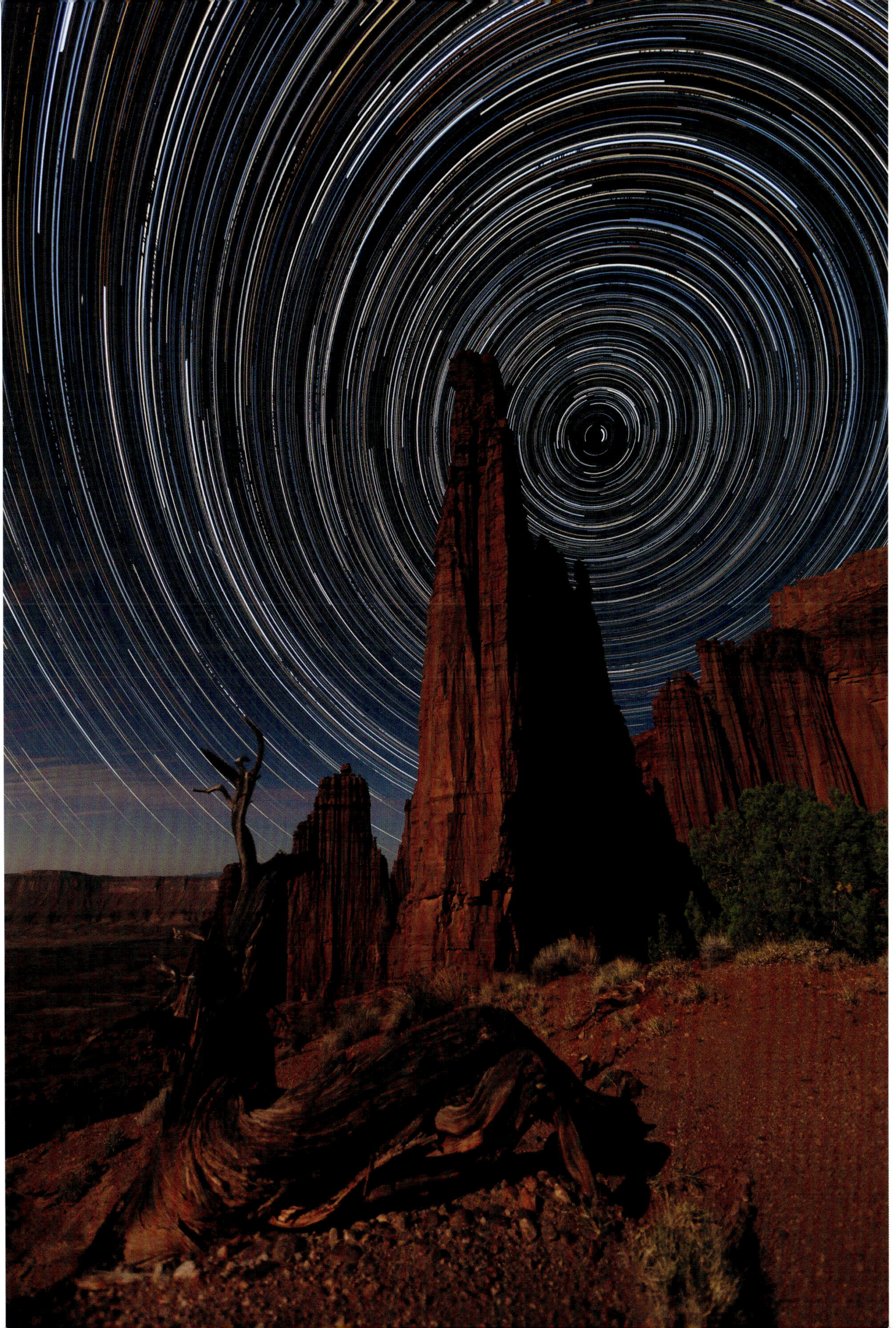

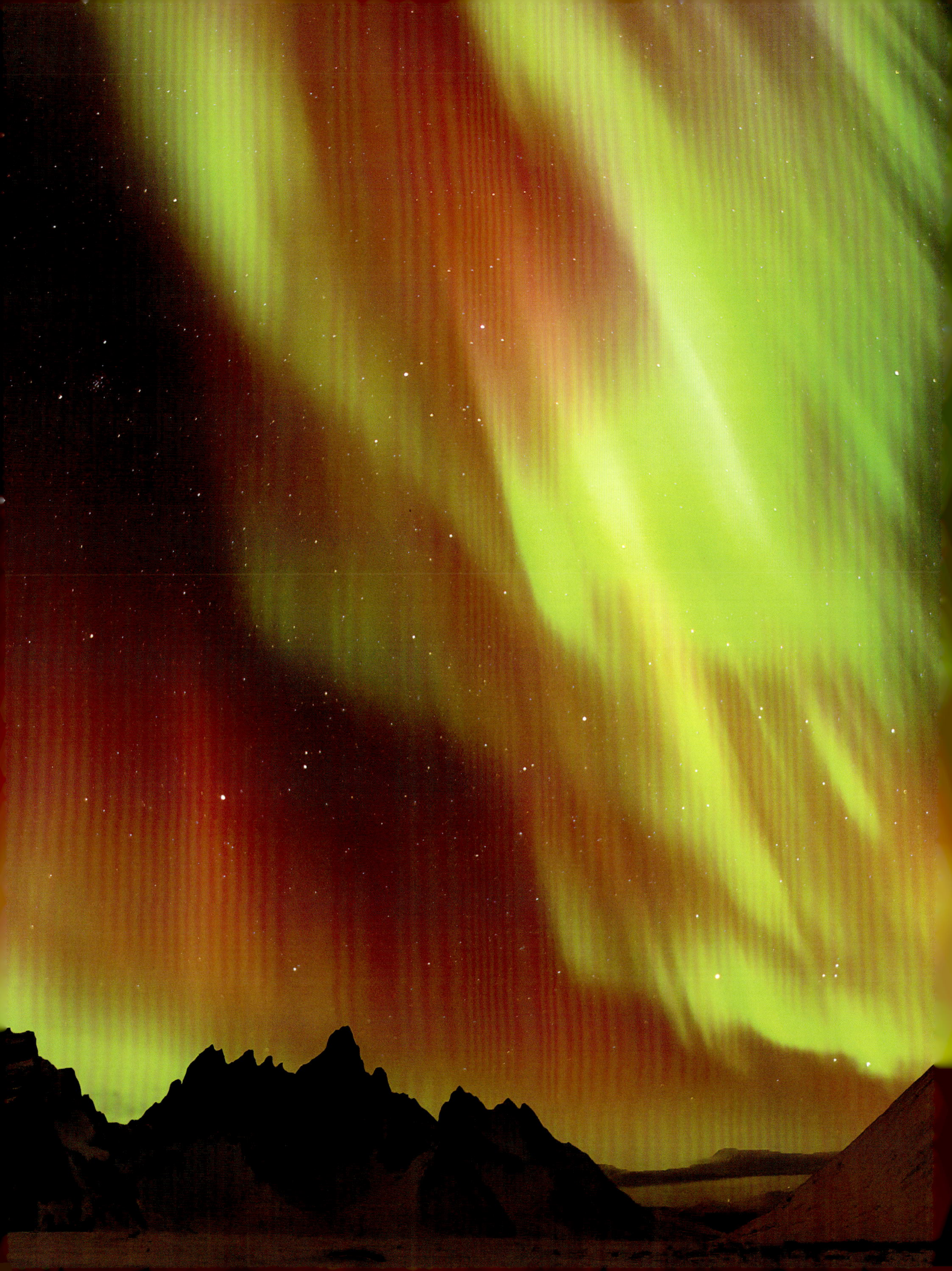

Shooting the Aurora

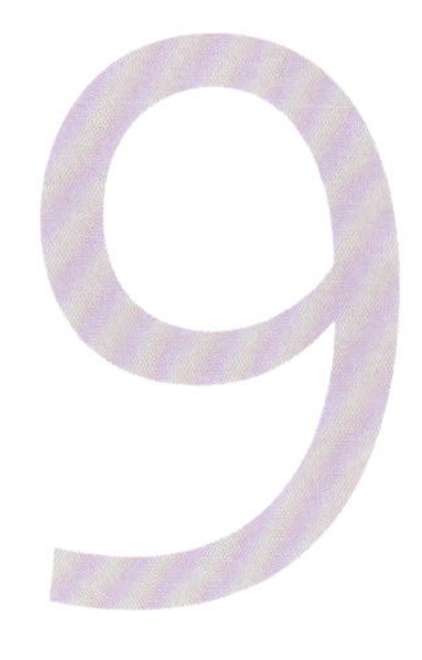

Every landscape photographer, at least once in their life, should make the long trek north to photograph the aurora. The entrancing sight of silvery curtains swirling across the sky is so otherworldly that your first reaction is likely to be disbelief. The shapes are ever changing and unpredictable, blossoming and fading in one quadrant of the sky, then erupting in a different direction. As in many other types of night photography, your camera will record the spectacle better than your eyes. Even when dark-adapted, your eyes may only see arcs, ribbons, and rays of shimmering silver, perhaps with a greenish or reddish tint; your camera, however, will record far more vivid hues.

The origins of the aurora can be traced to the sun, 93 million miles away. In addition to visible light and other forms of electromagnetic radiation, the sun constantly emits a stream of energetic particles—electrons and protons. Some of these particles become entrapped in Earth's *magnetosphere* and are eventually funneled down toward the surface, following paths dictated by Earth's magnetic field. The structure of Earth's magnetic field causes the aurora to be seen most frequently in the auroral zones, doughnut-shaped regions centered on the magnetic poles, as shown in figures 9-2 and 9-3. Both the southern and northern auroral zones offer an excellent chance to see the aurora, but the northern zone is far more accessible to photographers.

◄ FIGURE 9-1: Aurora over Tombstone Mountain, Tombstone Territorial Park, Yukon Territory, Canada. March 17, 2015, 2:00 a.m. Canon 5D Mark III, Canon EF 16-35mm f/2.8L II USM at 16mm. 8 seconds, f/2.8, ISO 3200.

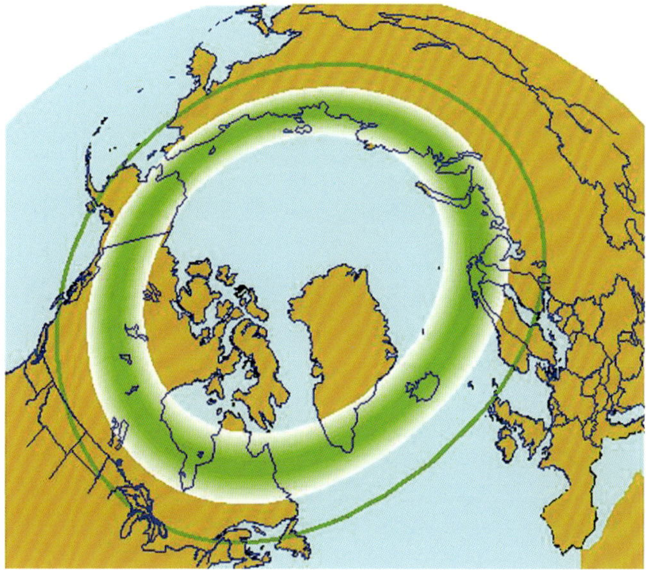

◄ FIGURE 9-2: A forecast for the extent of the auroral zone encircling the North Magnetic Pole on a night of average auroral activity. The region where auroral activity will be visible, weather permitting, expands and contracts depending on the level of geomagnetic activity. Illustration courtesy of the Geophysical Institute, University of Alaska Fairbanks.

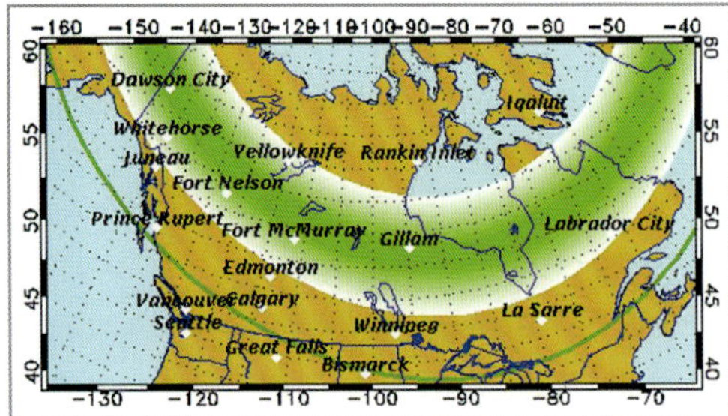

▲ FIGURE 9-3: A forecast for the extent of the auroral zone in North America on a night of average auroral activity. The region where auroral activity will be visible, weather permitting, expands and contracts depending on the level of geomagnetic activity. Illustration courtesy of the Geophysical Institute, University of Alaska Fairbanks.

▶ FIGURE 9-4: The long-term percentage of clear, dark nights during which the aurora can be seen at locations in North America. Figure derived from *The Aurora Watcher's Handbook* by Neil Davis, published by University of Alaska Press Fairbanks. Used with permission.

These energetic particles eventually collide with atoms and molecules in Earth's upper atmosphere, roughly 60 to 120 miles above the surface. Green, the most common auroral color, occurs when an energetic particle strikes an oxygen atom. If the energetic particle has the right amount of energy, it can cause one of the oxygen atom's electrons to jump to the second excited state. Such a configuration is unstable. When the electron falls back to the first excited state, that excess energy is released in the form of a photon of 577.7 nanometer green light. For oxygen atoms at the 60-mile level, the remaining excess energy is usually released through collision with another atom. At higher elevations, the atmosphere is so rarified that such collisions are uncommon. In that case, the remaining excess energy can be released in the form of a photon of red light, creating a red fringe atop arcs, bands, or curtains of green light. The red light sometimes seen at the bottom of green auroral curtains is most often caused by excited nitrogen molecules lower in the atmosphere.

First-time aurora watchers are often convinced that the aurora extends all the way down to the ground, perhaps even reaching the ground in front of a nearby mountain. In truth, all auroral activity occurs high above the earth's surface. A green aurora that appears to touch the horizon is actually at least 660 miles away, measured horizontally, and high in the sky.

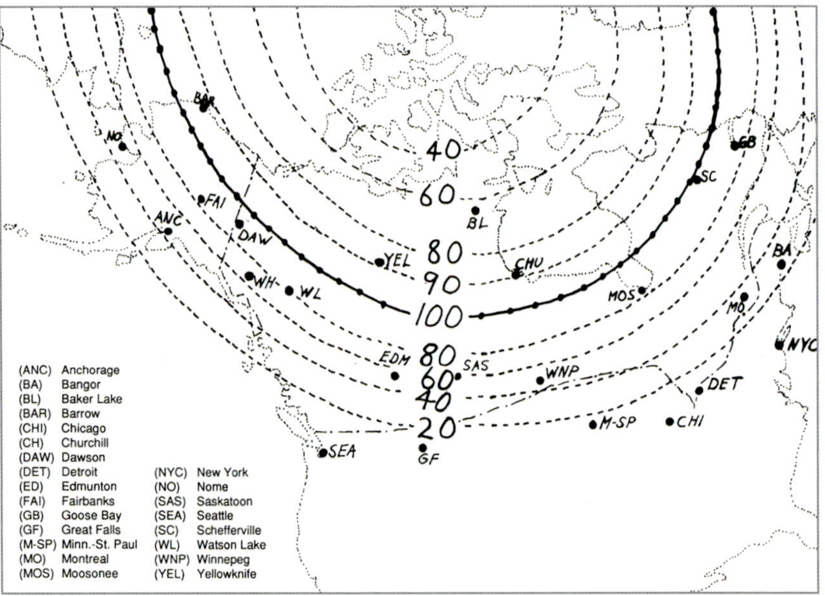

(ANC)	Anchorage
(BA)	Bangor
(BL)	Baker Lake
(BAR)	Barrow
(CHI)	Chicago
(CH)	Churchill
(DAW)	Dawson
(DET)	Detroit
(ED)	Edmunton
(FAI)	Fairbanks
(GB)	Goose Bay
(GF)	Great Falls
(M-SP)	Minn.-St. Paul
(MO)	Montreal
(MOS)	Moosonee

(NYC)	New York
(NO)	Nome
(SAS)	Saskatoon
(SEA)	Seattle
(SC)	Schefferville
(WL)	Watson Lake
(WNP)	Winnepeg
(YEL)	Yellowknife

The chances of seeing the aurora, even within the auroral zone, vary depending on your precise location within the zone. According to the late Neil Davis, who was emeritus professor of geophysics at the University of Alaska Fairbanks and author of *The Aurora Watcher's Handbook*, in the very center of the zone the odds of seeing the aurora on a clear, dark night are 100 percent. The aurora may be faint and low on the horizon if the night is extremely quiet, magnetically speaking—but it will still be visible.

As you can see in figure 9-4, the line of most-frequent auroral activity passes just north of Fairbanks, Alaska, one of the most convenient destinations for U.S.-based photographers. The Brooks Range is an even better destination than Fairbanks because it's even closer to the heart of the auroral zone and offers the possibility of photographing the aurora over dramatic, snow-capped peaks. To reach the Brooks Range, drive north about 270 miles on the Dalton Highway, the haul road for the Prudhoe Bay oil fields. Two tiny hamlets along the Dalton Highway, Coldfoot and Wiseman, just south of the Brooks Range, provide the only lodging. In Canada's Yukon Territory, Dawson, the epicenter of the Klondike gold rush in the 1890s, is the jumping-off place for another great aurora destination, Tombstone Territorial Park just to the north. Tombstone Territorial Park is a largely undeveloped wilderness park that looks like an Arctic version of Patagonia. Farther east, Yellowknife, the capital of Canada's Northwest Territories, is a small but modern city that is also close to the center of the auroral zone. Iceland and numerous locations in northern Norway and Sweden are other possible destinations.

To see the aurora most vividly, the sky must be totally dark, which precludes arctic destinations in the summer months. Figure 9-5 shows that auroral activity tends to peak around the fall and spring equinoxes, which means late September and late March are good times for a trip. In Alaska and western Canada, September has relatively mild temperatures but more cloudy skies. In Fairbanks, for example, the average low in September ranges from 43° F on September 1st to 31° F on September 30th, but the sky is mostly cloudy or overcast 63 percent of the time. I enjoyed completely clear skies for only two nights during a 10-night shoot in Yellowknife in September 2013. I was able to make a few other shots during one partly cloudy night and was shut down completely on the remaining nights. On the plus side, the mild nighttime temperatures meant the abundant lakes near Yellowknife weren't frozen, offering the possibility of capturing reflections.

March is much colder than September in Alaska and western Canada but has somewhat clearer skies. The average low in Fairbanks in March, for example, ranges from –5° F on March 1st to 10° F on March 31st, but the sky is mostly cloudy or overcast 54 percent of the time. During an eight-night shoot in Tombstone Territorial Park in March 2015, my companion and I were able

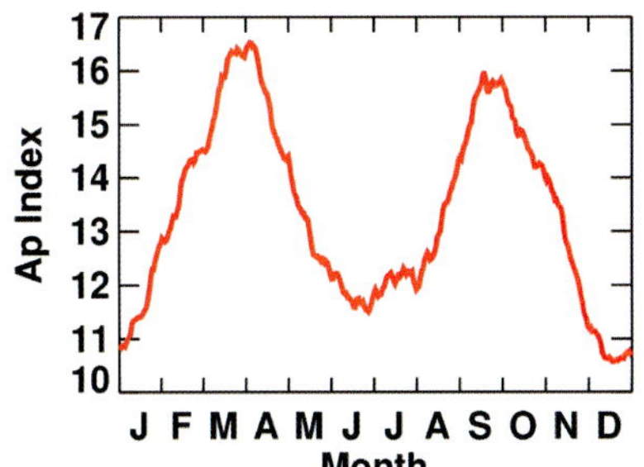

▾ Figure 9-5: The AP index, a proxy for auroral activity, varies throughout the year. This chart aggregates data from 1932 through August 2023. Note the increase in auroral activity around the spring and fall equinoxes. Illustration courtesy of Dr. Cora Randall, University of Colorado Boulder.

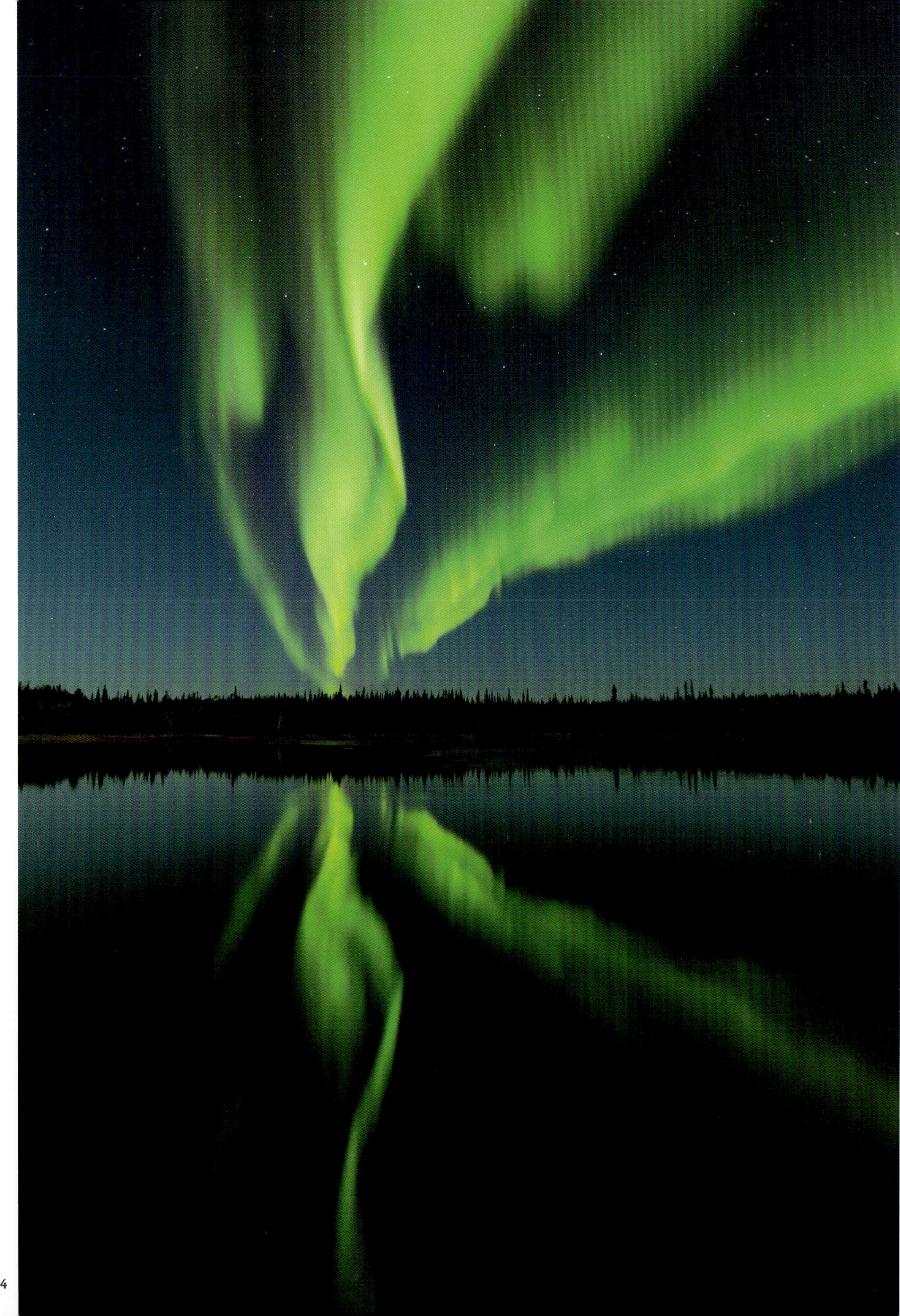

to shoot the aurora for six nights in a row. The coldest temperature, however, was –29° F. Iceland's location in the middle of the Atlantic Ocean means it has milder winters than the interior of Alaska or western Canada, but it is often windy and cloudy throughout the fall, winter, and spring, the only seasons when it becomes dark enough to see the aurora. Northern Scandinavia is also frequently cloudy during the seasons when the aurora can be seen.

The most vivid auroral displays often erupt in the hours around midnight, but they can occur at any time of night. In western Canada and Alaska the aurora most commonly appears in an arc of sky from northwest to southeast (moving clockwise around the compass). The ideal shooting location allows you to photograph in any direction within that 180-degree arc.

Moon phase is another factor to consider when planning an aurora shoot. Moonlight presents a tradeoff. If you have a full moon, faint auroras will not stand out prominently against the bright sky, but it will be much easier to hold detail in the land. Bright auroras are spectacular even in a moon-drenched sky. If the moon appears within your frame, however, expect it to be rendered as a completely white disk. Lens flare can also be a problem. Without moonlight, even faint auroras are easy to capture, but you may struggle to hold adequate detail in the land. I've photographed successfully under all phases of the moon, so moon phase is no excuse to sleep in. If possible, plan your trip so you will be able to photograph on both moonlit and moonless nights.

The Geophysical Institute at the University of Alaska Fairbanks offers forecasts of auroral activity. Visit www.gi.alaska.edu/AuroraForecast or search for "geophysical institute aurora forecast." The forecast is updated at midnight Universal time. Forecasts rely on the fact that light from the sun reaches us in about eight minutes, but the energetic particles that cause the aurora take two or three days to enter Earth's atmosphere. We can see the solar activity that presages a good auroral display before the energetic particles that cause the aurora actually reach us. If you live in the auroral zones, the forecast can help you decide whether to stay up all night, hoping to photograph the aurora. If you've traveled hundreds or thousands of miles to reach a good destination for aurora shooting, however, my advice is to invert your waking/sleeping schedule. Sleep during the day, and stay awake all night, or at least until 2 or 3 a.m. Auroral activity often occurs in bursts followed by lulls. Asking the hotel clerk to wake you when the aurora begins streaming across the sky rarely works. By the time you get dressed for the cold, go outside, and get your tripod set up, you've usually missed the best part of the display. Prepare yourself mentally and physically to stand outside in the cold next to your tripod-mounted camera all night. Sooner or later, the reward will be memories and photographs that will last a lifetime.

◄ FIGURE 9-6: Aurora over Prosperous Lake, Prosperous Lake Territorial Park, along the Ingraham Trail near Yellowknife, Northwest Territories, Canada. September 22, 2013, 10:32 p.m. Canon EOS 5D Mark III, Canon EF 16-35mm f/2.8L II USM at 17mm. 5 seconds, f/2.8, ISO 3200.

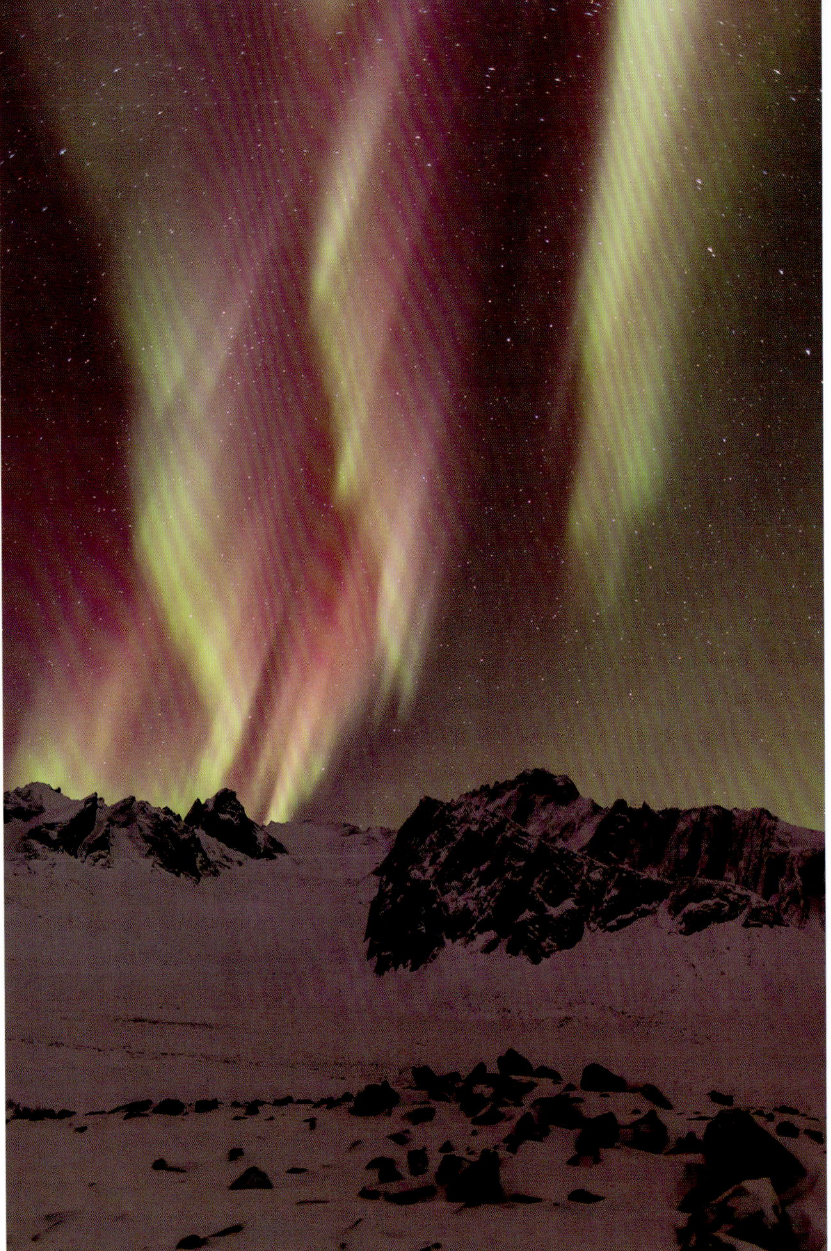

▸ Figure 9-7: Aurora over the Tombstone Range, Tombstone Territorial Park, Yukon Territory, Canada. March 17, 2015, 11:14 p.m. Canon EOS 5D Mark III, Canon EF 24mm f/1.4L II USM lens. 10 seconds, f/2.0, ISO 3200.

Preparing for an Aurora Shoot

The night-photography techniques you've learned elsewhere in this book are equally applicable to shooting the aurora. Use the techniques I describe in chapter 3 to set your lens to infinity focus. If you have an older lens with a mechanical connection between the focus ring and the lens elements, tape the lens so it stays focused at infinity throughout the night. When the aurora is good, it fills the sky. You'll probably use the widest, fastest lens you own. I used my Canon 16-35mm f/2.8 lens almost exclusively when shooting the aurora, with the majority of images at 16mm. I occasionally used my

24mm f/1.4 for very faint, smaller displays. A 35mm lens is usually not wide enough to include all of a good auroral display. If I am so fortunate as to shoot the aurora again, I would use my Sony 14mm f/1.8. Be sure to remove all filters from your lens, including UV filters you may be using primarily to protect the front element. Filter coatings can generate interference patterns in your image that are difficult or impossible to remove. In cold weather, avoid breathing on either the viewfinder or the front element of your lens, and check both frequently for frost or condensation. As with other night photographs, I always shoot with a daylight white balance.

Exposure for the Aurora

Unlike the Milky Way, which moves very slowly, the aurora is in constant motion. Use the shortest shutter speed you can, consistent with good overall exposure, to keep the fine structure in the aurora from becoming smeared. With an aurora of average brightness, a good starting-point exposure is about 10 seconds, f/2.8, ISO 3200. However, the correct exposure varies widely. My collection of aurora photographs includes photos taken at 2 seconds, f/2.0, ISO 800 and at 30 seconds, f/2.8, ISO 6400, a difference of six stops. Check your histogram to be sure you are capturing adequate detail without blowing out the highlights (which is surprisingly easy to do). Engage the blinking highlight warning to double-check that you aren't clipping the highlights. Turn on image review, the setting that causes the camera to display the captured image for a set period after each exposure. During the day, I find this setting annoying, but at night, particularly when it's very cold, it will save you a lot of time fumbling with buttons. I set the length of review time to infinite and cycle through the playback modes until the histogram is displayed. Now after every shot I get a quick check on exposure via both the blinking highlight warning and the histogram. A light tap on the shutter release with my heavily gloved hand turns off the LCD so I'm ready to compose the next shot. Turn down your LCD brightness to avoid getting a false impression about how much detail you've actually recorded. As always, your histogram is your best guide to correct exposure, not the image on your LCD.

In chapter 5 I urged you to shoot two frames when photographing the Milky Way, one exposed for sky, one exposed for land. It's certainly possible, but not necessarily advisable, to adopt the same strategy when shooting the aurora. The very best auroral forms often last only long enough for one exposure. You never know, from one minute to the next, how good it's going to get. You probably won't want to waste time shooting good-land images (which may overexpose the aurora) when the aurora is at its peak. And by

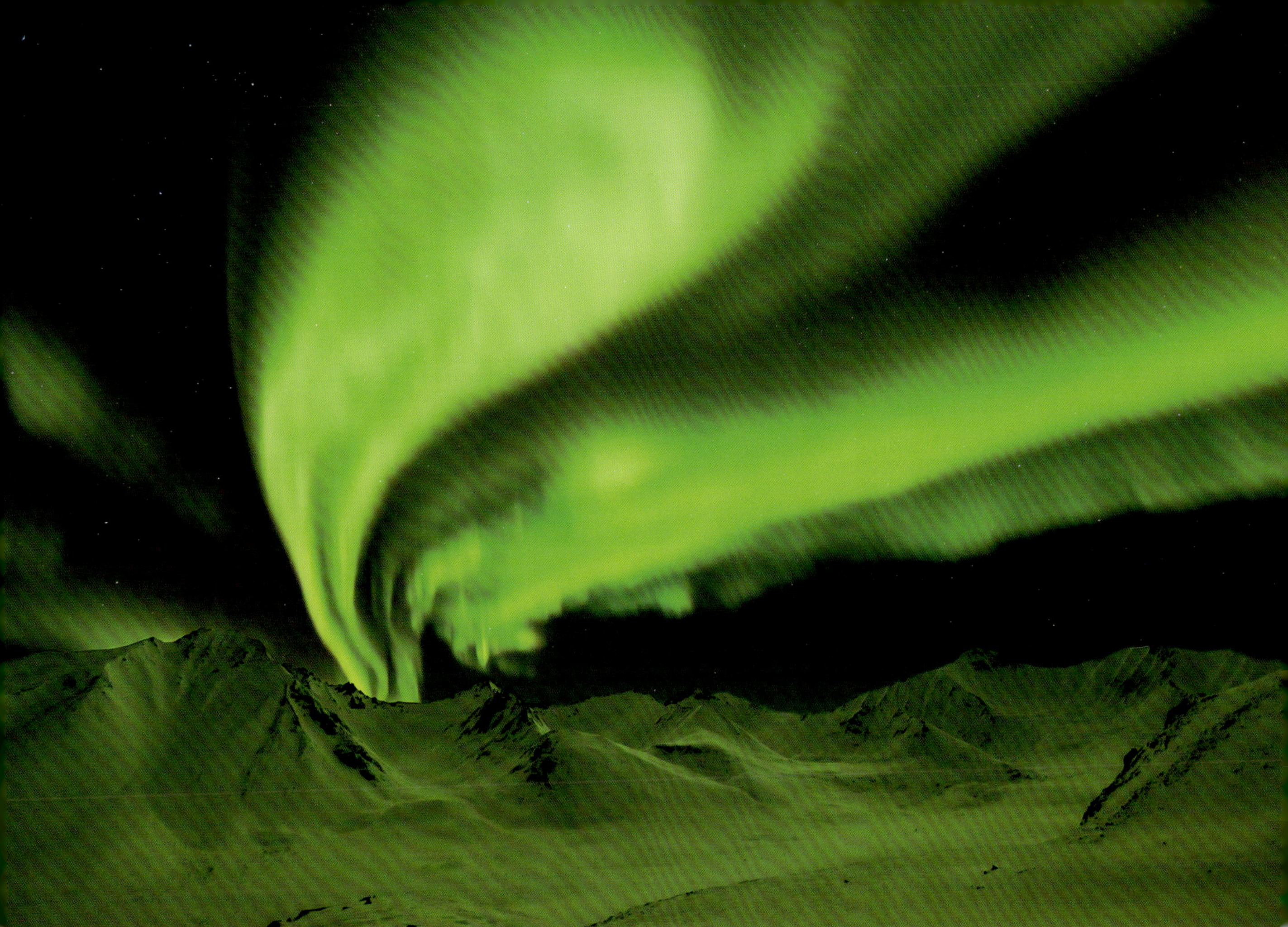

the time the aurora fades, you'll have shot so many different compositions of the aurora you won't know how to position the camera to shoot the corresponding good-land images.

Composing Photographs of the Aurora

The aurora's constant motion means you'll need to compose each shot separately while looking through the lens. You can't just point the camera in the general direction of the aurora and leave it set to that position. In order to see through the lens, your eyes must be as dark-adapted as possible, and that in turn means it's even more important than usual to use a headlamp with red LEDs. Turn your headlamp to a dim setting, use it sparingly, and be sure to turn it off before making the exposure. At high ISOs, the light of your headlamp will turn your foreground red.

When I'm shooting daylight landscapes, my usual strategy is to find the best possible combination of an interesting foreground, mid-ground, and background, refine my composition, wait for the perfect light, then (I hope) nail the shot. Unfortunately, the unpredictable, incessant motion of the aurora makes this traditional approach to composition problematic. For starters, you'll probably be shooting wide open, which limits your depth of field. When shooting with a wide-open 16mm f/2.8 lens focused at infinity, your depth of field extends from 15 feet to infinity. Even if you can find a great foreground that begins 15 feet away, you may not want to use it. Here's the problem: if you commit yourself to a composition with a close-in foreground, you are forced to wait until a good aurora appears within your frame. While you wait, great auroras may be swirling across the sky outside your viewfinder. Waiting for a great auroral form to position itself perfectly within your frame can be a frustrating experience. For your first aurora shoot in particular, and perhaps for many more, the best strategy is to choose an interesting background, such as a mountain range, then recompose each shot as the aurora ebbs and flows. It's difficult enough to capture a great auroral form perfectly positioned over a dramatic group of peaks without trying to include a well-composed, close-in foreground as well. A calm lake that offers the possibility of reflections is another great option. Reflections of very distant objects, such as the aurora, are also at infinity focus, so both the aurora and its reflection will be sharp regardless of how close the reflection appears to be.

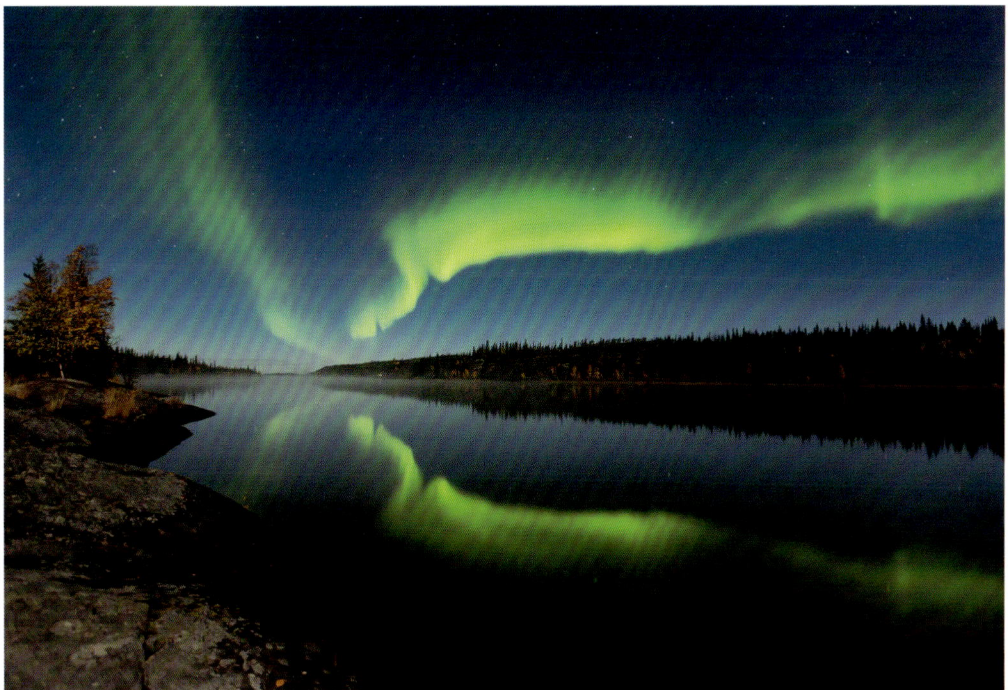

◄ FIGURE 9-9: Aurora at Powder Point, along the eastern shore of Prelude Lake, Hidden Lake Territorial Park, along the Ingraham Trail near Yellowknife, Northwest Territories, Canada. September 23, 2013, 2:03 a.m. Canon EOS 5D Mark III, Canon EF 16-35mm f/2.8L II USM at 16mm. 8 seconds, f/2.8, ISO 3200.

Processing Photographs of the Aurora

The first steps in processing an image of the aurora are similar to those for processing other night photographs, as described in chapter 6. In Lightroom's Lens Corrections panel, check Remove Chromatic Aberration and Enable Profile Corrections. In the Detail panel, try Lightroom Denoise or use the Luminance and Color sliders to reduce noise as necessary. Most aurora photos benefit from a significant boost in contrast to help separate the aurora from the background sky. The easiest method is to use the Contrast slider in the Basic panel. If that makes the land too dark, use the Brush or Select Sky in the Masking panel to add contrast to just the sky. While in the Basic panel, increase saturation to taste. I find a setting of about 10 produces rich but believable color (as if anything about the aurora is believable until you see it with your own eyes!). A generous dose of Clarity (20-30) can help the aurora stand out even more and brighten the stars. A small dose of Dehaze can also be helpful.

If you made your aurora image on a moonlit night using a daylight white balance, the sky will already be a pleasing blue. There's no need to apply any of the Tone Curve presets you may have created to shift the sky blue while preserving the colors of the stars and Milky Way. If you shot the image on a moonless night, you may find that the aurora is enough brighter than the sky that adding contrast makes the aurora stand out strongly against a black sky. In that situation, there may be no need to adjust the color of the sky. If, on the other hand, the sky comes out a muddy deep green, the aurora may not stand out sufficiently even after adding a lot of contrast. Pull the Blacks slider down to further darken the sky, either in the Basic panel (to create a global correction) or by adding a mask with the Brush or Select Sky in the Masking panel and using the Blacks slider to confine the correction to the sky. Or try one of your Milky Way blue sky Tone Curve presets as described in chapter 6.

For all aurora shots, you may wish to jump over to Photoshop and add some local contrast by using Unsharp Mask with a low Amount (around 30) and high Radius (again around 30), as described in chapter 6. You can also try adding local contrast with the High Pass filter technique, again as described in chapter 6. Both techniques will add still more zip to the aurora and brighten the stars.

The last night of my Yellowknife aurora shoot was forecast to be cloudy, just like the six cloudy nights in a row that had preceded it. I was astonished when the clouds parted just after sunset. For four glorious hours I shot the aurora reflected in a rippled pond in Prelude Lake Territorial Park. At 2 a.m., with the aurora still dancing across the sky, I had to head toward the airport to catch a very early flight. By the time I dropped off the rental car, the sky

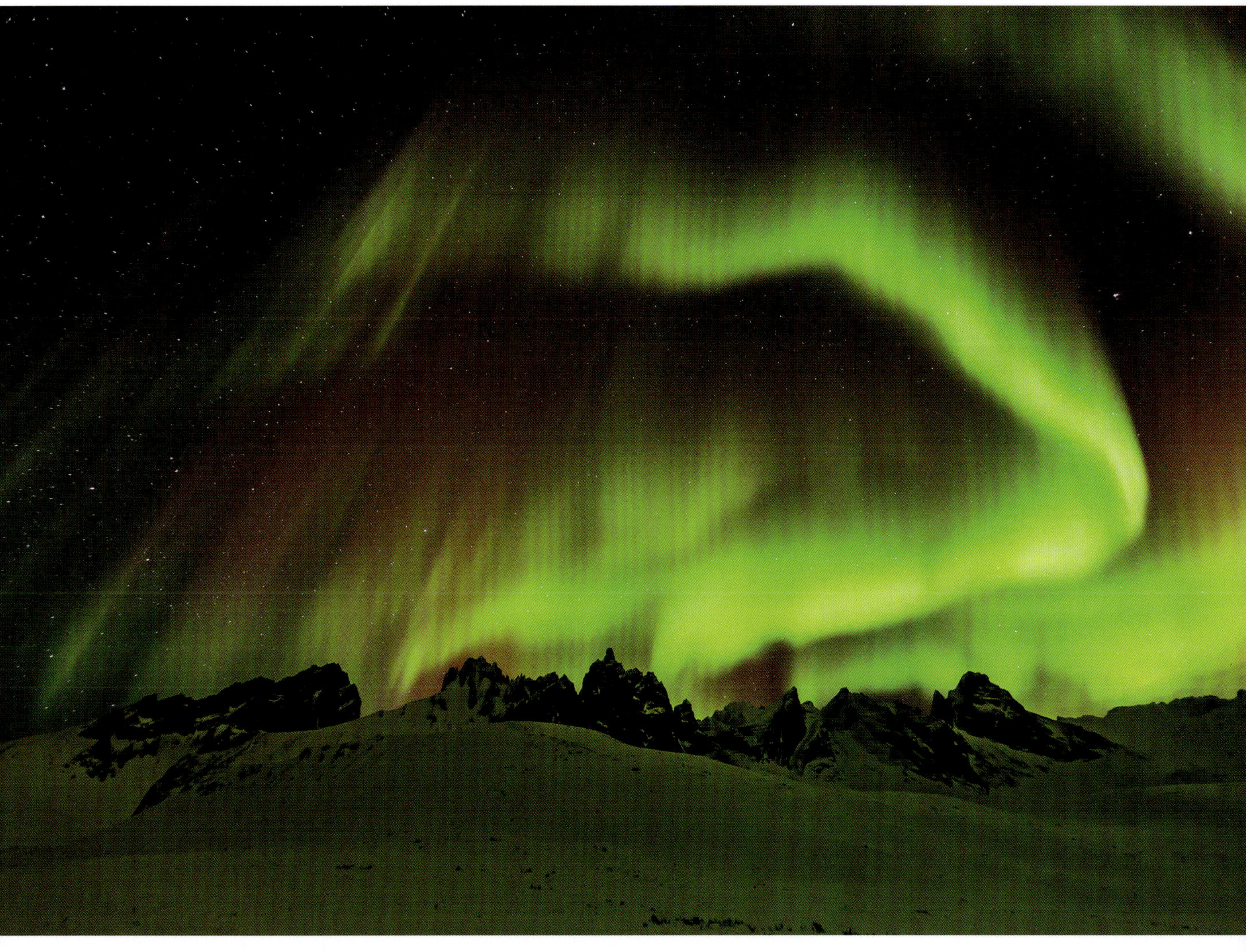

▲ FIGURE 9-10: Aurora over Mt. Monolith, Tombstone Territorial Park, Yukon Territory, Canada. March 17, 2015, 2:33 a.m. Canon 5D Mark III, Canon EF 16-35mm f/2.8L II USM at 16mm. 6 seconds, f/2.8, ISO 3200.

was overcast once more. We took off and the plane climbed into the clouds. Yellowknife vanished like it had never existed. It was like leaving some enchanted kingdom, a mythical place where dragons soared across the sky. That's what it feels like to witness and photograph the aurora—like you've been privileged to witness something so unearthly it can only exist in fantasy. Yet it's real, and every photographer should experience it at least once.

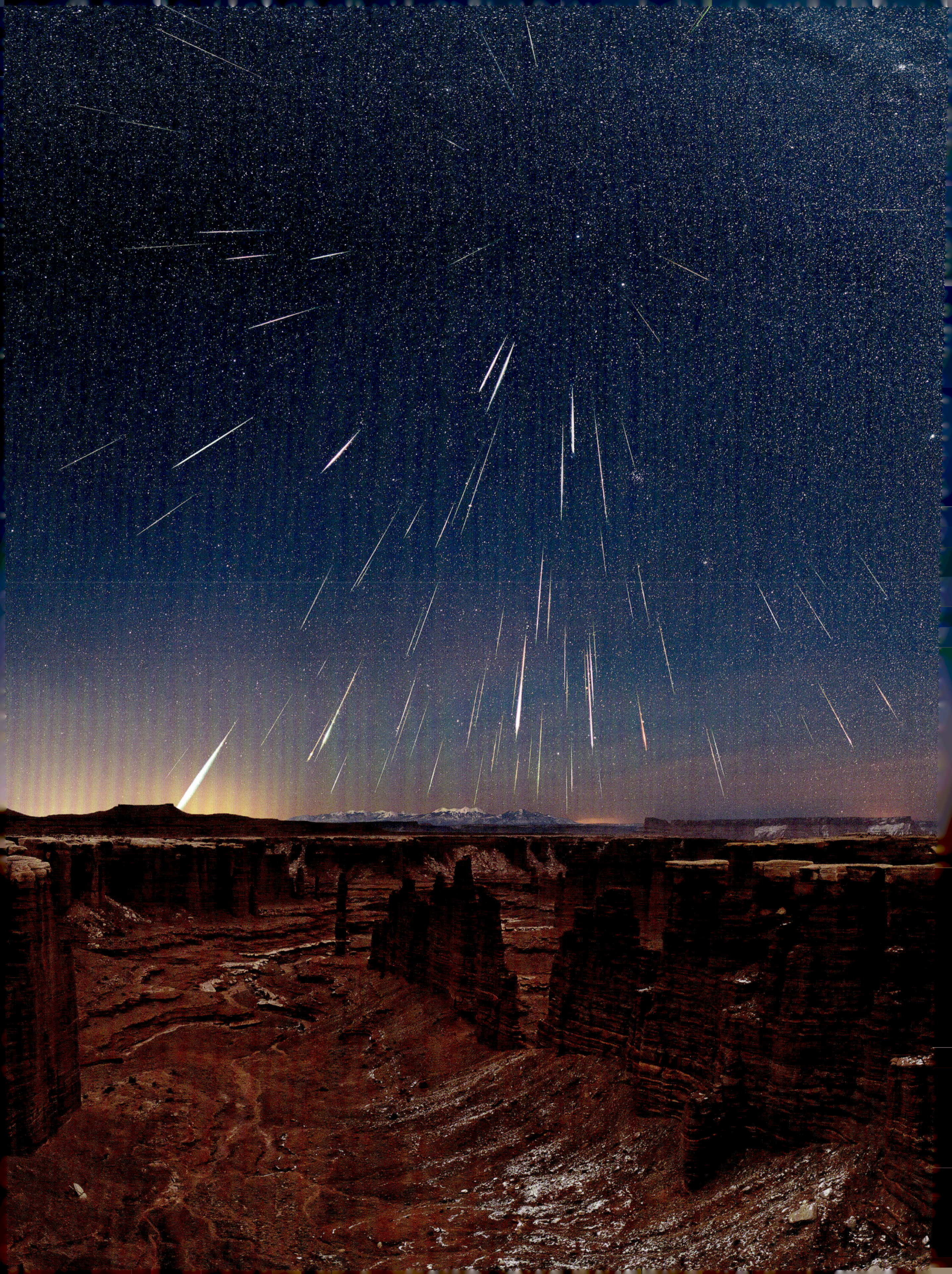

Photographing Meteor Showers, Comets, the Zodiacal Light, and Noctilucent Clouds

The Milky Way and star trails are the two night-photography subjects that are available most frequently. You can shoot star trails on any clear night. You can shoot the Milky Way's galactic core on any clear, moonless night during the Milky Way season for your latitude, as explained in chapter 4. The subjects described in this chapter, by contrast, are available much less frequently. Meteor showers occur at predictable times, but there are only two showers per year that are truly photogenic. The length of time between comets bright enough to be photographed with an ordinary DSLR or mirrorless camera (as opposed to a telescope) can be years or even decades. The zodiacal light, an eerie pillar of light visible to the west after sunset in the spring or to the east before sunrise in the fall, is an easily overlooked subject that is nonetheless fascinating to observe and photograph. Noctilucent clouds ("night-shining clouds") are shimmering, evanescent clouds in the mesosphere that are only visible from certain latitudes for a month or two in midsummer. The skills you learned when shooting the Milky Way can be applied equally well to shooting these subjects. Pursuing them will give you another compelling reason to get outside and photograph the wonders of the night sky.

Meteor Showers

Everyone who has been outside on a clear, moonless night has seen it happen: soundlessly and without warning, a bright streak splits the sky, then vanishes a second later. You've just witnessed a "falling star"—a meteor. The sight can be breathtaking.

Meteors occur when a bit of debris shed by a comet or asteroid enters Earth's atmosphere at speeds ranging from 25,000 to 160,000 miles per hour. At those speeds, friction with the air 50 to 75 miles above Earth's surface heats the *meteoroid*, as the bit of debris is known, to a temperature that can reach thousands of degrees Kelvin. The tremendous heat causes the gases along the meteoroid's path to ionize and glow, creating a momentary streak of bright light. These gases come both from the atmosphere and from bits of vaporized meteoroid. The column of excited gas may be only three feet

◄ Figure 10-1: Geminid meteor shower over Monument Basin, Canyonlands National Park, Utah, December 13-14, 2018. This composite image shows 86 meteors captured over period of nine hours and 15 minutes. All told, this image required 958 miles of driving, 10 hours of four-wheeling, and three days of processing in Photoshop. Land and sky: Canon EOS 5D Mark IV, Canon EF 35mm f/1.4L II USM. Land: one row, four camera positions per row, four frames per camera position, images stacked in Photoshop, noise reduced with Stack Mode>Median, 60 seconds, f/1.4, ISO 6400. Sky: two rows, four camera positions per row, four frames per camera position, images aligned and noise reduced in RegiStar, 10 seconds, f/1.4, ISO 6400. Meteors: 2702 frames exposed with two cameras (Canon EOS 5D Mark IV and Canon EOS 5D Mark III) each fitted with a Canon EF 24mm f/1.4L II USM lens. The cameras were mounted side-by-side using the setup shown in figure 10-10. Meteor exposures: 20 seconds, f/1.4, ISO 2000.

across, but it can stretch for 10 miles or more. Most meteoroids are tiny, ranging in size from a grain of sand to a small pebble, and burn up completely before smashing into the ground. Those that do reach Earth's surface are called *meteorites*.

Meteors fall every night of the year. By one estimate, as many as 25 million visible meteors fall worldwide every day. If you're outside long enough, you're bound to see a few. These sporadic meteors, as they're called, fall more frequently in the hours before dawn than they do right after sunset. They're also more common during early fall, around September, than they are in the spring, around March. Even under good viewing conditions, you might see only two to four meteors per hour in early evening in March, but you might see as many as eight to 16 meteors per hour just before dawn in September.

You can dramatically increase your odds of seeing lots of meteors if you go out during a *meteor shower*, a period when meteors rain down much more frequently than normal. Most meteor showers are associated with comets, which are often described as dirty snowballs because they are made up of ice, rocky debris, and a variety of gasses. As comets come close to the sun during their orbits, they shed large quantities of debris. This stream of debris spreads out slowly along the comets' orbits. If Earth passes through a debris stream, we experience a meteor shower as innumerable bits of debris burn up in Earth's atmosphere.

Meteor showers have a radiant, a point in the sky where all the meteors appear to originate. Meteors appear to radiate from a single point for the same reason railroad tracks seem to converge in the distance when viewed while standing between the tracks. The visible meteor streak may not begin at the radiant. Meteors often travel 30 degrees or more from the radiant before becoming bright enough to see. In fact, meteors can appear in any part of the sky. If you trace all the meteor streaks back to their origin, however, they all appear to begin at the radiant. Meteor showers are named for their radiants. The Perseids, for example, appear to radiate from a point in the constellation Perseus (although some authorities say the radiant is actually now in Cassiopeia). The stars, of course, are far more distant than the bits of comet debris that create meteors. A number of meteor showers occur every year, but the best two are the Perseids, which peak between August 11 and August 13 every year, and the Geminids, which peak around December 13 or 14.

The number of meteors you will see per hour depends on many factors. For starters, you need to seek out a dark location, just as you do when you're shooting the Milky Way. A moonless night is ideal. The full moon will drown out all but the brightest meteors. In fact, don't bother going out to shoot if 50 percent or more of the moon is illuminated. The Perseid meteor shower in August 2016 was supposed to be exceptional, with a peak rate of 200 meteors

▶ FIGURE 10-2: Perseid meteor shower over the Titan, Fisher Towers, Utah. August 11-12, 2016, 8:32 p.m. to 5:08 a.m. Canon 5D Mark III, Canon EF 14mm f/2.8L II USM. Land: 10 seconds, f/16, ISO 100 (shot 17 minutes after sunset). Sky: composite of 73 frames, 30 seconds, f/2.8, ISO 6400. The meteor-containing layers have been rotated around Polaris so that all Perseid meteors appear to originate at the radiant. Some meteors were sporadics.

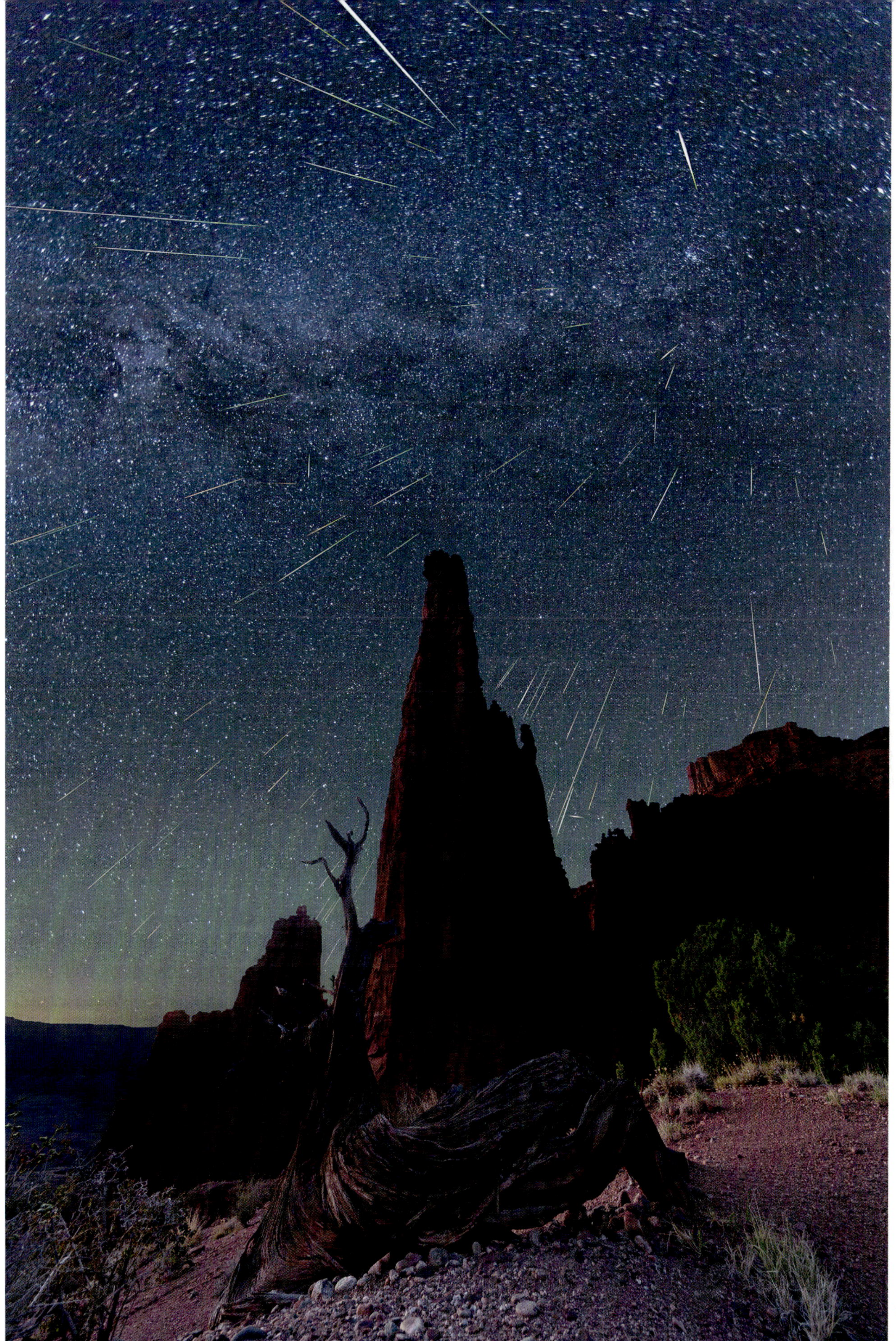

► FIGURE 10-3: During the hours between sunset and midnight, observers are facing away from the direction of Earth's motion as it orbits the sun. Meteoroids that enter that part of Earth's atmosphere have "overtaken" Earth, which means they are moving relatively slowly in relation to Earth. Slower speeds mean less heating, which means that the meteoroid is less likely to generate a visible meteor. During the hours between midnight and dawn, observers are facing toward the direction of Earth's motion as it orbits the sun. Meteoroids that enter that part of Earth's atmosphere hit Earth "head-on" and are moving very fast in relation to Earth, which means they are more likely to become visible meteors.

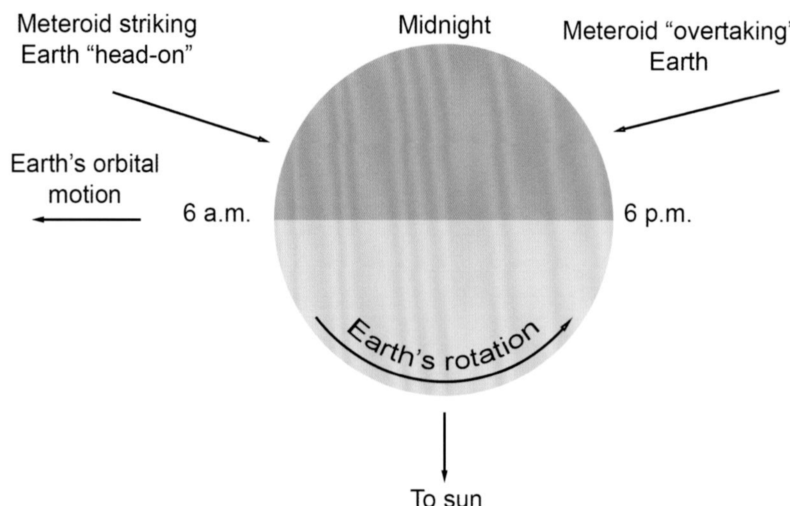

per hour. Unfortunately, the moon, which was 50 percent illuminated, was above the horizon during the first half of the night. I only recorded 13 meteors, all pretty faint, while making back-to-back exposures for four hours and 22 minutes. Fortunately, the moon set just before 1 a.m., and I was able to record many more meteors during the remainder of the night.

Most showers peak in the early morning hours before dawn, for two major reasons.

The first is that the radiant for most showers is highest in the sky after midnight. You'll see more meteors when the radiant is high in the sky because more meteors will become visible before they disappear below the horizon. In addition, when the radiant is low in the sky, even the meteors you can see will be near the horizon. Those meteors are much farther away than meteors that occur directly above you. Distance attenuates the light, as does the scattering caused by the additional miles of atmosphere.

The second major reason you'll see more meteors after midnight concerns the direction an observer is facing in relation to the path of Earth's orbit around the sun (figure 10-3). During the evening hours, an observer is facing away from the direction of Earth's motion through space as it orbits the sun. Meteors you see during evening hours must have "overtaken" Earth. Although meteoroids are generally traveling faster than Earth's motion through space, the difference is relatively small, so the meteoroid enters Earth's atmosphere at a relatively slow speed. The brightness of a meteor depends strongly on the speed of the corresponding meteoroid, so evening meteors are usually dimmer, if they can be seen at all. To make this clearer, imagine you're in a car driving 60 mph. There's a car behind you that is traveling in the same direction at 70 mph. It will catch up to you, but only at a rate of 10 miles per hour.

The situation is different during the early morning hours before sunrise. Now an observer is facing toward the direction of Earth's motion as it orbits the sun. The speed of Earth's motion adds to the speed of the meteoroid, which smashes into Earth's atmosphere at very high speed, increasing the chance it will become a bright meteor. It's as if you were driving at 60 mph and had a head-on collision with a car traveling in the opposite direction at 70 mph. The combined speed of the two vehicles—the rate at which they are approaching each other—would be 130 mph. Obviously, the collision would be catastrophic.

The rate at which meteors are expected to fall is often given as a *zenithal hourly rate*. This is the rate an observer would see if the radiant was directly overhead, at the observer's zenith. As a practical matter, the radiant is never quite directly overhead for the Perseids and Geminids as seen from the middle latitudes in North America. In Boulder, for example, the radiant for the Perseids reaches a maximum altitude of 62 degrees at astronomical dawn during the peak night of the shower. The radiant for the Geminid meteor shower reaches an altitude of 83 degrees at about 2 a.m. during the peak night. As a result, zenithal hourly rates are usually higher than most observers will actually see. The American Meteor Society puts the zenithal hourly rate for the Perseids at 100 but estimates that only 50 or so will actually be visible even for observers viewing the shower on a moonless night from a dark sky location. Similarly, the zenithal hourly rate for the Geminids is 120, but only about 75 meteors per hour will actually be visible even under ideal conditions.

Planning an Image of the Perseid or Geminid Meteor Shower

Witnessing a meteor shower is amazing; creating a compelling photograph of that experience is a challenge. Even the most active meteor showers, the Perseids and Geminids, produce just one or two meteors per minute. Those numbers refer to meteors visible anywhere in the sky. Even an ultra-wide 16mm lens on a full-frame camera can only see roughly one-third of the sky at best, less if part of the frame is occupied by land. The longest exposure you can use with a 16mm lens before the stars begin to make obvious streaks is about 30 seconds. Put all those figures together, and it's clear you're unlikely to capture more than one meteor in a single exposure—if you even capture one.

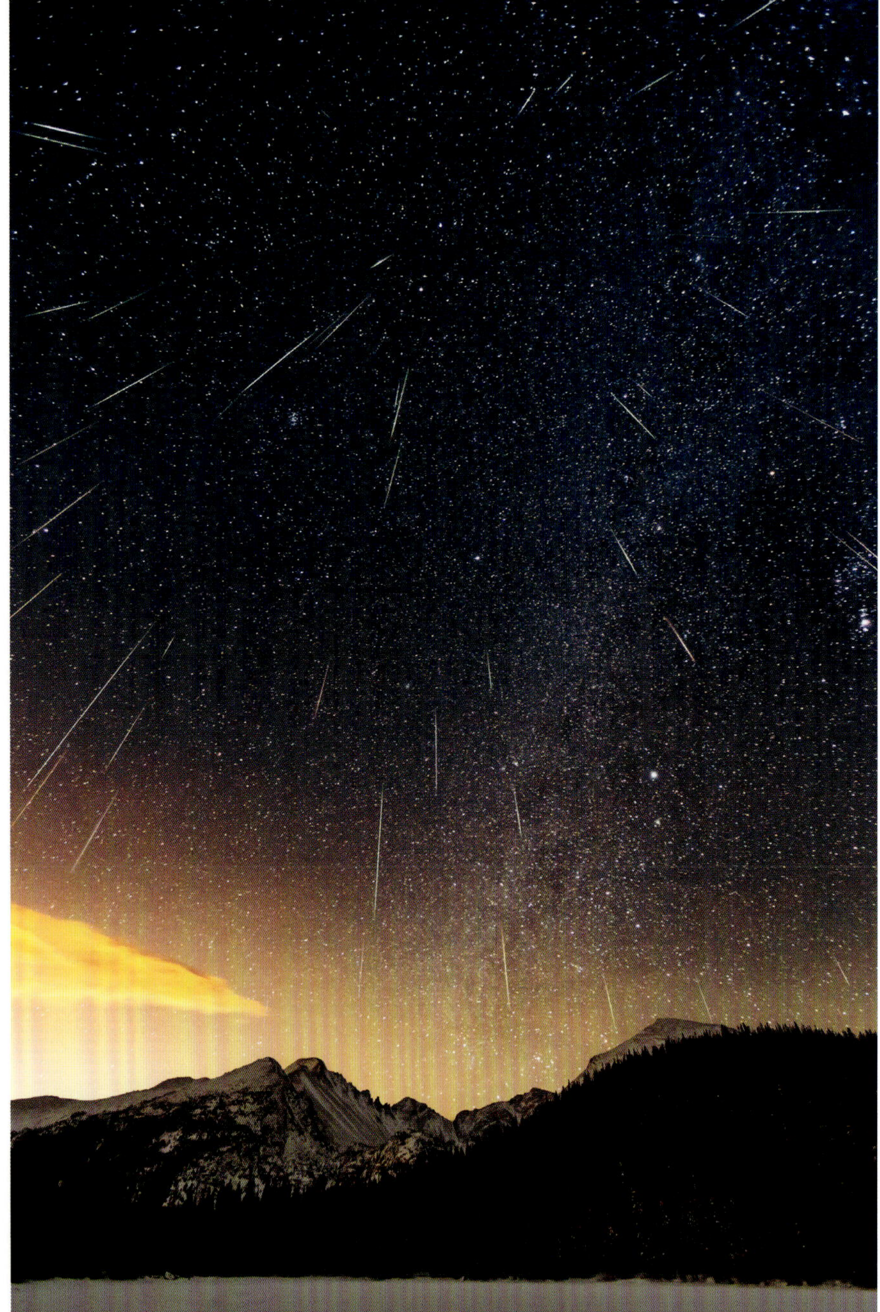

► FIGURE 10-4: Geminid meteor shower over Longs Peak and Bear Lake, Rocky Mountain National Park, Colorado. December 12-13, 2015, 9:40 p.m. to 5:44 a.m. Canon 5D Mark III, Canon EF 16-35mm f/2.8L II USM at 16mm. Land: one frame, 2 minutes, f/2.8, ISO 6400. Sky and meteors: 30 seconds, f/2.8, ISO 6400. This image is a composite of 54 images (one land image, 53 meteor images). I moved all of the Geminid meteors so they appeared to be radiating from the radiant, which is near the star Castor in the constellation Gemini. Three meteors were sporadics that did not originate in Gemini.

So how do you make a photograph that evokes the feeling of watching an active meteor shower?

One way to make a good meteor-shower photograph is to compose your image to include an interesting subject, then shoot back-to-back exposures all night with an ultra-wide-angle lens. It's not essential to include the radiant in your frame since meteors can appear in any part of the sky. Use an exposure that keeps the stars from making obnoxious streaks. For example, if you're shooting with a 16mm f/2.8 lens, your exposure should be 30 seconds, f/2.8, ISO 6400. While you're on location, be sure to make some longer exposures (in this example, usually 2 minutes, f/2.8, ISO 6400) that will record good detail in the land. Once you return home, sift through your images to locate the frame with the brightest meteor that fits into the frame compositionally. Combine that frame with the good-land frame, and you've created an image that evokes at least some of the feelings you experienced.

That approach is simple enough, but it doesn't fully capture the excitement of watching shooting stars fall from the heavens for hours on end. To do that, you may want to combine all the meteors you capture into one frame, then composite that image with a background sky frame and a second frame exposed for the land.

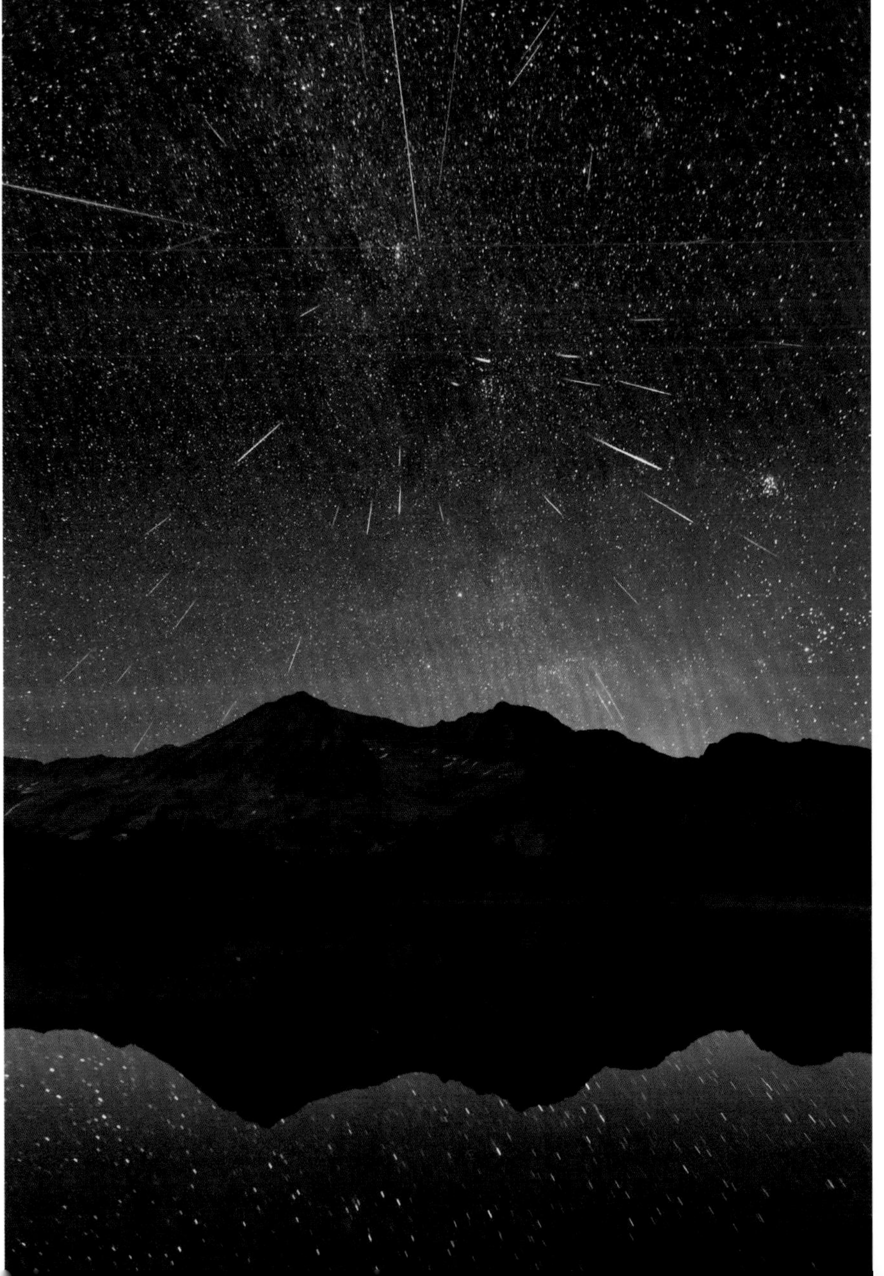

◄ FIGURE 10-5: Perseid meteors over Snowmass Mountain and Snowfield Lake, Maroon Bells-Snowmass Wilderness, Colorado. August 12-13, 2015, 9:09 p.m. to 4:52 a.m. Canon 5D Mark III, Canon EF 16-35mm f/2.8L II USM at 16mm. Land: 2 minutes, f/2.8, ISO 6400. Sky and meteors: 30 seconds, f/2.8, ISO 6400. This image is a composite of 40 images (one land image, 39 meteor images). One meteor-containing image also provided the background sky. For this image I needed two versions of the land image (which included the reflection of the sky). In Lightroom, in the Library Module, I created a virtual copy of the land image (Photo>Create Virtual Copy). I edited the first version for correct color in the mountains and the reflection of the mountains. I edited the second version for correct color in the reflection of the sky. To create the first version I set Temp to 4600K in the Basic panel in Lightroom. This slightly cooled off the land to preserve the nighttime feel. To create the second version I applied the same Milky Way blue-sky preset I applied to the sky images. This preset shifts sky (and the reflection of the sky) toward blue while preserving star colors (see chapter 6). I blended the two versions of the land-plus-reflection image with a layer mask.

The first step in planning such a shot is to decide if you want to include the radiant in your image. While certainly not essential, including the radiant gives the image a strong point of interest, so I generally include it. If you do decide to include the radiant, consult Starry Night or the Planner module in PhotoPills for the azimuth and altitude of the radiant at specific times during the peak nights.

Once you know where the radiant will be, you can begin to identify your shooting location. Let's start by planning a Perseid meteor-shower shot. The Perseids peak every year in the early morning hours of August 11, 12, and 13. The radiant for the Perseids, as seen from Colorado, is *circumpolar*: it moves counter-clockwise along a giant circle centered on Polaris, and never sets. At astronomical dusk the azimuth of the radiant is roughly 22 degrees; the altitude is roughly 14 degrees. At astronomical dawn, the azimuth of the radiant is about 38 degrees; the altitude is about 61 degrees. In other words, you basically want to be looking northeast if you want to include the radiant. Use your knowledge of promising locations and Photo Ephemeris Web to identify places where you will be looking northeast at something interesting. PlanIt Pro has a cool virtual reality module that can help you visualize where the radiant will be in relationship to the land when using lenses of different focal lengths. The 3D module in Photo Ephemeris Web shows graphically the position of the radiant in relation to the land for various meteor showers; as of this writing, it doesn't include the azimuth and altitude of the radiant.

For example, for my photograph of the Perseids over Snowmass Mountain in the Maroon Bells-Snowmass Wilderness near Aspen (figure 10-5), I decided to shoot from Snowfield Lake. I planned to shoot the background sky image when the radiant was roughly over the saddle between Snowmass Mountain and Hagerman Peak. At 3 a.m. on August 13th, 2015, the radiant had an azimuth (compass bearing) of about 43 degrees and an altitude (angle above a level horizon) of 49 degrees, as shown in figure 10-6. The shot I took at 3 a.m. would become my background sky image, the one containing the stars that would fill the night sky. That image would also contain the radiant. I would arrange all the meteor-containing layers so that the meteors would appear to originate at the radiant.

My approach to planning an image of the Geminid meteor shower is similar to that for my images of the Perseids, but with one important difference. The radiant for the Perseids is in the northeast sky throughout the night as seen from Denver. The radiant for the Geminids, which is near the star

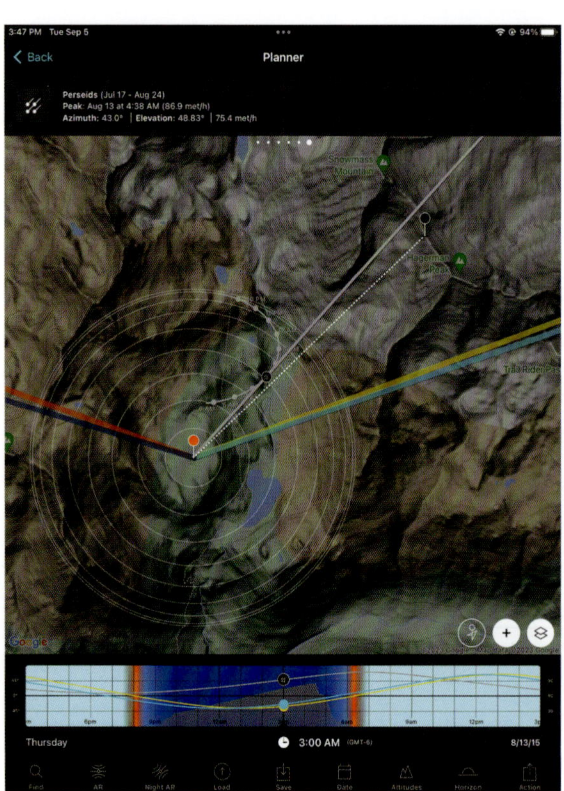

▼ FIGURE 10-6: Screenshot from Photo-Pills showing the altitude and azimuth of the radiant of the Perseids meteor shower at 3:00 a.m. on August 13, 2015, as seen from Snowfield Lake. The red pin is at Snowfield Lake. The black pin is on the saddle between Snowmass Mountain and Hagerman Peak. In the top-left corner you'll find the name of the meteor shower, the date and time when it peaks as seen from Snowfield Lake, the azimuth and altitude of the radiant at the date and time set, and the predicted number of meteors per hour.

Castor in the constellation Gemini, is not. It rises to the northeast a few minutes before astronomical dusk at about 6:15 p.m., is due east with an altitude of about 55 degrees at about 11:15 p.m., transits (reaches its highest altitude, 82 degrees) when it is due south at about 2 a.m. and is setting to the west with an altitude of about 47 degrees at astronomical dawn. No lens except an 8mm fisheye with a 180-degree angle of view can encompass such a wide swath of sky.

One good solution to this dilemma is to choose a composition where you are looking roughly east or west at some interesting geographic feature. If you choose a composition looking south, the radiant will be very high in the sky, which will crowd the radiant against the top of the frame if you also include an interesting land element. The ideal composition would not have any high mountains or canyon walls blocking your view of the sky along an arc from northeast, through south, to west. As you plan your composition, consider where you want to place the radiant in the frame. Let's say you want to place it over Longs Peak as seen from your shooting location at Bear Lake in Rocky Mountain National Park. Use Photo Ephemeris Web, Sun Surveyor, or Photo-Pills to determine the azimuth of Longs Peak from Bear Lake, then PhotoPills or Starry Night to determine when the radiant will be in that direction. PhotoPills or Starry Night will also tell you the altitude of the radiant at that time, so you can determine how wide a lens you'll need to include the desired amount of land while still placing the radiant roughly one-quarter to one-third of the way down from the top of the frame. The frame you shoot at that time will become the background sky layer in the final image. That frame will also contain the radiant, which will become the origin of all the meteors you capture during the night when you finish editing the image.

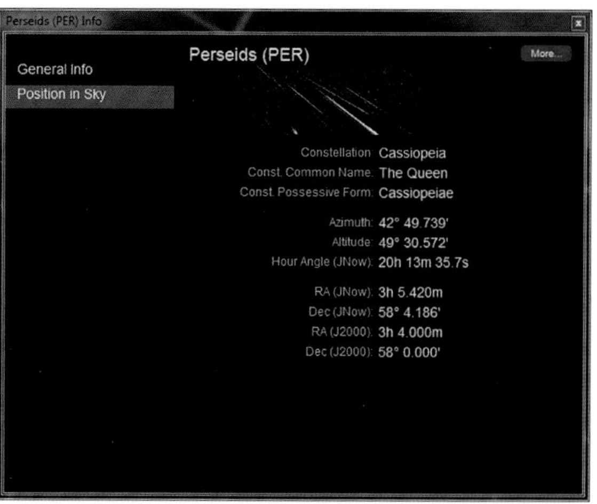

▲ FIGURE 10-7: Information about the azimuth and altitude of the radiant can also be found in Starry Night, as shown in this screenshot showing the position of the Perseids radiant at 3 a.m. on August 13, 2015, as seen from Snowfield Lake.

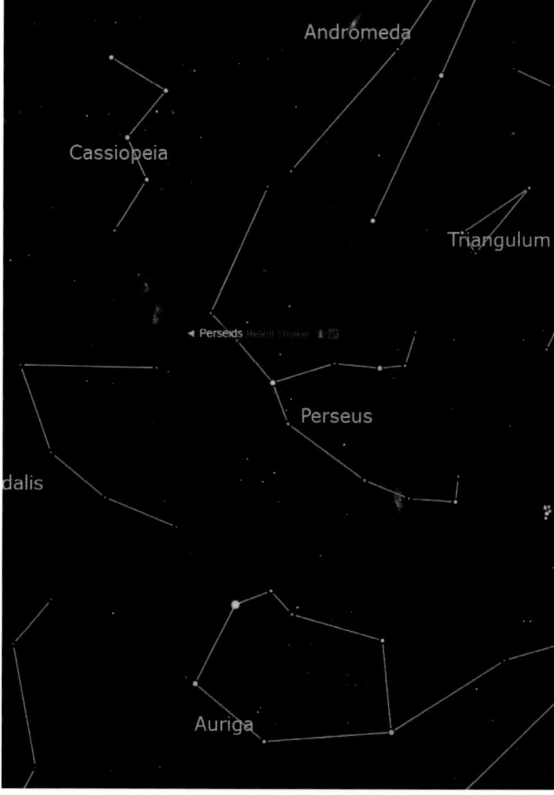

▶ FIGURE 10-8: The star map in Starry Night can help you locate the radiant in the sky. This screenshot shows the location of the radiant for the Perseid meteor shower at 3 a.m. on August 13, 2015, as seen from Snowfield Lake. I always take a screenshot of the star map, print it, and bring it with me to my shooting location.

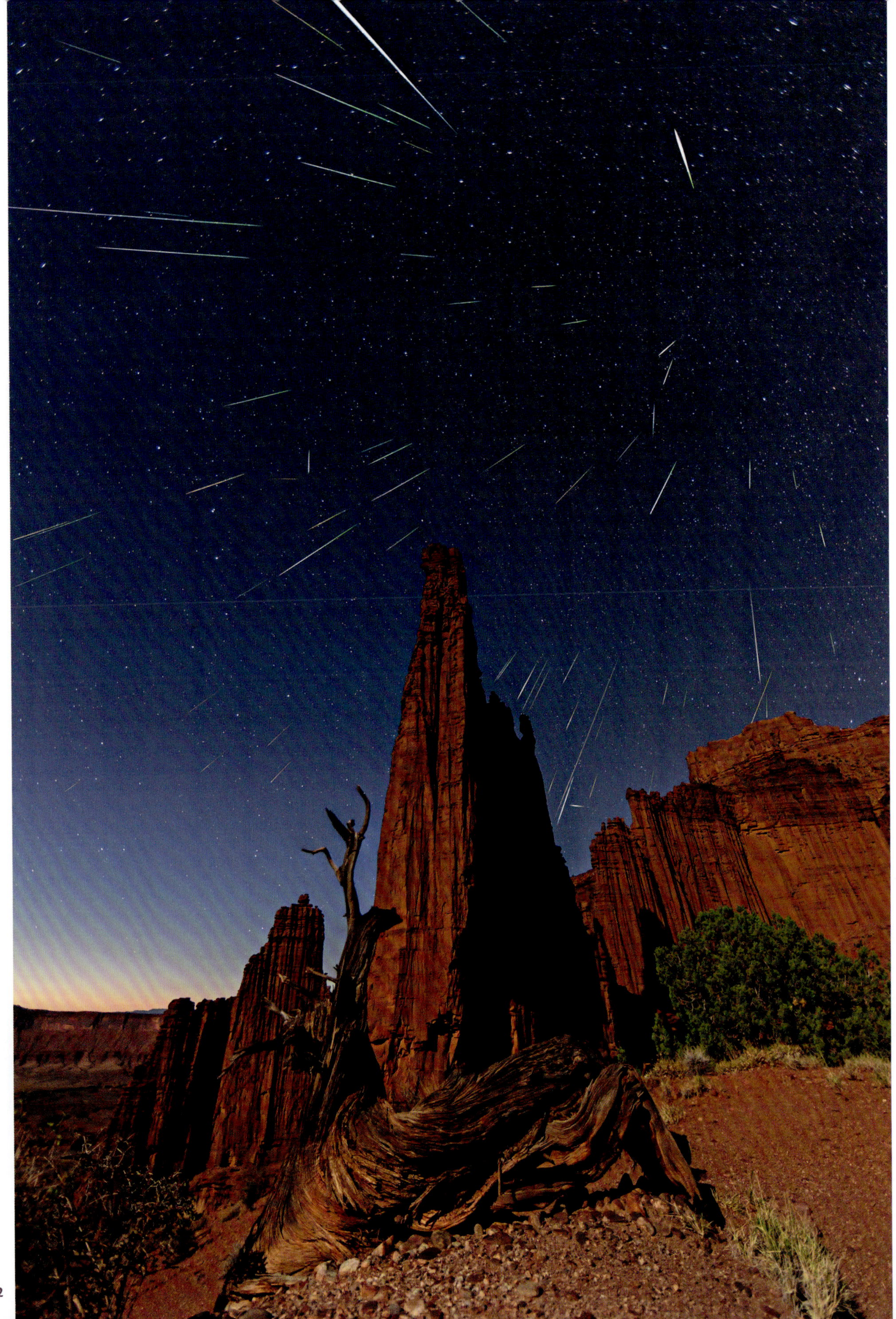

Shooting a Meteor Shower

Once you arrive at your shooting location, check that the camera's clock is set to the right time. It's easier to identify constellations and stars in the frame if the capture time embedded in the metadata is accurate. For the Perseids, I compose the image, lock down the tripod, and don't touch the controls again for the entire night. For the Geminids, I center the radiant in the frame left-to-right, then move the camera every 10 minutes or so to keep the radiant roughly centered, being sure that one of the compositions I use will be the one where the radiant is in the correct position in relationship to the land. At astronomical dusk, use an intervalometer to start making back-to-back exposures. Be sure you have enough extra batteries on hand to shoot continuously for hours and enough memory cards to hold all the data. To conserve space on my memory card, I use the 500 rule to choose the shutter speed when shooting meteors. The slight streaks made by the stars won't matter, since I'll be hiding everything from each meteor-containing image except for the meteor itself. I use a shorter shutter speed to reduce star trailing and shoot multiple identical frames when I'm shooting the background sky image. I then stack the frames to reduce noise, as explained in chapter 7. For reasons I'll explain later, I choose an ISO that's about 2/3 of a stop darker than I would use for a good Milky Way photograph at that location, then set the aperture to wide open. For example, with a 16mm lens I would shoot at 30 seconds, f/2.8, ISO 4000. Track the radiant until astronomical dawn, when the brightening sky begins to wash out the meteors. During the night I also make at least one good-land exposure and preferably more so I can use Stack Mode>Median to reduce noise, as described in chapter 7. I also make a reference photo (which won't appear in the final image) that is deliberately underexposed by 2 or 3 stops when the radiant is in the right position in my frame. This frame will show far fewer stars and make it easier to identify which stars belong to a constellation. When assembling the final composite, I compare the stars in this image to a star chart such as Starry Night to help locate the radiant.

If you have the luxury of owning two camera bodies with good high-ISO performance, two tripods, and two fast, wide lenses (perhaps an ultra-wide-angle, moderately fast lens, and a moderately wide, ultra-fast lens), you can improve your odds of catching lots of bright meteors. (If you don't own that much hardware, consider renting.) Normally you'll use your widest lens, perhaps a 14mm or 16mm f/2.8, to shoot the land and the background sky images. After shooting the background sky image, reposition that camera every 10 minutes or so to ensure that the radiant remains in the same location within the frame throughout the night, as described previously. Position your ultra-fast, moderate wide-angle lens, such as a 35mm f/1.4 or

◄ FIGURE 10-9: Perseid meteor shower over the Titan, Fisher Towers, Utah. August 11-12, 2016, 9:44 p.m. to 5:07 a.m. Canon 5D Mark III, Canon EF 14mm f/2.8L II USM. Land: five focus positions, 30 seconds, f/2.8, ISO 3200. Sky: composite of 64 frames, 30 seconds, f/2.8, ISO 6400. A waxing gibbous moon (65 percent illuminated) provided the light on the land. Most meteors were captured after moonset. The meteor-containing layers have been rotated around Polaris so that all Perseid meteors appear to originate at the radiant. Some meteors were sporadics.

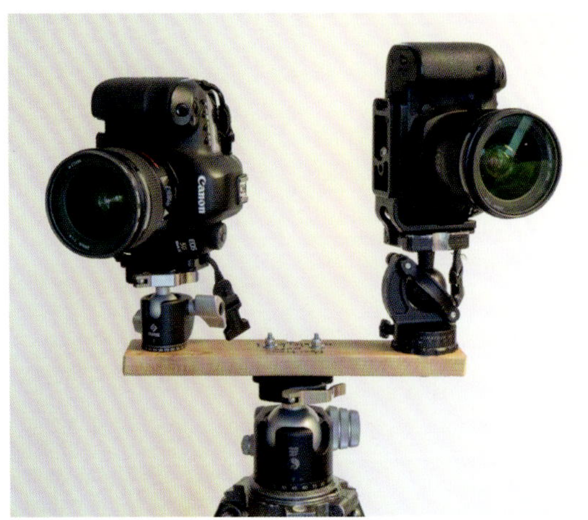

▲ Figure 10-10: My two-camera setup for shooting meteor showers. A 24mm f/1.4 lens is mounted on each camera.

24mm f/1.4, so that the radiant is centered in the frame. Reposition that camera every 10 minutes to keep the radiant centered throughout the night. The length of a meteor that appears close to the radiant is likely to be relatively short due to foreshortening. With luck, you'll capture the entire meteor within the field of view of your moderate-wide-angle lens. By using an f/1.4 aperture, you'll ensure that the meteor will be very bright, making it prominent in the completed image even though it is relatively short. Your ultra-wide-angle lens will capture meteors that begin farther from the radiant. These meteors are likely to be longer because they are less foreshortened. Although they may not be as bright because of the slower maximum aperture of f/2.8, their length will still make them prominent in the final composition.

An alternative two-camera approach is to use two 24mm f/1.4 lenses, which provide an excellent balance between wide angle of view and the light-gathering power of an aperture with a large area. I built a bracket to hold two tripod heads, which in turn was mounted on a single large tripod. I then mounted two cameras, each with a 24mm f/1.4 lens, on the heads mounted atop the bracket (figure 10-10). I positioned the cameras so the fields of views of the two lenses overlapped slightly, then moved the bracket to keep the radiant roughly in the middle of the combined fields of views throughout the night.

Assembling a Meteor Shower Image

Once you return home, use Lightroom to examine the images at 50 percent magnification and identify those images that contain a bright meteor. Don't bother examining the images at 100 percent magnification. You don't want to waste lots of time searching for meteors that are so faint they would never add significantly to the final image. Next, select all the good-sky images and use the Tone Curve panel in Lightroom to shift the color of the sky to a pleasing blue while preserving the colors of the stars and meteors, as described in chapter 6. Open the Lens Corrections panel and check the boxes labeled Lens Profile Corrections and Reduce Chromatic Aberrations. Reduce noise in the Detail panel using Denoise or the traditional noise-reduction sliders.

You'll find that many images contain the streaks made by passing jets and satellites. To separate these streaks from meteors, examine the images immediately preceding and following the image in question. If the streak appears in two or more successive images, it has to be a jet or satellite. Meteors only last a second or two, so they cannot appear in two successive

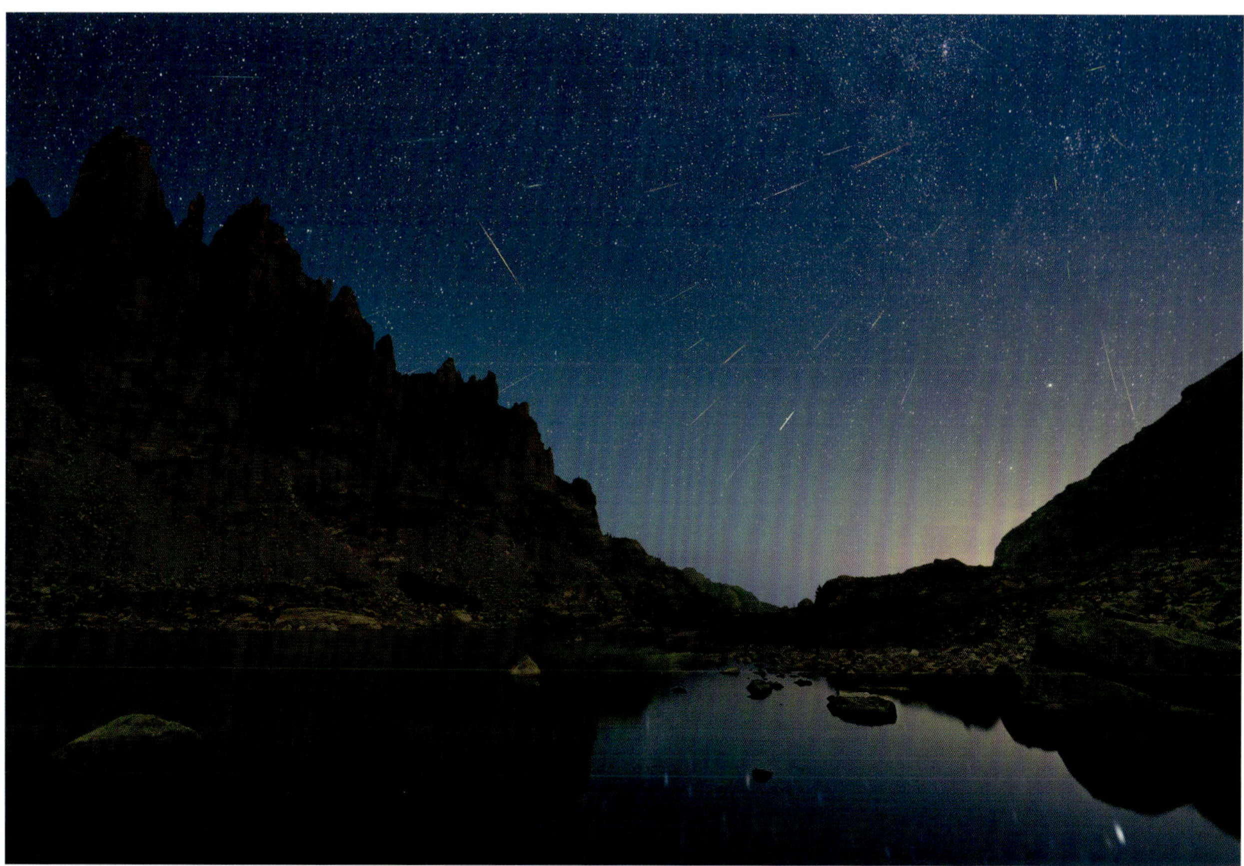

30-second exposures. Give each image containing a meteor a one-star rating, then do a second pass through all the images rated one star and give the brightest meteors a two-star rating. Next, select all the two-star meteor-containing images, open one in the Develop module, and make sure Auto Sync is selected. If necessary, darken all the meteor-containing images by .5 stops. You want to make sure the meteor-containing images are slightly darker than your background sky image. As you'll soon see, this will make it easier to select the meteors. Locate the background sky image and the image that was correctly exposed for the land and give them two stars as well.

Next, filter your meteor folder in Lightroom to show only the two-star images (the ones containing the brightest meteors, plus the background sky image and the land image), select all the images (Control+A), then choose Edit>Open as Layers in Photoshop. Drag the good land exposure to the bottom of the layer stack, then drag the background sky image to just above the good-land image.

The next task is to perfectly select the meteor in each meteor-containing image. Target the top layer in the layer stack, which should be the first layer containing a bright meteor. Add a layer mask. Activate the Brush tool and choose a soft, round brush a bit wider than the meteor. Set the foreground color to black. With the mask targeted, click once at the beginning of the meteor. Press-and-hold Shift and click again at the end of the meteor. Photoshop will draw a straight brush stroke between the two clicks. The meteor will disappear. Press Control+I to invert the mask, which will reveal the meteor streak once more (along with a narrow fringe of dark sky) and hide everything else on the meteor-containing layer. Change the blend mode of the meteor-containing layer to Lighten. By darkening all the meteor-containing images prior to loading them into Photoshop (either by underexposing them in the field or darkening them in Lightroom), you ensured that the sky surrounding the meteor would be darker than the background sky at that point. As I explained in chapter 8, the Lighten blend mode compares the pixel in the target layer to the pixel directly underneath. If the pixel underneath is lighter, Photoshop allows that pixel to shine through. The thin strip of sky surrounding the meteor is darker than the sky of the background star layer, so it will disappear.

If the halo of dark sky doesn't disappear completely, target the meteor layer (not the meteor layer mask) and darken the layer a bit further with a Curves adjustment (not a Curves adjustment layer) by choosing Image>Adjustments>Curves. Repeat this procedure for all the remaining meteor-containing layers.

You now have an image full of meteors that appear to crisscross the sky at random. This happened because the radiant, like all celestial objects, appears to move as the earth rotates. Simply compositing all the meteor-containing layers together makes the meteors look like they originate all over the sky rather than emanate from a single point.

The easiest way to fix this is to identify the radiant in both the meteor-containing image and the background sky layer, target the meteor-containing layer, activate the Move tool, and drag the meteor-containing layer until the two radiants coincide. If moving the meteor-containing layer positions the meteor outside the boundary of your image, or if you can't identify the radiant in both layers, you'll have to use your best judgment in placing the meteor so it appears to originate at the radiant.

Identifying the radiant in the meteor and background sky layers can be tricky because a correct exposure for the meteors will show so many stars it can be hard to identify constellations. Examine the deliberately underexposed frame you shot while in the field, which will show fewer stars, to identify constellations and then the radiant. Here's another tip: PhotoPills and Starry Night will give you the azimuth of the radiant at the time you shot

▶ FIGURE 10-12: Perseid meteors over Turret Arch, Arches National Park, Utah. This image is a composite of 49 meteors shot on the nights of August 10-11, 11-12, and 12-13, 2018. Almost all of the meteor images, plus the land image and background sky image, were shot from the same camera position on the west side of Turret Arch. A few of the meteors were shot from a second camera position, also on the west side of Turret Arch about 50 yards from the first camera position. Land and sky: Canon EOS 5D Mark III, Canon EF 35mm f/1.4L II USM. Land: one row, three camera positions, four frames per camera position, images stacked in Photoshop, noise reduced with Stack Mode>Median, 40 seconds, f/1.4, ISO 6400. Sky: two rows, three camera positions per row, four frames per camera position, images aligned and noise reduced in RegiStar, 10 seconds, f/1.4, ISO 6400. Meteors: Canon EOS 5D Mark IV with Canon EF 16-35mm f/2.8L III USM at 16mm, 30 seconds, f/2.8, ISO 6400, and Canon EOS 5D Mark III with Canon EF 24mm f/1.4L II USM lens, 20 seconds, f/1.4, ISO 3200. I shot a total of 3,780 frames over three nights to capture 49 bright meteors.

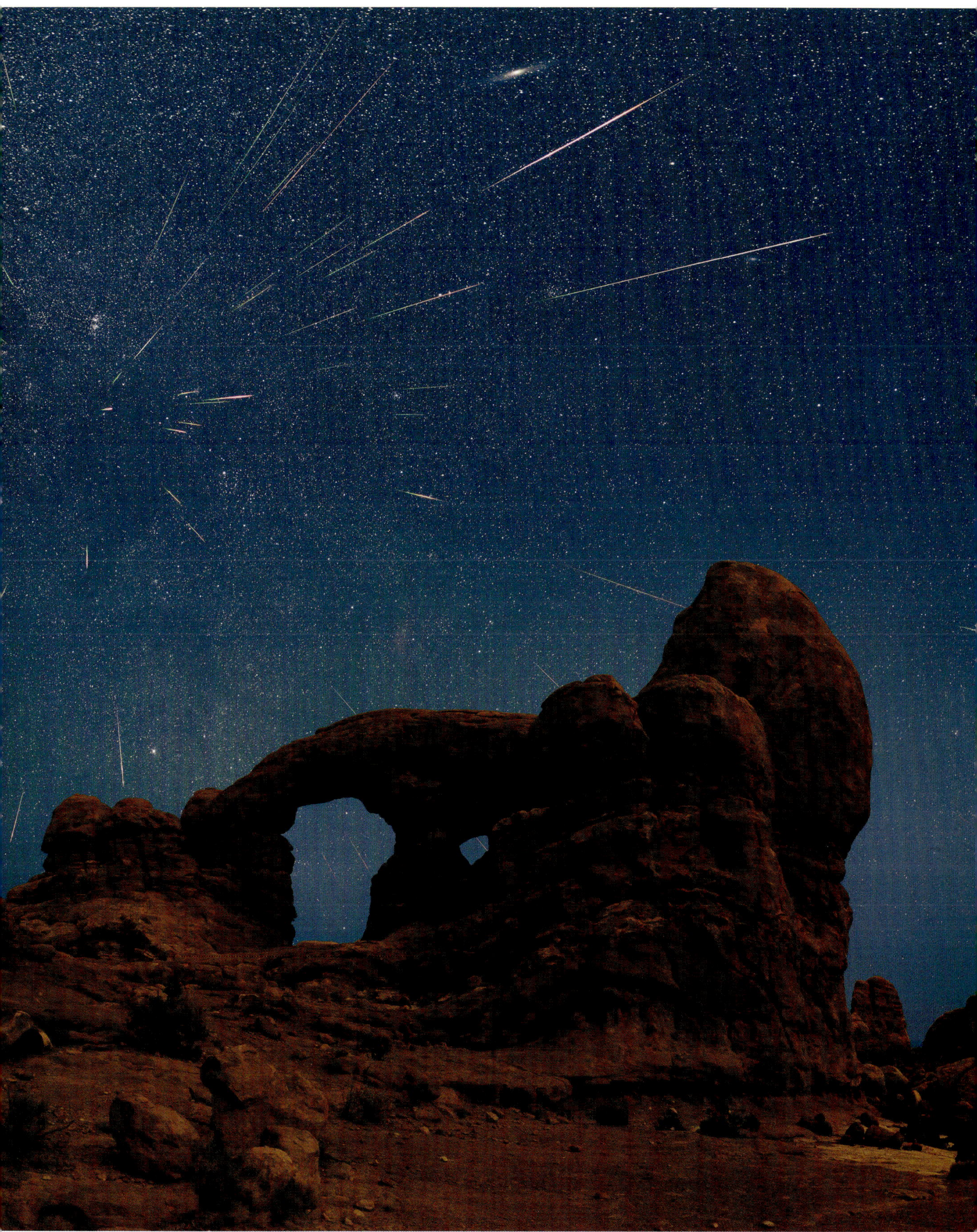

the background sky layer. You can take that information to Photo Ephemeris Web to see which geographic feature the radiant was above, which will help you identify the position of the radiant. For example, you might find that the radiant was directly above a summit, pass, or other geographic landmark that you can identify in your image. Once you've identified the radiant, mark it by dragging out a horizontal and vertical guide from the rulers displayed along the top and left side of the image window. If the rulers aren't visible, choose View>Rulers.

The disadvantage of this method of aligning the meteors with the radiant is that the meteors will not be passing by the same stars they passed in the original capture. The advantage is that the meteors will have the same orientation in the final image that they had when you saw them. In other words, a meteor that you saw traveling straight down from the radiant when you were in the field will still be traveling straight down from the radiant in the final image. There are elaborate methods of realigning the meteors so the stars they passed by in reality are the stars they pass by in the final image, but I no longer use these methods.

If you have so many good meteor shots that loading all of them simultaneously into a single Photoshop file brings your system to its knees, try this work-around. Open just the background sky and good-land images as layers in a Photoshop file. Move the background sky layer to the top of the layer stack if it isn't there already. Duplicate the background sky layer so you have clean background to use if you make a mistake (Layer>New>Layer Via Copy). Open the first meteor image as a separate file in Photoshop. (I'm assuming you're using the default tabbed interface; if you're not, choose Window>Arrange>Consolidate All to Tabs.) Target the meteor image and press Control+A to select all. Press V to get the Move tool. Press and hold the Shift key. Drag the meteor image to the tab for the background sky image, but don't try to drop it there. Instead, wait for Photoshop to switch to the background sky image, drag the meteor image back down into the window for the background sky image, and release the mouse button. Now—finally—you can release the Shift key. By holding down Shift, you are telling Photoshop to align the two images perfectly.

Proceed as before by masking out everything on the meteor layer except the meteor itself. Change the blend mode of the meteor layer to Lighten. Choose the Move tool, and align the meteor with the radiant in the background sky image. Now select the meteor layer and the copy of the background sky layer. Press Control+E to merge those two layers. Repeat this procedure to bring in all the remaining meteors. With this approach, you never have more than four layers in your file, which greatly reduces the demands on your computer. The disadvantage of this approach is that it is much harder to correct mistakes. Be sure your meteor is in the right position and blends perfectly with the background stars before merging the two layers.

If you used two different lenses on two camera bodies to capture the meteor images, you'll need to take one extra step before compositing them. The scale of an image shot with a 24mm or 35mm lens will differ from the scale of an image shot with a 16mm lens. A meteor captured with a 16mm lens will be only 67 percent as long as the same meteor captured with a 24mm lens, and only 46 percent as long as the same meteor captured with a 35mm lens. Let's assume for the moment that you shot the background sky and land with a 16mm lens, along with some of the meteor images. If you want to preserve the same scale for meteors shot with a 24mm or 35mm lens, you'll need to use Transform in Photoshop to scale the 24mm and 35mm meteor images down. Choose Edit>Transform>Scale and enter the correct scale (67 or 46 percent, respectively) in the options bar. Add the scaled-down meteor image to your composite image. In this example, meteor images captured with a 16mm lens already have the same scale as the background sky image, which was also shot with a 16mm lens, so they don't need to be scaled down.

The final step in creating your meteor-shower shot is to blend the good-land exposure with the rest of the image (see chapter 6 for two ways of doing that).

An active meteor shower is the ultimate celestial fireworks display. You never know exactly when or where the next meteor will appear. You'll spot some meteors only out of the corner of your eye. Others will erupt right in front of you. Creating a great image of that enthralling experience requires

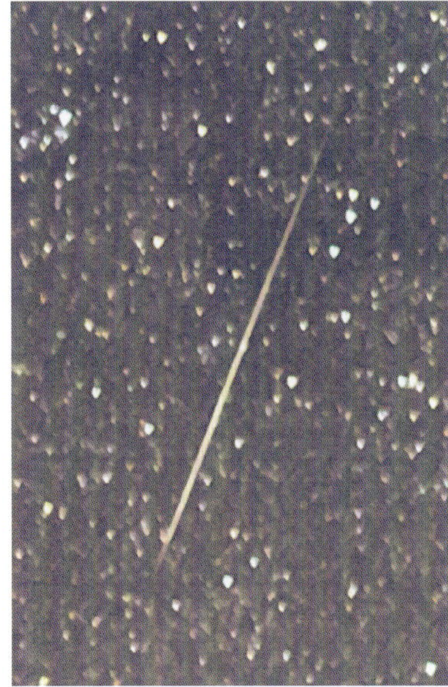

◄ FIGURE 10-13: A meteor captured by a Canon 5D Mark III and Canon EF 35mm f/1.4L II USM lens set to 10 seconds, f/1.4, ISO 6400.

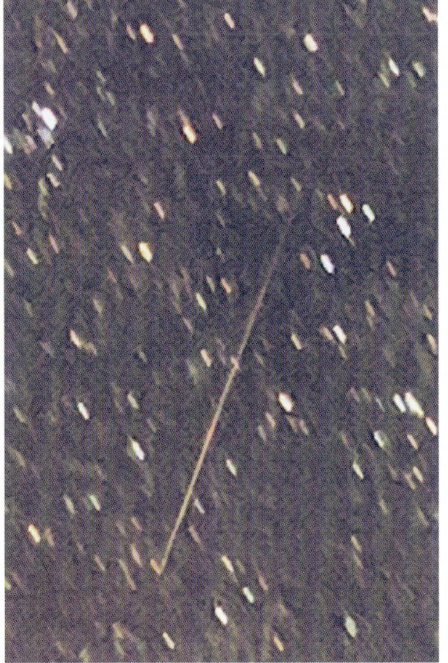

◄ FIGURE 10-14: The same meteor shown in figure 10-13, captured with a Canon 5D Mark III and Canon EF 16-35mm f/2.8L III USM lens at 16mm. I used an exposure of 30 seconds, f/2.8, ISO 6400. The meteor only lasted a second or two, so the shutter speed is actually irrelevant. The difference in brightness of the meteor was caused by the difference in the area of the aperture. The area of the aperture of the 35mm f/1.4 lens, shot wide open, is 19 times the area of the aperture of the 16mm f/2.8 lens, again shot wide open. During the meteor's brief life, the 35mm lens collected 19 times as much light as the 16mm. I scaled the 35mm shot so that the meteors are the same length.

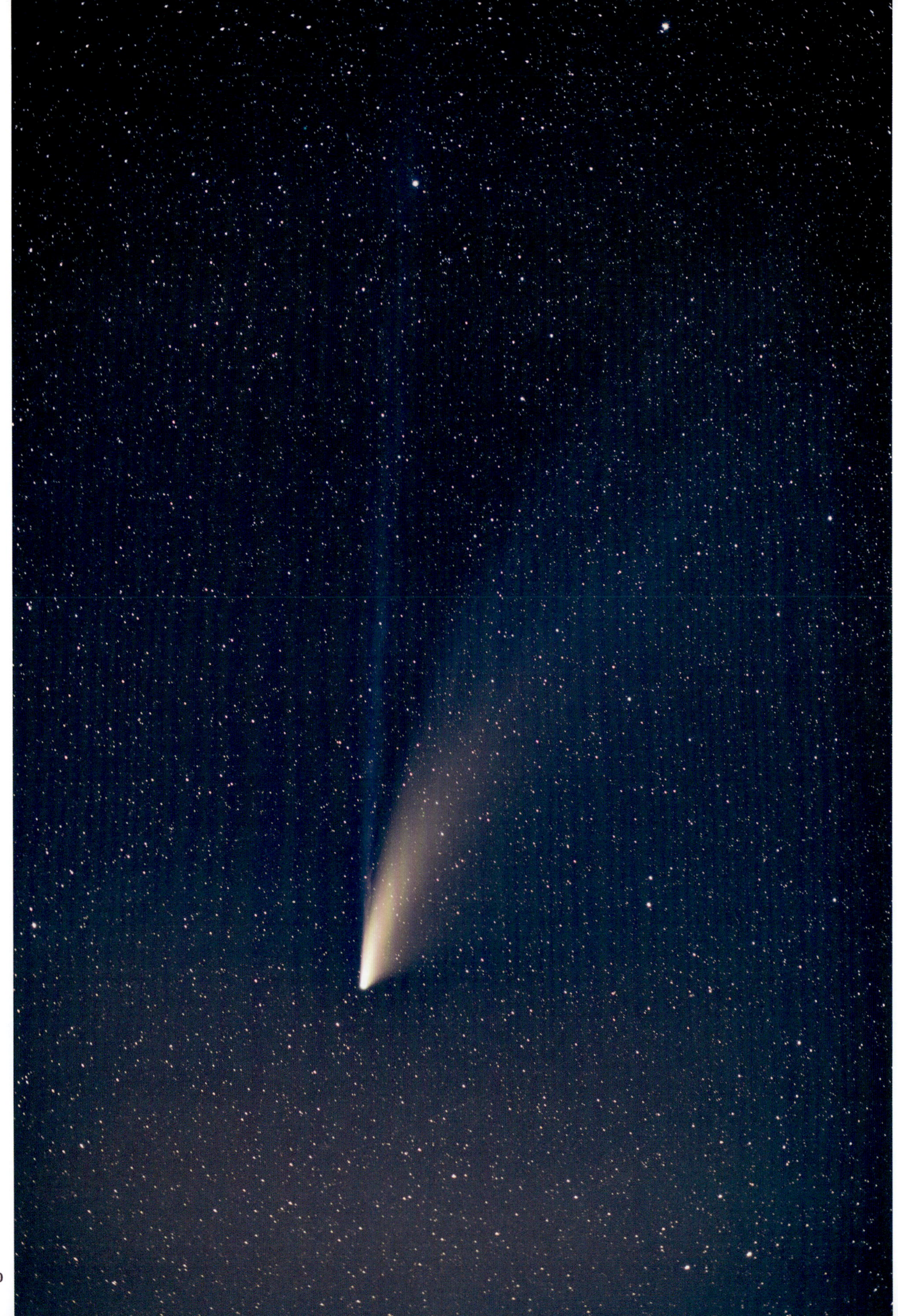

careful planning and patience both in the field and in front of the computer. It's certainly true that I didn't capture all the meteors my images show in a single 30-second exposure. However, I did see all those meteors fall, one by one, as I stood under a star-filled sky, awed at the wonders of our universe. The techniques I describe here are the best way I know to create an image that evokes that experience.

Photographing Comets

Comets are leftovers from the formation of our solar system some 4.6 billion years ago. Composed of frozen water, methane, ammonia, or carbon dioxide, plus dust and rock, they are often described as "dirty snowballs." Many originate in the Kuiper Belt, which lies outside the orbit of Neptune, 30 to 50 astronomical units from the sun. (One astronomical unit (AU) equals the distance from the earth to the sun.) The Kuiper Belt may contain as many as a billion comets more than six miles in diameter and 100,000 comets with a diameter greater than 60 miles. Most short-period comets (those whose orbits around the sun take less than 200 years) originate in the Kuiper Belt. Most of these comets travel in the same orbital plane as Earth and the other major planets. This plane is called the ecliptic. They also travel in the same counter-clockwise direction in their orbits as the planets.

Other comets originate in the Oort Cloud, which is still farther away. The Oort Cloud is theorized to be shaped like a giant spherical bubble surrounding our entire solar system. This region is dotted with billions, or perhaps trillions, of mountain-size objects. Its inner edge may be 2,000 to 5,000 AU from the sun. Its outer edge may be 10,000 or even 100,000 AU from the sun, or one quarter, perhaps even halfway, to the nearest star. The Oort Cloud marks the outer edge of our solar system. Comets originating in the Oort Cloud are said to be long-period comets because their orbits are so huge that it may be hundreds of thousands or millions of years before they reappear. Unlike Kuiper Belt objects, the orbital plane of Oort Cloud comets can be at any angle to the orbital plane of the major planets.

As comets approach the sun, the small, frozen core of the comet, called the nucleus, begins to release gases as the sun's heat vaporizes some of the ice. These gases expand to form the comet's coma, which can be hundreds of thousands of miles in diameter—larger in diameter than the earth. The solar wind then creates two tails. The ion or plasma tail, which is composed of vaporized gases, points straight away from the sun, regardless of the direction the comet is traveling. It can stretch for hundreds of thousands of miles; the longest comet tail on record stretched for 360 million miles. The second tail, composed of cometary dust, is usually shorter and can be curved. It also

◄ FIGURE 10-15: Comet NEOWISE over the Never Summer Range, Rocky Mountain National Park, Colorado. July 20, 2020, 10:30 p.m. Canon EOS 5D Mark IV, Canon EF 85mm f/1.4L IS USM. One camera position, nine frames, images aligned and noise reduced in RegiStar, 10 seconds, f/1.4, ISO 6400.

points roughly away from the sun. Comets typically lose about 1 percent of their ice each time they pass close to the sun. Sometimes the sun's heat is so intense that the comet breaks apart, and what seems like a promising comet for photographers proves to be a disappointment.

Contrary to what you might expect, you don't necessarily need a long telephoto to make strong images of a bright comet. My best comet shots were made with 35mm, 50mm, and 85mm lenses on full-frame cameras. (I used

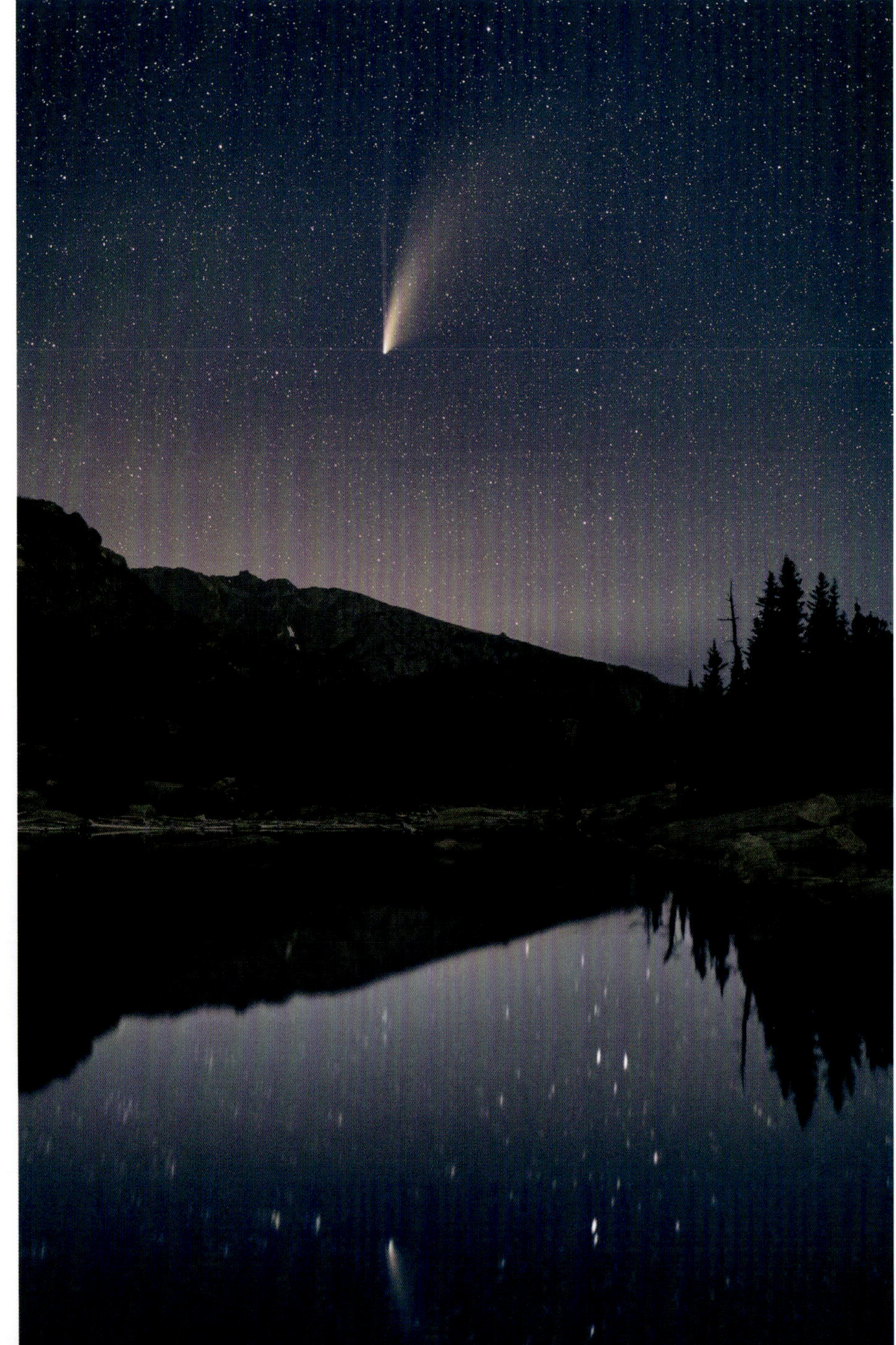

► Figure 10-16: Comet NEOWISE reflected in Mills Lake, Rocky Mountain National Park, Colorado. July 21, 2020, 10:12 p.m. Canon EOS 5D Mark IV, Canon EF 35mm f/1.4L II USM. Land: four frames, images stacked in Photoshop, noise reduced with Stack Mode>Median, 40 seconds, f/1.4, ISO 6400. Sky: nine frames, images aligned and noise reduced in RegiStar, 10 seconds, f/1.4, ISO 6400.

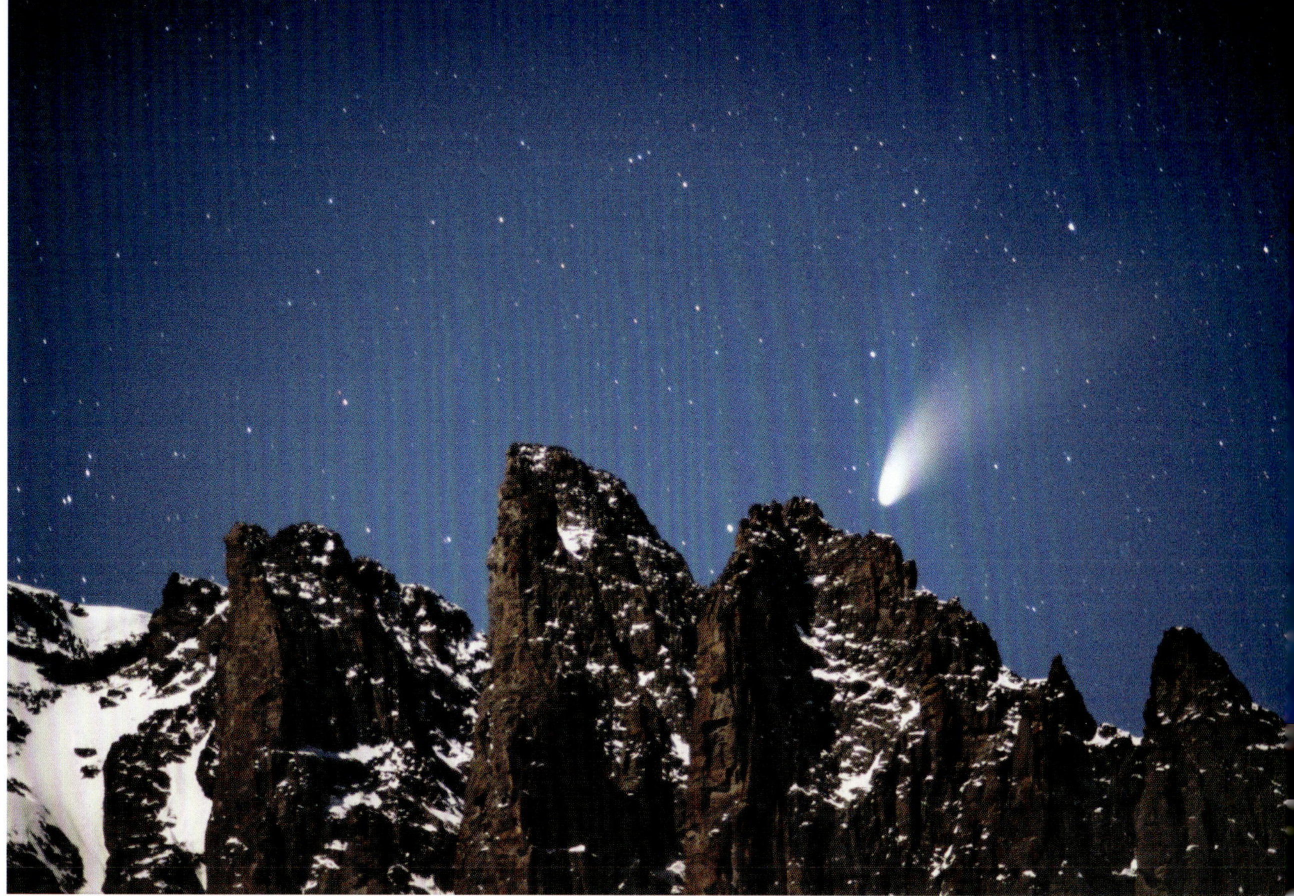

the 35mm lens when I was shooting Comet NEOWISE reflected in Mills Lake (figure 10-16).

Subscribe to an online astronomy newsletter to be alerted to the approach of a photogenic comet. I like the long-running newsletter from EarthSky (earthsky.org), but there are many to choose from. You're looking for an alert that a comet is becoming bright enough to be seen without optical aid. Starry Night will give you the azimuth and altitude of the comet at specific times during the night. That, in turn, will allow you to plan when and where to go. Comets are brightest when near the sun. If the comet is visible in the evening sky, you may have only a narrow window between the time when the sun is far enough below the horizon to see the comet and the comet setting. If the comet is visible in the morning sky, you may have only a short window between the time when the sun is still far enough below the horizon to see the comet and the time when the comet disappears into the brightening sky. If possible, shoot when the moon is below the horizon, particularly if the moon is more than 50 percent illuminated.

The correct exposure for a comet is typically about the same as the correct exposure for the Milky Way. As always, your histogram is your best guide to correct exposure. The comet's ion tail may appear longer in the photograph than it does to your eyes. Check your first images to be sure you've included the entire tail.

▲ FIGURE 10-17: Comet Hale-Bopp, the brightest comet of the 20th century, setting over the Saber in Rocky Mountain National Park in April 1997. Exact date, camera, lens, and exposure not recorded, but I believe I used an Olympus OM-4 and Olympus 85mm f/1.4 lens to expose Fujichrome Provia 400 (pushed two stops) for 15 seconds.

Comets that are bright enough to be photographed with ordinary cameras and lenses (as opposed to a telescope) are rare, which is all the more reason to be sure you get out and shoot them when they appear. For example, it won't be possible to photograph Comet Hale-Bopp again for more than 2,500 years. Don't miss what could be the opportunity of a lifetime!

Photographing the Zodiacal Light

The zodiacal light is an eerie pillar of white light that rises above the western horizon in the spring around astronomical dusk. In the fall the zodiacal light rises above the eastern horizon around astronomical dawn. At that time it is sometimes called the *false dawn*. This is true in both the Northern and Southern Hemispheres in terms of the season. The months, of course, are not the same, with springtime in the Northern Hemisphere arriving in March and arriving in the Southern Hemisphere in September. The zodiacal light is about the same brightness as the Milky Way, but it lacks the Milky Way's structure, so it is easily overlooked as a subject for night photography. Observers in the southern portions of the United States have an easier time spotting it than those farther north. Tropical observers can see it year-round. Even in the mid-latitudes, however, on moonless nights far from city lights, it is easily visible with dark-adapted eyes if you know when and where to look. I have seen it clearly from Canyonlands National Park in Utah at latitude 38 degrees N.

The zodiacal light is caused by sunlight scattering off a pancake-shaped cloud of interplanetary dust in the plane of the ecliptic that extends beyond the orbit of Mars. Astronomers are still debating the origin of the dust. Cometary debris and collisions between asteroids are two possible sources. Recently some researchers have theorized that Mars might also contribute. This dust cloud inhabits the same plane in space where the planets orbit. Ancient civilizations called the apparent path of the planets through the sky the *zodiac* or "circle of animals," a reference to the constellations visible along it. The zodiacal light also appears along this pathway, which gave it its name.

In the mid-latitudes, the zodiacal light is most visible in the spring around astronomical dusk and in the fall around astronomical dawn because that is when the plane of the ecliptic is nearly perpendicular to the horizon. Contrary to what you might expect, the opposite is not true. At astronomical dawn in the spring and astronomical dusk in the fall, the ecliptic rises diagonally from the horizon, so the zodiacal light tends to be lost in the band of relatively bright sky that always lurks along the horizon, day or night. At the mid-latitudes, the plane of the ecliptic also intersects the horizon at a diagonal in midsummer and midwinter, making the zodiacal light difficult to see at those times. At the equator, the plane of the ecliptic is nearly

▶ FIGURE 10-18: The zodiacal light over Cyclone Canyon, Needles District, Canyonlands National Park, Utah. March 17, 2023, 9:02 p.m. Sony Alpha 7R IVa, Sony FE 14mm f/1.8 GM. Land: four frames, images stacked in Photoshop, noise reduced with Stack Mode>Median, 1 minute, f/1.8, ISO 6400. Sky: four frames, images aligned and noise reduced in RegiStar, 14 seconds, f/1.8, ISO 6400.

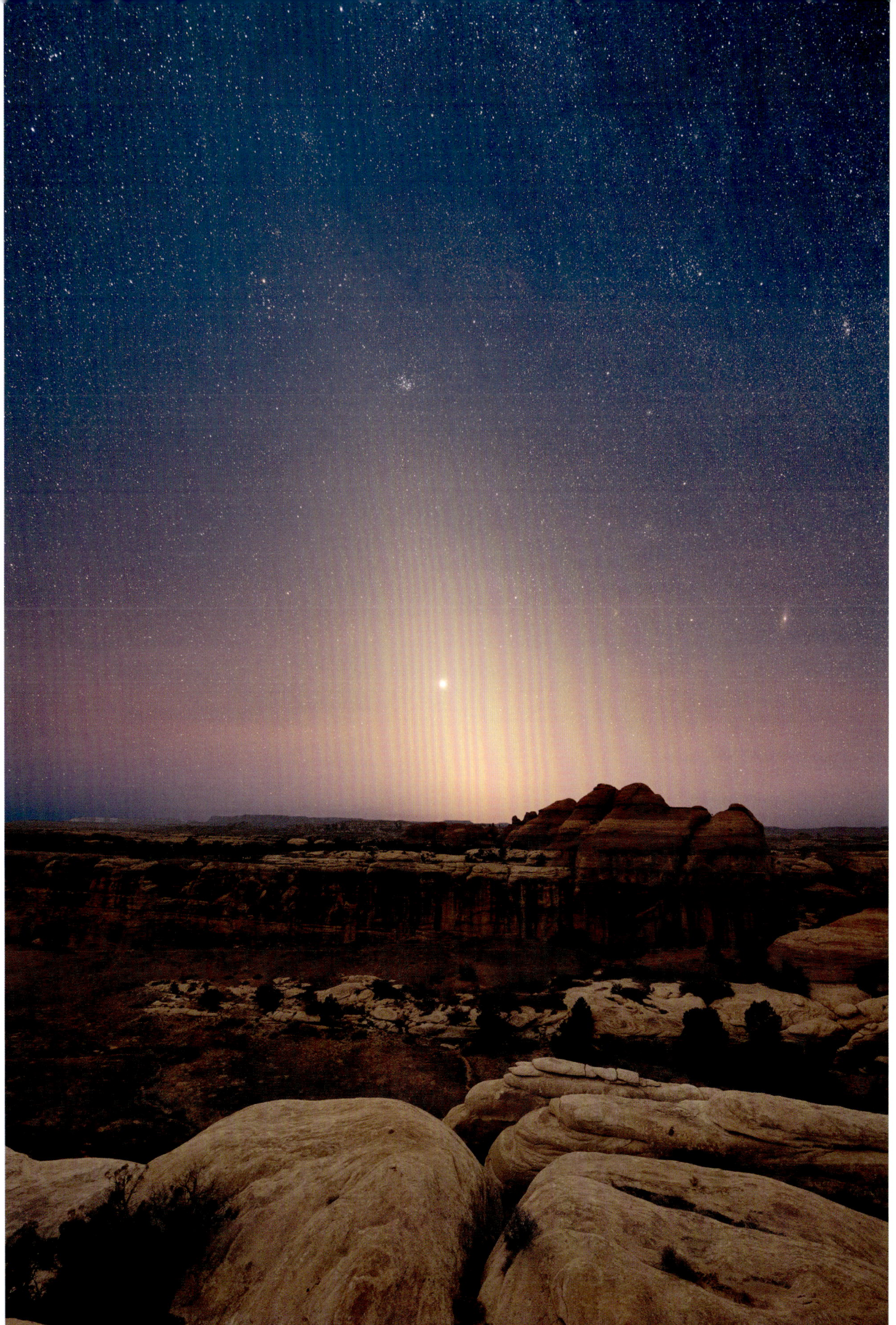

perpendicular to the horizon year-round, which means that the zodiacal light can be seen at both astronomical dusk and dawn throughout the year.

The pillar of light is tallest when the sun is just below the horizon. In the evening, it gradually shrinks as the sun continues its descent. In the morning, the pillar gradually grows as the sun resumes its ascent. The best time to shoot is when the sky is dark enough for the pillar to stand out, yet the pillar is as tall as possible. Usually that's around astronomical dusk and dawn.

The exposure for the zodiacal light is about the same as the exposure for the Milky Way, and all the techniques you learned for that subject are equally applicable to shooting the zodiacal light. As with many night subjects, the camera will record this phenomenon better than your eyes. You'll need a wider lens than you might expect. Most photos of the zodiacal light that include the entire pillar, plus some land, are shot with wide-angle lenses in the range 14mm to 20mm. As with the Milky Way, you'll probably need to make separate exposures for the sky and land if you want to hold good detail in both, then composite the two images in Photoshop.

Photographing Noctilucent Clouds

Noctilucent clouds (NLCs) are clouds made of tiny frozen water droplets in the mesosphere, 50 miles above Earth's surface, at the edge of space. When fully developed, these white or electric blue clouds take on wispy, evanescent shapes, sometimes resembling tropospheric cirrus clouds. They form when water vapor condenses onto tiny particles of dust created by the disintegration of meteoroids as they burn up in the atmosphere. In the Northern Hemisphere, NLCs only form from mid-May through August, peaking in early July, when temperatures in the mesosphere drop to –190 degrees F or lower. (Yes, that's right, the mesosphere is *colder* in the summer than in the winter, for complex reasons involving gravity waves and the way rising air expands and cools as it rises. Don't get me started.) Unlike stars, which emit light themselves, noctilucent clouds are only visible when lit by the sun. However, they are so faint that they can only be seen by earth-bound photographers when the lower atmosphere is in shadow. This means they can only be seen in deep twilight, after civil dusk or before civil dawn, when the sun is between 6 and 16 degrees below the horizon. In the terminology of atmospheric science, the *solar depression angle* (SDA) must be between 6 and 16 degrees. At SDAs in this range, the troposphere is in Earth's shadow, so it is dark, but the sun is still shining on the mesosphere, illuminating the clouds. If the SDA is less than 6 degrees, the sky is too bright, and these dim clouds are lost in the glare. If the SDA is more than 16 degrees, the sun will no longer be shining on the clouds.

NLCs are most commonly seen at latitudes from 50 to 65 degrees. Too far south in the Northern Hemisphere, and the clouds will be out of sight below your horizon to the north. Too far north, and the sky in midsummer never gets dark enough to see them. (The opposite would be true if you're in the Southern Hemisphere, in which case the peak of the season would be in January). The ideal latitude range is about 55 to 60 degrees. Exceptional displays have been seen as far south as Italy, at a latitude of 46 degrees, and in Seattle, at a latitude of 47 degrees. In 2019 they were even seen as far south as Joshua Tree, a town near Los Angeles, latitude 34.1 degrees, which is the current record for a low-latitude observation. Displays at the northern limit of the latitude band are most commonly seen late in the season, when

▾ FIGURE 10-19: Noctilucent clouds from the Peyto Lake overlook, Banff National Park, Canada. July 3, 2023, 4:11 a.m., one hour and 23 minutes before sunrise, SDA 9 degrees. Sony Alpha 7R IVa, Sony FE 35mm f/1.4 GM. 8 seconds, f/4.0, ISO 100.

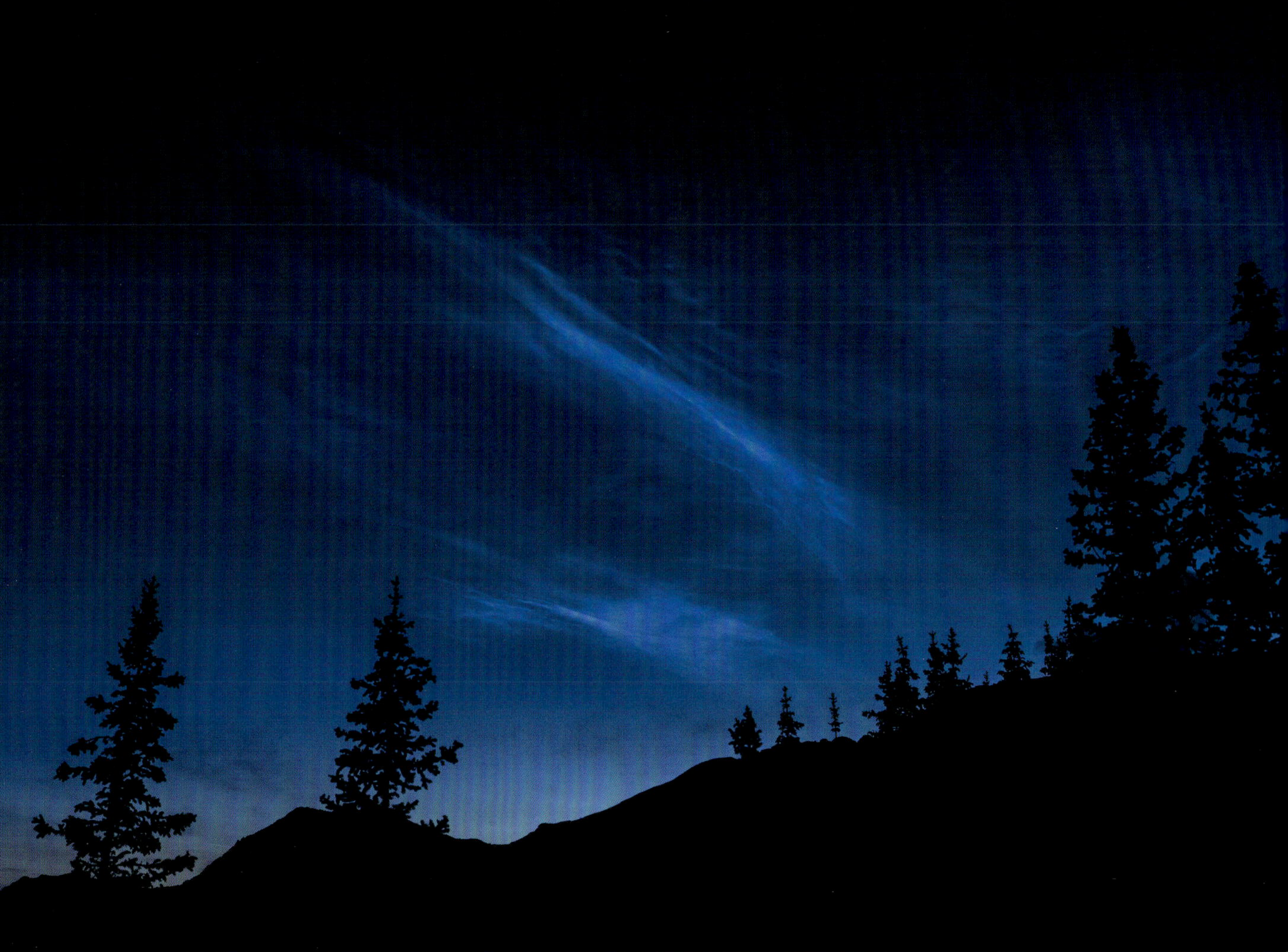

▸ FIGURE 10-20: This diagram is a two-dimensional representation of the hemispherical dome of the sky. The circle represents your horizon. The zenith is straight above you, in a direction at 90 degrees to the plane of the page. The gently curving lines crossing the circle represent the altitude of the uppermost edge of the visible band of NLCs at various SDAs. To put it another way, these lines represent the upper limit of the portion of the mesosphere that is lit by the sun at different SDAs. As SDA increases, the upper edge of visible clouds shrinks toward the horizon. Without sunlight shining on them, NLCs are invisible from the ground. One catch: at an SDA of 6 degrees, the sky is still so bright that NLCs are difficult to distinguish from the background sky. This diagram only shows where NLCs may be visible if indeed they are present. At high latitudes during the NLC season the sun is between northwest and northeast at SDAs greater than 6 degrees. Diagram based on work by dedicated NLC observer Mark Zalcik, which draws on *Noctilucent Clouds* by Benson Fogle, University of Alaska Press, 1966.

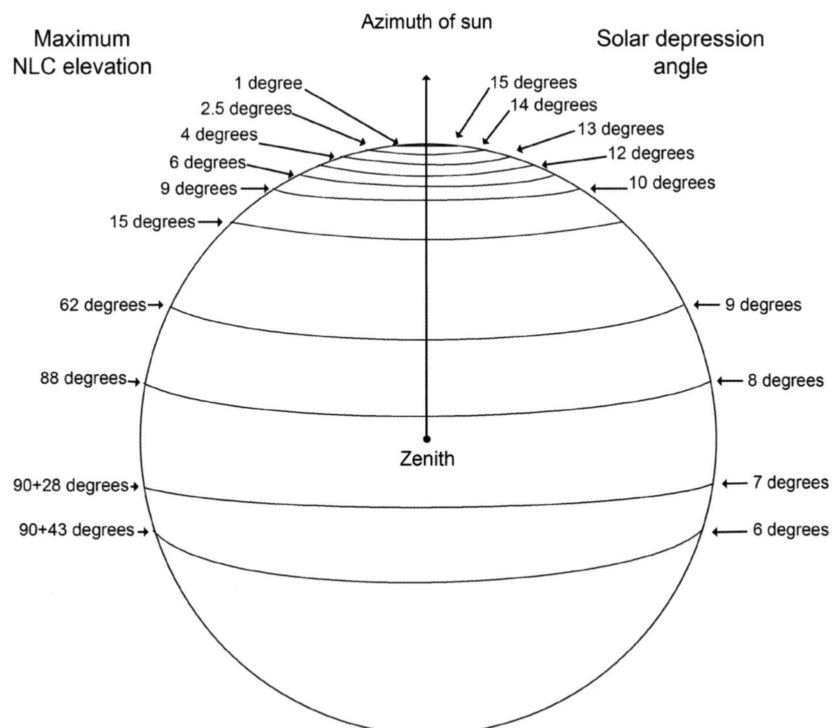

the maximum SDA during the night becomes greater and the sky briefly becomes dark enough to observe them.

The SDA also controls what portions of the mesosphere are lit, which in turn controls the perceived altitude of the upper edge of the clouds. At SDAs of 6 degrees or so, the mesosphere will be lit from directly overhead all the way to the northern horizon, so it is possible for visible clouds to cover the entire northern half of the sky or even a bit more. Unfortunately, the low contrast between the dim clouds and still-bright sky makes them difficult to see and photograph. As the SDA increases, the sky darkens, making the clouds easier to see, but less of the mesosphere is still lit, so the apparent altitude of the upper edge of the clouds decreases as the cloud band seems to shrink toward the horizon. (The clouds may still be present directly above you, but they become invisible because they are no longer lit.) An SDA of 9 degrees is probably the sweet spot. The clouds directly above you will have just started to go into shadow, but the sky is dark enough to see the remaining clouds clearly. At an SDA of 15 degrees at your location, the only clouds that are still lit are those far to the north, where the SDA at the same time is less. For example, on August 1st, when the SDA at 55 degrees N. latitude is 15 degrees, the SDA 250 miles to the north is only 11.6 degrees. NLCs are so high they would still be visible above the horizon even at that distance. At an SDA of

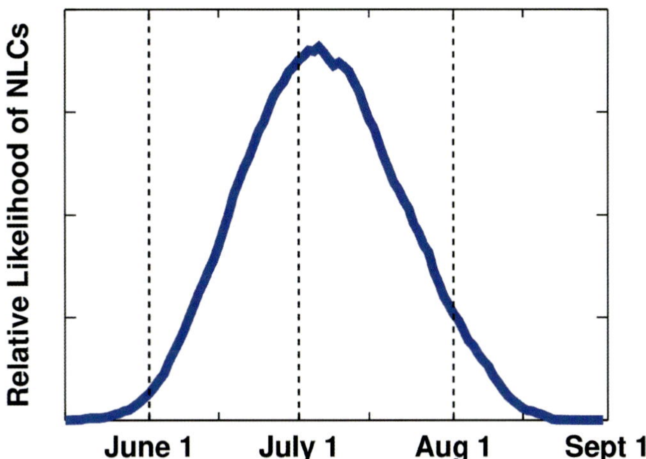

◄ FIGURE 10-21: Average daily variability in mesospheric cloud brightness in the northern hemisphere from 2007 to 2022. Data is from the NASA Aeronomy of Ice in the Mesosphere Cloud Imaging and Particle Size satellite instrument. Analysis covers a latitude band from 60 to 70 degrees. Courtesy of Dr. Cora Randall, University of Colorado Boulder.

15 degrees, the clouds may appear to extend only a degree or so above the horizon, making it difficult to photograph them unless you are in completely flat terrain and using a long lens. All of the photo-planning apps discussed in chapter 4 provide data on the SDA.

Exposures for photos of noctilucent clouds are usually considerably shorter than exposures for the Milky Way. I shot my best photo of noctilucent clouds from the Peyto Lake Overlook in Banff National Park (latitude 51.7 degrees N) at 12:29 a.m. Mountain Daylight Time on July 3, 2023, using an exposure of 1.6 seconds, f/1.4, ISO 1600. The moon was full (99.94% illuminated) but only 8 degrees above the horizon and almost directly behind me. The SDA was 13 degrees. Later that same night, from the same location, I saw another display of noctilucent clouds when the SDA was 8 degrees and the full moon was only 3 degrees above the horizon. My exposure at that time was 1.6 seconds, f/4.0, ISO 100—a difference of seven stops.

I processed my noctilucent cloud photos in Lightroom using simple adjustments to highlights, shadows, and contrast in an effort to accentuate the difference between the dim clouds and the relatively bright sky. I used the Select Sky tool in the Masking panel to add a generous dose of Clarity to the sky alone, which helped bring out the clouds still further.

Noctilucent clouds are one of the most elusive subjects you can tackle as a night photographer. At present there is no reliable way to predict accurately when they will appear, although scientists do think that they are more prevalent during periods near a minimum in the 11-year solar cycle (because less solar radiation will mean lower temperatures and more water vapor in the mesosphere). My trip to Banff in 2023 was unfortunately near a maximum in the 11-year solar cycle, and also during the worst wildfire season in recorded Canadian history. Smoke from wildfires often obscured the nighttime sky.

Even so, I was fortunate to be treated to two displays in the seven nights of my trip. If you're looking for a unique experience, travel to the right latitude, at the right time of year, wait for a clear night, set up, and hope. The rare

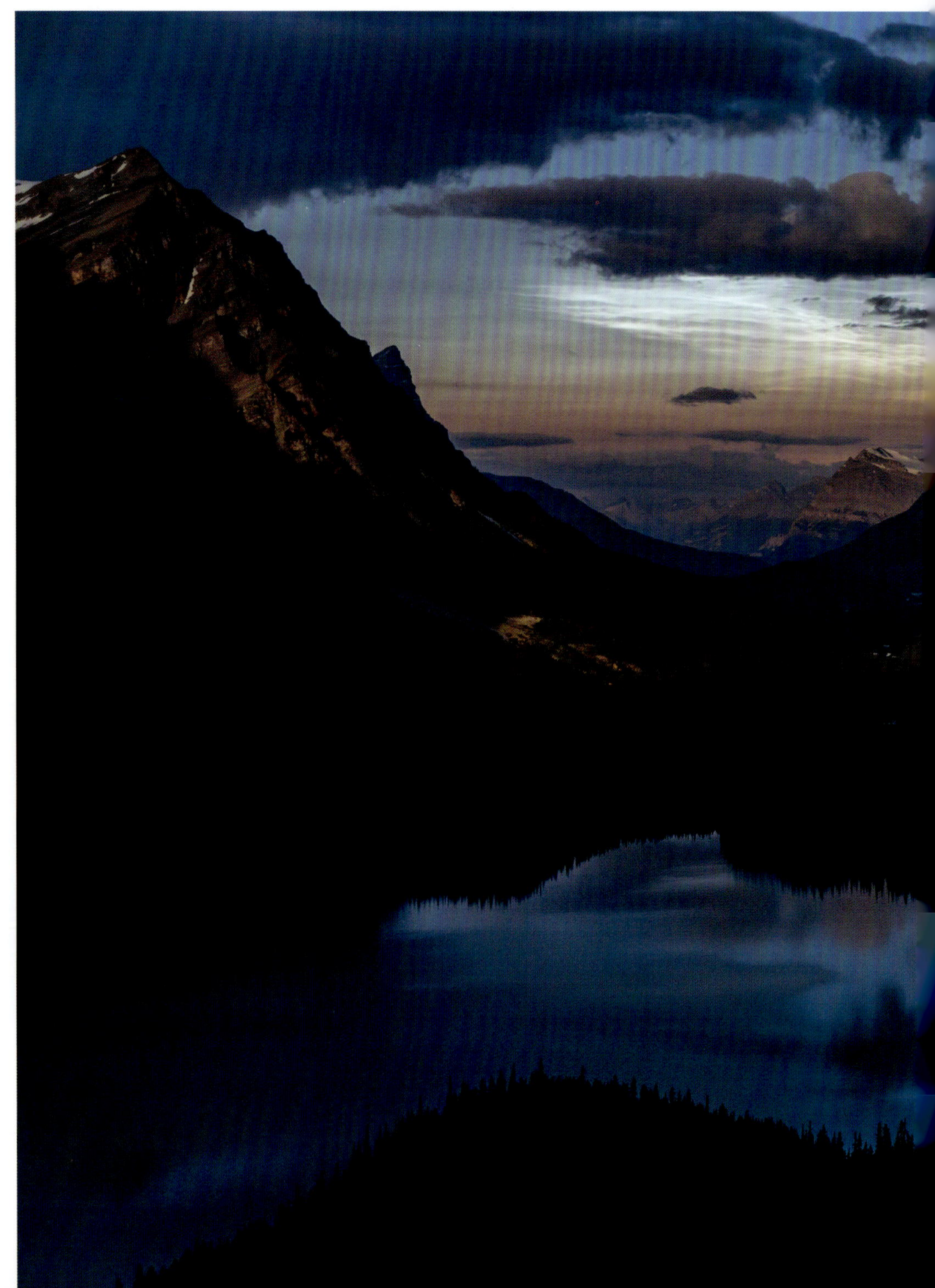

and astonishing photographs you will be able to make if you are fortunate enough to see a vivid display of NLCs will make all the waiting around in the dark worthwhile.

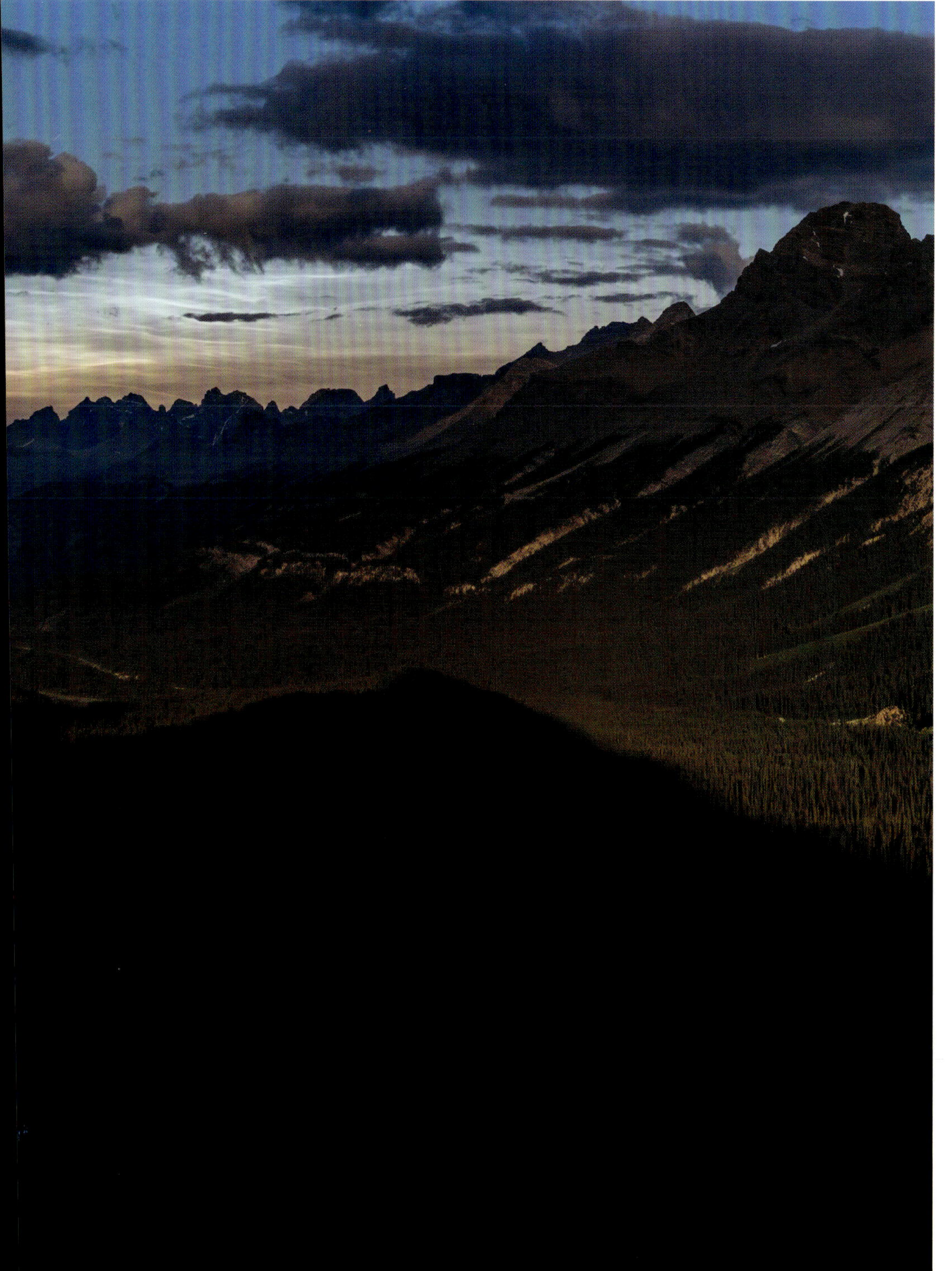

◄ FIGURE 10-22: Noctilucent and tropospheric clouds over Mt. Patterson and Peyto Lake, Banff National Park, Canada. The bright, bluish-white clouds near the horizon are noctilucent clouds. These are clouds in the mesosphere that are lit by the sun. The darker clouds are clouds in the troposphere that are lit by the moon. July 3, 2023, 12:29 a.m., SDA 13 degrees. Sony Alpha 7R IVa, Sony FE 35mm f/1.4 GM. 1.6 seconds, f/1.4, ISO 1600.

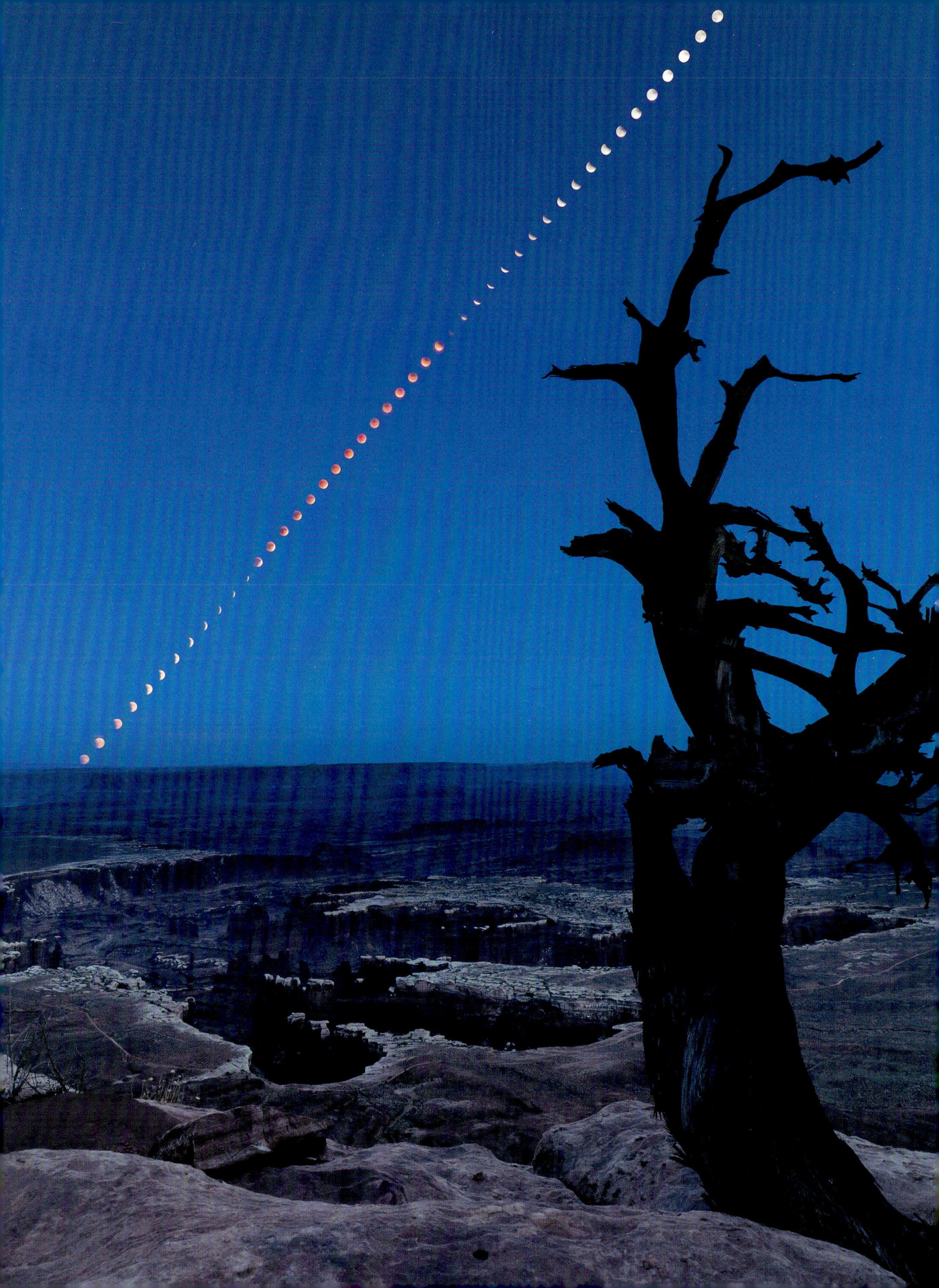

Photographing Lunar Eclipses

A total lunar eclipse occurs when the moon passes through Earth's shadow. That bland description utterly fails to do justice to this rare and spectacular event. Although astronomers can predict lunar eclipses accurately, there's no visible sign that one is about to begin. Sometimes the eclipse begins when the moon, which must be full, is riding high in the sky. At other times, the moon is already partially eclipsed when it rises. The first visible sign that an eclipse is beginning is a semi-circular notch that appears in the edge of the moon, as if some celestial Cookie Monster had taken a bite out of it. The notch grows until only a thin, crescent-shaped sliver of the moon is still lit. Then totality begins, and the moon turns a deep, eerie red. The sky darkens noticeably. More stars appear, along with the Milky Way. Totality can last as little as a few minutes and as long as an hour and 40 minutes. Then the moon begins to emerge from Earth's shadow. A thin crescent moon reappears, which then grows fatter and fatter until the moon once again appears full. Although as many as three total lunar eclipses can occur in one year, many years have none at all. An opportunity to see and photograph a lunar eclipse should not be missed.

Each total eclipse follows the same sequence. The key to understanding that sequence is found in figure 11-2, which shows the different types of shadows cast by the earth. If the sun was a point, then Earth would cast a single, hard-edged shadow. An observer on the moon would either see all of the sun or none of it. But the sun isn't a point. Like the moon, it subtends an angle of about 0.5 degrees. That means the shadow cast by the earth has two parts: the *umbra*, the region of complete shadow, and the *penumbra*, the region of partial shadow. An observer on the moon within Earth's umbra would see none of the sun. An observer on the moon in Earth's penumbra would see part of the sun; the remainder would be hidden behind the edge of the earth, which astronomers call the *limb*. An observer outside the penumbra would see the full disk of the sun.

Astronomers have given names to the various phases of an eclipse. The *penumbral phase* begins when the moon first enters the penumbra. Observers on Earth might notice a slight darkening of the face of the moon, but the effect is too subtle to be worth photographing. *First contact* is the moment when the limb of the moon enters Earth's umbra, and it looks like a small bite has been taken out of the moon. The partial phase of the eclipse has begun. Now is the time to start shooting. *Second contact* is the moment when the trailing edge of the moon enters fully into the umbra and *totality* begins. Although the moon is fully within Earth's shadow and no sunlight can reach

◄ Figure 11-1: Lunar eclipse over Monument Basin from Grand View Point, Canyonlands National Park, Utah. September 27, 2015, 7:04 p.m. to 11:52 p.m. Canon 5D Mark III, Canon EF 16-35mm f/2.8L II USM at 22mm. Land: .4 seconds, f/16, ISO 100 (shot one minute before sunset). Background sky: 20 seconds, f/16, ISO 800 (shot 31 minutes after sunset). Moon: 46 moon images, with exposures ranging from 1/125th, f/11, ISO 200 (full moon high in the sky) to 8 seconds, f/8, ISO 1600 (deepest totality).

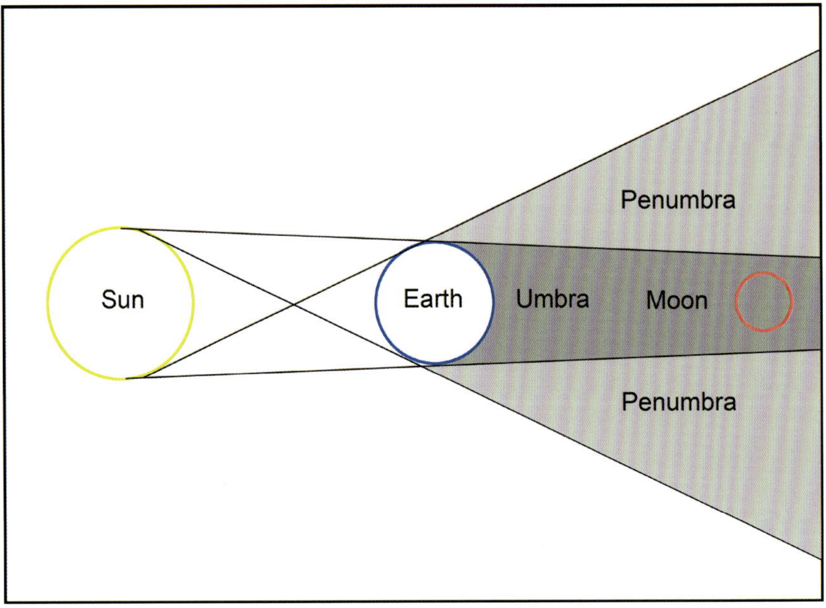

▸ FIGURE 11-2: The umbra is the region of complete shadow. An observer on the moon in Earth's umbra would see none of the disk of the sun. The penumbra is the region of partial shadow. An observer on the moon within Earth's penumbra would see part of the disk of the sun; the other part would be hidden by the edge of the earth.

it directly, it doesn't become invisible. Instead, it begins to glow red. Understanding why requires a brief foray into atmospheric optics.

Light as it comes from the sun is composed of all wavelengths, so we see it as white. When it encounters Earth's atmosphere, however, the light begins to scatter. As I mentioned in chapter 6, Rayleigh scattering causes the blue light to scatter much more strongly than red light. The amount of scattering is proportional to the distance the light travels through Earth's atmosphere. At noon, the path length is short, so we still see direct sunlight as white. At sunset and sunrise, the path length is much longer, so most of the blue light scatters out of the beam. The red light travels straight ahead and delights photographers by coloring clouds crimson and painting tall mountains with alpenglow.

That explains how sunlight can turn red, but how does it reach the moon, which, after all, is in Earth's shadow? The answer is refraction, the bending of light as it passes through the boundary between two mediums of different densities. If you've ever placed a pencil in a glass of water and observed how it appears to bend as it passes through the air-water interface, you've seen refraction. Most of sunlight's journey from the sun to the earth is through the vacuum of space. When it reaches Earth's atmosphere (a denser medium), it bends slightly toward regions of higher density, allowing a small portion of it to reach the moon, even during totality. During sunlight's long journey through Earth's atmosphere, the blue light scatters out of the beam and only reddish light reaches the moon, as shown in figure 11-3.

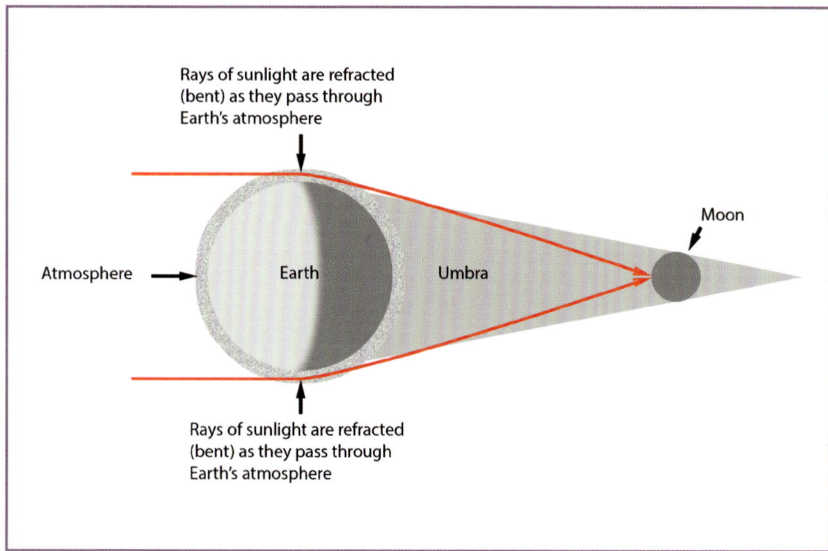

◄ FIGURE 11-3: Light from the sun refracts (bends) as it passes through Earth's atmosphere, allowing it to faintly illuminate the moon even though the moon is entirely within Earth's umbra, the region of complete shadow.

Third contact is the moment when the leading limb of the moon once again enters Earth's penumbra. Totality is over, and the moon again looks like a bite has been taken out of it. *Last contact* is the moment when the trailing limb of the moon exits the umbra. Although the moon is still inside the penumbra, the photogenic period of the eclipse is over.

From an angular perspective, the moon is very small, occupying just one quarter of the frame even with a 1000mm lens—an optic few photographers choose to buy. Unless you have a telescope, it's impossible to fill the frame with the moon. One solution is to find something interesting to occupy the rest of the frame. Locate a compelling landscape that you can photograph with a long lens while still including the moon. In this type of image, the land occupies most of the frame, and the eclipsed moon is just an added compositional element.

An alternative to this approach is to construct a composite image that shows all the phases of the eclipse. The idea is to shoot an image every five minutes, starting 10 or 15 minutes before first contact and ending 10 or 15 minutes after last contact, then combine the images in Photoshop, creating what some photographers call a string-of-pearls image. That's exactly how I made my image of a total lunar eclipse over Longs Peak (figure 11-4).

The first step was to find out when the eclipse would begin and end. That information is available in many places on the web, including the latest version of Photo Ephemeris Web. At the time, I used www.timeanddate.com. To be specific, I needed to know when the partial eclipse would begin (first contact), when totality would begin and end (second and third contact),

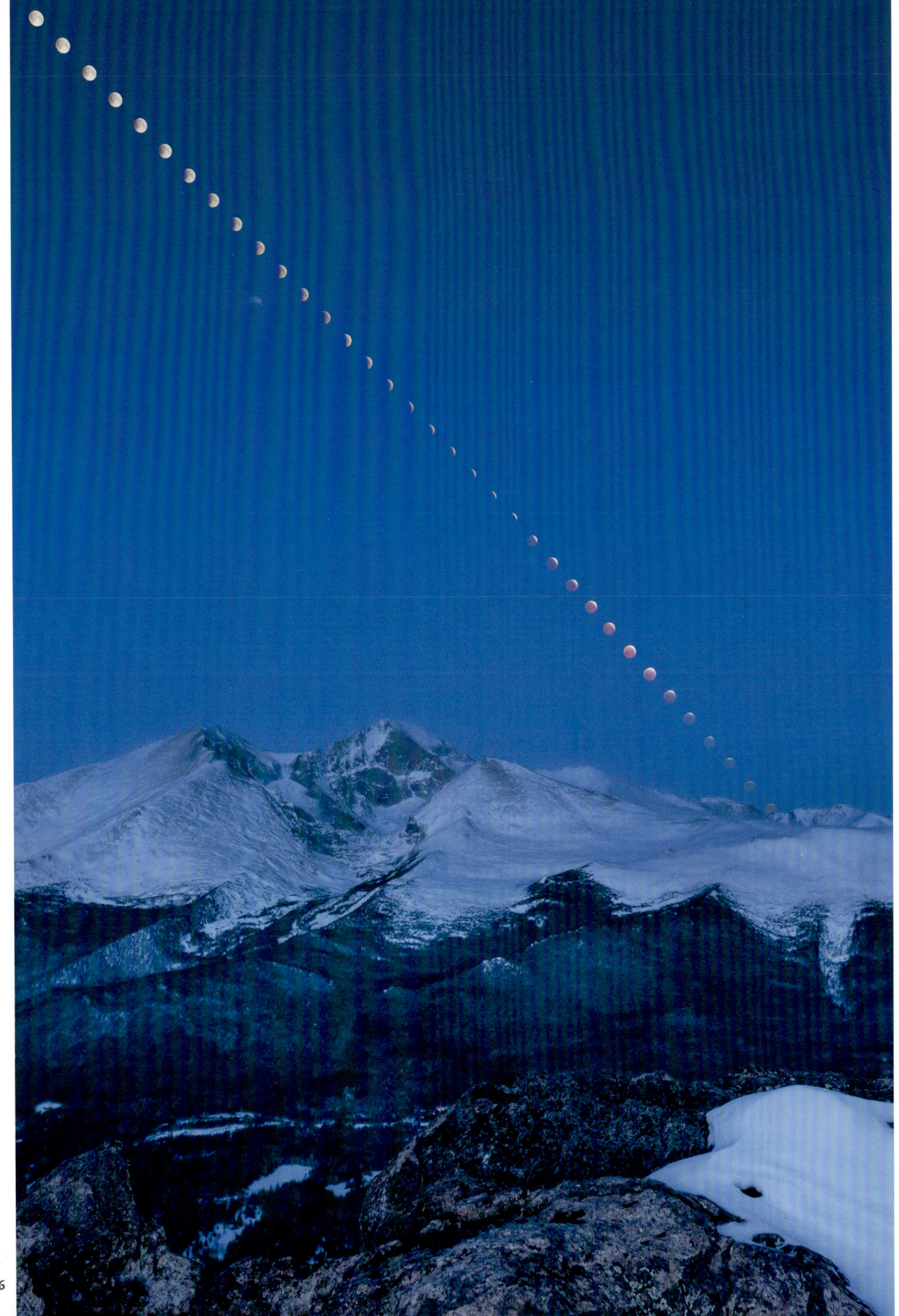

and when the partial eclipse would end (last contact), all for my location in Colorado. I wasn't concerned with the beginning and end of the penumbral phases of the eclipse.

Next, I needed to know where the moon would be, in terms of azimuth (compass bearing) and altitude (angular elevation above the horizon), at first and last contact. I also needed to know when the moon would set and when the sun would rise. For all that information, I turned to Photo Ephemeris Web (which was called The Photographer's Ephemeris at the time). I knew the partial eclipse would begin at 4:16 a.m. If I wanted to shoot one frame every five minutes, and I wanted six images of the fully illuminated moon before the partial eclipse began, I would need to start shooting at 3:45 a.m. So I set the date and time in Photo Ephemeris Web to April 4, 2015, 3:45 a.m., and saw in the information panel below the map that the moon would have an azimuth of 230 degrees and an altitude of 31 degrees, as shown in figure 11-5.

Further examination of Photo Ephemeris Web showed that at moonset at 6:47 a.m., the moon would be at azimuth 263 degrees. It also showed me that the moon would set just a few minutes before sunrise while it was still partially eclipsed. That meant that during the later stages of the eclipse the sky behind the moon would become increasingly bright and the land would be illuminated by twilight.

Putting all this together, I concluded that the ideal shooting location would be where I was looking at something interesting to the southwest and where I would be as high as possible, so the horizon to the west would be at my elevation (or close), and I could see as much of the eclipse as possible before moonset.

A little map work showed me that the logical place to go was the summit of Twin Sisters, which offers a great view of Longs Peak and Mt. Meeker to the southwest. I returned to Photo Ephemeris Web and activated the gray secondary marker by clicking it. I then dragged and dropped the secondary marker at the point where the thick blue line indicating moonset direction crossed the skyline ridge. The readout showed that the ridge was only 2 degrees above a level horizon as seen from Twin Sisters, so I would be able to see the moon until a few minutes before the almanac time of moonset. I dragged the timeline marker slowly back in time until the moon's altitude was 2 degrees, then read off the time. The moon would set behind the ridge at about 6:35 a.m. at an azimuth of 261 degrees. By dropping the secondary marker where the thin blue line indicating current moon position crossed the ridge, I confirmed that the altitude of the ridge at that point was still only 2 degrees. See figure 11-6.

I knew that my composition would need to span a left-to-right arc of 31 degrees, from 230 degrees to 261 degrees. A 35mm lens, set vertically, has

◄ FIGURE 11-4: Total lunar eclipse over Longs Peak from Twin Sisters, Rocky Mountain National Park, Colorado. Compare this image to PlanIt Pro's virtual-reality simulation of this image in figure 11-7. April 4, 2015, 3:44 a.m. to 6:34 a.m. Canon 5D Mark III, Canon EF 16-35mm f/2.8L II USM at 35mm. Land and background sky: 2 seconds, f/11, ISO 1600, shot at 6:09 a.m., 33 minutes before sunrise. Moon: 35 moon images, with exposures ranging from 1/125th, f/11, ISO 200 (full moon high in the sky) to 5 seconds, f/11, ISO 1600 (deepest totality).

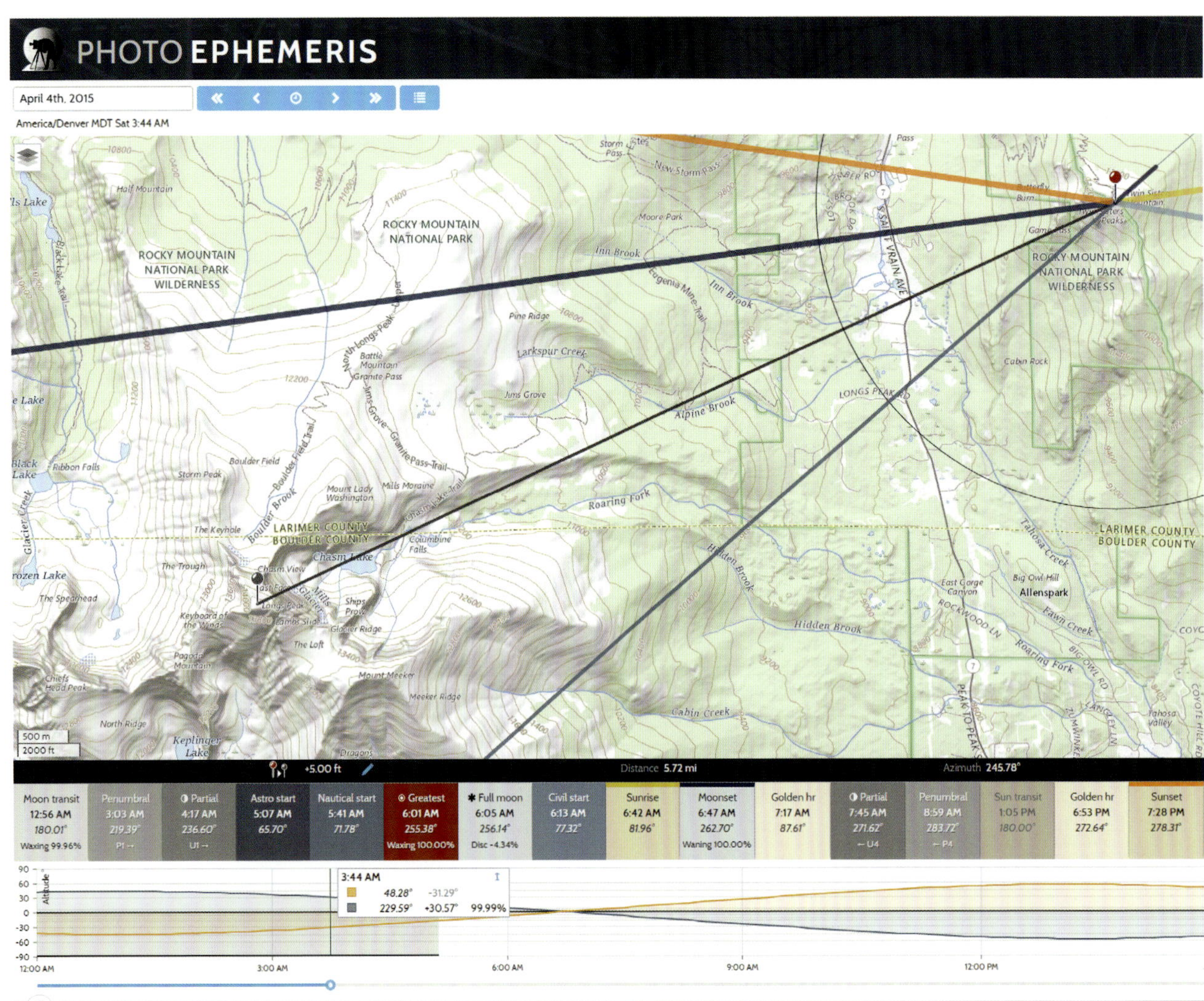

▲ FIGURE 11-5: This screenshot from Photo Ephemeris Web shows the moon position at 3:44 a.m., April 4, 2015, when I started my sequence of moon images. The red pin is atop Twin Sisters (my shooting location). The black pin is atop Longs Peak. The thin blue line shows that the moon was a bit left of Mt. Meeker at the time I started my eclipse sequence. The thick blue line shows where the moon would set if the terrain was flat. The timeline below the map shows the start and end times of the various phases of the eclipse.

an angle of view across the short dimension of 38 degrees. Its angle of view on the long dimension is 54 degrees—plenty to include both the moon (31 degrees above a level horizon when I started shooting) and some foreground. At 3:45 a.m., when I started the sequence of images, the moon would be just to the left of Mt. Meeker. It would move downward at roughly a 45-degree angle until it set to the right of Longs Peak.

Today when planning an image of a lunar eclipse I would continue to use Photo Ephemeris Web, but also turn to the Eclipse module in PlanIt Pro. PlanIt Pro has a marvelous tool for visualizing "string of pearls" shots of lunar eclipses. You begin by setting your shooting location and subject location on the map. Next, set the start and end times of the series of images

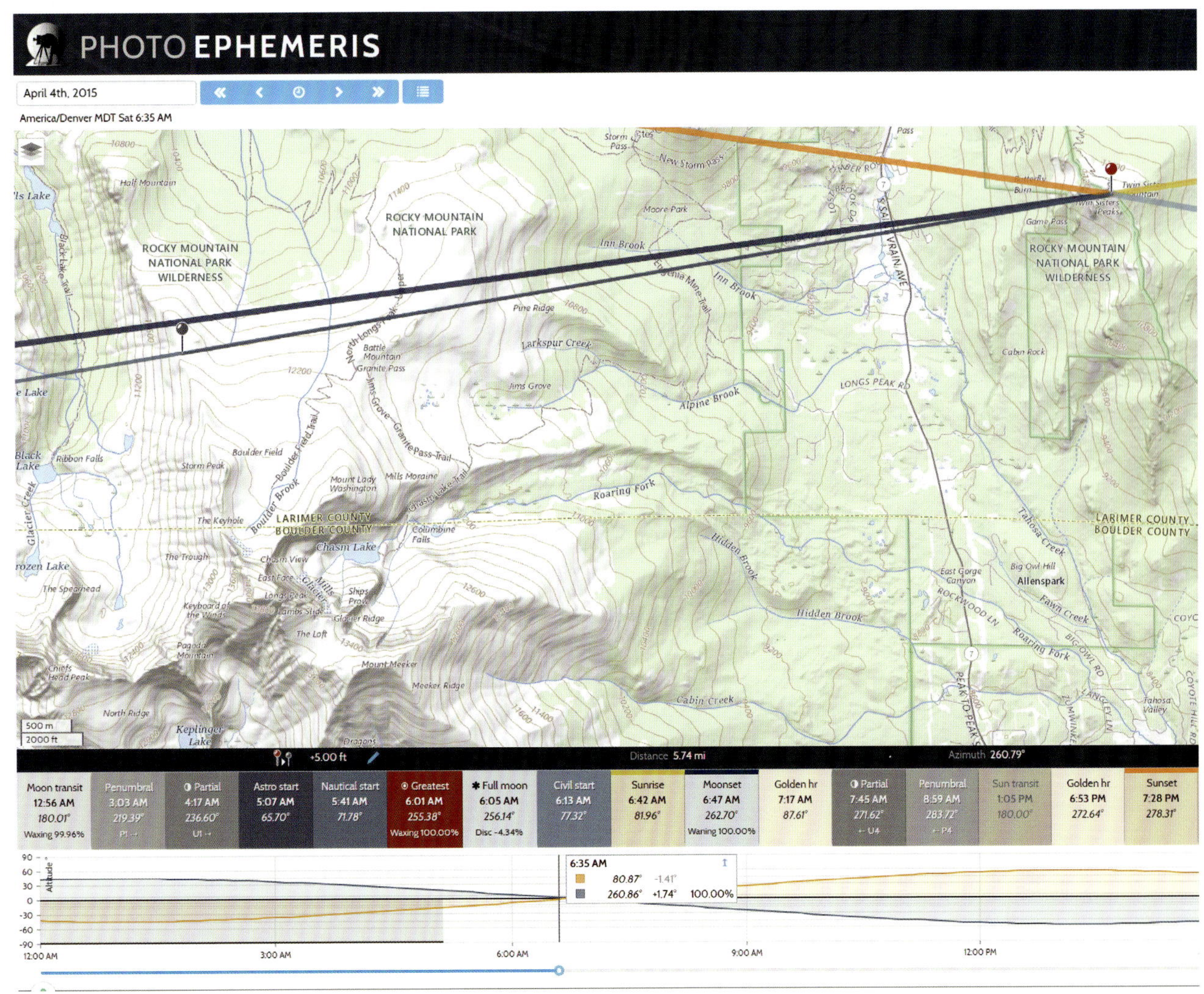

you plan to shoot. I like to start shooting 10 or 15 minutes before first contact so I have a few images of the completely full moon before the partial phase of the eclipse begins. I continue shooting for 10 or 15 minutes after last contact to again have some images of the full moon. On occasion, if the composition requires it, I'll start shooting even earlier or continue shooting even longer so the sequence of moons extends all the way to the edge of the frame. For example, if I want to include all of a particular mountain in the composition rather than cut it off

▲ FIGURE 11-6: This screenshot from Photo Ephemeris Web shows the position of the moon when it set below the skyline ridge at 6:35 a.m., a few minutes before the almanac time of moonset. The skyline ridge has an altitude of 2 degrees. The thin gray line extending from the red pin atop Twin Sisters toward the black secondary marker indicates the direction of the moon. This line obscures the thin blue line indicating current moon position. The altitude readout in the geodetics panel (not included in this screenshot) shows that the altitude of the black pin as seen from the red pin is 2 degrees—the same altitude as the moon at the time set, 6:35 a.m. In other words, 6:35 a.m. is the time the moon will set behind the skyline ridge, a few minutes before the almanac time of moonset. The thick blue line indicates where the moon would have set above a level horizon. The timeline below the map shows the start and end times of the various phases of the eclipse.

in the middle, I'll keep shooting until the moon exits the frame even if that means I continue shooting until well after the eclipse ends. PlanIt Pro also lets you set the interval between frames. I usually choose 5 minutes. You can then use the virtual-reality viewfinder to see what focal length of lens you need to include the full eclipse sequence, how much of the landscape below you'll be able to include when using that focal length, what the azimuth of the centerline of the field of view needs to be, and what the pitch of the camera should be. Once you're in the field, you can use your compass to identify the point on the horizon that should be in the exact center of your frame (left to right) and compose accordingly. You can use the inclinometer that is built into many good compasses to set the camera's pitch (the angle measured up or down). See figure 11-7 for a screenshot from PlanIt Pro of the April 4, 2015, lunar eclipse.

The correct exposure for the moon varies dramatically during an eclipse, from about 1/125 sec., f/11, ISO 200 when the moon is fully lit and high in the sky, to as much as 8 sec., f/8, ISO 1600, when it is totally eclipsed. (If I had used an exposure much longer than 8 seconds with my 35mm lens, the moon would have blurred due to the earth's rotation.) The brightness of the fully eclipsed moon varies considerably, depending on the moon's position within Earth's umbra and the extent of clouds along the limb of the earth as seen from the sun. Heavy clouds in that region can block some of the light that would otherwise refract and reach the moon. As insurance, I shoot a five-frame bracketed set with a one-stop bracket interval using the exposures below as a starting point, double-checking that I had some detail in the moon by examining the magnified moon image on the LCD. Since nearly all of the image will be black, the histogram is useless. If the entire eclipse takes place between astronomical dusk and astronomical dawn, I also shoot some images that are correctly exposed for the land. During that time interval, a correct exposure for the moon will render the sky and land black. Shooting good-land exposures wasn't necessary when shooting the lunar eclipse over Longs Peak, since I knew the eclipse would continue until just before dawn, when the land would be illuminated by twilight. Beware of flare if you do need to use the moon as the light source when shooting the land before or after the eclipse.

Here are my exposure recommendations in detail.

- Full moon, or moon more than half visible; moon high in the sky: 1/125 sec. at f/11, ISO 200 (open up two or three stops if the moon is very close to the horizon)

- Half to one-quarter of the moon visible: 1/60th, f/11, ISO 200

- Less than one-quarter of the moon visible: 1/30th, f/11, ISO 200

▸ Figure 11-7: Screenshot from PlanIt Pro's Eclipse module in virtual-reality mode showing the April 4, 2015, lunar eclipse over Longs Peak as seen from Twin Sisters. The start and end times of the simulation, as well as the time interval between moon exposures, are shown at the top of the screen. The elevation angle of the camera (how much it's pointing up or down from level), the azimuth of the camera (the direction it's pointing in the horizontal plane), the focal length of the lens, and the image's orientation (portrait or landscape) are also shown at the top of the screen. Compare this simulation to the image in figure 11-4.

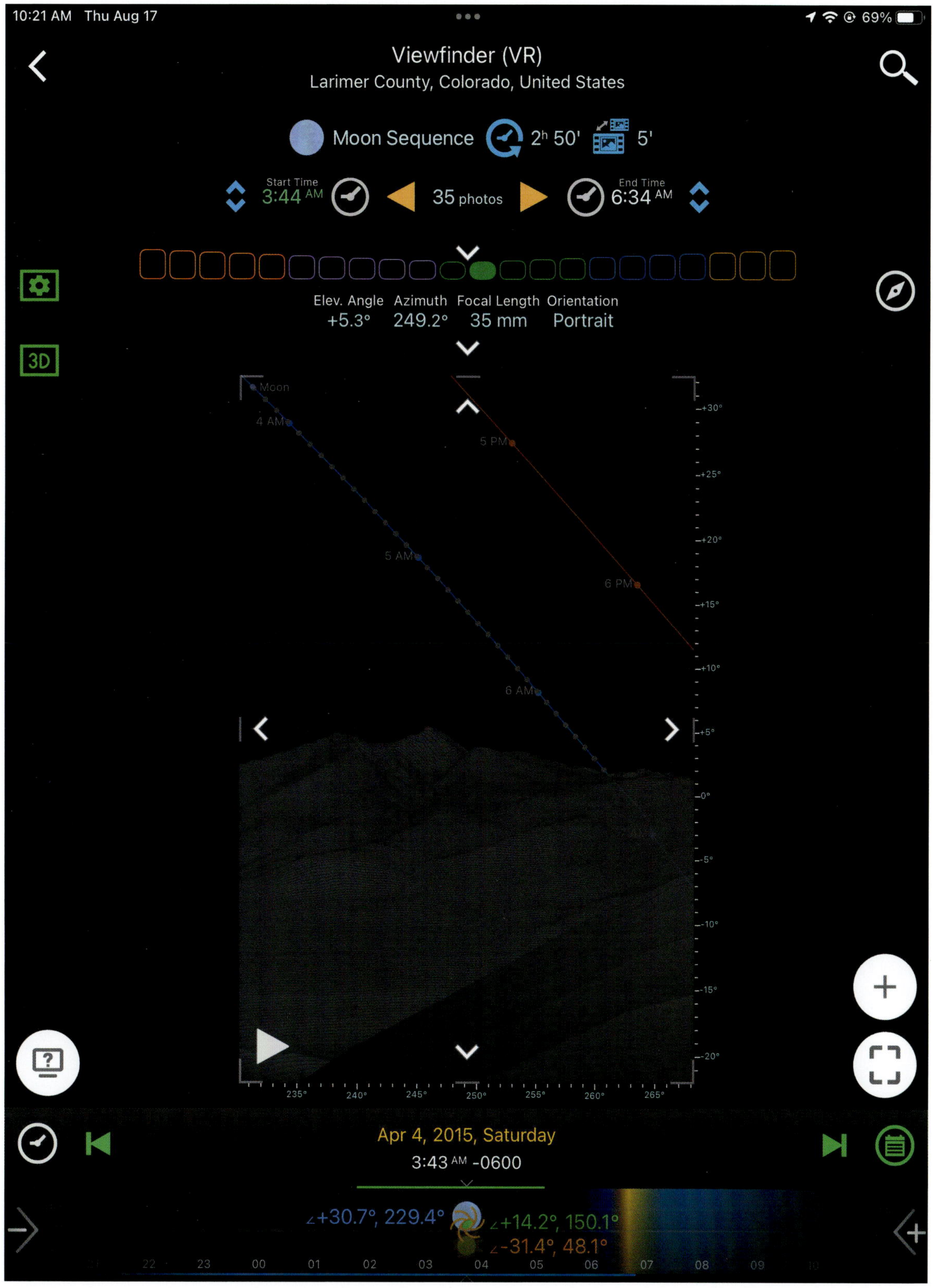

10:21 AM Thu Aug 17
69%
Viewfinder (VR)
Larimer County, Colorado, United States
Moon Sequence 2ʰ 50' 5'
Start Time
3:44 AM 35 photos 6:34 AM End Time
Elev. Angle Azimuth Focal Length Orientation
+5.3° 249.2° 35 mm Portrait
Moon
4 AM
5 PM
+30°
+25°
5 AM
+20°
6 PM
+15°
+10°
6 AM
+5°
0°
-5°
-10°
-15°
-20°
235° 240° 245° 250° 255° 260° 265°
Apr 4, 2015, Saturday
3:43 AM -0600
∠+30.7°, 229.4° ∠+14.2°, 150.1°
∠-31.4°, 48.1°
22 23 00 01 02 03 04 05 06 07 08 09

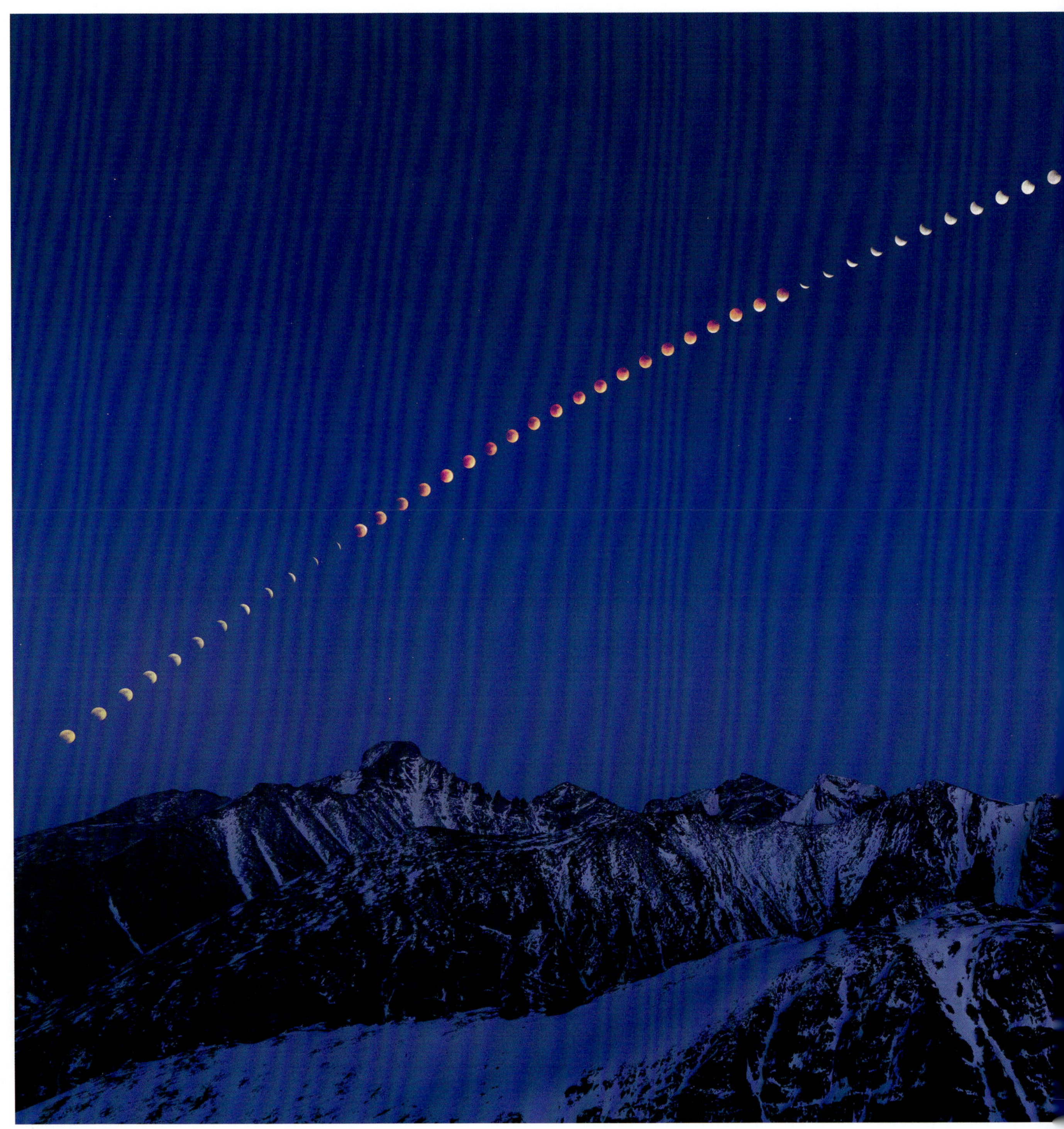

- Just the edge of the moon lit: $\frac{1}{15}^{th}$, f/11, ISO 200

- Fully eclipsed at the beginning and end of totality: 4 seconds, f/11, ISO 800

- Fully eclipsed, deepest totality: 8 seconds, f/8, ISO 1600

The hardest part of exposing correctly for a lunar eclipse is handling the transition from partial eclipse to totality. The sunlit portion of the moon is much brighter than the shadowed part. An exposure that provides detail in the sunlit portion will make the shadowed portion black. Conversely, an exposure that provides detail in the shadowed portion will make the sunlit portion blank white. The challenge is deciding when to stop exposing for the highlights and start exposing for the shadows. I usually make the switch while a thin crescent of lit moon is still visible because prior experience has shown that a very thin crescent of pure white next to a properly detailed, almost fully eclipsed moon was acceptable. I bracket widely during the transition so I have options when I put together my composite. With careful Photoshop work, you can composite two different exposures of the moon just before totality begins, one where you expose for the last sliver of sunlit moon, and one where you expose for the shadowed portion of the moon.

Assembling a Composite Image of a Lunar Eclipse

Once I get home, I use Lightroom to choose the best exposure from each bracketed set and give it a one-star rating. I then filter the view in Lightroom to show only one-star images, press Control+A to select all the

◄ Figure 11-8: Total lunar eclipse of May 15, 2022, over Longs Peak and the Continental Divide from the summit of Hallett Peak, Rocky Mountain National Park, Colorado. Sony Alpha 7R IVa, Sony FE 24-70mm f/4 ZA OSS at 30mm. Land and sky: 2 seconds, f/5.6, ISO 200, shot at 8:48 p.m., 37 minutes after sunset. Moon: 57 moon images, with exposures ranging from 1/125th, f/11, ISO 200 (full moon high in the sky) to 8 seconds, f/5.6, ISO 800 (deepest totality).

images, then load the images as layers in a new Photoshop document by choosing Photo>Edit In>Open as Layers in Photoshop. I select the top layer, then Shift-click the bottom layer to select all the layers simultaneously. In the Layers panel, I change the blend mode from Normal to Lighten. In this blend mode, Photoshop looks at every pixel in the top layer and compares its brightness to every pixel directly beneath it in the layer stack. It then lets the brightest pixel shine through. Since the moon is much brighter than the background (unless the eclipse begins or ends in twilight), the Lighten blend mode allows all of the moons to shine through. It also allows the brightest stars to shine through multiple times, so I use the Spot Healing Brush to remove the duplicate stars. If necessary, I also bring in a correctly exposed land image and blend the good-sky and good-land images using the techniques described in chapter 6.

Achieving the correct density in the land and in the moons that were near the horizon in my image of the lunar eclipse over Longs Peak required some additional Curves adjustment layers accompanied by layer masks to confine my adjustments to selected areas of the frame. Although the moon was shining brightly in a black sky at the beginning of the eclipse, the sky was blue and the land was softly illuminated by the time the moon set shortly before sunrise. I decided to use that twilight rendition of the sky and land behind the series of moons as they changed slowly from the brilliant white of full illumination to the ruddy red of total eclipse.

String-of-pearls images are clearly composites. My camera can't record dozens of moons in a single exposure. Obviously, it would be far easier to photograph eclipses from my backyard, then drop all those moons into an image that I took at some other time and place. For me, however—and I hope for my viewers—the fact that I shoot lunar eclipses from the location shown in the images gives those images the ring of authenticity that they would otherwise sorely lack.

▸ Figure 11-9: Lunar eclipse of January 31, 2018, over Star Dune, Great Sand Dunes National Park, Colorado. Canon EOS 5D Mark IV, Canon Compact-Macro EF 50mm f/2.5. Land and sky: 2 seconds, f/4.0, ISO 1600 at 6:31 a.m., 36 minutes before sunrise. Moon: 24 moon images, with exposures ranging from 1/60th, f/11, ISO 200 (full moon high in the sky) to 2 seconds, f/5.6, ISO 800 (deepest totality, moon in clear sky). One additional moon image at 2 seconds, f/4.0, ISO 1600 as the moon began disappearing into thin clouds. The moon vanished completely before moonset.

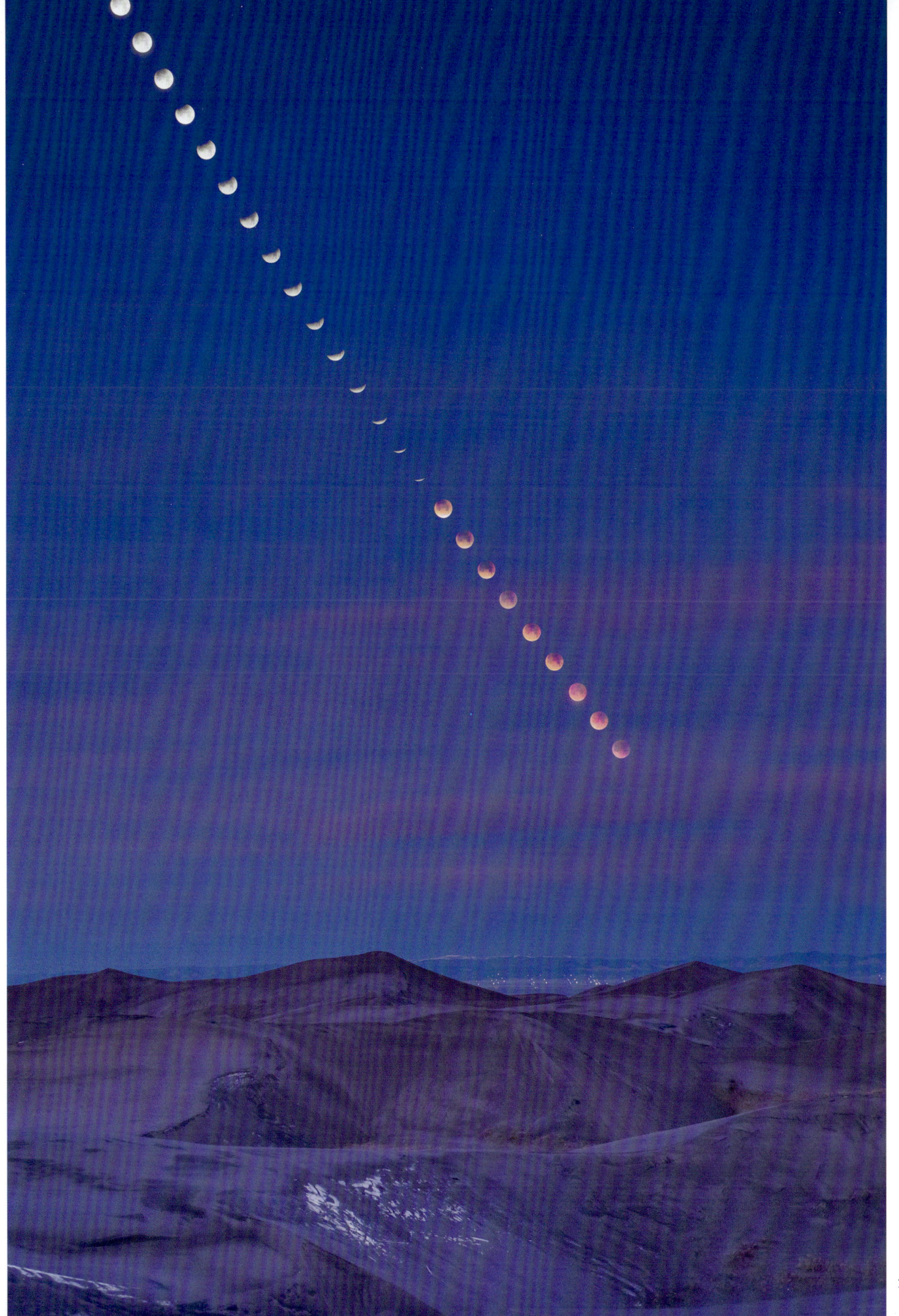

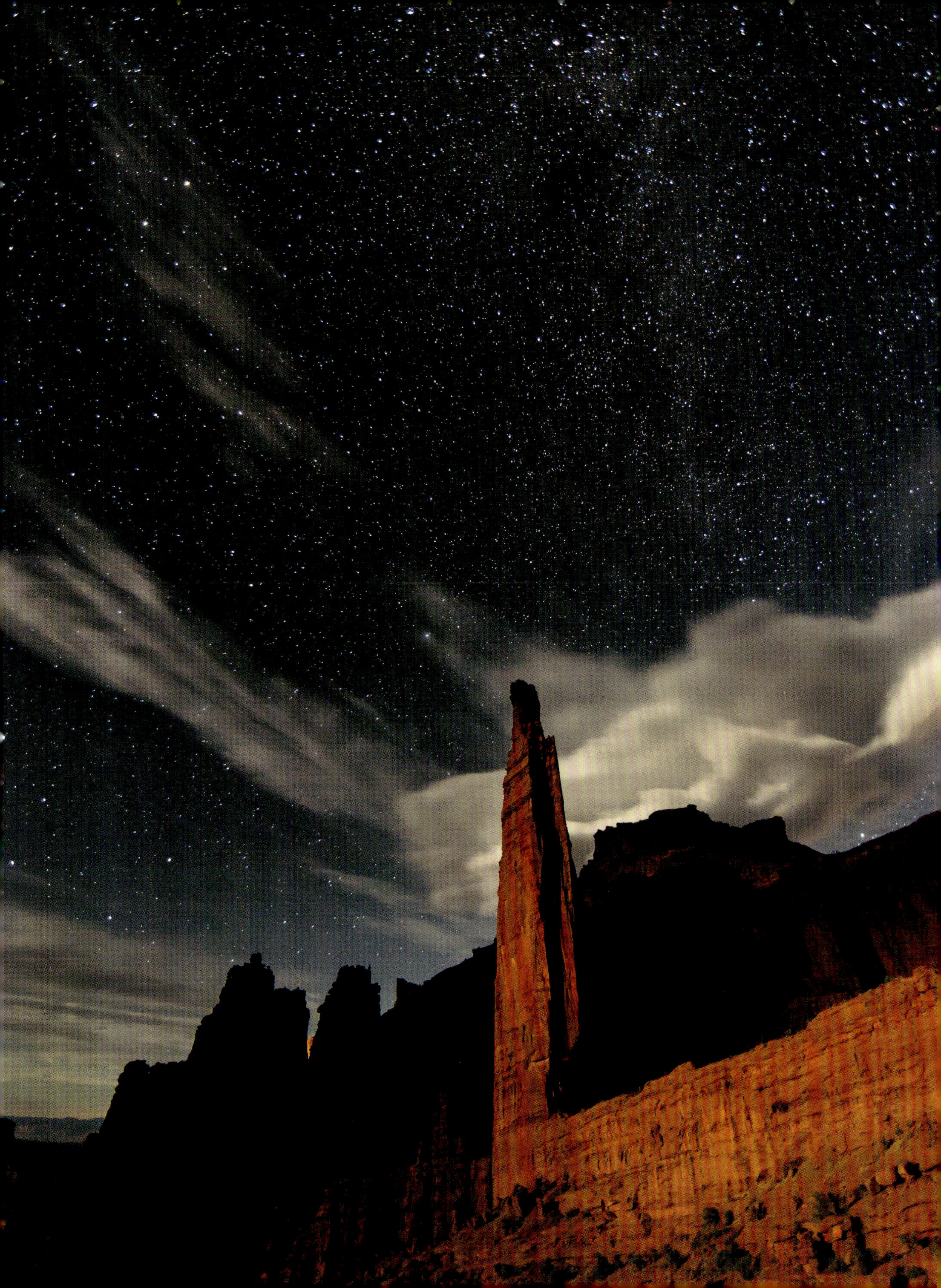

Photographing Moonlit Landscapes

A moonlit walk in the wilderness is an enchanting experience. The world is familiar yet transformed. The light seems to have a silvery, bluish quality. Shadows are inky black. When the moon is full, the beam of your headlamp becomes a barrier between you and the magic of moonlight. Turn your headlamp off and pause for a few minutes. Once your eyes have dark-adapted, a headlamp is only necessary if you're hiking through a forest or through deep shade in the depths of a canyon. Learning to make evocative images by the light of the moon opens up yet another realm of nighttime landscape photography.

In this chapter I'll concentrate on techniques for creating images where the stars are rendered as points rather than long streaks or trails. See chapter 8 for a full discussion of shooting star trails, which can be shot regardless of the phase of the moon.

As always, good planning will help ensure a successful shoot. Photo Ephemeris Web, Sun Surveyor, PhotoPills, and any number of mobile apps and internet sites can provide information on moonrise and moonset times. Photo Ephemeris Web, Sun Surveyor, and PhotoPills go beyond such basic information by giving you the azimuth and altitude of the moon at any time or place. They also provide information on the phase of the moon, usually expressed as the percentage of the moon's disk that is illuminated.

The day-to-day change in the time of moonrise and moonset is very different from the day-to-day change in the time of sunrise and sunset. In the Northern Hemisphere, from the winter solstice until the summer solstice, the sun rises earlier and sets later on successive days. From the summer solstice to the winter solstice, the sun rises later and sets earlier on successive days. The change in the time of sunrise and sunset is small, only a minute or two per day.

The moon, by contrast, always rises and sets later on successive days. The change in the time of moonrise and moonset is much larger and more variable than it is for sunrise and sunset. For example, in the northern part of the United States, the delay in moonrise from one day to the next ranges from a few minutes to well over an hour. To make things still more confusing, the difference between moonrise times on successive days is not necessarily the same as the difference between moonset times on those same successive days. If you need the moon to be in a very specific location (shining through an arch, for example), there may be only a few days in an entire year when the shot works. Use the position search capabilities in Photo Ephemeris Web or Sun Surveyor to identify those days.

◄ FIGURE 12-1: Milky Way and lenticular clouds over the Titan, Fisher Towers, Utah. The land was lit by the moon, which was 65 percent illuminated. August 10, 2016, 11:54 p.m. Canon EOS 5D Mark III, Canon EF 14mm f/2.8L II USM. 30 seconds, f/2.8, ISO 6400.

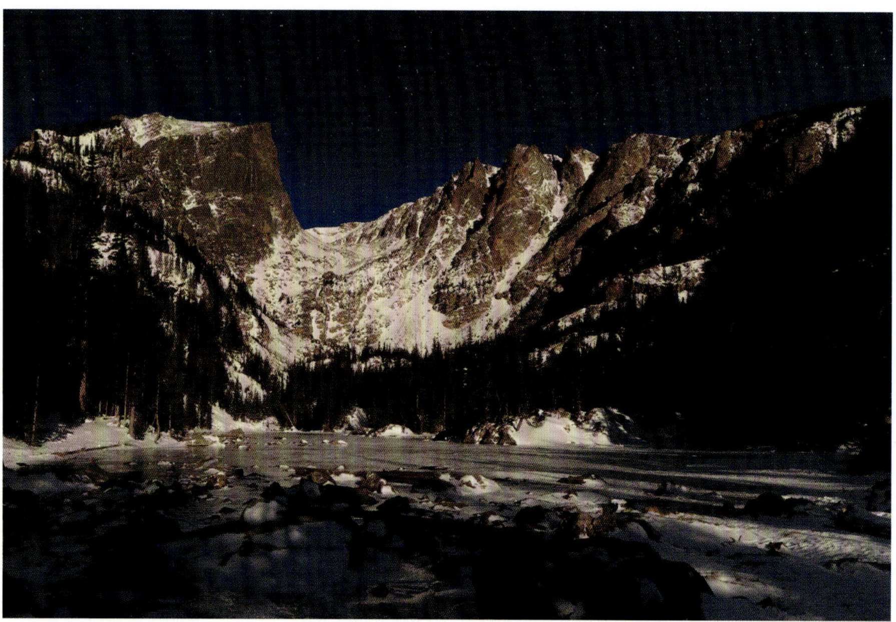

▸ Figure 12-2: Hallett Peak and Dream Lake by moonlight, Rocky Mountain National Park, Colorado. December 5, 2017, 8:26 p.m. Canon EOS 5D Mark IV, Canon EF 16-35mm f/2.8L III USM at 31mm. Land and sky: 15 seconds, f/5.0, ISO 4000. Land: two focus positions, four frames per focus position, images stacked in Photoshop, noise reduced with Stack Mode>Median. Land images blended manually in Photoshop. To create the sky I darkened one of the land exposures that was focused at infinity, converted it to a Smart Object, and applied the High Pass filter, radius 180, with the Overlay blend mode.

The azimuth of moonrise and moonset varies tremendously throughout the year. At the latitude of Denver, in the summer, when the sun rises well to the north of east and sets well to the north of west, the full moon rises well to the *south* of east and sets well to the south of west. Conversely, in the winter, when the sun rises well to the south of east and sets well to the south of west, the full moon rises well to the north of east and sets well to the north of west. This makes sense when you consider that the moon is full when it is directly opposite the sun as seen from Earth. If the sun rises to the southeast, the full moon will set to the northwest. If the ideal sunrise light on your subject occurs at summer solstice, the ideal moonrise light on your subject occurs at winter solstice.

The angle of moonlight as it illuminates your subject at night is just as important as the angle of sunlight during the day. The best angles during the day are generally those that produce sidelight, which creates texture, form, and volume; and backlight, which often adds drama, particularly if the sun is in the frame and right on the horizon. Front light, which occurs when the sun is directly behind you, is usually the least interesting direction of light unless the light itself is strongly colored at sunrise or sunset.

The best angles for moonlight are a bit different. During the day we easily see detail in most shadows; at night, even well-adapted human eyes can rarely penetrate dense shadows, and our cameras struggle to record much detail there if the exposure is correct for the highlights. Try to compose with the moon roughly 30 to 60 degrees right or left of a straight-behind-you position. A scene that is perfectly front-light (moon straight behind you) looks flat, just like it does in daytime. Front-lit scenes can also create problems with your own shadow intruding into your composition. Perfect sidelight, however, with the moon at exactly 90 degrees left or right of the camera axis, can create too large an area of black shadow to be pleasing. Backlight exacerbates the excessive-shadow problem. Backlight can also create unmanageable flare, particularly if the moon is in the frame and high in the sky. Backlit daylight scenes seem acceptable if the sun burns out to blank white. After all, we can't look directly at the sun. But a blank-white, irregularly shaped region of flare where a perfectly round and detailed moon should be seems unnatural.

▾ FIGURE 12-3: Sand dunes, lenticular clouds, and the Sangre de Cristo Range by moonlight, Great Sand Dunes National Park, Colorado. December 15, 2016, 5:18 a.m. Canon 5D Mark III, Canon EF 50mm f/1.4 USM. 30 seconds, f/1.4, ISO 100. A nearly full moon (97 percent illuminated) provided the light on the land.

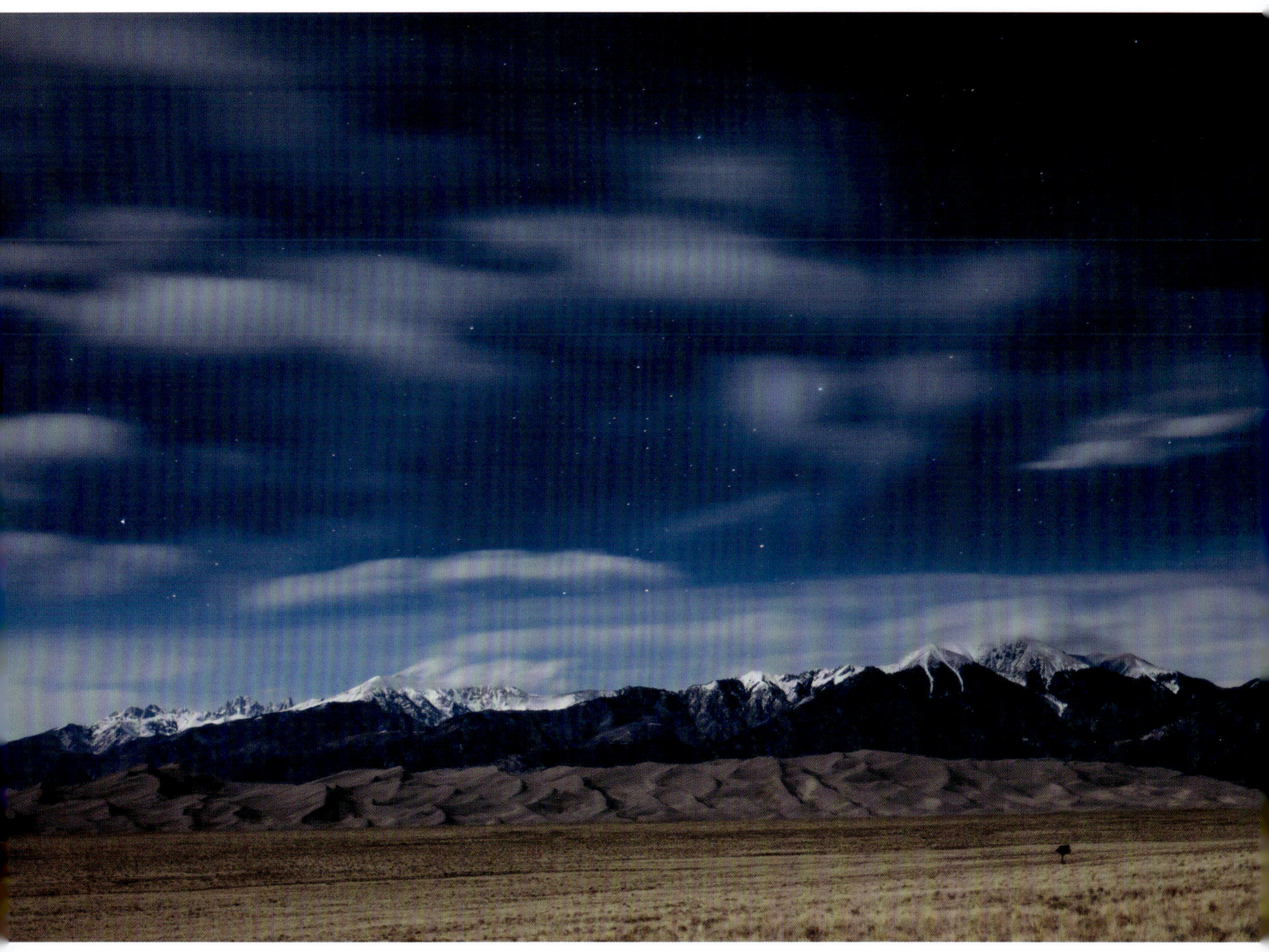

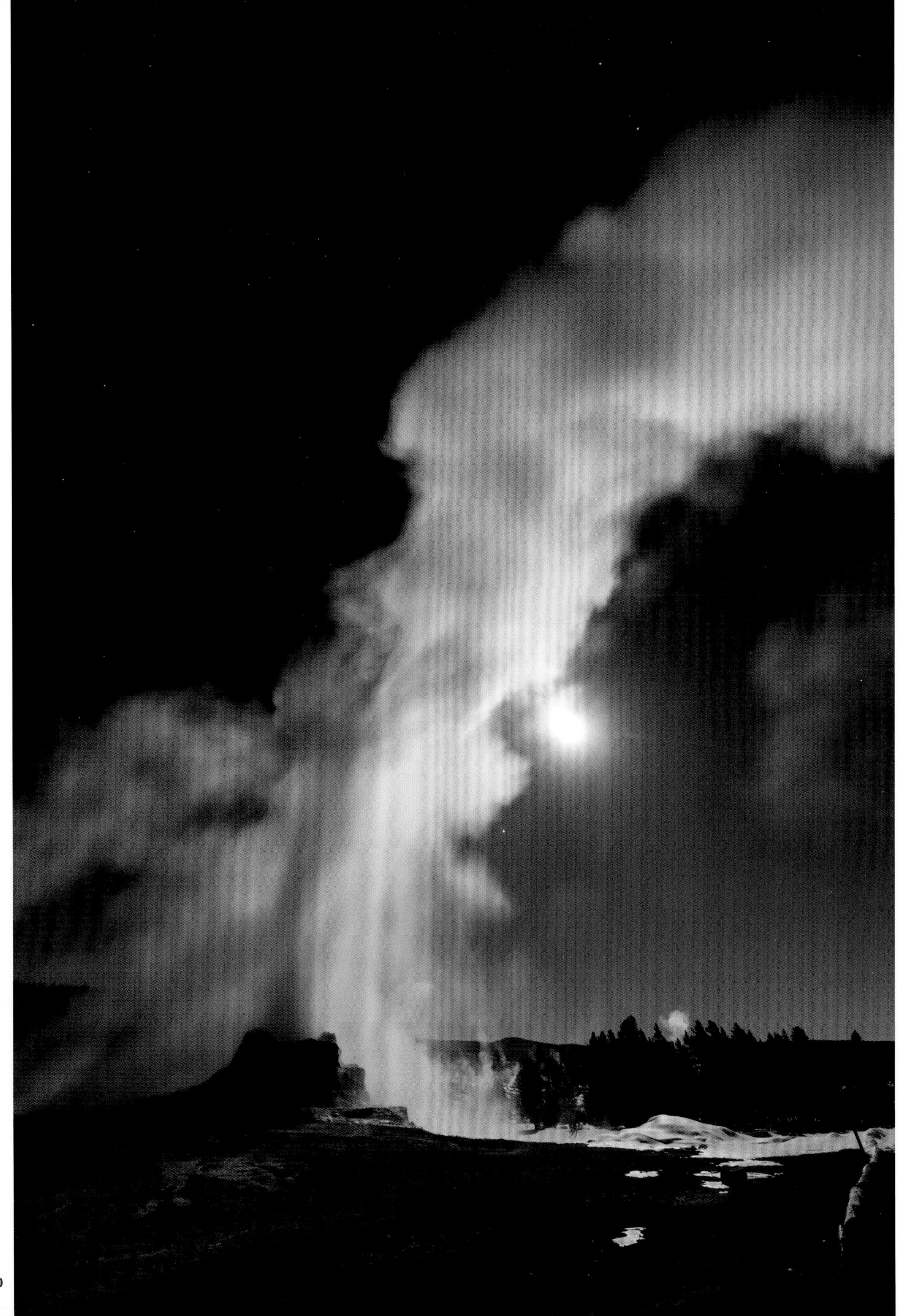

Once you're in the field, try to find compositions that require you to look up steeply. On moonlit nights, the sky near the horizon may be so bright that you see only a few stars. If the horizon is at the same elevation as you, and your composition includes only a narrow strip of sky, the photo may look like you shot it in daylight, then forgot to retouch those last few pesky white specks in the sky. The sky well above the horizon is much darker, which means you see more stars. As a rule, it doesn't work well just to include lots of sky because the sky, all by itself, is not interesting enough to carry the shot without the Milky Way, which is invisible on nights with a full moon. Try to fill part of the sky with something interesting. Clouds with interesting shapes can add a lot of appeal. Arches, sandstone towers, sea stacks, or other kinds of rock spires, interesting trees, and very dramatic peaks can all make good subjects. You can increase the number of stars in your image if you shoot the sky before or after moonrise, when the sky is dark, and shoot the land when the moon is above the horizon. Shooting when the moon is not completely full will also allow you to record more stars.

Exposure for Moonlit Landscapes

Even the light of a full moon is too dim for most camera meters to function. Exposure, therefore, becomes a matter of guess-and-check. As a rule of thumb, the correct exposure for a landscape lit by a full moon differs by about four stops from the correct exposure for the Milky Way. As you'll recall from chapter 5, the classic dark-sky exposure for the Milky Way is 30 seconds, f/2.8, ISO 6400. That means a good starting point for a full-moon exposure is about 30 seconds, f/2.8, ISO 400, or the equivalent. However, the brightness of the light from the full moon can vary by several stops, depending on the moon's position in the sky. When it's near the horizon, your exposure will need to be longer. In addition, the moon is *retroreflective*, which means that much of the light that reaches it from the sun bounces straight back toward the sun. The result is that the drop-off in brightness when the moon is not precisely full is much greater than you would expect based on the percentage of the moon's surface that is illuminated. For example, when the moon is full, 100 percent of its visible surface is illuminated. At first and last quarter, 50 percent is illuminated, so you might expect that the moon's light would be half as bright, meaning you would need to increase your exposure by just one stop. As it turns out, you'll need to increase your exposure by three stops or a bit more. Shooting under a crescent moon could mean you need to increase your exposure by another three stops.

Fortunately, your camera's histogram still works even if its meter won't. Your best bet is to use the guidelines above to decide on a starting point,

◄ FIGURE 12-4: Castle Geyser backlit by the full moon (100 percent illuminated), Yellowstone National Park, Wyoming. February 22, 2016, 9:07 p.m. Canon EOS 5D Mark III, Canon EF 16-35mm f/2.8L II USM at 16mm. 2 seconds, f/2.8, ISO 1250.

shoot a test frame, examine the histogram (not the captured image), and adjust accordingly. Of course, if you want to keep your stars reasonably round, you'll have to remember to employ the 500 rule discussed in chapter 3. If you want still rounder stars, you'll have to reduce the shutter speed and increase the ISO to compensate, or, better still, shoot multiple frames with a shorter exposure, then stack them to reduce noise, as discussed in chapter 7.

Processing Moonlit Landscapes

As I explained in chapter 6, we see moonlit scenes as bluish, but the color of moonlight is actually warmer than noon daylight. That presents you with a dilemma that is similar to the one you faced when processing Milky Way shots: do you accept the daylight white-balance rendition of the scene, which doesn't correspond with your expectations and experience, but does record the actual color of the light, or do you alter the color balance to more closely correspond with the way the scene felt? In this case, however, the issue is

▾ Figure 12-5: Comet NEOWISE over Mt. Wilson, Gladstone Peak, Lizard Head, and Wilson Peak, San Juan Mountains, Colorado. A waxing gibbous moon (69 percent illuminated) provided the light on the land. July 28, 2020, 11:27 p.m. Canon EOS 5D Mark IV, Canon Compact-Macro EF 50mm f/2.5. 20 seconds, f/1.4, ISO 1250.

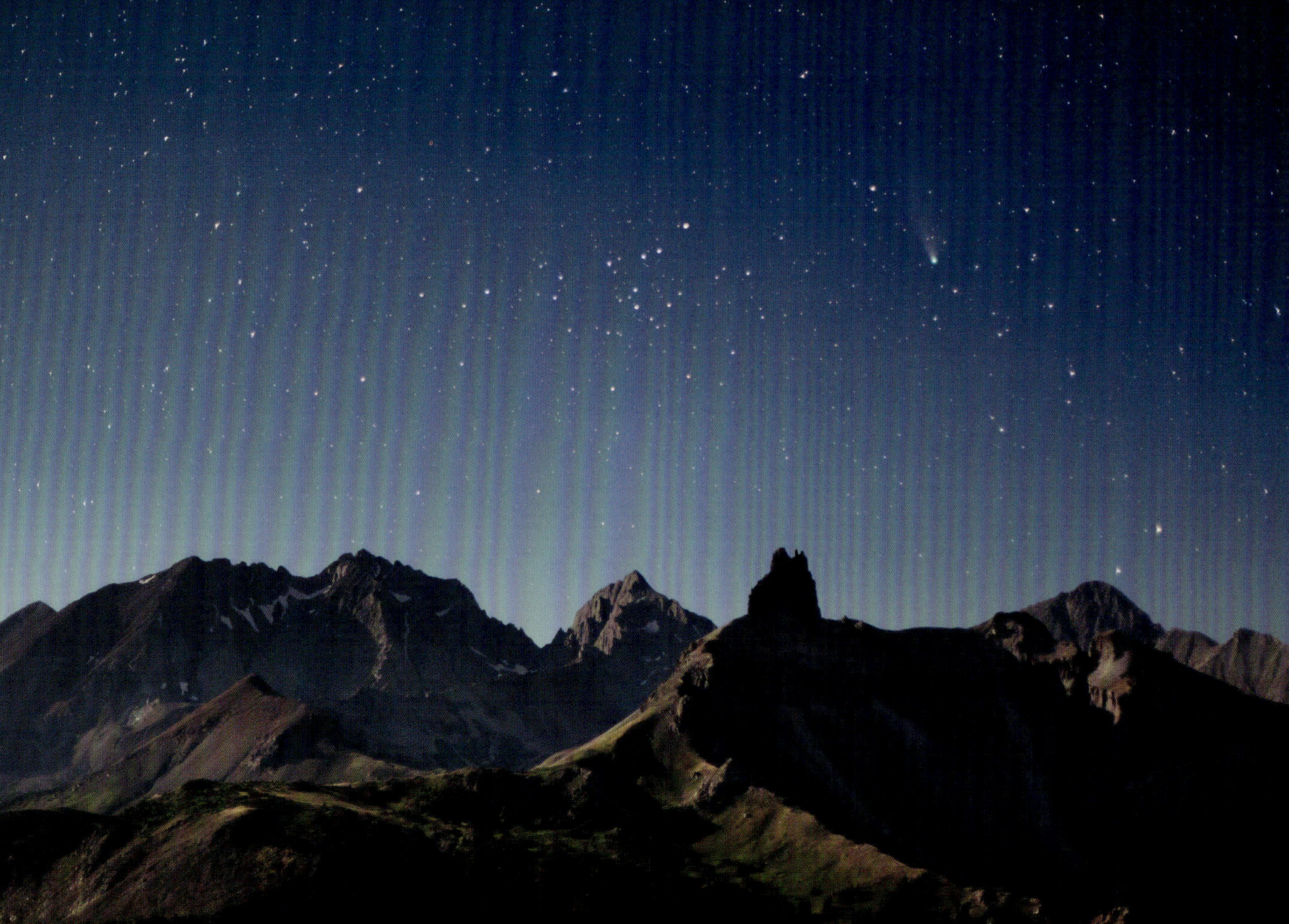

land color, not sky color. As I explained in chapter 6, on moonlit-drenched nights, the sky really is blue, and your camera will record it as such if you use a daylight white balance. Moonlight, however, has a color temperature of roughly 4100 degrees Kelvin, so the land will have an overall yellow colorcast compared to a shot of the same scene taken under clear skies at noon, when the light has a color temperature of roughly 5500 degrees Kelvin. (Remember that lower color temperatures correspond to warmer tones. An old-fashioned tungsten (incandescent) bulb has a color temperature of around 3200 degrees Kelvin, which corresponds to a very warm, orange-colored light.)

The contrast of warm-toned land and cool blue sky is very appealing, but it doesn't really evoke the feeling of moonlight. Here's how to give your image a moonlit feel, if indeed that's your goal.

First, give the image an overall bluish cast. I suggest using the Temp slider in the Basic panel in Lightroom to change the color temperature to between 4200 and 4800 Kelvin. The exact value will vary depending on the image and personal taste. I find I cool off snow scenes more than summer scenes. It's important to remember the counter-intuitive way that Lightroom interprets the temperature setting. This slider was designed to give images a neutral white balance. An image shot with a daylight white balance under tungsten light bulbs will have a strong orange cast. To correct that colorcast in Lightroom and make whites appear white again, set the temperature to the color of the light source—3200 degrees Kelvin—not to the color you want the image to be. Setting the Temp slider to a warm color like 3200 degrees Kelvin does not make the image look like it was lit with that color of light, but rather takes an image shot under that color of light and makes it neutral by cooling it down.

Even on a moonlit night, the sky is so dark it looks nearly black. You can help create a nighttime feel by darkening the sky until it is significantly darker than a daylight sky. Remember, however, that the sky near the horizon is always brighter than the land just below the horizon. If you make the sky just above the horizon very dark, the land will have to be darker still, and that may result in the land being too dark to be acceptable. Lightroom's Linear Gradient and Brush tools (both found in the Masking panel) are two good ways to darken the sky without darkening the land. You can also use Select Sky, also found in the Masking panel, to select just the sky, then the Exposure slider to darken the sky.

It may be tempting to darken the image overall in hopes of creating a nighttime feel. After all, it's dark out there! It's all too easy, however, to create an image that is so dark it becomes muddy and unappealing. A better solution for moonlit scenes is to add contrast to the land so that only the shadows become very dark, while keeping the moonlit portions of the land close to midtone. A good first step is to set a solid black point. In Lightroom's

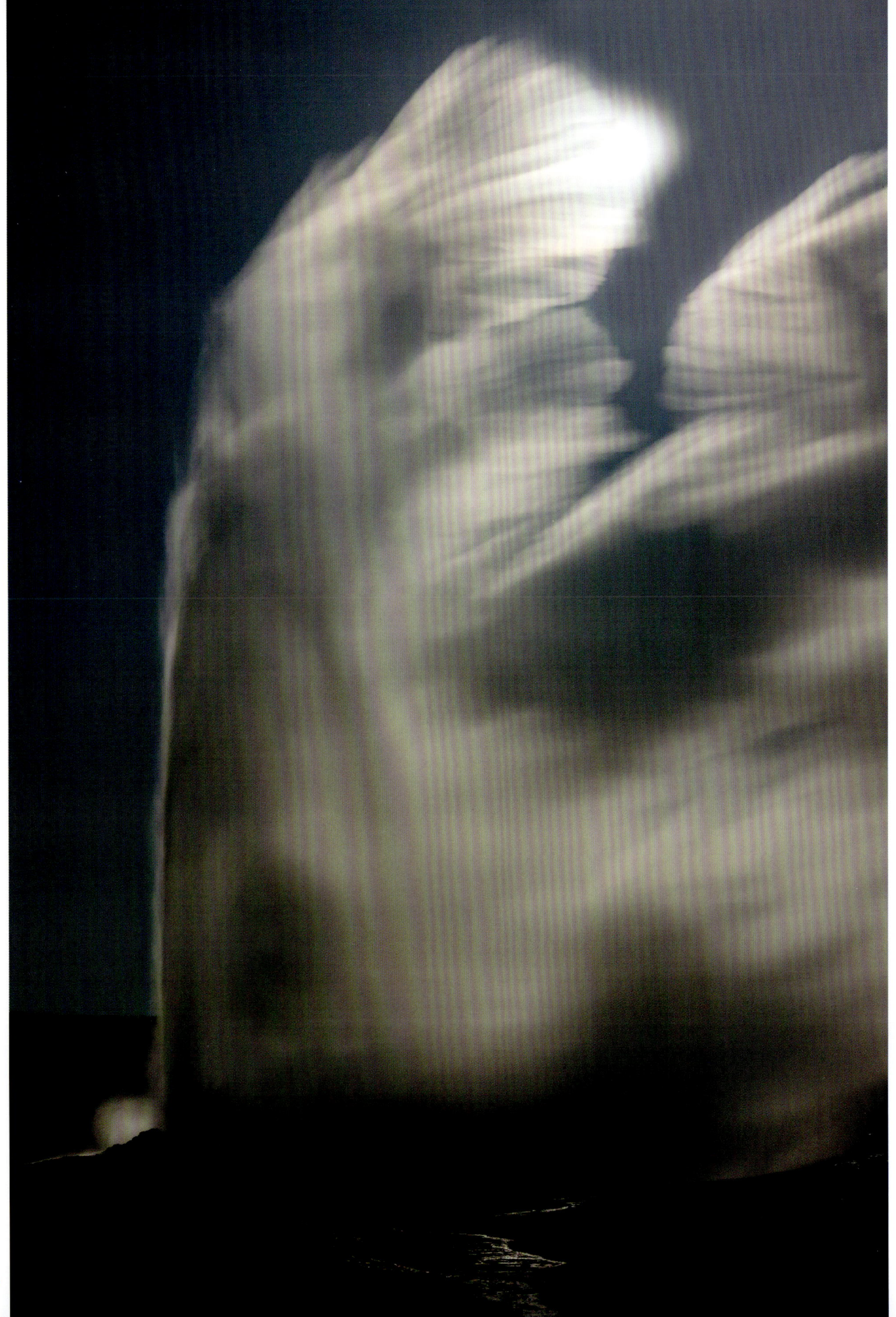

Basic panel, hold down Shift and double-click either the Blacks slider nub or the word "Blacks." You've essentially told Lightroom, "Find the darkest pixel in the image and make it pure black, then distribute all the remaining tones evenly through the tonal scale to prevent harsh transitions." You can also add contrast globally with the Contrast slider or locally with the Linear Gradient or Brush tools in the Masking panel.

Even if you have followed my suggestion to find a composition that allows you to look up steeply, you may find you have so few stars in images shot under a full moon that the image still looks like it was shot in daylight. If that's the case, you can increase the number of stars visible and brighten them with a variation on the High Pass technique described in chapter 6.

First, do all you can to create a nighttime feel in Lightroom. Now open the image as a Smart Object in Photoshop (right-click the image, then choose Edit In>Open as Smart Object in Photoshop). If the image is already open in Photoshop as a layered file, target the top layer and press Control+Alt+Shift+E. This invokes the Stamp Visible command, which combines all the layers into one new layer at the top of the layer stack. Now right-click the Stamp Visible layer and choose Convert to Smart Object.

Next, choose Filter>Other>High Pass. Set a high radius; 180 pixels often works well. Click okay. The image will look awful. In the Layers panel, double-click the tiny icon in the bottom-right corner of the Smart Object layer, as shown in figure 12-7. Change the Mode to Overlay. Adjust the Opacity to taste. I find a setting of 100 is often pleasing for the sky, but way too much for the land. If necessary, use the layer mask that comes with the Smart Filter to restrict the effect to the desired areas. Use the Brush tool and paint on the layer mask with black to hide the effect. To preserve some of the effect, reduce the Opacity to 25 to 50 percent before painting. Beware of haloes in the sky along the horizon. You may need to mask out the effect there as well.

Mastering the techniques I describe in this book will open up a whole new realm of landscape photography for you. Armed with these tools, you'll be able to plan, execute, and process exciting images of the landscape at night regardless of where you live or the current phase of the moon. As camera technology evolves, making photographs at night will keep getting easier, while the results will keep getting better. Venture into the dark tonight, and you'll never look back.

◄ FIGURE 12-6: Old Faithful backlit by the full moon (100 percent illuminated), Yellowstone National Park, Wyoming. February 22, 2016, 8:05 p.m. Canon EOS 5D Mark III, Canon EF 70-200mm f/4L IS USM at 93mm. 2 seconds, f/4.0, ISO 800.

▼ FIGURE 12-7: A Smart Object layer in the Layers Panel with the Blending Options icon circled.

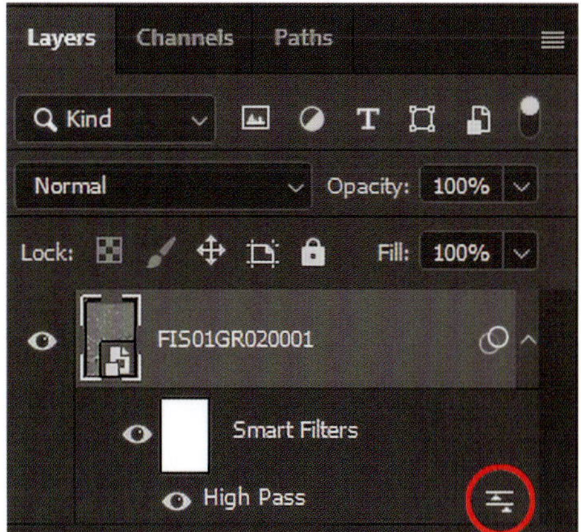

Index

3D models of Earth, 1, 90, 92-93, 96-98, 100, 220
3D module (Photo Ephemeris Web), 90, 97, 100, 220
500 rule, 67, 223

A
aberrations
  chromatic, 131, 138, 196, 224
  optical or stellar, 23, 39
accessories for night photography, 43-49
ACR. *See* Adobe Camera Raw
adaptation of visual system to darkness, 43-44
Adjustment Layers (Photoshop), 136, 152, 254
Adobe Camera Raw, 65-66, 69
AF. *See* auto-focus
airglow, vii, 127-128, 132
Alaska, 14, 31, 52, 70, 84, 203, 205
Alberta Falls, 150-151
Aldebaran, 128
Alma, 186
alpenglow, 244
American Meteor Society, 217
Android apps for night photographers. *See* PhotoPills; PlanIt Pro; Sun Surveyor
angle of view
  calculating pan angles for panoramas, 113
  crop sensor versus full-frame sensor, 31
  lenses and relationship to shutter speed, 29
  lenses and relationship to vignetting, 130
  selected lenses, 67
  table with relationship of aperture to, 36
angular elevation, 84, 94, 247
Antares, 128
Antero, Mount, 126-127
anti-aliasing (Photoshop), 141
AP index, 203
aperture
  brightness of meteors, 223-224, 229
  brightness of star trails, 189, 192
  depth of field table, 58
  exposure at night, 28, 30, 32, 35-37, 62, 64
  hyperfocal distance, 59
  relationship to noise, 24-25
  relative size for selected lenses, 36, 181

apps for night photographers. *See* Photo Ephemeris Web; PhotoPills; PlanIt Pro; Sun Surveyor
APS-C sensors, 27, 31, 67
Arca-Swiss standard for tripod heads, 41, 43
Arches National Park, 13, 16, 53, 119, 192, 226
Arcturus, 128
Ashcroft, x, xi
asteroids, 213, 234
astigmatism (lens aberration), 38
astronomical dusk and dawn
  best times to shoot, 76-78, 80, 83, 86, 90, 96, 98, 100, 234, 236
  defined, 21, 96
astronomy programs for night photographers, 88. *See also* Starry Night; Stellarium
astrophotography, 7
Atlantic Ocean, 205
atmosphere
  airglow, 127-128
  auroras, 202, 205
  lunar eclipses, 245
  meteors, 213-214, 216-217
  noctilucent clouds, 236
  Rayleigh scattering, 127, 244
  transparency and seeing, 19
atmospheric optics, 244. *See also* atmosphere
Auriga Software, 174
auroras
  aurora destinations, 203, 205
  aurora forecasts, 201-202, 205
  auroral zones, 201-203
  cause, 201
  composition, 208-209
  exposure, 207-208
  photographs of, front cover, 12, 15, 18, 29, 31, 41, 44-45, 48-49, 52, 56, 60, 70, 200-201, 204-206, 208-209, 211
  photographing, 21, 28, 62, 201-211
  processing, 210
  seasonal variation, 203
Aurora Watcher's Handbook, 202
authenticity in night images, 7-8, 125-129, 254
Auto-Align (Photoshop), 168-170
Auto Crop, for panoramas (Lightroom), 155
auto-focus, 52-55
Auto-Blend Layers (Photoshop), 168-170
Auto Sync (Lightroom), 176, 225
auto white balance, 70
AWB. *See* auto white balance
azimuth
  galactic center, 83, 97-98, 101
  mapping apps, 94-96, 220-221, 226, 233, 250

Milky Way arch, 101
  moonrise and moonset, 247, 257-258
  panoramas, 176
  Polaris, 180

B
backlight, 258-259
Bailey, Scott, vii, 128
Bair, Royce, vii
Bahtinov mask, 1, 56-58
Bahtinov, Pavel, 56
Balanced Rock, 192-193
ball head, for tripod, 40
Banff National Park, 10-11, 237, 239-241
Basic panel (Lightroom), 130, 132, 134, 137, 151, 194, 196, 210, 219, 263, 265
Bear Lake, 86-87, 90-96, 98-99, 187-189, 218, 221
bearings, compass, 83, 220, 247
bears, 13-14
Betelgeuse, 128
Big Dipper, 180
Big Spring Canyon, 116-117
black-and-white versus color at night, 7-8
Blacks slider (Lightroom), 210, 265
blend modes (Photoshop)
  Color, 154
  Lighten, 191, 195, 226, 254
  Normal, 135, 254
  Overlay, 149, 154, 258, 265
  Screen, 196, 198
  Soft Light, 154, 171
Blending Options icon for Smart Objects (Photoshop), 154, 265
blinking highlight warning, 207
Boulder Mountain Park, 9
Boundary Warp (Lightroom), 123, 156
Breugel, Floris van, vii, 186-187, 189-190, 192-193, 195-199
Bridge (Adobe software), 138
Brimhall Point, 182-183
Brooks Range, 31, 52, 70, 203
Brush tool (Lightroom), 133-134, 171, 210, 263, 265
Brush tool (Photoshop), 135, 143, 149, 153-154, 226, 265
bubble levels, 40, 60, 108-109
buffer, camera, 72

C
cable release, 16-17, 46. *See also* intervalometer
Camera Raw, Adobe. *See* Adobe Camera Raw
cameras
  best cameras for night photography, 3, 7, 23, 26-28
  double-exposure mode, 162
  DSLRs versus mirrorless cameras, 1, 23, 28